W9-ARH-236

LONGWOOD
C O L L E G E

LIBRARY

Longwood College
Farmville, Virginia 23909-1897

A center for learning. A window to the world.

Abraham Pizam, PhD
Yoel Mansfeld, PhD
Editors

Consumer Behavior in Travel and Tourism

Pre-publication
REVIEW

"**A** s technology and economics allow people to increasingly experience other nations and other cultures, it is important for students to appreciate the international perspectives of the travel and tourism industry. This is one of the major benefits of this book. Outstanding authors from Israel to Australia have contributedto the understanding of travel and tourism behavior from their global perspective. Such a unique combination makes the book a must for anyone who wants to take advantage of new global opportunities in this growing industry."

Bonnie J. Knutson, PhD
School of Hospitality Business,
Michigan State University

NOTES FOR PROFESSIONAL LIBRARIANS AND LIBRARY USERS

This is an original book title published by The Haworth Hospitality Press, an imprint of The Haworth Press, Inc. Unless otherwise noted in specific chapters with attribution, materials in this book have not been previously published elsewhere in any format or language.

CONSERVATION AND PRESERVATION NOTES

All books published by The Haworth Press, Inc. and its imprints are printed on certified pH neutral, acid free book grade paper. This paper meets the minimum requirements of American National Standard for Information Sciences–Permanence of Paper for Printed Material, ANSI Z39.48-1984.

Consumer Behavior
in Travel and Tourism

Consumer Behavior in Travel and Tourism

Abraham Pizam, PhD
Yoel Mansfeld, PhD
Editors

The Haworth Hospitality Press
An Imprint of The Haworth Press, Inc.
New York • London • Oxford

G
154.7
. C66
1999

Published by

The Haworth Hospitality Press, an imprint of The Haworth Press, Inc., 10 Alice Street, Binghamton, NY 13904-1580

© 1999 by The Haworth Press, Inc. All rights reserved. No part of this work may be reproduced or utilized in any form or by any means, electronic or mechanical, including photocopying, microfilm, and recording, or by any information storage and retrieval system, without permission in writing from the publisher. Printed in the United States of America.

Cover design by Marylouise E. Doyle.

Library of Congress Cataloging-in-Publication Data

Consumer behavior in travel and tourism / Abraham Pizam, Yoel Mansfeld, editors.
    p. cm.
   Includes bibliographical references and index.
   ISBN 0-7890-0610-3 (alk. paper)
   1. Tourism. 2. Travel. 3. Consumer behavior. I. Pizam, Abraham. II. Mansfeld, Y. (Yoel).
G154.7.C66   1999
338.4'791—dc21
                                                         99-17251
                                                              CIP

LONGWOOD COLLEGE LIBRARY
FARMVILLE, VIRGINIA 23901

CONTENTS

LONGWOOD LIBRARY

1000330411

ABOUT THE EDITORS

Abraham Pizam, PhD, is Professor of Tourism Management in the Department of Hospitality Management and Director of the Dick Pope Sr. Institute for Tourism Studies at the University of Central Florida in Orlando. Previously, he served as Director of Graduate Programs in the Department of Hotel, Restaurant, and Travel Administration at the University of Massachusetts. Widely known in the field of hospitality and tourism management, Dr. Pizam has conducted several international research projects, and served as a consultant in more than thirty countries. He has held various academic positions in the United States, United Kingdom, France, Austria, Australia, New Zealand, Singapore, Israel, and Switzerland. In addition, Dr. Pizam is the author of more than 100 scientific publications and four books and is on the editorial boards of ten academic journals in his field.

Yoel Mansfeld, PhD, is Chair of the Center for Tourism, Pilgrimage, and Recreation Research and Senior Lecturer in the Department of Geography at the University of Haifa. He is the author of more than twenty refereed publications and numerous technical reports, and serves on the editorial boards of several journals.

Contributors

John L. Crompton is Professor of Recreation, Park, and Tourism Sciences in the Department of Recreation, Park, and Tourism Sciences, College of Agriculture and Life Sciences, Texas A&M University, College Station.

John C. Crotts is Associate Professor and Director of the Hospitality and Tourism Management Program in the School of Business and Economics, College of Charleston, Charleston, South Carolina.

Alain Decrop is a Research Assistant in the Department of Business Administration, University of Namur, Belgium.

Maureen F. Devitt is with The Cadmus Group, Waltham, Massachusetts.

Ngaire Douglas is Senior Lecturer and Director of Studies in the School of Tourism and Hospitality Management, Southern Cross University, Lismore, NSW, Australia.

Norman Douglas is Director of Research Consultancy, Pacific Profiles, Australia.

Gordon Ewing is an Associate Professor in the Department of Geography, McGill University, Montreal, Quebec, Canada.

Jaishankar Ganesh is Assistant Professor of Marketing, Department of Marketing, College of Business Administration, University of Central Florida, Orlando.

Charles E. Gengler is Associate Professor in the Department of Marketing, School of Business at Baruch College, City University of New York, New York.

Peter Gillett is Professor of Marketing, Department of Marketing, College of Business Administration, University of Central Florida, Orlando.

Jurgen Gnoth is a Senior Lecturer in the Department of Marketing, University of Otago, Dunedin, New Zealand.

Wolfgang Haider is Assistant Professor in the School of Resource and Environmental Management, Simon Fraser University, British Columbia, Canada.

Monica Hanefors is Senior Lecturer in Tourism and Travel/Social Anthropology, School of Transportation and Society, Darlarna University College, Borlänge, Sweden.

Douglass K. Hawes is a retired Professor who previously taught at the University of Wyoming, Laramie, Wyoming.

J. S. Perry Hobson is Senior Lecturer in Marketing, School of Tourism and Hospitality Management, Southern Cross University, Lismore, NSW, Australia.

Simon Hudson is Senior Lecturer in the School of Service Management, University of Brighton, Eastbourne, United Kingdom.

Rajshekhar G. Javalgi is Professor of Services Marketing, James J. Nance College of Business Administration, Cleveland State University, Cleveland, Ohio.

John M. Jenkins is Senior Lecturer in the Department of Leisure and Tourism Studies at the University of Newcastle, Callaghan, Newcastle, NSW, Australia.

Bharath M. Josiam is Associate Professor in the Department of Hospitality and Tourism, University of Wisconsin-Stout, Menomonie, Wisconsin.

Biljana Juric is Senior Lecturer in the Department of Marketing, University of Otago, Dunedin, New Zealand.

David B. Klenosky is Assistant Professor in the Department of Health, Kinesiology, and Leisure Studies, Purdue University, West Lafayette, Indiana.

Robert Lawson is Professor of Marketing at the University of Otago, Dunedin, New Zealand.

Michael Luckett is Assistant Professor of Marketing, Department of Marketing, College of Business Administration, University of Central Florida, Orlando, Florida.

Lena Larsson Mossberg is Senior Lecturer in Marketing, School of Economics and Commercial Law, Goteborg University, Goteborg, Sweden.

Michael S. Mulvey is Assistant Professor in the Department of Marketing, School of Business, Rutgers University, New Brunswick, New Jersey.

Catherine M. Nichols is with the University of Alaska, Fairbanks.

S. R. Rao is Executive Director of Academic Programs and Associate Professor of Marketing, James J. Nance College of Business Administration, Cleveland State University, Cleveland, Ohio.

Chris Ryan is Editor in Chief, *Tourism Management,* and Professor in the Tourism Program, Center for Management Studies, University of Waikato, Hamilton, New Zealand.

David J. Snepenger is Associate Professor of Marketing in the College of Business, Montana State University, Bozeman, Montana.

Silvia Sussmann is Senior Lecturer in Management Computing, School of Management Studies for the Service Sector, University of Surrey, Guildford, Surrey, United Kingdom.

Edward G. Thomas is Professor of Marketing in the James J. Nance College of Business Administration, Cleveland State University, Cleveland, Ohio.

Maree Thyne is a Research Fellow working on a tourism research program at Otago University that is funded by the New Zealand Foundation for Research, Science and Technology, University of Otago, Dunedin, New Zealand.

Timothy J. Tyrrell is Professor of Tourism Economics, Department of Environmental and Natural Resource Economics, University of Rhode Island, Kingston.

Seoho Um is Associate Professor in the Department of Tourism and Recreation, Kyonggi University, E-We-Dong, South Korea.

Arzu Ünel has recently completed an MSc in Tourism Marketing at the University of Surrey, Guildford, Surrey, United Kingdom.

David J. Walmsley is Professor of Geography and Planning, School of Geography, Planning, Archaeology, and Palaeoanthropology, University of New England, Armidale, NSW, Australia.

Tracy Young is a Research Fellow working on a tourism research program at Otago University that is funded by the New Zealand Foundation for Research, Science, and Technology, University of Otago, Dunedin, New Zealand.

Introduction

Abraham Pizam
Yoel Mansfeld

The question of how people consume travel and tourism products has become a focal point in tourism research in the past two decades. Efforts to unveil the determinants that shape travel behavior stemmed not only from pure academic interest, but from practical business considerations as well. The evolving marketplace of the travel industry has realized that understanding travel behavior is imperative in today's highly competitive business environment. After all, in such circumstances the ability to compete effectively is highly correlated with the ability to tailor the travel product to tourists' needs, expectations, and desires. This mutual interest forms the raison d'etre for *Consumer Behavior in Travel and Tourism.*

In recent years, a growing number of published research works have improved our body of knowledge in this highly important domain. However, these scholarly studies are scattered in numerous journals and have never been incorporated into a single volume that summarizes all explored and, as yet, not fully explored issues in tourists' consumer behavior. The aim of this volume is twofold. First, it represents for the first time an attempt to explore, define, analyze, and evaluate the state of the art in this multifaceted phenomenon of consuming tourist and travel products. Second, it packages the various issues and aspects of consumer behavior in travel and tourism in the form of a textbook, to be used by both students and practitioners. Thus, each chapter includes learning objectives, main concept definitions, and review questions.

The book comprises five main sections. In search of improved approaches to marketing tourist products, Part I consists of a comprehensive discussion of the main factors that affect consumer behavior in travel and tourism. This discussion unveils, in a critical manner, the relationship between travel motivation, destination choice, and the consequent travel behavior. While evaluating these relationships, the chapter stresses the as-yet undiscovered issue of nonparticipants and their reluctance to travel.

Part II explores in greater detail the manner in which different consumers go through various decision-making processes that lead to consequent destination choices and spatial behaviors. Using various case studies such as a ski destination choice or decisions to visit Disney World in Florida, the section defines the unique characteristics of the tourist product, followed by an analysis of the major factors and constraints that shape each stage in the decision-making process. Based on observations illustrating the "push" and "pull" factors as well as various constraints imposed on potential travelers, this section also makes some marketing recommendations. It suggests that to succeed in this highly competitive environment, the tourism industry must improve the level of compatibility between tourists' expectations and their actual travel experience.

Because tourism is an intangible product, and since there normally is a time lag between the purchase of this product and its actual consumption, travelers develop a cognitive image of the product they bought. Part III of this book demonstrates how this image is created, developed, and changed as the traveler moves from a decision-making stage to a traveler stage. It is suggested in this section that the changing image of a given destination and the evolving travel experiences can have a major effect on travelers' satisfaction levels. Today, tourism practitioners and destination managers have at their disposal a variety of research techniques that enable them to measure the gap between expected and actual travel experience. Thus, one can evaluate the extent to which the quality of a given tourist product meets customer expectations and from this find ways to constantly improve it.

The availability of sophisticated research techniques aimed at understanding destination choice and tourists' spatial behaviors is imperative in a growing competitive business environment. Part IV discusses some selected research tools and evaluates the marketing implications of using qualitative and/or quantitative research techniques.

Finally, Part V, which concludes this book, examines the relationships between consumers' characteristics and their behavior as tourists. The section portrays possible environmental, socioeconomic, cultural, and/or demographic influences on how potential tourists select from among travel alternatives, choose their preferred destination, and behave while on site. It shows that consumer behavior in travel and tourism is shaped, after all, by both individual and environmental factors. We hope that after reading this book, students, practitioners, and fellow researchers will be better equipped to detect and analyze the relative roles of these two major types of behavioral determinants.

Consumer Behavior in Travel and Tourism would not have been possible without the commitment and dedication of our colleagues who contributed their valuable academic and industrial experience in this field. We would like to thank all of them—those who wrote their chapters specifically for this book and those who kindly allowed us to republish their outstanding research findings and theoretical developments. Special thanks go to Charles Goeldner, editor of the *Journal of Travel Research*, who gave us permission to use some articles that were previously published in his journal. We would also like to express our gratitude to the many colleagues and practitioners who strongly supported our initiative to edit this volume. The evident lack of such a textbook deterred many of them from teaching this highly practical topic as a full-fledged course. We believe that with this book, that opportunity can be realized. We are also grateful to the Research Authority of the University of Haifa, which financially supported the production of this book. Finally, a word of appreciation for three special women: Olga Sagi, who was responsible for the English editing, Genoveba Breitstein, who was responsible for typing and arranging the book according to the publisher's requirements, and Shoshi Mansfeld, who (re)produced all the graphic work for this book. By extending their professional skills they have contributed immensely to the successful production of this book.

PART I: OVERVIEW

In recent years, a substantial quantity of research has been conducted in the area of consumer behavior in tourism. While results varied greatly, most studies determined that motivation played a major role in determining tourists' behavior. Accordingly, motivation determines not only if consumers will engage in a tourism activity or not, but also when, where, and what type of tourism they will pursue.

In Chapter 1, Hudson summarizes some of the most popular theories that have been proposed for describing how consumers' motivation affects their tourism behavior and actions. Among the theories discussed in detail are Maslow's Hierarchy of Needs, Murray's Classification Scheme, Dann's Tourism Motivator, Crompton's Nine Motives, and Plog's Tourism Motivation Model. All of these models focus on the needs and motivations of individuals and the influence these needs have on their tourism behavior.

Findings based on surveys conducted by Perreault and the Gallup Organization which questioned the travel behavior of thousands of people, support the long-held belief that travelers can be divided into numerous categories, based on their reason and motivation to travel.

In addition to travel motivation, Hudson also discusses the traveler's destination choice process. Under this category fall theories such as those of Muller, Um, and Crompton, Woodside and Lysonski, and Mansfeld. Finally, Hudson presents some comprehensive models of consumer behavior in tourism. Models such as Wahab, Crampon, and Rothfield's, Mayo and Jarvi's, and Moutinho try to analyze the effects that the individual, environmental, and situational factors have on tourists' behavior and choice.

The chapter concludes with the observation that while extensive research has been conducted on why, where, and when individuals travel, there still is a lack of understanding of why some consumers do not travel. Hudson contends that the subject of nonusers in tourism is a relatively unexplored area partly because of the difficulty of properly researching it.

Chapter 1

Consumer Behavior Related to Tourism

Simon Hudson

LEARNING OBJECTIVES

By the end of the chapter the reader should:

- Understand the importance of consumer behavior within tourism marketing
- Have a broad grasp of the part played by motivational factors in tourism behavior
- Understand why tourism researchers have tried to explain tourist behavior by developing typologies of tourist roles
- Be familiar with various studies that have attempted to understand the destination choice process
- Have a general understanding of the usefulness and limitations of consumer behavior models developed over the years

MOTIVATION OF TOURISTS

Many authors see motivation as a major determinant of the tourist's behavior. Central to most content theories of motivation is the concept of need. Needs are seen as the force that arouses motivated behavior and it is assumed that, to understand human motivation, it is necessary to discover what needs people have and how they can be fulfilled. Maslow in 1943 was the first to attempt to do this with his needs hierarchy theory, now the best known of all motivation theories (see Figure 1.1).

FIGURE 1.1. Maslow's Hierarchy of Needs

Physiological needs	Hunger, thirst, sex, sleep, air, etc.
Safety needs	Freedom from threat or danger
Love (social) needs	Feeling of belonging, affection, and friendship
Esteem needs	Self-respect, achievement, self-confidence, reputation, recognition, prestige
Needs for self-actualization	Self-fulfillment, realizing one's potential

Source: Maslow, 1943.

Maslow's theory was originally developed in the context of his work in the field of clinical psychology, but has become widely influential in many applied areas such as industrial and organizational psychology, counseling, marketing, and tourism. One of the main reasons for the popularity of Maslow's hierarchy of needs is probably its simplicity. Maslow argues that if none of the needs in the hierarchy were satisfied, then the lowest needs, the physiological ones, would dominate behavior. If these were satisfied, however, they would no longer motivate, and the individual would move up to the next level in the hierarchy, safety needs. Once these were satisfied, the individual would move up to the next level, continuing to work up the hierarchy as the needs at each level were satisfied.

Maslow's theory has received little clear or consistent support from research evidence. Some of Maslow's propositions are totally rejected, while others receive mixed and questionable support. Witt and Wright (1992) criticize the theory for not including several important needs, perhaps because they do not fit conveniently into Maslow's hierarchical framework. Such needs are dominance, abasement, play, and aggression. They prefer Murray's (1938) classification scheme, suggesting that from the point of view of tourist motivation it provides a much more comprehensive list of human needs that could influence tourist behavior. Murray listed a total of fourteen physiological and thirty psychological needs, from which it is possible to identify factors that could influence a potential tourist to prefer or avoid a particular holiday. However, due to its complexity, Murray's work is not as easy to apply as Maslow's hierarchy, and has therefore not been adopted by tourism researchers.

Other attempts to explain tourist motivation have identified with Maslow's needs hierarchy. Mill and Morrison (1985), for example, see travel as a need or want satisfier, and show how Maslow's hierarchy ties in with travel motivations and the travel literature. Similarly, Dann's (1977) tourism motivators can be linked to Maslow's list of needs. He argued that there are basically two factors in a decision to travel, the push factors and the pull factors. The push factors are those that make you want to travel and the pull factors are those that affect where you travel. In his appraisal of tourism motivation, Dann proposed seven categories of travel motivation:

1. Travel as a response to what is lacking yet desired. We live in an anomic society and this, according to Dann, fosters a need in people for social interaction that is missing from the home environment.
2. Destination pull in response to motivational push, already discussed.
3. Motivation as a fantasy.
4. Motivation as a classified purpose, such as visiting friends and relatives or study.
5. Motivational typologies, which will be studied in depth later in this chapter.
6. Motivation and tourist experiences.
7. Motivation as auto-definition and meaning, suggesting that the way tourists define their situations will provide a greater understanding of tourist motivation than simply observing their behavior.

Crompton (1979) agreed with Dann, as far as the idea of push and pull motives was concerned. He identified nine motives, seven classified as sociopsychological or push motives and two classified as cultural or pull motives. The push motives were escape from a perceived mundane environment, exploration and evaluation of self, relaxation, prestige, regression; enhancement of kinship relationships, and facilitation of social interaction. The pull motives were novelty and education. Crompton identified these motives from a series of in-depth interviews with a group of people and found that the push motives were difficult to uncover. He pointed out that people may be reluctant to give the real reasons for travel if those reasons are deeply personal or intimate.

Mannel and Iso-Ahola (1987) identify two main types of push and pull factors, personal and interpersonal. They suggest that people are motivated to travel to leave behind the personal or interpersonal problems of their environment and to obtain compensating personal or interpersonal rewards. The personal rewards are mainly self-determination, sense of competence, challenge, learning, exploration, and relaxation. The interpersonal rewards arise from social interaction (see Figure 1.2).

Krippendorf (1987), in an enlightening book on tourism, sees a thread running through all these theories of tourism motivation. First, travel is motivated by "going away from" rather than "going toward" something; second, travelers' motives and behavior are markedly self-oriented. The author classifies these theories into eight explanations of travel: recupera-

FIGURE 1.2. The Escaping and Seeking Dimensions of Leisure Motivation

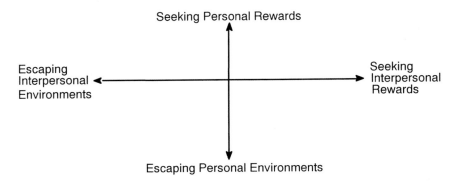

Source: Mannel and Iso-Ahola, 1987.

tion and regeneration, compensation and social integration, escape, communication, freedom and self-determination, self-realization, happiness, and travel broadening the mind.

The tourist motivation model proposed by Plog (1974) has been one of the most widely cited. According to Plog, travelers may be classified along two dimensions: allocentrism/psychocentrism and energy. Travelers who are more allocentric are thought to prefer exotic destinations, unstructured vacations rather than packaged tours, and more involvement with local cultures. Psychocentrics, on the other hand, are thought to prefer familiar destinations, packaged tours, and "touristy" areas. Later, Plog added energy, which describes the level of activity desired by the tourist; high-energy travelers prefer high levels of activity while low-energy travelers prefer fewer activities.

Plog's findings evolved from syndicated research for airline companies that were interested in converting nonflyers into flyers (recently the airlines have taken to giving a free experimental flight to nonflyers!). He found that the majority of the population were neither allocentric nor psychocentric, but "midcentric"—somewhere in the middle. It has been argued, however, that Plog's theory is difficult to apply as tourists will travel with different motivations on different occasions (Gilbert, 1991). There are many holidaymakers who will take a winter skiing break in an allocentric destination, but will then take their main holiday in a psychocentric destination.

Smith (1990) has also criticized the model. Using data from seven nations, he tested the model's basic hypothesis as well as its applicability to other countries. He concluded that his test of the allocentric/psychocentric model failed to support the hypothesized association between personality types and destination preferences. He even criticized tourism researchers for relying on untested hypotheses for explanations about how the tourist system works.

TYPOLOGIES OF TOURISTS

Besides Plog, other tourism researchers have tried to explain tourist recreational behavior by developing typologies of tourist roles. Most are based on empirical data obtained from questionnaires and/or personal interviews. One of the first—Cohen (1972)—proposed four classifications of tourists: (1) the organized mass tourist, highly dependent on the "environmental bubble," purchasing all-inclusive tours or package holidays; (2) the individual mass tourist, who is more autonomous and free than the previous group; (3) the explorer, who seeks new areas but would sometimes opt to step back into comfortable accommodation, etc.; and (4) the drifter, who avoids any kind of "tourist establishment." Cohen also introduced a differentiation between the "institutionalized" and "noninstitutionalized" forms of tourism. The first two tourist roles can be regarded as institutionalized types, as they deal with the institutionalized tourist system. The latter two roles are categorized as noninstitutionalized types, because they do not depend on the services offered by the tourist establishment.

Following Cohen, other researchers have developed different typologies of tourist roles. Perreault, Darden, and Darden (1977) questioned 2,000 households and found evidence of five distinct groups or types of vacation orientation: (1) the budget travelers (28 percent), whose interests are economy-oriented; (2) adventurers (24 percent), who exhibit a relatively low desire for relaxing travel and a relatively high disposition for venturesomeness; (3) homebodies (20 percent), who enjoy relaxing travel, but have no interest in vacation travel, do not seek travel information, and are not venturesome; (4) vacationers (7 percent), who plan ahead more, but are undecided about their vacations; and (5) moderates (21 percent), who have a high predisposition to travel, but are not interested in weekend travel or sports.

A Belgian study in 1986 by Westvlaams Ekonomisch Studiebureau questioned 3,000 adults about their demographic and socioeconomic characteristics and their behavior and expenditure during their holidays. Respondents were grouped on the basis of a cluster analysis and seven clusters were formed: the active sea lovers, the contact-minded holidaymakers, the nature viewers, the rest seekers, the discoverers, the family-oriented sun and sea lovers, and the traditionalists.

The Gallup Organization (1989) also attempted to develop traveler classifications, based on interviews with 4,000 adults. They found that there were five distinct groups of travelers, who experience travel differently, regardless of their origin, destination, or the frequency of their trips. These five groups they called the adventurers, the worriers, the dreamers, the economizers, and the indulgers.

It appears that although the above typologies represent different numbers of types (from four to seven types of tourist), the same characteristics appear in each of the types described: looking for adventure; discovering new cultures versus accustomed daily habits; the budget spent on the holiday; the importance attached to nature and authenticity; and seeking relaxation, sun, sand, and sea. Lowyck, Van Langenhove, and Bollaert (1992) criticize such typologies for this very reason, and suggest that it is possible to establish a typology of tourists not based on psychographic research. Thinking only about how the supply side is structured is sufficient to develop a classification.

Lowyck, Van Langenhove, and Bollaert, along with Urry (1990) and MacCannel (1976), suggest there should be more intensive design studies, with increased emphasis on the individual and how people experience tourist settings. Lowyck and colleagues also propose two alternative forms of typology: one developed in the context of personality theory, called the Matrix Typology Approach; and the second in the context of criminology, called the Processual Typology Approach, that can be formally transposed to questions of tourism behavior. Both methods call for the use of supplementary psychological approaches as well as the more classical socioeconomic approach when attempting to understand tourism consumer behavior.

Recently, the Henley Centre has carried out research on the changing needs and aspirations of U.K. holidaymakers (Stewart, 1993). As part of this work they developed a model of holidaytaking. The model is built on the empirical observation that as people become more affluent they tend to travel more, and that the experience of travel is cumulative. The more leisure travel people undertake, the more they tend to want to do. They also tend to become more adventurous and confident as their level of affluence and travel experience increases.

For individual holiday consumers, the model distinguishes among four different phases of holidaytaking, which are related to levels of affluence and travel experience. In each phase different destinations become more or less popular, but more important is the way in which the underlying motivation for travel changes across the phases and hence the demand for different types of holiday product.

Phase 1—The Bubble Travelers

Tourists in this initial phase of international travel are characterized by relatively low affluence and low travel experience. Their motivation for travel to foreign countries is very much one of curiosity, and the traditional package holiday concept is an ideal product for consumers in this phase. The Henley Centre borrowed Urry's theory of "bubble travel" (Urry, 1990), where the tourist has the opportunity to observe a foreign culture without having to become immersed in it. This bubble insulates the consumers from the difficult aspects of life in a foreign environment and gives them the basic confidence to travel.

Phase 2—Idealized-Experience Seekers

Consumers in this phase are more affluent and have a base of overseas travel experience upon which to draw. With this experience comes greater confidence, which manifests itself in a desire for more adventurous, more flexible, and more individually orientated types of travel. They will tend to look further afield in either cultural or geographical terms for their holiday destinations.

Phase 3—Wide-Horizon Travelers

Phase 3 travel marks a further progression in affluence and travel experience. Consumers have the confidence to experiment with and experience a wider range of cultural environments, both similar and dissimilar to their own. Their desire for independence and flexibility manifests itself in more individually oriented travel to a wider range of destinations.

Phase 4—Total Immersers

Finally consumers reach a stage that is almost beyond tourism as it is currently understood. Their travel motivation is not one of wanting to experience an idealized version of a foreign culture, but rather to reproduce the cultural experience of a native of that country; to become exposed to and fully immersed in its language, culture, heritage, and patterns of life.

In effect, in this model increasing experience of leisure travel is taken as a crucial determinant of the dominant type of travel product consumers will demand. Travel from the United Kingdom provides obvious examples of Phase 1 behavior in the dominant form of packaged holidaytaking to Spain and other Mediterranean countries. Relatively few international tourists are operating in Phase 4 at the present time, but in the German market in particular (which is the most advanced in the world), there are indications that this type of travel motivation is beginning to manifest itself in various ways. The Henley Centre hypothesizes that by the turn of the century, about half of British holidaymakers abroad will be Phase 2, one-third Phase 1 and the rest Phase 3. This augurs well for holidays based around a particular activity such as skiing.

Many of these studies of tourism motivation and typologies, particularly Plog's and Cohen's, see a direct link between behavior of individuals in their own environment and the destinations they choose to visit. Other researchers have investigated this area in more depth.

DESTINATION CHOICE

Many studies of destination choice have analyzed personal values to determine why consumers choose a particular destination. Muller (1991) developed profiles for various segments in an international tourism market. He surveyed U.S. residents planning a pleasure trip to Toronto in 1987. The aim was to demonstrate the usefulness of profiling visitor segments in such a way that the importance of various tourism destination criteria could be attributed to specific value orientations. He believed that value-based data are easier to obtain than lifestyle profiles because a value survey is considerably shorter than a lifestyle questionnaire. The approach taken was to:

   a. isolate segments in the market, based on the importance visitors attach to several attributes of a city visit;
   b. develop value-based profiles of these segments; and
   c. assess the marketing implications of the value profiles for tourism product development and promotional strategies.

Analysis of his survey results produced, by way of cluster analysis, three distinct segments. Examination of the value orientations of people in the three tourism segments supported Muller's hypothesis that international visitors to Canadian cities can be meaningfully segmented by the importance they attach to touristic attributes, and such segments have distinctive personal value orientations.

Muller concluded that when the consumer is free to choose, personal values determine the choice of vacation destination. However, he does acknowledge that there are methodological limitations in collecting such personal data. People are reluctant to assign a low priority to what are obviously supposed to be important things in life to many people. Muller suggests that a creative breakthrough for teasing out real differences in value priorities (for telephone and mail surveys) would be a very welcome contribution to value-based market research.

In 1986, Shih reviewed the concept of Values and Lifestyles (VALS) and its use as an aid to Pennsylvania's tourism market research. VALS can be a useful tool for tourism market research. Lifestyle variables reveal something beyond demographics and are real, meaningful, and relevant. Shih found that the key VALS segments—belongers, achievers, and the socially conscious—provide valuable information about market segmentation, advertising copy appeals, and media selection.

Shih focused on perceptions and image as determinants of destination choice. Previous research has shown how perceptions of tourist regions strongly influence the choice of vacation destinations (La Page and Cormier, 1977). In many cases, it is probably the image of a place more than the factual information that produces a tourist's decision on where to travel. Shih's study attempted to determine how residents in the primary market area perceive Pennsylvania as a travel destination. Overall, Pennsylvania received favorable ratings on almost all important travel selection criteria by the key VALS segments, when it was compared with other states in the prime tourism market region. For example, the "friendly people factor" was rated highly for Pennsylvania by belongers, achievers, and the socially conscious. The image of the state perceived by the respondents was further analyzed by examining the differences between mean importance and mean performance rating on eight primary travel selection criteria. The smaller the differences, the more positive the image Pennsylvania has achieved on a particular travel selection factor. The beautiful scenery factor had the smallest difference, while the reasonable price factor had the largest difference.

Um and Crompton (1990) tested the role of attitudes in the pleasure travel destination choice process. Destination choice has been conceptualized as having two phases (Crompton, 1977). The first is a generic phase that addresses the fundamental issue of whether or not to have a vacation at all. Once the decision in favor of a vacation is made, the second phase is concerned with where to go. Um and Crompton explored the second phase, developing a framework of travel destination choice to provide a context for the study (see Figure 1.3).

The concepts used in the framework were described as external inputs, internal inputs, or cognitive constructs. External inputs were viewed as the sum of social interactions and marketing communications to which a potential traveler is exposed. Internal inputs derived from the socio-psychological set of a potential traveler, which includes personal characteristics, motives, values, and attitudes. Cognitive constructs represent an integration of the internal and external inputs into the awareness set of destinations and the evoked set of destinations.

The authors used a two-stage approach to travel destination choice based on the construct of this evoked set. The two stages were the evolution of an evoked set from the awareness set, and destination selection from the evoked set. A longitudinal approach was used to collect survey data from respondents at both stages in their decision process. Results of

FIGURE 1.3. A Model of the Pleasure Travel Destination Choice Process

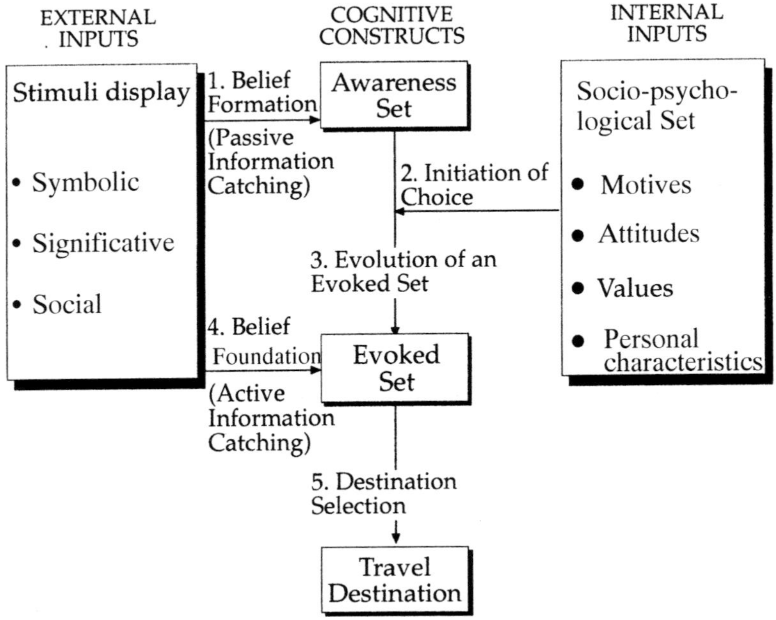

Based on: Um and Crompton, 1990.

the test suggested that attitude was influential in determining whether a potential destination was selected as part of the evoked set and in selecting a final destination.

Woodside and Lysonski (1989) also presented a model of traveler destination and choice. The model was built on the work of several propositions and research findings from cognitive and behavioral psychology, marketing, and travel and tourism (see Figure 1.4).

FIGURE 1.4. General Model of Traveler Leisure Destination Awareness and Choice

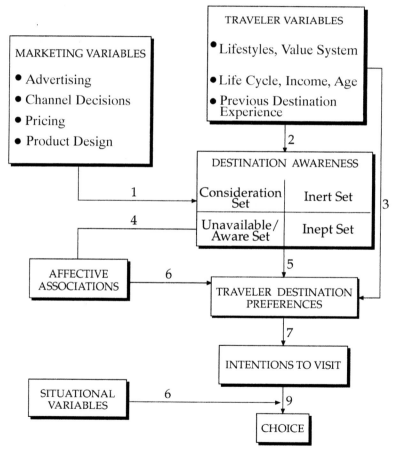

Based on: Woodside and Lysonski, 1989.

The authors tested the model with a small-scale, cross-sectional survey using students as respondents. The empirical evidence supported the basic accessibility hypotheses; the service or product that a consumer transfers from long-term memory into working memory in response to awareness is likely to be considered, and possibly chosen, for purchase. They concluded therefore that tracking target market populations' awareness of and preference for competing destinations should be recognized as a wise investment for measuring market performance and planning marketing actions. However, longitudinal research, using large samples of representative nonstudent populations, is needed before this conclusion can be universally accepted.

The need to study the destination-choice process has become more important in recent years as a result of the rapid growth of both travel demand and the tourist industry. Mansfeld (1992), in a review of the body of knowledge forming the basis of a theoretical framework for tourist destination choice processes, found a lack of a sound theoretical base for the issues involved. The majority of studies have narrowed their research perspective by investigating only tourists' preferences and destination-choice behavior. He believes that they need to go further and examine whether similar destination-choice patterns lead to similar spatial behavior among these tourists.

Concluding his review, Mansfeld recommends that future research in this area should incorporate two prevailing research strategies. One is the study of tourists' stated preferences; the other is the study of actual choice.

MODELS OF CONSUMER BEHAVIOR IN TOURISM

Zaltam and Burger (1975) define a model as a simplified but organized and meaningful representation of an actual system or process. It specifies both the key elements in a system—such as consumer beliefs and attitudes, situational factors, and purchasing behavior—and the relationships between these elements. The "grand models" of consumer behavior have been utilized or transformed by authors interested in the tourism choice process. They recognize that buyer behavior models are an extremely useful tool for planning and coordinating research studies.

An early attempt to provide some understanding of tourist purchase behavior was made by Wahab, Crampon, and Rothfield (1976). They acknowledge that the holiday purchase is unique in that there is (a) no tangible return on investment, (b) considerable expenditure in relation to earned income, (c) a purchase that is not spontaneous, and (d) an expenditure that involves saving and preplanning. The tourist is therefore resigned to a reduction of financial reserves and expects no economic return on the purchase of an intangible satisfaction. They stress however that this makes the tourist all the more sensitive to being disappointed. He or she will be embittered by anything or anybody who shatters the illusion.

They saw the tourist purchase decision based on the stages presented in the flow chart below (see Figure 1.5). They believed that all decision making goes through the same process, which may be instantaneous or take years, but which goes through the same steps. To conquer buying decisions, particularly the repeat buying decision that builds loyalty, the seller must "accompany" the buyer through the buying process, and adapt the marketing effort to that end.

Schmoll (1977) built a model based on the Howard and Sheth (1969) and Nicosia (1966) models of consumer behavior. Schmoll's model was based upon the following premises:

1. The decision process and its eventual outcome are influenced by four sets of variables: customer goals, travel opportunities, communications effort, and intervening or independent variables.
2. It is possible to identify these sets of variables and their individual components.
3. The eventual decision is in fact the result of a distinct process involving several successive stages or phases.

The model (see Figure 1.6) is composed of four fields:

Field 1: External stimuli such as trade publications
Field 2: Travel needs and desires determined by personality, socioeconomic factors, attitudes, and values
Field 3: External variables such as confidence in the travel agent, destination image, previous experience, and cost and time constraints
Field 4: Destination- or service-related characteristics that have a bearing on the decision process and its outcome

FIGURE 1.5. The Wahab, Crampon, and Rothfield Model of Consumer Behavior (1976)

FIGURE 1.6. The Travel Decision Process: A Model

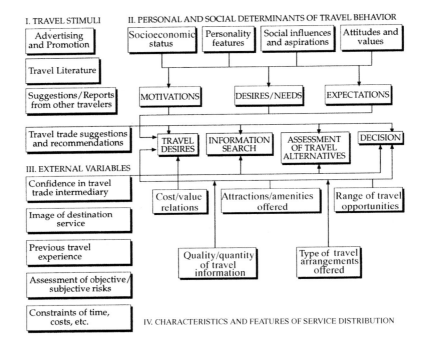

Based on: Schmoll, 1977.

Schmoll's model is descriptive—its purpose is to show the relevant variables and their interrelationships—but it cannot be quantified. Furthermore, the model is not a tool for prediction. It cannot serve as a basis for the forecasting of demand for a given destination or service. The author, however, sees real value in creating a model of the travel decision process, and believes it can be utilized in the following areas:

a. It indicates where marketing action can be used to influence the decision process.
b. It shows which factors have a bearing on travel decisions.
c. It can be used in research planning.
d. The model can be used to determine the criteria by which target markets of special interest to a tourism enterprise or destination can be identified.

Furthermore, Schmoll's is the only model that pays attention to constraints and their impact on the decision-making process.

Mayo and Jarvis (1981) believe that individual travel behavior can be explained by the length of the decision process and by the influence of psychological factors on a person's choices. After the decision to leave home has been made, other decisions such as where to go and what to do are made, utilizing several different decision-making approaches, ranging from the highly routine to the very extensive (see Figure 1.7).

When the traveler uses a routine decision-making approach, decisions are made quickly and with very little mental effort. At the other end of the continuum, extensive decision makers will spend considerable time and effort seeking information and evaluating the alternatives available.

According to Mayo and Jarvis, understanding how individual travelers make decisions also requires an insight into the psychological and social factors that influence their choices. Figure 1.8 illustrates that the decision-maker, located in the center of the diagram, is affected by both internal and social influences. The internal psychological factors that influence travel behavior are perception, learning, personality, motives, and attitudes. Perception is the process by which an individual selects, organizes, and interprets information to create a meaningful picture of the world. Learning refers to changes in an individual's behavior based on experiences. Personality is associated with the patterns of behavior and the mental structures that relate behavior and experience in an orderly way. Motives are thought of as internal energizing forces that direct a person's behavior toward the achievement of personal goals. Attitudes consist of knowledge and positive or negative feelings about an object, an event, or another person.

FIGURE 1.7. The Decision-Making Continuum

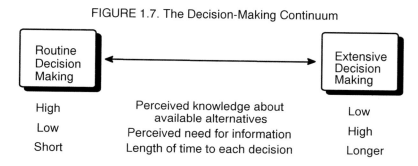

Based on: Mayo and Jarvis, 1981.

FIGURE 1.8. Major Influences on Individual Travel Behavior

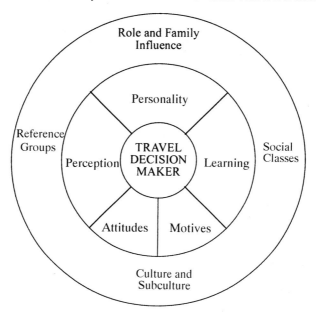

Based on: Mayo and Jarvis, 1981.

These psychological forces do not operate in a vacuum. Travel decisions are also affected by forces outside the individual, and by other people as well. Mayo and Jarvis's model groups these social influences into four major areas: role and family influences, reference groups, social classes, and culture and subcultures. However, the model does ignore external stimuli prominent in the other models, such as the market variables in the Woodside and Lysonski model and Schmoll's travel stimuli and external variables.

In the behavioral framework presented by Mathieson and Wall (1982), the decision-making process, as seen in Figure 1.9, involves five principal phases:

1. Felt need or desire for travel
2. Information collection and evaluation
3. Travel decisions
4. Travel preparations and travel experience
5. Travel satisfaction evaluation

FIGURE 1.9. The Tourist Decision-Making Process

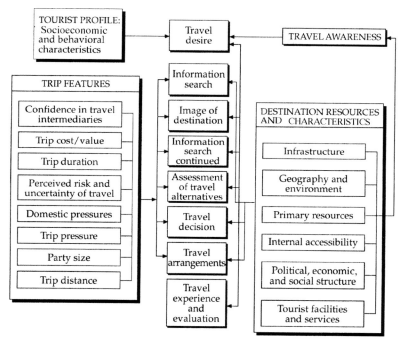

Based on: Mathieson and Wall, 1982.

The components that are itemized in the framework, and their interrelationships, influence each of the five decision phases. In their book, mainly dedicated to the impacts of tourism, the authors consider the framework under four major headings:

1. *The Tourist Profile.* This is viewed under the categories of the tourists' socioeconomic and behavioral characteristics.
2. *Travel Awareness.* Potential tourists may be motivated to travel but, unless they are informed about available opportunities, they may be unaware of the means of meeting their requirements. A tourist image is conjured up from the information received, as interpreted through the personal and behavioral characteristics of the tourist.
3. *Trip Features.* These include such factors as distance, duration of stay, time constraints, trip cost, party size, and perceived risk.

4. *Resources and Characteristics of Destinations.* These include types of attraction, the availability and quality of services, environmental conditions, the attributes of the host population, and their political organization.

Gilbert (1991) has criticized this model for omitting the important aspects of perception, memory, personality, and information processing, which is the basis of traditional models (although Mathieson and Wall could argue that these aspects are part of Travel Awareness in their model). Also, this, and other models, seem to ignore "type of holiday" in their trip features. With the increase in special interest and activity holidays, future models should take into account the plethora of holiday options available to the consumer. Despite its limitations however, the framework was designed solely to indicate that the impacts of tourism are the consequence of tourist decisions, and it recognizes that the impacts of tourism are dynamic, changing with corresponding changes in destination features, trip characteristics, and the personal and behavioral attributes of tourists.

One of the most recent models of vacation tourist behavior was presented by Moutinho in 1987 (see Figure 1.10). The model consists of a flow chart with three parts: (1) predecision and decision process, (2) postpurchase evaluation, and, (3) future decision making. Each part is composed of fields and subfields, linked by other concepts related to the tourist's behavioral process.

Part 1—Predecision and Decision Processes

This part is concerned with the flow of events, from the tourist stimuli to purchase decision. The fields included are preference structure (as a major process in the predecision phase), decision, and purchase. As the last two phases are outcomes of predecision, the model is more detailed in respect to this process, and its analysis includes the following subfields: stimulus filtration, attention and learning process, and choice criteria.

Moutinho saw the decision process as a series of conflicts with decisions based on perceived images, information from tourism destination promotion, previous experience, image of potential destinations, travel intermediaries, advice, or social interaction.

Part 2—Postpurchase Evaluation

This has three major purposes. First, it adds to the tourist's store of experiences. Second, postpurchase assessment provides a check on market-related decisions. Third, it provides feedback to serve as a basis for adjusting future purchase behavior.

FIGURE 1.10. Vacation Tourist Behavior Model

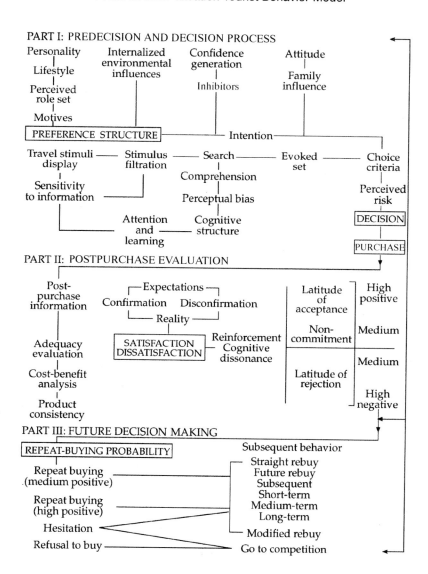

Based on: Moutinho, 1987.

Part 3—Future Decision Making

This is mainly related to the study of the subsequent behavior of the tourist by analyzing different probabilities for repeat buying.

The inclusion of postpurchase evaluation and future decision making in this model was an attempt by Moutinho to contribute to a global analysis of tourist behavior. But Gilbert (1991) has suggested that the last stage could have been incorporated in the first part of the model where issues of attitude, evoked set, and perception can be treated in a more complex way. He also argues that the subsequent behavior subfield is already encompassed in Part 2 of the model within the attitude outcome field of satisfaction or dissatisfaction.

A less comprehensive model of tourist-buyer behavior was presented by Middleton a year later (1988), which he called a "stimulus-response" buyer behavior model (see Figure 1.11). Middleton's diagram has four interactive components, with the central component identified as "buyer characteristics and decision process," which incorporates motivation. The first two components are inputs, most of which can be manipulated by marketing managers, while the final component represents the purchase output. The author has recognized the importance of friends and reference groups within the communication pro-

FIGURE 1.11. A Stimulus-Response Model of Buyer Behavior

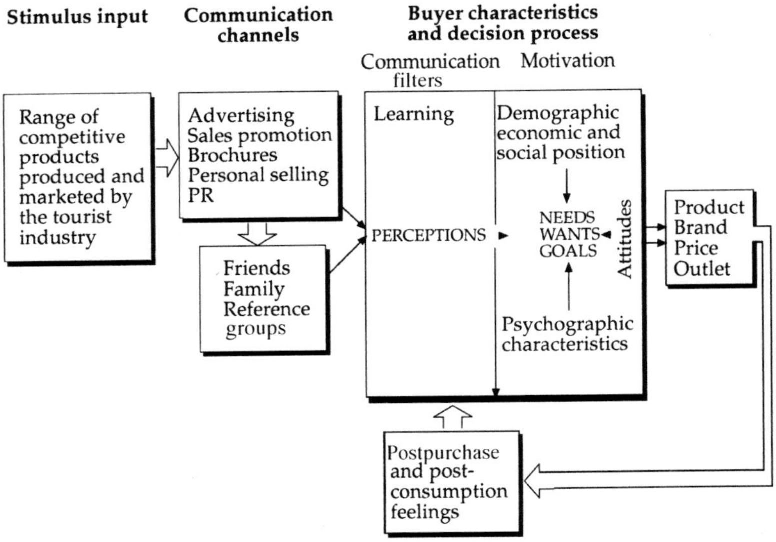

Based on: Middleton, 1988.

cess. Research suggests that information accessible to individuals through family, friends, and work colleagues can be extremely influential on purchase decisions (Wells and Gubar, 1966).

Middleton sees motivations as the dynamic process in buyer behavior, bridging the gap between the felt need and the decision to act or purchase. He emphasizes that actions on purchase are linked directly to motivations, which in turn are linked to the buyers' characteristics defined earlier in the model. The author also sees product satisfaction as the most powerful means of influencing future buyer behavior and provides a link in his model between postpurchase and the decision process. Moutinho has also provided this link in his model, but there is very little research into how much product satisfaction influences buyer behavior, and brand loyalty in tourism is very weak (Hodgson, 1991).

THE NONUSER

Not only is there a lack of research into the link between satisfaction and repeat purchase (or nonpurchase), the knowledge of the nonuser and the constraints facing this group is virtually nonexistent. In a wider context, authors on consumer behavior have occasionally referred to this group, usually during a discussion of user segmentation. For example, Evans, Moutinho, and Van Raaij (1996) distinguished among brand-loyal users, brand switchers, new users, and nonusers. However, they paid scant attention to the latter group, suggesting that they are an unattractive target group for marketers. Likewise, Loudon and Della Bitta (1993), in a section on usage segmentation, advise that marketing efforts should generally be aimed at light to heavy users rather than at nonusers. However, they do acknowledge that for many products, nonusers may represent a significant marketing opportunity, and with increased application of marketing research to understanding the motivations of different segments, greater success in converting nonusers to users should occur in the future.

For tourism, while research on nonusers is difficult, it is vital for marketers. Discovering why people are not purchasing the services provided by an organization is important, as most tourism organizations need to attract new customers if they are to thrive, or even survive. One should note the difficulty and high cost of finding out about nonusers as a major marketing challenge for those in the tourism industry. However, such research can help marketers identify different types of nonusers for whom different marketing messages need to be developed and transmitted. Such groups may be ex-users who need to be tempted back, those who are aware of the product but need to be persuaded to buy it, and those who are not aware of the product's existence.

Furthermore, an understanding of the constraints facing these groups can only help transform potential demand into purchase decisions.

Some authors have attempted to segment the travel market based on their constraints to travel. First, Stemerding et al. (1996) have suggested that travel segmentation models take constraint behavior explicitly into consideration. They propose a new integrated method that elicits the factors and constraints influencing leisure consumers' choice behavior, and on the basis of this, derives consumer segments. This involves (1) measuring the attributes influencing the respondents' leisure travel decisions, (2) identifying the role these attributes play in the decision-making process (constraints/rejection inducing attributes or tradeoff attributes), (3) deriving a preference function that allows positioning of leisure destinations on a preference scale, and (4) using the results to identify consumer segments. To this end, they developed a method derived from elements of the Repertory Grid methodology, the Decisions Plan Nets approach, and a choice-based scaling model. Four market segments resulted from this procedure, and the derived knowledge of the relevant preferences, constraints, and background profiles of the segment members enabled the authors to suggest relevant, segment-specific marketing strategies.

Second, Norman (1995) tried to identify homogeneous groups of individuals based on their perception of the influence of constraints to travel, as well as describing these market segments based on their motives for travel, level of involvement, past travel experience, travel intention, and a number of sociodemographic variables. To achieve these objectives, 544 individuals were questioned about the influence of perceived constraints on their decision to take a summer vacation trip. Factor analysis with a varimax rotation of the thirty-five constraints resulted in seven factors that accounted for 66.8 percent of the variance. A nonhierarchical cluster analysis procedure of the seven perceived constraint dimensions revealed a four-cluster solution.

Each cluster perceived different constraints on their travel decisions. For example, the largest group, Cluster IV (33.3 percent of respondents), identified the combination of friends and family and work commitments as having an influence on the generic travel decision. In addition, the results identified groups of respondents that were relatively unconstrained, those that were highly constrained, and those that report a high level of constraints but continue to participate at an unconstrained level.

SUMMARY AND CONCLUSIONS

Understanding the consumer's needs and buying process is the foundation of successful marketing. By understanding how buyers proceed through the decision-making process, the various participants in the buying procedure, and the major influences on buying behavior, marketers can acquire many clues about how to meet buyer needs.

Consumer behavior research in tourism has focused on motivations, typologies, destination choice, and the decision process itself. The "grand models" of consumer behavior have been transformed by authors interested in the tourism choice process. From a marketing point of view however, all of these models are not predictive, for two reasons. First, they are stereotypical and generalized whereas, in reality, the decision process will vary significantly among different groups of tourists. Second, they have no time dimension, so they do not indicate to the practitioner when to intervene in the process to influence the decision. In addition, just as in the marketing of consumer goods, people with a lack of motivation are ignored, typologies do not include the nonparticipant or nonuser, and the models (with the exception of Schmoll's) do not take into account the constraints facing consumers in the decision-making process. All of the models of consumer behavior in tourism assume that purchase is the outcome, and there is no reference to the negotiation of constraints. This lack of research into the nonuser and the associated constraints represents an important gap in consumer behavior research.

CONCEPT DEFINITIONS

Attitude: A person's enduring favorable or unfavorable cognitive evaluations, emotional feelings, and action tendencies toward some object, event, or another person.

Belief: A descriptive thought that a person holds about something.

Constraint: Any factor that comes between the preference for a product or an activity, and the purchase or participation.

Consumer: The person who uses a product or service.

Consumer behavior: The study of why people buy the products they do, and how they make decisions.

Learning: Changes in an individual's behavior arising from experience.

Model: A representation that seeks to illustrate and/or explain something.

Motive: A need that is sufficiently pressing to direct the person to seek satisfaction of that need.

Perception: The process by which an individual selects, organizes, and interprets information to create a meaningful picture of the world.

Personality: The patterns of behavior and the mental structures that relate behavior and experience in an orderly way.

Postpurchase behavior: The stage of the buying decision process in which consumers take further action after the purchase based on their level of satisfaction.

Psychographic: The analysis of people's lifestyles, perceptions, and attitudes as a method of segmentation.

Purchase decision: The stage of the buyer decision process in which the consumer actually buys the product.

Segmentation: The practice of dividing total markets up into subgroups that have similar characteristics.

Tourism: The activity in which people spend a short period of time away from home for business or pleasure.

Tourist: A consumer of tourism products.

REVIEW QUESTIONS

1. Discuss the main factors that might motivate tourists to take the following types of holiday:
   a. Snowboarding holiday in a fashionable mountain resort
   b. A cultural tour of Great Britain
   c. A beach holiday in the Caribbean
   d. Orangutan spotting in Borneo
2. Briefly review Maslow's motive hierarchy of needs. Cite three tourism products that might appeal to an individual at each stage of the hierarchy. Can you suggest any tourism product for which a marketer might be able to appeal to at least three stages at the same time?
3. Evaluate the potential applications of the main typologies of tourists and tourist behavior to the marketing of tourism products.
4. Of all the contemporary consumer behavior models summarized in the text, which do you think would be most valuable to the tourism marketer?
5. Why is the postpurchase behavior stage included in most models of the buying process?

REFERENCES

Cohen, E. (1972). Toward a Sociology of International Tourism. *Social Research,* 39(1), 164-182.

Crompton, J.L. (1977). A Systems Model of the Tourist's Destination Selection Process. Unpublished doctoral dissertation, Texas A&M University.

Crompton, J.L. (1979). Why People Go on Pleasure Vacation. *Annals of Tourism Research,* 6(4), 408-424.

Dann, G. (1977). Anomie, Ego-Enhancement and Tourism. *Annals of Tourism Research*, 4, 184-194.

Evans, M.J., Moutinho, L., and Van Raaij, W.F. (1996). *Applied Consumer Behavior.* Cornwall: Addison-Wesley.

Gallup Organization. (1989). *Unique Four Nation Travel Study Reveals Traveler Types.* London: American Express.

Gilbert, D.C. (1991). An Examination of the Consumer Behavior Process Related to Tourism. In Cooper, C. (Ed.), *Progress in Tourism*, 3, 78-105.

Hodgson, P. (1991). Market Research in Tourism: How Important Is It? *Tourism Management,* 12(4), 274-279.

Holloway, J.C. (1990). The Business of Tourism. Plymouth, UK: MacDonald and Evans.

Howard, J.A. and Sheth, J.N. (1969). *The Theory of Buyer Behavior.* New York: John Wiley.

Krippendorf, J. (1987). *The Holidaymakers.* London: Heinemann.

LaPage, W.F. and Cormier, P.L. (1977). Image of Camping—Barriers to Participation. *Journal of Travel Research,* 15(4), 21-25.

Loudon, D.L. and Della Bitta, A.J. (1993) *Consumer Behavior: Concepts and Applications.* London: McGraw-Hill.

Lowyck, E., Van Langenhove, L., and Bollaert, L. (1992). Typologies of Tourist Roles. In Johnson, P. and Thomas, B. (Eds.), *Perspectives on Tourism Policy,* 13-32. London: Mansell.

MacCannel, D. (1976). *The Tourist: A New Theory of the Leisure Class.* London: Macmillan.

Mannel, R.C. and Iso-Ahola, S.E. (1987). Psychological Nature of Leisure and Tourism Experience. *Annals of Tourism Research*, 14(3), 314-331.

Mansfeld, Y. (1992). From Motivation to Actual Travel. *Annals of Tourism Research*, 19(3), 399-419.

Maslow, S.H. (1943). A Theory of Human Motivation. *Psychological Review,* 50, 370-396.

Mathieson, A. and Wall, G. (1982). *Tourism: Economic, Physical and Social Impacts.* Harlow, UK: Longman.

Mayo, E. and Jarvis, L. (1981). *The Psychology of Leisure Travel.* Boston: CBI Publishing.

Middleton, V.T.C. (1988). *Marketing and Travel and Tourism.* Oxford, UK: Heinemann.

Mill, A.S. and Morrison, A.M. (1985). *The Tourism System: An Introductory Text.* Englewood Cliffs, NJ: Prentice-Hall.

Moutinho, L. (1987). Consumer Behavior in Tourism. *European Journal of Marketing,* 21(10), 1-44.

Muller, T.E. (1991). Using Personal Values to Define Segments in an International Tourism Market. *International Marketing Review,* 8(1), 57-70.

Murray, H.A. (1938). *Explorations in Personality.* New York: Oxford University Press.

Nicosia, F.M. (1966). *Consumer Decision Process: Marketing and Advertising Implications.* Englewood Cliffs, NJ: Prentice-Hall.

Norman, W. (1995). Perceived Constraints: A New Approach to Segmenting the Vacation Travel Market. Paper presented at the NRPA Symposium on Leisure Research, San Antonio, Texas.

Perreault, W.D., Darden, D.K., and Darden, W.R. (1977). A Psychological Classification of Vacation Life Styles. *Journal of Leisure Research,* 9, 208-224.

Plog, S.C. (1974). Why Destination Areas Rise and Fall in Popularity. *Cornell Hotel and Restaurant Quarterly,* 14(4), 55-58.

Schmoll, G.A. (1977). *Tourism Promotion.* London: Tourism International Press.

Shih, D. (1986). VALS as a Tool of Tourism Market Research. *Journal of Travel Research,* 26(4), 2-11.

Smith, S.L.J. (1990). A Test of Plog's Allocentric/Psychocentric Model: Evidence from Seven Nations. *Journal of Travel Research,* 28(4), 40-43.

Stemerding, M.P., Oppewal, H., Beckers, T.A.M., and Timmermans, H.J.P. (1996). Leisure Market Segmentation: An Integrated Preferences/Constraints-Based Approach. *Journal of Travel and Tourism Marketing,* 5(3), 161-185.

Stewart, F. (1993). UK Leisure Trends and the Prospects After Skiing. Paper presented at the 1993 National Ski Conference, Olympia, London.

Um, S. and Crompton, J.L. (1990). Attitude Determinants in Tourism Destination Choice. *Annals of Tourism Research,* 17(3), 432-448.

Urry, J. (1990). *The Tourist Gaze.* London: Sage.

Wahab, S., Crampon, L.J., and Rothfield, L.M. (1976). *Tourism Marketing.* London: Tourism International.

Wells, W. and Guber, G. (1966). Life Cycle Concepts in Marketing Research. *Journal of Marketing Research,* November, 355-363.

Westvlaams Ekonomisch Studiebureau, Afdeling Toeristisch Onderzoek. (1986). *Toeristische Gedragingen en Attitudes van de Belgen in 1985.* Brussels: Reeks Vakantieonderzoeken.

Witt, A. and Wright, P.L. (1992). Tourist Motivation: Life After Maslow. In Johnson, P. and Thomas, B. (Eds.), *Perspectives on Tourism Policy,* 33-55. London: Mansell.

Woodside, A.G. and Lysonski, S. (1989). A General Model of Traveler Destination. *Journal of Travel Research,* 27(4), 7-14.

Zaltam, G. and Burger, P.C. (1975). *Marketing Research—Fundamentals and Dynamics.* Hinsdale, IL: The Dryden Press.

PART II: DESTINATION SELECTION AND PRODUCT CHOICE

As discussed in Part I of the book, the process of destination selection is a crucial part of the study of tourism. Not only is destination selection important for the study of tourism, but it is perhaps the most important decision that any traveler must make. Part II highlights some of the reasons a particular destination is chosen, and also describes some marketing strategies used to make a destination desirable to potential customers.

Naturally, a destination must have something to attract travelers to it. Customers are usually pulled toward a destination with offerings to suit their needs and desires. Therefore, it is critical for marketing professionals to make the destination's offerings known to customers. Simultaneously, travelers will often research a destination on their own before making a purchase decision. In Chapter 2, Ewing and Haider describe one method used by tourists to make destination choices, called the Discrete Choice Experiment. This statistical modeling approach, which is based on utility theory, allows destination marketers to understand what customers prefer in a destination.

Likewise, customers must have a positive view of a particular destination to choose it above others. In short, the destination must maximize consumer benefits and minimize undesirable outcomes. The Means End Theory presented by Klenoski, Gengler, and Mulvey in Chapter 3 examines both the tangible and intangible attributes of the tourism product and measures their relative importance in influencing travelers to choose a particular destination.

Although it is of great importance to identify the factors that attract tourists to a destination, it is of even greater importance to identify those that inhibit potential tourists from selecting a particular destination. Chapter 4, written by Um and Crompton, explores the role of perceived inhibitors and facilitators in formulating a late evoked set of destinations from an early evoked set, and in selecting a final destination from the late evoked set of destinations.

Decrop, in a comprehensive review of the recent literature on tourist decision making (Chapter 5), describes and critiques the classical positivist methods of conceptualizing the decision-making process and discusses some of the more recent interpretivist and neomodern approaches.

In Chapter 6, the influence and relative weight of the husband versus wife in family tourism decision making is examined by Nichols and Snepenger, who studied the decision-making process of families who vacationed in Alaska. Based on the results of their study, the authors discovered significant behavioral differences among the three decision-making modes of "husband-dominant," "wife-dominant," and "joint decision making."

The process of communicating information to potential tourists in the prepurchase stage and the role of information in influencing tourist behavior are discussed by Crotts in Chapter 7. Based on an extensive review of current and past literature, Crotts examines the quantity, intensity, and type of information that tourists seek, the time when it is acquired, the credibility of the sources, and other relevant factors.

Although marketing plays an important role in determining whether a destination becomes or remains a success, it may be surprising to find that financial aspects do not play as great a role as one may believe. As Josiam and Hobson demonstrated in their Decoy Effect (Chapter 5), low prices are not always a deciding factor in destination selection.

Finally, as suggested by Hanefors and Mossberg in Chapter 9, once a destination has been chosen, especially in an all-inclusive package, future customer-loyalty may or may not occur. The effect of customer satisfaction on loyalty—along with the impact of a few other factors such as steady prices and quality of service—are analyzed and critiqued in this chapter.

Obviously, identifying the effects of every conceivable variable on destination selection and product choice is close to impossible. Instead, this part of the book has concentrated on describing and analyzing the most important and influential factors. It should be remembered while reading the following that many variables play a role in destination selection, but most are interrelated and therefore should not be thought of independently.

Chapter 2

Estimating What Affects Tourist Destination Choice

Gordon Ewing
Wolfgang Haider

LEARNING OBJECTIVES

By the end of the chapter the reader should:

- Understand the steps required to design a discrete choice experiment (DCE)
- Know how to make operational different types of attributes (product characteristics, environmental attributes) in a single discrete choice experiment
- Appreciate alternative methods of stimulus representation, written and pictorial, in a DCE
- Know how to use evidence from consumer choice behavior to estimate the importance of different features of a tourist destination
- Know how to estimate the monetary value of unpriced "goods," including attributes of a tourist destination or activity
- Know how to use the results of a discrete choice model to design a decision support system (DSS)
- Know how to use a DSS to estimate the sensitivity of demand to changes in a tourist destination's features
- Know how to use a DSS to show how attributes of alternatives are traded off by consumers

INTRODUCTION

How do tour operators or resort planners know which elements of a destination will appeal to clients and how can they determine the optimal price at which to market them? Expert judgment is the most common guide in making such decisions. As tourists become more sophisticated and suppliers try to cater to more specialized niche markets, expert judgment is often not enough. When a new or different product is being tried, or is transferred to a different country, past experience may be insufficient, because that kind of facility in that particular region or country has no track record. Also, in the case of many refinements to a facility that developers may consider, they will have no way of estimating whether they will attract sufficient users in a particular setting to make the investment worthwhile. For example, would the addition of a casino be an asset to a Caribbean island targeting affluent, empty-nester tourists interested in unspoiled natural landscapes? Again, there is unlikely to be enough experience to say with certainty. In each of the above cases a method exists that is widely used in market research to estimate the likely demand for a new or improved product, called stated preference analysis.

Stated preference research asks survey respondents to evaluate imaginary alternative products or services. This contrasts with revealed preference methods, which rely on consumers' actual past choices among alternative products. In both cases, researchers then infer statistically what features of the alternatives influence the different choices. The inference is based on knowing what alternatives each consumer had and what the attributes of each alternative were, including price. Of course revealed preference methods cannot be used if the products being evaluated are not available in the marketplace. This is where stated preference methods come into play. Put simply, researchers use stated preference methods to mimic the kinds of alternatives consumers face in the real world. The difference is that the alternatives may contain new attributes or new ranges of attribute values or new combinations of attributes not found in the real world. In stated preference research, many different sets of imaginary alternatives are designed, each containing two or more alternatives, each of which has different values or levels of a set of attributes that the researcher thinks may influence choice. Of the different stated preference methods involving preference ratings, rankings, or choices, the discrete choice experiment (DCE) is nowadays the most popular. Its major advantage is that it comes closest to mimicking the real world by asking each respondent to select one alternative from each of several sets of alternatives presented. Based on the choices made by many respondents among the hypothetical alternatives, the same statistical approach as in revealed preference analysis is used to infer the relative importance of each attribute in influencing choice.

This chapter describes the results of two DCEs used to assess the importance of various attributes of destinations to tourists in the Caribbean and northern Ontario, Canada. In the Caribbean study (Haider and Ewing, 1990) the emphasis is on estimating the relative importance of attributes concerning hotel proximity to beach, accommodation type, accessibility by air, hotel facilities, local area facilities, and price. These attributes are often called generic variables in the literature, because they are properties of all alternatives. In addition, it is often important to estimate the importance to tourists of labels identifying a destination, such as its country or the name of the hotel chain. We call these alternative-specific variables. In this study the interest was in country names, to know whether some countries had an advantage over others that was not related to any of the generic variables in the study. The statistical estimation method used, which is called multinomial logit regression, can be used to estimate the influence of these alternative-specific variables.

The second study (Haider and Carlucci, 1994), based in northern Ontario, focuses on how recreational anglers seeking a wilderness experience at remote fly-in fishing camps react to different degrees of presence of logging operations near the "remote" lake. It is the more complex of the studies and looks at the effect of twenty-two attributes on choice, including some depicted pictorially. Besides accommodation type, the attributes include accessibility, the quality and quantity of fish by species, crowding, the naturalness of the setting, and various measures of the presence of logging near the lake. This study also shows how the results of the statistical analysis of choice data can be used to design a decision-support system (DSS). This allows facility managers to simulate how changes in the values of the same attributes in real-world alternatives as were studied in the DCE are likely to affect a facility's competitiveness. The DSS can also be used to estimate the effect of introducing new types of alternative on the relative demand for other alternatives in a real choice set, if the alternatives are defined by the same attributes as in the DCE.

THEORETICAL BACKGROUND OF DISCRETE CHOICE EXPERIMENTS

The behavioral theory underlying discrete choice experiments is discrete choice theory, which is based on random utility theory (see Ben-Akiva and Lerman, 1985; McFadden, 1981; and Wrigley, 1985 for a fuller treatment). "Utility" is the economist's term for the desirability or attraction of some course of action or product. Briefly, random utility theory posits that the attraction or utility (U) of any object or course of action is made up of a "systematic" (V) and a "random" (ε) component, which is typically expressed as:

$$U = V + \varepsilon$$

The systematic component, V, is some function of the attributes of an alternative that most individuals consider and weigh when making a choice between alternatives. The random component, ε, relates to several factors that make it impossible to consider choice as a wholly deterministic process, as might be implied if there was only a systematic component. It includes idiosyncratic influences on choice, transitory influences, myriad small influences whose combined effect appears random, and other random effects that could result in the same individual not making the same invariable choice under identical circumstances. Given this random component, the probability of an individual choosing one alternative over another will depend on the relative sizes of the systematic components of their utilities compared with the size and sign of their random components. Also the more the systematic plus random components of one alternative's utility equal the sum of these two components in another alternative, the more equal is the chance of each being chosen. But the greater the difference in systematic components compared with the difference in random components, the more likely is the alternative with the larger systematic component to be chosen.

Clearly we need a formal rule that defines how the probability of choosing one alternative over one or more others is affected by their relative utilities. The most widely used is based on Luce's choice model (1959). It states that the probability of an alternative m being chosen from a set of M alternatives equals the size of m's utility to a respondent expressed as a ratio of the sum of the utilities of all M alternatives in the choice set. This can be written as:

$$p_m = \frac{U_m}{\sum\limits_{m=1}^{M} U_m} \tag{1}$$

where U_m is some function of attributes of alternative m and of the random component ε, typically of the form:

$$U_m = e^{\,a_m + \sum\limits_{k=1}^{K} b_k X_{km} + \varepsilon_m} \tag{2}$$

where

e is the base of natural logarithms and equals 2.718
a_m is the alternative-specific constant for alternative m
b_k is the generic effect of attribute k on an alternative's utility
X_{km} is the quantity of attribute k in alternative m
ε_m is the random component of alternative m's utility

Once choice information has been collected from a sufficient number of respondents, a form of multiple regression analysis, called multinomial logit regression, is used to estimate the coefficients a_m and b_k, $k = 1, \ldots, K$ in Equation (2). It is beyond the scope of this chapter to discuss the actual estimating equation, but note that it is the estimated coefficients, b_k, $k = 1$, $\ldots$, K, which are used to measure the effects of each attribute. If, as often, an attribute is defined in terms of $n \geq 2$ discrete levels, a separate coefficient can be estimated for $n - 1$ of the levels. If the mth alternative in every choice set is always associated with the same unique feature such as the name of a country or hotel chain, the coefficient a_m, $m = 1, \ldots, M$, can be estimated for all but one country or hotel chain. By definition the coefficient for the remaining alternative is zero. Equation 2 can be rewritten as:

$$U_m = e^{a_m} e^{b1\ X_{1m}} \ldots e^{b_K\ X_{Km}} + \varepsilon_m \tag{3}$$

Each term with the base e in Equation (3) is called a part-worth and refers to the contribution that a particular attribute value, X_k, makes to the utility of an alternative. Note that the part-worths are multiplicative. If, for example, the part-worth associated with a particular level of an attribute equals 1.2, this means that it multiplies the utility of an alternative by 1.2, or put another way, it increases the alternative's utility by 20 percent.

A MODEL OF CHOICES OF HYPOTHETICAL DESTINATIONS ON FIVE CARIBBEAN ISLANDS

In the winter of 1985-1986, 159 respondents in Ottawa, Ontario, were recruited by travel agents to complete a survey that included a discrete choice experiment. The sample cannot be considered random because agents were free to forward the questionnaire to any of their clients whom they knew had previously taken a package vacation trip to the Caribbean. Each respondent was required to complete one of six versions of a questionnaire, each containing a different group of nine choice sets.

An issue facing island states in the Caribbean is how to ensure that more of the economic benefits of tourism remain within the local economy. Often, local developers have access neither to the substantial amounts of capital required to build large hotels, nor to sophisticated international marketing and reservation systems. At the same time, foreign developers from North America or Europe do have the capital, and tour operators typically find it easier to deal with a few large hotels than many small ones. Given this context of local needs and the global economic system, the question emerged whether alternative and smaller types of accommodation, combined with locally provided auxiliary services, would be attractive to tourists. Consequently, an experiment needed to be designed that would allow for the modeling of both the standard large-scale type of development and the small-scale adaptive types of development. This task was accomplished by specifying attributes related to accommodation size, amenities offered on the premises, amenities found in the vicinity of the accommodation, location of the accommodation in relation to the beach and local residences, convenience of access by air, and price.

Therefore a concern in the study by Haider and Ewing was to estimate the part-worth of different hotel sizes as defined by three different numbers of rooms. As can be seen in Table 2.1, the larger hotels, as measured by the number of rooms, are only marginally less attractive to respondents than the twelve-room hotel and the difference is not statistically significant. Note also that one level of this and the other three-level attributes is, with no loss of generality, implicitly equal to zero and therefore its part-worth is equal to one.

TABLE 2.1. Estimated Regression Coefficients and Part-Worths of Attributes and Countries

	Level	Reg. Coefficient	t statistic[a]	Part-worth
Accommodation				
Hotel size	12 rooms 60 rooms 250 rooms	[b] 0 − .055 − .063	 − 1.04 − 1.21	1 .95 .94
Hotel facilities	restaurant (r) r, shops and entertainment (r, se) r, se, sport facilities (r, se, s)	− .428 − .211 [b] 0	− 7.86 − 4.12	[c] .65 [c] .81 1
Area around accommodation				
Location	in a town close to a town in a rural area	[b] 0 .075 .117	 1.42 2.20	1 1.08 [c] 1.12

Proximity to beach	on beach 10-minute walk 30-minute walk	[b] 0 − .741 − 1.11	 − 14.80 − 17.75	1 [c] .48 [c] .33
Access by air	must change to a local flight 1-hour drive from direct flight 25-min. drive from direct flight	[b] 0 .027 .18	 .50 3.46	1 1.03 [c] 1.20
Other hotels within 3 miles	none few many	[b] 0 .137 .097	 2.58 1.88	1 [c] 1.15 [d] 1.10
Walking time to other restaurants	none within 30 minutes 30 minutes 10 minutes	[b] 0 .125 .235	 2.32 4.44	1 [c] 1.13 [c] 1.26
Walking time to other shops & entertainment	none within 30 minutes 30 minutes 10 minutes	[b] 0 .137 .152	 2.75 2.90	1 [c] 1.15 [c] 1.16
Walking time to other sport facilities	none within 30 minutes 30 minutes 10 minutes	[b] 0 .001 .164	 .06 3.14	1 1 [c] 1.18
Package price		− .00279	− 15.95	[c,e] .76
Destination country				
Barbados		.742	3.33	[c] 2.10
Cuba		.057	.08	1.06
Jamaica		.276	1.11	1.32
Martinique		.834	3.81	[c] 2.30
St. Vincent		.647	2.93	[c] 1.91

[a]   − 1.96 ≥ t ≥ 1.96 is statistically significant at the 5% level; − 1.64 ≥ t ≥ 1.64 is significant at the 10% level.
[b]   Implicit default value of coefficient for base level of that attribute (not estimated in regression), against which estimated coefficients of other levels are compared.
[c]   Significantly different from 1 at the 5% level.
[d]   Significantly different from 1 at the 10% level.
[e]   Part-worth of CAN$100 in 1985.

By contrast, the nature of facilities does make a difference. Compared with a hotel having not only its own restaurant but also shops and entertainment and sports facilities (r, se, s), one with only a restaurant (r) has a part-worth that is .65 of the former. Put another way, the odds of the average respondent choosing a restaurant-only hotel are about two-thirds that of choosing a hotel with the maximum range of facilities, other things being equal. Of course, generally, other things, particularly price, are not equal, assuming two hotels of otherwise equal quality have different levels of facilities. A useful aspect of these regression coefficients is that they can be used to estimate the equivalent monetary value of additional facilities. In other words, we can estimate how much more can be charged for additional facilities without making a hotel less attractive than its competitor with fewer facilities. To do so, we write an equation setting the part-worths of, say, the lowest level of facilities (r) equal to the part-worth of price *(Price)* and solve for the value of price that makes the two sides of the equation equal. Therefore, we write:

$$\exp(-.428) = \exp(-.00279 \, Price) \qquad (4)$$

Since both sides have a common base, *e*, it is simpler to equate the exponents and solve for the value of *Price* as follows:

$$-.428 = -.00279 \, Price$$

$$\therefore Price = -\frac{.428}{-.00279} = 153.41$$

Therefore, we can estimate that a hotel with shopping, entertainment, and sports facilities in addition to its restaurant could charge about CAN$153 more per client per week in 1986 than an equivalent quality of hotel that had only a restaurant. As we will see below, we can repeat this simple exercise of estimating the monetary value of an amenity for any of the other attributes including the country effect.

Regarding a hotel's location, if it is away from any town its utility increases by 12 percent (part-worth = 1.12). Of course in real life there may be other amenities, such as varied shopping, bars, and restaurants typically associated with towns, which would compensate for staying in a hotel that was close to or in a town. We will find whether that is the case when we look at the separate part-worths of these amenities. The part-worth of 1.12 for a hotel in a rural area tells us that, other things being equal, the average respondents would prefer a rural setting for their hotel. The odds are some 12 percent higher that they will choose a rural rather than an urban hotel, other things being equal.

A primary reason many tourists go to the Caribbean is to be able to relax on an oceanside beach. Just how important is it for their hotel to be on the beach rather than, say, ten minutes' walk from it? The answer can be found in the difference in the part-worths of the two locations. A hotel that is ten minutes' walk from the beach is less than half as likely to be chosen (part-worth = 0.48) as one on the beach. Of course, Caribbean destinations promote themselves largely as beach vacation destinations and the respondents surveyed were people who had presumably responded to that image. Therefore we should bear in mind that this finding should not be generalized to the entire population. Nevertheless, for that fraction of the population that visits the Caribbean to enjoy the beach, a major penalty is associated with hotels not on the beach. Again, we can easily calculate the price premium people are willing to pay to have a hotel on the beach rather than ten minutes' walk away. It turns out to have been worth CAN$266 in 1986 dollars, which is calculated using Equation (4) by dividing the regression coefficient for a ten-minute walk to the beach ($-.741$) by the regression coefficient for price. Put otherwise, a hotel ten minutes from the beach would have had to charge $266 less than its equivalent on the beach to be equally attractive. A hotel half an hour from the beach would have had to charge almost $400 less. Given that prices in the experiment ranged from $690 to $1,450, these results mean the price penalty for owners of hotels not on the beach is high if they are to compete for the attention of beach-oriented tourists.

Some Caribbean islands can be reached by direct flight from major cities such as Toronto and Montreal. However, to reach some islands it is necessary to change planes in the region and complete the journey by a local carrier. In addition some hotels are closer to the destination airport than others. Due to one or other of these circumstances, difficult access reduces the enjoyment of a vacation. The part-worths in Table 2.1 show that changing planes and long rides from the airport to the hotel both reduce the utility of the vacation by about 20 percent compared with a destination less than half an hour's ride from an airport with a direct flight home (whose part-worth is 1.20). This translates into a premium of about $65 in the price of a package to the more conveniently located hotel twenty-five minutes from the flight home.

Clients do not always prefer the maximum or minimum quantity of an attribute. For example, people generally prefer an intermediate quantity of beverage sweeteners. The same would appear to be the case for the number of hotels within three miles. The most preferred of the three levels was "a few" (part-worth = 1.15) rather than "none" or "many" (the part-worth is one for the former and not significantly different from one for the latter). This may be caused by tourists feeling insecure in a wholly nontourist environment while not enjoying densely developed resorts. An advantage of defining an attribute categorically by levels rather than as a single continuous variable is that it allows this type of nonmonotonic preference to be detected.

As for proximity to other services, respondents were progressively more satisfied the closer other restaurants were to their hotel. Indeed, of the three sets of other facilities mentioned, restaurants were the ones to which proximity mattered most (see part-worths in Table 2.1). This may partly reflect the fact that they were told the vacation package did not include meals. By contrast, with shopping and entertainment, people simply wanted them within a half-hour's walk (part-worth = 1.15) but attached no additional premium to their being closer than that. This may be because an activity such as shopping on a Caribbean vacation is associated in people's minds with strolling around a town center. By contrast, trips to restaurants may be seen as both more purposeful and more frequent and therefore should be more convenient to the tourist's hotel.

Sports facilities that were half an hour's walk away from the hotel were just as bad as having none within that distance. Being within a ten-minute walk made a significant difference (part-worth = 1.18). So although a hotel with off-site restaurants within a half hour's walk was preferred over one that had none within that distance, there was no advantage to a hotel whose nearest sports facilities were a half-hour's walk distant versus one where they were even farther away. In this sense, tourists are less likely to choose or return to a hotel where the nearest sports facilities are half an hour away than one where the nearest restaurant is that far away.

These results give the impression that people do not mind a stroll of up to half an hour to reach restaurants, shops, and entertainment, but that they find such a distance inconvenient if they plan to use sports facilities, for which a handy location is more important. For eating out, given its more frequent occurrence, they preferred restaurants to be even closer, although willing to walk up to half an hour.

The part-worth of price is best envisaged as the disutility of a higher price, which in Table 2.1 is set at $100 for the sake of realism. The part-worth of .76 is simply the base e raised to the power of the regression coefficient ($-.00279$) times 100. In an experiment where prices ranged from $690 to $1,450, a part-worth of .76 for a $100 price difference means that if two travel agencies were selling the same package vacation to the same hotel at a $100 price difference, the dearer would attract .76/(1 + .76) or 43 percent of clients and the cheaper would attract the balance, 57 percent.

The part-worths of the five countries show their relative desirability as tourist destinations in the mid-1980s. Martinique, with a part-worth of 2.30 was preferred by over twice as many respondents as Cuba, the least preferred of the five islands. Barbados and St. Vincent were the other two preferred destinations. Jamaica, with its reputation at that time for a high crime rate, was much less attractive. The fact that Cuba rated lowest of the five islands in the mid-1980s with the Canadian sample possibly relates to the image of Cuba as providing cheap but lower quality accommodation and food. It is also the only one of the five islands where Spanish is the local language. On the other four English or French is the language, both of which residents of Ottawa would either speak or have some knowledge of. Being seen as a communist dictatorship may also have adversely affected Cuba's attractiveness to Canadian tourists. Again the regression coefficients can be used to estimate how much cheaper a Cuban vacation package, for example, would have to be to be equally preferred to a package vacation in Martinique. We simply have to calculate what amount of money saved by choosing a cheaper package compensates for the difference in Cuba's utility or part-worth compared with Martinique's. The latter difference is .057 − .834, i.e., − .777. We then solve for *Price* in the following equation:

$$-.00279 \, Price \; = \; -.777$$

$$\therefore Price \quad = \frac{-.777}{-.00279}$$
$$= 278.49$$

The Cuban package would have to be priced $278 cheaper than the equivalent Martinique package to be equally attractive.

The above results show not only how much insight can be gained into the relative weight tourists place on various destination factors, but also how price can be adjusted to compensate for negative factors or to capitalize on positive ones.

A DISCRETE CHOICE EXPERIMENT ON REMOTE FLY-IN RECREATIONAL ANGLING IN NORTHERN ONTARIO

The second example represents an application of the DCE in resource-based tourism. It will show how this stated preference method can be applied beyond market research to resource management, if a series of environmental variables is included.

Remote fly-in tourism in northern Ontario is a distinctive form of resource-based tourism and makes a significant contribution to the northern Ontario economy. Remote fly-in tourism relies mostly on the consumptive activities of fishing and hunting in pristine, roadless forest settings. Accommodations are provided in the form of lodges or outpost camps, both of which are accessible by float plane only. Because of the emphasis on proximity to nature and perceived wilderness, this form of tourism is particularly sensitive to disturbances by other land uses, of which logging is the most common. The major effects of logging activities on remote tourism are noise from harvesting equipment and forest road traffic, aesthetics from cut areas that are visible from the ground, lakes, or air, and access from newly constructed forest roads that provide access for road-based anglers and hunters to previously remote areas.

Such a multivariate phenomenon cannot be researched adequately with a revealed preference approach as long as no comprehensive database exists about remote tourism establishments, and given the impracticality of collecting and measuring actual information about relevant environmental aspects. The vastness and inaccessibility of the landscape in northern Ontario further exacerbate the difficulty of doing revealed preference research.

Table 2.2 shows the experimental attributes and their respective levels used in this study. Most of these attributes and their levels were determined from focus group sessions with actual remote anglers (Daniel and Orland, 1995), and in meetings with representatives of the tourism sector and resource managers. Some attributes describe the type and quality of the accommodation, the price for such a vacation, and the travel distance from home to the destination. The majority of attributes describe activity-specific resource characteristics or the environmental setting. For remote fly-in fishing, fishing quality, defined by the type and number of fish and associated catch restrictions, is of prime importance, together with an indication of the intensity of other tourists' use of the destination lake. The subset of attributes describing logging begin with the presence/absence of logging in the vicinity of the destination lake, and then distinguish among a number of important logging-related attributes in more detail. A pre-survey (Haider and Carlucci, 1994) proved the difficulty of developing meaningful profiles about logging in written form. Therefore, these attributes were presented visually in an oblique aerial perspective, in which the salient attributes were controlled digitally (Orland, Daniel, and Haidler, 1995). Thus, each hypothetical profile combined written and visual stimuli (see Figure 2.1). Two such profiles were combined in one choice set and respondents simply selected between the left and right alternatives. If neither of these alternatives was acceptable, the respondents also had the option of selecting another "nonremote" fishing trip, or not to go fishing at all. The design required a total of 128 choice sets for the estimation of all main effects and selected interaction effects. These 128 choice sets were divided into eight blocks of 16 choice sets each, so that each respondent evaluated 16 choice sets (Anderson et al., 1995).

Data were collected in the winters of 1994 and 1995 at eight travel trade shows in the American Midwest (Michigan, Illinois, Wisconsin, and Min-

TABLE 2.2. Sensitivity Table for American Plan Lodge for Remote Tourism DSS

Attribute	Level	Lodge A	Lodge B	Other	No fish
Base case		*47.8%*	*47.8%*	*3.4%*	*1.0%*
Price	$590	5.7%	− 5.2%	− 0.4%	− 0.1%
	$725	3.7%	− 3.4%	− 0.2%	− 0.1%
	$860[1]	0.0%	0.0%	0.0%	0.0%
	$995	− 4.8%	4.4%	0.3%	0.1%
	$1,130	− 9.8%	9.0%	0.6%	0.2%
Wildlife	*frequent wildlife along shore*	0.0%	0.0%	0.0%	0.0%
	occasional wildlife along shore	− 2.1%	2.0%	0.1%	0.0%
Crowding	*small lodge only*	0.0%	0.0%	0.0%	0.0%
	large lodge only	− 7.4%	6.8%	0.5%	0.1%
	small lodge, occasional fly-in users	− 3.9%	3.6%	0.3%	0.1%
	large lodge with another lodge on lake	− 8.8%	8.0%	0.6%	0.2%
Travel distance	500 km	1.2%	− 1.1%	− 0.1%	− 0.0%
	750 km	0.0%	0.0%	0.0%	0.0%
	1000 km	− 3.1%	2.9%	0.2%	0.1%
	1250 km	− 8.1%	7.4%	0.5%	0.2%
Fly time	15 min	2.9%	− 2.7%	− 0.2%	− 0.1%
	30 min	0.8%	− 0.7%	− 0.1%	0.0%
	37.5 min	0.0%	0.0%	0.0%	0.0%
	45 min	0.6%	0.6%	0.0%	0.0%
	60 min	− 1.3%	1.2%	0.1%	0.0%W
Walleye	*excellent*	0.0%	0.0%	0.0%	0.0%
	good	5.3%	4.8%	0.3%	0.1%
Pike	*excellent*	0.0%	0.0%	0.0%	0.0%
	good	− 4.2%	3.8%	0.3%	0.1%
Trout	*good*	0.0%	0.0%	0.0%	0.0%
	none	− 4.2%	3.8%	0.3%	0.1%
Bass	*good*	0.0%	0.0%	0.0%	0.0%
	none	− 2.3%	2.1%	0.2%	0.0%
Limits	*6 fish limit, no size restrictions*	0.0%	0.0%	0.0%	0.0%
	6 fish limit,1 trophy	− 0.7%	0.6%	0.0%	0.0%
	3 fish limit, 1 trophy	− 6.6%	6.1%	0.4%	0.1%
	catch and release only, 1 trophy	− 15.2%	13.9%	1.0%	0.3%

TABLE 2.2 (continued)

Attribute	Level	Lodge A	Lodge B	Other	No fish
Size	mostly moderate size fish, occasional trophy	−2.8%	2.5%	0.2%	0.1%
	mostly moderate size fish, often a trophy	−3.4%	3.1%	0.2%	0.1%
	moderate to large size fish, occasional trophy	−3.8%	3.4%	0.2%	0.1%
	moderate to large size fish, often a trophy	0.0%	0.0%	0.0%	0.0%
Noise	no shore noise	0.0%	0.0%	0.0%	0.0%
	occasional noise in the distance	−6.0%	5.4%	0.4%	0.1%
	occasional noise near the lake	−7.9%	7.3%	0.5%	0.1%
Buffer	100 m	−6.5%	5.8%	0.6%	0.2%
	500 m	−6.3%	5.6%	0.5%	0.2%
	1000 m	−6.1%	5.4%	0.5%	0.1%
	3000 m	0.0%	0.0%	0.0%	0.0%
Residual	none	−5.7%	5.1%	0.5%	0.1%
	hardwood	−5.4%	4.8%	0.5%	0.1%
	conifer patches	0.0%	0.0%	0.0%	0.0%
	conifer single	−6.3%	5.6%	0.5%	0.2%
Road	none	0.0%	0.0%	0.0%	0.0%
	50-100 m	−7.0%	6.3%	0.6%	0.2%
	500 m	−0.2%	0.2%	0.0%	0.0%
	2000 m	2.0%	−1.8%	−0.2%	−0.0%
Forest	conifer	0.3%	−0.3%	−0.0%	−0.0%
	mixed wood	0.0%	0.0%	0.0%	0.0%
Cut size	large	0.0%	0.0%	0.0%	0.0%
	small	−0.3%	0.3%	0.0%	0.0%
Cut shape	irregular	2.3%	−2.1%	−0.2%	−0.1%
	regular	0.0%	0.0%	0.0%	0.0%
Cut number	single	−0.0%	0.0%	0.0%	0.0%
	multiple	0.0%	0.0%	0.0%	0.0%
Cut age	fresh brown	0.0%	0.0%	0.0%	0.0%
	greened-up	0.6%	−0.5%	−0.0%	−0.0%

[1] Italicized items represent the default attribute levels used to calculate the base case's market shares.

FIGURE 2.1. Sample Choice Set from Vincent's Ontario Study

Area immediately around your facility on the destination lake

Example: view 4-6 miles away

Example: shoreline view

Accommodation:
American plan lodge
4-day $530, 7-day $725
Only lodge on the lake, small
(20-30 people)
30 minute fly-in time

Setting:
Frequent wildlife along shore
Occasional noise near the
lake

Fishing:
Excellent walleye fishing
Excellent northern pike fishing
No lake trout fishing
Good bass fishing

Limits and Expectations:
3 fish possession limit, only
one trophy size
Mostly moderate size fish,
often a trophy

Distance:
375-525 miles (long day
drive)

nesota) and in Ontario. A total of 1,059 visitors were recruited for the study, and they completed a self-administered survey instrument on-site.

The results are presented differently from the first case study. Because the model is so large and involves twenty-two attributes with seventy-three estimated parameters, b_k, we do not report them here (see Haider and Carlucci, 1994 for details). If we insert each of the estimated parameters, b_k, into Equation 2 and multiply each by any desired level of the kth attribute, X_{km}, we obtain the estimated utility, U_m, of an imaginary alternative. If we then calculate U_m for a different alternative, i.e., one with a different amount or level of at least one attribute from the first alternative, Equation 1 can be used to calculate what proportion of anglers is likely to choose each alternative or neither. Hence the part-worths, $e^{b_k X_{km}}$, can be used to calculate market shares of alternatives in hypothetical scenarios. Based on this principle, exploring the changes associated with many different scenarios is possible in a PC-based decision support system (DSS), in which calculations of market shares are performed instantaneously. The DSS runs as a standalone Windows application and therefore can be distributed widely and used by virtually anybody interested; e.g., tourist operators, resource managers, and other stakeholders. Figure 2.2 shows the user interface of this DSS. As in the survey instrument, the DSS compares two remote destinations and calculates the associated market shares. The user can alter profiles for either of the lodges to discover how their market shares will change.

Each row of percentages in Table 2.2 shows how market shares change as the level of one attribute of Lodge A is changed while the values of Lodge B's attributes remain fixed at the base case's levels. In the base case each lodge has the attribute levels shown in italics. Generally speaking, these are the most preferred level of each attribute, except for price, travel distance, and flying time where an intermediate level is used. In effect each row of Table 2.2 shows the sensitivity of market share to change in any attribute of Lodge A. Of course if the change increases Lodge A's market share, Lodge B's will decrease, as will the support for both other alternatives, namely another type of angling trip or not angling. Note that changes associated with any one attribute are proportional changes, and will be largest when a market share is around 50 percent, and will decline as a market share approaches either zero or 100 percent.

In the base case, each lodge would receive 47.8 percent market share, while 3.4 percent of clients would select another type of fishing trip, and 1.0 percent would not fish. Readers are reminded that the model presented here is a probabilistic model and, therefore, even under optimal conditions, a small portion of respondents will still choose neither lodge alternative.

FIGURE 2.2. OMNR Fly-In Fishing Share Simulator

	OUTPOST 1	OUTPOST 2	OTHER	DO NOT GO
Water:	running water	running water		
Price 4 Day/7 Day:	$590 $854	$590 $854		
Recreation:	frequent wildlife along shore	frequent wildlife along shore		
Crowding:	no other fishermen on the lake	no other fishermen on the lake		
Fishing:				
Walleye/N. Pike:	excellent excellent	excellent excellent		
Lake Trout/Bass:	good good	good good		
Limits:	6 fish; no size restrictions	6 fish; no size restrictions		
Fish Size:	large; often trophy	large; often trophy		
Travel Distance:	875-1125 miles	875-1125 miles		
Fly-in Time:	60 minutes	60 minutes		
Noise:	no shore noise	no shore noise		
Pristine:	YES	YES		
Share 4 Day/7 Day:	26.03% 21.04%	26.03% 21.04%		
Total Market Share:	47.07%	47.07%	4.03%	1.82%
Base Share:	47.07%	47.07%	4.03%	1.82%
Change in Share:	0.00%	0.00%	0.00%	0.00%
Change %:	0.00%	0.00%	0.00%	0.00%

Source: Ontario Ministry of Natural Resources   Intelligent Marketing Systems Inc.

Among the attributes of the tourism product, vacation price is one of the most significant. An increase of $135 for a seven-day package decreases market share by 2.0 percent in the lowest price range ($590 to $725), and 5.0 percent in the highest price range ($995 to $1,130). Respondents also prefer a small lodge (twenty to thirty clients) over a large lodge (sixty to eighty clients), as is evident by a 7.4 percent drop in Lodge A's market share when it is changed from small to large. Interestingly, adding occasional fly-in day users in the case of a small lodge, and adding a second lodge on the same lake in the case of a large lodge have little effect on preferences. Each 250-kilometer increment in travel distance has a progressively more negative impact on market share. At one extreme, the increase from 500 to 750 kilometers decreases market share by 1.2 percent. At the other, an increment from 1,000 to 1,250 kilometers decreases it by 5.0 percent. Increasing fly-in time from the airbase to the remote lake by float plane is associated with a decay in market share of approximately 1 percent for every 15 additional minutes of flying time.

Attributes relating to fishing quality and the fishing experience indicate that a decline in the numbers of any one of the fish species is associated with a significant decline in market share. Among these fish species, walleye is an essential prerequisite for remote tourism and any decline in the abundance of this species will contribute to a significant decline in market share. During the interviews, a glossary explained to respondents that excellent fishing quality implied a catch rate of twenty to twenty-five walleye per day, while a good catch rate referred to ten to twelve walleye a day. Pike is considered almost equally important. The two other species in the model, lake trout and bass are of generally lesser importance and were, therefore, modeled as being either available or not available. As such, having either one of those species available will add to the desirability of the experience.

Most anglers prefer the current possession limit of six fish per day. Anglers are not sensitive to being allowed only one trophy fish, but are to a reduction of the possession limit to three fish a day (− 6.6 percent) and even more so to being restricted to catch-and-release fishing only (− 15.2 percent). Changes to the expected catch size of fish, by contrast, cause no more than a modest decline of 3.8 percent. These findings suggest that reducing the possession limit would be an unpopular management action with most remote anglers, presumably because one of the primary reasons for visiting these remote locations is a superb fishing experience that includes keeping fish.

Finally, the effects of different types of logging on an angler's choice of destination is indicated by a last set of attributes. All the differences in logging methods show the expected effects. Noise at some distance from the lake causes a 6 percent decline in visitation, while noise close to the lake increases that decline to 7.9 percent. Among the visual attributes, decreasing the buffer size (i.e., distance between the fishing lake and the clearcut) from 3,000 m to 1,000 m is associated with a 6.1 percent decline of visitors.

In this overall model, the market share does not decline much further if the buffer is narrowed to 500 m and even to 100 m. Conifer patches are the most preferred type of residual. The presence of a primary logging road within 100 m of the lake is perceived as highly detrimental to the angling experience. A regularly shaped cut block is less preferred than an irregular cut block. The size and the number of cutovers did not produce any significant results. The preference for a greened-up cut over a fresh brown cut is small in the case of a 3,000 m buffer, but changes dramatically in the narrower buffer situations, as is explained in Figure 2.3.

All these findings are intuitively plausible and by and large confirm many of the arguments that typically emerge during land-use planning conflicts, during which these effects are acknowledged in the form of

FIGURE 2.3. Interaction Between Buffer Size and Age of Cut on Market Share

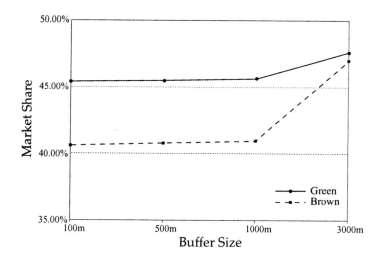

anecdotal evidence. However, this study is the first to provide quantitative evidence of the effects of logging activities on remote tourism.

The interactive nature of the DSS can be utilized to evaluate several changes simultaneously. A typical question may relate to the relationship between the price and any other attribute. For example, a lodge operator may desire to know how much to adjust the price for a week-long package if the fishing quality for walleye declines from "excellent" to "good." By applying a trial-and-error approach, the user of the DSS can quickly establish that such a decline in walleye fishing quality would have to be matched by a $105 decline in the price of a seven-day package.

Simulations can be pushed further: the previous example of a reduction in price because of poorer fishing quality may only be the first step in a more complex process. After an operation has reduced its price to offset declining fishing quality, it will find that overall revenue has now declined. If this change threatens the viability of the operation, one likely response may be to contemplate expansion of the business. The DSS suggests that for lodge-based remote tourism such an expansion may not be an appropriate alternative, because larger lodges are less preferred.

Another question relates to the effect of logging activity on the clients. The DSS reveals that the width of the buffer is the single most crucial logging attribute affecting the choice behavior of remote tourists, followed by the existence of a primary logging road in close proximity to the destination lake, and cutover age, which has been modeled only as a brown (fresh) clearcut versus a greened-over (ten to twenty year old) clearcut. This finding would suggest that the effects of past logging on remote tourism diminish over time. Such a finding should lead to further discussions about mitigating effects.

The model also accounts for several important interactions among attributes, which are more appropriately represented graphically. For example, the effect of the age of a cutover depends on the width of the buffer. Figure 2.3 depicts this relationship; as is to be expected, for any buffer width, a green cutover is preferred to a brown one. For buffers of 100 m to 1,000 m a green buffer, when compared to a brown buffer, contributes approximately 5 percent more to market share. However, at a distance of 3,000 m from the fishing lake, that difference is negligible.

Modeling the choice behavior of remote fly-in tourists using a DCE has, for the first time, produced results that systematically and quantitatively document the likely effects of logging on this type of tourism. These findings alone will contribute significantly to the discussions of land use issues in northern Ontario. Besides the focus on the relationship between logging and tourism, the study also produces a wealth of information about the importance of the main product characteristics such as package price, type of accommodation, travel distance, crowding, and fishing quality. All that information is relevant to the marketing efforts of tourist establishments and to managing the fishery. The discussion above focused on evaluating the results in terms of market share, which makes the results of a complex study design and rigorous statistical analysis more transparent. The major attraction of the DSS is that its interactive nature permits users to evaluate instantaneously many possible management options as well as future development scenarios, including nonexisting alternatives. The DSS can be used to document the importance of the respective levels of single attributes, as well as to explore the trade-offs clients are willing to make under a wide range of suboptimal conditions.

SUMMARY AND CONCLUSIONS

This chapter has illustrated one method of deciphering tourist choice behavior to discover what influences destination choice in a strict quantitative sense. It is one thing to claim to know what factors influence choice in a qualitative sense. Discrete choice modeling replaces that general knowledge with much more exact information on the relative impact of particular quantities of different attributes on destination choice. The power of the discrete choice experiment lies in its careful control of the combinations of attribute quantities that are presented to respondents. Such factorial designs allow much more information to be gleaned from the respondents' choices than could be obtained from real-world choices. Despite the complexity of the alternatives in both case studies, it is telling that respondents did not answer at random. If they had, none of the attributes would have shown any significant effect on choice. In fact, quite the opposite was true. Therefore, although care has to be taken not to exhaust respondents by presenting them with too many choice sets, it appears that quite complex and realistic choice sets can be used, incorporating visual as well as verbally defined attributes.

Having estimated the relative utility of each level of each attribute defining alternative destinations, the second case study showed how the logit regression modeling results made it feasible to build a decision support system. It allows planners to evaluate the impact of making specific changes to attributes of destinations over which they have control. This makes the DCE a key tool for those planning tourist destinations and for those designing tour packages. With a sufficiently large sample and sufficient information about respondents, the DCE can also be used to estimate different market segments' response to given destination attributes. Such intelligence is of growing importance as destination planners refine their products and target particular segments of the market. But the most distinctive feature of the DCE is that it allows the planner to evaluate the likely impact of a novel feature or combination of attribute levels on the drawing power of a destination. Given the great expense and risk involved in testing innovative products, the DCE provides an inexpensive first step in test-marketing a new tourist product.

CONCEPT DEFINITIONS

Alternative: In a choice set, a combination of quantities of different attributes that make up one distinct entity that may be chosen by a respondent. It may also be referred to as a *profile* or *scenario*.

Attribute: Any identifiable characteristic of an alternative in a choice set.

Attribute levels: Two or more different qualitative or discrete quantitative descriptors of one attribute; any given alternative possesses only one level of a particular attribute.

Choice set: In a choice experiment, any set of alternatives within which a respondent must make a choice. In revealed preference analysis, the definition is more problematic, because one cannot always be sure what alternatives each respondent is aware of, or can afford to consider.

Destination (demand-side): Any location to which a trip is made, defined in terms of attributes viewed as relevant by tourists.

Destination (supply-side): Any facility catering to tourists, defined in terms of attributes relevant to its management.

Discrete choice experiment (DCE): An experiment in which respondents are presented with carefully designed multiattributed alternatives from which to choose according to their preferences.

Market-share decision support system (DSS): Permits instantaneous evaluation of the competitiveness of alternatives with different attribute scores or levels. A user interface allows the user to set the attribute scores or levels of each alternative. An algorithm, based on the part-worth of each attribute or attribute level as obtained from a choice model, calculates the market share of each alternative. As such, the DSS helps the planner reach an informed decision in cases where there are many ways to design or redesign a destination. The DSS merely indicates the competitiveness of any particular design rather than defining the best possible design.

Part-worth: That component of an alternative's utility which is attributable to the quantity it possesses of a particular attribute.

Revealed preference analysis: Differs from a discrete choice experiment in that preferences are inferred from actual choices made by different respondents from among real-world alternatives.

Stated preference analysis: Any procedure whereby subjects' preference ratings, rankings, or choices from a set of two or more hypothetical alternatives are used to estimate, usually statistically, the importance of each attribute or attribute level of the alternatives.

Trade-off: Occurs when a user/client accepts less of one desired attribute if compensated by a particular additional amount of another desired attribute and experiences no reduction in satisfaction as a result of the trade-off.

Utility: The term used in economics to describe the satisfaction derived from the use or consumption of some object.

REVIEW QUESTIONS

1. In what situations would an analyst have to resort to a discrete choice experiment rather than a revealed preference approach?
2. Explain how the results of a DCE that includes price can be used to estimate how much the average respondent would be willing to pay for any specified increment in the quantity of a desirable attribute in an alternative.
3. Explain how market share is calculated in a DSS.
4. Explain how the results of a DCE can be used in a decision support system by facility managers or developers who want to know what impact a particular feature associated with an alternative will have on its competitive position.
5. Why would one want to include visual stimuli in a choice experiment rather than the usual written statements?

REFERENCES

Anderson, D.A., Williams, M.J., Haider, W., and Louviere, J.J. (1995). Efficient experimental designs for the study of remote tourists' destination choice. In M.J. Power, M. Strome, and T.C. Daniel (eds.), *Proceedings—Decision Support 2001. Proceedings of the 17th Annual Geographic Information Seminar and the Resource Technology '94 Symposium,* Toronto, Ontario, September 12-16, 1994. Bethesda, MD: American Society for Photogrammetry and Remote Sensing, pp. 909-918.

Ben-Akiva, M. and Lerman, S. (1985). *Discrete Choice Analysis: Theory and Application to Travel Demand.* Cambridge, MA: MIT Press.

Daniel, T.C. and Orland, B. (1995). Identifying and scaling factors affecting remote tourists' experiences. In M.J. Power, M. Strome, and T.C. Daniel (eds.), *Proceedings—Decision Support 2001. Proceedings of the 17th Annual Geographic Information Seminar and the Resource Technology '94 Symposium*, Toronto, Ontario, September 12-16, 1994. Bethesda, MD: American Society for Photogrammetry and Remote Sensing, pp. 897-908.

Haider, W. and Carlucci, L. (1994). *Remote Tourism in North Algoma—Visitor Survey 1991*. Thunder Bay, Ontario: Centre for Northern Forest Ecosystem Research, Ontario Ministry of Natural Resources.

Haider, W. and Ewing, G. (1990). A model of tourist choices of hypothetical Caribbean destinations, *Leisure Sciences,* 12, 33-47.

Luce, R.D. (1959). *Individual Choice Behavior: A Theoretical Analysis*. New York: John Wiley and Sons.

McFadden, D. (1981). Econometric models of probabilistic choice. In D. McFadden and C.F. Manski (eds.), *Structural Analysis of Discrete Data with Econometric Applications*. Cambridge, MA: MIT Press.

Orland, B., Daniel, T.C., and Haider, W. (1995). Calibrated images: Landscape visualizations to meet rigorous experimental design specifications. In M.J. Power, M. Strome, and T.C. Daniel (eds.) *Proceedings—Decision Support 2001. Proceedings of the 17th Annual Geographic Information Seminar and the Resource Technology '94 Symposium*, Toronto, Ontario, September 12-16, 1994. Bethesda, MD: American Society for Photogrammetry and Remote Sensing, pp. 909-918.

Wrigley, N. (1985). *Categorical Data Analysis for Geographers and Environmental Scientists*. London: Longman.

Chapter 3

Understanding the Factors Influencing Ski Destination Choice: A Means-End Analytic Approach

David B. Klenosky
Charles E. Gengler
Michael S. Mulvey

LEARNING OBJECTIVES

By the end of the chapter the reader should be able to:

- Characterize the range of factors influencing destination choice examined in previous research
- Describe the key features and theoretical basis of means-end theory
- Define attributes, consequences, and values
- Explain the concept of a means-end chain
- Describe the general methodology used to assess means-end relationships
- Demonstrate the use of the methodology in a destination choice context
- Describe and demonstrate an approach for identifying the dominant means-end chains involved in destination choice
- Discuss the applied and theoretical implications offered by the means-end approach for future leisure and tourism research

INTRODUCTION

Research has detailed a variety of factors that influence destination choice behavior. In general, these factors can be placed along a continuum

This chapter was previously published in the *Journal of Leisure Research,* *25*(4), 1993. Reprinted with permission.

ranging from the concrete or tangible attributes of the destinations at one extreme (Gearing, Swart, and Var, 1974; Goodrich, 1977; Var, Beck, and Loftus, 1977) to the abstract or intangible benefits, needs, motivations, or personal values travelers seek to satisfy at the other extreme (Crompton, 1979; Dann, 1981; Fisher and Price, 1991; Lounsbury and Hoopes, 1985; Muller, 1989; Pitts and Woodside, 1986). Although some have recently noted the conceptual relationship among several of these factors (Muller, 1989; Pitts and Woodside, 1986), researchers typically treat the extremes of this continuum as distinct and independent of each other in empirical studies of tourism choice behavior.

A recently developed theoretical perspective provides a way to integrate these concrete and abstract entities in a single framework. This perspective, termed means-end theory (Gutman, 1982), focuses specifically on the cognitive linkages between the relatively concrete aspects or attributes of products or services (the "means"), the more abstract consequences these attributes provide for consumers, and the highly abstract personal values (the "ends") these consequences help reinforce. Examining these means-end relationships (called means-end chains) provides a useful way to understand the fundamental relationship between consumers and the products they purchase and consume. This type of analysis provides an insightful complement to other, more-established research approaches. As such, it holds important implications for researchers and practitioners interested in understanding and influencing destination choice behavior.

The purpose of this paper, therefore, is to present the basic conceptual and methodological features of means-end theory and to demonstrate its usefulness for leisure and tourism research. We begin with an overview of means-end theory. Then, we describe the general methodology used to measure and analyze means-end relationships. Next, we demonstrate the use of this methodology in an empirical study of ski destination choice. We also provide an extension of this basic analysis, using a cluster analytic technique, that enhances the interpretability, and thus the usefulness, of the empirical results. Finally, we discuss some of the implications offered by the means-end approach for future leisure and tourism research.

MEANS-END THEORY

Broadly speaking, the focus of means-end theory is on understanding how consumers think about products. More specifically, the focus is on examining the important meanings that consumers associate with the products they purchase and consume. In means-end theory, it is useful to distinguish among three levels of abstraction or categories of meaning that are typically associated with a concept such as a product (cf. Olson and Reynolds, 1983). These categories are product attributes, consequences of product consumption, and personal values relevant to the consumer. Product attributes are relatively concrete meanings that represent the physical or observable characteristics of a product. For example, a ski area might be described in terms of the "number of expert trails" it has. Consequences are more abstract meanings that reflect the perceived benefits (or costs) associated with specific attributes. "Expert ski trails," then might lead to the consequence of "feeling challenged." Finally, personal values are highly abstract meanings that refer to centrally held, enduring beliefs or end-states of existence that consumers seek to achieve through their purchase and consumption behavior (Rokeach, 1973). Continuing the previous example, "feeling challenged" while skiing might allow one to experience a sense of "achievement" or "excitement." Taken together, this pattern of associations from attributes to consequences and from consequences to personal values represents a special type of knowledge structure called a means-end chain (Gutman, 1982; Howard, 1977; Olson and Reynolds, 1983):

Attribute → Consequence → Personal Value

This means-end chain model provides a simple way of characterizing the basic pattern of relationships by which the physical features or attributes of products gain personal relevance or meaning for consumers.

Simply stated, the rationale underlying the means-end model is that people choose products with attributes that produce desired consequences and minimize undesired consequences (Gutman, 1982). The desirability or importance of these consequences is, in turn, determined by the personal values they are associated with. Gutman (1982), following Rokeach (1973), suggests that consequences have positive or negative valences, depending upon their relationship to personal values. Thus, from a means-end perspective, values are the key factor underlying preferences and choice behavior (cf. Homer and Kahle, 1988; Henshel, 1971; Rokeach, 1973; Rosenberg, 1956; Wickert, 1940a, 1940b).

The emphasis of the means-end model is different than that of more traditional multiattribute models of choice. The traditional multiattribute approach concentrates on determining *if* and *to what degree* particular product attributes are important. The means-end approach, in contrast, focuses on *why* and *how* product attributes are important. Why and how attributes are important is addressed by assessing the sequence of means-end relations that link product attributes to personal values. In the next section we discuss the procedures used to identify these concepts and linkages.

GENERAL METHODOLOGY FOR ASSESSING MEANS-END RELATIONSHIPS

Reynolds and Gutman (1988) offer a methodology for assessing means-end knowledge structures. The procedure, known as laddering, involves a series of one-on-one in-depth interviews. Initially, respondents are given a simple categorization or sorting task. This task is designed to elicit the basic concepts or distinctions consumers use to differentiate between the stimuli (e.g., products or brands) within the domain of interest. These basic distinctions are typically made at the relatively concrete product attribute level, although distinctions at the other higher-order consequence and value levels are also possible.

The interviewer then asks the subject a series of probing questions designed to uncover the higher-level meanings and associations related to these basic distinctions. These questions are open-ended and designed to encourage the subject to give an answer specific to his or her own particular thoughts, and in his or her own words. Specifically, the respondent is presented with one of the distinctions elicited from the categorization task and asked "Why is (this distinction) important to you?" The response is then used as the focus of the next "Why is that important . . . ?" question. This questioning process continues until the subject can no longer provide an answer. This procedure is called "laddering" because it forces the respondent up the "ladder of abstraction," bridging relatively concrete product meanings at the attribute level to more abstract meanings at the consequence and personal-value levels. A thorough review of this approach can be found in Reynolds and Gutman (1988).

Analysis of the responses gathered from these individual laddering interviews involves several steps. First, the data are reviewed to develop/ define appropriate categories of meaning. Then, the verbatim responses are classified using these categories of meaning. Based on this content analysis, the structural relationships between specific attributes, consequences, and values are aggregated across respondents in an asymmetric implication matrix. This matrix is then used as the basis for constructing a summary chart called a Hierarchical Value Map (HVM) (Reynolds and Gutman, 1988). The HVM is a network diagram that characterizes the key meanings associated with a particular product domain. Note that the objective in the content and structural analyses of the data is not to portray every individual's ladders but rather to develop an aggregate representation that is reasonably faithful to the means-end knowledge structures of most of the individuals interviewed.

In the following sections, we demonstrate the use of the above methodology in an empirical study designed to identify the patterns of meanings involved in choosing among competing alpine ski destinations. In addition, we show how the data from this study can be further analyzed using cluster analysis to help reveal the major groupings among the chains of meaning represented in the summary HVM.

STUDY OBJECTIVES AND METHODOLOGY

A study was conducted to assess the means-end structural relationships downhill skiers perceive as relevant in selecting a destination for a getaway ski vacation. The data was collected during a ski show held in Ottawa, Canada over a three-day period in November 1991. A total of ninety subjects participated in one-on-one in-depth interviews using the laddering approach described above. Ski show attendees passing by a booth set up for the study were approached by one of four interviewers (two male and two female). Interviewers identified themselves as researchers from a local university and not affiliated with any ski resort. Only attendees who were at least twenty-two years old and had been on at least two overnight ski vacations in the past five years were asked to participate in the study. Each subject received a coupon book (provided by the ski show) as compensation for participating in the study. A demographic profile of these subjects is presented in Table 3.1. Note that all of the ninety subjects used in this analysis spoke English as their primary language.

Subjects were questioned individually in an interview lasting approximately twenty to thirty minutes. After collecting initial demographic information, a preference-oriented sorting task (Reynolds and Gutman, 1988) was used to elicit the basic concepts or distinctions subjects use when choosing among alternative ski resorts. In this task, subjects were presented with a list of the thirty-three largest ski resorts in the surrounding area and asked to indicate which resorts on that list they had visited (in the past five years). The interviewer randomly selected three of the resorts the subject had been to, and asked which of the three he or she preferred. The interviewer then asked the subject why he or she preferred that resort over the other two. This procedure typically elicited one or two reasons (or basic distinctions) from the subject.

The laddering process described earlier was then employed for each distinction the subject mentioned to elicit the higher-level concepts to

TABLE 3.1. Sample Profile (n = 90)

Gender:	
Male	64
Female	26
Number of Days Skiing Per Year:	
1-5	3
6-10	1
11-14	10
15-19	12
20 or more	64
Number of Ski Trips Per Year:	
0-1	22
2-3	45
4-5	11
6 or more	12
Lodging Most Frequently Used:	
Friends/Relatives	10
Private Cottage/Condominium	31
Hotel/Motel/Lodge	49
Age Group:	
Under 34	43
34-44	28
44-54	12
55 or over	7
Household Income (in Canadian $'s):	
Up to $29,999	5
$30,000-39,999	17
$40,000-54,999	22
$55,000-69,999	14
$70,000 or more	27
No Response	5

which it was associated. Depending on the subject's initial response, the interviewers probed for the other dimensions of meaning that completed a means-end chain. For example, if a subject's initial response was "can meet people easily," the interviewer would recognize this as a consequence and probe for both the supporting attribute and the relevant personal value. The attribute would be probed for with questions such as, "What is it about the resort that makes you feel you can meet people easily?" The personal-value-level meanings would be elicited by probing with questions of "Why is meeting people easily important to you?"

This process of eliciting distinctions and laddering from those distinctions was then repeated using the two remaining resorts. On average, these procedures resulted in 3.4 "ladders" per subject for a total of 310 ladders elicited across the ninety study participants.

ANALYSIS AND RESULTS

Content Analysis

The LadderMap computer software developed by Gengler and Reynolds (1989) was employed to facilitate the data analysis. The initial task of the analysis was to enter the verbatim responses for each subject's ladders into the computer. Each ladder was entered, making a separate entry for the individual elements within the ladder. As each element was entered, it was given an initial classification as being either an attribute, consequence, or value. After all of the verbatim responses were entered, and content categories were established to allow aggregation of the responses across subjects and further quantitative analysis. An analyst familiar with the topic developed a set of codes. Then that analyst and another experienced analyst coded the data independently. A comparison of the coding results indicated intercoder agreement of 87 percent. All disagreements between the two coders were resolved jointly. The content categories used in the study are given in Table 3.2. Note that of the twenty-four categories in Table 3.2, thirteen represent concepts at the attribute level, seven at the consequence level, and four at the personal-value level.

The four values identified through the content analysis differ only slightly from those used in previous personal values research. For example, the values "belonging," "achievement," and "safety" use different labels but are semantically equivalent to "sense of belonging," "sense of accomplishment," and "security," which are given in the List of Values (LOV) developed by researchers from the University of Michigan's Survey Research Center (Kahle, 1983; Veroff, Douvan, and Kulka, 1981). The other value, "fun and excitement," is a combination of "fun and enjoyment in life" and "excitement" from the LOV. These two values were combined because they tended to be mentioned together during the laddering interviews and because previous research in tourism indicated that they were strongly related. In particular, Muller's (1989) study of international tourism identified a market segment characterized by their

TABLE 3.2. Implication Matrix for Ski Destination Choice (n = 90)

FROM	N	A1	A2	A3	A4	A5	A6	A7	A8	A9	A10	A11	A12	A13	C1	C2	C3	C4	C5	C6	C7	V1	V2	V3	V4
Attributes																									
A1 Ski Packages	8						1									1	7	2							2
A2 Familiarity	9						1									1		1	1	2	3		1		6
A3 Local Culture	11		2																7						4
A4 Grooming	15									2			6											9	4
A5 Close to Home	16											2				5	4	9						1	6
A6 Lodging	16									1	3	2				1	6	2	2			1		1	
A7 Friendly People	17										2						1	1	14			4			7
A8 Crowding	17								2							2		13					1	4	8
A9 Difficulty	25								2					3		1	1	3		14	3	1	8	4	11
A10 Resort Services	30					1	1					2		2	2	1	2	2	3	2	1	1	2	9	5
A11 Entertainment	31			1						1	2				2	1	1	1	16			6	2	2	16
A12 Snow Conditions	32				3					3				1				1			1		1	11	17
A13 Hill & Trail Quality	41		1						2	9	2	1			1	2	1	3		20	12	1	7	5	19

TO — Attributes · Consequences · Values

FROM	N	Attributes													Consequences							Values			
		A1	A2	A3	A4	A5	A6	A7	A8	A9	A10	A11	A12	A13	C1	C2	C3	C4	C5	C6	C7	V1	V2	V3	V4
Consequences																									
C1 Choice	10																					1			4
C2 Save Time	14										2	1						9				2	1	1	6
C3 Save Money	26											1						7							5
C4 Ski More	30								1	1							2								4
C5 SocialAtmosphere	40										1									1		12		2	15
C6 Challenging	41							1										1			1		12	1	16
C7 Ski Variety	51								1	3			1		9	1	2	4		21		1	1	3	28
Values																									
V1 Belonging	14																								
V2 Achievement	17																								
V3 Safety	27																								
V4 Fun & Excitement	64																								

Notes: N refers to the number of subjects mentioning each concept. The entries in the matrix indicate the total number of times each concept (the rows) directly or indirectly elicited each of the other concepts (the columns).

interest in seeking fun and excitement while on vacation. The other values from the LOV ("self-respect," "warm relationships with others," "self-fulfillment," and "being well-respected") were not mentioned during the laddering interviews.

Structural Analysis

The concepts identified in the content analysis represent the key meanings underlying subjects' ski destination choices. Structural analysis was then used to identify the linkages or interrelationships among these concepts. The first step in this analysis was to construct an aggregate implication matrix. This is a square matrix in which the rows and columns refer to the concepts developed in the content analysis. The entries in the matrix consist of the number of times each pair of concepts was associated together in the laddering interviews. These associations may be either direct or indirect. To illustrate this distinction between direct and indirect associations, consider a means-end chain of A→B→C. This chain consists of direct associations from A to B and from B to C, and an indirect association from A to C.

Although one could argue that direct and indirect associations are different measures of interconcept association, we prefer to treat them as equivalent measures and sum the number of direct and indirect associations between concepts when aggregating across respondents. Our rationale for doing so stems from the observation that some respondents tend to elaborate more than others during the laddering interviews and mention more intervening meanings between concepts. This point is best illustrated by an example. Suppose that two respondents both differentiated ski areas in terms of "slope grooming" (i.e., the extent to which the slopes are maintained or groomed). The first respondent, when asked why "grooming" is important, responds that "better grooming means the snow conditions will be better"; and then when asked why having "better snow conditions" is important, responds that "I feel safer skiing when the snow conditions are good." This respondent would then have direct associations between "grooming" and "snow conditions" and between "snow conditions" and "safety", and an indirect association between "snow conditions" and "safety." In contrast, suppose we spoke to another less-talkative respondent who simply responded that "grooming" is important because it means the "skiing will be safer." This respondent would have only a direct association between "grooming" and "safety." In this example, the key factor affecting whether these associations linking "grooming" and "safety" are classified as direct or indirect is the amount of elaboration elicited during the interview. Treating them as different types of measures or focusing solely on the number of direct associations, as some have suggested (e.g., Olson and Reynolds, 1983), would bias the results by underweighting the importance of the associations recorded for the more verbose respondents (who would tend to have longer ladders and more indirect associations between concepts).

The implication matrix constructed from the 310 ski destination ladders is given in Table 3.2. As noted previously, the entries in the matrix indicate the number of times a concept (the rows) directly or indirectly elicited each of the other concepts (the columns). These entries provide the basis for constructing the Hierarchical Value Map or HVM. The first step in constructing an HVM involves selecting a cutoff value to determine which relations should be represented on the map and which should not. In practice, an implication matrix typically consists of a large number of cells that are either zero or near zero. Thus, the idea in selecting a cutoff is to select a value that captures the dominant relations represented in the matrix (Olson and Reynolds, 1983). One heuristic that can be used is that the concepts represented in the HVM should be mentioned by at least 5 percent of the study respondents. Thus, for the present study a cutoff of five relations was selected (5 percent of 90 = 4.5, or 5 rounded to the next whole number).

Based on this cutoff, a binary matrix was then created where a cell received a one if the corresponding element of the implication matrix was greater than or equal to the cutoff value and a zero otherwise. These binary flags indicate which associations should be illustrated on the graph. In the interest of constructing a meaningful, uncluttered graph, however, not all of the marked associations are actually drawn as individual lines. Some of the connections indicated in the binary matrix are considered redundant and therefore are not illustrated on the map. If, for instance, the matrix indicates X→Y, X→Z, and Y→Z; then the connection X→Z is redundant since it is captured in the X→Y and Y→Z relationships. After all the redundant relationships were eliminated, the binary matrix was then used to draw the graph.

The final step in constructing the HVM involved representing the number of subjects mentioning each concept and the relative strength of association between concepts. The number of subjects mentioning a concept was represented on the graph by varying the size of the node (or circle) on the map; the relative strength of association between concepts was represented by varying the width of the line connecting related concepts. This approach for constructing an HVM is based on recommendations made by Gengler, Klenosky, and Mulvey (1992).

The final HVM for the ski destination study is illustrated in Figure 3.1. Note that the value-level concepts (represented by black-filled circles and labeled using all capital letters) are positioned near the center of the diagram to reflect the core role they play in defining the meaning of the other less-abstract concepts. The more-concrete attribute concepts (represented by white-filled circles and labeled using all lowercase letters) are posi-

FIGURE 3.1. Hierarchical Value Map for Ski Destination Choice

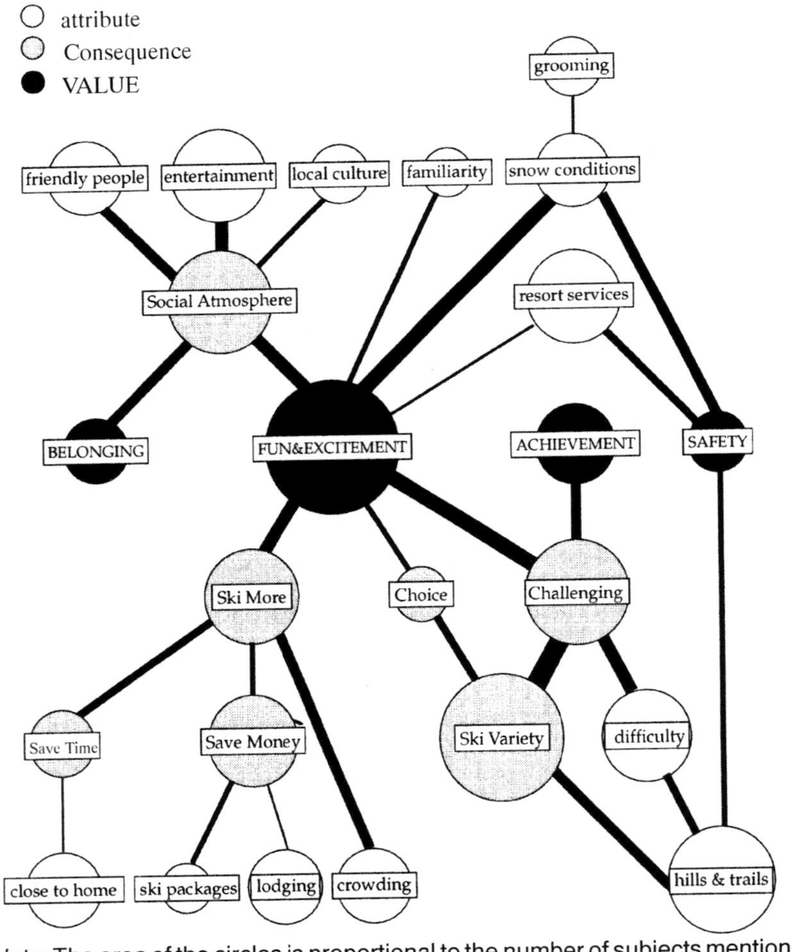

Note: The area of the circles is proportional to the number of subjects mentioning concepts. The width of the lines is proportional to the number of subjects associated with the linked concepts.

tioned around the perimeter of the HVM since they typically began (or occurred early in) the laddering process. Finally, concepts reflecting consequences (represented by shaded circles and labeled using initial capital letters are positioned between these two extremes. It should be noted that traditionally in means-end research, the HVM is structured vertically so that values appear at the top of the map, consequences near the middle, and attributes at the bottom. Our "centralized" format for the HVM was used partly to avoid a cluttered map (that would have had only a few values at the top of the diagram and a large number of attributes at the bottom, with a large number of crossing lines connecting the concepts) and partly to reflect the centrality of the values concept in cognitive structure.

Cluster Analysis

The HVM illustrated in Figure 3.1 suggests a large number of pathways from the attributes, consequences, and values elicited during the laddering interviews. More specifically, the HVM shows twenty-one unique paths that can be traced between elements at the attribute level and elements at the personal-values level, any or all of which may be worthy of further consideration. Reynolds and Gutman (1988) present one approach for determining which pathways in the HVM are the most important or dominant. In their approach, the analyst simply totals the number of associations linking the different concepts in each chain represented in the HVM. In this paper, we present an alternative approach that uses cluster analysis to identify the dominant pathways or groupings of concepts in the HVM.

The first step in the cluster analysis involved creating a similarities matrix. This matrix was constructed by combining the entries in the asymmetric implication matrix above and below the diagonal to create a symmetric matrix of associations between concepts. Thus, each entry in the similarities matrix gives the total times each concept elicited or was elicited by each of the other concepts. Since the clustering procedure used in the analysis (described in SAS Institute, 1990) required the use of dissimilarity measures rather than similarities, each entry in the similarities matrix was then converted to a dissimilarity score using a transformation that subtracted the entry from a constant representing a number larger than the maximum value in that matrix. Thus, each entry in the similarities matrix was subtracted from twenty-nine (one more than the largest value in that matrix, twenty-eight). This final dissimilarities matrix was then input into an agglomerative hierarchical clustering algorithm, using the average-linkage method of computing between-cluster distances.

An analysis of the pseudo-F and pseudo-t^2 statistics (discussed in SAS Institute, 1990, pp. 98) indicated a six-cluster solution. The six clusters are listed in Table 3.3 (employing the convention of using all lowercase letters for attributes, initial capitals for consequences, and all capital letters for values). In general, each of the six clusters appears to capture a different aspect or chain of meaning skiers use when selecting among competing ski resorts. Cluster 1 appears to capture the most dominant chain in the HVM (i.e., many of its concepts were among the most frequently mentioned across the respondents). It includes concepts that link concern about the hills and trails making up a ski resort to the personal values FUN &

TABLE 3.3. Cluster Analysis of Ski Destination HVM Data

Cluster 1
hills & trails
difficulty
Ski Variety
Choice
Challenging
ACHIEVEMENT
FUN & EXCITEMENT

Cluster 2
grooming
snow conditions
SAFETY

Cluster 3
friendly people
entertainment
Social Atmosphere
BELONGING

Cluster 4
close to home
crowding
Save Time
Ski More

Cluster 5
ski packages
lodging
resort services
Save Money

Cluster 6
familiarity
local culture

EXCITEMENT and ACHIEVEMENT. The patterns of associations in the HVM involving this cluster's concepts suggest that skiers are concerned about the hills and trails at a ski area for two interrelated reasons. The first appears to reflect a concern for the difficulty of the terrain and the benefit of feeling Challenged; the second involves the opportunity to have some Variety and Choice. Note that several of these concepts were among the most frequently mentioned during the laddering interviews, reflecting the central role of these concepts in the ski destination choice process.

The next cluster, Cluster 2, focuses on skiers' concern with the grooming and snow conditions at a resort. Interestingly, skiers' attention to these attributes appears to be driven by a concern for personal SAFETY, on the one hand; and, as reflected in the HVM, by meanings associated with the personal value FUN & EXCITEMENT, on the other. The next cluster includes concepts that reflect the social benefits associated with a ski vacation. In particular, Cluster 3 suggests that the attributes friendly people and entertainment create a Social Atmosphere, which ultimately leads to a feeling of BELONGING. The fourth Cluster includes the attributes crowding and close to home and the benefits Save Time and Ski More. These meanings are all strongly linked in the HVM, apparently reflecting a general concern for some of the temporal or convenience aspects (travel and lift lines) that can potentially detract from the fun and excitement of a ski outing. Whereas Cluster 4 appears to capture concepts related to how skiers spend their time on a ski trip, Cluster 5 appears to capture concepts related to how they spend their money. More specifically, this cluster includes the attributes lodging, ski packages, and resort services and the consequence Save Money. Interestingly, as shown in the HVM, Saving Money is important because it allows one to Ski More, thus allowing one to have more FUN & EXCITEMENT. The final cluster, Cluster 6, links the two remaining attributes local culture and familiarity. Although not reflected in the HVM, the association between these concepts may reflect the novelty associated with being in a particular resort environment.

Taken together, the laddering procedure and subsequent analyses provide considerable insight into the major means-end knowledge structures skiers use when choosing among competing ski destinations. The content and structural analyses, as summarized in the HVM, reflect the complex patterns of interrelationships among the concepts in these structures; and the cluster analyses reveal the dominant chains of meaning connecting those concepts.

IMPLICATIONS FOR LEISURE
AND DESTINATION RESEARCH

In general, the data from a means-end study can be used to address a broad range of applied and theoretical problems facing leisure and tourism researchers. At an applied level, these problems range from developing and evaluating advertising strategy, to segmenting markets, to positioning products (for more detailed discussions of these and other applications see Gengler and Reynolds, in press; Gutman, 1982; Olson and Reynolds, 1983; Reynolds and Gengler, 1991; Reynolds and Gutman, 1984, 1988). As one illustration of these potential uses, the different patterns of means-end associations identified in the present ski destination study can be used to develop positioning and promotion strategies for a ski resort. For instance, a strategy could be developed that emphasized the Challenge and FUN & EXCITEMENT associated with the trails at the resort or, alternatively, the unique Social Atmosphere and SENSE OF BELONGING associated with the friendly people who work and ski there.

Another use of the technique could be in helping leisure and tourism-service providers better understand how their clientele think about their product offerings. Means-end theory and the laddering methodology could be used to identify differences in the means-end structures associated with these two groups. For example, the dominant chains of meaning uncovered in the present study of skiers could be contrasted with those identified in a subsequent study of ski-area operators. Once identified, this information could serve as the basis for a training or management program in which service providers are made aware of how their views match or differ from the consumers they seek to serve.

In addition to their tremendous potential for applied uses, means-end theory and the laddering methodology hold important implications for addressing a variety of theoretical issues in leisure and tourism research. One such issue concerns the impact of situational factors on leisure choice behavior (e.g., Filiatrault and Ritchie, 1988; June and Smith, 1987). In general, previous research has shown that the way in which a situation is defined has a strong influence on how people evaluate the importance of different attributes and attribute levels. The bases of these situational effects, however, still remain as an important research question. The means-end approach outlined in the present research may prove useful for enhancing our understanding of this issue. In particular, it is quite possible that the situational differences in attribute importances may be driven by differences in the consequences and personal values that are salient in a given situation.

In a different direction, means-end research can be used to assess the means-end knowledge structures of leisure and tourism phenomena that exist among people with different levels of experience or personal involvement. Recent leisure and tourism research (Bloch, Black, and Lichtenstein, 1989; Bloch and Bruce, 1984; Havitz and Dimanche, 1990; Pearce, 1982; Schreyer, Lime, and Williams, 1984; Watson, Roggenbuck, and Williams, 1991) suggests that differences in one's level of experience or involvement often have a strong impact on a variety of information-processing and behavioral measures. These effects may be productively examined using the means-end approach. For example, people with high levels of experience (or involvement) may have more complex and better established means-end knowledge structures relative to those with low levels of experience (or involvement).

Finally, our study focused on active skiers (i.e., those who had been on at least two ski trips in the past five years). An interesting future study would be to replicate the procedure on a sample of inactive skiers (i.e., those who have not been on a ski vacation in the past five years) or nonskiers. As one anonymous reviewer pointed out, the means-end approach outlined in this paper may be just as useful for exploring why people *do not* engage in particular activities or visit certain sites, as for exploring why they *do* participate or visit. Such an analysis would be of considerable interest given the number of recent studies on leisure constraints/constrained leisure behavior (excellent overviews of this research can be found in Jackson, 1991; and in recent reviews by Goodale and Witt, 1989 and Jackson, 1988).

As with all research, care should be taken in generalizing the results beyond the sample of active skiers interviewed in this research. There may be important differences in the means-end structures of the present sample of skiers and those in different markets. Additional research should be conducted to determine the extent of these differences.

In conclusion, the aim of this research was to introduce means-end theory and to demonstrate its basic methodology in a destination choice context. Another goal was to show one way in which the basic analysis of means-end data can be extended. Hopefully, this paper will inspire additional research on means-end analysis to refine and extend the methodological and analytical procedures and examine other important leisure and tourism research issues.

CONCEPT DEFINITIONS

Attributes: The physical or observable characteristics that can be used to describe a product or service.

Consequences: The perceived benefits (or costs) associated with a specific attribute.

Hierarchical value map: A graphical summary that illustrates the main relationships between the attributes, consequences, and values in the implication matrix.

Implication matrix: An aggregate summary of the number of times each attribute, consequence, and value was associated together during the laddering interviews.

Laddering: A semistructured interview procedure for uncovering means-end chains.

Means-end chain: A special type of knowledge structure or model that summarizes the pattern of relationships among attributes, consequences, and values.

Values: Centrally held, enduring beliefs or end-states of existence that consumers seek to achieve through their purchase and consumption behavior (Rokeach, 1973).

REVIEW QUESTIONS

1. Describe the structure of a means-end chain and explain the basic rationale underlying the means-end approach.
2. Compare the emphasis of the means-end model to that of more traditional multiattribute choice models.
3. Describe the laddering procedure for measuring means-end chains.
4. Explain the key steps involved in analyzing laddering data.
5. Discuss the implications of the means-end approach for hospitality and tourism practitioners and researchers.

OPTIONAL PROJECT:
MEASURING MEANS-END CHAINS

- Find two people whom you can talk to separately for about five to ten minutes each. Try to find a quiet place where you won't be interrupted. Then use the procedure below to measure each person's means-end chains for the following context: *choosing a destination for a spring break vacation.*
- Begin the interview by stating: "Assume that you are planning a spring break vacation. What different destinations would you consider going to for this vacation?" Try to get the interviewee to mention about three to six destinations.

- Randomly select three of the destinations (it is best to select destinations that differ) and ask the respondent which of the three he or she prefers. Then ask why that destination is preferred over the other two. Ask if there are any other reasons. Record the factor(s) they mention. If necessary, select another set of three destinations and repeat this process until you have identified three to four factors.
- Tell your respondents that you will be asking several questions about the reasons or factors they mentioned. Warn them that some of the questions may seem obvious. Tell them that it's not that you don't understand the obvious, it's just that you want to hear things in their own words to know exactly what they mean.
- Then select one of the factors they mentioned, *other than price,* for the laddering task. Begin the laddering session using this factor . . .

  "Why is _____ important to you?" (or, "Why is _____ important?" or, "What does _____ give you?" or "Why would it be bad if _____ happened?")

NOTE: You are looking for responses that refer to consequences or values associated with choosing a vacation destination. Not everything they say will be relevant to the destination. Don't let them ramble on and on. Try to get them to focus on things related to the destination—that is, the consequences of the factor they mentioned, and the higher-level meanings (values) associated with those consequences.

After recording their response, use it as the focus of the next "why" question. Continue this questioning process until the respondent cannot go on. (Note: you do not need a transcript of your interview, just a record of the responses [the meaningful responses] they give you.) Then repeat the process for one other (nonprice) factor. You should get a total of four ladders or means-end chains (two for each person).

- Then, draw out the means-end chains you measured for each respondent.
- Discuss what you learned about these individuals and how they think about spring break destinations. Then, discuss the implications of your findings for developing promotional strategies. Be specific, provide examples of how your results could be used in an advertisement, etc.
- Finally, describe any problems you had with the laddering procedure and discuss your view concerning the strengths and weaknesses of this measurement technique.

REFERENCES

Bloch, P.H., Black, W.C., and Lichtenstein, D. (1989). Involvement with the equipment component of sport: Links to recreational commitment. *Leisure Sciences, 11*, 187-200.

Bloch, P.H. and Bruce, G.D. (1984). The leisure experience and consumer products: An investigation of underlying satisfactions. *Journal of Leisure Research, 16*(1), 74-88.

Crompton, J.L. (1979). Motivations for pleasure vacation. *Annals of Tourism Research, 6*(4), 408-424.

Dann, G.M.S. (1981). Tourism motivation: An appraisal. *Annals of Tourism Research, 8*(2), 187-219.

Filiatrault, R. and Ritchie, J.R.B. (1988). The impact of situational factors on the evaluation of hospitality services. *Journal of Travel Research, 26*(4), 29-37.

Fisher, R.J. and Price, L.L. (1991). International pleasure travel motivations and post-vacation cultural attitude change. *Journal of Leisure Research, 23*(3), 193-208.

Gearing, C.E., Swart, W.W., and Var, T. (1974). Establishing a measure of touristic attractiveness. *Journal of Travel Research, 12*(4), 1-8.

Gengler, C.E., Klenosky, D.B., and Mulvey, M.S. (1992). A note on the representation of means-end study results. Unpublished manuscript.

Gengler, C.E. and Reynolds, T.J. (1989). Means-end structural analysis: Computer-generated hierarchical value maps. Paper presented at EIASM Workshop on Consumer Behavior: Extending the Cognitive Structure Perspective, Brussels, Belgium.

Gengler, C.E. and Reynolds, T.J. (in press). A structural model of advertising effects. In A.A. Mitchell (Ed.), *Advertising Exposure, Memory, and Choice.* Hillsdale, NJ: Lawrence Erlbaum.

Goodale, T.L. and Witt, P.A. (1989). Recreation non-participation and barriers to leisure. In E.L. Jackson and T.L. Burton (Eds.), *Understanding Leisure and Recreation: Mapping the Past, Charting the Future* (pp. 421-449). State College, PA: Venture Publishing, Inc.

Goodrich, J.N. (1977). Benefit bundle analysis: An empirical study of international travelers. *Journal of Travel Research, 16*(2), 6-9.

Gutman, J. (1982). A means-end chain model based on consumer categorization processes. *Journal of Marketing, 46*(2), 60-72.

Havitz, M.E. and Dimanche, F. (1990). Propositions for testing the involvement construct in recreational and tourism contexts. *Leisure Sciences, 12,* 179-195.

Henshel, A.M. (1971). The relationship between values and behavior: A development hypothesis. *Child Development, 42*, 1997-2007.

Homer, P.M. and Kahle, L.R. (1988). A structural equation test of the value-attitude-behavior hierarchy. *Journal of Personality and Social Psychology, 54*(4), 638-646.

Howard, J.C. (1977). *Consumer Behavior: Application of Theory.* New York: McGraw-Hill.

Jackson, E.L. (1988). Leisure constraints: A survey of past research. *Leisure Sciences, 10*, 203-215.

Jackson, E.L. (1991). Leisure constraints/constrained leisure: Special issue introduction. *Journal of Leisure Research, 23*(4), 279-285.

June, L.P. and Smith, S.L.J. (1987). Service attributes and situational effects on customer preferences for restaurant dining. *Journal of Travel Research, 26*(2), 20-27.

Kahle, L.R. (1983). (Ed.). *Social Values and Social Change: Adaptation to Life in America*. New York: Praeger.

Lounsbury, J.W. and Hoopes, L.L. (1985). An investigation of the factors associated with vacation satisfaction. *Journal of Leisure Research, 17*(1), 1-13.

Muller, T.E. (1989). Using personal values to define segments in an international tourism market. *International Marketing Review, 8*(1), 57-70.

Olson, J.C. and Reynolds, T.J. (1983). Understanding consumers' cognitive structures: Implications for advertising strategy. In L. Percy and A. Woodside (Eds.), *Advertising and Consumer Psychology*, Vol. 1. Lexington, MA: Lexington Books, 77-90.

Pearce, P.L. (1982). Perceived changes in holiday destinations. *Annals of Tourism Research, 9*(2), 145-164.

Pitts, R.E. and Woodside, A.G. (1986). Personal values and travel decisions. *Journal of Travel Research, 25*(1), 20-25.

Reynolds, T.J. and Gengler, C.E. (1991). A strategic framework for assessing advertising: The animatic vs. finished issue. *Journal of Advertising Research, 31*(5), 61-71.

Reynolds, T.J. and Gutman, J. (1984). Advertising is image management. *Journal of Advertising Research, 24*(1), 27-36.

Reynolds, T.J. and Gutman, J. (1988). Laddering theory, method, analysis and interpretation. *Journal of Advertising Research, 28*(1), 11-31.

Rokeach, M.J. (1973). *The Nature of Human Values*. New York: Free Press.

Rosenberg, M. (1956). Cognitive structure and attitudinal effect. *Journal of Abnormal and Social Psychology, 53*, 367-372.

SAS Institute. (1989). *SAS/STAT User's Guide, Version 6, Fourth Edition, Volume 1*. Cary, NC: SAS Institute, Inc.

Schreyer, R., Lime, D.R., and Williams, D.R. (1984). Characterizing the influence of past experience on recreation behavior. *Journal of Leisure Research, 16*(1), 34-50.

Var, T., Beck, R.A.D., and Loftus, P. (1977). Determination of touristic attractiveness of the touristic areas in British Columbia. *Journal of Travel Research, 15*(3), 23-29.

Veroff, J., Douvan, E., and Kulka, R.A. (1981). *The Inner American*. New York: Basic Books.

Watson, A.E., Roggenbuck, J.W., and Williams, D.R. (1991). The influence of past experience on wilderness choice. *Journal of Leisure Research, 23*(1), 21-36.

Wickert, F. (1940a). The interrelations of some general and specific preferences. *Journal of Social Psychology, 11*, 275-302.

Wickert, F. (1940b). A test for personal goals. *Journal of Social Psychology, 11*, 259-274.

Chapter 4

The Roles of Image and Perceived Constraints at Different Stages in the Tourist's Destination Decision Process

Seoho Um
John L. Crompton

LEARNING OBJECTIVES

By the end of the chapter the reader should:

- Understand the stages through which tourists pass in making a high-involvement decision about which destination to visit for a vacation
- Demonstrate the sequential nature of the decision process
- Illustrate the different roles played by image and constraints at different stages in the decision process
- Illustrate the challenges associated with undertaking longitudinal research
- Introduce the notion that destination choice is a satisfying behavior which is constraint driven, rather than an optimizing behavior that is attribute driven

INTRODUCTION

Potential tourists frequently have limited knowledge about a destination that they have not previously visited. This knowledge often is confined to

This chapter was previously published in the *Journal of Travel Research, 30*(3), 1992. Reprinted with permission.

symbolic information acquired either from media or from their social groups. From this information, tourists formulate images of alternative destinations, so image emerges as a critical element in the destination choice process. For this reason, a substantial number of studies concerned with destination choice have focused upon identifying the dominant attributes of destination image and exploring their role in the selection of a travel destination (e.g., Mayo, 1973; Hunt, 1975; Crompton, 1979; Keown, Jacobs, and Worthley, 1984; Gartner, 1986; Fakeye and Crompton, 1991).

The emphasis on image has gradually evolved from including only destination attributes to incorporating constraints that are conceptualized as a mechanism for reducing desired alternatives (Jackson and Searle, 1985). As Jackson (1991) notes, "barriers and perceptions of barriers enter, both overtly and covertly, into the decision-making process of individuals at all stages of leisure engagement" (p. 280). The inclusion of constraints that were specific to a tourist's decision-making context has been found to reduce the unexplained variance in models and to increase the management value of research in this area.

Crompton (1977) suggested a two-stage model to describe a tourist's destination choice process that emphasized the roles of perceived constraints and image. In his study, destination choice behavior was characterized as a function of the interaction among perceived constraints such as time, money and travelability, and destination image. He suggested that destination images were first prioritized in terms of ideal preference and the prioritization was then amended by the impact of perceived constraints. More recently, Crompton and Ankomah (1993), based on their review of the choice set literature, developed a proposition that stated, "The criteria used to evaluate alternatives in the early consideration set will primarily focus on the relative merits of the destinations' attributes, while the criteria used to evaluate alternatives in the late consideration set will primarily focus on the constraints associated with each of the alternative destinations" (p. 469). Hence, the critical role of the interaction between constraints and image is now widely accepted in the tourism area (for example, see the general models of traveler destination choice proposed by Moutinho (1986), Woodside and Lysonski (1989), and Um and Crompton (1990).

The destination choice process has received similar attention in the outdoor recreation literature, where destination choice has been characterized as the result of individual cognitive evaluations of both social and physical environmental attributes of the alternatives (Fesenmaier, 1988; Iso-Ahola, 1980; McCool, Stankey, and Clark, 1985). It has been suggested that individuals integrate their subjective impressions (evaluations) of each attribute in different ways so they have distinctive preferences for alternative sites

(Holbrook, 1981; Young and Kent, 1985). In other words, the attributes are perceived to be input factors that produce utility. The maximization of utility over all choice alternatives is reported to be the most common decision rule (Corstjens and Gautschi, 1983; Peterson et al., 1985). Brown and Ross (1982) suggested that different desired experiences are relevant in formulating different preferences for recreation sites. This is consistent with the notion that different attributes of different destinations form the basis for different experience expectations.

In reality, limits are considered in the selection of any destination and most of the outdoor recreation studies have included constraints such as travel distance and available time and money (Harris, Driver, and Bergersen, 1985; Krumpe and McLaughlin, 1982). Among these constraints, the primary emphasis has been placed on travel distance as a determinant of recreation site choice. Krumpe and McLaughlin (1982) emphasized the role of constraining attributes associated with the recreation site in the process of reaching a reduced set of alternatives in destination choice. They proposed that the destination choice process can be conceptualized as a constraint-driven conditional and sequential elimination model. They envisioned the choice process as an alternative-reducing process, followed by sequential selection of a final single choice from the remaining alternatives. Constraining attributes were valued either negatively or positively depending upon the situation and the number of them perceived to be present. Finally, after evaluating remaining alternatives, an alternative that had the fewest constraining attributes was chosen as the preferred recreation site.

Harris, Driver, and Bergersen (1985) suggested that the recreation destination finally chosen represents a decision-maker's set of preferences for site attributes constrained by situational factors. In their words, "Constrained demand is emphasized because the model recognizes that most human decisions are strongly influenced by limited money, time, and other personal resources and capabilities" (p. 46). They found that choices of fishing sites were influenced both by facilities that were viewed as constraining attributes and by setting attributes that were viewed as facilitating attributes. Unconstrained preferences for alternative destinations are analogous to the concept of a utility function, but these preferences are modified by inhibitors:

> The site finally chosen represents the decision maker's constrained set of preferences for site attributes. This concept of constrained preferences parallels the concept of demand as formulated in microeconomic theory; demand curves are, in theory, derived by tracing out these price-quantity points where each individual's indifference curve (which

reflects that individual's utility, or unconstrained preferences) intersects his/her budget constraint function (Harris, Driver, and Bergersen, 1985, p. 47)

A destination choice decision reflecting these constraints may be conceptualized as emerging from the interaction of an individual's beliefs about a destination's attributes with his or her motives for pleasure travel and constraint factors. Those beliefs about a destination's attributes which help to satisfy a potential traveler's specific motives constitute "image" and in this study they are termed "facilitators," whereas attributes which are not congruent with his or her motives are viewed as "constraints" and in this study are termed "inhibitors." Perceived inhibitors and facilitators were operationalized as consisting of two components: (1) the extent to which prospective destinations were believed to possess certain attributes, and (2) the relative strength or intensity of beliefs about each attribute as either an inhibitor or a facilitator in evaluating each place as a possible destination. Thus, a choice of whether an alternative is selected as a travel destination may be expressed as a function of the interaction of perceived facilitators and perceived inhibitors.

THE STRUCTURE OF DESTINATION CHOICE SETS

The notion of choice sets is central to most models of the pleasure traveler's destination choice process, and it was the conceptual underpinning in the study reported here. They are most likely to be applicable when the purchase task is a new or modified one in which individuals typically seek information and evaluate alternatives, and when the purchase entails some degree of high risk (Spiggle and Sewall, 1987). It seems likely that many vacation destination selection decisions will meet these two criteria, and it is in these high-involvement situations that the choice set structure described and tested in this chapter is likely to be most useful.

In the context of tourism, there appears to be general agreement that selection of a vacation destination goes through three central core stages (see Figure 4.1): development of an initial set of destinations that has traditionally been called the awareness set, a discarding of some of those destinations to form a smaller evoked or late consideration set, and a final destination selected from those in the late consideration set (Thompson and Cooper, 1979; Woodside and Lysonski, 1989; Woodside and Sherrell, 1977; Um and Crompton, 1990).

Conceptualization of the decision process as a narrowing down of alternatives was articulated by Nicosia (1966) who, in his theory of buyer behavior, presented the final purchase act as "emerging from a funneling

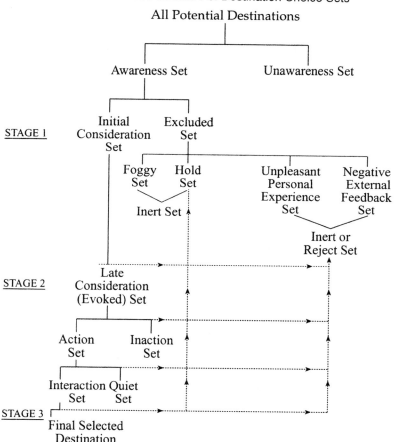

FIGURE 4.1. The Structure of Destination Choice Sets

process." However, he offered no explanation for this process. The notion of choice sets provided an explanation. It was first introduced into the consumer behavior literature by Howard (1963) and later elaborated upon by Howard and Sheth (1969). It offers a conceptualization of how potential tourists narrow down the number of destinations considered and how they then reach a final decision. The process explains how the decision is simplified, so a potential tourist is required to process only a fraction of the destination-related information to which he or she is likely to be exposed. The approach assumes that individuals seek information and evaluate the destination alternatives that are available to them.

Extensions of Howard's original conceptualization of awareness and evoked sets have been suggested by Narayana and Markin (1975), Brisoux and Laroche (1980), and Spiggle and Sewall (1987). They are shown in Figure 4.1, but since they were not tested in the study reported in this chapter they are not discussed further here. A full description of them was provided by Crompton (1992). The discussion here is limited to formation of the initial consideration set, late consideration set, and final selected destination.

The first stage of Howard's (1963) original paradigm suggested that all destinations could be categorized as belonging either in an individual's *awareness set* or in his or her *unawareness set*. The awareness set was defined as being composed of all the destinations of which an individual may be aware at any given time. The unawareness set consisted of all the destinations of which individuals are unaware.

The concept of awareness and unawareness sets was originally developed and tested on products such as toothpaste, automobiles, and beer where the number of brands is limited. Although it is effective in those contexts, operationalizing it in the context of tourism is challenging. In contrast to a product category of consumer goods, there are likely to be a prodigious number of destinations of which potential tourists are aware. Conceivably, each individual's list could consist of hundreds of such destinations. The notion of an unawareness set seems even more inappropriate to tourist decision making, given that there are an infinite number of potentially unknown destinations. To address this problem, Woodside and Sherrell (1977) discarded the notion of an unawareness set and suggested that it should be divided into an awareness-available set and an awareness-unavailable set: "The available set includes the travel destinations which the traveler believes he or she has the ability to visit within some period, for example, a year. Determining travelers' available sets may be more reasonable because of the infinite number of destinations possible in awareness set." (p. 15). The introduction of the phrase, "the ability to visit," substantially modifies and narrows the original definition of awareness set.

However, the phrase, "ability to visit," may be ambiguous. Some may interpret it to mean all those places travelers have the resources to visit, irrespective of whether they have any inherent appeal for them as a vacation destination. An alternative operationalization of this set would be "the destinations which a traveler is *considering as possible* vacation destinations within some period, e.g., a year." Given this definition, an appropriate descriptive nomenclature for this set is the *initial consideration set* (Woodside and Lysonski, 1989). Hence, this term was adopted in the study reported here, rather than the more traditional term of awareness set. Those destinations of which an individual is aware, but is not considering as a possible destination within a given period, constitute *the excluded set* (see Figure 4.1).

The second stage of Howard's (1963) original paradigm was the formulation of an *evoked set* of destinations, which consisted of those remaining from an initial awareness set after some reduction process has been implemented. Howard borrowed the term evoked set from March and Simon (1958), who had introduced it earlier to the field of organization theory and rather crudely defined it as "the part of the memory that is influencing behavior at a particular time." According to Howard and Sheth's (1969:26) operationalization, "The brands that become alternatives to the buyer's choice decision are generally a small number, collectively called his evoked set." In the context of tourism, this stage could be defined as "the destinations which a traveler is *considering as probable* destinations within some period of time," and should more appropriately be termed the *late consideration set*. A key conceptual differentiating element between the initial and late consideration sets is that a period of time elapses between them that is sufficiently long to enable individuals to evaluate and reduce their list of destinations from a broad set of possibles to a narrower set of probables.

Acceptance of the choice sets structure recognizes that there is an initial active search to reduce the number of alternative destinations in the initial consideration set to a smaller number of destinations that constitute the later consideration set. This approach then recognizes that a second search is undertaken to select a final destination from the late consideration set.

STUDY HYPOTHESES

Four hypotheses were developed and tested:

1. The mean score (perceived importance) of the magnitude of inhibitors among the alternative destinations which were not selected for inclusion in the late consideration set was greater than that among the alternatives which were selected for the late consideration set.
2. The mean score (perceived importance) of the magnitude of facilitators among the alternative destinations which were selected for inclusion in the late consideration set was greater than that among the alternatives which were not selected for the late consideration set.
3. The mean score (perceived importance) of the magnitude of inhibitors among the alternative destinations which were not selected the from the late consideration set was greater than that of the alternative(s) which was selected as the destination.
4. The mean score (perceived importance) of the magnitude of facilitators of the alternative(s) which was selected as a travel destination(s)

from the late consideration set was greater than that of the alternatives which were not selected from the late consideration set.

DATA COLLECTION

Constraints of time and financial resources led to the decision to use a convenience sample to serve as the panel of respondents. This meant that the study's findings could not be generalizable. However, this was not considered a major limitation because the intent was to test the structure of theoretical relationships, rather than to test the generalizability of those relationships. The total sample (n = 359) consisted of undergraduate college students from a variety of majors (n = 152) and recreation and park professionals (n = 207) who were attending a professional development program at the university (see Table 4.1).

Data collection was implemented in two stages. First, data concerning the early consideration sets of prospective summer pleasure travel destinations were collected in February from all 359 respondents using a self-administered questionnaire. Respondents were asked "Please list the names of all the out-of-state or foreign places which you are considering as possible destinations for a pleasure trip this summer." They were

TABLE 4.1. Summary of the Sampling Process

	Students	Nonstudents	Combined
Initial respondents (stage 1)	152	207	359
Incomplete or no intention to travel respondents	59	103	162
Qualifiers for stage 2 respondents	93	104	197
Unable to contact for the second survey	30	0	30
Returns from stage 2 respondents	63	75	138
Changed plans: no longer intending to travel	23	15	38
Usable sample	40	60	100

requested to evaluate each of these possible destinations using the set of scale items shown in Table 4.2. Twenty-five out of the 359 respondents provided incomplete responses and were discarded from further analysis. In addition, forty-five students and ninety-two nonstudents indicated in this first survey that they did not intend to take a pleasure vacation in the summer.

The second stage of data collection took place in May and included only those respondents who had indicated in the first survey that they intended to take a pleasure vacation. However, because of low class attendance at the end of the semester when the second survey was administered, thirty students who qualified for the second survey had to be dropped since they could not be contacted. Mail surveys were sent to all members of the nonstudent groups (n = 104). Out of the seventy-five nonstudent responses returned, sixty were usable for data analysis; fifteen responses were discarded because respondents indicated they no longer intended to take a vacation trip. The student group was given surveys to complete and forty of the sixty-three qualified students' responses were usable. The remaining twenty-three also indicated they no longer intended to go on a vacation. Thus, a total of 100 responses, sixty from nonstudents and forty from students, were used to test the hypotheses.

In the second survey instrument, respondents were asked two questions: (1) "Please write down the name of the place(s) which you have selected for your vacation trip this summer (vacation trip refers to an out-of-state or international pleasure trip which does *not include* travel in which the main purpose of the trip is to visit family, friends, relatives, or for business purposes)"; and (2) "Please list other out-of-state or foreign places which were close to being selected before you made your final selection decision."

If they had not yet decided upon a vacation destination, then respondents were asked to "Please list the names of *all the out-of-state or foreign places which you are still considering as possible destinations* for a pleasure trip this summer. In addition, please place in the parentheses (provided) the rank of each place in the order in which you are most likely to travel to it this summer." In this case, the place ranked first was considered the selected destination. Respondents were then asked to respond to the scale items measuring their beliefs about all the destinations that they listed, both close selections and likely final destination(s). Given that respondents completed the second stage survey before they had actually gone on their trips, the study measured intent to purchase rather than actual choice.

The decision to consider the highest ranked destination as the choice in situations where respondents had not selected their final destinations was made on the basis of findings reported by Axelrod (1968) and Woodside and Wilson (1985). In both of these studies it was reported that the brand

TABLE 4.2. Coefficients of Variations of the Scale Items and Their Mean Scores (n = 334) on the Facilitator-Inhibitor Instrument

	Scale with which item is associated	Mean	C.V. (%)
1. A trip to_____will be a lot of fun.	N.S.	4.21	27.92
2. It will cost more money to travel to _____than I can afford.	T	−2.16	−116.42
3. _____ is physically accessible only at certain times during each year.	T	−.16	−1168.52*
4. Others have recommended that I select _____ as a place to go.	S.A.	2.08	100.84
5. Climate is a major factor in my decision to visit _____.	N.S.	3.35	60.89
6. I can do a wide variety of things in_____.	N.S.	3.64	46.57
7. A trip to _____ is likely to enhance my feelings of well being.	N.S.	3.32	58.41
8. I can participate in outdoor recreation activities which I particularly enjoy in_____.	N.S.	3.26	61.19
9. I will travel to _____ because a friend or family member wants to go there.	S.A.	1.69	133.21
10. Others in the travel group with whom I usually travel agree with my selection.	S.A.	1.72	121.11
11. A trip to _____ is likely to improve togetherness with my family and friends.	S.A.	2.95	72.43
12. I want to travel to _____ because that is where everyone goes.	S.A.	−.41	−596.77*
13. I consider a trip to _____ to be challenging.	N.S.	2.58	80.57
14. Potential health problems are a concern if I go on a trip to _____.	T	−.76	−237.29
15. I am likely to meet many people with different interests and lifestyles in _____.	N.S.	2.63	80.69
16. _____ is likely to be a good place for me to relax.	N.S.	3.75	45.44
17. The time spent to get to _____ is longer than other places I considered going to.	T	−1.17	−174.20
18. It is not absolutely safe for me to travel to _____.	T	−1.01	−198.63
19. The attractive natural environment is the major reasons for selecting _____ as a destination.	N.S.	−1.01	−198.63
20. _____is not a place everyone would enjoy.	S.A.	.40	506.96*

N.S. = Need Satisfaction
S.A. = Social Agreement
T = Travelability
* These items were deleted

that received first mention by respondents was the most preferred and received the highest intention-to-purchase ratings. Similar findings were reported in the context of tourism by Bronner and de Hoog (1985).

OPERATIONALIZING FACILITATORS AND INHIBITORS

Multi-item scales were developed to measure three image and constraint dimensions that were consistently reported in the literature as affecting travel decisions. They were need satisfaction, social agreement, and travelability. The conceptualization that guided selection of the dimensions used in the scale was reported by Um and Crompton (1990). The need satisfaction dimension incorporated a set of benefits sought from a vacation that included novelty, challenge, relaxation, learning, and curiosity (Crompton, 1979), which the potential tourist would seek to fulfill by interacting with a destination's attributes. The social agreement dimension reflected potential travelers' inclinations to act in accordance with their social groups' opinions. The travelability dimension described an individual's capability to travel to a place in terms of such variables as money, time, skill, and health.

To operationalize the three dimensions, a pool of items was generated by an interacting panel of five individuals whom the authors believed to be knowledgeable of this literature. The researchers selected forty items from this pool based on face validity, and their content validity was checked by a different team of five knowledgeable individuals (Kerlinger, 1986). These judges were asked to ascertain with which of the three dimensions each item was associated and to consider: (1) clarity of the items, (2) readability of the items; and (3) likelihood of the items being objectionable to respondents.

Internal reliability of the scale items was pretested by using data collected from a sample of undergraduate students. Cronbach's alpha coefficient was computed separately for each dimension and items were deleted to improve the alpha values. This process reduced the number of items from forty to twenty. The Cronbach alphas for each of the three dimensions, need satisfaction, social agreement, and travelability were .80, .65, and .73, respectively. The twenty items and the image or constraint dimension with which they were associated are shown in Table 4.2.

Perceived inhibitors and facilitators were operationalized as consisting of two components: (1) the extent to which prospective destinations were believed to possess certain attributes, and (2) the relative strength or intensity of beliefs about each attribute as either an inhibitor or a facilitator in evaluating each place as a possible destination. Two different instruments were developed to measure each of these two components.

In the first instrument, all respondents were instructed to "Please list the names of all out-of-state or foreign places which you are considering as destinations for a pleasure trip this summer." They were then presented with sets of Likert-type scale items using five-point "strongly agree-strongly disagree" responses that were developed to measure the extent of each item's association with each of the destinations that respondents cited as being in their choice sets. The set of items is presented in Table 4.2. Each set of items was identical and was reproduced on a single page. Respondents were given several sets of items (pages) and the following directions: "Please write down the name of each of the places you just listed, at the top of each of the next pages." The researchers verbally reinforced this instruction by checking with each group that this was done. That is, if five places were listed by a respondent, then he or she had five sets of scale items with a different place listed at the top of each sheet. It was explained verbally that the blanks in the scale items (Table 4.2) represented the name of the place listed at the top of the sheet.

The wording of the second instrument and the format used are shown in Table 4.3. Respondents were asked to check each item on a three-point scale as being a "perceived inhibitor," "neither perceived inhibitor nor perceived facilitator," or "perceived facilitator," and then to evaluate its relative strength on a five-point "very weak-very strong" continuum. This process yielded an eleven-point, Likert-type scale ranging from minus five for very strong inhibitor to plus five for very strong facilitator with "neither perceived inhibitor nor perceived facilitator" representing zero. In this way, respondents evaluated each item in terms of its relative strength as either an inhibitor or a facilitator.

The survey took approximately fifteen minutes to complete. The researchers had a long-established positive rapport with both the student and the recreation and park professional respondents. There was enthusiastic respondent cooperation and the researchers did not observe any indication of respondent fatigue.

The second column in Table 4.2 reports the mean scores of the twenty items on the eleven-point facilitator—inhibitor scale. It shows that the strongest facilitators were the items: a lot of fun (item number 1); attractive natural environment (19); relaxation (16); and a wide variety of things to do (6). Five of the six inhibitors were the items that made up the travelability scale: high monetary cost (2); long time to get there (17); not absolutely safe (18); potential health problems (14); and physically accessible only at certain times (3). The only other inhibitor item was: a vacation place where everyone goes (12).

TABLE 4.3. The Format Used to Measure the Relative Strength of Each Scale Item As a Perceived Facilitator or Inhibitor

When you evaluated the possible destinations for your summer vacation travel, how strongly did you consider each of the following to be either an inhibitor (negative factor) or facilitator (positive factor) in your evaluations? First identify whether each item is an inhibitor, neither inhibitor nor facilitator, or facilitator, and then indicate its relative strength. (If an item is identified as neither inhibitor nor facilitator, do not answer the question about its relative strength.)

Inhibitor	Neither Inhibitor nor Facilitator	Facilitator	Very Weak	Weak	Neutral	Strong	Very Strong

1. A lot of fun
2. Higher monetary cost than you can afford .
   .
   .
   .

20. Not a place which everyone would enjoy

RESULTS

Out of the initial set of 359 study respondents, there were 334 completed responses to the twenty scale items. Based on these responses, three of the twenty items were deleted from the instrument because their high coefficients of variation suggested low content validity (that is, these three items were perceived inconsistently across respondents). The coefficients of variation are reported in the third column of Table 4.2. The seventeen items were subjected to a factor analysis that confirmed the differentiation of the three dimensions: need satisfaction, social agreement, and travelability. However, it suggested that the need satisfaction dimension could be further specified into active needs, passive needs, and intellectual needs. The total variance explained by the factors was 51 percent. Details of this factor analysis procedure are reported in Um and Crompton (1991).

The predictive validity of the multi-item scales was checked by testing for significant differences between scores toward the potential destination that respondents ranked first in their early consideration sets and scores toward the potential destination they ranked last in their early consideration sets in terms of their likelihood of traveling to them. Table 4.4 illustrates how scores were calculated between the places a respondent listed as "the most likely to visit place" and "the least likely to visit place." For example, for subject 1, the overall score for Colorado (123) was compared with the score for Hawaii (110), and, for subject 2, the score for Florida (142) was compared with the score for Europe (115). Related sample t-tests revealed significant differences between first- and last-ranked destinations in the early consideration set in the scores of both perceived facilitators and perceived inhibitors as well as in the overall scores (Table 4.5). These results provide evidence suggesting there was criterion-related validity of the multi-item scales measuring perceived facilitators and inhibitors.

The hypotheses were designed to explore the roles of perceived inhibitors and facilitators at the two different stages in the destination choice process. Related sample t-tests were used for testing the hypotheses. The procedures adopted for testing the hypotheses were as follows:

1. Each respondent's mean scores of inhibitors and facilitators across items were calculated for the group of selected alternatives (and first ranked places) (χ_1) and the group of nonselected alternatives (χ_2) at each stage of the destination choice process.
2. The difference (d) between the mean scores of the two groups of alternatives was calculated for each respondent and then the mean score across respondents ($\overline{d}$) of those differences was calculated (see Table 4.4).

$$d = \chi_1 - \chi_2$$

3. The standard error of the differences between the mean scores of the two groups of alternatives was estimated from:

$$S_\delta = (3[\overline{d} - d]^2/n[n-1])^{1/2}$$

where: n is the number of pairs.

4. The t value was calculated by:

$$t = \overline{d}/S_{\overline{d}}$$

5. The calculated t was compared to the tabled value at the .05 level of significance and with degrees of freedom equal to $n-1$. If the calculated statistics equalled or exceeded the tabled value, the null hypothesis was rejected and the alternative hypothesis was accepted.

TABLE 4.4. Illustration of How Facilitator and Inhibitor Scores Were Used to Quantify Destination Evaluation Divisions

Respondent Number	Preference Rank	Set of Destinations	ΣPF - ΣPI [1]	PI [2]	d (PI) [3]	PF [4]	d (PF) [5]
1	1.	Colorado	123	23		146	
	2.	Hawaii	110	48	25	158	12
2	1.	Florida	144	12		156	
	2.	Canada	113	21		134	
	3.	Mexico	110	68		178	
	4.	Europe	115	76	64	191	35
3	1.	Disney World	101	11		112	
	2.	Los Angeles	98	23		121	
	3.	Alaska	110	16	5	127	15
	.	.	.	.	.	.	.
	.	.	.	.	.	.	.
	.	.	.	.	.	.	.
			91	21	–	113	–

1. The scores are the summed scores of items that were perceived as facilitators (PF) minus the summed scores of items perceived as inhibitors (PI).

2. and 4. The scores of both perceived inhibitors and perceived facilitators were calculated based on the formulas given in the paper.

3. and 5. d represents the different in magnitude of PI and PF between the first-ranked place and the last-ranked place.

Table 4.6 shows the results of the t-tests performed to test hypotheses 1 and 2 concerned with the magnitude of perceived inhibitors and facilitators at the stage of evolving a late consideration set from an early consideration set. The results indicate that the mean score of the magnitude of facilitators among the alternative destinations which were selected for inclusion in the late consideration set was significantly (.05 level) greater than that of the alternatives not selected in the late consideration set. No significant difference was found in the mean score of inhibitors between selected alternatives and nonselected alternatives in the late consideration set.

Table 4.7 shows the results of the related sample t-tests performed to test hypotheses 3 and 4 concerned with the magnitude of inhibitors and facilitators at the stage of selecting a destination from the late consideration set. The results indicate that the mean score of the magnitude of inhibitors which were

TABLE 4.5. Results of Related Sample t-Test Seeking Differences Between First- and Last-Ranked Destinations in Respondents' Early Evoked Sets

	N	Mean $(\bar{d})$	t value[1]	Probability
Perceived Inhibitors	261	3.48	5.76	.001*
Perceived Facilitators	291	3.21	2.32	.020*

[1] $t = \bar{d}/S\bar{d}$ where $d = \chi_1 - \chi_2$
* Significant at the 0.5 level.

TABLE 4.6. Results of Related Sample t-Test for Differences in the Mean Scores of Facilitators and Inhibitors Among Alternative Destinations in the Early Evoked Set Which Were, and Were Not Included in the Late Evoked Set

Type of Variable	n	Mean $(\bar{d})$	STD Error	T Value	Probability
Perceived Inhibitors	50	7.25	2.36	3.07	.004*
Perceived Facilitators	41	1.27	.91	1.55	.128

*Significant at the 0.5 level.

TABLE 4.7. Results of Related Sample t-Test for Differences in the Mean Scores of Facilitators and Inhibitors Among Alternative Destinations in the Late Evoked Set Which Were Not, and the Alternative(s) Which Were, Selected As Final Destination

Type of Variable	n	Mean $(\bar{d})$	STD Error	T Value	Probability
Perceived Inhibitors	84	3.18	2.24	1.42	.160*
Perceived Facilitators	41	1.27	.91	1.55	.036*

*Significant at the 0.5 level.

associated with destinations not selected as the destination from the late consideration set were significantly (.05 level) greater than that of the alternative(s) selected as the travel destination. Interestingly, no significant difference was found in the mean score of perceived facilitators between selected alternatives and nonselected alternatives.

CONCLUDING COMMENTS

The literature relating to human judgment and decision making from which the conceptual framework in this chapter emerges is substantial. Useful reviews of the early work can be found in Rapoport and Wallsten (1972), Lee (1971), and Slovic and Lichtenstein (1971). It is apparent from this literature that beliefs and attitudes have been used most frequently in efforts to predict behavioral responses (Bass and Talarzyk, 1971). This literature also suggests that in the early stages of making a decision, belief or attitude is related to preference rather than to the act of purchasing a vacation at a destination (Assael, 1984; Tuck, 1973). The evolution of a late consideration set and ultimate selection of a destination is a function of the interaction between attitude toward the alternative destinations and constraints acting on a potential traveler at the time of the destination selection decision (Hansen, 1976). This is consistent with findings reported in the consumer behavior literature (Belk, 1975; Park, 1978), in the tourism literature (Woodside and Lysonski, 1989; Tian, Crompton and Witt, 1996), and in the recreation choice literature (Harris, Driver, and Bergersen, 1985), which suggest that constraints should be integrated into the cognitive choice process. In this study, this was achieved by operationalizing perceived inhibitors and facilitators and relating them to destination attributes.

Two hypotheses concerned with identifying the roles of inhibitors and facilitators were tested at two stages of the decision process. The results of the hypotheses testing suggested that whereas at the early stage of selecting a destination, magnitude of the perceived facilitators (image) was a significant indicator in predicting which destinations evolved to a late consideration set from an initial consideration set, at the later stage this changed and it was magnitude of perceived inhibitors (constraints) that was the significant indicator of destination selection.

Far-reaching suggestions based on this preliminary study should be avoided since the results were based on a relatively small convenience sample. Two preliminary implications were suggested by the study's findings. First, the decision process in the structure of the model was conceptualized as being sequential. The results showing the greater importance of facilitators in the earlier stage of formulating a late consideration set and of inhibitors in the later stage of making an actual choice, provided evidence to suggest that this conceptualization was appropriate.

Second, the results were consistent with the notion that choice is a satisfying behavior (Simon, 1957) which is constraint driven, rather than an optimizing behavior which is destination-attribute driven. Selection of a vacation destination is likely to be a decision made under conditions of uncertainty, since knowledge of a destination's ability to meet needs is likely to be based on indirect symbolic or social information. An optimal decision maximizes the payoff, but it may require disregarding constraints, which involves a considerable investment of risk. The greater importance of image at the early stage in the decision process reflects optimization, but people tend to be risk reducers and the study suggests that at the final decision stage it is constraints which prevail. To reduce risk, the potential tourist requires only that the destination appears to offer a satisfactory payoff that can be attained within perceived constraints. This suggests models of tourism behavior should reflect that it is the risk reduction constraint factors which are likely to be deterministic, rather than the attributes of the amenities or attractions of a destination.

CONCEPT DEFINITIONS

Constraints: Barriers or perceptions of barriers that militate against potential tourists selecting a destination for their vacation.

Facilitators: Attributes that operationalize the image construct.

Image: A holistic construct which is derived from attitudes toward a destination's perceived tourism attributes.

Inhibitors: Perceptions of barriers that operationalize constraints.

Initial consideration set: Comprises the set of destinations a tourist is considering as *possible* vacation destinations within some time period.
Late consideration set: Comprises the set of destinations a tourist is considering as *probable* destinations within some time period.

REVIEW QUESTIONS

1. Describe the structure of destination choice sets and define how the alternative sets may be operationalized in a way that is meaningful to managers.
2. Describe what is meant by "facilitators" and "inhibitors." Discuss how their roles in the decision process differ at each stage in the decision process. What are the implications for managers of these differences?
3. What weaknesses in the design of this study can you identify? Describe how you would design the study to improve on this exploratory effort, if you were given a substantial budget to do it.
4. Distinguish between "satisficing" and "optimizing" behavior. Is optimizing behavior likely to lead to greater satisfaction than satisficing behavior?
5. Identify factors beyond facilitators and inhibitors that are likely to be influential in a decision to select a particular destination for a pleasure vacation. Develop a model of the decision process that incorporates both choice sets and these other factors.

REFERENCES

Assael, H. (1984). *Consumer Behavior and Marketing Action.* Boston: Kent Publishing Company.

Axelrod, J.N. (1968). Attitude measures that predict purchase. *Journal of Advertising Research* March, 3-17.

Bass, F M. and Talarzyk, W. (1971). Using attitude to predict individual preference. *Advertising* 4, 63-72.

Belk, R.W. (1975). Situational variables and consumer behavior. *Journal of Consumer Research* 2, 157-164.

Brisoux, J.E. and Laroche, M. (1980). A proposed consumer strategy of simplification for categorizing brands. In *Evolving Marketing Thought for the 1980s, Proceedings of the Southern Marketing Association Annual Meeting,* New Orleans, Louisiana, pp. 112-114.

Bronner, F. and de Hoog, R. (1985). A recipe for mixing decision ingredients. *European Research* July, 109-115.

Brown, P.J. and Ross, D.M. (1982). Using desired recreation experiences to predict setting preferences. In *Forest and River Recreation Research Update*, Agricultural Experiment Station Miscellaneous Publication 18, University of Minnesota, St. Paul, MN, pp. 105-110.

Corstjens, M.L. and Gautschi, D.A. (1983). Formal choice models in marketing. *Marketing Science* 2, 19-56.

Crompton, J.L. (1977). A systems model of the tourist's destination selection decision process with particular reference to the role of image and perceived constraints. Unpublished doctoral dissertation, Texas A&M University, College Station, TX.

Crompton, J.L. (1979). Motivations for pleasure vacation. *Annals of Tourism Research* 6, 408-424.

Crompton, J.L. (1992). Structure of vacation destination choice sets. *Annals of Tourism Research* 19(3), 420-434.

Crompton, J.L. and Ankomah, P.K. (1993). Choice set propositions in destination decisions. *Annals of Tourism Research* 20(3), 461-476.

Fakeye, P.C. and Crompton, J.L. (1991). Image differences between prospective, first-time, and repeat visitors to the Lower Rio Grande Valley. *Journal of Travel Research* 30 (Fall), 10-16.

Fesenmaier, D.R. (1988). Integrating activity patterns into destination choice models. *Journal of Leisure Research* 20(3), 175-191.

Gartner, W.C. (1986). Temporal influences on image change. *Annals of Tourism Research* 13(4), 635-643.

Hansen, F. (1976). Psychological theories of consumer choice. *Journal of Consumer Research* 3, 117-142.

Harris, C.C., Driver, B.L., and Bergersen, E.P. (1985). Do choices of sport fisheries reflect angler preferences for site attractions? In G.H. Stankey and S.F. McCool (Eds.) *Proceedings of the Symposium on Recreation Choice Behavior*, USDA Forest Service, Intermountain Research Station General Technical Report INT-184, Ogden, UT, pp. 46-53.

Holbrook, M.B. (1981). Integrating compositional and decompositional analyses to represent the intervening role of perceptions in evaluative judgments. *Journal of Marketing Research* 18, 13-28.

Howard, J.A. (1963). *Marketing Management Analysis and Planning*. Homewood, IL: Irwin.

Howard, J.A. and Sheth, J.N. (1969). *The Theory of Buyer Behavior*. New York: John Wiley and Sons, Inc.

Hunt, J.D. (1975). Image as a factor in tourism development. *Journal of Travel Research* 13, 18-23.

Iso-Ahola, S.E. (1980). *The Social Psychology of Leisure and Recreation*. Dubuque, IA: William C. Brown Company.

Jackson, E.L. (1991). Leisure constraints/constrained leisure: Special issue introduction. *Journal of Leisure Research* 23(4), 279-285.

Jackson, E.L. and Searle, M.S. (1985). Recreation non-participation and barriers to participation: Concepts and models. *Loisir et Societe* 8, 693-707.

Keown, C., Jacobs, L., and Worthley, R. (1984). American tourists' perceptions of retail stores in 12 selected countries. *Journal of Travel Research* 22(Winter), 26-30.

Kerlinger, F.N. (1986). *Foundations of Behavioral Research* (Third Edition) New York: Holt, Rinehart and Wilson, Inc.

Krumpe, E.E. and McLaughlin, W.J. (1982). A model of recreationists' decision making process. In *Forest and River Recreation Research Update*, Agricultural Experiment Station Miscellaneous Publication 18, University of Minnesota, St. Paul, MN, pp. 94-99.

Lee, W. (1971). *Decision Theory and Human Behavior.* New York: Wiley.

March, J.G. and Simon, H.A. (1958). *Organization.* New York: John Wiley.

Mayo, E. J. (1973). Regional images and regional travel development. In *1973 Travel and Tourism Research Association Proceedings*, 211-217.

McCool, S.F., Stankey, G.H. and Clark, R.N. (1985). Choosing recreation settings: Processes, findings, and research directions. In G.H. Stankey and S.F. McCool (Eds.) *Proceedings of the Symposium on Recreation Choice Behavior,* USDA Forest Service, Intermountain Research Station General Technical Report INT-184, Ogden, UT, pp. 1-8.

Moutinho, L. (1986). Consumer behavior in tourism. *Management Bibliographies and Reviews* 12, 3-42.

Narayana, C.L. and Markin, R.J. (1975). Consumer behavior and product performance: An alternative conceptualization. *Journal of Marketing* 39, 1-6.

Nicosia, F.M. (1966). *Consumer Decision Processes: Marketing and Advertising Implications.* Englewood Cliffs, NJ: Prentice Hall.

Park, C.W. (1978). A conflict resolution choice model. *Journal of Consumer Research* 5, 125-137.

Peterson, G.L., Stynes, D.J., Rosenthal, D.H., and Dwyer, J.F. (1985). Substitution recreation choice behavior. In G.H. Stankey and S.F. McCool (Eds.) *Proceedings of the Symposium on Recreation Choice Behavior*, USDA Forest Service, Intemountain Research Station General Technical Report, INT-184, Ogden, UT, pp. 19-30.

Rapoport, A. and Wallsten, T.S. (1972). Individual decision behavior. *Annual Review of Psychology* 23, 131-176.

Simon, H.A. 1957. *Models of Man: Social and Rational; Mathematical Essays on Rational Human Behavior in a Social Setting.* New York: Wiley.

Slovic, P. and Lichtenstein, S. (1971). Comparison of bayesian and regression approaches to the study of information processing in judgment. *Organizational Behavior and Human Performance* 6, 649-744.

Spiggle, S. and Sewall, M.A. (1987). A choice sets model of retail selection. *Journal of Marketing* 51, 97-111.

Thompson, J.R. and Cooper, P.D. (1979). Attitudinal evidence on the limited size of evoked set of travel destinations. *Journal of Travel Research* 17, 23-25.

Tian, S., Crompton, J.L. and Witt, P.A. (1996). Integrating constraints and benefits to identify responsive target markets for museum attractions. *Journal of Travel Research* 35(2), 34-45.

Tuck, M. (1973). Fishbein theory and the Bass-Talarzyk problem. *Journal of Marketing Research* 10, 345-348.

Um, S. and Crompton, J.L. (1990). Attitude determinants in tourism destination choice. *Annals of Tourism Research* 17(3), 432-448.

Um, S. and Crompton, J.L. (1991). Development of pleasure travel dimensions. *Annals of Tourism Research* 18(1).

Woodside, A.G. and Lysonski, S. (1989). A general model of traveler destination choice. *Journal of Travel Research* 27(4), (Spring), 8-14.

Woodside, A.G. and Sherrell, D. (1977). Traveler evoked set, inept set, and inert sets of vacation destinations. *Journal of Travel Research* 16, 14-18.

Woodside, A.G. and Wilson, E.J. (1985). Effects of consumer awareness and brand advertising on preference. *Journal of Advertising Research* 25 (May-June), 44-53.

Young, R.A. and Kent, A.T. (1985). Using the theory of reasoned action to improve the understanding of recreation behavior. *Journal of Leisure Research* 17, 90-106.

Chapter 5

Tourists' Decision-Making and Behavior Processes

Alain Decrop

LEARNING OBJECTIVES

By the end of the chapter the reader should be able to:

- Define and describe the main components of tourists' decision-making and behavior processes
- Discuss how the interpretivist and constructivist approaches to science differ from the more traditional positivist and postpositivist views
- Discuss how the interpretivist view sheds new light on vacationers' decision-making processes
- Describe the components and explain the hypotheses (i.e., assumed relationships between components) of the three traditional models of vacationers' decision-making processes
- Compare the traditional models of Crompton, Moutinho, and Woodside (including both similarities and disparities)
- Discuss the sets of propositions and new frameworks emerging from interpretivist research about vacationers' decision-making processes
- Contrast the "rational" tourist with other types of tourists

INTRODUCTION

Many textbooks on consumer behavior start with the presentation of a general framework of the consumer's decision-making process, and only after this are its different components discussed. In this chapter, we will go the other way around. First, we describe the major aspects of tourists'

103

decision-making and behavior processes before looking at how those components relate to each other. The reason is that, instead of developing only one general model, we consider several approaches to decision making. This is introduced by a discussion of the major competing paradigms in the social sciences. On one hand, we present three traditional models that consider the tourist as being rational and a cognitive information processor. On the other hand, alternative frameworks are proposed that include sets of propositions which question classical assumptions. A new typology of tourists, based on their decision-making style, closes the chapter.

MAJOR ASPECTS OF TOURISTS' DECISION-MAKING AND BEHAVIOR PROCESSES

The Cognitive Tourist

Cognition pertains to brain processes or mental activities that involve information processing. We examine how the tourist perceives, thinks about, and understands information. Three core cognitive constructs deserve particular attention: perception, learning, and attitudes.

Tourist *perception* can be defined as the process of translating tourist information from the external world into the internal, mental world that each of us experiences. Three basic cognitive operations make perception a very selective process: sensation, attention, and memory. Tourist information originates from the marketer (through marketing-mix tools such as product design and advertising message) or from other sources (for example, our social network).

Learning is related to perception. Perceived information can be mentally assimilated or "learned" in order to develop knowledge and skills that give new responses to the environment. This process of knowledge acquisition consists of storing information in the memory in the form of associations. Those associations give birth to beliefs and feelings. For instance, a particular holiday destination may be connected with such different attributes as climate, culture, or nature, as well as with how the tourist feels about it.

Attitude is classically defined as the declared statement of a "learned predisposition to respond to an object or a class of objects in a consistently favorable or unfavorable way" (Allport, 1935). From this definition, some social scientists argue that attitudes include three components: cognitive (perception, belief), affective (evaluation, affect), and conative (action, intention). Following that multidimensional view, examples of a vacationer's attitude statements about destinations are:

- I think Greece has the most wonderful historical sites in the world (belief).
- I like Thailand very much (affect).
- I will choose Turkey for my vacation (behavioral intention).

Other authors prefer a unidimensional definition of attitude as "feelings of liking or disliking an object," limiting it to the affective component. Note that *preference* is a special case of attitudes where product alternatives are compared and the one is chosen over the other.

As far as tourist products and services are concerned, perception and preference judgments are often expressed in terms of the *attributes* the product/service possesses. A usual distinction (Lefkoff-Hagius and Mason, 1993) is made between:

- Characteristic or product referent attributes (e.g., mean temperature or spiciness of food at a tourist destination)
- Beneficial or outcome referent attributes (e.g., friendliness of the local people or tastiness of the food)
- Image or user referent attributes (e.g., vacationing in Monaco would give me a prestigious and rich image; going to Iraq would make a reckless adventurer of me)

Choice then consists of an evaluation and selection process where different product alternatives are compared by their attributes. Both perception and preference are involved in the following selection process. The *awareness set* (result of perception) includes all potential travel destinations the vacationer has in mind, independently, from a real decision process. The *consideration set* or *evoked set* (result of perceptions and preferences) only contains those destinations that the vacationer considers reasonable alternatives after deciding to go on holiday. The *final choice* of travel location is selected among those alternatives (result of preferences and situational variables).

The Personal Tourist

It is common sense to say that behavior is much more than the result of cognitive information processing. The tourist is a person who deserves to be considered as a human being with motivations, emotions, and lifestyle.

Personality and Self-Concept

Personality is a complex psychological phenomenon. Although consensus is lacking, it could be defined as the reflection of a person's enduring and unique characteristics that urge him or her to respond in persistent ways to recurring environmental stimuli. Personality is the result of a person's history and goes far beyond sociodemographics.

The individual's enduring characteristics are often called *traits*. Following this approach, vacation travelers could be characterized as reflective, active, sociable, outgoing, inquisitive, and confident. Air vacationers could be described as very active, very confident, and reflective while bus vacationers are dependent, apprehensive, sensitive, hostile, belligerent, and unrestrained (Canadian Government Travel Bureau, 1971 in Mayo and Jarvis, 1981). Traits together form personality *types*. One popular type-casting approach makes a distinction between psychocentric persons, who are more concerned with themselves (introverted), anxious, and inhibited, and allocentric persons, who tend to be more extroverted, self-confident, and adventurous. This useful model was first adapted in tourism by Plog (1972): "Travelers who are more allocentric are thought to prefer exotic destinations, unstructured vacations rather than package tours, and more involvement with local cultures. Psychocentrics, on the other hand, are thought to prefer familiar destinations, packaged tours, and touristy areas" (Ross, 1994, pp. 33-34).

The *self-concept* is another way to explain how personality influences behavior. The notion of self-concept, or self-image, derives from Freudian psychoanalytic theory and pertains to the concepts that the consumer believes characterize him or her. Authors generally deal with two levels of self-concept (e.g., Grubb and Stern, 1971):

1. The actual self-image refers to the individual's global perception of the self (including his or her descriptions and evaluations).
2. The ideal self-image is the person's perception of what (including who) he or she would like to be. Note that vacationing and traveling are often elicited as part of the ideal self.

Self-image is, like the other personality concepts, important in tourism marketing for the segmentation and positioning of destinations and services. For example, it would be very relevant to first promote a cruise for people who aspire to have an extraordinary experience characterized by prestige, luxury, and romance. When associated with product image, the self-concept helps in explaining tourist behavior.

Lifestyles

The term *lifestyle* refers to unique patterns of thinking and behaving (including daily life routine, activities, interests, opinions, values, needs, and perceptions) that characterize differences among consumers. Lifestyles (or "psychographics") are reflections of self-concept and offer insight into tourists' patterns of time, spending, and feeling. In contrast with the purely descriptive demographic data, lifestyles give indications about how people really live. Plog (1994) identifies eight psychographic/personality dimensions of the tourist: venturesomeness, pleasure-seeking, impulsivity, self-confidence, plan-making, masculinity, intellectualism, and people orientation. Another interesting typology comes from Mayo and Jarvis (1981). Based on a broad literature review, they describe five types of travelers: the "peace and quiet" traveler, the overseas traveler, the historian traveler, the recreational vehicle traveler, and the "travel now/ pay later" traveler. The Austrian National Tourist Office condensed sixteen styles from the *Eurostyles* typology into five socio-targets: the prudent relaxation-seeker, the young family, the young hedonistic vacationer, the demanding adventure-seeker and the classic culture-seeker (Mazanec, 1994).

Motivation and Involvement

Next to *how*, the question of *why* consumers behave as they do is of paramount importance to understand decision-making processes. It is important to notice that *motivation* and *motivation research* are generic terms. Four terms about which there is a lot of confusion deserve a close look: motives, needs, wants, and benefits.

A *motive* is a lasting disposition, an internal drive or "push factor" that "causes the tourist to search for signs in objects, situations, and events that contain the promise of reducing the prevalent drive" (Gnoth, 1997, pp. 290-291). Each motive has a different content in terms of goals of behavior. Motives and personal characteristics determine a person's disposition that leads to behavior. A *need* is the materialization (on the consumer plane) of a motive (on the psychological plane). In the same way, the *want* (manifestation of the need) is the goal object and the *benefit* (whatever consumers derive from products) is the goal of behavior (Foxall and Goldsmith, 1994). Next to general theories of motivation by Freud, Murray, and Maslow, many motivation typologies were specifically developed to explain tourist behavior (for a review, see Ross, 1994).

Involvement is another concept related to motivation. In contrast with basic motives and needs (see below), which characterize the consumer alone, involvement is the result of a consumer/product interaction. It is more precisely defined as "the level of perceived personal importance and/or interest evoked by a stimulus within a specific situation" (Antil, 1984, p. 204). The level of involvement (low/high) is used to categorize products or consumer behavior theories (see later). Its consequences are types of searching, information processing, and decision making.

Emotion

Vacation decisions are much more than a question of cognitive information processing, lifestyle, and motivation. Fantasies, feelings, and fun, encompassed by what is called the "experiential view," are part of tourist experiences. However, this aspect is often omitted in tourist behavior textbooks and articles. This is especially surprising since tourism destinations and services can be considered as part of those phenomena that include "various playful activities, sensory pleasures, daydreams, esthetic enjoyment, and emotional responses" (Holbrook and Hirschman, 1982, p. 132).

Emotion can be defined as "a state of arousal involving conscious experience and visceral, or physiological, changes" (Mullen and Johnson, 1990, p. 75). In consumer behavior, emotion is generally expressed in terms of feeling toward the product while for Holbrook (1984), it encompasses a wider range of phenomena that entail four interacting components: physiological response, cognition, behavioral expression, and feelings. Several typologies of emotions follow (see Holbrook, 1984) that can be used in tourism marketing and advertising. A few studies have proven that advertising effectiveness depends upon the emotional content of messages. The use of repetition, classical conditioning, humor, and fear appeals are particularly powerful in eliciting emotional responses toward products. Here are examples for Plutchik's (1980) eight primary emotions in the tourist experience:

- Acceptance: Deep personal liking for your favorite travel agent.
- Disgust: Discovering that your hotel room is infested with cockroaches.
- Fear: Being stung by a mosquito during a safari trip in Kenya when no antimalaria precautions have been taken.
- Anger: Being stuck in a traffic jam on the way to the airport as you leave for the holiday.
- Joy: Listening to exotic music played by the locals.
- Sadness: Being seven years old and finding that there is no swimming pool in your hotel.
- Surprise: Finding a bottle of champagne in your room which you did not ask for.
- Expectancy: Getting into the bus for the excursion to Egypt's pyramids.

The Tourist in Context

The previous paragraphs focused on the individual tourist and his or her cognition and personality. To come to a complete understanding of tourist decision-making processes, the context must be considered. The context refers to the external variables affecting what and how the tourist thinks, feels, learns, and behaves. We make a basic distinction between (1) environmental or situational influences and (2) social and cultural influences before (3) discussing the dimensions a group adds to the decision-making process.

Situational Influences

It is easy to argue that such environmental variables as time, money, health, or marketing pressure can intervene as either inhibitors or facilitators in making a vacation decision. Belk (1975) defines situations as "all those factors particular to a time and place of observation, which do not follow from a knowledge of personal (intra-individual) and stimulus (object or choice alternative) attributes and which have a demonstrable and systematic effect on current behavior" (p. 158). He distinguishes five types of situational variables. For each, we give an appropriate tourism example.

- *Physical surroundings* include weather, geographical location, decor, sounds, lights, aromas, tangible signs and displays of merchandise, and other materials. The weather in the home region, outdoor advertising, and the decor of a travel agency's window are part of the vacationer's physical surroundings.
- *Social surroundings* include other people and their characteristics, roles, and interactions. The social network is an important source of information and persuasion in selecting a particular travel destination. Crowding can also act as a situational variable: people living in crowded cities tend to spend their holiday in open spaces where they can rest and be alone for a while.
- *Temporal perspective* includes the period (from the time of day to season of the year), time constraints, and elapsed or expected time. This situational variable is very important in tourism since many vacationers are limited by the period (depending on the school holiday) and by the available time (paid holiday). The wish to go on holiday is also a positive function of the time elapsed since the last vacation travel.
- *Task definition* stands for the orientation, intent, role, or frame of a person, through which certain aspects of the environment may

become relevant. One would not use the same criteria in selecting a city trip for oneself or as a gift for one's parents.

- *Antecedent states* are momentary moods or conditions that "color" the perception, evaluation, and acceptance of the environment present. These conditions are stipulated to be immediately antecedent to the current situation. A person who has just inherited a large sum of money could suddenly decide to take a cruise vacation; a couple that is very tired after moving into a new home could choose a club vacation even if they usually prefer a more culturally active holiday.

Social and Cultural Influences

All the facets of the individual consumer discussed above, as well as situational influences on choice are influenced by the social and cultural structure in which the consumer is embedded. Because they are pervasive and intangible, the consumer is often unaware of those influences.

Groups are fundamental to the individual because they protect, they help solve problems, they allow interaction with certain types of people, and they provide models of behavior ("norms"). *Reference group* is defined as a collection of people used by the individual as a standard for his or her own attitudes, beliefs, values, and behavior (Sears, Peplau, and Taylor, 1991). For example, I could decide to spend my next holiday in such an exotic destination as Madagascar, just because all my friends are going to exotic destinations. Such a person can belong to the group or aspire to join it.

Culture can be considered as a broad, impersonal reference group consisting of the knowledge, behaviors, customs, and techniques socially acquired (i.e., learned) by human beings. It includes beliefs, values, norms, signs, habits, and nonnormative behavior. Thus, culture also influences the way a person behaves as a consumer or as a tourist. The single example of sport will make us understand how culture can influence travel behavior. Sport has become such an important cultural value in the Western countries that it has influenced the content of the holiday experience. Golf, tennis, skiing, and scuba diving are, among others, activities that are not accessory anymore but are the primary motives for pleasure travel of many Europeans and Americans. Cultures also exist within the overall culture. Those *subcultures* are groups based on region, race, language, religion, age, social class, or other factors. The point is that members of a subculture typically conform to many of the norms of the dominant culture, but deviate from other norms which are not compatible with those of their subculture.

Social classes are a special case of subcultures. Social classes are the consequence of the division of society on the basis of status and prestige. Education and occupation are the basic factors that explain the belonging to one social class. Wealth and income are less decisive determinants. "Each social class displays a distinctive life-style which is reflected in values, interpersonal attitudes, and self-perceptions that differ from those held by any other class" (Mayo and Jarvis, 1981). Many tourist destinations such as ski resorts have a definite social class orientation. For example, the Spanish Costa Blanca appeals to the lower middle class and the working class searching for sea, sun, and fun to escape the stress and grayness of everyday life. The Caribbean or the French Riviera are spots where higher social classes gather and feel at home. Other places, such as Florida, attract people from all social classes, but the different classes tend to separate and segregate once they arrive.

Group (Family) Decision Making

Family is a major reference group since it is the source of most of our norms. Also, the family functions as a decision-making unit (DMU) where the important decisions of life, including consumption choices, are discussed. Note that as far as vacation is concerned, parties of friends or special interest groups also represent relevant DMUs. The level of communication, the mode of decision making (consensus, bargaining, vote, dictatorship), and the result of confrontation (agreement versus conflict) are important determinants of group decision processes.

Role is a major variable when analyzing group decision making. The relevant questions are:

1. How are roles and tasks distributed within the DMU? Kotler (1997) distinguishes five buying roles (initiator, influencer, decider, purchaser, and user).
2. What is the relative influence of each member of the family (husband, wife, or children dominant, versus syncretic decisions)?
3. What is the specialization level (joint versus autonomic decisions, depending on the degree of dialogue)?

Note that vacation decisions are usually joint and syncretic.

THE NEED FOR RELATIVISM: COMPETING PARADIGMS IN THE SOCIAL SCIENCES AND IN DECISION THEORY

Before considering how the different elements presented in the previous section relate to each other in decision making, we want to insist on relativism." In contrast with many received ideas, there is not only one, but several ways of looking at tourists' decision-making processes. Differences are related to competing paradigms in the social sciences. Therefore, presenting the major existing paradigms used to describe consumer behavior and, in particular, decision-making processes is crucial.

Positivism and Postpositivism

First, there is the classical view, based on the positivist and postpositivist philosophies of science. Positivism postulates a "real" and apprehendable reality, driven by immutable natural laws and mechanisms. Postpositivism is more critical: reality is only imperfectly (and probabilistically) apprehendable because of "basically flawed human intellectual mechanisms and the intractable nature of phenomena" (Guba and Lincoln, 1994, p. 110). Based on those paradigms, classic conceptions of decision making postulate order and simplicity in the world. That order is based on three pillars: reality (there only exists an objective world that can be apprehended), causality (reality and history are structured by chains of causes and effects), and intentionality (human behavior is goal directed and decisions are instruments of purpose and self).

Decision-making processes are characterized by a logic of reason that encourages thought, discussion, and personal judgment. In the *classical theory of rational choice* (grounded in microeconomic theory), the consumer is considered a rational decision maker, a "homo economicus" who seeks to maximize personal utility or satisfaction. In this framework, the same actions lead systematically to the same consequences. This deterministic approach of "pure" rationality has been somewhat tempered by a more probabilistic approach. After introducing risk, or uncertainty about consequences, a decision is evaluated on the basis of not solely its expected value but, also, its degree of risk.

Limited or "bounded" rationality (March and Simon, 1958; Cyert and March, 1963) is a more realistic approach to decision processes. Even if individuals are intrinsically rational, they are constrained by limited cognitive capabilities and incomplete information. Consumers' attention, memory, comprehension, and communication all have a selective effect on information. This results in actions that are not (always) completely rational. The goal is to choose an alternative that is "good enough" rather than "the best possible." The satisfaction principle replaces that of maximization. Experience and history influence the threshold of acceptability (or aspiration level).

Rule following (Anderson, 1983; March, 1994) is another popular paradigm in the postpositivist view. It parallels the rationality paradigms in that it also implies a logic of reason and order. However, in rule following, the reasoning process does not consist of evaluating alternatives in terms of expected consequences for preferences. It rather pertains to establishing identities and matching rules to recognized situations. There is a logic of appropriateness instead of expectation. In that sense, rule following is more retrospective (one learns from the past to form useful identities) while rationality is clearly future oriented (one anticipates the future to form useful preferences).

Interpretivism and Constructivism

Regarding tourist decision making from the positivist and postpositivist perspectives, the questions raised are of this kind: what are the decisions tourists make, in what sequence are they made, how are they related to actual behavior, and how to predict them? The more recent *interpretivist* and *constructivist* views on science depart dramatically from this approach. The focus is no longer on explanation in order to predict and control but rather on understanding and interpretation. To understand the world, one must interpret it. Hence, the relevant question is how tourists come to particular decisions and why. Both philosophies of science emphasize relativism: there are only local and specific constructed realities. Reality is not objective, single, and divisible but rather socially constructed, multiple, holistic, and contextual (Ozanne and Hudson, 1989). This implies the use of a very different methodology. Instead of a rigid separation between the investigator and the object of investigation, constructivism and interpretivism propose an interactive and cooperative relationship. The focus is no longer on the quantity of the gathered information but rather on its quality (richness). All points of observation are worthwhile: the interpretive inquirer watches, listens, feels, asks, records, and examines. In-depth interviews, participant observations, or archival research are privileged tools for this.

This renewed view on social sciences has opened the way for sharp critiques on the rationality and rule-following theories of human decision making. New paradigms have been developed to take relativism into account. Decision makers live in worlds that are systematically less ordered, more ambiguous, and more symbolic than the world portrayed in classical theories. Reality is not unique, causality is often unclear, and intentionality is a weak predictor of behavior.

The *political model* of decision making (Pettigrew, 1973; Pfeffer, 1981) starts from the fact that most human decisions are not individual but involve groups. Theories of teams and games have first been proposed to explain group decision making but they rest on weak (because unrealistic) assumptions, that is:

1. Theories of teams: individuals have consistent preferences and (or) identities so that no conflict can occur.
2. Game theories: preferences and identities are inconsistent but partners strive to solve conflict since they behave rationally.

In contrast, the political decision-making paradigm assumes that multiple inconsistent actors are less inclined to emphasize eliminating conflict in preferences or identities (March, 1994). Struggle for power (through force or exchange) and coalition formation (through bargaining) are two common expressions of political decision processes.

The *garbage can model* (Cohen, March, and Olsen, 1972) integrates the ambiguity and uncertainty that are observed in the world. This suggests that decisions are analogous to garbage cans into which problems, solutions, choice opportunities, and decision makers are dumped. Decision making is not a question of logical relationships from causes to effects but rather a function of exogenous time-dependent arrivals. Problems and solutions are attached to choices because of their temporal proximity. This paradigm has important implications for consumer decision making (see Wilson and Wilson, 1988):

- Problem definitions are variable (changing as new problems or people are attached to choice opportunities).
- Information is often collected but not used.
- Preferences are unclear and may have little impact on choice.
- Evaluation criteria are discovered during and after the decision-making process.
- A particular choice can be made without a problem being noticed or with problems related to other choice opportunities (no choice is made when a number of problems are attached to the choice opportunity because it exceeds the energy of the decision maker).

THE POSITIVIST VIEW: THE RATIONAL TOURIST

After the critical perspective introduced in the previous section, we now describe how the different elements presented in the first section relate to each other to form global frameworks of tourist decision-making processes. According to the paradigmatic taxonomy we have just described, we start with models that are anchored in the postpositivist view on science and the human rationality paradigm. This was and still is by far the dominant tradition in consumer and tourist behavior research. Most of the authors consider tourist decision making as a sequential or hierarchical process. Some authors lean heavily on classical buyer behavior theory (see Howard and Sheth, 1969; Engel, Kollat, and Blackwell, 1973) where decisions are thought to evolve in sequential steps. Typically these are problem identification, information search, evaluation of alternatives, and choice and postchoice processes. Other authors refer to the "hierarchy of effects" model (Lavidge and Steiner, 1961) where six "layers" are distinguished: awareness, knowledge, liking, preference, conviction, and purchase.

The particular topic of the tourist's decision-making process has been investigated in several papers and monographs in the past two decades. The great majority of these, however, are restricted in scope since they are limited to some specific macro or micro aspect of the decision process (for a review, see Brent Ritchie, 1994). General models are rare. Efforts to integrate the elements described in the first section in a global decision-making process come, to a large extent, from three authors: Crompton, Moutinho, and Woodside.

Crompton's Model

Crompton (1977) presents a system model of the tourist's destination choice process in two steps. First, there is the generic decision of whether to have a holiday. If the answer is yes, then a second decision follows: where to go? He suggests that destination choice should be conceptualized as the result of the interaction of perceived constraints (such as time, money, and skills) and destination images. Broadening Crompton's conceptualization, Um and Crompton (1991) develop a more complete framework. The model is based on three sets of variables:

1. *External inputs* represent influences from both the social and marketing environment. They are classified into significative (destination attributes), symbolic (promotional messages), and social stimuli, according to Howard and Sheth (1969).
2. *Internal inputs* derive from the vacationer's sociopsychological characteristics (personal characteristics, motives, values, and attitudes).
3. *Cognitive constructs* represent the "integration of the internal and external inputs, into the awareness set of destinations and the evoked set of destinations" (Um and Crompton, 1991, p. 436).

There is thus a cognitive evolution which Um and Crompton materialize in five sets of processes, which are represented by arrows in Figure 5.1:

1. The formation of beliefs about destination attributes (through passive information catching or incidental learning).

2. The initiation of the destination choice process after the generic decision to go on holiday has been made (include the consideration of situational constraints).
3. The evolution of an evoked set from the awareness set of destinations.
4. The formation of beliefs about evoked destinations attributes (through active information search).
5. The selection of a specific travel destination from the evoked set.

FIGURE 5.1. Um and Crompton's Model of the Pleasure Travel Destination Choice Process

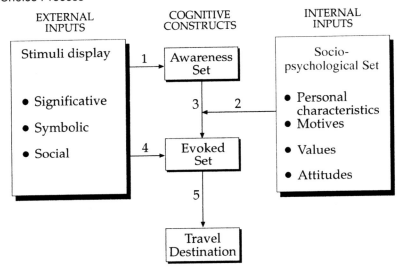

Moutinho's Model

In his investigation of vacation tourist behavior in Portugal, Moutinho (1982) makes a comprehensive overview of the literature in the field of the tourist's decision-making process and expands it to the proposition of a general flowchart model. An initial extremely complex framework (occupying three full pages) is simplified into a more manageable, although still very detailed, vacation tourist behavior model (Moutinho, 1987) and is revisited by Teare (1994).

As can be seen in Figure 5.2, the model is divided in three parts based on the usual distinction between pre- and postpurchase phases in consumer decision processes (e.g., Wilkie, 1991):

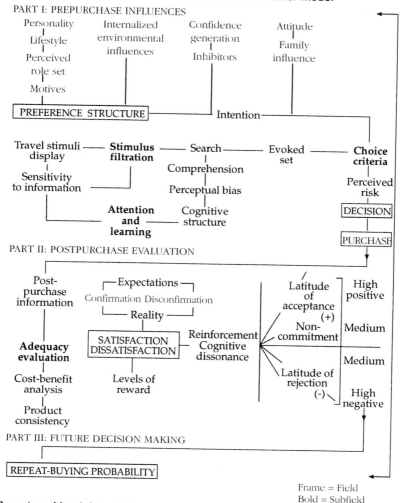

FIGURE 5.2. Vacation Tourist Behavior Model

Based on: Moutinho, 1987.

Predecision and Decision Processes

This involves "the flow of events, from the tourist stimuli to purchase decisions" (Moutinho, 1987, p. 39). Three fields are included: preference structured, decision, and purchase. The last two phases are outcomes of the first and are easily defined: a decision is "a psychological predisposition in terms of intention toward the buying act" and purchase is "the act of buying a vacation destination." Note that Moutinho rightly indicates that the total tourist product is often purchased in a sequence and not always as a tour package. The preference structure for a particular destination is based on a set of factors, including internalized environmental influences (cultural norms and values, reference groups, social class) and individual determinants (personality, lifestyle, motives). Attitude and family influence also contribute framing the preference structure. Intention to purchase depends on the tourist's degree of certainty toward the destination ("confidence generation") and on inhibitors, which can cause the tourist to respond differently from what his or her attitudes dictate. The psychological analysis of the preference structure is split into three subfields:

1. *Stimulus filtration:* filtering travel marketing stimuli enables the vacationer to organize information in a meaningful way. If some stimuli are ambiguous, he or she may feel the need to search for additional information.
2. *Attention and learning:* refer to the process of comparison whereby inputs are confronted with information stored in memory, fashioning the individual's cognitive structure.
3. *Choice criteria:* refer to the tourist product attributes that are important to the vacationer when evaluating the different alternatives that constitute his or her evoked set.

Postpurchase Evaluation

The tourist's purchase assessment process is fundamental since it adds to his or her store of experiences and provides feedback by adjusting the frame of reference for future purchase intentions. In the model, the postpurchase evaluation field is labeled "Satisfaction/Dissatisfaction." That dimension is considered in relation to the cognitive dissonance mechanism and results in three zones ("latitudes") of commitment to subsequent behavior: positive (acceptance), negative (rejection), and neutral (noncommitment). Moutinho further introduces "Adequacy Evaluation" as a subfield. This factor, resulting from a mental comparison process of costs and benefits, is related to "the 'ideal' point of each attribute of the tourist product as perceived by the tourist" (Moutinho, 1987, p. 42). We can interpret this as a kind of quality/price ratio.

Future Decision Making

The last part of Moutinho's model can be seen as the practical interface with marketing decision planning. This is concerned with the study of subsequent behavior of the tourist by analyzing repeat buying probabilities of tourist products and services. Depending on return prospect, three cases are possible: straight rebuy, future rebuy, and modified rebuy behavior (change to new products or search for better quality). The fourth case, that is, going to the competition, results from either hesitation or a refusal to buy the product again.

Moutinho does not especially focus on the destination choice process. He considers destination choice as a compulsory subdecision among other travel decisions. He places it in a group of other subdecisions (travel mode, timing, budget, intermediaries) that come as a third step after tourism need has been aroused and gathered information has been deliberated on, and before travel preparation. He often takes vacation destination as one of the possible examples of tourist products. But he sometimes also explains it separately (e.g., when describing the evoked set theory and the tourist product utility concept). In doing so, he implicitly recognizes the special case of destination decisions.

Woodside's Model

More recently, Woodside and Lysonski (1989) proposed another general model of traveler destination choice. To a large extent, this model is in line with Um and Crompton's model. Marketing variables (coming from the marketing mix's four P's) stand for the external inputs; traveler variables (previous experience, sociodemographics, lifestyles, and value system) represent the internal inputs; and Woodside and Lysonski's evolution from destination awareness to choice can be compared with Um and Crompton's progression from awareness set to the final location choice. However, Woodside and Lysonski are more precise since destination awareness is seen as the mental categorization process between consideration set (spontaneously evoked destinations), inept set (rejected destinations), inert set (destinations that are not actively considered), and unavailable/aware set. They also add important variables that are not isolated in Um and Crompton's model:

- *Affective associations:* specific feelings linked with a specific destination by a traveler.
- *Traveler destination preferences:* influenced by both destination awareness categorizations and affective associations, and result in a ranking of destinations.

- *Intentions to visit:* perceived likelihood of visiting a specific destination within a specific time period.
- *Situational variables* (Belk, 1975).

The arrows in Figure 5.3 indicate how the variables are connected to each other.

Destination awareness and, in particular, the categorization process in four sets, is influenced by both marketing mix and the traveler's own (especially, previous experience) variables (arrows 1 and 2). More pre-

FIGURE 5.3. Woodside and Lysonski's General Model of Traveler Leisure Destination Awareness and Choice

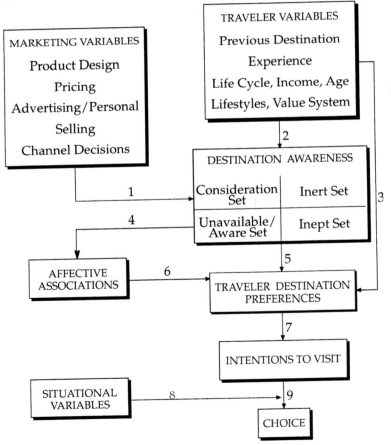

cisely, they increase the destination's likelihood of being included in the vacationer's consideration set. Affective associations are usually positive for a destination which is part of the evoked set ("Spain has breath-taking beaches and a wonderful nightlife") and usually negative for a destination that is in the inept set ("there is nothing to do in Austria") (arrow 4). Tourists' preferences for particular destinations are a positive function of the rank order of those destinations in tourists' consideration sets (arrow 5). Intention to visit a specific destination is influenced positively by the consumer's preference for the destination (arrow 9). Woodside and Lysonski found empirical support for those hypotheses. Another interesting finding is that the average size of the consideration is small (three to five destinations on average; see also Woodside and Sherell, 1977). Although the other relationships were not tested, it is argued that:

- Preferences are (at least partly) positively influenced by affective associations and are also affected by some of the traveler's variables.
- Choice is predicted to be affected by the interaction of intention to visit and situational variables.

THE INTERPRETIVIST VIEW: THE OTHER ASPECT OF THE TOURIST

Critique on the Traditional Models

The reader can realize that quite a substantial amount of work has already been done in the study of the tourist's decision-making process. But so far, the models have developed a view of the tourist's behavior that is very rational and sequenced. However, we think that the tourist's decision-making process is more than a purely formalized multistage process. Phillips, Olson, and Baumgartner (1995) point out that traditional decision-making models are relatively irrelevant for describing choices "for which consumers have little experience, or where the problem is less well-defined, or where emotional considerations play an important role" (p. 280). Woodside and MacDonald (1994) also recognize that "while useful, such models fail to capture the rich interactions of decisions and behaviors of the travel party and the destination environment experienced by the travel party" (p. 32). A more situational and experiential vision of behavior is thus needed as a complement. Attention should be paid not only to psychobehavioral variables as such, but also to the way consumers come to have cognitive and affective judgements, intentions, and practices and post-purchase evaluations. It is the only condition to capture fantasies, feelings, and fun (Holbrook and Hirschman, 1982) which can be very influential in tourism. Therefore, we need "thick descriptions about what, when, where, how did what and with what outcomes in the traveler's own language and cultural interpretations" (Woodside and Mac Donald, 1994, p. 32).

New Frameworks

Woodside and MacDonald (1994) fill the gap to some extent, as they use qualitative data to describe a general systems framework of how leisure visitors may make choices. What is new here is that they identify eight choice subsets which can be activated by four principal "start nodes" related to the information acquisition and processing sequence. Double-sided arrows indicate that causality is not a priori imposed but depends on each individual tourist. This is in sharp contrast with the rationality paradigm. The framework gives insight into how decisions, interactions between members of a travel party, and activities or events that occur during pleasure trips are related to each other and lead to other activities or events. An important assumption of the model is that activation of initial travel choices (due to "triggering events") spreads over time to related travel choices. The model is displayed in Figure 5.4 and the accompanying set of propositions.

Teare (1994) conducted a case study of consumer decision making in the U.K. hotel leisure market. After reviewing prepurchase and purchase studies, he concludes that prior product experience and product involvement lie at the core of the decision-making process. This is especially in line with Reid and Crompton's (1993) taxonomy of leisure purchase decision paradigms that is based on the level of involvement. Starting from the belief that these two variables are interrelated, Teare summarizes their potential explanatory value in six research propositions. Four other propositions arise from the review of consumption and postconsumption studies. Prior experience is still an important factor: it influences the formation of expectations, assessment criteria, and finally, the tourist's personal rating system (derived from experience-based norms).

Teare's ten propositions (see Table 5.1) can be better understood when looking at his full consumer decision process flowchart (Figure 5.5). The propositions were examined in a longitudinal study conducted over a three-year period. He used Glaser and Strauss's (1967) grounded-theorizing approach to analyze the data gathered on the basis of participant observations and personal interviews.

FIGURE 5.4. General Systems Framework of Customer Choice Decisions of Tourism Services

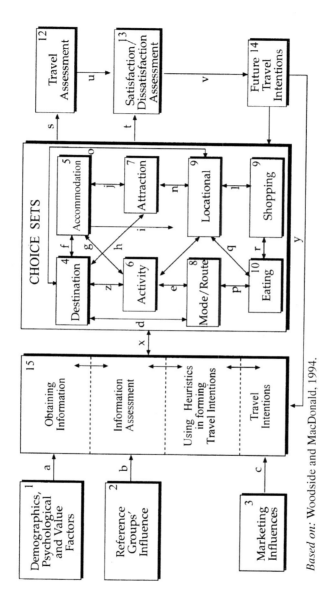

Based on: Woodside and MacDonald, 1994.

123

TABLE 5.1. Teare's Set of Propositions (1994)

P	Proposition
1.	The propensity of consumers with extensive prior experience to engage in high-involvement decision making is related to the perceived importance of the product.
2.	The propensity of consumers with extensive prior experience to engage in low-involvement decision making is related to product familiarity and personal confidence in product class decision-making ability.
3.	The propensity of consumers with limited prior experience to engage in high-involvement decision making is related to perceived risk, and limited personal confidence in product class decision-making ability.
4.	The propensity of consumers with limited prior experience to engage in low-involvement decision making is related to preknowledge of product suitability and low perceptions of risk.
5.	The uses of prepurchase decision rules, and their relative effectiveness during the assessment of choice criteria, are positively related to the consumer's prior product experience.
6.	Confidence in joint decision making is positively related to product role specialization.
7.	The correlation between product expectations and experience is positively related to product familiarity.
8.	The degree of sophistication inherent in the operation of the consumer's personal rating system is positively related to the extent of prior product experience.
9.	Satisfaction during product consumption is a function of many differently weighted impressions and experiences that are cumulative, and which are continually being integrated into the consumer's personal rating system.
10.	Satisfaction during postconsumption evaluation represents the sum total of individual assessments made during consumption. This evaluation reinforces or modifies the consumer's preference structure and influences future decision making.

FIGURE 5.5. Teare's Consumer Framework for Assessing and Evaluating Hotels

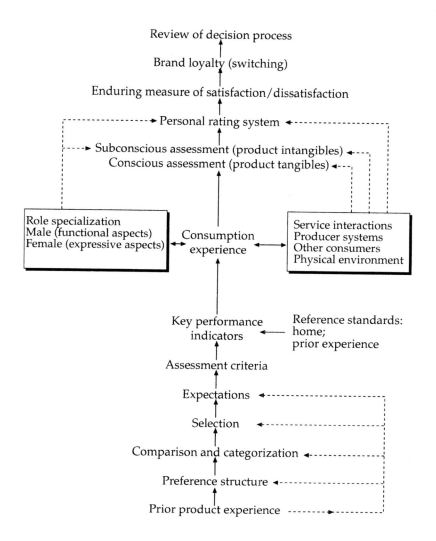

Toward a New Typology of Tourists

Instead of developing another general framework of the tourist's decision-making process, we prefer to close the chapter by giving some reflections that have emerged from qualitative data we have gathered in the course of a year. We followed the vacation decision-making process of twenty-seven Belgian households by interviewing them in depth up to four times; three times before their summer holiday and one time after. In the wake of those interviews, we propose a new typology of tourists based on their decision-making process style (see Table 5.2).

According to the previous propositions, it is no longer reasonable to speak of one universal decision-making process. Depending on the individual and the circumstances, more decision-making processes are possible, which can be used as a basis for distinguishing different tourist types. Sproles and Kendall (1986) and Lysonski, Durvasula, and Zotos (1996) support this approach.

The *alternative tourist* plans a participant observation, extended stay. The trip is well prepared, not as much for its practical aspects as for the information about the history, culture, and way of life in the visited regions. In this respect, alternative tourists are intellectuals who read a lot. They plan to meld into the value system and live the life of the local. They want to lose their home-identity and create a new self-identity, to live a second life, even if for only one season or year. Alternative tourists are mass-tourism aversive. They do not attach any importance to the material conditions of their trip. They go backpacking in search of authenticity.

Surrogate tourists like speaking about vacations and they (most of the time, he) do not hesitate to prompt friends to go on holiday and to recommend particular destinations. They grasp any occasion to collect tourist information. They are so optimistic that they often neglect the importance of situational constraints. As a consequence, theye rehearse both planning and experiencing the "dream" trip but: (1) they never actually make the trip or (2) they substitute a proxy destination experience.

The *unplanned tourist* minimizes cognitive thinking and planning, either as a strategy or because of time pressures. The desire for flexibility is one important reason for this strategy. The unplanned tourist often looks for an opportunity (e.g., last-minute offer or invitation by a friend) or anticipates potential situational constraints (e.g., children's summer activities, payment of vacation nest egg, or a threatening illness). There is a desire to stay "free" as long as possible. Heavy professional activities and the resulting lack of time for leisure are another reason for being unplanned. Information is ver limited and not actively searched. For example, this tourist

TABLE 5.2. Set of Propositions for a Renewed Perspective on Vacationers' Decision-Making Processes

P	Proposition
1.	Vacationers' decision-making processes are much less rational than described in the traditional models. Reference to alternative paradigms such as those proposed in the second section of this chapter should be invoked to explain decision-making and behavior processes of certain vacationers, in certain circumstances.
2.	For many tourists, information search is not that intensive and purposive as usually recognized. The vacationer is not a cognitive animal: the largest part of information is acquired incidentally and through noncommercial stimuli (internal information and social contacts).
3.	An important distinction is to be made between intervening conditions and situational variables. While the latter are specific to a time and place of observation, the first are more lasting, structural conditions that intervene either as facilitators or inhibitors of decisions and behaviors.
4.	For a substantial number of persons, moderate involvement as well as limited problem solving and decision planning characterize vacation decisions. The willingness not to be forced into commitments is an important explicative reason for this.
5.	Emotion, feelings, and (day)dreams are important constructs in the vacation decision process (in particular, for destination evaluations).
6.	The so-called "generic" decision on whether or not to go on holiday does not always precede vacation and destination decisions.
7.	Destination does not matter that much in vacation decisions. Time period, accompaniment, and financial constraints as well as the presence of generic attributes (sea, sun) are much more relevant issues.
8.	An important determinant of the decision-making process style is the individual's life cycle. Transition moments (from single to couple; the birth of a baby; children leaving the family decision-making unit; the death of the partner) can be identified.

may find herself or himself in Vienna for two days, with only the prior knowledge that Vienna is in Austria.

The *unwilling tourist* is required to make the trip and visit the destination because of work or family demands. This can be the case of the whole decision-making unit (a family going to Italy for the funeral of a parent) or of particular individuals within the decision-making unit. Children are often unwilling tourists because the destination chosen by their parents does not match their favorite activities or their favorite attributes (e.g., sea and not mountains; sunny climate but not too hot). Women also become unwilling tourists when they realize that the choice of accommodation (apartment renting) will force them to do the housework as they do at home.

The *homebody tourist* is not really involved in a vacation decision-making process, since he or she goes each year to the same place out of habit or by owning a second house. In many instances, this type of tourist is risk aversive (they cannot allow themselves to "miss" their holiday) and likes to feel at home for the holidays. Optimizing the holiday time is another possible motive of homebody tourists: by always going to the same spot, they avoid spending time in familiarizing themselves with a new environment. It is not surprising that their information search is limited to new possible activities or cultural visits in the region.

The last two types of tourists we describe here are "new modern" in the sense that they merge both positivist and interpretivist theories in more synthetic tourist types. The *Adaptable tourists* (inspired by Payne, Bettman, and Johnson's *Adaptive Decision Maker*, 1993) combine planning and situational contingencies for revising decisions and modifying behaviors, and are adaptable in two ways. On one hand, they adapt the decision-making process to new situations, such as the birth of a baby or the death of the usual travel partner. On the other hand, they adapt to the decision-making unit. Adaptable tourists (usually married) go on holiday sometimes with their families (including children), sometimes with friends. Occasionally, they also look for romantic trips with their partners. Each time, they adapt to the different circumstances affecting the decision mode.

Gestalt tourists combine propositions from plans and environments to direct trip behaviors. They are Gestalt (from the German for "whole" or "entirety") for several reasons. First, travel and vacation are not everything in their lives; they are not prepared to make sacrifices to allow themselves to go on holiday or to spend a lot. Second, a holiday is not only a question of spatial and temporal distance; it is first and overall a state of mind. Gestalt tourists can escape everyday life and feel as if they are on vacation when reading, watching television, talking with friends, wandering in the nearby countryside, or visiting a church. Finally, Gestalt tourists are by nature variety seekers when considering travel formulas, destinations, and activities. They want to taste a bit of everything and they especially hate missing any interesting opportunity. As a consequence, they always lie in wait for new information and are willing to revise heuristics and behaviors.

SUMMARY AND CONCLUSIONS

In this chapter, we warn against intellectual myopia. There is not one but several ways of looking at vacationers' decision-making and behavior processes. Traditional models, like those developed by Um and Crompton (1991), Moutinho (1982, 1987), and Woodside and Lysonski (1989) are based on such pervasive paradigms as positivism, (limited) rationality, and cognitive information processing. Until now tourism behavior literature and practice have leaned heavily on those models. While useful, they fail in translating the complexity of real life (the problem of attitude—behavior discrepancy is the most glaring example) and in addressing such important issues as the role of emotion and feelings, low involvement and passive information search, nostalgia and daydreaming, etc. These problems have urged a more naturalistic and experiential vision of tourist behavior. The reference to the interpretivist and constructivist paradigms paves the way for alternative frameworks and propositions. Major contributions by Woodside and MacDonald (1994) and Teare (1994), as well as our own set of propositions, have been presented. Taking relativism and complexity into account, we have developed other types of tourists in addition to the rational tourist. It is important to remember that there are more possible decision-making processes, depending on the individual, the group, and the moment in time.

CONCEPT DEFINITIONS

Attitude: The statement of a general evaluation of some object.
Attribute: A characteristic or property possessed by a product.
Consideration (or evoked) set: The set of product alternatives the consumer considers for a particular choice.
Decision-making unit: A group in which the important decisions of life (including consumption choices) are discussed.
Emotion: A state of arousal involving conscious experience and physiological changes.

Gestalt psychology: A theory that focuses on how people organize and combine stimuli into a meaningful whole.

Involvement: The perceived personal relevance of a stimulus in a particular context.

Learning: The relatively permanent change in behavior as a result of knowledge acquisition.

Lifestyle: Someone's unique pattern of thinking, feeling, and behaving.

Motive: A state of tension within the individual that arouses, directs, and maintains behavior toward a goal.

Perception: The mental processing of information received by the senses.

Personality: The reflection of a person's enduring and unique characteristics.

Preference: An attitude resulting from an explicit comparison process by which one object is chosen over the other.

Reference group: A collection of people the individual uses to match attitudes and behavior.

Self-concept: The image that a person believes characterizes him or her.

Situational influence: The influence arising from time- and place-specific factors that are independent of consumer and object characteristics.

Social class: A subculture based on education and occupation and characterized by a distinctive status and lifestyle.

REVIEW QUESTIONS

1. Identify the interrelated elements involved in tourists' decision-making processes. Give examples of each.
2. Describe what characterizes the cognitive tourist.
3. Explain the benefits a tourism researcher can obtain from studying lifestyles.
4. Name and briefly discuss the environmental influences on tourist decision making.
5. Compare positivism and interpretivism regarding their epistemological stances and the different assumptions they entail for decision making.
6. Discuss the particularities of the garbage can model.
7. Discuss the common variables and hypotheses (i.e., assumed relationships between variables) of the traditional models of Crompton, Moutinho, and Woodside.
8. Describe the predecision and decision processes in Moutinho's vacation tourist behavior model.

9. Explain Woodside and Lysonski's operationalization of destination awareness.
10. Do you think the tourist is rational? Give an argumentative answer.
11. Describe vacationers' decision-making processes based on Woodside and MacDonald's, and Teare's frameworks.
12. What is meant by "the other side of the tourist"? Explain a new typology of tourists.

REFERENCES

Allport, G.W. (1935). Attitudes. In C.A. Murchinson (Ed.), *A handbook of social psychology.* (pp. 798-844). Worcester, MA: Clark University Press.

Anderson, J.R. (1983). *The architecture of cognition.* Cambridge, MA: Harvard University Press.

Antil, J.H. (1984). Conceptualization and operationalization of involvement. *Advances in Consumer Research*, 11.

Belk, R.W. (1975). Situational variables and consumer behavior. *Journal of Consumer Research*, 2, 157-167.

Brent Ritchie, J.R. (1994). Research on leisure behavior and tourism—state of the art. In R.V. Gasser and K. Weiermair (Ed.), *Spoilt for choice. Decision-making processes and preference change of tourists: Intertemporal and intercountry perspectives* (pp. 2-27). Thaur, Germany: Kulturverlag.

Cohen, M.D., March, J.G., and Olsen, J. (1972). A garbage can model of organizational choice. *Administrative Science Quarterly*, 17, 1-24.

Crompton, J.L. (1977). A systems model of the tourist's destination selection decision process with particular reference to the role of image and perceived constraints. Unpublished doctoral dissertation, Texas A&M University, College Station, TX.

Cyert, R.M. and March, J.G. (1963). *A behavioral theory of the firm.* Englewood Cliffs, NJ: Prentice Hall.

Engel, J.F., Kollat, D.T., and Blackwell, R.D. (1973). *Consumer behavior.* New York: Holt, Rinehart and Winston.

Foxall, G.R. and Goldsmith, R.E. (1994). *Consumer psychology for marketing.* London: Routledge.

Glaser, B.G. and Strauss, A.L. (1967). *The discovery of grounded theory.* Chicago: Aldine.

Gnoth, J. (1997). Tourism motivation and expectation formation. *Annals of Tourism Research*, 24, 283-304.

Grubb, E.L. and Stern, B.L. (1971). Self-concept and significant others. *Journal of Marketing Research*, 8, 382-385.

Guba, E.G. and Lincoln, Y.S. (1994). Competing paradigms in qualitative research. In N.K. Denzin and Y.S. Lincoln (Eds.), *Handbook of Qualitative Research* (pp. 105-117). Thousand Oaks, CA: Sage.

Holbrook, M.B. (1984). Emotion in the consumption experience: Toward a new model of the human consumer. In R.A. Peterson, W.D. Hoyer, and W.R. Wilson (Eds.), *The role of affect in consumer behavior: Emerging theories and applications* (pp. 17-52). Lexington, MA: Lexington Books.

Holbrook, M.B. and Hirschman, E.C. (1982). The experiential aspects of consumption: Consumer fantasies, feelings and fun. *Journal of Consumer Research*, 9, 132-140.

Howard, J.A. and Sheth, J.N. (1969). *The theory of buyer behavior.* New York: John Wiley and Sons.

Kotler, P. (1997). *Marketing management: Analysis, planning, implementation, and control.* Englewood Cliffs, NJ: Prentice Hall International.

Lavidge, R.J. and Steiner, G.A. (1961). A model for predictive measurements of advertising effectiveness. *Journal of Marketing*, 25, 59-62.

Lefkoff-Hagius, R. and Mason, C.H. (1993). Characteristics, beneficial, and image attributes in consumer judgments of similarity and preference. *Journal of Consumer Research*, 20, 100-110.

Lysonski, S., Durvasula, S., and Zotos, Y. (1996). Consumer decision-making styles: A multi-country investigation. *European Journal of Marketing*, 30, 10-21.

March, J.G. (1994). *A primer on decision-making: How decisions happen.* New York: The Free Press.

March, J.G. and Simon, H.A. (1958). *Organizations.* New York: Wiley.

Mayo, E.J. and Jarvis, L.P. (1981). *The psychology of leisure travel.* Boston: CBI.

Mazanec, J.A. (1994). Segmenting travel markets. In R. Teare, J.A. Mazanec, S. Crawford-Welch, and S. Calver (Eds.), *Marketing in hospitality and tourism: A consumer focus* (pp. 99-166). London: Cassell.

Moutinho, L. (1982). *An investigation of vacation tourist behaviour.* Unpublished PhD Dissertation, University of Sheffield, Sheffield, UK.

Moutinho, L. (1987). Consumer behaviour in tourism. *European Journal of Marketing*, 21, 2-44.

Mullen, B. and Johnson, C. (1990). *The psychology of consumer behavior.* Hillsdale, NJ: Lawrence Erlbaum Associates.

Ozanne, J.L. and Hudson, L.A. (1989). Exploring diversity in consumer research. In E.C. Hirschman (Ed.), *Interpretive Consumer Research* (pp. 1-9). Provo, UT: Association for Consumer Research.

Payne, J.W., Bettman, J.R., and Johnson, E.J. (1993). *The adaptive decision maker.* Cambridge, UK: Cambridge University Press.

Pettigrew, A. (1973). *The politics of organizational decision-making.* London: Tavistock.

Pfeffer, J. (1981). *Power in organizations.* Boston: Pittman Publishing.

Phillips, D.M., Olson, J.C., and Baumgartner, H. (1995). Consumption visions in consumer decision-making. *Advances in Consumer Research*, 22, 280-284.

Plog, S.C. (1972). Why destination areas rise and fall in popularity. Paper presented to the Travel Research Association (Southern California Chapter), Los Angeles, October.

Plog, S.C. (1994). Developing and using psychographics in tourism research. In J.R. Brent Ritchie and C.R. Goeldner (Eds.), *Travel, Tourism, and Hospitality Research* (pp. 209-218). New York: John Wiley and Sons.

Plutchik, R. (1980). *Emotion: A psychoevolutionary synthesis.* New York: Harper and Row.

Reid, I.S. and Crompton, J.L. (1993). A taxonomy of leisure purchase decision paradigms based on level of involvement. *Journal of Leisure Research,* 25, 182-202.

Ross, G.F. (1994). *The psychology of tourism.* Melbourne: Hospitality Press.

Sears, D.O., Peplau, L.A., and Taylor, S.E. (1991). *Social psychology.* Englewood Cliffs, NJ: Prentice Hall.

Sproles, G.B. and Kendall, E.L. (1986). A methodology for profiling consumer decision-making styles. *The Journal of Consumer Affairs,* 20, 267-279.

Teare, R. (1994). Consumer decision-making. In R. Teare, J.A. Mazanec, S. Crawford-Welch and S. Calver (Eds.), *Marketing in hospitality and tourism: a consumer focus* (pp. 1-96). London: Cassell.

Um, S. and Crompton, J.L. (1991). Development of pleasure travel attitude dimensions. *Annals of Tourism Research,* 18, 374-378.

Wilkie, W.L. (1991). *Consumer behavior.* New York: John Wiley and Sons.

Wilson, E.J. and Wilson, D.T. (1988). "Degrees of freedom" in case research of behavioral theories of group buying. *Advances in Consumer Research,* 15, 587-594.

Woodside, A.G. and Lysonski, S. (1989). A general model of traveler destination choice. *Journal of Travel Research,* 27, 8-14.

Woodside, A.G. and MacDonald, R. (1994). General system framework of customer choice processes of tourism services. In R.V. Gasser and K. Weiermair (Eds.), *Spoilt for choice. Decision-making processes and preference change of tourists: Intertemporal and intercountry perspectives* (pp. 30-59). Thaur, Germany: Kulturverlag.

Woodside, A.G. and Sherrell, D. (1977). Traveler evoked, inept, and inert sets of vacation destinations. *Journal of Travel Research,* 16, 14-18.

Chapter 6

Family Decision Making and Tourism Behaviors and Attitudes
Catherine M. Nichols
David J. Snepenger

LEARNING OBJECTIVES

By the end of this chapter the reader should:

- Understand family decision making within the vacation context
- Understand the three types of family decision-making styles
- Be aware of how most families make decisions while on vacation
- Gain insight into how decision making influences vacation planning, on-site behaviors, participation in leisure activities, and evaluation of the vacation experience
- Understand how vacation marketers could position offerings to families

INTRODUCTION

The family remains the predominant social group in which people choose to spend their free time, particularly their vacations (Crompton, 1981; Cheek, Field, and Burge, 1976; Kaplan, 1975; Dumazedier, 1967). Thirty-nine million or 60 percent of all families in the United States took a vacation in 1984 (Davidson, 1985).

Tourism researchers have viewed family decision making operationally as being one of three types; husband-dominant, wife-dominant, or a joint decision between husband and wife (Sharp and Mott, 1956; Blood and

This chapter was previously published in the *Journal of Travel Research, 26*(4), 1988. Reprinted with permission.

Wolfe, 1960). Characteristically, two-thirds or more of all vacation decisions such as problem recognition, information search, and the final destination decision are shared by the husband and wife (Sharp and Mott, 1956; Kenkel, 1961; Cunningham and Green, 1974; Davis and Rigaux, 1974). Furthermore, specific decisions such as travel routes and commercial lodging are also made by the couple (Myers and Moncrief, 1978). The other one third of family decision making has been either husband- or wife-dominant.

Although several studies have examined family decision making within the vacation context the topic has not received a great deal of attention over the past decade. However, the recent marriage and family literature indicates changes in husband and wife relationships. The increased participation of women in the workforce along with the blurring of sex roles will profoundly affect vacation behavior by families (Waite, Goldscheider, and Witsberger, 1986; Lipman-Blumen and Tickamyer, 1975). Current and future vacation planning may be less likely to be a joint decision than in the past owing to changing sex roles. Consequently, decision making should be monitored and similarities and differences identified.

The purpose of this article is to replicate and extend research on family decision making as it relates to vacations. This study evaluates husband-dominant, wife-dominant, and joint decision-making couples on socio-demographic characteristics and prior travel behavior. In addition, comparisons between family vacationers are made across anticipation and planning, travel to the destination, on-site behavior, and evaluation of the travel experience as suggested by Clawson and Knetsch (1966).

DATA AND METHOD

A 1983 exit survey collected for the Alaska State Division of Tourism provided the data for analysis. Travelers who left Alaska by highway, scheduled airline, ferry, or cruise ship completed a self-administered questionnaire. One individual from each travel party completed the survey form, providing the information for the entire group. Of the 3,717 travel parties that visited Alaska strictly for pleasure, 1,753 identified themselves as families and made up the data set examined here.

"The family" is defined here as a husband and wife, traveling with or without children. Consistent with prior research, decision making within the family was viewed as husband-dominant, wife-dominant, and joint (Davis, 1977; Wolfe, 1959).

In this sample, the husband filled out the survey instrument in 70 percent of the families. The proportion of males providing the information was stable across the joint decision-making and husband-dominant decision-making parties. However, slightly more wives answered the survey instrument when the wife made the final decision to travel to Alaska.

According to Kenkel (1961), the use of direct questions concerning the relative influence of each spouse in decision making assumes that individuals (1) know the relative amount of influence they have, (2) are willing to admit it to themselves and others, and (3) are able to recall with accuracy how influence was distributed in some past decision making. Although these assumptions are not always met, direct questions about specific decisions still represent the best approach for identifying roles (Engel, Kollat, and Blackwell, 1973).

The three decision-making modes were compared on several variables. The three sociodemographic variables used for comparative purposes were the average age of the couple, the difference in age between the spouses, and the household income of the family. Prior research indicates that middle-aged couples are more likely to make joint vacation decisions than either younger or older couples (Filiatrault and Brent Ritchie, 1980; Erickson, Yancey, and Erickson, 1979; Davis, 1977; Scanzoni, 1977; Myers and Moncrief, 1978; Komarovsky, 1961). With respect to household income, the literature suggests that low-income families are more wife-dominant, middle-income families employ more joint decision making, and high-income families utilize husband-dominant decision making (Filiatrault and Brent Ritchie 1980; Erickson, Yancey, and Erickson, 1979; Davis, 1977; Scanzoni, 1977; Myers and Moncrief, 1978; Komarovsky, 1961). Prior trip behavior variables under study include the presence of children, the prior number of long-distance vacations by the couple, and the number of previous visits to Alaska.

Several vacation-specific comparisons were also investigated across the three decision-making modes. For the trip decision-making phase, the planning time horizon and the number of information sources utilized in planning the vacation were studied. Three measures of travel to and within Alaska described transportation preferences by the three travel modes. Several on-site variables were analyzed: total monetary expenditures, number of cities visited, number of nights spent in Alaska, and the number of nights by accommodation type. In addition, three Likert scale items measured the visitors' evaluation of the trip: value received for money spent, overall rating of trip, and intentions of returning to Alaska.

One-way analysis of variance and Scheffe's multiple range test were utilized with each of the quantitative descriptor variables. For the qualitative descriptors, the K-sample binomial test for equal proportions along with post hoc multiple comparisons were employed (Marascuilo and

McSweeney, 1977). Tests for differences of means or proportions were undertaken only when the one-way analysis of variance test or its nonparametric counterpart was statistically significant. For the test of proportions, the stated assumptions regarding sufficient sample size as discussed in Siegel (1956) were observed. For all statistical tests, a significance level of .05 was employed.

FINDINGS

Almost one-half of all vacationers to Alaska were families (47 percent). A majority of the families employed a joint decision making mode (66 percent): wife-dominant and husband-dominant decision-making households made up 13 percent and 21 percent of the sample, respectively.

In an effort to describe those utilizing the three decision-making modes, the household characteristics and sociodemographics of each travel mode were evaluated (see Table 6.1). The average ages of families were remarkably similar. Yet, when the three modes were compared on the age difference between the husband and the wife, it was found that husband-dominant decision-making parties were more likely to have spouses that differed in age.

Slightly more husband-dominant family travel parties were accompanied by children than were either wife-dominant or joint decision-making families; however, no significant difference was observed. In addition, no statistically significant difference was observed when the household income index was evaluated. The average income of all families exceeded $30,000 annually. Also, all families exhibited similar long-distance travel patterns. Each family group averaged a little over two trips in the past three years.

In contrast to the background variables, the planning variables revealed differences across the three decision-making modes (Table 6.1). Joint decision makers tended to plan their vacation earlier than the other two modes (twenty-five weeks). The utilization of information sources when planning the trip also varied, with joint decision makers using slightly more sources than the others (see Table 6.2). Those families utilizing joint decision making consulted friends and relatives more than wife- or husband-dominant families. A higher percentage of husband-dominant (14 percent) and joint decision-making families (12 percent) used information gathered from a prior visit to Alaska in making their travel plans. This contrasted with 6.5 percent of wife-dominant families using this information source. Other information sources, such as travel agents, the State Department of Transportation, convention and visitor's bureaus, chambers of commerce, airlines, brochures and guidebooks, and advertising produced by the state showed no differences in use among the three travel groups.

TABLE 6.1. Sociodemographic and Prior Trip Variables Across the Three Family Vacation Decision-Making Modes

Variable	Joint Decision (n = 1,151)	Wife Dominant (n = 230)	Husband Dominant (n = 372)	Test Stat.	Sig. Level
Average spouse age index[1]	5.70	5.73	5.61	0.96	0.3843
Difference in spouse age index[1]	0.07[a]	0.09[ab]	0.15[b]	3.38	0.0342
% of families traveling with children[2]	8.1%	7.0%	9.1%	0.93	0.6278
Total household income[1]	6.32	6.34	6.59	1.90	0.1501
No. of trips over 4,000 miles past 3 yrs.[1]	2.38	2.07	2.46	2.68	0.0688
Previous no. of trips to Alaska[1]	0.64	0.72	0.86	0.65	0.5226

[1] One-way analysis of variance and Scheffe's multiple range test employed to compare means. All tests conducted at an alpha level of .05.

[2] K-sample binomial test for equal proportions with post hoc multiple comparisons of sample proportions utilized. All tests conducted at an alpha level of .05.

[a,b] Means and percentages with different superscripts are significantly different from each other.

Travel behaviors within the state are displayed for each of the vacation decision-making groups in Table 6.3. The three groups were similar in the total amount of money they spent on their vacations. Joint decision-making families averaged $3,878, while wife-dominant families averaged $3,792 and husband-dominant families $4,180 on their trips. Family groups visited approximately the same number of cities while in Alaska.

A slight difference in the number of nights spent in Alaska was observed across the three decision-making modes (see Table 6.3). Joint-decision and husband-dominant families averaged twelve nights, while wife-dominant families averaged only ten nights. Overall, lodging patterns for these family vacationers were alike. No statistically significant differences were observed for the selection of hotels, private residences, camping, or cruise ships. On average, each segment spent six to seven nights at a hotel, motel, or lodge, eight to eleven nights at a private residence,

TABLE 6.2. Planning Variables Across the Three Family Vacation Decision-Making Modes

Variable	Joint Decision (n = 1,151)	Wife Dominant (n = 230)	Husband Dominant (n = 372)	Test Stat.	Sig. Level
No. of weeks spent planning trip[1]	25.12[a]	21.55[b]	22.97[ab]	5.37	0.0047
No. of information sources consulted[1]	2.30[a]	2.04[b]	2.13[ab]	6.52	0.0015
% Friends/relatives consulted[2]	38.1%[a]	33.0%[ab]	29.0%[a]	10.68	0.0048
Travel agent used[2]	41.5%	36.5%	42.7%	2.49	0.2876
Alaska Dept. of Tourism used[2]	18.8%	12.2%	17.2%	5.80	0.0551
Prior visit[2]	12.0%[a]	6.5%[b]	13.7%[a]	7.55	0.0230
Convention and Visitors Bureau used[2]	2.7%	2.6%	3.0%	0.09	0.9560
Chamber of Commerce used[2]	3.6%	2.2%	3.8%	1.28	0.5264
Airlines used[2]	3.0%	2.6%	3.8%	0.81	0.6655
Brochures/guidebooks used[2]	39.9%	32.2%	36.8%	5.21	0.0740
State of Alaska ads used[2]	53.5%	49.1%	48.7%	3.48	0.1753

[1] One-way analysis of variance and Scheffe's multiple range test employed to compare means. All tests conducted at an alpha level of .05.

[2] K-sample binomial test for equal proportions with post hoc multiple comparisons of sample proportions utilized. All tests conducted at an alpha level of .05.

[a,b] Means and percentages with different superscripts are significantly different from each other.

thirteen to seventeen days camping or in an RV, and approximately four days on a cruise ship or the ferry.

Leisure activity participation patterns are shown in Table 6.4. Joint-decision families participated in the most leisure activities, while wife-dominant families participated in the fewest. Thirty-five percent of joint-decision families, 30 percent of wife-dominant, and 23 percent of husband-dominant visited friends and relatives. Only 15 percent of the wife-dominant families camped or hiked, which differed from the 24 percent of husband-dominant and 25 percent of the joint-decision families. Slightly more joint-decision

TABLE 6.3. On-Site Behavior Variables Across the Three Family Vacation Decision-Making Modes

Variable	Joint Decision (n = 1,151)	Wife Dominant (n = 230)	Husband Dominant (n = 372)	Test Stat.	Sig. Level
Total monetary expenditures[1]	$3877.53	$3791.53	$4179.87	1.39	0.2492
No. of cities visited[1]	4.83	4.48	4.65	1.74	0.1763
No. of nights in Alaska[1]	12.86[a]	10.32[b]	12.17[ab]	3.29	0.0374
No. of nights in hotel/motel/lodge[1]	6.46	7.81	6.14	2.52	0.0811
No. of nights in private residence[1]	10.87	10.95	8.02	1.71	0.1819
No. of nights in camping/RV[1]	15.76	12.97	17.37	0.65	0.5216
No. of nights in cruise ship/ferry[1]	4.56	4.39	4.58	0.30	0.7441

[1] One-way analysis of variance and Scheffe's multiple range test employed to compare means. All tests conducted at an alpha level of .05.

[a,b] Means and percentages with different superscripts are significantly different from each other.

travel parties (65 percent) visited national parks and monuments than the other two travel groups (58 and 59 percent).

The proportion of each group participating in sightseeing activities, taking short educational courses and visiting museums, and attending concerts and the performing arts were similar (see Table 6.4). In addition, the three decision-making modes did not differ significantly in the number participating in sport fishing, other winter sports, small pleasure boating, and learning about different cultures.

There was insufficient participation to conduct statistical tests for hunting, skiing, snowmobiling, and other winter sports. However, the data revealed that these activities occurred more often among husband-dominant decision-making groups. Husband-dominant travel groups were the only groups to ski or snowmobile during their vacations.

Evaluations of the vacation experience by wife-dominant, husband-dominant, and joint-decision travelers are displayed in Table 6.5. All segments agreed that the value received given the money spent was above average, with joint decision makers giving the most favorable responses.

TABLE 6.4. Leisure Activity Participation Across the Three Family Vacation Decision-Making Modes

Variable	Joint Decision (n = 1,151)	Wife Dominant (n = 230)	Husband Dominant (n = 372)	Test Stat.	Sig. Level
Leisure activity index[1]	3.50[a]	3.16[b]	3.26[ab]	5.37	0.0047
% Visiting friends/ relatives[2]	35.2%[a]	30.4%[ab]	22.8%[b]	19.96	0.0000
Camping/hiking[2]	24.8%[a]	14.8%[b]	23.7%[a]	10.76	0.0046
Visiting national parks and monuments[2]	65.4%[a]	57.8%[b]	59.1%[ab]	7.91	0.0191
Sightseeing[2]	97.0%	97.8%	94.9%	5.14	0.0765
Taking short educational courses[2]	2.6%	2.6%	2.7%	0.01	0.9962
Museums/concerts/ performing arts[2]	54.2%	52.6%	48.4%	3.83	0.1472
Sport fishing[2]	24.2%	17.8%	26.3%	6.93	0.0514
Small pleasure boating[2]	9.7%	7.0%	10.5%	2.21	0.3306
Cultural education[2]	35.8%	36.5%	33.9%	0.589	0.7484
Hunting[2]	0.8%	0.4%	2.2%	N.A.	N.A.
Skiing[2]	0.0%	0.0%	0.5%	N.A.	N.A.
Snowmobiling[2]	0.0%	0.0%	0.5%	N.A.	N.A.
Other winter sports[2]	0.2%	0.0%	0.5%	N.A.	N.A.

[1] One-way analysis of variance and Scheffe's multiple range test employed to compare means. All tests conducted at an alpha level of .05.

[2] K-sample binomial test for equal proportions with post hoc multiple comparisons of sample proportions utilized. All tests conducted at an alpha level of .05.

N.A., not applicable owing to insufficient participation.

[a,b] Means and percentages with different superscripts are significantly different from each other.

In their overall rating of the trips, all groups agreed that their trips were good to excellent. Nevertheless, wife-dominant families rated their vacations significantly higher than did husband-dominant families. The three travel modes were basically in accord on their intentions of returning to Alaska. On average, the families in each segment reported that they might visit Alaska again.

TABLE 6.5. Evaluation of the Trip Across the Three Family Vacation Decision-Making Modes

Variable	Joint Decision (n = 1,151)	Wife Dominant (n = 230)	Husband Dominant (n = 372)	Test Stat.	Sig. Level
Value received for money spent[1]	3.73[a]	3.59[b]	3.61[b]	1.11	0.0449
Overall rating of trip[1]	4.30[ab]	4.32[a]	4.18[b]	3.62	0.0271
Intentions of returning to Alaska[1]	3.27	3.13	3.17	2.58	0.0758

[1] One-way analysis of variance and Scheffe's multiple range test employed to compare means. All tests conducted at an alpha level of .05.

[a,b] Means with different superscripts are significantly different from each other.

MARKETING IMPLICATIONS

For tourism providers targeting families, the following recommendations are suggested. When efforts are directed toward joint-decision-making families, promotion should appeal to both spouses and be aimed at spouses of about the same age. To time promotion effectively one should be aware that these tourists plan their trip sooner than the others and use the largest number of information sources in their vacation planning. Therefore, promotion materials must be dispersed broadly and made available early in the season. Joint-decision-making families participate in many leisure activities. Consequently, advertisements should incorporate families engaging in such activities as visiting friends and relatives, camping, hiking, and visiting national parks and monuments. Joint-decision families have reported the strongest intentions of returning to visit Alaska, and hence may be viewed as potential repeat customers and may also be important in terms of word-of-mouth promotion.

The second largest family segment consists of those in which the husband makes the vacation destination decision. These families are characterized by spouses with greater differences in ages and they utilize more information acquired from prior visits to Alaska. Promotional information should emphasize outdoor sports participation. A greater number of husband-dominant families enjoy camping, hiking, and hunting than for the other family segments. This segment is particularly important since husband-dominant families spend the largest amount of money on their vacations.

Families characterized by the wife making the final vacation decision were the smallest segment. They planned their trips with the shortest time horizon and used the fewest information sources in the planning process. These families spent the smallest amount of time and money on their vacations and participated in the fewest leisure activities. Although this segment may be difficult to target, it may become increasingly important to tourism marketers owing to changing family relationships. Currently, these families give the lowest ratings for the value received for money spent, and they were the least likely to return to Alaska. This would suggest that the industry may not be doing an effective job of catering to these people.

RECOMMENDATIONS FOR FUTURE RESEARCH

Nearly one-half of the visitors to Alaska were families. The proportion of families utilizing husband-dominant, wife-dominant, and joint decision making was consistent with previous findings on family decision making. For vacation decisions, the overwhelming majority of families utilized joint decision making. The proportion of families utilizing joint decision making corresponds to findings by Sharp and Mott (1956), Blood and Wolfe (1960), and Myers and Moncrief (1978). Across four decades, joint decision making by the husband and wife remains the predominant form of vacation decision making.

Although this article has adopted the prevalent research tradition of viewing family decision making as joint, husband-dominant, or wife-dominant, a fourth role structure exists that may become more relevant to both tourism marketers and scholars. Autonomic decision making occurs when either the husband or the wife makes the decision and either one is equally likely to make the decision. For instance, the selection of lodging may be-made by either spouse and the choice is likely to be made by either spouse. It may be difficult to predict lodging preferences without knowing who the decision maker will be. Other vacation decision-making behavior may become more difficult to model with the increased potential for autonomic decision making.

The overall findings indicate that family decision making may lack utility as a behavioral basis for understanding tourism behavior. There are at least two possible reasons for these results; one is conceptual, the other methodological. The conceptual issue focuses on the phenomena under investigation. The number of face-to-face interactions between family members more often than not overshadows the single vacation family decision. Furthermore, the families in this study were relatively homogeneous with respect to age and income. This may be due to the travel distance required to get to Alaska. Consequently, their similarities in sociodemographics resulted in restricting the range of variance for many of the variables which may have produced few statistically significant differences (Bollen and Barb, 1981).

Methodologically, the models tested here utilized variables that were not at the same level of abstraction or discourse. Household characteristics such as age, income, and presence of children are at the population level of discourse since they apply to all members of society. For instance, travelers and nontravelers can respond to the question, "How old are you?" In contrast, the decision-making mode variable, family decision making, was relevant only to a subset of the total population since a minority of the population travels to Alaska on vacation. When attempting to analyze the family vacation market by sociodemographics, the model shifts level of discourse by employing population-level variables such as age with the subpopulation-level segmentation variable, family decision making. Similarly, the travel behavior and attitudes variables also had a slightly larger level of discourse than did the family decision-making variable. This also resulted in a shift in level of discourse.

Future research in the area of vacation decision making should consider using descriptor variables that are consistent with the level of discourse of the segmentation variable. It is probably necessary to expand the universe of discourse for the segmentation variable by incorporating both family and nonfamily vacationers. Then, benefits received or sought from the travel experience may prove to be a fruitful means of describing the travel modes. It is anticipated that substantive differences would more likely result between travelers based upon this model formulation. For further discussion regarding level of discourse and tourism models, see Schul and Crompton (1983) and Snepenger and Crompton (1984, 1985).

The study of family decision making could help tourism marketers in the development and facilitation of exchange based upon product decisions, price structures, promotional campaigns, and distribution channels. More research in this area is needed to assess whether family decision making segmentation would be useful in understanding the vacation market.

CONCEPT DEFINITIONS

Autonomic decision making: Individualized decision making.

Family decision making: Involvement in the vacation decision-making process. The level of involvement and the role specialization by each spouse dictates the family decision-making style.

Husband-dominant decision making: The husband is the predominant decision maker.

Joint decision making: Both husband and wife are involved in the decision-making process.

Sex roles: A prescribed pattern of behavior in a given situation based on gender.

Social groups: The members of the vacation party. Social groups include couples, families, single parents with children, and multiple generations including grandparents, parents, and children. Another important social group is friends traveling together. An emergent social group is constructed by marketers, consisting of singles. For example, companies develop vacation packages for individuals and then groups form based on shared experiences.

Wife-dominant decision making: The wife is the predominant decision maker.

REVIEW QUESTIONS

1. With whom do most people vacation and why? How should marketers cater to this social group?
2. What are the three predominant decision-making styles used by families on vacation? Based on the Alaska study, do the styles vary by tourism behaviors and attitudes? Can the family vacation market be segmented by decision-making style?
3. What is autonomic decision making and how would a marketer develop a strategy to cater to families using this style?
4. How might the increase in single-parent households affect vacation behaviors and attitudes? Should marketers target single-parent households? How?
5. How might the presence or absence of children impact husband and wife decision making concerning vacation choices? Give an example of a vacation package targeted toward a childless couple, a couple with one or more children under six, a couple with children between six and twelve, and a couple with teenagers?

REFERENCES

Blood, Robert O., Jr. and Donald M. Wolfe (1960). *Husbands and Wives: The Dynamics of Married Living*, Glencoe, IL: The Free Press of Glencoe.

Bollen, Kenneth A. and Kenny H. Barb (1981). "Pearson's R and Coarsely Categorized Measures," *American Sociological Review* (April), 232-239.

Cheek, Neil H., Jr., Donald R. Field, and Rabel J. Burge (1976). *Leisure and Recreation Places*, Ann Arbor, MI: Ann Arbor Science Publishers, Inc.

Clawson, M. and L. Knetsch (1966). *Economics of Outdoor Recreation*, Baltimore: Johns Hopkins.

Crompton, John L. (1981). "Dimensions of the Social Group Role in Pleasure Vacations," *Annals of Tourism Research* 8(4), 550-567.

Cunningham, Isabella C. M. and Robert T. Green (1974). "Purchasing Roles in the U.S. Family, 1955 and 1973," *Journal of Marketing* 36(October), 61-81.

Davidson, Thomas Lea (1985). "Outlook for Family Vacation Market Segments," *1985-86 Outlook for Travel and Tourism,* Proceedings of the U. S. Travel Data Center's Eleventh Annual Travel Outlook Forum (September). 102-111. Travel and Tourism Research Association.

Davis, Harry L. (1977). "Decision Making Within the Household," in *Selected Aspects of Consumer Behavior,* ed. R. Ferber. Washington, DC: U.S. Government Printing Office, pp. 73-97.

Davis, Harry L. and Benny P. Rigaux (1974). "Perception of Marital Roles in Decision Processes," *Journal of Consumer Research* 1 (June), 51-62.

Dumazedier, Joffre (1967). *Towards a Society of Leisure.* New York: Free Press.

Engel, J. F., D. J. Kollat, and R. D. Blackwell (1973). *Consumer Behavior.* Second Edition, New York: Holt, Rinehart and Winston, Inc.

Erickson, J., L. Yancey, and E. Erickson (1979). "The Division of Family Roles," *Journal of Marriage and the Family* 4, 301-312.

Filiatrault, Pierre and J. R. Brent Ritchie (1980). "Joint Purchasing Decisions: A Comparison of Influence Structure in Family and Couple Decision Making Units," *Journal of Consumer Research* 7 (September), 131-140.

Kaplan, Max (1975). *Leisure Theory and Policy,* New York: John Wiley and Sons, Inc.

Kenkel, William F. (1961). "Husband-Wife Interaction in Decision Making and Decision Choices," *The Journal of Social Psychology* 54, 225-262.

Komarovsky, Mirra (1961). "Class Differences in Family Decision-Making on Expenditures," in *Household Decision Making,* ed. Nelson Foote, New York: New York University Press, pp. 255-265.

Lipman-Blumen, Jean and Arm R. Tickamyer (1975). "Sex Roles in Transition: A Ten Year Perspective," *Annual Review of Sociology,* 297-337.

Marascuilo, Leonard A. and Maryellen McSweeney (1977). *Nonparametric and Distribution-Free Methods for the Social Sciences,* Monterey, CA: Brooks/ Cole Publishing Company.

Myers, Paul B. and Lewis W. Moncrief (1978). "Differential Leisure Travel Decision-Making Between Spouses," *Annals of Tourism Research* 5, 157-165.

Scanzoni, J. (1977). "Changing Sex Roles and Emerging Directions in Family Decision Making," *Journal of Consumer Research* 4, 185-188.

Schul, Patrick and John L. Crompton (1983). "Search Behavior of International Vacationers: Travel-Specific Lifestyle and Sociodemographic Variables," *Journal of Travel Research* 22, 25-34.

Sharp, Harry and Paul Mott (1956). "Consumer Decisions in the Metropolitan Family," *Journal of Marketing* 21, 149-156.

Siegel, Sidney (1956). *Nonparametric Statistics for the Behavioral Sciences,* New York: McGraw-Hill Book Company.

Snepenger, David J. and John L. Crompton (1984). "Leisure Activity Participation Models and Level of Discourse Theory," *Journal of Leisure Research* 16, 22-33.

Snepenger, David J. and John L. Crompton (1985). "A Review of Leisure Models Based on the Level of Discourse Taxonomy," *Leisure Sciences* 7, 443-465.

Waite, Linda J., Frances Kobrin Goldscheider, and Christina Witsherger (1986). "Nonfamily Living and the Erosion of the Traditional Family Orientations Among Young Adults," *American Sociological Review* 51 (August), 541-554.

Wolfe, D. M. (1959), "Power and Authority in the Family," in *Studies on Social Power,* ed. D. Cartwright, Ann Arbor, MI: University of Michigan Press.

Chapter 7

Consumer Decision Making and Prepurchase Information Search

John C. Crotts

LEARNING OBJECTIVES

By the end of the chapter the reader should be able to:

- Describe the role information search has in consumer decision making
- Distinguish between internal and external sources of information
- Grasp the four major categories of external information commonly available to consumers (e.g., personal, neutral, marketer-dominated, experiential)
- Recognize when consumers acquire information and its implication for the timing of promotional efforts
- Compare and contrast consumer's inert, inept, and evoked sets in terms of consumer decision making and the influence of external information
- Distinguish among habitual, limited, and extensive decision making and the influence the marketer can have in the purchase deliberations

MARKETING COMMUNICATIONS IN THE TRAVEL AND TOURISM INDUSTRY

Reaching today's consumers is an extremely difficult and expensive task. Since 1988, travel advertisement expenditures in the United States alone have exceeded $1 billion annually (see Figure 7.1). Airlines accounted for $574 million of travel advertising expenditures, followed by

FIGURE 7.1. Advertising Expenditures in the United States

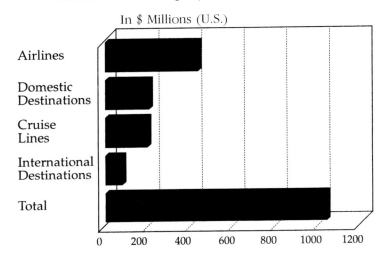

Source: Ogilvy and Mather (1996).

domestic destinations at $216 million, cruise lines at $195 million, and other countries at $90 million. It should be noted that these expenditures do not account for local and regional cooperative advertising programs and trade papers, nor the production, sales promotion, or public relations costs associated with promotional campaigns (Ogilvy and Mather, 1996).

Once information is developed and transmitted by the marketer, consumers must acquire the information and be influenced by it for the expenditure to make sense. Marketing programs that do not directly or indirectly influence consumer decisions are by definition failures. An old marketing adage is "I know that half my promotional efforts are effective—the problem is I don't know which half it is." Decision making is the very heart of the study of consumer behavior and marketing communications is considered one of the principal means to influence consumer decision making.

Marketing managers use their advertising dollars for three general purposes. First they attempt to recognize what problems consumers are facing and then develop the promotional message (supported by the appropriate marketing mix) to solve those problems. United Airlines' advertisement, in which they promise to take the business traveler "above the storm in today's global competitive environment," is such a problem identifying and solving approach. In this case, problems confronting business travel- ers are identified, promises are made by the airline, and a fulfillment strategy supported by market mix variables is put into place to deliver upon these promises. Second, marketing managers may often wish to cause consumers to recognize problems. Florida television and radio advertisements triggered to air by snowstorms in Canada and snowbelt states are designed to create discrepancies between a consumer's desired state and actual state, in an effort to arouse and activate the travel decision- making process (e.g., Figure 7.2). Third, marketing managers may use their promotional dollars at times to suppress consumer decision making.

FIGURE 7.2. "Return to Your Senses"—A Good Example of an Advertisement Designed to Create a Discrepancy Between a Consumer's Desired State and Actual State

For your free Florida Vacation Kit call (904) 487-1462 ext. 21

Source: Reprinted with permission from Visit Florida, Inc.

"Create and keep customers" is a central tenet of relationship marketing, where one firm attempts to conceive mechanisms where a customer repurchases the same service without considering the alternatives, due to either an emotional attachment to the brand or marketing inducements that create brand loyalty. Airlines' frequent flier programs are a good example of suppressing consumer decision making. By rewarding a consumer for making a repeat purchase, in the form of free airline tickets, the airline is in effect attempting to suppress consumer decision making when airline travel becomes necessary. Others attempt to create brand loyalty by encouraging an emotional attachment to the individual service and/or destination.

The term travel decision making connotes an image of a consumer or group of travelers (e.g., family, etc.) carefully evaluating the attributes of a set of tourism destinations and travel services and rationally selecting the one that most clearly solves a clearly recognized need for the least cost. It has a rational and functional connotation. However, although consumers do make decisions in this manner, many others make purchase decisions with little apparent mental effort.

THE NATURE OF PREPURCHASE
INFORMATION SEARCH

Once a consumer recognizes a need or a problem, relevant information from long-term memory is used to determine if satisfactory alternatives exist. This is called internal information search, which is nothing more than retrieving decision-relevant information stored in an individual's long-term memory. The internal information may have been actively acquired at one time from past information searches or passively through low-involvement learning, where consumers are repeatedly exposed to marketing stimuli. In addition, prior experience with the destination or service provides a consumer with a wealth of information that is not available to first-time visitors (see Figure 7.3).

When internal search proves inadequate to make a purchase decision, then the search process focuses on acquiring information from external sources. This is called external information search. Sources of external information available to consumers have generally been organized into four basic categories. They commonly appear in the literature as (1) personal (e.g., advice from friends and relatives), (2) marketer-dominated (e.g., brochures, advertisements in print and electronic media), (3) neutral (travel clubs, travel guides, travel agents), and (4) experiential sources (inspections, prepurchase visits, or store contacts) (Beatty and Smith,

FIGURE 7.3. A Model of Prepurchase Information Search

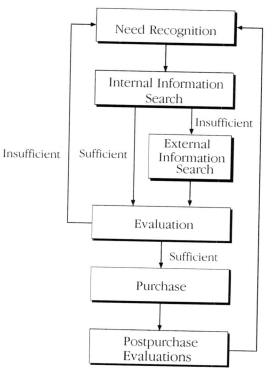

1987; Assael, 1987; Hawkins, Best, and Coney, 1995). Many consider the Internet (e.g., World Wide Web) as a fifth uniquely interactive source of external information, while others would assign homepages to marketer-dominated or neutral sources depending upon their purpose or content.

It should be noted that consumers often engage in external information search in the absence of purchase deliberations. Ongoing search for information is conducted both to acquire information for later use and because the process itself can be so pleasurable. Viewing a cable travel channel, reading a travel magazine, talking to friends who have just returned from a vacation, or surfing the travel destinations on the World Wide Web provides consumers with a source of vicarious pleasure, as well as information available for later use. Determining when a purchase deliberation actually begins is a critical issue for researchers attempting to distinguish between prepurchase and ongoing information search.

TYPES OF INFORMATION SOUGHT

Hawkins, Best, and Coney (1995) suggest that consumer decisions require the following types of information:

- The appropriate evaluative criteria for the solution of a problem
- The existence of various solution alternatives
- The characteristics of each alternative on each of the evaluative criteria

Suppose you won the grand prize in a sweepstakes awarding you a cruise for two of your choice. Your first thought (and that of your travel partner) would probably be, "What do I want in this vacation? Do I (we) want to escape and relax, to experience the new and different, and so on?" To begin, you would engage in an internal information search to determine the features and characteristics that meet your needs. These desired characteristics of your preferred state are your evaluative criteria. If you have limited experience with this preferred state, you may also engage in an external information search to learn what characteristics a good cruise should have. You could check with friends, meet with a travel agent, and so on to determine the appropriate evaluative criteria.

While you are searching for the appropriate evaluative criteria, you are probably seeking appropriate alternatives—in this case cruises in the Mediterranean, Caribbean, Alaska and so on.

The number of vacation destinations you are aware of (let alone the vacation alternatives that actually exist) is likely to be substantial and difficult to evaluate mentally. As a result, the consumer considers only a limited number of these alternatives in planning a vacation (Woodside and Sherrell, 1977; Woodside and Ronkainen, 1980). The concept of the evoked set in the tourism literature is defined as the "Travel destinations of which the consumer is aware and has some likelihood greater than zero of visiting (selecting)" (Woodside and Ronkainen, 1980, p. 7). This set of travel destinations becomes the list of alternatives that the potential traveler has reached positive conclusions on and is most likely to draw from in reaching a purchase decision.

The inept set is composed of those alternatives the consumer dislikes and therefore is unworthy of further consideration. Information about these destinations will not likely be processed by the consumer even when it is readily available. Destination alternatives toward which the consumer is basically indifferent are known as the inert set. Consumers will generally accept information about alternatives in their inert sets, although they do not actively seek such information. The challenge for marketers is to move their product from the inert set to the evoked set.

To choose among the destinations in the evoked set, a consumer compares each on the relevant evaluative criteria. This process requires that the consumer acquire information about each alternative on each of the pertinent evaluative criteria. In our example, you may collect information on cabin availability, onboard activities, ports of call, etc. of your most preferred cruise lines on which to base your final decision (see Figure 7.4).

Woodside and Ronkainen (1980) found that travelers initially consider a limited range of destinations when planning a vacation trip. Their study of a 400-person sample drawn from a population of 2,200 personal inquiries for travel information about the state of South Carolina revealed an evoked set size of 4+ or −2. To date, there has been little additional research into the evoked sets of travel consumers to validate their findings by using different sampling frames.

FIGURE 7.4. Traveler's Evoked, Inert, and Inept Sets

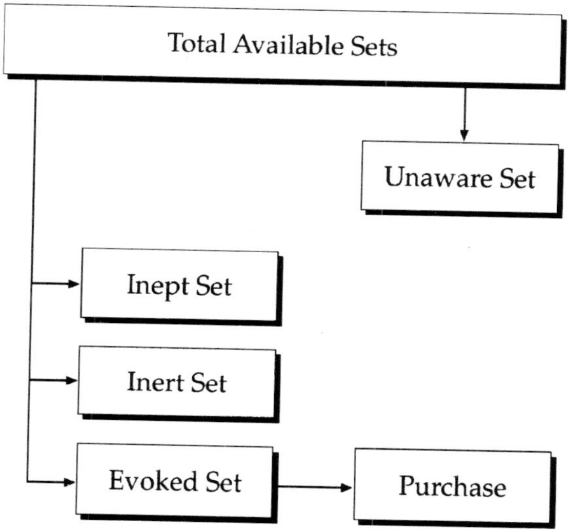

AMOUNTS AND SOURCES OF EXTERNAL INFORMATION SEARCH

Marketing managers are particularly interested in both the amount of information consumers are acquiring and where they are acquiring the information, because it gives them direct access to consumers.

Not all travelers can be expected to actively engage in external information search. In a survey of 331 visitors to a historic attraction known as Old Salem (Crotts, 1992), 39 percent of the respondents reported that they did not acquire information prior to their vacation purchase decision, while 29 percent collected information from one to three sources, and 32 percent from four to thirty-five sources. Subjects in the no information search group apparently relied on internal information in making their trip decisions. However, at some point in time, information stored in long-term memory must have been acquired from external sources.

Figure 7.5 shows the initial sources of internal information. Information retrieved from long-term memory could have been actively acquired from past information searches or past personal experiences with the destination. In addition, information may have been passively acquired through low-involvement learning gleaned from external sources.

The information seekers indicated that they actively acquired external information from personal sources, followed by neutral, experiential, and marketer-dominated sources of information. Marketer-dominated sources of information are often found to have the least direct influence on consumer decision making. Instead, advice from friends and relatives—or what many call word-of-mouth advertising—generally tops the list as the most frequently acquired and influential source of information available to the traveler. Unfortunately, word of mouth can be good or bad and intuitively must be based on the friends' and relatives' previous experience with the destination or its promotions. Success therefore depends on a destination's ability to create satisfied customers due to its impact on repeat patronage and positive word of mouth.

Travel guides, travel agents, and other sources of neutral or unbiased information have considerable impact on the travel and tourism industry. Like word of mouth, neutral sources can be positive or negative. Destination travel guides, such as those from the Lonely Planet, are generally based upon the travel writer's unannounced visit and interaction with the destination. Seldom will a destination know exactly when and where a visit will take place. Likewise, many hotels and resorts will subscribe to a quality rating scheme such as those sponsored by the AAA and Mobile Club. One to five diamonds (or stars) will be awarded to a property based upon an unannounced inspection. Travel destinations will periodically sponsor familiarization tours—or FAM tours—targeted to specific groups of travel writers or travel agents. FAM tours are designed to influence theinformation customers will ultimately receive from neutral sources. FAM tour participants are provided a complimentary package of first-class accommodations or travel agency and share favorable impressions with consumers through

FIGURE 7.5. Sources of Prepurchase Information

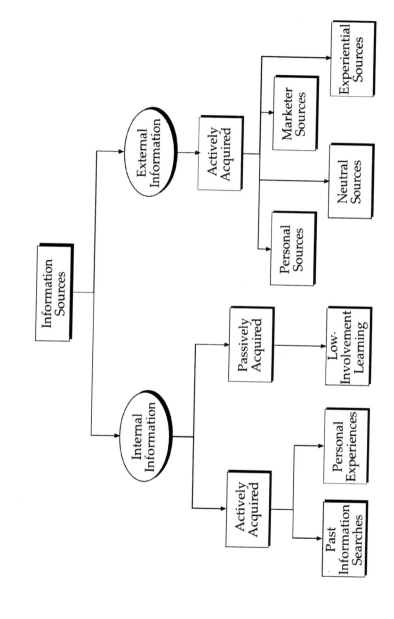

their respective medium.and itineraries in the hope that they will return to their newspaper, magazine, or travel agency and share favorable impressions with consumers through their respective media.

Understandably, you might question why it is important to advertise if marketer-dominated information is only one of many sources of information available to the consumer. Many well-established tourism businesses spend very little on advertising (Crotts and Guy, 1993), relying instead on their reputations to create and retain satisfied customers. However, most firms find that advertising provides them additional means to create consumer awareness and distinguish themselves from the competing alternatives.

Most consumers can be expected to acquire information from external sources and it is these consumers who are the audience for advertising and promotional efforts. Understandably, marketing managers continually evaluate and refine their promotional efforts on the basis of their ability to reach and influence their target audiences in a cost-effective manner. Figure 7.6 illustrates where major travel and tourism industry groups used their advertising dollars in the United States.

The largest share of the U.S. airlines' travel advertising dollar in 1996 went to newspapers (40 percent of the total), followed by magazine (28 percent), television (23 percent), radio (7 percent), and outdoor billboards (2 percent). States put their advertisement dollars in magazines (45 percent), television (41 percent), newspapers (11 percent), and radio (3 percent). Cruise lines spent their budgets on newspapers (45 percent), television (32 percent), magazines (20 percent), outdoor billboards (2 percent), and radio (1 percent). Other countries advertised in the United States in magazines (40 percent), television (32 percent), newspapers (23 percent), outdoor billboards (4 percent), and radio (1 percent).

Marketing managers often reallocate where they spend their advertising dollars, based upon an understanding of their customers' media preferences, as well as tracking each medium's performance in generating awareness and demand in a cost-effective manner. Advertising tracking and conversion studies are the most frequently used means of determining what works—and does not work—in tourism advertising.

The Timing of Information Acquisition

To effectively and efficiently promote a destination to potential visitors, it is critical not only to identify the types of information sources visitors use during their trips but also when the sources are used. In other words, one should understand if the promotional strategy being employed conforms with the timing of visitors' need for information. An important but

FIGURE 7.6. Distribution of Media Dollars in the United States by Travel Categories

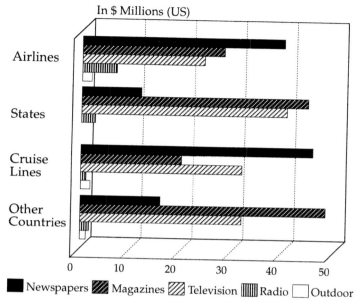

Source: Ogilvy and Mather (1996).

relatively underresearched area has specifically focused on the timing of visitors' activity decisions to assess whether promotional efforts are being channeled in ways that conform to the timing of visitors' information needs and decision making. Much more research is needed.

Perdue and Pitegoff (1990) suggest that a destination's promotional activities can be organized into three general types. They are: (1) promotions aimed at influencing potential visitors before they leave their homes, (2) promotions aimed at influencing the traveler while enroute from home to a destination area, and (3) those aimed at influencing visitors after they arrive at the destination.

Reserving an airline seat or a suite in a particularly popular resort are prudently all done well in advance of a trip. However, there are many subdecisions that can reasonably be delayed, such as where to eat and what to do and see. Although some travelers may take great pleasure in planning every detail of their trips before leaving home, others will enjoy the freedom of acting more impulsively. Conforming your firm's promotions to when consumers have a need for—and therefore are receptive to—the information will improve its success.

To illustrate, a resort on a remote barrier island would likely focus the majority of its advertising and promotional dollars at consumers several months prior to the vacation season. When to launch the preseason campaign should be based upon some understanding of the consumer's need for information. Launch the campaign too early and the chance that the information will be forgotten by the consumer is great. Run it too late and its impact will be minimal since most consumers will have confirmed their travel itineraries. In contrast, a transit motel located along a major highway would likely concentrate its promotional efforts on billboards, travel guides, and in-tour promotional media to capture customers en route to their ultimate destinations.

Knowing when visitors are making their decisions across an entire range of purchase decisions has important implications for an entire region's tourism economy. In a study of 546 respondents to a survey of visitors to a Florida county (Crotts and Reid, 1993), respondents were asked to first identify the recreational activities they and their travel party members engaged in during their visits and then asked to indicate the timing of their decisions to participate in those activities. The results were that 71.5 percent of the respondents decided which recreational activities they would engage in prior to leaving home, 3.7 percent made that decision en route to the county, and 24.9 percent after arriving in the county. For comparison purposes, the destination was channeling 83.4 percent of its promotional budgets to "at home before trip" strategies, 11.8 percent to en route promotions, and 4.7 percent to after-arriving strategies.

Further analysis revealed several important insights. First, the 25 percent of the respondents who made their activity decisions after arriving in the county were typically a part of the long-haul market. These visitors on average traveled greater distances from their homes to reach the destination and stayed significantly longer in the county. As a result of their tendency to stay longer, these visitors spent, on average, twice as much on food and supplies bought in stores; twice as much on food and beverages in eating and drinking establishments; and three times as much on paid forms of lodging. Such findings do not prove that in-tour promotional efforts influence the visitor's decision to stay longer and engage in additional unplanned activities—this would require an experimental design to prove such cause and effect. Instead the findings simply identify an important segment of visitors, namely the long-haul, long-stay visitor market—who made their generic decision to visit the destination and after arriving decided what they would do and see. As a result of these findings, many of the area's attractions began allocating more resources to deliberately target this market with promotional activities designed to get them out of their hotel rooms (or friends' and relatives' homes) and interacting even more with area businesses.

DETERMINANTS OF INFORMATION SEARCH

Do certain types of consumers ordinarily seek more information than others? An enduring component of the travel and tourism literature is research that has attempted to describe the extent to which travelers acquire information in their purchase deliberations and the degree to which the use of these sources may be influenced by selected explanatory variables. Such studies have often drawn upon the findings in the consumer behavior literature related to information source use of consumers of durable and nondurable products. Such cross-product comparisons create a basis for understanding why some resort travelers conduct more prepurchase search for information than others.

One striking conclusion has emerged from this research: Though age, income, and education have often been found to influence the amount of prepurchase information in consumer durables, seldom have they done so in the case of experience goods such as tourism. Instead, trip-specific variables such as the size of a vacationer's evoked set (i.e., the number of vacation alternatives seriously considered), amount of pretrip planning time available, distance traveled, and the frequencies of repeat visitation to a destination have proven to be far more productive in explaining the total amount of information collected and each source's subsequent degree of influence on vacation decision making.

However, the decision making consumers engage in when deciding where to spend their vacations should not be thought of as a uniform process. Deciding where to spend the family's annual vacation is a different process from deciding where to spend a weekend get-away. The degree to which the consumer is concerned for or interested in the purchase process will likely influence the amount and importance of information search.

PURCHASE INVOLVEMENT AND INFORMATION SEARCH

Purchase involvement is a behavioral concept used to describe a temporary state of an individual, family, or household triggered by a need for a particular purchase. It is useful to consider purchase involvement as a continuum. On one end of the continuum is habit; on the other is extended (complex) decision making. Limited decision making incorporates the middle ground. All three describe the processes that occur along various points on the continuum.

Habitual, limited, and complex decision-making processes are composed of two behavioral constructs. First, they involve the presence or lack of consumer evaluations of destination alternatives in their prepurchase decisions. In evaluating which destination alternative to purchase, consumers base their judgments on certain decision criteria. Two of the more important criteria for pleasure travelers are quality and price. At the same time, consumers may engage in active external information search. Consumers may not have enough good information in their memories to make adequate vacation purchase decisions. In such cases, they will seek to acquire additional information to evaluate the possible alternatives.

One extreme of the purchase involvement continuum is habit. Habitual decision making involves no decision per se. According to Markin (1969), habit refers to the elimination of all cognitive activities connected with making a decision. Prior satisfaction with a vacation destination may lead to repeat purchases and eventually purchases based on habit. The consumer may find little need to evaluate vacation alternatives and search for additional information beyond what has been previously processed. Recognizing a need or desire to vacation leads directly to internal information search and the eventual purchase—and in this case repurchase—of a vacation experience. Purchasing through habit is a way of ensuring satisfaction based on past experiences and of simplifying decision making by reducing the need for information search and evaluating alternatives.

Habitual decisions can be broken down into two distinct categories: destination-loyal decisions and repeat purchase decisions (Hawkins, Best, and Coney, 1986). At one time a consumer may have been heavily involved in selecting a vacation destination, using an extensive decision-making process. Having selected the resort previously and being satisfied with that purchase decision, the consumer will repurchase the same experience without further consideration of other options. This person is a loyal patron because of his or her high commitment to one destination. In contrast, one may believe that all resort properties along a vacation corridor are about the same. Having spent a vacation at one of them and finding it satisfactory, this traveler will repurchase the same experience using habitual decision making. This visitor is a repeat customer who has no loyal commitment to the resort in question.

Although decisions to purchase the same vacation appear identical across the repeat visitors using habitual decision making, differences do exist in terms of their loyalty to the vacation destination. Repeat purchasers can be induced to change their purchase habits because they possess little commitment to the destination. On the other hand, destination-loyal visitors are highly committed to their preferred destination and will not change easily.

Limited decision making covers the middle ground on the purchase involvement continuum. In its simplest form, limited decision making is similar to habitual decision making. For example, while reading the Sunday newspaper a person turns to the travel section and says, "Gee, I have not taken the family to the coast for a long time." The consumer may recall previous vacation experiences and decide to purchase one of them with or without further information beyond what can be recalled from memory.

On the opposite end of the continuum from habit is complex decision making. In complex decision making, consumers are highly involved in the purchase process and evaluate the alternatives in a detailed and comprehensive manner. More information is sought and more alternatives are considered than in limited decision making. Assael (1987) theorized that complex decision making is more likely for (1) high-priced products, (2) products associated with performance risks, (3) specialty purchases, and (4) products associated with one's ego. A search of the travel and tourism literature reveals an assumption that vacation purchase decisions involve complex decision making. According to Schul and Crompton (1983) and Gitelson and Crompton (1984), vacation consumers are generally expected to actively search for information and evaluate several alternatives during their vacation deliberations. Since a vacation is assumed to be a relatively expensive product involving significant amounts of a person's discretionary time (McIntosh and Goeldner, 1986) and income (Gitelson and Crompton, 1984), requires purchases to be made on symbolic communications alone (Gitelson and Crompton, 1984), and is viewed by most people as an extension of their personality (Mill and Morrison, 1985), complex decision making should be the rule, not the exception.

In a survey of 189 visitors to a resort located on the Oregon coast (Crotts, 1990), 63 percent of the respondents were repeat visitors to the destination area. If commitments to the destination area were measured entirely by repurchase behavior, 63 percent were loyal and 37 percent nonloyal. When both the presence of external information search behavior and evaluation of nonpurchased alternatives are considered, the percentage of customers who probably should be regarded as at least moderately loyal to the vacation destination area dropped to 18 percent. Thus the repeat visitor phenomena described by Gitelson and Crompton (1984) may not as stable an occurrence as one might think.

Many repeat customers do routinize their decision making processes but seldom to the point of loyalty. According to Assael (1987), consumers of this nature are not resistant to persuasion and can be induced to change their decision-making behaviors through marketing efforts. Perhaps the need for novelty (Snepenger and Snepender, 1993) and the enjoyment of problem solving (Crotts, 1990) explains why most travelers will expend effort on vacation deliberations.

STRATEGIC IMPLICATIONS

Understanding consumers' prepurchase information search behavior is an important concern of researchers on both theoretical and applied grounds. Every human community develops a system whereby goods and services are produced and distributed. Among technologically advanced societies, the system is complex and the range of available goods and services is wide. The search for and use of information obtained from both marketer-dominated and non–marketer-dominated sources becomes the one activity in which people understand the alternatives to perceived problems, the characteristics and attributes of these alternatives, and their relative desirability. Because consumption of goods and services is prevalent throughout nearly every activity in which human beings are involved, research in this area attempts, in a broad sense, to understand a fundamental aspect of modern, industrialized society.

Of practical concern to the tourism marketer is the role an understanding of consumers' prepurchase information search behavior can play in the design of efficient marketing strategies. By understanding the types of information and the depth at which consumers use it, channels of influence can be designed in a cost-effective manner. For the marketing manager this means getting the right message, in the right place, at the right time to the consumer.

CONCEPT DEFINITIONS

Awareness set: The vacation destinations (or brands) that a consumer thinks of when a need arises. The awareness set is composed of three subcategories of importance to marketers: the evoked, inept, and inert sets.

Brand loyalty: A brand to which a consumer has formed an emotional attachment or commitment. The brand is consistently repurchased without consideration of the alternative brands, its price, or other relevant factors. A consumer who is brand loyal to a particular airline cannot be easily influenced to switch to another.

Complex decision making: The response to a high level of purchase involvement, characterized by extensive internal and external information search followed by a complex evaluation of the competing alternatives.

Consumer decision making: A consumer decision process that is activated or aroused by a discrepancy between a consumer's desired state and actual state, and the relative importance of the need or problem. When the discrepancy is sufficient, it can lead to internal and external information search, evaluation of competing alternatives, and eventually to a purchase. Consumer decision making can be described as habitual, limited, and complex.

Evoked set: The subcategory of travel destinations (or brands) that a consumer has reached positive conclusions on and is most likely to draw from in making a purchase decision.

External information search: Information the consumer acquires from external sources after information stored in memory proves insufficient to make a purchase decision. Sources of external information are generally characterized as (1) personal (e.g., advice from friends and relatives), (2) marketer-dominated (e.g., brochures, advertisements in print and electronic media), (3) neutral (travel clubs, travel guides, travel agents), and (4) experiential (inspections, prepurchase visits or contacts).

Habitual decision making: Habitual decisions in effect involve no decision per se. When a consumer need or problem is recognized, internal information search provides a single preferred solution that is purchased without further consideration of competing alternatives. Habitual decisions can either be brand-loyal or repeat purchases depending on the level of commitment.

Inept set: A subcategory of the awareness set of destinations or brands that a consumer dislikes or feels is unworthy and will have little chance of purchasing. Positive information about brands in the inept set will not likely be acquired and processed.

Inert set: A subcategory of the awareness set of brand alternatives including destinations or brand alternatives a consumer is basically indifferent toward. Consumers will generally accept information about alternatives in their inert sets, although they do not actively seek such information.

The challenge for marketers is to move their products from the inert set to the evoked set.

Internal information search: Relevant information stored in long-term memory used to assess whether a satisfactory alternative exists once a consumer need is activated. Internal information may have been actively or passively acquired by the consumer.

Purchase involvement: The level of concern for, or interest in, the purchase process triggered by the need to consider a particular purchase.

Repeat purchase: A form of habitual decision making in which a brand is purchased again without any emotional attachment or commitment to it. Competitors can influence repeat purchases to brand switch.

REVIEW QUESTIONS

1. What is the difference between internal and external information search?
2. What are the principal sources of information available to consumers?
3. When does external information search occur? Why does it occur?
4. Why are some alternatives in a consumer's evoked set and others in the inert and inept sets? What role does information search play in the formation of the evoked, inert, and inept sets?
5. How do habitual, limited, and extensive decision makers differ? What category appears most rational to you?
6. Would you expect the prepurchase search efforts of a couple planning a honeymoon to differ when planning a weekend holiday? Why?
7. Why advertise if consumer research shows that it is the least often acquired and least influential source of information available to consumers?

BIBLIOGRAPHY

Assael, Henry. (1987). *Consumer behavior and marketing action*. Boston: Kent Publishing.

Beatty, Sharon E. and Smith, Scott. (1987). External information search: An investigation across several product categories. *Journal of Consumer Research, 14* (June), 83-95.

Bettman, James R. (1978). Consumer information acquisition and search strategies. In Andrew A. Mitchell (ed.), *The effect of information on consumer and market behavior*, Chicago: American Marketing Association, 35-48.

Claxton, John, Fry, Joseph N., and Portis, Bernard. (1974). A taxonomy of prepurchase information gathering patterns. *Journal of Consumer Research, 1* (December), 35-42.

Crotts, John. (1990). Purchase involvement of repeat visitors to a destination environment. *Visions in Leisure and Business, 10* (1).

Crotts, John (1992). Information search behaviors of free and independent travelers. *Visions in Leisure and Business, 11* (3).

Crotts, John C. and Guy, Bonnie S. (1993). The relationship between retail advertising and published quality ratings of hotels and motels. *Proceedings of the 1993 Academy of Marketing Sciences Conference*, Miami Beach, FL, May 26-29.

Crotts, John and Reid, Laura. (1993). Segmenting the visitor market by the timing of their recreation decisions. *Visions in Leisure and Business, 12* (3).

Donohew, Lewis and Tipton, Leonard. (1973). A conceptual model of information seeking, avoiding, and processing. In Peter Clark (ed.), *New models of communications research*, Beverly Hills, CA: Sage Publications, Inc., 243-268.

Francken, Dick A. and van Raaij, W. Fred. (1979). *A longitudinal study of vacationers' information acquisition behavior.* Paper on Economic Psychology (No. 2), Erasmus University: Rotterdam, Netherlands, July.

Gitelson, Richard J. and Crompton, John L. (1984). Insights into the repeat vacation phenomenon. *Annals of Tourism Research, 11*(2), 199-217.

Hawkins, Del I., Best, Roger J., and Coney, Kenneth A. (1986). *Consumer behavior: Implications for marketing strategy*, Fourth edition. Chicago: Irwin, Inc.

Hawkins, Del I., Best, Roger J., and Coney, Kenneth A. (1995). *Consumer behavior: Implications for marketing strategy*, Sixth edition. Chicago: Irwin, Inc.

Markin, R.J. (1969). *The psychology of consumer behavior.* Englewood Cliffs, NJ: Prentice Hall.

McIntosh, R.W. and Goeldner, C.R. (1986). *Tourism: Principles, practices and philosophies.* New York: John Wiley and Sons.

Mill, R.C. and Morrison, A.M. (1985). *The tourism system.* Englewood Cliffs, NJ: Prentice Hall.

Moore, William L. and Lehmann, Donald R. (1980). Individual differences in search behavior for a non-durable. *Journal of Consumer Research, 7* (December), 296-307.

Newman, Joseph W. and Staelin, Richard. (1972). Prepurchase information seeking for new cars and major household appliances. *Journal of Marketing Research, 9* (August), 249-257.

Nolan, Sidney D., Jr. (1976). Tourists' use and evaluation of travel information sources. *Journal of Travel Research, 14* (3), 6-8.

Ogilvy, David and Mather. (1996). *Trends in travel and tourism advertising in the United States measured media, 1991-1996.* New York: Author.

Perdue, R.R. and Botkin, M.R. (1988). Visitor survey versus conversion study. *Annals of Tourism Research, 15* (1), 76-87.

Perdue, R.R. and Pitegoff, B.E. (1990). Methods of accountability research for destination marketing. *Journal of Travel Research, 28*(4), 45-49.

Schul, Patrick and Crompton, John L. (1983). Search behavior of international vacationers: Travel-specific lifestyle and socio-demographic variables. *Journal of Travel Research, 22* (Fall), 25-30.

Snepenger, D. and Snepenger, M. (1993). Information search by pleasure travelers. In M. Khan, M. Olsen, and T. Var (eds.), *Encyclopedia of hospitality and tourism.* New York: Van Nostrand Reinhold.

Van Raaij, W. Fred. (1986). Consumer research on tourism: Mental and behavioral constructs. *Annals of Tourism Research, 13* (1), 1-9.

Westbrook, Robert A. and Fornell, Claes. (1979). Patterns of information source usage among durable goods buyers. *Journal of Marketing Research, 16* (August), 303-312.

Woodside, Arch G. and Ronkainen, Ilkka A. (1980). Tourism management strategies for competitive vacation destinations. In D. E. Hawkins, E. L. Shaffer, and J. M. Rovelstad (eds.), *Tourism marketing and management issues* Washington, DC: George Washington University, 3-19.

Woodside, Arch G. and Sherrell, Dan. (1977). Traveler evoked, inept, and inert set of vacation destinations. *Journal of Travel Research, 16* (Summer), 14-18.

Chapter 8

Consumer Choice in Context: The Decoy Effect in Travel and Tourism

Bharath M. Josiam
J. S. Perry Hobson

LEARNING OBJECTIVES

By the end of the chapter the reader should be able to:

- Understand the assumptions underlying models of consumer choice. Some important assumptions are rational person, value maximization, perfect information, information overload, and cognitive miserliness
- Understand the theories underlying models of consumer choice. Some important theories are proportionality model and the similarity hypothesis
- Understand how the regularity assumption underpins both the choice models described above
- Understand how the decoy effect violates the regularity assumption
- Illustrate how the combination of price and quality of new products introduced into the market affect the decision-making process of the consumer

INTRODUCTION

One of the basic assumptions that economists make about consumer choice is that individual consumers behave rationally. Further, economists

This chapter was previously published in the *Journal of Travel Research*, *34*(1), 1995. Reprinted with permission.

assume that consumers make choices best suited to their goals, budget constraints, and earning power and are primarily interested in value maximization (VM). However, this theory presumes that consumers have specific preferences and are then consistent with their choice among alternatives (Robertson, Zielinski, and Ward, 1984). But economists also assume that consumers have perfect information about market offerings. This assumption is rarely true, since most consumers make a choice from a limited contextual set.

One of the critical factors in consumer decision making is the range of choices presented to the consumer in the information search stage. The two fundamental issues are how many choices should be offered and what should be the nature of the choices offered?

Too many choices overwhelm the consumer, leading to information overload and poorer choice decisions (Jacob, Speller, and Kuhn, 1974). Consumers attempt to limit the time and effort spent in processing information (Payne, Bettman, and Johnson, 1988). This means that a limited choice set should be presented to the consumer. What then should be included in such a limited choice set? Should the choice set consist of similar or dissimilar items?

In the consumer behavior literature, one well-known concept is the proportionality model (Luce, 1959). This model assumes that a new market offering will attract defectors from their initial choices in proportion to the original shares of the existing items. This suggests that any item introduced to the choice set will attract customers because it expands the range of available choices. What this model leaves unanswered is why some customers defect.

The similarity hypothesis proposes that customers defect to items similar to existing offerings (Tversky, 1972). This suggests that designing a new product or service to be as dissimilar from a company's current offering as possible can minimalize cannibalization. Based on these assumptions, alternative choice theories have been developed (Batsell, 1980; Tversky, 1972).

Both the similarity and the proportionality models share the assumption of regularity, which claims that the introduction of a new alternative cannot increase the probability of choosing a member of the original set (Luce, 1959).

The basis of an effective marketing strategy is an understanding of how consumers make choices between alternatives within such a contextual set. VM implies that the consumer opts for the choice that maximizes value, independent of the other available choices. In other words, if a traveler chooses a Marriott hotel over a Hyatt hotel in one context (when Marriott is cheaper), then the traveler is very unlikely to prefer Hyatt over Marriott if a third, more expensive hotel (such as a Ritz Carlton) is introduced into the choice set.

However, Huber, Payne, and Puto (1982) proposed that under certain conditions the similarity hypothesis and the regularity model can be violated by the addition of an asymmetrically dominant alternative. They called this the "decoy effect."

In the marketplace customers are normally offered a choice of items varying in price and quality. The higher-priced items are perceived to be of higher quality. This scenario is referred to as symmetrical domination. Customers maximize value by making choices that balance their ability to pay with their need for a certain quality level. Huber, Payne, and Puto (1982) suggested an alternative to this scenario with the introduction of an asymmetrically dominated item. An asymmetrically dominated alternative is one that is higher in some important attributes, such as price, but is lower in other equally valuable attributes, such as quality. This item is referred to as the "decoy." It is not expected to be chosen because it offers low value. The only purpose of introducing the decoy into the choice set is to shift the consumers' selection in favor of the target (an item high in price and quality) that dominates the decoy. The "option" is the third item in the choice set and is low in both price and quality. Figure 8.1 represents the position of the target, decoy, and option in terms of the price/quality relationship.

Huber, Payne, and Puto (1982) tested and found support for the following hypothesis:

FIGURE 8.1. Asymmetrical Domination

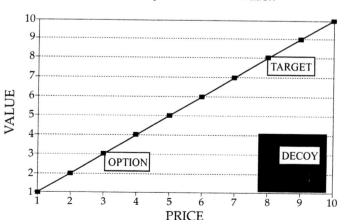

(H1) In a two-item choice set, the introduction of a third item, which is an asymmetrically dominated item (the decoy), will shift the selection in favor of the high price-high quality item (the target).

They tested six products with a student sample using a test-retest design. They asked student respondents to indicate their preferences within a choice set, first without and then two weeks later with a decoy. Their study showed that on average 9.2 percent of the students had shifted their selection to the target after the decoy was introduced into the choice set.

However, the study had many limitations. They used a convenience sample of students in laboratory conditions and the products tested were defined with only two attributes.

If this asymmetrical domination choice model can be supported with additional evidence, the results can be applied with greater confidence and the marketing implications could be very significant. Further, the application of this theory in the field of tourism has not been tested, but was suggested as an area for future research.

PURPOSE OF THE STUDY

This study, with features that overcome the limitations of the study by Huber, Payne, and Puto (1982), is intended to test the application of the decoy effect in tourism. It tests the following hypothesis:

(H1) The introduction of a third item, which is asymmetrically dominated (the decoy), into the choice set of tour packages to Walt Disney World and Las Vegas will shift the selection in favor of the high price-high quality item (the target) from the low price-low quality item (the option).

METHODOLOGY

Sample Selection

To test the hypothesis in a real-world situation, the cooperation of a Midwestern travel agency was obtained. The agency agreed to distribute survey sets to customers as they came in to make inquiries or bookings.

The sample was divided into two equal groups by giving out two different survey sets alternately. Surveys were given to customers who agreed to cooperate and were completed while they waited to see a travel agent. A total of 136 usable responses were collected over a period of two months.

Survey Administration

Recognizing the limitations of the original study by Huber, Payne, and Puto (1982), it was decided to use customers who were actually inquiring about or buying travel products. To avoid bias, respondents were not told their answers would be used as part of an academic exercise. They were informed verbally and also by means of a cover letter (see Exhibit 8.1) that the agency was seeking their input into developing attractive travel packages. The letter asked respondents to indicate their preferences from the packages offered.

Two popular travel destinations, Las Vegas, Nevada, and Walt Disney World in Orlando, Florida, were identified. In collaboration with the travel agent and using existing prices and amenities, three packages were developed for each destination. Each package was specifically developed to act as either the option (low price-low value), the target (high price-high value), or the decoy (high price-low value).

The need for a realistic field study design did not permit the use of a test-retest model. The disadvantages of a test-retest model of the same choice set are that consumers have already been made aware of the first choice set before the decoy is added. As Huber, Payne, and Puto (1982) note in their findings:

> Within the same subjects the decoy effect was significant, but not strongly so . . . the relative weakness of the distortion can be attributed to a carryover effect in which subjects simply repeated choices made two weeks earlier. Indeed, the cross-subject analysis, which does not share pretest sensitization, resulted in a much stronger decoy effect. (p. 94)

Accordingly, for this study a split-half model was developed and used. The advantages of such a model were that it allowed the researchers to survey a larger sample, in a more realistic setting, without prior sensitization to a choice set.

Survey Instrument

As shown in Exhibits 8.2 and 8.3, the tour packages were actual packages. In fact, had any customer so indicated, the travel agency was fully prepared

EXHIBIT 8.1. Cover Page

---

100 Main Street
Anytown, USA

We at XYZ Travel Agency are constantly seeking ways to improve your travel experiences and provide you with attractive packages to suit every budget.

This time, we have put together a choice of 5 packages to two of *America's Favorite* vacation spots.

—DISNEY WORLD AND LAS VEGAS—

Enclosed is a checklist. Please make your choice of one Disney vacation and one Las Vegas trip that you might consider for your next vacation.

Thanks for your time!

Whether you travel for business or pleasure—please call (123) 456-7890.

Thanks again,

Jane Doe

(NAME AND ADDRESS HAVE BEEN CHANGED
TO MAINTAIN CONFIDENTIALITY.)

EXHIBIT 8.2. Survey Set A—Las Vegas/Walt Disney World Vacation Packages

LAS VEGAS

☐ TOUR #1 $365.50 INCLUDES

♥ Roundtrip airfare from St. Louis to Las Vegas on nonstop charter.

♦ Three nights' hotel accommodation at the Flamingo Hilton (garden section), located on the Strip.

♣ Transfers between airport and hotel.

♠ Las Vegas Fun Book with discounts on shows and meals for use in Las Vegas' favorite night spots.

☐ TOUR #2 $449 INCLUDES:

♥ Roundtrip airfare from St. Louis on scheduled American Airlines flight.

♦ Three nights' luxury hotel accommodation in the tower section of the Flamingo Hilton Hotel, located on the Strip.

♣ Buffet breakfast or lunch daily at the Flamingo's Crown Room or Food Fantasy.

♠ Transfers between airport and hotel.

♥ City Lights Revue at the Flamingo including 2 drinks

♦ All gratuities on the above features.

♣ Las Vegas Fun Book with discounts on shows and meals for use in Las Vegas' favorite night spots.

> All prices are per person based on double occupancy. Prices quoted are subject to change and availability. Restrictions may apply.

WALT DISNEY WORLD

☐ TOUR #1 $805 INCLUDES:

• Roundtrip airfare from St. Louis to Orlando on nonstop service.

• Five nights' accommodation at the Caribbean Beach Hotel located on the grounds of Walt Disney World.

• Hotel taxes are NOT included.

• Use of compact car for five 24-hour periods. Taxes are not included.

• Four-day passport providing use of the three main Disney theme parks, Disney World, Epcot, and Disney MGM Studios.

• Magic Morning breakfast feature.

☐ TOUR #2 $1,073 INCLUDES:

• Roundtrip airfare from St. Louis to Orlando on nonstop service.

• Five nights' accommodation at the Grand Florida Hotel (water view) located on the grounds of Walt Disney World.

• Five-day SUPERPASS providing unlimited use of all Disney theme parks as well as Pleasure Island, Typhoon Lagoon, River Country, and Discovery Island.

• Magic Morning breakfast feature.

☐ TOUR #3 $1,273 INCLUDES:

• Roundtrip airfare from St. Louis to Orlando on US Air via Charlotte.

• Five nights at the Holiday Inn Maingate located close to Walt Disney World. Two-room suite accommodation.

• Hotel taxes are NOT included.

• One-day admission to your choice of the Magic Kingdom, Epcot Center, or MGM Studios.

• Steve Birnbaum guide to Walt Disney World.

• Use of intermediate car for three 24-hour periods.

> All prices are per person based on two to a room. Car rental Collision Damage Waiver insurance is not included. Prices are subject to change and availability. Some restrictions may apply.

EXHIBIT 8.3. Survey Set B—Walt Disney World/Las Vegas Vacation Packages

WALT DISNEY WORLD

☐ TOUR #1 $805 INCLUDES:

- Roundtrip airfare from St. Louis to Orlando on nonstop service.

- Five nights' accommodation at the Caribbean Beach Hotel located on the grounds of Walt Disney World (garden view).

- Hotel taxes are NOT included.

- Use of compact car for five 24-hour periods. Taxes are not included.

- Four-day passport providing use of the three main Disney theme parks– Magic Kingdom, Epcot, and Disney MGM Studios.

- Magic Morning breakfast feature.

☐ TOUR #2 $1,073 INCLUDES:

- Roundtrip airfare from St. Louis to Orlando on nonstop service.

- Five nights' accommodation at the Grand Floridian Hotel (water view) located on the grounds of Walt Disney World.

- All hotel taxes ARE included.

- Five-day SUPERPASS providing unlimited use of all Disney theme parks as well as Pleasure Island, Typhoon Lagoon, River Country, and Discovery Island.

- Magic Morning breakfast feature.

> All prices are per person based on two to a room. Car rental Collision Damage Waiver insurance is NOT included. Prices are subject to change and availability. Some restrictions may apply.

LAS VEGAS

☐ TOUR #1 $365.50 INCLUDES:

- ♥ Roundtrip airfare from St. Louis to Las Vegas on nonstop charter service.
- ♦ Three nights' hotel accommodation at the Flamingo Hilton (garden section), located on the Strip.
- ♣ Transfers between airport and hotel.
- ♠ Las Vegas Fun Book with discounts on shows and meals for use in Las Vegas' favorite night spots.

☐ TOUR #2 $449 INCLUDES:

- ♥ Roundtrip airfare from St. Louis on scheduled American Airlines flight.
- ♦ Three nights' luxury hotel accommodation in the tower section of the Flamingo Hilton Hotel, located on the Strip.
- ♣ Buffet breakfast or lunch daily at the Flamingo's Crown Room or Food Fantasy.
- ♠ Transfers between airport and hotel.
- ♥ City Lights Revue at the Flamingo including 2 drinks.
- ♦ All gratuities on the above features.
- ♣ Las Vegas Fun Book with discounts on shows and meals for use in Las Vegas' favorite night spots.

☐ TOUR #3 $525 INCLUDES:

- ♥ Roundtrip airfare from St. Louis to Las Vegas on Southwest Airlines.
- ♦ Three nights at the luxury Las Vegas Club hotel located off the Strip in downtown Las Vegas.
- ♣ Hotel taxes are NOT included.
- ♠ Transfers between airport and hotel.
- ♥ One buffet lunch.
- ♦ 10% discount on a rental car.
- ♣ Las Vegas Fun Book with discounts on shows and meals for use in Las Vegas' favorite night spots.

> All prices are per person based on double occupancy. Prices quoted are subject to change and availability. Restrictions may apply.

to make the bookings. Table 8.1 gives a synopsis of the pricing and grouping of the packages.

FINDINGS

Preferences of the respondents are summarized in Table 8.2. Table 8.3 indicates the results of introducing a decoy into the choice set in the context of a given destination. Figures 8.2 and 8.3 give a graphical representation of the findings. As shown by the tables and graphs, in the case of Disney World the shift is in favor of the target, with 9.1 percent of the respondents opting for it. A chi-square test revealed a Pearson value of

TABLE 8.1. Price and Nature of Tour Packages in the Choice Sets

SET A			SET B		
Destination	**Package**	**Price**	**Destination**	**Package**	**Price**
Disney World	Option	$805	Las Vegas	Option	$365
	Target	$1,073		Target	$449
Las Vegas	Option	$365	Disney World	Option	$805
	Target	$449		Target	$1,073
	Decoy	$525		Decoy	$1,273

TABLE 8.2. Summary of Preferences

SET A (N = 69)				SET B (N = 67)			
Destination	**Pkg.**	**No.**	**Percent**	**Destination**	**Pkg.**	**No.**	**Percent**
Disney World	Option	31	44.9	Las Vegas	Option	19	28.4
	Target	38	55.1		Target	48	71.6
Las Vegas	Option	19	27.5	Disney World	Option	17	25.4
	Target	43	62.3		Target	43	64.2
	Decoy	7	10.1		Decoy	7	10.4

TABLE 8.3. Summary of Shifts Resulting from Decoy Introduction

Choice in Context– Las Vegas (N = 68)				Choice in Context– Disney World (N = 68)			
Destination	**Package**		**Percent**	**Destination**	**Package**		**Percent**
Las Vegas	(O1)	Option	28.4	Disney World	(O1)	Option	44.9
	(T1)	Target	71.6		(T1)	Target	55.1
Las Vegas	(O2)	Option	27.5	Disney World	(O2)	Option	25.4
	(T2)	Target	62.3		(T2)	Target	64.2
	(D2)	Decoy	10.1		(D2)	Decoy	10.4

Shift = (O1) – (O2)	=	0.9%	

Shift = (O1) – (O2)	=	19.5%
Shift to Target	=	9.1%
Chi-square = 5.69	=	
Sig. = .01		

FIGURE 8.2. Las Vegas—Choice in Context

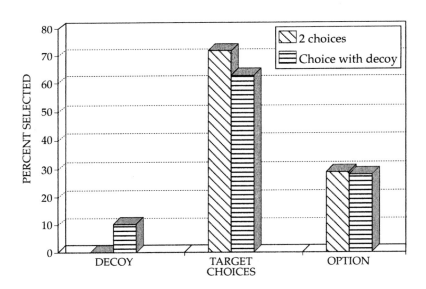

FIGURE 8.3. Disney—Choice in Context

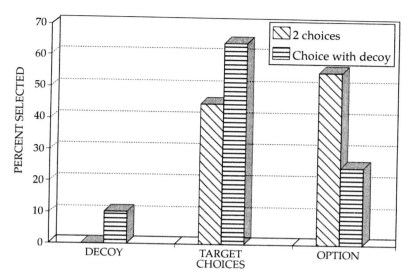

5.69, which was significant at the .01 level, indicating that this was not a chance occurrence. This is consistent with the findings of Huber, Payne, and Puto (1982), which shows an average shift of 9.2 percent within contextual choice sets of cars, beer, restaurants, lotteries, films, and TV sets in a laboratory setting.

In the case of Las Vegas, when the decoy was added to the choice set, a minor shift from the option was seen. A chi-square test showed that this shift was not significant. In addition, a more pronounced shift from the target to the decoy was observed. This shift to the decoy was not expected. It can be accounted for by the fact that the decoy was offering more value than had been expected either by the travel agent or the researchers. In addition, an overall trade-up effect was observed, with a 10 percent shift in favor of the higher-priced decoy.

This study found that in both cases more than 10 percent of the respondents opted for the decoy, while the 1982 study found that only 2 percent actually selected the decoy. This apparent discrepancy merits further explanation. As noted by Huber, Payne, and Puto (1982), "it is expected that increasing the complexity of the decision task would increase the error in the choices and thereby limit the effect of adding any alternative" (p. 94).

Further, the 1982 study was undertaken in a laboratory, offering decoys that were obviously of low value, while high in price. This field study, on the other hand, was conducted using realistic multidimensional offerings, increasing the complexity of the decision-making process.

In the competitive travel and tourism business, it is unlikely any company would realistically be willing to offer a package with zero value. As this study was conducted with customers of a reputable travel agency, the field setting precluded offering any items that would be considered totally lacking in value. Therefore, the researchers and the travel agent made every effort to offer packages that could be construed as decoys, while still retaining elements of value.

IMPLICATIONS

Travel agents are paid on a commission basis. This means that there are two basic ways to generate additional revenue: first, sell more tickets and tours; second, sell the same number, but higher-priced ones that are more profitable.

If the first option is selected, additional customers are needed. Further, each ticket or tour sold has variable costs such as employee time, telephone calls, computer time, and documentation that affect its ultimate profitability. This option is not very attractive, and may not be feasible in a saturated market.

The second option, selling higher-priced tours, is more attractive. This option does not need more customers, nor are there are any additional variable costs. Hence, travel agents are constantly seeking ways to promote higher-priced tours.

The findings of this study have far-reaching implications for travel and tourism companies that offer a range of products and services. Instead of offering limited choices to the market at random, a decoy choice may shift customer purchase patterns to more expensive or more profitable items. In this case, had customers' purchases followed the preferences indicated, revenue would have increased without any additional costs to the agency.

Revenues were projected for each survey set at the prices indicated. Even with this small sample, the revenue projections indicate a total increase of approximately US $4,500. For a large travel agency with hundreds of customers, implementation of these findings could increase revenue by thousands of dollars per month.

Simonson and Tversky (1992) reported similar findings. But their study also found that customers have an inclination to stay away from extreme options. The introduction of the decoy as a third choice would make the low price-low value option an extreme choice. This addition would reinforce the tendency of the customer to shift toward the high price-high value target, which is no longer seen as an extreme. This study supports the concept of introducing a decoy to the choice set.

However, two other points must be remembered. First, as noted earlier, information overload is to be avoided and a limited choice set carefully constructed. Second, a true decoy with minimal value can destroy the credibility of the agency.

When considering the choice set, the agency will also have to consider the positioning of all its products and ensure they are in tune with its image. The choice set of option, target, and decoy should be viewed as a portfolio and presented within a systems framework.

This study has implications for many areas of the travel and tourism industry. For example, restaurants could increase their profitability by introducing decoy choices in their menus and wine lists to influence consumers. Souvenir vendors could also employ this concept to increase their revenues.

Clearly, all companies want to present their products and services in a way that will appeal to their target markets. When considering the decoy technique, marketers must be mindful of the ethical implications of this promotional method. Marketing has been defined as "communicating to and giving the target market customers what they want, when they want it, and at a price they are willing to pay" (Lewis and Chambers, 1989, p. 9). Shaw (1992) has noted that "the marketing tools used to accomplish this include advertising and personal selling. Because we use these techniques, we have an ethical responsibility about what we say and how we say it" (p. 150).

Essentially, the decoy method is one way of presenting perceived value options. It should be noted that a similar effect may be achieved without using a decoy through carefully worded advertisements, imagery, and other tools. What is clear is that all pricing and presentation issues should be carefully considered in a holistic manner. In the long run it will be counterproductive to offer zero-value items. Given the complexity of the issues behind consumer decision making, value perception will ultimately be decided by the customer.

LIMITATIONS

Before the decoy effect can be widely implemented, it needs further testing. This study has its limitations in terms of both methodology and application. As in the study by Huber, Payne, and Puto (1982), this study was limited by the use of a nonrandom sample. Further, demographic data was not gathered. It is not known what effect, if any, demographics may have on the propensity of individual consumers to make choices. This study was done at one location with a relatively small sample. Furthermore, the two destinations selected, Disney World and Las Vegas, are not comparable. They draw travelers from market segments that differ in demographics, psychographics, and benefits sought. The decoy effect could have been tested with greater rigor had two directly comparable destinations been used in this study.

CONCLUSIONS

Since Huber, Payne, and Puto (1982) offered decoys with virtually zero value in a laboratory setting, the decoy effect was magnified. The current realistic field study, conducted with greater rigor than the 1982 study, demonstrated a strong decoy effect in one of the two cases. In the other case, the introduction of the decoy led some customers to trade up. In both cases projected revenue increased on introducing the decoy into the choice set.

Future research should use random samples, a large sample size, multiple locations, and comparable destinations. Future studies should not only address the limitations of this study but also seek a better understanding of the conditions under which decoys can be effectively deployed.

CONCEPT DEFINITIONS

Asymmetrical domination: An item in a choice set that is superior in some important attributes, such as price, but is lower in other equally valuable attributes, such as quality.

Cognitive miserliness: Consumers attempt to limit the time and effort spent in processing information to cope with information overload.

Decoy: An asymmetrically dominated item in a choice set that is high price, but low quality. It is not expected to be chosen by the customer, because it offers low value. The only purpose of introducing the decoy into the choice set is to shift the consumers' selection in favor of the target.

Decoy effect: A model of consumer behavior, which hypothesizes that the introduction of a carefully constructed decoy into a choice set will result in a segment of consumers shifting their choice to a higher-price targeted item.

Information overload: Too many choices and excessive information overwhelm the consumer, leading to poorer choice decisions.

Option: The low price-low quality item in the choice set.

Proportionality model: A new market offering will attract defectors from their initial choices in proportion to the original shares of the existing items. This suggests that any item introduced to the choice set will attract customers because it expands the range of available choices.

Regularity assumption: The introduction of a new alternative cannot increase the probability of choosing a member of the original set.

Similarity hypothesis: Customers defect to items similar to existing offerings.

Symmetrical domination: Higher-priced items are perceived to be of higher quality. Customers maximize value by making a choice that balances their ability to pay with their need for a certain quality level.

Target: The high price-high quality item in the choice set that dominates the decoy.

REVIEW QUESTIONS

1. Give examples from different sectors of the tourism and hospitality industry of the proportionality model and similarity hypothesis.
2. How can marketers reduce information overload in materials targeted at consumers? Analyze brochures of three attractions/destinations to identify strategies used by marketers to use cognitive miserliness to the advantage of the seller.
3. Give specific examples of how the decoy effect can be used to the advantage of a seller in a restaurant menu, wine list, clothing store, or mail-order catalog. Clearly identify the items specified by you as target, decoy, and option. Give product attributes and prices in all cases.
4. Why do some rational customers select the decoy?
5. The decoy is introduced into the choice set, despite the fact that it is *not* intended to be sold. It serves to induce customers to buy the target and spend more money than they originally intended. Therefore, is the use of decoys *unethical*?

REFERENCES

Batsell, R.R. (1980). "A Market Share Model Which Simultaneously Captures the Effects of Utility and Substitutability." Working paper 80-007. Philadelphia: Wharton School, University of Pennsylvania.

Huber, J., J.W. Payne, and C. Puto (1982). "Adding Asymmetrically Dominated Alternatives: Violations of Regularity and the Similarity Hypothesis." *Journal of Consumer Research*, 9 (June): 90-98.

Jacob, J., D.E. Speller, and C.A. Kuhn (1974). "Brand Choice Behavior as a Function of Information Load: Replication and Extension." *Journal of Consumer Research*, 1 (June): 69.

Lewis, R.C., and R.E. Chambers (1989). *Marketing Leadership in Hospitality.* New York: Van Nostrand Reinhold.

Luce, R.D. (1959). *Individual Choice Behavior.* New York: John Wiley and Sons.

Payne, J.W., J.R. Bettman, and E.J. Johnson (1988). "Adaptive Strategy Selection in Decision Making." *Journal of Experimental Psychology: Learning, Memory, and Cognition*, 14: 534-552.

Robertson, T.S., J. Zielinski, and S. Ward (1984). *Consumer Behavior.* Glenview, IL: Scott Foresman and Company.

Shaw, M. (1992). "Hospitality Ethics: A Marketing Perspective." In *Ethics in Hospitality Management*, ed. S.J. Hall. East Lansing, MI: American Hotel and Motel Association, p. 150.

Simonson, I., and A. Tversky (1992). "Choice in Context: Tradeoff Contrast and Extremeness Aversion." *Journal of Marketing Research*, 29 (August): 281-295.

Tversky, A. (1972). "Elimination by Aspects: A Theory of Choice." *Psychological Review*, 79 (July): 281-299.

Chapter 9

Package Tourism and Customer Loyalties

Monica Hanefors
Lena Larsson Mossberg

LEARNING OBJECTIVES

By the end of the chapter the reader should be able to:

- Describe the tourism package
- List and understand the various loyalties to be found in package tourism
- Understand package tourism loyalty descriptors
- Understand the relative importance of word of mouth, and personal bonds
- Discuss the importance of customer satisfaction for package tours
- Recognize why supply has to be considered in relation to tourists' loyalties
- Understand the complexity of the tourists' combination of travel motives.

CHAPTER AIM AND STRUCTURE

Modern tourist behavior is far more complicated than tourism consumer behavior of the past, partly due to the variety of possibilities available to individuals. Therefore, it is important to take advantage of several disciplines, in this case marketing and social anthropology, among others. Through such an approach more can be learned about the tourism encounter and the tourist.

This chapter will present a brief introduction to package tourism, and will then refer more specifically to the loyal traveler (see e.g., Pritchard and Howard, 1993), through the effects of the rapid changes of "tourism consumer behavior" during the past decade (see e.g., Moutinho, 1987; Ryan, 1995; Hanefors and Larsson Mossberg, 1998). Thereafter, it focuses more specifically on package tourists' different loyalties (Hanefors and Larsson Mossberg, 1997a). Two particular questions are discussed in this chapter: what is loyalty in a package tourism context, and what factors lead package tourists to become loyal? More precisely, it will discuss loyalty to tour operators.

Throughout, this chapter will follow the tourist David and his decision-making process. Starting with David's experiences during his last trip to Gran Canaria, it continues discussing his different loyalty considerations. Thereby it becomes clear what factors influence loyal attitudes and behavior, for David and in general. Especially, travel motives will be dealt with at some length. Finally, a new package tourism loyalty model is presented.

PACKAGE TOURISM

David is a forty-four-year-old, divorced man, from a small town in Sweden. He has a son, who lives with his mother, not far away from David. David has started to think about the annual winter holiday. He desperately needs a break, wants to get some sun, and to get to know some new people.

David works in computer engineering, and travels a lot through his work—both nationally and internationally. A travel agency, with which his company has an agreement, takes care of all those arrangements. But, when David travels privately, he has to count both his money and his time. Besides, he prefers to travel as effortlessly as possible. Therefore, he always chooses a package tour when going on a holiday.

The package tour, package holiday, and package travel are all-inclusive tours, often with flight transportation, all with limited flexibility, and with the same purpose. For example, they have a number of common characteristic features such as being effective, safe, and less expensive, in comparison to buying a flight and a hotel stay separately, and individually (Enoch, 1996). This gives the tourist on a package tour the possibility to visit a large number of sites in a short period of time, needing neither time nor skill to arrange the tour personally, and to be able to take advantage of the tour organizer's lower prices, through their clever economic negotiations.

The tourist can even use the package to "travel to far away countries with strange cultures, unreliable transportation, and doubtful standards of hygiene" (Enoch, 1996, p. 601). Besides, when buying the package, the tourist feels sure to receive everything promised, for example, in the catalogue that he or she read prior to the tour (see also Hanefors and Larsson, 1993; Dann, 1997). As early as the time of purchase of the holiday trip, the tourist may have a set of expectations about its nature and performance, and the anticipated benefits (Lewis, 1994).

The World Tourism Organization (WTO) recommendation says: "The tour type can be either package or non-package. The package refers to the purchase of a package of travel services including transport and accommodation. All other types of trips are non-package tours" (cf. Yale, 1995). According to the European Union the package stands for at least two of the following services that are sold or offered for sale at an inclusive price: (a) flight transport, which most of the time is chartered; (b) accommodation, e.g., hotel or resort; (c) guides; (d) activities; and (e) sometimes food (HMSO, 1993). One has to remember, though, that a package tour also may mean transportation by bus, ship, or train.

TRAVEL EXPERIENCES AND LOYALTIES

David spent his last holiday together with his son on Gran Canaria. That was his first time on the island, and his initial idea for the holiday had been to visit Madeira, because of his interest in flowers. However, he had to compromise on his travel plans because his young son was accompanying him. David's ex-wife did not think Madeira was a suitable place for children. David felt very satisfied with his holiday, and he really enjoyed Gran Canaria and its people, the few he met. Even the hotel with its service-minded personnel was excellent, according to David.

On arrival at the island, David and his son at first were informed that the prebooked hotel was completely full. The tour operator's representative offered them a room in another hotel, even more luxurious. David got upset because one of his friends at home had recommended this particular hotel. After complaining to the guide, they were able to stay at the hotel David originally booked. They received a very nice room with a balcony, costing much more than David actually paid for. Even though they had to wait a couple of hours to get into the room, eventually they were pleased with the arrangement.

The holiday time went slowly—it floated away. David and his son went swimming every day. They also participated in some excursions arranged by the tour operator, during one of which they went up to the mountains and stopped at sites where they could see a variety of rare plants. The guide was very knowledgeable on this subject.

The tourist's experiences of the various ingredients of the package tour affect his or her perception of the service quality of the tour. Many approaches have been used to evaluate consumers' views of a company's services. The most commonly used models, within the area of marketing, are multiattribute ones. With these, a customer's assessment of service quality is often considered the result of a comparison between the customer's expectations and actual perceptions of the service, based upon a number of service quality attributes.

A number of interactive perspectives have also been proposed. These perspectives originate from a variety of behavioral sciences, primarily anthropology, psychology, and sociology. The interactive perspectives have been chosen to give a deeper understanding of behavior. The participants' roles, their statuses, and the personalities of the personnel are discussed, and assumed to influence the behavior of those involved in the service encounters.

Within the package context, service satisfaction can be evaluated either at specific service encounters, or for a whole tour. Service encounter satisfaction can be defined as "The customer's dis/satisfaction with a discrete service encounter" (Bitner and Hubbert, 1994, p. 76). It reflects the customer's feelings about discrete encounters with the personnel, and will result from the evaluation of the events and behaviors that occur during a definable period of time, in this case the tour in question. Discrete service encounters with parts of the product (e.g., hotel, or air transportation) can also be evaluated. For example, if a tour operator has received many complaints related to hotel employees' performance, an assessment of the tourists' perceptions of these particular service encounters may be carried out.

The overall service satisfaction with the tour operator, based on experiences from at least one tour, can be examined as well. Overall service satisfaction is defined as: "The customer's overall dis/satisfaction with the organization based on all encounters and experiences with that particular organization" (Bitner and Hubbert, 1994, p. 77). These multiple service encounters may include several interactions with many individuals during one or more tours. Service quality, on the other hand, is seen as a higher-order construct than overall service satisfaction and is defined as: "The customer's overall impression of the relative inferiority/superiority of the organization and its services" (Bitner and Hubbert, 1994, p. 77). This means that the overall service satisfaction is based on the tourist's experiences of the tour operator in question and of at least one tour, while an individual tourist can have perceptions of a tour operator's service quality, without taking part in any of their tours. If service quality should be evaluated in connection to package tours, other variables have an influence, such as advertising, service encounters with competing tour operators, word of mouth, and public relations (see also Bitner, 1990).

Servqual, the most cited and used technique for assessing customers' perceptions of service quality, measures expectations and perceptions at the same time (Parasuraman, Zeitmal, and Berry, 1988). For package tours, if data from the tourist's expectations and perceptions instead are collected and measured separately, changes in opinions at the individual level can be analyzed for each of the different attributes (such as friendliness, helpfulness, and security)—an advantage (see e.g., Larsson Mossberg, 1994). This way of measuring can be difficult to carry out in other service organizations, such as bank services, post office services, and so on, when the time of consumption is shorter. It is hardly recommended to deliver a questionnaire at the entrance to the bank, and another at the exit, when the service encounter is over.

An important prerequisite in order to keep tourists as customers is, to maintain the quality of the package tours can be maintained at a constant and high level without any price increase, as the market is relatively price sensitive. The goal for the tour operator must be to build and maintain a basis of committed customers who stay loyal. Even though clarification of the relationship between loyalty and service quality, in tourism contexts, has been asked for (Dimanche and Havitz, 1994), quality of service is generally assumed to affect business performance and loyalty in a positive way. Dissatisfied customers are said to be more willing to change to another provider than satisfied ones. However, satisfaction alone is not a sufficient guarantee of customer loyalty.

From the one true loyal customer to the one who will never use the service provider again, service loyalty is a matter of degree. Loyalty differs considerably from simple repeat purchase behavior, because attitudes always have to be considered as well, since customers can buy any service regularly, without being positive toward the specific organization (Pritchard, Howard, and Haviz, 1992). To use both attitude and behavior in the loyalty definition increases its predictive power, according to Day (1969). Gremler and Brown (1996) define service loyalty as "the degree to which a customer exhibits repeat purchasing behavior from a service provider, possesses a positive attitudinal disposition toward the provider, and considers using only this provider when a need for this service arises" (p. 173). That definition includes three dimensions—behavioral, attitudinal, and cognitive. To explain the dimensions, the following example is given. Our friend David has used the same travel agency for his last ten journeys, when traveling for work. Therefore, we might be inclined to think of him as a loyal customer. If we only consider the behavioral dimension, that is, a form of customer behavior directed toward a particular service provider over time, this is true. David, however, is not particularly positive about this travel agency, because they have recently made many mistakes. As his employer has a special agreement with the travel agency including better airfares, David is obliged to use it. But if he could choose by himself he would have a strong preference (attitudinal dimension) for another agency, where he always books his holiday trips. Some researchers also talk about the cognitive dimension (see e.g., Lee and Zeiss, 1980). It can be a brand or a store that appears first in a consumer's mind when the need arises, or is the first choice among alternatives. For David the particular travel agency he has to use for business is either the first one in his mind, or his first choice.

For package tourism destinations, hotels and travel agencies must be considered when it comes to loyalty, and not just the tour operator. For example, some tourists who always choose to go to the same specific destination because they wish to visit friends there, or because they own property, are considered *destination loyal.* Others go with the same tour operator all the time *(tour operator loyalty)*, while still others are on the outlook for better offers and if they find one, they gladly change. Loyalty to a specific hotel or hotel chain is also found *(hotel loyalty)*. For instance, certain tourists stay at a Holiday Inn whenever possible, e.g., for safety or comfort reasons. Others always buy their tickets at a specific travel agency *(travel agency loyalty),* because they know someone who works there, but the tour operator they actually end up with might vary from one trip to another.

DESCRIPTORS OF PACKAGE TOURISM LOYALTIES

One day after work David visits the travel agency he used the last time to talk to Christine, the sales representative, who was very pleasant and helpful when he booked his trip to Gran Canaria. She is a member of the Orchid Club, just like David, and shares his great interest in flowers. Christine has a few different suggestions this time, and provides David with some relevant catalogs. When looking into them he thinks all destinations look the same, and are presented in a similar way. A mixture of hotels and resorts, beach activities, and traditional food are presented. But between the lines David can also see promises of new social relations, excitement, adventure, and self-fulfillment. When reading the catalogs at bedtime, he starts to dream about them.

The next time he sees Christine at the Orchid Club, she tells him about a new video from one of the major tour operators. It presents various sun packages offered during the winter season, in both Gran Canaria and Madeira, but also several others including Thailand, The Gambia, Morocco, and Egypt.

For a whole month David thinks about his alternatives. He consults his friends, colleagues, and relatives, and scrutinizes newspaper advertisements, the video, and the catalogs he received from Christine. David still prefers a green destination, but he also wants to fulfill his other wishes. Finally, he decides to go back to Gran Canaria, with the same tour operator, and to stay at the same hotel, but this time without his son. He contacts Christine for the booking and is disappointed when she tells him that every tour to Gran Canaria is fully booked for the time he likes to travel. She convinces him that Madeira is a good alternative, especially since he had that destination in mind in the previous year's holiday planning. He agrees with her suggestion, and still feels happy to be able to stay with the same tour operator, and with the same hotel chain as in Gran Canaria.

It is not easy to explain more precisely what it means to be a loyal customer. Even though it is a goal in marketing to have loyal customers, it is still not clear what factors lead to customer loyalty. Research shows that for services in particular it is troublesome, since an organization's offer could be difficult to evaluate, for the researcher as well as for the customer, due to the service characteristics (Gremler and Brown, 1996). It is pointed out here that for the tour operator it is even harder, as was shown in the story about David (see also Pritchard and Howard, 1993).

Gremler and Brown (1996) create a framework for examining service loyalty in general that includes three antecedents—satisfaction, switching costs, and interpersonal bonds. Satisfaction is seen as the customer's overall evaluation of the quality of the core service. The nature of the relationship between satisfaction and loyalty is influenced by a number of factors, and the relationship is assumed to differ in strength from one context to another. For example, it is frustrating if the customers are satisfied, based on customer satisfaction (CS) evaluations, but do not use the same provider again (e.g., Larsson Mossberg, 1994). Switching costs includes the investment in time, money, and effort required to change to another organization. Interpersonal bonds can include a customer's personal, sociable relationships with a service provider's employees, and feelings of familiarity, care, friendship, rapport, and trust. Another study, examining loyal travelers, argues that the antecedent descriptors of loyalty are: satisfaction, involvement, and perceived differences in service quality (Pritchard and Howard, 1993). In a study of package tourism loyalty and travel motives (Hanefors and Larsson Mossberg, 1997a, 1997b, 1997c) somewhat different antecedents were pointed out, and it became clear that the link between satisfaction and loyalty was valid in this context as well.

The advantage with comprehensive qualitative research, before selecting the scale items in a questionnaire, is obvious. Some of the scale items used in previous loyalty studies are irrelevant in this context. Involvement items, such as "Which airline I fly with gives a glimpse of the type of person I am," or "The airline you fly with when traveling tells something about you" (Pritchard and Howard, 1993), are not suitable for package tours. This is difficult to capture, because for some segments package tours have a negative touch. Tourists sometimes do not admit that they go on this kind of tour. Instead of telling their friends the took the ordinary "sun and warmth-package" to Majorca, they call it a "golf tour to Spain." As was mentioned earlier in the text, Gremler and Brown (1996) emphasize switching costs, but that is of limited importance here, since it is very easy for a tourist to switch between one tour operator and another. There are no contractual costs nor setup costs, which can be the case for many other services. The investments in time, or the effort to leave one company for another, compared to, for example, banks, insurance companies, or dentists, are also limited. Some tour operators, especially when they belong to the same owner group, which is a common phenomenon in Scandinavia, work very closely together. They use the same planes, transfer buses, hotels, and sometimes also the same guides. The tourists do not often realize these close bonds, and are surprised to see the same guide wearing one tour operator's uniform one day, and another's the next. Also, when booking trips a similar confusion is common. One surprised tourist said, "I called two different tour operators for inquiries, but I spoke to the same person!"

In factor analyses (in the package tourism study) three dimensions appeared: satisfaction, supply, and personal bonds, (see Table 9.1). These dimensions are supported by qualitative data. The first dimension was named *satisfaction*. It relates to a tourist's perception of the importance of the guide's performance, as well as safety reasons for returning to the same tour operator. These service quality attributes also proved to be the most

TABLE 9.1. Tour Operator Loyalty Scales: Rotated Factor Loadings with Three-Component Solution*

Label	Scale Item	Comp. 1	Comp. 2	Comp. 3
Satisfaction	Guides are:			
	reliable	**0.885**	0.283	0.084
	knowledgeable	**0.903**	0.263	0.089
	pleasant and helpful	**0.907**	0.293	0.065
	easy to reach	**0.907**	0.264	0.089
	It feels safe	**0.606**	0.570	0.157
Supply	Great supply of			
	destinations	0.367	**0.823**	0.167
	hotels	0.291	**0.883**	0.201
	tours	0.271	**0.889**	0.161
	Well-organized arrangement	0.536	**0.641**	0.130
Personal bonds	Friend at tour operator	0.121	0.215	**0.792**
	Closeness to booking office	0.093	0.209	**0.648**
Variance Explained (%)		52.2	10.6	10.3
Eigenvalue		6.79	1.38	1.33

*The data are collected from Swedish tourists going on package tours to London and Gran Canaria.

important for tourist satisfaction in an earlier study in a similar package tourism context (Larsson Mossberg, 1994).

The second dimension was called *supply*—a dimension not seen in other studies. It relates to whether the tourists perceive the tour operator to have a good supply of destinations, hotels, and tours. For example, David has used a particular tour operator many times, he holds a positive attitude toward this operator, and would only use this provider the next time he travels. Now he wishes to go to Gran Canaria, and learns that the tours are sold out, so that he has to change either his destination or the tour operator. Variety of destinations, hotels, and types of trips are all important. Some tourists have to travel with a certain tour operator, since it is the only one operating to that specific destination. Others are loyal to their tour operator because of the variety of tours and destinations offered.

The third dimension was related to *personal bonds.* The first two scales, "friend who works for the tour operator" and "closeness to the booking office," are connected to friendship and familiarity. The latter relates to personal bonds, because the tourists who are close to the office at home often walk in, chat, and become friendly with the personnel there. Two scales—"well-organized arrangement," and "feels safe"—correspond both to "satisfaction" and "supply."

An interesting issue is whether age, gender, and educational background have any effect on the underlying factors (satisfaction, supply, and personal bonds), and may lead customers to become loyal to the tour operator. The result of this study shows that they do not. Older tourists with different educational levels have the same perceptions as younger ones, and these do not vary because of gender. The underlying factors are the same for all the package tourists in this study.

Of course, the frequency of package tour consumption has to be considered when studying loyalty. The tours are very different in this sense, in comparison to bank and post office services, hairdressing, and bus rides for commuting, because we use these services frequently. We also know what to expect when using them, and in many cases it is a question of lifelong relationships—especially so with banks and dentists. Besides, it is felt that expectations, dreams, and also the special novelty aspects must be taken into account, and therefore travel motives will be discussed next.

Travel Motives

When asking tourists why they travel, we find answers differing from individual to individual, and from one trip to another. However, reviewing many studies of motives by both academics and industrial researchers, the answers, far too often, seem simple and clear-cut. Admittedly, the discussions of motives have become more complex since it was suggested that human needs are organized hierarchically, even though they are embedded in one another. It is, however, still possible to trace Abraham Maslow (e.g., 1954) in many of the discussions, and his work is obligatory in textbooks for students. The first phase of theory development was relatively slow, partly because understanding motives is complicated, and partly as a result of strong ongoing interest not to look for any deeper understanding, but mainly to list motivational factors. "Thomas (1964) for example, listed

18 reasons, Gray (1970) discussed just two distinct motivations, 'wanderlust' and 'sunlust,' and Lundberg (1972) identified 20 factors, while Crompton (1979) recognized nine different motives" (Shaw and Williams, 1994, p. 75). It has also been argued that the tourists themselves are to blame: they may not be able, or prepared, to articulate why they travel (Dann, 1981).

Through the more focused and recent research it has become clear that tourists' reasons for traveling constitute a complex of several motives working simultaneously (see e.g., Dann, 1981; Iso-Ahola, 1982, 1991; Harré, Clarke, and de Carlo, 1985; Mannel and Iso-Ahola, 1987; Pearce, 1988; Dunn Ross and Iso-Ahola, 1991). Two dominating traits are found: tourists travel away *from* something or some place ("escape"), at the same time as they travel to something or some place ("compensation"). Graham Dann (1981) assures us that escape motives deal with tourist motivation per se. Furthermore, Neil Leiper (1983), for example, agrees that all traveling involves a temporary escape of some kind.

In the study on Swedish package tourists, referred to previously (Hanefors and Larsson Mossberg, 1997a), a new motive model was presented and tested. It leans toward the idea that every tourist has a situational combination of interacting escape and compensation motives, both of which direct and limit the tourist's travel. Furthermore, it emphasizes that the motive combination is nourished in the course and change of ordinary everyday life. The importance of this becomes evident when, for instance, Jafar Jafari (1987) discusses the tourism system, and compares the structure of a tourist trip to the structure of a ritual (see also, e.g., Graburn, 1989). At the same time he also introduces the concept of "touristhood," being the state of the "nonordinary," equal to the liminality phase of the ritual, where norms of everyday life can be challenged and changed. Being a tourist means a life of nonordinary flotation, and "the nonordinary of here and now becomes the new reality" (Jafari, 1987, p. 153). By traveling the tourist has "stepped beyond the bounds of ordinary social reality" (Crick, 1989, p. 332)—he is outside social time and space (Wagner, 1977). Hanefors (e.g., 1994) adds to the discussion, talking about the tourists' apparent lack of responsibility during the holiday time away from home, and the possibilities for "selective normlessness" offered as well (see also Hanefors and Larsson Mossberg, 1998). Obviously, this has to do with the tourist's great urge to escape everyday life.

Such escape motivations conceal the tourist's individual characteristics and social and cultural background. The individual characteristics are age, gender, education, occupation, travel experience, and so on. The ordinary social context may include family and work situation, a variety of reference groups, and the like, while the cultural background may show, for example, whether the tourist is an open-minded "cosmopolitan," or a more culturally encapsulated "local" (Hannerz, 1993). The compensation motives allude to a destination's possibilities for attracting the tourist—to what that tourist does not have at home, but what he or she possibly can seek elsewhere. A number of preconditions attract the tourist: a destination's own characteristics, possible activities there, and various attributes (see Figure 9.1). The characteristics may be described as a backdrop—what kind of background suits the tourist? Some tourists prefer nature—mountains, desert, beach, or jungle; others prefer urban environment—a quiet small rural town or the pulse of the big city. Activities relate to what the tourist wants to do on vacation—maybe swimming, visiting museums, or learning about flowers. Finally, a destination's attributes mean what the tourist prefers, and wants to obtain, e.g., a certain kind of climate, a specific hotel, or a level of service.

In the study the tourists express their escape motives in various ways, e.g., "I want to take a step out of the gray," "I want to let go of all responsibilities at home," and "I want to turn a page." Also, it became perfectly clear that tourists travel both in order to leave home for a limited period of time, and to go to a specific destination, just as other earlier studies have pointed out. A young couple with a small baby, traveling to Gran Canaria, were asked about their motives, and answered: "We want summer, sun, and swimming. To be able to luxuriate, and be together. We wouldn't like it to rain, but a few clouds are all right, because we're here mainly to take it easy. We feel safe here, that is with the resort possibilities. We don't want it to be more Spanish." Another couple, middle-aged with a teenage daughter, on their visit to London, got the same question during an

FIGURE 9.1. Tourists' Combination of Travel Motives

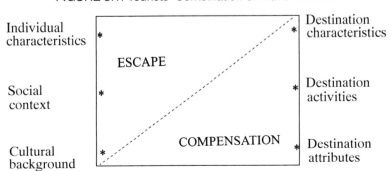

interview: ". . . change of environment. See different things, and meet other people. To store impressions in our heads, to be able to think about later. Relaxation."

In both these quite different destinations, Gran Canaria and London, the escape motives are remarkably strong in the motive combination. In a comparison between the two, 81 percent of the tourists in Gran Canaria (n = 265) agree or strongly agree (7-point Likert-type scale questions) to the statement "I travel this time to leave everyday life, to get a break, and relax." In London, on the other hand, 75 percent (n = 293) agree or strongly agree. With the statement "I wanted to visit this destination, because it has something special to offer that I cannot find at home" 67 percent of the same tourists in Gran Canaria agree or strongly agree, while 76 percent of the tourists in London do the same.

Motives to escape the home environment aside, the remains of the motive combination, shown by the Gran Canaria tourists, includes "sun/warmth," "beach," "eat and drink well," "luxuriate," "socializing," and "see/learn something new." In London there are even more motives in the combination. Some similarities to Gran Canaria were shown in this particular study, except for the strong escape motives, namely the motives to "see/learn something new," "eat and drink well," and to "socialize." In the London motive combination are also found some destination attributes: "famous buildings," "sights," "language," and some destination activities, such as sport. "To be able to talk about the trip afterward" is also important here.

Interestingly enough, the tourists of this particular study in general rank safety-related motive alternatives very high, for example, "I feel more safe if I travel with a group," "I enjoy interacting with other tourists," and "A package tour is the only thing for me" (see also, e.g., Schmidt, 1979; Quiroga, 1990). This could be a cultural prerequisite, just as it is when Japanese package tourists say that their preferred activity at a destination is shopping (Hanefors and Larsson Mossberg, 1995; cf. JTB Report '94, 1994). Another interesting finding, especially derived from the qualitative part of the study, which included depth interviews with 142 tourists in eight destinations with different characteristics, is that motives are not necessarily ego-centered. The social context factor is important and, more often than not, the situational motive combination is the result of a compromise between the motives of individuals traveling together. For example, when David is planning to travel with his son, his motive combination looks different than when he travels alone. His son wants to swim, to play with other children, and to see camels, while David needs a break, wants to meet new people, and prefers a destination with a great botanical garden.

Together they leave home to reach a destination that can offer the most to both of them, but one of them traveling alone could go to quite another destination.

Dann (1981) discusses motivation and satisfaction, and argues that they differ in many ways, yet they are often confused. He also states that it makes little sense to study the two in isolation from each other, since they are intimately linked together, i.e., motives occur before an experience and satisfaction after it—"people seek a variety of satisfactions, each in its own way contributing to the richness of the travel experience" (p. 203). Iso-Ahola (1982) agrees that the two cannot be equated, but adds that psychologists probably would offer an approach-avoidance model, such as the one offered above, as another explanation of the reason why motives are aroused when individuals think of a coming holiday, and this is potentially satisfaction-producing (p. 258). Whatever the explanation may be, the link between the two concepts is interesting here, because just as we can see motives as linked to satisfaction, we also saw earlier in this chapter how satisfaction links to loyalty—satisfied tourists will become loyal to a much greater extent than dissatisfied ones. Moreover, it is important to remember that since the tourism experience is a package of several products, satisfaction or dissatisfaction can occur many times during a trip. Therefore, if motives are measured before and after an experience the data can be very different from each other, especially if the experience has been clearly positive or negative (see Dunn Ross and Iso-Ahola, 1991), and it has to be analyzed accordingly.

SUMMARY AND CONCLUSIONS

This chapter discusses customer loyalty in package tourism, partly based on research on Scandinavian package tourists, and points out that an understanding of loyalty must consider both loyal attitudes and behavior. Loyalties to tour operators, destinations, hotels, and travel agencies must also be involved in such an understanding. In this chapter empirical data about tour operator loyalty is presented. The antecedent descriptors of tour operator loyalty are shown in Figure 9.2. In addition, it can be seen that the tourist's combined travel motives indirectly influence loyalty to a tour operator.

One of the dimensions in the model is *satisfaction.* A prominent reason why a package tourist returns to a specific tour operator is positive experiences of the service encounters with the operator's guides, for example. The service quality characteristics—reliability, responsiveness, assurance, and empathy—have been assessed, and prove to be important. This means

FIGURE 9.2. Tour Operator Loyalty

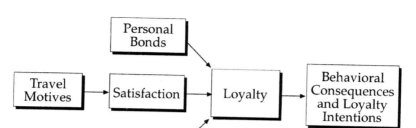

that a tour operator that provides good service through caring personnel who in turn make the tourists feel safe is much more likely to have loyal customers.

The variety and richness of offerings of tours, destinations, and hotels, affect loyalty. This is a *supply* dimension—a new concept. A tourist who uses the tour operator often, and holds a positive attitude toward the operator, preferably chooses destinations available through this tour operator. If everything is sold out, and the tourist cannot find good alternatives, he or she might change to another tour operator. This suggests that tour operators that aim to develop loyalty should consider the number of destinations and hotels as well as available seats, not just destinations suitable to a particular market segment. Sometimes it seems as though the most effort is put into selecting new and attractive destinations, but a loyal tourist who tries to book one several times without success becomes disappointed, and goes elsewhere.

For personnel involved in booking tours the third dimension—*personal bonds*—plays an important role. Clearly, this is related to safety, because for the tourist making a reservation entails making an important and sometimes expensive decision, furthermore one that is made only infrequently. Several related decisions must also be made about the proposed holiday, e.g., when, where, traveling companions, length of stay, etc., and for this the tourist needs a variety of trustworthy information. In this event, if the travel agent or tour operator has an office close to where the presumptive tourist lives or works, the latter is quite likely to drop in and visit, and probably knows the names of the office staff. This may play a decisive part in establishing personal bonds and loyalty.

This chapter also contributes to the understanding of travel motives. By taking into account earlier research attempts and adding new findings, it not only verifies the complexity of motives and the importance of escape motives, but shows what motive combinations look like. As a surprising example we see that the combination for tourists traveling to Gran Canaria shows a similarity to the combination of motives for tourists going to London. The latter, however, show greater variation. Moreover, tourists talk about how they usually compromise on their own travel motives, and take into consideration also the travel companion's wishes and needs, and the combination of motives thereby becomes even more complex.

Motives are potentially satisfaction-producing, which means that a specific, situational combination of travel motives will result in either satisfied or dissatisfied tourists. The individual tourist has created the basis for satisfaction. In the model above it is shown that loyalty leads to behavioral consequences and loyalty intentions. A satisfied package tourist may become loyal (i.e., repeats a purchase), and holds a positive attitude to a travel agency, tour operator, destination, or hotel.

CONCEPT DEFINITIONS

CS evaluation: Customer satisfaction evaluation.

Interpersonal bonds: When a tourist (1) perceives having a personal relationship with a service provider employee(s) and (2) has feelings of familiarity, care, friendship, rapport, and trust.

Package travel: At least two of the following services offered for sale at an inclusive price: (1) transport, (2) accommodation, (3) guides, (4) activities, and (5) food.

Service loyalty factors: Include satisfaction, switching costs, and interpersonal bonds.

Supply: The supply of destinations and hotels when a tourist wants to book a tour.

Switching costs for package tourists: Investments of time, money, or effort, perceived by a tourist as factors that make it difficult to purchase from a different tour operator.

Tourist satisfaction: The tourist's overall evaluation of the quality of the core service being provided, and the potential result of aroused travel motives.

Tour operator loyalty: When a tourist (1) exhibits repeat purchasing behavior from a tour operator, (2) possesses a positive attitudinal disposition toward the tour operator, and (3) considers using only this tour operator.

Tour operator loyalty factors: Made up of satisfaction, supply, and interpersonal bonds.

Travel motives: A tourist's situational combination of several interacting motives that make the tourist travel away from home to a certain destination.

REVIEW QUESTIONS

1. Think about different types of package tours, and how they differ. Relate to motives and loyalty.
2. How can you increase tourist loyalty? Discuss and give suggestions.
3. Think about the important factors for tourist loyalty discussed in this chapter. Try to add to the proposed list by continued discussion.
4. What can possibly interfere with a tourist's loyalties?
5. Having the tourism package in mind, how can you further develop the model on travel motives?

REFERENCES

Bitner, M.J. (1990, April). Evaluating Service Encounters: The Effects of Physical Surroundings and Employee Responses. *Journal of Marketing,* 54, 69-82.

Bitner, M.J. and Hubbert, A.R. (1994). Encounter Satisfaction Versus Overall Satisfaction Versus Quality: The Customer's Voice. In T. Rust, and R. Oliver (Eds.), *Service Quality: New Directions in Theory and Practice,* (pp. 72-94). Thousands Oaks, CA: Sage Publications.

Crick, M. (1989). Representations of International Tourism in the Social Sciences: Sun, Sex, Sights, Savings, and Servility. *Annual Review of Anthropology,* 18, 307-344.

Crompton, J.L. (1979). Motivations for Pleasure Vacation. *Journal of Lesisure Research,* 6, 408-424.

Dann, G.M.S. (1981). Tourism Motivation: An Appraisal. *Annals of Tourism Research,* 9 (2), 187-219.

Dann, G.M.S. (1997). *The Language of Tourism. A Sociolinguistic Perspective.* Wallingford, UK: CAB International.

Day, G.S. (1969, September). A Two Dimensional Concept of Brand Loyalty. *Journal of Advertising Research,* 9, 29-35.

Dimanche, F. and Havitz, M.E. (1994). Consumer Behavior and Tourism: Review and Extension of Four Study Areas. In J.C. Crotts and W.F. van Raaij (Eds.), *Economic Psychology of Travel and Tourism,* (pp. 37-57). New York: The Haworth Press.

Dunn Ross, E.L. and Iso-Ahola, S.E. (1991). Sightseeing Tourists' Motivation and Satisfaction. *Annuals of Tourism Research,* 18 (2), 226-237.

Enoch, Y. (1996). Contents of Tour Packages: A Cross-Cultural Comparison. *Annuals of Tourism Research,* 23 (3), 599-616.

Graburn, N.H.H. (1989). Tourism: The Sacred Journey. In V.L. Smith (Ed.), *Hosts and Guests. The Anthropology of Tourism.* Second Edition, (pp. 21-36). Philadelphia: University of Pennsylvania Press.

Gray, H.P. (1970). *International Travel: International Trade.* Lexington, UK: Heath Lexington Books.

Gremler, D. and Brown, S. (1996). Service Loyalty: Its Nature, Importance, and Implications. In B. Edvardsson, S. Brown, R. Johnston, and E. Scheuing (Eds.), *Advancing Service Quality: A Global Perspective.* New York: ISQA.

Hanefors, M. (1994). Travelling in the Periphery of Culture. *Third Annual International Seminar on Tourism Development,* May 29-June 4, Phoenix, Arizona, 166-171.

Hanefors, M. and Larsson, L. (1993). Video Strategies Used by Tour Operators: What Is Really Communicated? *Tourism Management,* 14 (1), 27-33.

Hanefors, M. and Larsson Mossberg, L. (1995). *Den paketresande japanen— en studie av köpbeteende och resmotiv.* Göteborg: Forskning Turism—Utbildning.

Hanefors, M. and Larsson Mossberg, L. (1997a). *Resmotiv och Kundlojalitet—rapport från en studie om paketturister.* Högskolan Dalarna.

Hanefors, M., and Larsson Mossberg, L. (1997b). Travel Motives and Loyalties. *TTRA 28th Annual Conference "The Evolution of Tourism: Adapting the Change,"* June 15-18, Norfolk, Virginia, 21-30. Travel and Tourism Research Association.

Hanefors, M. and Larsson Mossberg, L. (1997c). Travel Motives and Loyalties in Package Tourism: Safety and Trust. In T. Flognfeldt Jr. and H. Holmengen (Eds.), *TTRA European Chapter Conference,* Aug. 17-20. Conference Report 2. Lillehammer, Norway, 79-94. Travel and Tourism Research Association.

Hanefors, M. and Larsson Mossberg, L. 1999. The Travel and Tourism Consumer. In H. Hogg and M. Gabbott (Eds.), *Consumers and Services.* West Sussex, UK: John Wiley.

Hannerz, U. (1993). Cosmopolitans and Locals in World Culture. In M. Featherstone (Ed.), *Global Culture. Nationalism, Globalization and Modernity.* London: Sage.

Harré, R., Clarke, D., and de Carlo, N. (1985). *Motives and Mechanisms.* London: Methuen.

HMSO (1993). *The Package Travel Regulations.* Guidance Notes. Department of Trade and Industry. Brussels: European Union.

Iso-Ahola, S.E. (1982). Toward a Social Psychological Theory of Tourism Motivation: A Rejoinder. *Annuals of Tourism Research,* 9 (2), 256-262.

Iso-Ahola, S.E. (1991). Sightseeing Tourists: Motivation and Satisfaction. *Annuals of Tourism Research,* 18 (2), 256-262.

Jafari, J. (1987). Tourism Models: The Socio-Cultural Aspects. *Tourism Management,* 8 (2), 151-159.

JTB Report '94. (1994). *All About Japanese Overseas Travelers.* Tokyo: JTB Overseas Travel Department.

Larsson Mossberg, L. (1994). *Servicemöten och deras betydelse vid charterresor.* Göteborg: Bas.

Lee, B. and Zeiss, C. (1980, April). Behavioral Commitment to the Role of Sport Consumer: An Exploratory Analysis. *Sociology and Social Research,* 64, 405-419.

Leiper, N. (1983). Why People Travel: A Causal Approach to Tourism. Working Paper. Sydney, Australia: Sydney Technical College.

Lewis, B.R. (1994). Qualitative of Service and Customer Care. In S.F. Witt and L. Moutinho (Eds.), *Tourism Marketing and Management Handbook,* Second Edition. (pp. 285-290). New York: Prentice Hall.

Lundberg, D.E. (1972). *The Tourist Business.* Boston: Cahners.

Mannel, R.C. and Iso-Ahola, S.E. (1987). Psychological Nature of Leisure and Tourism Experience. *Annuals of Tourism Research,* 14 (2), 314-331.

Maslow, A. (1954). *Motivation and Personality.* New York: Harper.

Moutinho, L. (1987). Consumer Behavior in Tourism. *European Journal of Marketing,* 21 (10), 3-44.

Parasuraman, A., Zeithmal, V., and Berry, L. (1988, Spring). SERVQUAL: A Multiple-Item Scale for Measuring Consumer Perceptions of Service Quality. *Journal of Retailing,* 64, 12-40.

Pearce, P.L. (1988). *The Ulysses Factor.* New York: Springer-Verlag.

Pritchard, M.P. and Havitz, M.E. (1997, Spring). The Loyal Traveler: Examining a Typology of Service Patronage. *Journal of Tourism and Travel Research,* 2-10.

Pritchard, M.P. and Howard, D.R. (1993). Measuring Loyalty in Travel Services: A Multi-Dimensional Approach. *Proceedings of the World Marketing Congress,* 6, 115-119.

Pritchard, M.P., Howard, D.R., and Havitz, M.E. (1992). Loyalty Measurement: A Critical and Theoretical Extension. *Leisure Sciences,* 14, 155-164.

Quiroga, I. (1990). Characteristics of Package Tours in Europe. *Annuals of Tourism Research,* 17 (2), 185-207.

Ryan, C. (1995). *Researching Tourist Satisfaction.* London: Routledge.

Schmidt, C.J. (1979). The Guided Tour: An Insulated Adventure. *Urban Life,* 7 (4), 441-467.

Shaw, G. and Williams, A.M. (1994). *Critical Issues in Tourism. A Geographical Perspective.* Oxford, UK: Blackwell.

Thomas, J. (1964, August). What Makes People Travel? *Asia Travel News,* 64-65.

Wagner, U. (1977). Out of Time and Place—Mass Tourism and Charter Trips. *Ethnos,* 41 (1-2), 38-52.

Yale, P. (1995). *The Business of Tour Operations.* Essex, UK: Longman.

PART III: PERCEPTIONS, EXPECTATIONS, AND SATISFACTION

Part III of this book discusses the perceptions, expectations, and resulting satisfaction of tourist activities. In the following chapters several interesting studies are presented and though some of the results may be surprising, their explanations provide an excellent basis for understanding the processes of tourist expectations, perceptions, and satisfaction.

It is very important to understand, while reading the following chapters, that people develop images of destinations from personal characteristics such as their motivation and past experiences. Although these factors alone do not create expectations, they as well as many others play a crucial role in what travelers tend to expect from a particular location. As demonstration by Sussman and Ünel in Chapter 10, while travelers' expectations about a particular destination are often positive, they can also be negative. Fortunately, it has been shown that the use of proper marketing techniques can change negative perceptions. However, the most significant changes in the perception of a destination will occur with the actual experience.

The expectations tourists hold regarding a particular destination can play an important role in determining their satisfaction with travel to that location in the long run. Gnoth, in a study on travel to New Zealand via camper vans, found that tourist expectations vary by type of transportation. The study is described in Chapter 12.

Not only does mode of travel affect tourist expectations and satisfactions, but also so do the facilities available on the road to the destination. For example, in a study conducted by Tyrrell and Devitt on scenic byways in Vermont (Chapter 11) it was found that the most desirable characteristics of these roads to travelers were availability of rest areas and the possibility of traveling at higher speed limits.

In Chapter 13, Ryan reviews and critiques the current state of the art in the measurement of service quality and customer satisfaction, and discusses its relevance to the tourism and hospitality industry. The chapter also analyzes the evolution of gap analysis, and reports some research findings from a sample of 1,100 U.K. tourists showing that perceptions correlated highly with other measures of satisfaction. The findings show that past experience is important in that tourists learn what features of a holiday are more likely to provide them with satisfactory experiences. Hence, the proposition arises that more experienced tourists may score marginally higher on measures of satisfaction than less experienced ones.

Related to the way in which travel occurs is the distance one must travel to reach a desired location. Cognitive distance is the impression of distance that is formed in the mind of an individual. This perceptual distance is often different from the objective distance and is usually overestimated. Nevertheless, as demonstrated by Walmsley and Jenkins in Chapter 14, cognitive distance is an important antecedent of tourism because it plays a significant role in destination choice and travel behavior. Unfortunately, the only measures of distance for tourism purposes are maps, as brochures usually make little or no mention of distance factors. Knowing this, it is not hard to imagine the confusion occurring in estimating actual distances and the avoidance of certain destinations that are perceived to be remote.

Chapter 10

Destination Image and Its Modification After Travel: An Empirical Study on Turkey

Silvia Sussmann
Arzu Ünel

LEARNING OBJECTIVES

By the end of the chapter the reader should:

- Have an understanding of the concept of destination image and of the process leading to its formation
- Review the usage of destination image as a differentiating marketing tool and review image modification techniques
- Have an understanding of the different methodologies available for image assessment and to measure the modification induced by a visit to the destination
- Have an awareness of the need for both a control and an experimental group in this type of pre- and after-travel analysis of destination image through an understanding of the empirical study
- Have an appreciation of the limitations of this type of empirical study, and of the potential for further research in the area

DESTINATION IMAGE

A traveler's choice of destination is influenced by a variety of personal and environmental factors. The organizations attempting to promote a particular destination need to have an understanding of the *perceptions, attitudes,* and *motivations* of the market sectors they address, and also of their image of that destination. The following paragraphs will attempt to define these concepts, with specific reference to the tourism field. It is important to point out that perception, attitude, and image are sometimes used interchangeably in the marketing literature, but in what follows we will attempt to distinguish image from perception and attitude, while trying to establish their causal relationship.

Perception

Perception has been defined as "the process by which an individual receives, selects, organizes and interprets information to create a meaningful picture of the world" (Mayo and Jarvis, 1981, p. 67). In relation to the tourism product, it is the process of sorting and filtering the vast array of information about a particular area.

Given that each individual's psychological makeup is unique, so too will be perceptions of similar sets of attributes. This poses a potential problem for marketers; the same message may be interpreted differently by different audiences, or even individual members of the same audience. Marketers require an understanding of the concept of *perceptual bias*, that is, the distortion of information that results from the way in which it is perceived by the receiver. The mechanism of perceptual bias allows individuals to cope with information that is inconsistent with what they prefer, know, or believe. In direct relation to the tourism product, no amount of positive coverage will render a destination attractive to a market segment looking for a completely different set of attributes.

One way in which stimuli are filtered is by categorizing people, behavior, objects, places, or areas of the world. This process is commonly called *stereotyping* and allows people to perceive according to "preconceived categories of meaning" (Mayo and Jarvis, 1981, p. 42). Stereotyping is undoubtedly convenient in terms of simplifying the process of choice, and making quick categorical judgments. It is this speed of judgment that renders the job of the tourism marketer more difficult when trying to rectify a negative image.

According to Engel (1993), when people are faced with information about a place or a product, perceptual distortion may take place in three ways:

1. Distortion and misinterpretation of appeals to make them consistent with attitudes
2. Rejection of the message and its source as being biased
3. Absorbing factual information but ignoring persuasive appeals

Finally, another fact marketers need to consider together with perceptual bias is *selective retention*, because only retained information is capable of influencing buying behavior.

Attitude

A conclusive definition of attitude has been given by the social psychologist G.W. Allport (1954), as follows: "A mental and neural state of readiness, organized through experience, exerting a directive or dynamic influence upon the individual's response to all objects and situations with which it is related" (p. 505). To this we could add "in a predetermined manner." Moreover, it is held to be enduring by nature, but not innate. It is a learned mental state that could be modified slightly through a process of relearning. Chisnall (1985) further adds that an *opinion* is the verbal expression of an attitude.

Attitudes tend to form selectively—according to needs, past and present—and arise from four main sources:

1. Information exposure
2. Group membership
3. Environment
4. Satisfaction of needs

Information sources are categorized in terms of their credibility. We will see later that a similar process occurs in image formation. It is important to note that when facts are not known they tend to be invented, in accordance with preexisting beliefs. A negative disposition will fill any gaps in information with negative attributes.

Attitudes are also the product of group affiliation, where a group is defined as any number of people who interact with each other. The opinions of the group tend to become a standard for self-evaluation. Nevertheless, most people tend to pick and choose those group standards that are suitable for their needs. Therefore, the link between group membership and attitude formation can be said to be indirect and complex.

A change of environment and individual wants may also influence the formation and development of attitudes. Attitudes serve people's needs by simplifying their responses to complex information stimuli or decision making. In this way, attitudes may govern buying decisions, for example, about a holiday destination. It can thus be said that developing a favorable image of a place, service, or product is largely dependent on attitude formation or, perhaps, its change.

It is of paramount importance to understand how and why attitudes change, as well as the constraints that prevent certain types of attitudinal change, when trying to influence behavior. For instance, attitudes based on deep personal values will be less likely to change than those passed down by environment or culture. Mayo and Jarvis offered the marketers' view of inducing attitude change as follows: "An individual with strong attitudes must be exposed to new information repeatedly until gradually his defence mechanisms weaken" (Mayo and Jarvis, 1981, p. 215).

There are two types of attitude change: congruent and incongruent. The first type of change is a reinforcement of the initial attitude, from positive to very positive or from negative to very negative. Incongruent attitude change (Chisnall, 1985) is a move in the opposite direction from existing attitudes, e.g., a shift from positive to negative. Though this is generally the marketer's objective, it is more difficult to achieve than congruent change.

Communication factors are of paramount importance in attitude change. Hovland (1957) stresses the importance of *who* says it (the communicator), *what* is said (the communication), and to *whom* it is said (the audience). Word of mouth, for example, is incredibly effective. The credibility of the communicator is held to be critical to the success of communication. However, follow-up studies have revealed that within approximately four weeks, the respondents no longer associate the information with its source, be it credible or not. This seems to indicate the need for regular reinforcement of the message.

By far the most important factor in potential attitude change in terms of the tourism product is the travel experience itself. Ideally, insofar as negative attitudes are concerned, it is hoped that the experience of the tourism product would lead to an incongruent change. Nevertheless, it has already been stated that congruent attitude changes are more likely or at least easier to bring about.

There are several studies of the role of tourism as a mediator of attitude change among countries who had long-standing conflicts: Anastasopoulos (1992) Greeks visiting Turkey; Milman, Pizam, and Jafari (1991) U.S. students visiting the former Soviet Union; and Milman, Reichel, and Pizam (1990), Israelis visiting Egypt. Interestingly, their findings have very often displayed a reinforcement of the stereotype, undermining the common belief that tourism broadens the mind and acts as a peace mediator. Moreover, they highlight the difficulty of the marketer's task, since visitors will very often see what they want to see, and this is determined by attitudes, prejudices, and needs, along with cultural and stimuli factors.

Image

There are different definitions of image throughout the marketing literature, and in some cases, perception and attitude are used as a substitute for image. The authors, while acknowledging their proximity, believe that they are quite different: images are the result of composite perceptions which are, in turn, dictated by attitudes to result in a positive or negative image. We will, therefore, propose two of the many definitions of image as the most suitable. Image, according to Kotler (1994, p. 223) is the "net result of a person's beliefs, ideas, feelings, expectations and impressions about a place or an object." Gensch (1978, p. 384) states that image is "an abstract concept incorporating the influences of past promotion, reputation and peer evaluation of the alternative. Image connates the expectation of the user."

In terms of image formation, Gartner (1986, p. 635) says that "Every person perceives a certain image of an object by relating it to similar objects within a determined cognitive structure." It could be argued that a destination a tourist knows nothing about would be perceived in terms of the attributes of the immediate region. That is, a tourist who frequents Greece and knows very little of Turkey is likely to have an image of the latter that is based on his or her knowledge of the former.

Gunn's (1988) exploration of the image phenomenon revealed that an area's image exists on two levels. Her study has become very popular and the terms *organic* and *induced* are commonly used when referring to image formation. A definition of each follows.

Organic image is the product of noncommercial sources: newspapers, periodicals, and books, including geography and history books. In relation to a destination, and more specially a country, it would include history, politics, natural and human catastrophes, etc. This image is mostly maintained through stereotypes and prejudices and is therefore very difficult to change.

Induced image is the result of conscious promotional effort and advertising. An example would be image enhancement of a destination as a consequence of television promotion. The alteration of the induced image is of primary interest to tourism marketers.

Destination information comes from many sources, but mainly from national tourist organizations (NTOs). Their information, however, is often seen as biased, so they tend to concentrate their promotional efforts on "brand identification and image enhancement" (Gartner, 1986, p. 636). Crompton (1979, p. 20) indicates that some sources are seen as "superior in credibility, such as news media." Direct experience and personal recommendation are perceived as the most credible sources. The effects of direct experience will be considered in detail when describing the empirical study.

Image and Holiday Buying Behavior

Goodall and Ashworth (1988) have described how holiday choice is based on person-specific motivation and destination-specific attributes, commonly known as the push/pull factors. The motivation to take a holiday *pushes* the potential tourist into a decision, while the attraction of the holiday images *pulls* the holidaymaker to a particular destination.

Many alternatives will be weighed when making the holiday decision, but the most relevant among them will be the image of each alternative and its perceived ability to satisfy a potential tourist's needs (Mayo and Jarvis, 1981).

Pizam, Neumann, and Reichel (1978, p. 315) give a measure of tourist satisfaction as follows: "When the weighted total sum of experiences compared to the expectations results in feelings of gratification, the tourist is satisfied; when the tourist's actual experiences compared with his expectations result in feelings of distance, he is dissatisfied." A satisfied tourist not only comes again, but also "spreads the word." Our empirical study has shown the influence of word of mouth opinion on the choice to travel to Turkey.

Recollection and Image Modification

After the visit, the tourist will evaluate the experience against the previous destination image. According to Chon (1990, p. 7) this evaluation process can take four sets of comparisons:

- If the individual's destination image was negative, while the reality was perceived to be positive, a *positive incongruity* would occur, which provides the highest possible satisfaction.
- *Positive congruity* would result in moderate satisfaction. An "as expected" outcome is a less positive evaluation than "doing better than expected."
- *Negative congruity* results from low discrepancy between a negative image and a negative experience. Here the individual is moderately dissatisfied.
- *Negative incongruity* arises from a significant discrepancy between a positive expectation and a negative outcome. The individual experiences high dissatisfaction to the point of frustration.

The conclusions of the evaluation process will greatly reinforce or modify the destination image. This modified afterimage will determine whether the same destination may be considered for a future purchase, and for recommendation to friends and relatives.

IMAGE AND MARKETING

The tourism product is a set of experiences identified with a destination and marketed through images of that place. This link between tourist and destination is what makes image an invaluable element in marketing. We will therefore introduce in this section the need for product *differentiation* and the crucial role that image modification plays in this context.

First, it is important to review the well-known characteristics of the tourism product (Middleton, 1994) that distinguish it from most other products marketed. The primary factors are generally held to be *perishability, inseparability,* and *intangibility*. Perishability means that consumption and production must occur simultaneously, since the service cannot be stored. Therefore, production and consumption are inseparable; in the absence of a client the production potential is lost forever. Finally, tourism products are largely intangible and cannot be sampled in advance, which makes the tourist's image of the product a fundamental component of the decision-making process.

Product differentiation (Echtner and Brent-Ritchie, 1991, 1993) is the search for recognition of the product's uniqueness, with the aim of achieving sustainability. In the specific case of Turkey, which was the object of our study, a number of countries are situated in the same geographical area which offer similar characteristics, such as sea, good climate, and a rich cultural heritage. Turkey's main competitors are in the Mediterranean basin: Greece, Spain, Italy, and Malta. If all competing destinations are seen as largely offering the same attributes, Turkey must, in some way, differentiate itself. Gartner (1986, p. 643) identified this need: "Maintaining or increasing market share requires that perceptions of brand quality be easily differentiated."

This indicates the need for research into the images held by prospective travelers so that, if the images are not realistic, strategies can be devised to move them closer to reality. Although very little can be done to alter the physical product, it is potentially possible to find an attribute unique to the destination that can be marketed successfully. Success will depend on moving the image of the product into a gap in the market that meets unfulfilled needs of a significant group of consumers (Assael, 1984).

Image Modification

The first decision to be taken is the development of the *desired image*, which should clearly be feasible in terms of present reality and resources. Second, the image gaps need to be identified. This points to the need for an overall image modification plan and an awareness that images cannot be changed overnight. Images tend to be long-lasting, even after real changes in the destination, since people, as explained above, have difficulty changing their preexisting perceptions. Actual experience should be the most effective image modifier, since personal experience has been shown to be the most credible information source.

Although a region may contain high quality tourist-recreation resources, a distorted image may detract from its potential. For instance, in countries where violence has occurred, or in any place that has suffered a natural disaster, extensive corrective marketing may be needed. Correcting a negative image is, however, an arduous task. Ahmed (1991, p. 25) exemplifies some negative images that, although incongruent with reality, were widely held to be true: "Lake Erie is a dead lake; Israel is wholly consumed with Palestinian terrorism; New York City languishes in filth and unemployment." He further states that many tourists from the United States believed that a holiday in the third world must necessarily be third rate. He remains optimistic, however, that such negative images may be corrected with the appropriate techniques. He proposes the following six steps to reposition a destination's image:

1. Capitalize on positive images of component parts: differentiate components from the overall image and emphasize the positive ones.
2. Schedule mega-events: sport and cultural festivals, ethnic and food fairs, will focus media attention on the destination and also bring resources to the improvement of the tourism infrastructure.
3. Organize familiarization tours: hosting selected opinion leaders, such as travel writers, travel agents, or tour operators, whose advice is crucial in helping the tourist's choice.
4. Use selective promotion: apply the differentiation suggested in step 1 to all promotional efforts and literature.
5. Bid to host international travel and tourism conventions: here he offers the example of India, which successfully hosted the ASTA (American Association of Travel Agents) convention in New Delhi in 1988 and increased tourist arrivals afterward.
6. And, if all else fails, take advantage of a negative image.

Before any image modification technique is applied, it is necessary to conduct an accurate assessment of the current image. The next section will review the main methodologies available for this purpose.

Image Assessment Methodologies

Prior to undertaking the empirical study described in the next section, assessing the image of Turkey held by British tourists and its modification after travel, it was necessary to conduct a review of the available techniques.

They were found to fall into two basic approaches: unstructured and structured. *Unstructured* methodologies use free-form descriptions to measure image (Boivin, 1986). Data may be gathered via focus group discussions, in-depth interviews, or open-ended questionnaires. This approach is more suited to capturing the holistic components of images and unique individual features that a highly structured technique might possibly miss. Its success depends upon the verbal and or writing skills of the individuals participating in the study, their knowledge of the product, and their willingness to provide multiple responses (McDouglas and Fry, 1974).

Structured methodologies incorporate various image attributes into a standardized instrument, usually a set of semantic differential or Likert-type scales. Products or places are rated by respondents and an image profile is derived. They are easier to administer, simple to code, and results can be analyzed using statistical packages. Moreover, they allow comparisons among several product image profiles. The principal structured techniques are described briefly below, followed by an explanation of the reasons for choosing the semantic differential technique for the study.

Kelly's Construct Theory and the Repertory Grid

The repertory grid technique is based on George Kelly's personal construct theory. Kelly (1991, p. 69) believed that each person "invents and re-invents an implicit theoretical framework which is a *personal construct* system." Kelly postulated that individuals behave and interpret the world around them in terms of this system. The repertory grid technique was developed in order to explore such personal construct systems, that is, to see other people's worlds as they see them. It therefore appears to be well suited to exploring the individual perceptions leading to a destination image.

The keystones of this methodology are *elements* and *constructs.* Embacher and Buttle (1989), who applied the technique to assessing the image of Austria as a summer vacation destination, explain that elements are the objects to be considered (countries in their case) and constructs are the qualities that people attribute to such objects.

Moreover, three types of *sets* can be identified in this context, according to Woodside and Sherrel (1977): the *evoked set,* which includes all the destinations considered; the *inert set,* comprising those destinations of which the tourist is aware but cannot evaluate for lack of data; and the *inept set,* which includes all those rejected.

Kelly (1991, p. 106) defined a construct as: "in its minimum context, a way in which two elements are similar and contrast with the third." The respondent is then presented with three elements and asked to say which two are alike and how they differ from the third. This process is repeated until no new construct can be elicited or until the researcher feels that a sufficiently representative set of constructs has been identified. Limitations of this methodology are the danger of value judgment and descriptive or irrelevant responses.

Multidimensional Scaling

There are numerous examples of the application of multidimensionalscaling (MDS) in the tourism literature (Fenton and Pearce, 1994, provide a comprehensive review). It is particularly useful where a comparison is sought between the image of one destination and its competitors, since respondents are asked to compare countries or areas and rate them in respect of a set of attributes.

Computer analysis of the resulting similarity matrices produces a two- or three-dimensional plot of the rated destinations. Destinations perceived as similar cluster, while those classified as dissimilar are dispersed over separate parts of the computer-generated space. This permits an analysis of the degree of image separation, which could help in suggesting differentiating strategies. Limitations of this methodology are that respondents are asked to make relatively complex judgments, and that the interpretation is open to errors.

Free Elicitation of Descriptive Adjectives

This method, propounded by Reilly (1990) is based upon the respondent answering questions such as "What three words best describe Turkey as a destination for vacation or pleasure travel?" Replies are coded into similar categories and recorded according to frequency. The aim of this free-form style is to allow individuals to describe stimuli in terms that are relevant to themselves, rather than to the researcher. The limitations of this methodology are similar to those of the unstructured techniques: it is heavily dependent on the ability of the respondents to express their ideas clearly. Moreover, researcher bias could occur when grouping and analyzing responses and there are difficulties in constructing comparative image profiles.

Attitude Scaling Techniques

Images have been assessed by tourism researchers using attitude scales and related techniques such as semantic differential scales. The principal type of scales available are ordinal, interval, and ratio. These may be verbal, such as "I strongly agree"/"I strongly disagree," diagrammatic, or numerical. Chisnall (1992) includes an in-depth treatment of scales. The principal scaling methods are Thurstone's or equal appearing intervals, Likert summated ratings, Guttman's scales, and the semantic differential.

Thurstone's or Equal Appearing Intervals

These methods are rarely used in commercial practice due to sophisticated mathematical procedures and elaborate preparation. A large number (between 100 and 150) of favorable and unfavorable statements are collated, which are then assessed by a large number of judges and ranked into eleven groups from most to least favorable. Finally, twenty to twenty-five of these are selected and presented, in random order, to respondents, who are asked to indicate which ones they agree with. Total scores are calculated by taking the mean or median of the median values of the confirmed statements. For a critical appraisal of this method see Chisnall (1992) and Aaker and Day (1990).

Likert Scale or Summated Ratings

The verbal rating scale was developed in the 1930s by Rensis Likert and is still widely used in all areas of market research. Again, a large number of statements relating to the object under study are assembled by the researcher and administered to a representative sample of the people whose attitudes are being investigated, who are asked to respond to each statement by indicating whether they: *strongly agree, agree, are uncertain, disagree,* or *strongly disagree.* These categories are usually scored from five to one and individual scores totaled for each statement. It is accepted that the midway point on a Likert scale is not necessarily the precise middle between the two extreme scores. Likert's scale is quite popular, since it has been shown to be reliable, is easy to construct, and gives more information about the respondent's feelings than Thurstone's simple *agree/disagree.* Again, a critical review can be found in Chisnall (1992).

Guttman's Scales

Guttman's scales attempt to define more accurately the neutral point of an attitude scale. After a respondent is presented with attitude questions, intensity of feelings is registered using the question: *"How strongly do you feel about this?,"* where degrees of intensity may be *strongly agree/agree/*

undecided/disagree/strongly disagree. Favorable statements are then scored 4 to 0 and each individual's content score is computed. As previously, the maximum will be the number of statements times the highest intensity score, that is, if there are seven statements the scores will lie between 0 and 28. The scores are then plotted and the resulting curves are termed *intensity curves.* A flat bottomed, U-shaped curve would indicate a wide area of neutral attitudes.

Semantic Differential Scaling

Semantic differential scaling (SDS) is a well-accepted and reliable method of measuring attitudes (Osgood and Snider, 1969). In this technique, each statement is measured on a bipolar adjectival scale, usually with seven or five points. The stages of this methodology, which was the one finally chosen for the empirical study, are as follows:

1. *Develop a set of relevant dimensions.* These emerge ideally from focus groups, where participants could be asked questions such as, "What things do you think of when you consider Turkey as a holiday destination?" An example could be "friendliness of locals," which in *bipolar* terms would be translated as "locals are friendly"—"locals are hostile," or in *monopolar* terms: "locals are friendly"—"locals are unfriendly." The latter example, in which the attribute is simply negated, may in many cases be preferred, since finding the exact opposite could be the subject of semantic argument. In fact, Chisnall (1992, p. 174) states that "descriptive phrases instead of bipolar adjectives can be particularly effective in measuring the acceptability of certain features of a destination."

2. *Administer the instrument to a sample of respondents.* It is advised that the bipolar adjectives be rotated so as not to load the negative adjectives all on one side, which could create a halo effect. It will be seen in the next section that the pilot study disproved this recommendation in our case.

3. *Average the results.* The before and after images are represented by a vertical "line of means" that summarizes how the average respondent sees each attribute. Tull and Hawkins (1990) argue that the semantic differential data can be evaluated either by aggregate analysis, which requires the scores across all adjective pairs to be summed for each individual, who is assigned a summated total score; or by profile analysis, which allows isolation of strong and weak attributes. Since this is the method chosen for the analysis in our empirical study, it will be described in the next section.

4. *Check on the image variance.* The image profile is a line of means. If the majority of respondents have an image that coincides with the means line, the image is said to be highly *specific.* If there is considerable variation, the image would be highly *diffused.*

The following section will explain the parameters of the empirical study and attempt to justify the choice of methodology.

AN EMPIRICAL STUDY OF THE IMAGE CHANGE INDUCED BY ACTUAL EXPERIENCE OF TURKEY

The aim of this section is to describe the objectives of the study, the rationale for the choice of methodology, from among the ones described above, and the process of sample selection and instrument administration. Finally, the main conclusions will be given, together with the study's limitations and suggestions for further research. It is beyond the scope of this chapter to give a comprehensive description of the analysis carried out. For a detailed description of the results of the primary research, as well as a comprehensive review of all the sources of opinion about Turkey consulted for the selection of the attributes, the reader is directed to Ünel (1995).

The study was designed to monitor the *image change* that actual experience of Turkey effects on British first-time travelers to Turkey. The authors accept that the images these travelers have will differ considerably, as will the changes, if any, induced by actual experience. Like any other small empirical study, this one was aimed at providing a partial picture from which comparisons could be drawn.

The *main objectives* the research hoped to carry out were to:

- Ascertain the *pretravel image* of Turkey held by first-time British visitors
- Determine the *importance* of the attributes measured
- Measure the *after-travel image* of Turkey in the *same subjects* to identify any trends, either in the positive or negative direction
- Infer any *high-priority areas* for future marketing strategies
- Discover the *main influencing factors* in the choice of destination
- Obtain a general profile of *Turkey's market segment*

Choice of Methodology

The use of both *repertory grid* and *free elicitation of descriptive adjectives* was ruled out because of the impossibility of establishing direct contact with first-time travelers in the numbers required. Besides, a before and after survey could not have been simply administered.

Multidimensional scaling is, as described above, not suitable for first time visitors, as respondents are required to make a large number of similarity or dissimilarity judgments that require the type of knowledge that first-time visitors are unlike to have.

It was decided that the most effective and appropriate method would be semantic differential, because of its inherent simplicity and efficacy, in view of temporal (short period) and financial constraints of the study. The criticism by Reilly (1990) that dimensions considered crucial to the respondent could be omitted is mitigated by the fact that attributes were modified in response to direct feedback from the pilot study. Another significant advantage was the ease with which respondents could convey their images before and after traveling to Turkey. They would receive a single envelope with the two questionnaires, involving only one prepaid envelope, and it was hoped that the simplicity of the method would encourage a good response.

Sample Population and Frame

It was decided to focus on passengers already booked to travel to Turkey, since this would allow the pre- and posttravel image assessment within a relatively short time span. As mentioned before, they were required to be first-time visitors.

In view of security difficulties confronting the initial plan of approaching visitors in departure lounges, the use of a postal questionnaire was chosen. The sample frame of 102 tour operators dealing with Turkey was obtained from the Turkish Tourist Office. Of these, thirty-three operators were selected based on geographical location within London. The Turkish Tourist Office deputy director agreed to supply signed and headed letters to the researcher, personally addressed to managers or marketing directors, requesting them to give the researcher as much assistance as possible.

Each tour operator was personally visited by the researcher, who in all cases explained the nature of the research and its potential advantages for their marketing, promising a summary of the findings once completed. The intention was to persuade them to send the questionnaires with the wallet of travel documents.

Twenty-three out of the thirty-three tour operators agreed to help—three were out of business and seven either had insufficient bookings to Turkey or had already sent out the travel documents. Finally, the average number of questionnaires given to each tour operator was twelve and the total number was 296.

Control Group

A control group of 17 percent was used to monitor the bias caused by preexposure to the questionnaire; respondents contemplating their after-travel responses while on holiday. To minimize this type of bias, the mean results of the after-travel questionnaires were compared with those of the controlled after-travel questionnaires to acknowledge any explicit biases. The control group were given an identical cover letter with shorter instructions, and an identical after-travel questionnaire.

Questionnaire Design and the Pilot Study

The questionnaire consisted of twenty-one bipolar and monopolar statements whose subject matter covered local people, entertainment and things to do, personal and national safety issues, and cultural/ethnic and socio-economic issues. The dimensions were the product of extensive library research. An attempt was also made to include topical issues that had been subject to recent media coverage, to ascertain the extent to which they had affected the holidaymaker's image of Turkey. A complete description of both the library research and the questionnaire dimensions can be found in Ünel (1995).

A simple introduction and a real example explained the nature of the survey to the potential respondent. The respondents were asked to rank each of the attributes in terms of their importance to them, from extremely important to not at all important. This was considered fundamental to understanding the meaning of either positive or negative responses to attributes.

A pilot study was conducted with the help of sixteen individuals, to test both the physical presentation of the questionnaire and the clarity of the statements included, as recommended by Aaker and Day (1990) and Chisnall (1992). As a result, changes were made to the wording, and a vertical line was introduced to separate the main part of the questionnaire from the numbers indicating importance, to separate both scales visually and avoid confusion. Also, as explained previously, the favorable and unfavorable statements were changed and put all on the same side, against advice from the literature which suggests a random placing to avoid the "halo effect," because the pilot questionnaire respondents expressed confusion. In practice, moreover, none of the usable questionnaires obtained displayed a complete adherence to one dimension or the other—answers appeared randomly.

Limitations of the Research

In using a mail questionnaire, the response is the most critical limitation. In this particular case, this was compounded by the fact that the researcher could not follow up, because of the anonymity of the respondent due to the method of distribution. All potential negotiating tools were used in this case (good, clear presentation and inclusion of a friendly cover letter explaining the objectives of the research).

Because mail questionnaires can be read through completely before being answered, responses may thus be premeditated and not spontaneous. If the interval between pretravel and posttravel questionnaire completion is too short, there may be an attempt to remember the responses from the first test. A "date completed" question was included to identify any major correlation between interval lengths.

Mail questionnaires may sometimes represent the views of more than one person. In this case, it was thought that even if people traveling together might join in the reply, they might also have been exposed to similar stimuli.

A limitation of the sampling method was the inability of the researcher to obtain lists of people traveling to Turkey. Therefore, she was unable to control the balance of the sample characteristics, such as gender, age groups, etc. The sample was well varied in terms of tour operator, which in turn includes type of holiday and price; however, the fact that probability sampling could not be used seriously limits the reliability of the statistical conclusions drawn.

Brief Summary of Findings

The total response rate was 27 percent. This included some unusable questionnaires, either because they arrived after the deadline set by the researcher or because they were incomplete. The percentage of usable responses was thus 18 percent, with 24 percent for the control group. The female to male group ratio was 60:40. The largest age group was 45-54.

As explained above, *profile analysis* was employed. Weights were assigned to continuum positions for each scale interval (-2 to $+2$) and scores for each attribute were totaled and averaged in order to present image profiles. For the purpose of interpretation, the reliability of transport, for example, would appear as follows:

Very reliable	2
Reliable	1
Slightly reliable	0.1 to 0.5
Neither reliable nor unreliable	0
Slightly unreliable	-0.1 to -0.5
Unreliable	-1
Very unreliable	-2

An analysis was then carried on the pre- and after-travel profiles, as well as on the importance ratings, by gender and age group. Very little difference appeared between the sexes. After-travel images were slightly more positive than pretravel images and at least a little importance was attached to most of the attributes chosen. The control group showed slight differences in five out of the twenty-one attributes, and none of them were incongruent. The variances remained within the same part of the positive area. The two extreme age groups (18-25 and 55-64) displayed more negative congruent changes than the 26-55 group. A summary of the congruity of the pre- and posttravel images, by subject and age group, is given in Table 10.1.

CONCLUSIONS

This chapter has attempted to explain the concept of *destination image,* and its distinction from and links with the concepts of *perception* and *attitude.* Furthermore, it provided a review of *image assessment techniques.* Finally, a small empirical study of the image of Turkey among first-time British travelers was used to provide an illustration of one such technique in operation.

CONCEPT DEFINITIONS

Attitude: A learned mental state that conditions an individual's response to all objects and situations in a predetermined manner. It is held to be enduring, but not innate.

Destination image: The result of a person's beliefs, ideas, feelings, expectations, or impressions about a tourist destination. Frequently substituted by perception or attitude.

Image modification: The result of the evaluation of the direct experience of a destination against a previously held image.

Perception: A process by which an individual selects information to create a meaningful picture of the world.

TABLE 10.1. Congruity of Pre- and Posttravel Images by Subject and Age

Attribute		Mean Congruence					
		18-25	26-34	35-44	45-54	55-64	65+
SAFETY	Personal safety	0.79-	0.7+	0.83+	0.93+	0.8+	0
	Treatment of females	0.2-	0.8+	0.37+	0.87+	1.17-	0.33-
	Terrorism	0.02+	0.4+	0.83+	1.18+	0	0.34+
LOCAL LEVEL	Helpfulness of police	0.08-	0.7+	0.8+	0.56+	1.33+	0
	Local temperament	0.2-	0.3+	0.17+	0.39+	0.17+	0.33+
	Hospitality	0.63+	0.4+	1.43+	0.92+	0.33+	0.34+
	Friendliness	0.36-	0.3+	1.17+	0.77+	0.17+	0.33+
	Reliability of transport	0.23+	0.9+	0.17-	1.25+	0.17-	1.0+
	Religiousness	0.69-	1+	0.5+	0.92+	1.17+	1.0-
	Understanding English	0.04-	0.5+	0.17+	0.6+	1.33+	0.33-
	Honesty of locals	0.1-	0.9+	0	0.53+	0.5+	1.0+
	Traffic congestion	0.33-	0.5-	0.37-	0.16+	1.0-	1.34+
NATIONAL LEVEL	Natural disasters	0.38-	0.5+	0.5-	0.5+	0.67-	0.67-
	Treatment of Kurds	0.01+	0.1-	0.5+	0.47+	1.0+	0.33+
	Environment protection	0.14+	0.4+	0.7+	0.29+	0.83+	0.33+
	Development	0.01+	0.7+	0.5+	0.61+	1.0+	0.67-
TO DO	Atmosphere of markets	0.46-	0.3-	0.84-	0.17+	0.17+	0.67-
	Museums —availability	0.07+	0.3+	0.18+	0.27-	1.33-	0.34-
	Archaeological sites	0.67-	0.3+	0.33+	0.33-	1.0-	0.33-
	Attractions signposting	1.22+	1.9+	0	1.2+	0.67+	0
	Evening entertainment	0.89-	0.3+	0.53+	0.46-	0.67-	0
SUMS	Pretravel image	8.3	5.0	2.0	2.6	6.7	15.0
	After-travel image	6.0	15.0	9.5	15.0	10.5	12.0

REVIEW QUESTIONS

1. Explain the difference between perception and image, and the concept of perceptual bias.
2. Analyze the characteristics of attitude change, and their application to travel experiences.
3. Differentiate between induced and organic images, and explain the importance of each in the marketing of a destination.
4. Give some reasons for the importance of image modification in terms of product differentiation.
5. Provide a critique of the different techniques of image assessment described in the chapter.

REFERENCES

Aaker, D.A. and Day, G.S. (1990) *Marketing Research*, Fourth Edition. New York: John Wiley and Sons.

Ahmed, Z.U. (1991) Marketing your community: Correcting a negative image. *The Cornell H.R.A. Quarterly* 31(4): 24:27.

Allport, G.H. (1954) *Nature of Prejudice*, Reading, MA: Addison-Wesley.

Anastosopoulos, P.G. (1992) Travel in Turkey—negative impact on Greek tourist perception of the host population. *Annals of Tourism Research* 19(4): 629-642.

Assael, H. (1984) *Consumer Behaviour and Marketing Action*, Second Edition. Boston: Kent Publishing Company.

Boivin, Y. (1986) A free response approach to the measurement of brand perceptions. *International Journal of Research in Marketing* 3: 11-17.

Chisnall, P.M. (1985) *Marketing: A Behavioral Analysis*, Second Edition. Maidenhead, UK: McGraw-Hill.

Chisnall, P.M. (1992) *Marketing Research*, Fourth Edition. London: McGraw-Hill Book Co.

Chon, K.S. (1990) The role of destination image in tourism: A review and discussion. *The Tourist Review* 2: 2-9.

Crompton, J.L. (1979) An assessment of the image of Mexico as a vacation destinaton and the influence of geographical location upon that image. *Journal of Travel Research* 18 (Fall): 18-23.

Echtner, C.M. and Brent-Ritchie, J.R. (1991) The meaning and measurement of destination image. *The Journal of Tourism Studies* 2(2): 2-12.

Echtner, C.M. and Brent-Ritchie, J.R. (1993) The measurement of destination image: An empirical assessment. *Journal of Travel Research* (Spring): 3-13.

Embacher, J. and Buttle, F. (1989) A repertory grid analysis of Austria's image as a summer vacation destination. *Journal of Travel Research* 27(3): 3-7.

Engel, J.F. et al. (1993) *Consumer Behaviour*, Seventh Edition. New York: Holt, Rinehart and Winston, Inc.

Fenton, M. and Pearce, P. (1994) "Multidimensional Scaling and Tourism Research" in Brent-Ritchie, J.R. and Goeldner, C.R. (eds.) *Travel and Tourism Research Handbook for Managers,* Second Edition. New York: Wiley and Sons Inc.

Gartner, W.C. (1986) Temporal influences on image change. *Annals of Tourism Research,* 13(4): 635-644.

Gensch, D. (1978) Image-measurement segmentation. *Journal of Marketing Research* 15 (August): 384-394.

Goodall, B. and Ashworth, G.J. (eds.) (1988) *Marketing in the Tourism Industry: The Promotion of Destination Regions.* London: Croom Helm.

Gunn, C.A. (1988) *Vacationscope—Designing Tourist Regions,* Second Edition. New York: Van Nostrand Reinhold Company.

Hovland, C.I. (ed.) (1957) *The Order of Presentation in Persuasion.* New Haven, CT: Yale University Press.

Kelly, G.A. (1991) *The Psychology of Personal Constructs Vol. 1—A Theory of Personality.* London: Routledge.

Kotler, P. (1994) *Marketing Management: Analysis, Planning, Implementation and Control,* Eighth Edition, Paramus, NJ: Prentice Hall International.

Mayo, E.J. and Jarvis, L. (1981) *The Psychology of Leisure Travel: Effective Marketing and Selling of Travel Services.* Boston: CBI Publishing Co., Inc.

McDouglas, C.H.G. and Fry, J.N. (1974) Combining two methods of image measurement *Journal of Retailing* 50 (Winter): 53-61.

Middleton, V.T.C. (1994) *Marketing in Travel and Tourism,* Second Edition. London: Butterworth-Heinemann Ltd.

Milman, A., Pizam, A., and Jafari, J. (1991) Influence of tourism on attitudes— US students visiting USSR. *Tourism Management* 12(3): 47-54.

Milman, A., Reichel, A., and Pizam, A. (1990) The impact of tourism on ethnic attitudes: The Israeli-Egypt case *Journal of Tourism Research* 29(2): 45-49.

Osgood, C.E. and Snider, J.G. (eds.) (1969) *Semantic Differential Technique: A Source Book.* Chicago: Aldine Publications.

Pizam, A., Neumann, Y., and Reichel, A. (1978) Dimensions of tourist satisfaction with a destination area. *Annals of Tourism Research* 5(3): 314-322.

Reilly, M.D. (1990) Free elicitation of descriptive adjectives for tourism image assessment. *Journal of Travel Research* 28-29 (Spring): 21-26.

Tull, D.S. and Hawkins, D.I. (1990) *Marketing Research, Measurement and Method,* Fifth Edition. New York: Maxwell MacMillan International Editions.

Ünel, A. (1995) The image of Turkey and its modification after travel, MSc dissertation, University of Surrey, Guildford UK.

Woodside, A.G. and Sherrell, D. (1977) Traveler evoked, inept and inert set of vacation destinations. *Journal of Travel Research* 20: 2-6.

Chapter 11

Valuing Changes to Scenic Byways

Timothy J. Tyrrell
Maureen F. Devitt

LEARNING OBJECTIVES

By the end of this chapter the reader should:

- Be familiar with the "scenic byways" concept and the value assigned to them by tourists
- Understand the effect of willingness to pay on consumer behavior
- Understand the logit model as a concept and methodology

INTRODUCTION

Scenic byway plans serve to guide travelers through communities that have historical, cultural, and natural qualities to be enjoyed by visitors. Thus, byway planning has the potential to help boost a state's economy, and the travel and tourism industry in particular.

The overall objective of this study was to provide Vermont planners with a means of evaluating alternative byway designs. The tools developed from the study are intended to be used in decisions regarding scenic byway designation and roadway investments. Specifically, the core of the project was a traveler survey designed to:

- identify traveler types and their byway preferences, and
- identify economic impacts of different types of travelers

From the results of the traveler survey, an applications workbook was developed for use by state and local planners in making roadway design decisions by assisting them in determining the economic impacts of different byway treatments. The workbook specifies the input that is needed from planners and illustrates by example how to predict the potential impact of a roadway change on area revenues, wages, and employment.

ECONOMICS OF TRAVEL CHOICE BEHAVIOR

The analysis of economic impacts of scenic byways begins with the traveler who generates the impacts. It is important to understand reasons for travel and how these relate to the reasons for the choice of a roadway. Obviously, business travelers look for different roadway characteristics than vacationers or local residents who are running errands.

If roadway characteristics change, the traveler may alter travel behavior, and thus, the travel service supplier in the local community may notice an increase (or decrease) in sales from different customer segments. In economic terms, this might be described as a shift in the demand for travel on specific roadways. The response by local businesses will determine the consequences of the demand shift. Businesses might simply increase (or reduce) prices to equilibrate demand and supply. On the other hand, the number of businesses and availability of travel services might be increased (or decreased) while maintaining the original price level. More likely, we expect some combination of price and quantity response by business. It is this supply response that will determine job, wage, profit, and tax impacts on the community. In the long run, roadway characteristics, travel services availability, and prices will determine the image travelers form about the region.

Linking Economic Impacts to Scenic Byways

Scenic byways are described in the National Scenic Byways program as having six major "intrinsic" characteristics: scenic, cultural, natural, archaeological, historic, and recreational. Travelers, however, consider a much longer list of characteristics when they choose a road to travel. Some of these characteristics, such as roadside views and distant views, can be closely linked to the intrinsic qualities of the byway. Another set of characteristics, including the availability of rest areas, average speed limits, and shoulder widths, are associated with personal comfort and safety. A third set, including shopping, eating, and entertainment opportunities, are associated with economic behavior and economic impacts. The linkage between the intrinsic qualities of scenic byways and economic impacts is one of the trade-offs—the traveler will trade some less-valued characteristics for greater-valued characteristics in order to obtain a most preferred travel experience.

Alternatives for Measuring the Impacts of Scenic Byways

Total Expenditures by Tourists Traveling Scenic Byways

A study by the U.S. Travel Data Center (1990) estimated the current economic value of scenic roadways by asking travelers about expenditures and multiplying average expenses by traffic volume. However, this method did not provide a way to estimate the potential change in expenditures that might be achieved through various roadway planning decisions.

Traffic Comparison Before and After
Scenic Byway Designation

The Urban Institute (1990) measured impacts of scenic designation by comparing traffic volumes on highways before and after the scenic byway designation, and contrasted these with similar roadways that had received no such designation. Although some of the Urban Institute results suggested a 2 to 3 percent difference in volume, a wide range of exogenous factors makes it difficult to establish a causal relationship between scenic designation and growth.

Contingent Valuation/Willingness to Pay
for Scenic Byway Characteristics

A California State University study of scenic byways commented that:

> The purest measure of the economic impact of scenic highways would be to measure the dollars brought into the regional economy by the scenic designation. These would be the dollars spent by tourists who choose to travel the scenic highway over another because of the designation. This is difficult to accomplish in California because there are few alternative routes to the same destination where clear consumer choice can be measured. (Real Estate and Land Use Institute, 1994, p. 19)

In a step toward this "purest measure," this pilot study of Vermont scenic byways assessed relative preferences for highway characteristics by asking survey respondents to make trade-offs between two roadway scenarios. Specifically, each interviewee was asked to make a series of choices between pairs of roadway scenarios. Each route scenario comprised a different set of seven roadway characteristics, including toll cost for use of the road. This approach enabled us to estimate a minimum dollar value (via the toll) for each change in a roadway characteristic.

Estimating Economic Impacts

The potential economic impact of a roadway change for the surrounding community will be determined by shift in demand attributed to the roadway change. If a roadway change is found to be associated with an increase in demand for use of the roadway, area businesses can respond to this demand shift, and capture some of the increased willingness to pay from roadway users. This section explains in economic terms how local businesses may benefit from traveler preferences.

New revenues generated by increased quality, for example, may be received by firms in the form of increased prices at constant quantity of supply (volume), as an increase in volume at constant prices, or in the form of a combination of increased prices and volumes. The relationship between changes in price and volume is characterized by the elasticity (δ) of the supply curve for the industry. Figure 11.1 illustrates the combination case where demand shifts from *D1* to *D2*.

The shaded area between *P3* and *P1* out to the supply curve *S* represents new revenue received because of increased prices by firms. The rest of the shaded area, below *S*, between *T1* and *T3*, represents new revenues attributable to greater volume of output. The horizontal area can be associated with profits and returns to investments; the vertical area can be associated with costs, including wages and salaries.

FIGURE 11.1. Shift in Demand

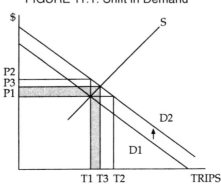

The intersection of supply and demand curves at the point (*T3, P3*) can be determined for specific functional forms of demand and supply. Equilibrium prices, quantities, and revenues can be shown to be:

$$P_3 = P_1 \left(\frac{P_1}{P_2}\right)^{\frac{\eta}{\delta-\eta}}$$

$$T_3 = T_1 \left(\frac{P_1}{P_2}\right)^{\frac{\delta\eta}{\delta-\eta}}$$

$$R_3 = R_0 \left(\frac{P_1}{P_2}\right)^{\frac{\delta(1+\eta)}{\delta-\eta}}$$

Assuming a constant supply elasticity of δ, the portion of total revenues going to the cost of production can be shown to be $\delta/(1+\delta)$. Thus, if we can select appropriate values of demand elasticity (η) and supply elasticity (δ), a vertical shift in the demand curve can be translated into economic impacts measured by changes in revenues (*R*), costs (*C*), and profits, (Π):

$$R_3 - R_0 = R_0 \left(\left(\frac{P_1}{P_2}\right)^{\frac{\delta(1+\eta)}{\delta-\eta}} - 1\right)$$

$$C_3 - C_0 = \left(\frac{\delta}{1+\delta}\right)(R_3 - R_0)$$

$$\Pi_3 - \Pi_0 = \left(\frac{1}{1+\delta}\right)(R_3 - R_0)$$

Revenues R_3, costs C_3, and profit Π_3, result from changes in both price, *P*, and quantity, *T*. These equations were used to create a set of multipliers for the planners' workbook, so that planners could estimate the potential benefits that a specific community may realize from roadway improvements or scenic preservation.

SURVEY METHODOLOGY

Experimental Design

The format for the questions to determine travel preferences was a comparison between a pair of roadway scenarios that might have been used for one day's travel. In this paired comparisons approach, respondents chose one of two specifically defined roadway scenarios to reveal trade-offs between roadway characteristics.

To determine the full range of traveler trade-offs, a large number of pairs of comparisons (2,430) must be evaluated. Given time and budget constraints, this number of comparisons was clearly not feasible. Instead, a subset of roadway comparison scenarios was used to estimate the main effects of roadway characteristics (how a single characteristic would affect traveler preferences) and some two-characteristic interactions. Three types of modifications to the original (complete) sampling design were tested for minimum variance to determine the most efficient sampling design for the survey:

1. It was determined that, due to time and patience limitations, the most comparisons that a respondent can be expected to make in one survey is between five and seven.
2. A second modification was made to eliminate the possibility that respondents might see any pattern between the panels which described roadway scenarios (e.g., always the "best" scenario first).
3. Finally, the design was modified to eliminate noncomparison trials (where almost all characteristics are the same) and difficult trials (where almost none of the characteristics are the same).

For a more thorough discussion of the experimental sampling design see Tyrrell and Devitt (1996a).

Implementation

The survey was implemented at four sites around Vermont over three days: Friday through Sunday, August 11-13, 1995. After discarding unusable surveys, there were 752 respondents, including 68 state residents. Travelers interviewed in the Vermont study were characterized by: residence and distance traveled that day, reasons for travel, and activities enjoyed. The focus of the study, as discussed above, was the assessment of travel choice trade-offs.

In the hypothetical comparisons of roadways in the survey, roadways were characterized by intrinsic qualities including distant and roadside views. They were also characterized by safety and comfort qualities, including speed limit, availability of rest areas, and size/availability of shoulders. To identify the importance of scenic byway designation, each roadway choice was either described as designated as scenic on a map, or not. And finally, to estimate traveler willingness to pay for trade-offs between byway characteristics, a hypothetical toll cost was attributed to each travel scenario. The specific characteristics (factors) and their levels that were used in the survey are shown in Table 11.1.

THE LOGIT MODEL

To represent the probability of roadway choice for each of the traveler groups identified above, a binomial logit analysis was used. The analysis determined the parameters that best described the probability of a roadway choice for each group as a function of roadway characteristics. The trade-offs are measured between each roadway characteristic and its dollar value (willingness to pay) through a hypothetical toll cost that was attributed to each roadway scenario in the surveys.

The binomial logit model is given by an equation that describes the probability that the ith respondent will choose the first alternative (W^1) over the second (W^2) as a function of the difference between quality characteristics and the dollar difference in tolls. For a single quality difference the model is given by:

$$\text{Prob}(W^1 \text{ is chosen by } i) + \left[\frac{1}{1 + e^{\ [\beta_0^0 - \beta_0^1 + \beta_q(q^0 - q^1) + \beta_c(c^0 - c^1)]}}\right]$$

Where: $q^0 - q^1 =$ byway quality differences
$c^0 - c^1 =$ toll difference (in $)

and the parameters are estimated by a maximum likelihood estimation procedure using survey data.

To determine the willingness to pay for a roadway characteristic change by the average individual, it is only necessary to find the amount of money that keeps the probability constant. That is, in order to balance the probability equation when roadway quality changes from q^0 to q^1, the increase in cost would need to be:

$$-\frac{\beta_q}{\beta_c}\ (q^0 - q^1)$$

Thus, this can be interpreted as the individual's willingness to pay for a roadway characteristic change from q^0 to q^1.

TABLE 11.1. Roadway Characteristics for Survey

Characteristic	Level Description
Distant View	mostly forest
	1/2 forest, 1/2 farms & fields
	mostly farms & fields
Designated Scenic on Map	no
	yes
Roadside View	occasional houses and businesses
	infrequent small towns
	little to no development
Speed Limit	25 mph
	35 mph
	50 mph
Roadside Rest Areas	not available
	available, no restroom
	available, with restroom
Shoulders	no shoulder
	1-2 ft shoulder
	2-4 ft shoulder
Toll Cost Per Trip	$4.00
	$3.00
	$2.00
	$1.00
	$0.00

MAXIMUM LIKELIHOOD ESTIMATES

Maximum likelihood estimates for three basic models are shown in Table 11.2. Although five levels of toll were used in the survey (and thus, four possible incremental changes), only a single coefficient (the same for each change) was used to measure the influence of a $1 increase in a toll (that is, the difference between $0 and $1 equals the difference between $1 and $2, etc.). Each of the remaining coefficients corresponds to a specific change between two levels of a specific factor.

For the nonresident model, most factor changes were significant at traditional levels of 1 and 5 percent (significant results shown in bold). The exceptions were: changes in distant views, an increase in the speed limit from 35 mph to 50 mph for long-distance travelers, and the change from no rest areas to rest areas without restrooms. Overall, the statistics for nonresidents and total sample are marginally acceptable, but the residential model is unacceptable. Larger samples would improve all models. The number of observations used in the model reflects the number of comparisons made by all respondents (usually seven per respondent).

WILLINGNESS TO PAY FOR ROADWAY CHANGES

A variety of analyses of the relative values of roadways were conducted for different types of travelers. The results presented here are for all respondents and a comparison of Vermont residents and nonresidents.

Distant View

As seen in Table 11.3, preferences for distant view (mostly forest, half farm/half forest, mostly farms) were different for residents and non-residents. Although results were not highly significant (primarily due to small sample size), residents tended away from choosing a farm and forest mix, rather choosing the mostly forest or mostly farm scenarios. That is, residents had a negative willingness to pay of $1.66 for travel with a distant view of the farm and forest mix compared to travel with a distant view of mostly forest, and a positive willingness to pay of $0.67 to travel along the mostly farm view road, as opposed to one with a distant view that was mixed (see column two of the results in Table 11.3). In contrast, nonresidents tended to choose the mix over the farm- or forest-dominated landscape, with a positive willingness to pay of $0.39 for the farm and forest mix over the mostly forest view, and a negative willingness to pay of $0.72

TABLE 11.2. Maximum Likelihood Estimates of Logit Model for All, Residents, and Nonresidents

Change in Roadway Characteristic			All	Vermont	Nonresident
	From	*To*			
Intercept			**− 0.1409**	**− 0.0110**	**− 0.1546**
			(0.0000)	*(0.9183)*	*(0.0000)*
Distant View	*Mostly Forest*	*1/2 Farms 1/2 Forests*	0.0598	− 0.2449	0.0904
			(0.5259)	*(0.4203)*	*(0.3631)*
	1/2 Farms 1/2 Forests	*Mostly Farms*	− 0.1388	0.0986	− 0.1642
			(0.2340)	*(0.7886)*	*(0.1829)*
Scenic Designation	*No*	*Yes*	**0.1694**	0.1333	**0.1742**
			(0.0180)	*(0.5719)*	*(0.0207)*
Roadside View	*Occasional Houses and Businesses*	*Infrequent Small Towns*	**0.3286**	0.0343	0.3570
			(0.0007)	*(0.9117)*	*(0.0005)*
	Infrequent Small Towns	*Little to No Development*	**− 0.2634**	0.0707	**− 0.3004**
			(0.0067)	*(0.8127)*	*(0.0036)*
Speed Limit	*25 mph*	*35 mph*	**0.4129**	0.5355	**0.3976**
	(Where Total Miles Traveled 250 or less)		*(0.0013)*	*(0.1842)*	*(0.0034)*
	25 mph	*35 mph*	0.3359	**0.6368**	0.3156
	(Change in Willingness to Pay Where Total Miles Traveled >250)		*(0.0157)*	*(0.2564)*	*(0.0286)*
	35 mph	*50 mph*	**0.7964**	0.2962	**0.8521**
	(Where Total Miles Traveled 250 or less)		*(0.0000)*	*(0.5091)*	*(0.0000)*
	35 mph	*50 mph*	0.0747	0.3978	0.0480
	(Change in Willingness to Pay Where Total Miles Traveled >250)		*(0.5655)*	*(0.4445)*	*(0.7222)*
Rest Areas	*None*	*Rest area without Restrooms*	0.0146	− 0.2620	0.0442
			(0.8767)	*(0.3995)*	*(0.6558)*
	Rest area without Restrooms	*Rest area with Restrooms*	**0.7134**	**0.6957**	**0.7183**

Change in Roadway Characteristic			All	Vermont	Nonresident
	From	*To*			
Shoulders	*None*	*Shoulder of 1-2 ft.*	*(0.0000)* **0.4891**	*(0.0457)* 0.0281	*(0.0000)* **0.5403**
	Shoulder of 1-2 ft.	*Shoulder of 2-4 ft.*	*(0.0000)* −0.2492	*(0.9328)* 0.0844	*(0.0000)* −0.2869
Toll increase of $1			*(0.0043)* −0.2208	*(0.7589)* −0.1471	*(0.0019)* −0.2289
Chi-Squared (Likelihood ratio) Probability			*(0.0000)* 50.16 15.45%	*(0.0204)* 36.22 68.28%	*(0.0000)* 48.24 20.35%
Number of Observations			5014	454	4560
Degrees of Freedom Used			41	41	41

Note: Probabilities of obtaining test statistics under null of zero are reported below parameter estimates.

for a move from the mixed distant view to a mostly farm view (column three).

Responses indicate that residents prefer a view of forests over farms, since the relative magnitude of willingness to pay for the move from mostly forest to a forest-farm mix is greater than that for the move from a mix to mostly farms. Thus, from the survey results, it can be said that the resident willingness to pay for a change from mostly farms in the distant view to mostly forest is $0.99 (calculated by: $1.66 − $0.67). Calculated in the same way, the nonresident willingness to pay for a move from mostly forests to mostly farms is $0.33.

Scenic Designation

It was found that as a whole, respondents were willing to pay approximately $0.77 per trip to use a roadway that is designated as "scenic" on the map over one that is not. When resident choices were analyzed separately, results show that these respondents have a positive willingness to pay of $0.91 for traveling on a scenic-designated road over one that is not. However, this figure is not bold in Table 11.3 because the coefficient on the choice variable was not significant at the 10 percent level. In the last column of Table 11.3, corresponding to scenic byway designation, it is

TABLE 11.3. Willingness to Pay for Roadway Changes: All Respondents, Residents, and Nonresidents

Change in Roadway Characteristic			All	Vermont	Nonresident
	From	*To*			
Distant View	*Mostly Forest*	*1/2 Farms, 1/2 Forests*	$0.27	–$1.66	$0.39
	1/2 Farms, 1/2 Forests	*Mostly Farms*	–$0.63	$0.67	–$0.72
Scenic Designation	*No*	*Yes*	$0.77	$0.91	**$0.76**
Roadside View	*Occasional Houses and Businesses*	*Infrequent Small Towns*	**$1.49**	$0.23	**$1.56**
	Infrequent Small Towns	*Little to No Development*	–**$1.19**	$0.48	–**$1.31**
Speed Limit	*25 mph (Where Total Miles Traveled 250 or less)*	*35 mph*	**$1.87**	$3.64	**$1.74**
	25 mph (Where Total Miles Traveled >250)	*35 mph*	**$1.52**	$4.33	**$1.38**
	35 mph (Where Total Miles Traveled 250 or less)	*50 mph*	**$3.61**	$2.01	**$3.72**
	35 mph (Where Total Miles Traveled >250)	*50 mph*	$0.34	$2.70	$0.21
Rest Areas	*None*	*Rest area without Restrooms*	$0.07	–$1.78	$0.19
	Rest area without Restrooms	*Rest area with Restrooms*	**$3.23**	**$4.73**	**$3.14**
Shoulders	*None*	*Shoulder of 1-2 ft.*	**$2.22**	$0.19	**$2.36**
	Shoulder of 1-2 ft.	*Shoulder of 2-4 ft.*	–**$1.13**	$0.57	–**$1.25**

Note: Numerator (likelihood estimate of roadway characteristic) and denominator (likelihood estimate of toll cost) of bold figures are significant at 10% level.

shown that nonresidents were willing to pay $0.76 to travel on the scenic designated roadway.

Roadside View

Willingness to pay for a change from "occasional houses and businesses" in the roadside view to "infrequent small towns" was consistently positive (although only significant for some of the groups), and willingness to pay was negative for a subsequent change from "infrequent small towns" to "little to no development." Thus, infrequent small towns were significantly preferred over both the little to no development and the occasional houses and businesses scenarios. Resident preferences were not statistically significant.

Overall, respondents were willing to pay $1.49 for travel on a road with infrequent small towns over one with occasional houses and businesses. Furthermore, it is estimated that respondents were willing to pay $1.20 for roadway travel with the infrequent small towns instead of little to no development.

Speed Limits

Preferences for higher speed limits yielded the second highest willingness to pay responses of all the roadway characteristics comparisons. The general respondent was willing to pay up to $1.87 for an increase in speed limit from 25 mph to 35 mph, and $3.61 for an increase from 35 to 50 mph.

Respondents that had driven 250 miles or less were willing to pay approximately $5.48 ($1.87 + $3.61) per trip to travel on a roadway with a 50 mile per hour speed limit over one with a 25 mile per hour speed limit. Surprisingly, responses indicate that those who traveled more than 250 miles that day were willing to pay only $1.86 for this same variance in speed limit (although the preference for 50 mph over 35 mph was not significant).

Rest Areas

Preference for availability of rest areas equipped with restrooms was consistently strong and positive. In fact, this was the only roadway characteristic that was found to be significantly preferred by resident respondents as a whole.

All respondents were willing to pay more than $3.00 for travel along a roadway where restrooms are available over travel with no restrooms available. No significant preferences were found for the change from no rest areas to rest areas without restroom facilities, thus indicating that respondents found almost no difference between no roadside rest area provisions, and a rest area without restrooms.

Roadway Shoulders

Model results show that most respondents prefer shoulders that are 1 to 2 feet in width. When asked to choose between a roadside shoulder of 1 to 2 feet versus none at all, respondents were found to have a positive willingness to pay of $2.00 or more. Choices made by respondents overall indicate an aversion to the 2 to 4 foot shoulder, with negative willingness to pay of $1.13 for a move to the 2 to 4 foot shoulder from a 1 to 2 foot shoulder.

AN APPLICATIONS WORKBOOK

Considerable effort was put into translating the econometric results into a useful tool for byway planners. It was assumed that the economic impacts of a byway change could be estimated through predicted shifts in demand and the ability of local business to respond to the change in demand (supply shift).

The increase (or decrease) in traveler willingness to pay associated with each roadway change, as calculated for different types of travelers, represents a positive shift in demand for businesses in this area. This demand shift can be translated into percentage changes in local area sales volume and prices and ultimately into local economic impacts. A planners' workbook was developed to guide users through these impact calculations. In it, planners are asked to provide estimates of numbers of travelers of all major types for a particular roadway. In addition, it is necessary that planners make rough estimates of the responsiveness of the local business community to an increase (or decrease) in business. Together, this information and the estimates of the willingness to pay are used to compute local impacts on sales volumes, prices, wages, and jobs.

The four outputs from the workbook that can be used in making roadway planning decisions are:

1. Current expenditure estimates for each type of user,
2. Predicted traveler volume after byway changes for each type of user,
3. Predicted traveler expenditures after byway changes for each type of user, and

4. Predicted changes in employment and wages caused by byway changes.

A two-page worksheet in the workbook summarizes the calculations to be made in evaluating byway changes. It makes reference to five notes that provide data and discussions about selecting values for the worksheet. In almost every case where user input was required a default value was suggested. A default supply elasticity of 1 was suggested to approximate balanced increases in prices and volumes. Default demand elasticities of $-\frac{1}{2}$ for nonresidents and -1 for residents were suggested, based on available travel demand literature. Average daily expenditures, estimated from the travel survey, were \$58.65 for residents, \$117.42 for nonresident business travelers, \$159.79 for nonresident sightseers, and \$136.72 for nonresident shoppers. The translation of revenues to wages was accomplished using a multiplier. Default wage/sales and employment/sales ratios (0.226 and 0.022) were derived from a weighted average of seventeen Vermont travel and tourism-related industries, with the weights subjectively based on average tourism sales as a percent of total sales in each industry.

LIMITATIONS

Conceptual

There are a few major conceptual limitations in the study: first, the costs of roadway development are not measured, and thus a true benefit/cost analysis cannot be conducted. Second, the approach taken is "One road at a time" and does not account for simultaneous changes to other substitutable travel routes. Finally, the study does not provide an overall value of the image of a region, which can include many other factors that are important to travelers.

Statistical (Sample Size)

The study also has three important statistical limitations, all of which relate to the size of the sample taken. First, in order to efficiently estimate the effects of the seven roadway changes, the design of the questionnaire focused on the accuracy of the "main effects." A different design and more observations would be required to efficiently estimate interactions between effects. Second, even estimates of some of the main effects had large variances that could be reduced by more observations. Finally, only a few segments of the traveling population were sampled. Travelers in other regions of the state, traveling at other times of the day and other seasons of the year would most likely have different preferences.

CONCLUSIONS

An Assessment Methodology

This chapter has presented a methodology for assessing traveler trade-offs that can be determined from a survey method involving paired comparisons of roadways and analyzed using a conditional logit model.

Some Traveler Preference Estimates

The primary empirical results indicate that there is considerable variability in responses by different types of travelers who, generally speaking, want to drive fast and have restrooms available at rest areas. The designation of a highway as "scenic" appears to be worth $0.77 per day of travel.

A Planning Tool

A workbook was developed to enable Vermont planners to use the results from the survey to value alternative roadway improvements. These calculations can be valuable in several stages of the state scenic byways program. First, they can help promoters of the program by describing, in economic terms, the advantages of roadway design. Second, they can help state and local government agencies in evaluating specific roadway project proposals. Finally, they can assist with local economic development plans by describing the economic potential of business support of roadway changes and business responsiveness to growth.

CONCEPT DEFINITIONS

Economic impacts: The change in an area's supply or demand that occurs as a result of a change in an external influencing factor.

Elasticity: The sensitivity of supply or demand to respond to a change in price.

Logit model: Statistical model that estimates the probability of an event occurring as a logistic density function.

Maximum likelihood analysis: Estimation method that maximizes the probability of obtaining the sample of observations.

Scenic byway: Roadway with picturesque views; defined by the National Scenic Byways Program as possessing scenic, cultural, natural, archaeological, historic, and recreational characteristics.

REVIEW QUESTIONS

1. What are some ways that economic impacts of scenic byways were estimated prior to this study?
2. What were some of the problems with these estimation methods?
3. How were economic impacts of scenic byways and byway characteristics estimated in this study, and how are the economic impacts realized?
4. What were some of the problems with the estimation methods used in this study?
5. What are some of the uses of such a study to planners?

BIBLIOGRAPHY

Addelman, Sidney (1962a). "Orthogonal Main-Effect Plans for Asymmetrical Factorial Experiments," *Technometrics*, 4 (1), February, 21-46.

Addelman, Sidney (1962b). "Symmetrical and Asymmetrical Factorial Plans," *Technometrics*, 4 (1), February, 47-58.

Beaman, Jay, Sylvanna Hegmann, and Richard DuWors (1991). "Price Elasticity of Demand: A Campground Example," *Journal of Travel Research*, 30 (1), Summer, 22-29.

Cochran, William G., and Gertrude M. Cox (1957). *Experimental Designs*, Second Edition, John Wiley and Sons, New York.

Crouch, Geoffrey (1994). "Demand Elasticities for Short Haul versus Long Haul Tourism," *Journal of Travel Research*, 33 (2), Fall, 2-7.

David, H.A. (1963). *The Method of Paired Comparisons, Being Number Twelve of Griffin's Statistical Monographs and Courses*, Charles Griffin and Co., Ltd., London.

Maddala, G.S. (1986) *Limited-Dependent and Qualitative Variables in Econometrics*, Cambridge University Press, New York.

Mazzotta, Marisa J. and James J. Opaluch (1995). "Decision Making When Choices Are Complex: A Test of Heiner's Hypothesis," *Land Economics*, 71 (4), November, 500-515.

Real Estate and Land Use Institute (1994). "Economic Impact of Scenic Highways," School of Business Administration, California State University, Sacramento, CA, April 12.

Tyrrell, Timothy J., and Maureen F. Devitt (1996a). "An Analysis of the Economic Impact of Scenic Byway Treatments in Vermont: A Pilot Study," Impact Research Associates, Inc., Kingston, RI.

Tyrrell, Timothy J., and Maureen F. Devitt (1996b). "A Workbook and Guide for Valuing Vermont Byway Changes: Pilot Study Application," Impact Research Associates, Inc., Kingston, RI.

The Urban Institute (1990). "Economic Impacts of Scenic Byways," Final Case Study for the National Scenic Byways Study, Washington, DC.

The U.S. Travel Data Center (1990). "The Economic Impact of Travel on Scenic Byways," Final Case Study for the National Scenic Byways Study, Washington, DC.

Chapter 12

Tourism Expectation Formation: The Case of Camper-Van Tourists in New Zealand

Jurgen Gnoth

LEARNING OBJECTIVES

By the end of this chapter the reader should be able to:

- Define motives, motivations, values, and attitudes
- Differentiate expectations from attitudes
- Describe the construct of "cognitive structure"
- Describe expectations within the behavioral process
- Describe the value of expectation research

INTRODUCTION

New Zealand lies in the Southwest Pacific, some 2,000 miles off the coast of Australia. The North Island is the smallest of New Zealand's two main islands, yet two-thirds of its 3.5 million inhabitants live there. The largest group of New Zealanders—called Pakeha by the Maoris—are of European and, particularly, of British stock. Hence the Union Jack appears in one corner of New Zealand's flag.

New Zealand abounds in natural beauty and is similar in size to California. It stretches over some 1,300 miles from the tip of the North Island to the tip of the South Island. Both islands are rather narrow and it is easy to travel from coast to coast in one day or less. The North Island contains many scenic bathing beaches, vast areas of bushland, geysers, active volcanoes, and beautiful lakes.

The South Island offers spectacular coastlines. Whales can be seen close to the coast where snow-capped mountains meet the sea. The Southern Alps offer skiing and mountain-climbing opportunities in the winter and wilderness experiences in the summer. Hunting and fishing in bush-clad valleys are additional activities that add to a plethora of man-made attractions. Although the road system is extensive, vast areas can only be reached via dirt roads or by foot. No dangerous animals live on either of the islands. These are some of the features and attractions of New Zealand and reasons why traveling by camper van (recreational vehicle) is attractive and practical.

DEVELOPING AN UNDERSTANDING OF EXPECTATIONS

Consider the introduction above. Doesn't this conjure up lively pictures of scenery, people, and things to do? To explain the construct of expectations, we might as well begin with your own images of these descriptions. As you will learn, the way we obtain new knowledge depends on what we already know, so expectations are often reconfigured recollections of things we have already experienced.

The images in your mind, triggered by the introduction as well as things you already know about New Zealand, often contain motivations and attitudes. We find that expectations, too, often contain drives, emotions, and cognitions in conjunction with motives and attitudes.

In other words, thinking back to the time you learned about any of the images you now use to visualize and understand the scenic descriptions mentioned previously, you must have had some reason for paying attention to them. You must have learned the concepts and images in a particular context, then associated other pieces of knowledge and feelings with those concepts to form some opinion about the content or object of the image. In this way you have opinions and attitudes (cognitions and feelings) connected to entire images or elements thereof. You also have reasons for remembering these images, attitudes, and opinions. These reasons are often called motivations. Motivations contain drives and information, such as knowledge about the objects you might have in front of you or are thinking about. These are arranged in a way that is best suited to satisfy the need underlying the motivation. In other words, your mind has learned to organize everything that it deems important in a way that helps the satisfaction process. This may sound tautological, but it is based on the fact that you can think only with what you have already stored in your memory.

For the moment it is best to imagine any piece of knowledge and/or feeling you might have as a piece of information. Being aware of this knowledge (attitude, opinion) or feeling means that you use material stored in your memory to form this awareness or understanding. Encoded along with this piece of knowledge come data on when, where, and why you learned it, whether you like it, are indifferent to it, or dislike it, or even whether you dislike things that are related to the piece of knowledge or feeling. Also encoded with this information would be an evaluation of what you, your friends, family, or society in general may think of it. In short, whether conscious or not, once we begin thinking about holidays or travel, we would immediately have other associations flooding in through our memories. In the next few paragraphs, we will discuss both the reasons why we think about New Zealand in the way we do and how the associations and feelings we have affect us.

THE CONSTRUCTS OR TOOLS

The following is a description of a number of constructs. Constructs can be understood as concepts that are developed to the degree that they can be measured (Kerlinger, 1973). These constructs are all antecedents to behavior and cannot be observed. Yet knowing them, and understanding how they are linked together, facilitates a better understanding of behavior. In turn, this improved understanding can help in managing tourists and the resources they need and use as well as how best to market to them. Thus, if we know and understand people's expectations, we can advise them on who or what might satisfy them and whether their expectations are realistic. We can also evaluate the best way to satisfy those expectations or whether we can satisfy them at all. The detailed explanation of these constructs begins with an urge and ends with behavior and its outcome.

MOTIVES AND MOTIVATIONS

Before we know what we want, we feel a drive in the form of an energy compelling us to act. At this stage the drive is called an *urge* because it has no direction as yet. We feel an urge, for example, when we are restless. The urge can be seen as the center or generator of involvement. Depending on the emotional or instinctive strength of the urge, the level of involvement with a connected need or motive can be defined by the intensity and persistence with which it recurs.

As soon as we realize what the urge actually indicates, we can term it a *need* (see e.g., Maslow, 1954). If we act on it, the need has turned into a motive. A motive differs from a need in that need is a generic term. Needs are expressed in concepts such as "hunger" or "sleep" on which a person might act. As soon as a person acts on that need, he or she is propelled by a drive that stems from the urge. When we have a drive, a need, and a person acting on this, we can call it a motive.

At this point, it is valuable to differentiate between a motive and a motivation. Each motive has its distinct type of content in the form of behavioral goals whereby a person can choose from a learned or conceived repertoire of actions, which have these goals as outcomes. In turn, motivations contain results referring to specific person-situation interactions (Heckhausen, 1989).

The distinction is necessary because if a motive was meant to contain a limited set of goals *and* behavior, there would either be an immeasurable amount of needs and motives, or adaptation to different situations would be difficult and time consuming. On the other hand, when treating motivations as distinct from motives, we acknowledge the fact that each motive can trigger a variety of behaviors as much as each behavior can be triggered by a variety of motives (Murray, 1938).

If this were otherwise, we would be locked into an immutable stimulus-reaction type scenario in which only trial-and-error sequences of behavior (Thorndike, 1911) would help us adapt to new and changing situations. As it turns out, this distinction will also help us to understand expectations. We often act on mere motives, hoping that our action will result in the achievement of the goal. If the situation has not been appraised sufficiently, however, the adaptation process might not be complete and the action futile. Expectations, in this case, are more like hopes, which lack or are even contrary to evidence. Motivations, in turn, contain processes and effects with a higher degree of definition and adaptation. Expectations that follow cognitive motivation processes could therefore be deemed more "realistic." In actual fact, there appears to exist a continuum between these two concepts in terms of degree of abstractness and integratedness, which we will explain further later.

Since motives always occur within a given environment, it is this environment as well as our values and attitudes that shape and form our specific response to a need. Sometimes, a motive cannot be satisfied or come to fruition because the time and/or situation are not right. It may be that a need cannot be satisfied for physical reasons. For example, it is another hot day in your city (e.g., New York) and the hustle and bustle, the noise and crowds really get you down. You want to escape from noise and indifferent people—the motive. Slowly you start to dream of a quiet place with lots of green foliage, trees, and bushes around you. You even imagine hearing birds—the situation. "Would you mind?!" a voice suddenly says behind you and you are thrown back into the reality of being at the corner of seventh and fourteenth. You cannot act on your need and escape as yet. The need for peace and quiet therefore remains latent. Although the motive triggered the memory of some learned or conceived behavior to achieve the desired goal, it has not reached the stage at which plans are being made, tickets bought, and visa applications filled out.

When, finally, you find yourself in the airplane on the way to New Zealand, your motive has turned into a motivation because now not only is the basic need about to be satisfied, but the motive occurs within a set environment and defined situation. In other words, you have finally saved enough money as well as days off work and you find yourself traveling to New Zealand. A large number of activities have been performed to achieve the desired result. Each of these activities has its distinct meaning for the desired result, adding to the set of a tourist's expectations. Some of the observable as well as nonobservable behavior raises expectations that resemble a motive because the link to a situation is only abstract and more related to the process of "doing things" such as "being free and independent." Other behavior raises more definite expectations arising from concrete pieces of knowledge such as, for example, the expectation of receiving a rental vehicle at the destination, which has five square meters of floor space and 105 horsepower. Such knowledge and expectations are based on intensive person-situation interactions among tourist, travel agent, and information brochures.

In addition, you might also have other motives operating when dreaming about New Zealand. A need for peace and quiet with birds singing in the background does not just come from experiences in downtown New York. The desire to listen to birds without a noisy background might also stem from your interest in ornithology. All of these additional influences shape the configuration of the motivation that finally drives your behavior.

Thus, while we discuss a motive in a singular form, this is only so we can understand the concept with more clarity. In reality, several motives operate within the many actions that form our behavior. In this case we speak about motive bundling. For instance, in the example above, the desired place for peace and quiet is not the desert—where you would find a similar situation—but New Zealand's unique landscape. In addition, your image is also crowded with birds and your feet are treading soft ground. The image satisfies several motives. The objects that "fill the stage of dreams," like the one above, are linked to what people value and prefer.

As has been mentioned, at some point in the motivation process, attitudes and values help determine the actual shape and form of motivations and the resulting behavior. Since values are thought to control attitudes, we will deal with values first.

VALUES

In the process of adaptation to the environment, humans learn that similar situations often allow similar behavior. They also learn that when situations become too dissimilar, a different behavior has to be applied to solve a task or problem. Learning processes that cause people to adapt to differing situations in a controlled or conscious fashion utilize abstraction. This abstraction is necessary to form rules for behavior. While rules can be learned by copying, for example, at home through parental guidance or, at school, by copying teachers, rule learning can also be seen as a creative process.

If rules are learned by habit, then the behaviorists' stimulus-reaction theory applies (Hull, 1943). In this case, behavior is repeated over and over and is learned because it leads to a desired success, often facilitated by reinforcement (Thorndike, 1911). When rules are formed through creative processes, they are mostly cognitive (see Gestalt School; e.g., Wertheimer, 1945). Information acquired during several similar learning processes can be abstracted from the specific situations in which it has been learned. This information is then applied to new situations and becomes the basis for rule acquisition. When differing situations are tied with similar requirements, it may cause similar behavior. Thus we can say that a behavioral rule has been created.

We apply rules to satisfy our needs. If we learn that some rules apply more or better than others to particular situations, we learn to prefer them. In time, such rules become values in their own right, that is, principles according to which we wish to conduct our behavior. Values thus either describe a preferred way of conduct (instrumental value) or they represent a desirable end state (expressive value). Receiving value for money when going on holiday might therefore be an example of a desirable conduct, while being well respected by tourism hosts might be an example of an end state.

In this way, people have learned, for example, that holidays are an attractive way to recover from the toils of every day life. What they do on holidays, where they go, and how they travel can, on one hand, often be linked to the type of work they do, what hobbies and interests they have, their education, stage in the family life cycle, and the amount of money they earn. On the other hand, the destination they choose often reveals the choices they have to fulfill their motives and satisfy values that derive from tourists' psychographic profiles. Matching needs with destination attributes is therefore driven by the values tourists hold and their attitudes toward individual aspects of these attributes. In terms of adapting to the environment, values can be regarded as strategies by which the environment is adapted to suit one's motives, or we adapt to our environment to achieve instrumental and/or expressive goals.

THE "LOGIC" OF VALUES

Values are abstract and gain their expression in specific behavior. Once applied, we can often say that a value is operating and motivating behavior. But most of the time, it is difficult to find any true logic when values are applied. Let us couch this somewhat difficult argument in a discussion of some imaginary people. For example, take the value of "freedom": as a preferred value a person might say, "Freedom is good." "Good for what?" another person might ask. "Well, being free of a mortgage, for example," might be the answer. "Free" therefore means "without a mortgage" and is used synonymously. But "free," in this case, has nothing to do with the "freedom" above, which is an ideal value, quite distinct from "being free of mortgages." In terms of rhetoric and logic, a value thus lacks the second argument (Miceli and Castelfranchi, 1989), that is, what "freedom" is good *for*.

Measuring tourists' expectations, values, and attitudes therefore encounters a problem. Although we have seen the link between people's values and behavior, when looking at it more closely, we find that there is a logical gap. This dilemma can be expressed in another way: a motive or value can be satisfied in a number of ways (to satisfy one's desire for excitement, one might read a gripping novel, watch a movie, or go bungee-jumping off a bridge in New Zealand). One motive can therefore cause a variety of behavior. Conversely, a person jumping off a bridge tied to a flexible cord might have a number of differing motives. Maybe that tourist wants to overcome fear, impress someone, or just experience free fall. In any case, a behavior can be triggered by many motives (Murray 1938).

How tourists' values are satisfied can be determined by their attitudes toward the objects they choose or surround themselves with. Often, the link between the attitude object and the value may not be logical, yet the tourists' links drive their behavior (see the theory of attribution, Kelley, 1967). We therefore have to take note of this triad of value, attitude, and behavior.

As it turns out, instrumental values are modes of conduct such as "traveling fast, comfortably or leisurely," whereas expressive values represent end states (Rokeach, 1979) such as "traveling to be recognized" or "to become educated." The difference between these types of values can often be further characterized by the level of emotion they contain and the direction these emotions have (de Rivera, 1977; Gnoth, 1997). Thus, the value of "being recognized" very much depends on social conventions and how people in their respective cultures and subcultures express this concept. "Being recognized" is therefore an outer-directed value that aims at conventions and rituals as a social phenomenon. Conversely, "being educated" is mostly understood as an inner-directed or self-directed value because it is often pursued for its own sake rather than to satisfy any social norm.

To gain a deeper understanding of the quality of values, we now turn briefly to attitudes, because they form the link between behavior and its underlying values. It should be kept in mind, however, since attitudes are strongly bound to situations and therefore appear to change over time and because of different situations, the value structure tourists hold can give us a more stable reference system, by which the nature and quality of expectations and attitudes can be determined.

ATTITUDES

While values give us an idea of tourists' motivational structure, attitudes form the link between observable behavior and abstract values, that is, the rules by which tourists form attitudes and conduct their behavior. According to attitude research (Fishbein and Ajzen, 1975; McGuire, 1985) attitudes contain cognitions (things we know about an object) affect or an emotional liking or dislike, and conations, in other words, a measure of intensity according to which we are likely to act upon an attitude.

In the subsequent empirical example of camper-van tourists in New Zealand, tourists have been asked why they chose a camper van to travel through New Zealand. The qualitative research that preceded the questionnaire design produced many differing answers, all of which represent attitudes toward the camper van. For example, tourists stated that they chose a camper van because it "makes them feel free and independent" or because "it is a cheap way to travel" through the sparsely populated areas of the country. Others said that "it is a safe way to travel," "I do not have to book ahead for accommodation," or "I just owe myself something like a camper van," i.e., a comfortable and even luxurious way to travel given the fully equipped kitchen, the stereo, comfortable beds, and bathroom facilities.

In all of these and other statements, the tourists referred to something they know about their camper vans (cognitions). In some cases, however, these statements express more than just a piece of knowledge. Indeed, as in the case of "I owe myself something like this camper van," we also detect a fair amount of emotional or affective content. "Owing" oneself something expresses a feeling of indebtedness, of respect for oneself. While this feeling—the affective aspect of the attitude—might be easily appreciated, the (logical) link between the underlying value of "self-respect" and the concrete features of a camper van is harder to understand.

Last, the conational aspect of an attitude refers to the likelihood that a person acts upon the attitude. This aspect reveals an expectational content, because thinking that "I owe myself something like this" entails having a certain knowledge about the result of owning a product. This knowledge is "expected" to be true when the product is used or possessed.

Given that the questionnaire for the subsequent empirical section used a repeat-measurement method and asked tourists for reasons for choosing a camper van before they took possession of the vehicle, as well as after they returned, means that the researcher is asking for motivations and formed attitudes. The attitudes formed after the holiday can also be seen as performance evaluations because they have been formed on prior experiences. In any case, it can be seen that attitudes and expectations can share similar structures.

EXPECTATIONS

To understand expectations and before we can define them more closely, we have to grasp how attitudes, values, and other knowledge fit into the wider system of memory. In his effort to explain behavior, Tolman (1932) developed the concept of the *cognitive map,* which can be understood as what we usually term memory. The cognitive map is to be considered as containing cognitive systems, i.e., various distinct patterns of interrelated cognitive elements (e.g., means-end relations) that also include elements of affect. These cognitive systems carry four structural characteristics, a degree of complexity, consonance, abstractness, and realism, which are all concepts based on the School of Gestalt (e.g., Wertheimer, 1945).

The complexity of a given cognitive system refers to the number of elements and their degree of differentiation. Tourists who have never been to a destination will therefore have knowledge about this destination with only a minimal level of complexity. Although they might know, for example, that New Zealand has a network of roads much like anywhere else, tourists will not know how long it will take to get from Christchurch, the gate city of the South Island, to Queenstown or the Milford Sound, one of the country's foremost attractions. Nor will they know how it really feels to drive on the left side of the road—unless they are used to it—or what particular hazards are involved in driving on New Zealand's roads (e.g., sheep, opossums, rabbits, hedgehogs, flightless birds, and some farmers).

Degree of consonance relates to the level of harmony between elements of each system. Consonance refers to, for example, how the knowledge of having to drive on the left-hand side of the road links in with rules at crossings, motor skills such as shifting gears with the left hand rather than the right hand, or how the van has to be serviced, and how you pay for fuel. Each of these actions relates to particular systems of knowledge and behavior that have many missing links because the behavior has never been executed in these particular circumstances.

Moreover, because of a certain lack of harmony between knowledge systems, the systems lack the degree of abstractness that would allow rule and value formation, other than what we can infer from already existing knowledge. While it might therefore be possible to say that traveling on New Zealand's motorways can get you quickly across a city, that knowledge cannot be generalized because most of New Zealand's roads are considerably slower and narrower than New Zealand's few and short motorways. Abstractness, therefore, in conjunction with complexity and consonance, refers to the degree of differentiation and integratedness of the cognitive system. Another way of describing the level of abstractness would be to determine the level of either clarity or ambiguity of cognitive systems (see also Harvey, Hunt, and Schroder, 1961).

Realism denotes the individual's sincerity about his or her cognitive systems, for example, the degree to which a tourist who has never been to New Zealand truly believes that he or she will be able to cover a certain distance within a determined time period. In a different social scenario, realism would refer to a tourist's belief of how easy it would be to meet people and strike up friendships with Maoris, given that the tourist has never met a Maori before.

The detailed structural characteristics of cognitions render the first notions of what expectations are and that they must have a rather elusive quality. It will also have come to mind, given the only loosely connected pieces of information about unknown tourist destinations, that these cognitions have very much a hypothetical character. Before we explicate these aspects further, let us also include the notion of emotions. Emotions play an important role in tourism, since it is a hedonic activity or one that we pursue to derive pleasure.

EMOTIONS

If we consider all of the hitherto developed concepts and constructs in sequence, we can assume the following with regard to a deeper understanding of expectations. An urge indicates that a need will activate a person and compel him or her to act. A person can learn how to respond to a need through trial and error, or through modeling one's behavior on that of others. It can also be learned through word of mouth, advertising, and general learning at school or by reading nonfiction, or it can be conceived cognitively and uniquely by the persons themselves.

Before cognitions (the contents of the cognitive map) are activated, however, the person feels the urge as emotions, i.e., an energy that occurs with a measure of persistence and intensity. The more often an emotion occurs and/or the stronger this emotion is, the more likely it is that the person will get involved in some behavior. "A specific emotion sets up a specific action tendency—the first sign that emotion is working to organize your thought and action" (Izard, 1991, p. 23).

These emotions—as yet little understood by tourism scientists—activate a repertoire of behavior, with which the person has learned to satisfy needs within a given environment. In other words, the person has learned to channel needs and desires into certain, perceived as appropriate, situations, in a personally effective and socially acceptable or even desirable fashion. The activation thus involves emotions, past learning, and other aspects of memory and thereby values and attitudes. The combination of situation and behavior have mostly been learned in a defined social and cultural environment and behavior has turned into habit. Therefore, tourists can often appear to be out of place in other countries because, intuitively, they act and expect results like those they are used to at home.

In summary, we can define expectations as forward-directed, tentative attitudes containing a more or less definite element of knowledge about an object. They also contain an emotional charge expressing the intensity of the drive with which behavior, in reaction to the drive, is executed (demand for a goal). Both these elements can interact and influence each other.

Expectations are specific types of attitudes, both having either a negative or a positive direction and containing emotions, cognitions, and intentions. Expectations are motive-driven and dynamic, whereas motivations contain perceptions, judgments, and behavior (conation).

Finally, expectations are a specific type of attitude in that they have a temporally forward-directed intentional charge. Whereas an attitude refers to a latent state or condition that directs a mode of conduct when activated (adapted to a situation), expectations, while being based on attitudes, refer specifically to outcomes or future events particularly through their conational element. Expectations, which have the structure of attitudes, are henceforth called expectancies.

In other words, as multidimensional and interdependent structures (cognitive systems), attitudes differ from expectations in that they are stronger in their complexity, consonance, and abstractness. In contrast, expectations are less concrete, less interconnencted to other related aspects, and therefore more elusive; they are of a hypothetical character.

Expectations contain a certain strong emotional charge, representing the intensity of the drive with which behavior is pursued. It is related to, but can be distinct from, affect, which has a cognitive structure and is integrated in the cognitive map. Drive is forward-directed and energizes behavior which, in turn, seeks reduction in intensity. While drive denotes the energy, the emotion denotes the class of objects a person is driven toward.

Tomkins (1981) noted the particular strength of the emotional system to combine with messages from various other sources. It forms the basis for drive-based learning in that drive-stimulated behavior can result in associative learning. Over and above this type of learning, humans are capable of cognizing, reflecting, and rationalizing experiences, thus giving drive-based learning access to the cognitive system and part of subsequent evaluations and goal-oriented behavior. It must be emphasized, however, that the rationalization of experiences in such cases are cognitions of emotion awareness and an attempt to grasp a Gestalt rather than to generate premises for deductive arguments. In such cases it is important to note that, while an expectation contains a drive, the satisfied state following an experience must be void of that drive. Tourists can be aware of both, i.e., the presence or absence of drive.

In this sense, either by stimulus association and generalization (Pavlov 1927), or by cognitive attribution, emotions facilitate the arousal of motives and help generate the association between a need and certain objects the person has learned to perceive as means to satisfy the motive. These associations form the basis for expectations that anticipate results. A tourist perceives certain destinations, means of travel, and activities as satisfying felt needs. The expression of the need—now a motive—is based on values, attitudes, situations, and preferences. Once these elements interact within the mind of a decision maker, we are confronted with motivations. Yet, because the result of an action has not eventuated, expectations have a hypothetical character. The tourist's subsequent journey is thus a new learning process, in which expectancies are confirmed or altered and drives reduced. The consequence for tourism researchers is therefore to assume that expectations are not as strongly intercorrelated as performance experiences and that the links between expectations and performance experiences and evaluations are also not very strong. Furthermore, the role of drive reduction has to be considered within the processes between expectation and satisfaction formation during the experience. These are the challenges for the future.

EMPIRICAL INVESTIGATION OF EXPECTATIONS: CAMPER-VAN TOURISTS IN NEW ZEALAND

The following is part of a research project measuring expectations and satisfaction among camper-van tourists in New Zealand. In a longitudinal study, some 1,100 tourists were asked to fill in a questionnaire. The sample consists of 385 respondents from over 10 nations who answered two questionnaires, one filled in before obtaining their vehicles from the rental company and one after returning it at the end of their journeys.

Measuring the Complexity of Expectations

Asking tourists why they chose a destination or a special type of transport is a relatively easy question for tourists to answer when they are arriving at their holiday destination. We can assume this because they have been thinking carefully about how they will be traveling and achieving all their goals during their decision-making process. The present sample booked their camper vans, on average, 3.5 months prior to their holidays. Tourists' mind-sets (Boring, 1950) that contain the reasons and outcomes for why they choose a camper van can be assumed to be quite conscious. The mind-set resulting from the motivation process should therefore contain high "internal validity," as far as the perceived reasons for the choice are concerned. It can also be assumed that—despite the tourist's lack of actual experience of a new destination—these cognitions are interrelated.

One way of measuring the level of differentiation in the cognitive structure is by using Cronbach's (1951) alpha. This test is usually applied to test the internal validity of scale measures. As it computes the correlation of each item to the total scale, it reflects a measure of interrelatedness and harmony.

When comparing camper van users by experience, 149 reported that they had used the type of vehicle before, whereas 246 had not. Applying the Cronbach test to the list of motivations for choosing a camper van (see Table 12.1), it can be seen that tourists arriving in New Zealand who had used a recreational vehicle before produced an alpha value of .8414. Those without any such experience achieved an alpha value of only .8226. The difference in these groups can also be shown through multivariate analysis of variance. Using MANOVA in SPSS/PC, the difference in motivational structure between those with experience and those without is highly significant (Pillais value .5505; sig. F = .000). This difference became

TABLE 12.1. Motivations to Choose a Camper Van

ITEMS in SHORT	VALUE "I chose a camper van because....(strongly agree) 5 4 3 2 1 (strongly disagree)	Mean Value	Standard Deviation
CHEAP	To me it is the cheapest way to travel	2.777	1.2915
FUN TO DRIVE	Driving a van is fun and enjoyable	3.536	1.0712
FREE	I want to be free and independent	4.775	.4286
ADVENTURE	It gives me the feeling of adventure	3.712	1.0931
DO	I can really do what I want	4.553	.6619
OWE	I just owe myself something like this	2.532	1.3539
BELONG	I need a place where I belong	2.356	1.2659
STYLE	It suits my style	3.338	1.2860
EASY	It makes it easier to meet locals	1.413	.8998
TOURIST	I don't feel as if I am "just a tourist"	2.658	1.2226
NATURE	You get close to nature easily	4.231	.8986
ACHIEVE	I can achieve more than with any other form of holiday	4.115	.9464
BEST WAY	It is the best way to travel the country	4.146	.9165
SAFE	It is a safe way to travel New Zealand	3.348	.9632
NO BOOKING	I enjoy not having to book ahead for accommodation	4.204	1.0002
FUN & ENJOYMENT	It guarantees holiday fun and enjoyment	3.677	1.0595
POTENTIAL	I can live up to my full potential and be myself	3.340	1.1930

insignificant once all tourists had completed their holidays and returned the vehicles. At that time, tourists were asked to respond to the same set of statements as shown in Table 12.1. After their journey, the items were introduced by the leading sentence, "Choosing a camper van has proven to be right because. . . ." Whether the choice was right or not could then be answered with reference to each motivational statement.

Since the motivation has led to an experience and result, the tourist is now able to treat what was formerly a motivational statement as an attitude statement, from which we can expect a higher level of complexity, consonance, and abstractness. Accordingly, the Cronbach alpha test for the evaluation of all expectancies returned an overall value of .9057 after the trip. Those who had not had experiences with camper vans prior to the holiday returned an alpha of .8990 whereas those with prior experience returned an alpha of .9147. These latter alphas were not significantly different from each other.

Motivational Dimensions

The seventeen items of the motivation scale in Table 12.1 were generated from exploratory research. This involved interviewing camper van tourists at various stages of their trips. Statements are also referred to as "expectancies" and have been measured on five-point Likert-type scales. The items have then been selected according to both frequency and Lynn Kahle's (1983) list of values. This was achieved by interpretatively matching items with the nine abstract values of that list. In order to cover all these values as well as differentiating between instrumental and expressive values, two items are listed matching each of Kahle's values. Kahle's value of "warm and friendly relationships" has only one matching item (EASY) because respondents thought that seeking warm and friendly relationships was no reason at all to hire a recreational vehicle. Subsequently, EASY also had to be dropped from further analyses due to low item-to-total correlations.

In order to detect the underlying dimensions of the motivational items, the remaining sixteen items were factor analyzed (principal axis with varimax rotation). This resulted in four factors with 41 percent of the common variance explained (see Table 12.2).

The factor analysis of the same items after the holiday experience, but couched in an evaluatory phrasing ("It was right to choose a camper van because. . . .") resulted in almost 50 percent of the variance explained and only three factors (not tabled here). In this solution, FUN & ENJOYMENT became part of the Outer-Directed and Expressive factor while NO BOOKING joined ACHIEVE and BEST WAY to form a more general

TABLE 12.2. Motivational Dimensions for the Use of Camper Vans

Factor I: Outer-Directed & Expressive		Factor III: Inner-Directed & Instrumental	
OWE	.77260	ACHIEVE	.67780
BELONG	.70967	BEST WAY	.52384
STYLE	.61949		
TOURIST	.48822		
ADVENTURE	.48591		
POTENTIAL	.46543	Factor IV: Inner-Directed & Expressive	
FUN to DRIVE	.42774		
SAFE	.35302	DO	.54753
CHEAP	.33137	NATURE	.52026
		FREE	.48934
Factor II: Outer-Directed & Instrumental			
FUN & ENJOY	.76036		
NO BOOKING	.33970		

instrumental factor. Again, the increased explanation of common variance is a result of a cognitive map with a higher level of consonance and complexity. The former expectancy values have now turned into actual attitudes. It should be observed that the sequence of the factors itself is an indication of the strength these cognitions hold within tourists' minds. The names of the factors also reflect their decreasing cognitive strength, increasing affect, and characteristics of a Gestalt.

The increased complexity within the now-existing attitudes comes about through the actual experiences. Expectancies of an outer-directed nature are more cognitive and less emotional than inner-directed ones. Experiences therefore function as confirmations leading to an effect, whereby expectancies—by being confirmed and strengthened—turn into attitudes. It can be observed in the significantly increased means of the before and after measurements in Table 12.3. Those expectancies that are inner-directed and significantly different all had decreased means. This phenomenon can be interpreted by using drive theory (Hull, 1943). There is a strong possibility that the decrease occurred because of a reduction in drive regarding the underlying emotions of these items; after their trips tourists are simply aware of an absence of drives that motivated their holidays. The implications of this finding go beyond this chapter but should challenge further research.

The move of FUN & ENJOYMENT into the Outer-Directed and Expressive factor can be explained by considering that the experience is part of the long-term memory and linked (correlated) to all other experiences. At the

TABLE 12.3. The Changes in Means from Expectancy Values to Final Attitudes

VALUES	BEFORE	AFTER	MEAN of DIFFERENCE	SIGNIFICANCE of DIFFERENCE
CHEAP	2.8	3.1873	.387	.000
FUN to DRIVE	3.5418	3.7797	.238	.037
DO	4.6025	4.3215	−.281	.000
EASY	1.4328	3.038	1.605	.000
TOURIST	2.7241	2.7696	.046	ns
NATURE	4.2405	4.0177	**−.223**	.000
BEST WAY	4.1595	4.1899	.030	ns
NO BOOKING	4.2608	4.3595	.099	.085
POTENTIAL	3.3772	3.3975	.020	ns
FREE	4.7949	4.5342	**−.261**	.000
ADVENTURE	3.7013	3.6633	−.038	ns
OWE	2.5797	2.8911	.311	.000
BELONG	2.4405	3.3063	.866	.000
STYLE	3.3316	3.4633	.132	.05
ACHIEVE	4.1241	3.9722	**−.152**	.008
SAFE	3.4101	3.6861	.276	.000
FUN & ENJOYMENT	3.7165	3.7873	.071	ns

end of the holidays, the expectancy has become confirmed knowledge related to tangible and intangible objects and situations. Conversely, the move of NO BOOKING to the items of ACHIEVE and BEST WAY can be interpreted by the particular character of the experience. The fact that camper vans provide the opportunity to park anywhere over-night has been experienced. The freedom of not having to book accommodations is merely a cognized consequence of this fact. Since these tourists never had to book, this consequence is therefore more elusive within the cognitive structure.

From Motivations and Expectations to Intentions

Although a camper van can be an attraction in itself for many tourists, it is nevertheless merely the instrument by which a destination can be explored. However, the motives that led to the decision to travel, and the particular person-situation interaction that formed motivations, also reveal certain value structures. For example, tourists who are strongly outer-oriented find interest and attraction in the material aspects of the vehicle (see e.g., OWE) and can be assumed to have the tendency to target products of a similar nature (Prentice, 1987). The mere fact that some tourists strongly agree with the statement "I owe myself something like this van" indicates that these tourists imbue the vehicle with a symbolism whereby it represents this particular attitude.

In a similar way, we can expect that tourists who score strongly on STYLE ("it suits my style") are keen on doing things related to commercial attractions, sanctioned by important others. Since the notion of style conforms to a certain normative behavior (whether social or antisocial), it is always conceived of either in contrast to, or through processes and standards outside of the person portraying the style (style can therefore never be asocial). The particular character of the underlying values is formed under the influence of peers or relevant opinion leaders who helped frame the associations between the value and an object. In other words, targeted holiday activities are value expressive and relate back to motivations. A relative stability between peoples' value structures and behavior is due to their tendency to be consistent and to avoid disharmony within their own cognitive structures. It causes tourists to link certain values consistently with certain classes of activities.

Camper van tourists were also asked which activities they intended pursuing while traveling in New Zealand. In Table 12.4, a selection of eighteen activities are listed together with the motivational dimensions. The significant correlations reveal that (a) if positive, the more tourists score on that factor, the more likely they are to take on that activity. Conversely, (b) the more they load on a particular factor associated with a negative correlation, the less likely they are to pursue that activity. Since the correlations are bivariate, the argument is also true in reverse, i.e., if a tourist is likely to pursue that activity, then he or she loads high (or low, if the correlation is negative) on that factor.

Table 12.4 shows that certain motivations, with their respective sets of underlying emotions and values, tend to associate with particular activities. We can see, for example, that all types of walks, whether hiking, short or long are negatively correlated with the Outer-Directed and Expressive factor. In other words, the more tourists score on the motivational items of the first factor, the less likely they are to take longer walks. Conversely, visiting galleries is considered a priority by those who are strongly outer-directed in their motivational structure.

The Influence of Expectations on Satisfaction

Finally, expectations have an influence on satisfaction. Tourists were also asked how satisfied they were with their camper vans at the end of

TABLE 12.4. Correlations Between Activities and Motivational Dimensions

	Outer-directed & expressive	Outer-directed & instrumental	Inner-directed & instrumental	Inner-directed & expressive
Bungee jumping	-.093	.038	-.015	-.103*
Fly fishing	.095	-.040	-.112*	.007
Befriending locals	.120*	.182**	.047	.189**
Visiting galleries	.118*	.010	-.062	.050
Eating Hangi food	.119*	.120*	.030	.102*
Finding isolated country	-.033	.007	.091	.189**
Befriending Maoris	.166**	.178**	.047	.128*
Visiting Maori performances	.033	.133**	.054	.116*
Visiting museums	.057	-.008	-.059	.111*
Paragliding	.009	.114*	-.007	-.084
Pubs	-.001	.036	-.100*	.012
Restaurants	-.080	-.058	-.144**	-.049
Finding solitude	-.076	-.039	-.052	.138**
Specialty restaurants	-.032	.083	-.101*	.097
Hiking	-.099*	-.047	.015	.060
Water ski	.028	.115*	-.008	-.058
Short walks	-.105*	-.007	.055	.153**
Long walks	-.208**	-.104*	.028	.066

*Correlation is significant at the 0.05 level (2-tailed).
** Correlation is significant at the 0.01 level (2-tailed).

their holidays. Following Herzberg, Mausner, and Snyderman (1959), who proposed that satisfaction should be measured on two scales rather than just one, the satisfaction scales were split, asking for the intensity of satisfaction on one and dissatisfaction on the other.

As can be seen in Table 12.5, expectations do affect satisfaction judgments. While the correlations appear small, it can be attributed to the characteristics of expectancies, i.e., the low levels of complexity and consonance. The results show that satisfaction with the vehicle is significantly related with the inner- and outer-directed expressive expectations. While only twenty-two visitors were dissatisfied with the camper van, the stronger the dissatisfaction, the more this is due to unfulfilled inner-directed expressive expectations.

TABLE 12.5. Satisfaction with the Vehicle Correlated with Motivational Dimensions

	Outer-directed & expressive	Outer-directed & instrumental	Inner-directed & instrumental	Inner-directed & expressive
I am satisfied with the camper van (n=366)	.151**	Ns	.105*	.138**
I am dissatisfied with the camper van (n=22)	Ns	Ns	Ns	.462*

*Correlation is significant at the 0.05 level (2-tailed).
** Correlation is significant at the 0.01 level (2-tailed).

CONCEPT DEFINITIONS

Expectations: Forward-directed, tentative attitudes containing a more or less definite element of knowledge about an object (e.g., tourism experiences, destinations, objects, etc.). They contain an emotional charge expressing the intensity of the drive with which the behavior, in reaction to the drive, is executed.

Motivations: The results of specific person-situation interactions. They contain motives influenced and operationalized by persons' values and their perception of given situations.

Motives: The recognized drives that target particular classes of objects to satisfy the underlying need.

Values: Srongly held beliefs governing attitudes and behavior. They express strategies whereby objects are chosen and adapted to achieve the satisfaction of felt needs (motives) or according to which tourists adapt themselves to given situations in order to satisfy their motives.

REVIEW QUESTIONS

1. What is the practical consequence of differentiating between motives and motivations?
2. Explain the concept "values are strategies to adapt (to) situations." What impact does this have on tourists' motivation and behavior?

3. How do expectations differ from attitudes?
4. How can we describe tourists' cognitive structure?
5. How do the variables STYLE and DO differ in their emotional and object-related direction and content?

REFERENCES

Boring, E G. (1950). *A History of Experimental Psychology.* New York: Appleton-Century-Crofts.

Cronbach, L.J. (1951). Coefficient Alpha and the Internal Structure of Tests. *Psychometrica,* (16), 297-334.

de Rivera, J. (1977). *A Structural Theory of the Emotions.* Psychological Issues Monograph, 40. New York: International University Press, Inc.

Fishbein, M. and I. Ajzen (1975). *Belief, Attitude, Intention and Behaviour: An Introduction to Theory and Research.* Reading, MA: Addison Wesley.

Gnoth, J. (1997). Tourism Expectation and Motivation Formation. *Annals of Tourism Research, 24* (2), 283-304.

Harvey, O.J., D.E. Hunt, and H.M. Schroder (1961). *Conceptual Systems and Personality Organization.* New York: Wiley.

Heckhausen, H. (1989). *Motivation und Handeln* (Second Edition). Berlin: Springer.

Herzberg, F., B. Mausner, and B.B. Snyderman (1959). *The Motivation to Work* (Second Edition). New York: Wiley.

Hull, C.L. (1943). *Principles of Learning.* New York: Appleton-Century-Crofts.

Izard, C.E. (1991). *The Psychology of Emotions.* New York: Plenum.

Kahle, L.R. (Ed). (1983). *Social Values and Social Change: Adaptation to Life in America.* New York: Praeger.

Kelley, H.H. (1967). Attribution Theory in Social Psychology. In D. Levine (Ed.), *Nebraska Symposium on Motivation* (pp. 192-238). Lincoln, NE: University of Nebraska Press.

Kerlinger, F.N. (1973). *Foundations of Behavioral Research.* New York: Holt, Rinehart and Winston.

Maslow, A.H. (1954). *Motivation and Personality.* New York: Harper.

McGuire, W.J .(1985). Attitudes and Attitude Change. In G. Lindzey and E. Aronson (Eds.), *Handbook of Social Psychology* (Vol.2) (Third Edition, pp. 233-346). New York: Random House.

Miceli, M. and C. Castelfranchi (1989). A Cognitive Approach to Values. *Journal for the Theory of Social Behaviour, 19* (2), 169-193.

Murray, H.A. (1938). *Explorations in Personality.* New York: Oxford University Press.

Pavlov, I.P. (1927). *Conditioned Reflexes.* London: Oxford University Press.

Prentice, D.A. (1987). Psychological Correspondence of Possessions, Attitudes, and Values. *Journal of Personality and Social Psychology, 53* (6), 993-1003.

Rokeach, M. (1979). *Understanding Human Values, Individual and Societal.* New York: Free Press.

Thorndike, E.L. (1911). *Animal Intelligence.* New York: Macmillan.
Tolman, E.C. (1932). *Animals and Men.* New York: Century.
Tomkins, S.S. (1981). The Quest for Primary Motives: Biography and Autobiography of an Idea. *Journal of Personality and Social Psychology, (41),* 306-329.
Wertheimer, M. (1945). *Gestalt Psychology.* New York: Liveright Publishing Corporation.

Chapter 13

From the Psychometrics of SERVQUAL to Sex: Measurements of Tourist Satisfaction

Chris Ryan

LEARNING OBJECTIVES

By the end of this chapter the reader should:

- Be aware of the origins of services marketing theory
- Know what the concerns of services marketing are
- Know the distinguishing features of the holiday service situation
- Be familiar with the development of services marketing theory and measurement as applied to holiday taking
- Know the issues surrounding the form of service quality measurement known as SERVQUAL within the context of holiday taking

INTRODUCTION

Peterson and Wilson (1992) note that in the period 1970 to 1990 over 15,000 academic and trade articles on the subject of customer satisfaction have been published. To attempt a review of the development of even one part of the theory of the measurement of customer satisfaction, as it applies to tourist experiences, may be perceived as an act of insanity or megalomania. Yet such a review may be of use if it can identify at least some of the twists and turns in the debate; especially if it raises questions about whether the apparent ease of measurement makes us blind to the real nature of the experience tourists seek and often find. This chapter thus has a few basic themes. First it will briefly note the emergence of gap analysis as a form of consumer satisfaction measurement derived from theories of quality production, services management, and service quality. Second, it will discuss more fully the development of a specific form of gap analysis associated with the work of Parasuraman, Zeithaml, and Berry. Third, the question will be raised whether this form of measurement does in fact help us understand the nature and causes of satisfaction that arises from tourist experiences.

THE DEVELOPMENT
OF SERVICE QUALITY THEORY

Marketing is traditionally much more than simply promotion. The oft-quoted four "P's" of introductory textbooks in marketing point to "price," "product," "place," and "promotion" as making up the marketing mix, requiring entrepreneurs to get all four factors "right" if they are to be successful (e.g., Kotler, 1991). Hence, product planning and product quality are prerequisites for customer satisfaction. Substandard destinations and poor-quality attractions are not likely to elicit satisfaction from tourists. The adoption of quality production might be said to originate from the pioneering work of Shewhart who, in 1931, espoused the use of statistical process control. In the period after World War II, Deming drew attention to the role of the designer and the use of production specifications. With the successful resurgence of Japanese industry based on his policies, the concept of quality production spread to the United States and Europe (Deming, 1982). Two additional ideas associated with production quality were those of zero defects (Crosby, 1979) and fitness for purpose (Juran, 1974). The concepts are related to each other because a product technically free from defects, but not meeting the purpose of the consumer, cannot be said to possess quality.

While continuing to be strongly related to production engineering, these approaches have not been without their impacts on the delivery of services. A concern with specifications led to blueprinting as described by Laws (1990) with reference to airline service. It might also be said to have led to the development of ISO 9000 standards. Ryan (1996, p. 148) notes the definition of quality incorporated within these standards as "the total features and characteristics of a product or service that bear on its ability to satisfy stated or implied needs" and also describes the emergence of ISO 9001 pertaining to services such as travel agencies. Such a definition of quality neatly encapsulates the production engineering antecedents noted in the previous paragraph.

The emergence of the service sector, combined with traditional marketing approaches espoused by writers including Kotler, led in the 1970s to the development and description of a services marketing process. Fisk, Brown, and Bitner (1993) identify three stages in this literature. Prior to 1980, the debate was dominated by the question of to what extent was services marketing different from the marketing of fast moving consumer goods (FMCG), which had hitherto attracted most attention due to the postwar growth in consumer spending, branding, and supermarket sales that characterized that period. From this literature the oft-quoted characteristics of services as heterogeneous, intangible, and requiring the presence of the seller arise, and it is not coincidental that the early books on the marketing of tourism stem from this tradition (e.g., Middleton, 1988). In the second stage, between 1980 and 1985, attention begins to turn to questions of service encounters and service quality. Oliver's 1981 work is an early example. During this period the gap between customer expectation and perception appears as an important concept in measurements of client satisfaction and service quality. It is perhaps notable that Parasuraman, Zeithaml, and Berry's first statement of SERVQUAL occurred in 1985. The concept of gaps as a form of perceptual measurement was, of course, not new. In 1963 the American sociologist Rodman had described: first, a satisfaction gain (a gap between what one can tolerate and what one expects);second, a concept of reconciliation as the gap between achievable and nonachievable goals; and third, a "value stretch"—the sum of these two gaps, denoting a gap between minimum needs and the absolute quality of goals. By 1994 Parasuraman, Zeithaml, and Berry were making similar arguments with reference to service quality, while in 1995 Mansfeld applied Rodman's concept of value stretch to the tourist behaviors of London Jews. The third stage, since 1985, has seen an increasingly rigorous and academic debate about the nature of consumer satisfaction and service quality, and has merged the issue of services marketing into service quality theory.

Service quality theory might be described as an integration of quality theory and theories of marketing and services. Increasingly it is being subsumed into a management debate about the provision of quality for clients and the implications for management structures. Thus the terminology of this debate includes not only questions of gaps, but "moments of truth" (e.g., Normann, 1984; Carlzon, 1987), critical incidents (Bitner, Booms, and Tetreault, 1990) and staff empowerment (see Baum, 1997, for a discussion of this within the hospitality and tourism industries). Thus, within the tourist experience, there may be moments when the tourist receives a recognition of his or her individuality that complements an experience of the place, a critical incident of the unlooked-for service that "makes the day"—all delivered by staff trained to provide such occasions and empowered by management structures to show initiative because discretion is permitted whereby staff can act without reference to higher management. These notions have been fostered by different writers, including the "Nordic School." In 1982 Lehtinen and Lehtinen noted that customers judge the service they receive during and after the service, and thus distinguished between "process quality" and "output quality." Similarly, Gronross (1984) noted:

> The perceived service is the result of a consumer's view of a bundle of service dimensions, some of which are technical and some of which are functional in nature. When this perceived service is compared with expected service, we get the perceived service quality. (p. 39)

Gronross also drew attention to the importance of corporate image as a quality dimension that can moderate between technical and functional service quality and perceived service quality. Arguably this concept identifies a distinction between determining and moderating variables, which was later to play a role in the theory of service quality advanced by Taylor and Baker (1994). This view was subsequently developed by Taylor (1997), who emphasized the curvilinear as well as interactive foundations underlying both satisfaction judgments and quality perceptions.

THE DEVELOPMENT OF SERVQUAL

This brief review of the development of service quality/customer satisfaction theory has noted that its development is derived from many different perspectives with implications for service design, staff training, and management structures as well as the long-term retention of customers and thus profitability and/or enterprise sustainability. Because the issue is so important, a consistent theme in both academic literature and management practice has been the measurement of service quality and customer satisfaction. It is this concern that accounts for the widespread adoption of the SERVQUAL model, developed by Parasuraman, Zeithaml, and Berry (1985, 1986, 1988, 1994a, 1994b, 1994c), and the subsequent critical analysis of the model. SERVQUAL, as a means of measuring service quality, has been continually refined by its authors since 1983. The first phase consisted of focus group interviews which resulted in a conceptualization of ten determinants of service quality and the identification of five gaps that can occur in the provision of services. The second stage was based upon further qualitative research that led to a reduction from ninety-seven to the twenty-two items representing the five dimensions, which became the SERVQUAL questionnaire. Further qualitative research followed combined with quantitative research in five different service companies using the SERVQUAL measure. This stage was reported by Parasuraman, Zeithaml, and Berry in 1988 and 1991, alongside the results of a further qualitative study involving sixteen focus groups of customers in six service sectors. By 1993 the authors reconceptualized expectations as a dual-level variable, namely desired service expectations and adequate service expectations, and an expanded gap model of customer expectation/perception was introduced (Zeithaml, Berry, and Parasuraman, 1993, Parasuraman, Zeithaml, and Berry, 1994a, 1994b, 1994c).

The new model measured the difference between perceived and desired service described as the measure of service superiority (MSS), as well as the difference between perceived and adequate service described as the measure of service adequacy (MSA).

In consequence they recommended that SERVQUAL should be administered in a three-column format with each of the columns being headed for each of the items "My Minimum Service Level is . . . ," "My Desired Service Level is . . . ," and "My Perception of _____ 's Service Performance is . . ." (underlining in original, Parasuraman, Zeithaml, and Berry, 1994b, p. 46). The three-column approach is recommended as having greater diagnostic value because it indicates the perceived level of service relative to the minimum tolerance level of service. The authors also recommend that companies consider adopting a measurement system that provides separate measures of adequate-service and desired-service level expectations and perceptions.

Also, the research suggested the SERVQUAL item "Maintaining error-free records" could be eliminated, and two others ("Keeping customers informed about when services will be performed" and "Convenient business hours") could be reclassified from "responsiveness" to "reliability," and from "empathy" to "intangibles" respectively. Furthermore, the scale was increased from seven to nine intervals, offering respondents a wider range of choices.

In addition, the presence of five dimensions was tested by the use of confirmatory factor analysis using LISREL's unweighted least squares procedure. The conclusion was reached that while a five-dimension model was consistent across the different samples, the results also supported "the possibility of a three-dimensional structure wherein responsiveness, assurance and empathy meld into a single factor" (Parasuraman, Zeithaml, and Berry, 1994a, p. 211).

These changes in SERVQUAL are significant in view of the criticisms that have been levied at the model and may be interpreted as a specific response to such criticisms. The next section will outline some of these criticisms, indicate the actions underlying gap analysis, and begin to address the issue of whether such approaches can inform research into tourist satisfaction.

GAP ANALYSIS—MEASURES OF SATISFACTION AND SERVICE QUALITY

A two-stage model of consumer satisfaction is consistent with wider measurements of attitudes. Fishbein (1967) argued that the strength of attitudes was the product of the importance attached to an attribute, and an evaluation of the degree to which the object of the attitude possessed the attribute. The relationship was perceived as being multiplicative, although it might be argued that a gap between importance and evaluation might also be a measure of strength of attitude. The confirmatory/disconfirmatory analysis used in consumer gap analysis retains the evaluation of an object in terms of perceived quality of service, while "importance" is replaced by "expectation." Fishbein's earlier conceptualization of attitude also took into account expectation in an extended model of attitude measurement, by incorporating expected outcomes of a decision. Indeed, the three variables noted by Fishbein are echoed by the extended SERVQUAL model with its variables of desired outcome (importance), perception (evaluation), and tolerated outcome (expectation). However, the original concept of SERVQUAL that customer satisfaction could be conceived as being the gap between customer expectation (E) and perception (P) of the quality of the service, had been quickly questioned. Miller (1977) had previously noted that expectations reflected anticipated performance, and that four different types of expectations could be identified. These were "ideal," "expected," "minimum tolerable," and "desirable." Thus, the question of what *type* of gap was being measured was quickly raised. While P < E could be deemed to be "dissatisfaction," if E = P was "satisfaction," what was P > E? Much more than satisfied? The model also implied satisfaction could be created if expectations were low. It can also be stated that any uniform gap does not have a consistent meaning. For example, an "expectation score" of five and a "perception score" of four might not be the same as a gap between an "expectation score" of two and a "perception score" of three. Based on earlier research, Saleh and Ryan

(1992, p. 115) noted that "If customer tolerance of some deviation from expectation exists, and thus a level of service less than ideal does not generate dissatisfaction, this implies that the boundary between that which is acceptable and that which is not is 'fuzzy.' "

They suggested that "the just noticeable difference was a factor not only of past consumer experience, but also a structural component within the service delivery process" (Saleh and Ryan, 1992, p. 115) while drawing attention to a habituation effect in the formation of expectations and perceptions of service quality. Thus one issue was, what was the gap actually measuring? Indeed, what was SERVQUAL measuring—was it client satisfaction or service quality? What were the linkages between these two variables?

A further problem arose when other researchers, using the 1988 SERVQUAL model, were unable to replicate the five dimensions of tangibles, reliability, responsiveness, assurance, and empathy. Among the first to question this was Carman (1990). He sought to replicate the dimensions in different service industries and was unable to do so, suggesting that the factors were sensitive to changed wording in the questions as researchers amended the wording of the questionnaire to fit specific situations. A number of papers critical of SERVQUAL were soon published. Bakabus and Boller (1992, p. 259), in a study of users of a utility company, stated that "the proposed dimensionality of SERVQUAL is problematic . . . the model provided poor overall fit statistics." Brown, Churchill Jr., and Peter (1992, p. 138) concluded from their study that "not only did SERVQUAL fail to achieve discriminant validity from its components, but the perceptions score component by itself performed as well as the difference score on a number of criteria." More recently, Suh et al. (1997) have replicated this finding, arguing that the confirmation-disconfirmation is an inappropriate measure of service quality.

Other researchers noted the difficulty of the use of positively and negatively worded questions. Koelemeijer (1996) was one such researcher when she noted that "negative wording of some of the items seems to affect the factor structures of the scales used" (p. 742). Ryan and Cliff (1997) replicated the findings of Brown, Churchill Jr., and Peter when they reported from a study of clients of travel agents that most of the variance lay in the perception scores, and this was a major determinant of the gap. This was also something reported upon by Parasuraman, Zeithaml, and Berry (1994a, p. 213) who noted "This superior predictive validity of the perceptions-only scale," but both Parasuraman, Zeithaml, and Berry (1994a, p. 228) on the one hand and Danaher and Hadrell (1996, p. 16) on the other attribute the higher R^2 values to being "an artifact of the common method variance."

Among others, Ryan and Cliff (1997) could not replicate the five dimensions of the SERVQUAL scale. They had also earlier reported that the expectations scale tended to be constant when nonusers and infrequent and frequent users of travel agency services were compared (Ryan and Cliff, 1996). Another factor that bedeviled the analysis of data was the high level of skew noted in respondents' scores. Peterson and Wilson (1992, p. 69) had drawn attention to this, arguing that:

> given a skewed distribution . . . the arithmetic mean is no longer an appropriate measure of central tendency since it excludes considerable information about satisfaction. Indeed, in this instance, "average satisfaction" is a meaningless concept.

They argued that the very act of seeking satisfaction scores might in itself create a Hawthorn effect. While a number of researchers have noted the issue of skew (Ryan and Cliff, 1997; Peterson and Wilson, 1992; Danaher and Hadrell, 1996), Suh et al. (1997) picked up an implicit theme in some of the earlier research to argue that an important determinant of consumer satisfaction was customer involvement. In a study of users of twelve deluxe hotels in Seoul they devised an involvement scale that was found to have three dimensions—"perceived importance," "symbolic value," and "perceived risk." While the twenty-two items of the SERVQUAL scale were found to have four factors and not five, they nonetheless argued that "the casual order of the relationship between service quality, consumer satisfaction and (re)purchase intention existed, and the three factors were highly perceived when the level of consumer involvement was high" (Suh et al., 1997, p. 50).

However, while it may appear that the confirmation/disconfirmation gap may have little superior predictive ability in distinguishing client satisfaction scores, nonetheless the concept of the gap between expectation and perception as having significance remains conceptually appealing. To state that tourist satisfaction implies a comparison between what is found at a destination with a previous conceptualization or expectation of what that destination would be like, seems consistent with other approaches adopted by researchers in tourism and marketing. For example, Pearce's (1988) theory of the travel career ladder only makes sense in terms of the tourist evaluating experiences against internalized needs and the choice of a destination as meeting those needs.

To assess this more fully requires a discussion of a further question that has been associated with SERVQUAL, and that is, what is it measuring?

The terms "service quality" and "customer satisfaction" have been, in the past, used almost interchangeably. Parasuraman, Zeithaml, and Berry (1988) had written:

> Perceived quality is the consumer's judgement about an entity's overall excellence or superiority (Zeithaml, 1987). It differs from objective quality. . . . It is an attitude, related but not equivalent to satisfaction, and results from a comparison of expectations with perceptions of performance. (p. 15)

Thus, SERVQUAL might be said to be about service quality—but it is a quality that is closely linked to client satisfaction—it is a determinant of satisfaction. Whereas earlier research into clients' perceptions of quality viewed expectations as normative standards, i.e., a belief about what standards *should* be, the gap model attempts to establish what *will* be, i.e., it is predictive. For this reason, the debate about whether the gap or the perceptions scale is more closely correlated with an independent measure of satisfaction has occurred. While Parasuraman, Zeithaml, and Berry have strongly defended the nature of the gap as both an analytical tool for management and a predictive measure, it is fair to say that the debate has been characterized by claim and counterclaim. It is also clear, as shown above, that Parasuraman, Zeithaml, and Berry have been responsive to the criticisms that have been made of the SERVQUAL model. It might also be observed that while the journals include many articles that have been critical of the concept, it is the nature of academic journals that papers that simply confirmed SERVQUAL and its dimensions might be rejected as offering little new to the debate. SERVQUAL has certainly been adopted by management consultants and found to be useful in aiding management to analyze areas of strength and/or weakness.

Recently, research has taken the debate into a new area of work where the linear relationship of expectation, perception, quality, and satisfaction has been questioned, and where the gap between perception and expectation is seen not simply as an outcome but as a contributory factor to expectations and perceptions. Thus the relationship becomes one of higher orders and is reiterative in process.

The basis for such an approach is to note that customer satisfaction is not simply an outcome but an input variable into decisions to repurchase a service, revisit a destination, or repeat a specific type of holiday. So consumers make purchase decisions based upon expected quality, perceived quality, the perceived quality as against criteria of that which is thought to be ideal or tolerable, and past satisfaction with the service. Note that the gap between expectation and perception is also not only an outcome which is a measure of service quality, but is itself a *determinant* of future purchase decisions. Equally, satisfaction is not solely determined by the recent experience of purchase, but an appraisal of that satisfaction within an assessment of past satisfactions. A linear representation of the model might then be:

$$\text{Purchase} = a + b \text{ Expected Quality} + c \text{ Perceived Quality} + d \text{ Gap} + e \text{ Satisfaction Intention} \qquad (1)$$

where:

a = intercept term

b, c, d, and e are coefficients to be empirically determined

Such an approach is not far removed from the approach adopted by Bolton and Drew (1991) and Boulding et al. (1993). These researchers argue that customer satisfaction and service attributes are determinants of both service quality and customer behavior; that is, the formulation can be rewritten as:

$$\text{Purchase} + b \text{ Perceived Quality} = a + c \text{ Expected Quality} + d \text{ Gap} + e \text{ Satisfaction Intention} \qquad (2)$$

Statistically, such representation presents problems of interdependence of variables—the prime condition of regression analysis that the variables are independent is obviously broken (e.g., see Sincich, 1992). However, an alternative approach is to view the variables as being moderating, interventionist, or acting as antecedents. Such a view is not new. For example, in 1993 Oliver suggested the model shown in Figure 13.1. He proposed that while service quality is formed by a comparison between ideals and perceptions of performance on quality dimensions, satisfaction is a function of the disconfirmation of the predictive expectations regarding both quality dimensions and nonquality dimensions. Thus, perceived service quality is an antecedent to satisfaction. This is akin to the view of Taylor and Baker (1994) that disconfirmation moderates the quality-purchase intention relationship, implying a reiterative process as shown in formula (2).

Although these approaches are related, they are not exactly the same. Nonetheless they represent the direction that the SERVQUAL debate has been taking in recent years. Indeed Zeithaml and Bitner (1996) argued that a consensus is emerging whereby:

1. quality perceptions and satisfaction judgments exist at multiple levels of analysis;
2. the concepts may have fundamentally different underlying causes and outcomes; and
3. customer satisfaction is a superordinate construct to quality perceptions in the formation of purchase intentions.

While this may be and probably is true, it leaves Parasuraman, Zeithaml, and Berry's attempt at delivering a pragmatic tool for management purposes in limbo. Moreover, there is also the notion already alluded to that the relationship is both curvilinear and reiterative. Thus the type of model written in formula (1) needs to take the form of:

$$Y = a + b_1X + b_2X^2 + e \qquad (3)$$

Such a model refers to a single curvilinear independent variable and hence is insufficient on the premise that it lacks additional variables, and more importantly ignores the reiterative nature of the argument. To overcome these objections Aiken and West (1991) suggest that marketers should consider the use of hierarchical multiple regressions analysis (HMRA) using the unstandardized regression coefficients. They note that it is the shape rather than just the slope of the curve that is important and that "The simple slope of the regression of Y on X is the first (partial) derivative of

FIGURE 13.1. Modified Satisfaction-Service Quality Model (After Oliver, 1993)

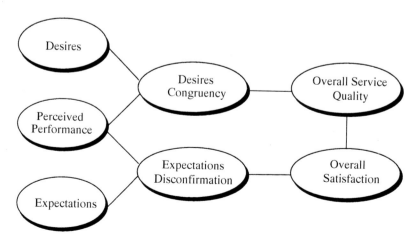

the overall regression equation with respect to the variable X" (Aiken and West, 1991, p. 75). This means that the slope of the derived regression equation at alternative levels of a moderating independent variable (e.g., satisfaction) can be determined on the basis of the first derivative of the obtained regression equations. This is the approach adopted by Taylor (1997) who, using seven-point Likert-type scales, questioned 937 respondents about their purchase intentions, level of satisfaction, perception of quality, and disconfirmation measures by comparing products to expectations and competitors. Clear evidence of higher-order and interactive effects were found. Thus, "the slope of the quality/satisfaction iteration appears to consistently decrease as satisfaction judgments increase" (Taylor, 1997, p. 149).

RELATIONSHIP BETWEEN GAP MODELS
AND TOURIST EXPERIENCE

From a conceptual viewpoint the recognition of higher-order and reiterative processes in models of consumer satisfaction and quality service theory begins to move the usefulness of such theories nearer to the reality of tourist experiences. The early debate about services marketing, revolving around the differences between the marketing of services and the marketing of fast-moving consumer goods, has been remarked upon earlier in this chapter. It might be said that a similar debate has been present, albeit perhaps in an implicit rather than explicit manner, about the nature of service quality in tourism. It is notable that most attempts at applying services marketing theory in the field of tourism have been directed toward specific components of the industry and not the totality of the holiday experience. The work of Ryan and Cliff (1997) and Suh et al. (1997) are examples of such attempts. These are typical of this research in that the subject has been the service provided by travel agencies and the hospitality sector. It is a cliché that tourism comprises a number of services—travel agencies, airlines, hoteliers, and attractions to mention just a few. Attractions themselves can range from the brothels of Bangkok to marvels of the Luxor Casino in Las Vegas via the peace of the English countryside. The numbers and types of such services are myriad. Yet, that there is a hierarchical and reiterative process in generating tourist satisfaction with and within a holiday can be easily established. Thus, for example, there may be initial satisfaction with the services provided by a travel agency in that service was prompt, friendly, and the documentation provided in due time. But what if there is a subsequent failure by a hotelier? Does a failure by the hotel to provide satisfactory service lead to recriminations against a travel agent for recommending such a hotel? To what extent does the failure of the hotel create dissatisfaction with the holiday?

Ryan (1996, 1997) has emphasized the opportunity that the tourist has to create satisfaction by being a major actor in the consuming experience. He argues that tourists retain their social and adaptive skills while on holiday and, being motivated to have a "good time," will adopt strategies necessary to achieve that goal. The constraints of limited time and the costs of taking holiday time to pursue a complaint will mean that many tourists will engage in value displacement—that is, downgrade the importance of that which is unsatisfactory in terms of its contribution to the overall holiday experience. The overall result is that satisfaction may be still be high even if an aspect of the service has failed to meet expectations. The question thus arises as to whether the holiday is experienced and assessed as a holistic experience, or as a sequence of experiences? Even if viewed as a holistic experience, it must be recognized that the "critical incident" of Bitner, Booms, and Tetreault (1990) still has the potential to make or mar the holiday—and whether any one incident has that potential is a function not solely of the nature of the incident, but its importance to the tourist. Arguably, the holiday experience differs from other service experiences by reason of the nature of involvement of the tourist. Unlike many service encounters described in the retail services literature, the holiday has:

a. Important emotional involvement.
b. A strong motivation for successful and satisfactory outcomes on the part of the client.
c. A significantly long period of interaction between the tourist on one hand and, on the other, the place and people in the holiday destination—a period wherein the tourist can manipulate his or her surroundings to achieve the desired outcomes.
d. Such manipulative processes are themselves part of the holiday experience and a source of satisfaction and need not require confrontation, which may not be acceptable to some.
e. As the holiday is made up of a number of holiday services, the tourist can select among alternatives—also, while a distribution chain may be said to exist between these services, in terms of satisfaction creation the direction of the chain may not be casual.
f. The tourist can play several different roles within a holiday—each role may have separate determinants of satisfaction; each role may have unequal contributions to total holiday satisfaction.
g. The holiday has a temporal significance not found in many service situations—it resides in the memory as a preparation for the

future, and is a resource for ego sustainment during nonholiday periods.

Arguably therefore, if services marketing is different from fast-moving consumer goods marketing, then the holiday/tourism product also differs from the service encountered when buying tires, cashing a check, or similar such situations described in the services quality literature. However, the distinguishing feature of SERVQUAL as a model was that it sought to identify factors common to *all* service situations. Certainly the dimensions of "tangibles," "assurance," "reliability," "empathy," and "responsiveness" are important in holidaymaking. Oddly enough though, a tourist may gain satisfaction when the tangibles are lacking in some part, the reliability is not entirely present, and the responsiveness is a shrug of the shoulders. By this is meant the case where the tourist encounters situations that may not run smoothly but, as they are deemed to be part of a "cultural experience" accompanied by other features which are thought attractive, the final experience of "difference" is found to be desirable. Indeed the tourist may take delight in his or her adaptability, and so long as the stress does not exceed competence to deal with the situation, the "flow" of events (to use Csikszentmihalyi and Csikszentmihalyi's [1988] terminology) produces arousal levels that are associated with optimal experiences.

It is possible to define and model the quality of the tourist experience and resultant satisfactions in the terminology of confirmation/disconfirmation paradigms. Following Taylor (1997), the purchase intention toward a given holiday can be derived whereby the relationship between quality and intention, and between satisfaction and intention are both of a higher order and are fully interactive. Such a quadratic relationship would take the form:

$$Y = \alpha + b_1X + b_2Z + b_3X^2 + b_4Z^2 + b_5XZ + b_6XZ^2 + b_7X^2Z + b_8X^2Z^2 + e \qquad (4)$$

where:

Y = purchase intention

X = quality perception

Z = satisfaction judgment

α = intercept and $b_1 \ldots b_8$ coefficients to be established empirically and the confirmation/disconfirmation paradigm is included by the satisfaction judgment being assessed by questions such as "I would generally character-ize this holiday as being . . . than expected" with the value being selected from a Likert-type scale.

However, a debate exists as to whether such global as against transaction-specific forms of quality perceptions and satisfaction judgments are valid. It may be, as already stated, that $X = \Sigma x_1, x_2, x_3 \ldots x_n$ and likewise with Z. Iacobucci, Grayson, and Ostrom (1994) argue that consumers do not make this type of distinction when assessing a consumer experiences, while Ryan and Glendon (1998) report that tourists had little difficulty in undertaking a global assessment of their holiday experiences when assessing levels of satisfaction. However, in the same article Ryan and Glendon note that:

> From a psycho-sociological perspective . . . the perceived importance of an activity in terms of self-development, self-enhancement, ego, role fulfillment, and responding to perceived requirements of significant others, can be argued to be important variables determining motivation, behavior, and derived satisfaction. (pp. 170-171)

This represents a very different view of the nature of the holiday experi-ence by emphasizing the nature of involvement and issues of status and ego enhancement in holiday taking. What the confirmation/disconfirmation model does not do, unless it is explicitly extended as done by Suh et al. (1997), is to specifically elicit these types of consideration. The nature of the issue may be shown by briefly assessing a not-uncommon holiday experi-ence—the search for sex. (While this may be thought to be an extreme example, there is sufficient evidence to suggest that it is not uncommon; e.g., Clift and Page, 1996; Clift and Grawboski, 1997). Any analysis of sex and tourism and the satisfaction derived from "holiday sex" needs to take into account a myriad of issues including sexual need, satisfaction, ego enhance-ment, self-identity, sexual identity, self-exploration, exploitation, the marginal and liminal natures of commercial sex and those who provide those services, issues of responsibility over sexually transmitted diseases, assessment of guilt—in short, a whole series of emotions and social issues. Obviously gap models are not designed to tackle these sorts of issues.

SUMMARY AND CONCLUSIONS

It is my view that as the gap model exemplified by SERVQUAL becomes more sophisticated and thus approaches reality, it paradoxically loses the assets that made it such a desirable tool of both management and practical market research. It is a traditional dictum of empirical science that good theory is economical. From the viewpoint of a manager seeking to ensure a satisfactory level of service for the tourist, the setting is not global but specific—the concern is a particular business setting. And while it is true that correlations between perception scales and indices of overall satisfaction are high, any manager will want to know how specific parts of the product are viewed by customers. To simply ask the equivalent of "How satisfied are you?" is insufficient—in Fishbein's terms the evaluations provided about an item may be high, but the item is not important to the consumer. Parasuraman, Zeithaml, and Berry were right to emphasize the human interaction between client and service provider—and if this is right for services in general, it is arguably even more right in the case of a business operating in a tourism setting. Thus, dimensions of empathy, assurance, and responsiveness, even if they often seem to collapse into one dimension, are appropriate. Given the concern about the constructs of the scale and psychometric measures, it is often overlooked by critics that the basic SERVQUAL model was based on qualitative research, including focus groups as previously described. It provides SERVQUAL with a strength other than that sought by more traditional quantitative techniques. In a sense it matters little if the dimensions cannot be replicated. What is of more importance is that it gives management a simple tool that produces results whereby they can tackle the areas of weakness in their company's service delivery. Indeed, the argument may be taken further by stating that management should feel free to amend the wording of the questions if such new wording addresses specific issues of concern to them. The promise gap models deliver is one of structured monitoring, and this perhaps is the major advantage of such approaches.

Yet there are caveats to the argument that if the approach is methodical, structured, and, when repeated over time, a useful means of management monitoring results and all is well. The results need to be interpreted carefully. It has, for example, been pointed out that a uniform gap may have different meanings if the expectations-perceptions values are of differing order. The results may provide an indicator of poor service, but do not of themselves provide the reason for such poor service, nor provide an answer as to how to address the issue. Of more importance is that the manager should be aware that service quality and customer satisfaction are more complex than even the 1994 extended version of SERVQUAL admits. As Brown (1995) has shown, consumers purchase and manipulate brands in the postmodern age. Urry (1995) has noted that tourists consume places and are consumed by them. It is difficult for any mathematical model to capture this level of experience, especially in the case of tourism, which is a complex mix of entertainment, education, self-discovery, and sheer fun. The mathematical modelers themselves recognize the limitations of the techniques. Iacobucci, Grayson, and Ostrom (1994, p.50) warn "while the technique of structural equations modelling is useful for many applications, it has no omniscient powers and cannot greatly aid researchers in making subtle distinctions between highly related constructs." Such a warning is even more pertinent in the field of tourism.

CONCEPT DEFINITIONS

Gap analysis: The analysis of service quality as being the difference between expectation and perception. A number of gaps exist—for example, between what clients expect and what they think is being offered, or between a manager's perception of client needs and the clients' own perceived needs.

Iterative processes: A process where people move backward and forward between attitudes and experiences to arrive at an outcome.

Linear processes: A process of progression in a straight line from start to finish.

Psychometrics: The measurement of attitudes through the use of questions in which respondents indicate levels of agreement with statements using a scale.

SERVQUAL: A scale of twenty-two items constructed on the premise of gaps in the dimensions of "tangibles," "assurance," "reliability," "empathy," and "responsiveness." The scale measures service quality.

REVIEW QUESTIONS

1. What processes led to the emergence of services marketing theory?
2. What are the advantages of gap analysis?
3. What are the disadvantages of gap analysis?
4. What is meant by "reiteration" and "higher order" relationships within the tourist services marketing relationship?
5. In what ways do tourist service relationships differ from other services marketing relationships?

REFERENCES

Aiken, L.S. and West, S.G. 1991, *Multiple Regression: Testing and Interpreting Interaction Effects*, Newbury Park, CA: Sage Publications.

Bakabus, E. and Boller, G.W., 1992, An empirical assessment of the SERVQUAL scale, *Journal of Business Research*, 24:253-268.

Baum, T., 1997, Making or breaking the tourist experience: The role of human resource management, pp. 92-111 in Ryan, C. (ed), *The Tourist Experience—a New Introduction*, London: Cassell.

Bitner, M.J., Booms, B.H., and Tetreault, M.S., 1990, The service encounter—diagnosing favorable and unfavorable incidents. *Journal of Marketing*, 54 (January):71-84.

Bolton, R.N., and Drew, J.H., 1991, A multistage model of customers' assessments of service quality and value, *Journal of Consumer Research*, 17 (March):375-384.

Boulding, W., Kalra, A., Staelin, R., and Zeithaml, V.A., 1993, A dynamic process model of service quality: From expectations to behavioral outcomes, *Journal of Marketing Research*, 30 (February):7-27.

Brown, S., 1995, Postmodern marketing research: No representation without taxation, *Journal of the Market Research Society*, 37(3):287-310.

Brown, T.J., Churchill Jr., G.A., and Peter, J.P., 1992, Improving the measurement of service quality, *Journal of Retailing*, 69(1) (Spring):127-139.

Carlzon, J., 1987, *Moments of Truth*, Cambridge, MA: Ballinger.

Carman, J.M., 1990, Consumer perceptions of service quality: An assessment of the SERVQUAL dimensions, *Journal of Retailing*, 66 (Spring):33-55.

Clift, S. and Grawboski, P., 1997, *Tourism and Health: Risks, Research and Responses*, London: Mansell.

Clift, S. and Page, S.J., 1996, *Health and the International Tourist*, London: Routledge.

Crosby, P.B., 1979, *Quality Is Free*, New York: McGraw-Hill.

Csikszentmihalyi, M. and Csikszentmihalyi, I.S., 1988, *Optimal Experiences: Psychological Studies of the Flow of Consciousness*, New York: Cambridge University Press.

Danaher, P.J., and Hadrell, V., 1996, A comparison of question scales used for measuring customer satisfaction, *International Journal of Service Industry Management* 7(4):4-26.

Deming, W.E., 1982, *Quality, Productivity, and Competitive Position*, Cambridge, MA: Massachusetts Institute of Technology.

Fishbein, M., 1967, *Readings in Attitude Theory and Measurement*, New York: John Wiley and Sons.

Fisk, R.P., Brown, S.W., and Bitner, M.J., 1993, Tracking the evolution of the services marketing literature, *Journal of Retailing*, 69(1): 61-103.

Gronross, C., 1984, A service quality model and its marketing implications, *European Journal of Marketing*, 18(4):36-44.

Iacobucci, D., Grayson, K.A., and Ostrom, A., 1994, The calculus of service quality and customer satisfaction: Theoretical and empirical differentiation and integration, pp. 1-67 in T.A. Swartz, D.E. Bowenand, and S.W. Brown (eds.) *Advances in Services Marketing and Management*, Vol. 3, Greenwich, CT: JAI Press.

Juran, J.M., (ed.) 1974, *Quality Control Handbook*, New York: McGraw-Hill.

Koelemeijer, K., 1996, Measuring perceived service quality in retailing: A comparison of methods, *American Academy of Marketing Sciences Conference*, pp. 729-744.

Kotler, P., 1991, *Marketing Management—Analysis, Planning, Implementation and Control*, Seventh Edition, Englewood Cliffs, NJ: Prentice Hall.

Laws, E., 1990, Effectiveness of airline responses to passengers during service interruptions—A consumerist gap analysis, *Proceedings of Tourism Research into the 1990s*, University College, Durham Castle, 10-12 December, pp. 124-137.

Lehtinen, J., and Lehtinen, J., 1982, *Service quality: A study of quality dimensions*. Research report, Helsinki, Service Management Institute.

Mansfeld, Y., 1995, The "value stretch" model and its implementation in detecting tourists' class-differentiated destination choice, *Journal of Travel and Tourism Marketing*, 4(3):71-92.

Middleton, V.T.C., 1988, *Marketing of Travel and Tourism*, Oxford, UK: Heinemann Professional Publishing.

Miller, J., 1977, Exploring satisfaction, modifying models, eliciting expectations, posing problems, and making meaningful measurements, pp. 72-91, in Hunt, H.K. (eds.), *Conceptualization and Measurement of Consumer Satisfaction and Dissatisfaction*, Cambridge, MA: Marketing Science Institute, May.

Normann, R., 1984, *Service Management*, New York: John Wiley.

Oliver, R.L., 1981, Measurement and evaluation of satisfaction processes in retail settings, *Journal of Retailing*, 57 (Fall):25-48.

Oliver, R.L., 1993, A conceptual model of service quality and service satisfaction: Compatible goals, different concepts, *Advances in Services Marketing and Management*, Vol. 2, 65-85, Greenwich, CT: JAI Press.

Parasuraman, A., Zeithaml, V.A., and Berry, L.L., 1985, A conceptual model of service quality and its implications for future research, *Journal of Marketing*, 49 (Fall): 41-50.

Parasuraman, A., Zeithaml, V.A., and Berry, L.L., 1986, *SERVQUAL: A Multiple-Item Scale for Measuring Consumer Perceptions of Service Quality Research*, Cambridge, MA: Marketing Science Institute, Report Number 86-108, August.

Parasuraman, A., Zeithaml, V.A., and Berry, L.L., 1988, SERVQUAL: A multiple-item scale for measuring consumer perceptions of service quality Research, *Journal of Retailing*, 64 (Spring):12-37.

Parasuraman, A., Zeithaml, V.A., and Berry, L.L., 1991, Refinement and reassessment of the SERVQUAL scale, *Journal of Retailing*, 67 (Winter):420-450.

Parasuraman, A., Zeithaml, V.A., and Berry, L.L., 1994a, Alternative scales for measuring service quality: A comparative assessment based on psychometric and diagnostic criteria, *Journal of Retailing*, 70(3):201-230.

Parasuraman, A., Zeithaml, V.A., and Berry, L.L., 1994b, *Moving Forward in Service Quality Research: Measuring Different Customer-Expectation Levels, Comparing Alternative Scales, and Examining the Performance-Behavioral Intentions Link*, Cambridge, MA: Marketing Science Institute Working Paper, report number 94-114, September.

Parasuraman, A., Zeithaml, V.A., and Berry, L.L., 1994c, Reassessment of expectations as a comparison standard in measuring service quality: Implications for further research, *Journal of Marketing,* 58 (January):111-124.

Pearce, P.L., 1988, *The Ulysses Factor: Evaluating Visitors in Tourist Settings,* New York: Springer Verlag.

Peterson, R.A., and Wilson, W.R., 1992, Measuring customer satisfaction: Fact or artifact, *Journal of the Academy of Marketing Science,* 20(1):61-71.

Rodman, H., 1963, The lower class value stretch, *Social Forces,* 45:205-215.

Ryan, C., 1994, Leisure and tourism—the application of leisure concepts to tourist behavior—a proposed model, pp. 294-307 in A.V. Seaton et al., (eds.) *Tourism—The State of the Art,* Chichester, UK:Wiley.

Ryan, C., 1996, Seeking quality in Pacific tourism, pp. 146-160, in C.M. Hall and S.J. Page (eds.), *Tourism in the Pacific—Issues and Cases,* London: International Thomson Business Press.

Ryan, C., 1997, *The Tourist Experience—A New Introduction,* London: Cassell.

Ryan, C., and Cliff, A., 1996, Users and nonusers on the expectation items of the SERVQUAL scale, *Annals of Tourism Research,* 23(4):931-934.

Ryan, C., and Cliff, A., 1997, Do travel agencies measure up to customer expectations? An empirical investigation of travel agencies service quality as measured by SERVQUAL, *Journal of Travel and Tourism Marketing,* 6(2):1-32.

Ryan, C., and Glendon, I., 1998, Tourist motives—An application of the leisure motivation scale to U.K. Tourists, *Annals of Tourism Research,* 25(1):169-194.

Saleh, F., and Ryan, C., 1992, Conviviality—A source of satisfaction for hotel guests? An application of the SERVQUAL model, pp. 107-122 in Johnson, P. and Thomas, B., (eds.) *Choice and Demand in Tourism,* London: Mansell.

Shewhart, W.A., 1931, *Economic Control of Quality of Manufactured Product,* New York: Van Nostrand.

Sincich, T., 1992, *Business Statistics by Example,* New York: Maxwell Macmillan International.

Suh, S.H., Lee, Y.H. Park, Y., and Shin, G.C., 1997, The impact of consumer involvement on the consumers' perception of service quality—Focusing on the Korean hotel industry, *Journal of Travel and Tourism Marketing,* 6(2):33-52.

Taylor, S.A., 1997, Assessing regression-based importance weights for quality perceptions and satisfaction judgments in the presence of higher order and/or interaction effects, *Journal of Retailing,* 73(1):135-159.

Taylor, S.A. and Baker, T.L., 1994, An assessment of the relationship between service quality and customer satisfaction in the formation of consumers' purchase intentions, *Journal of Retailing,* 70(2):163-178.

Urry, J., 1995, *Consuming Places,* London: Routledge.

Zeithaml, V.A., Berry, L.L., and Parasuraman, A., 1993, The nature and determinants of customer expectations of service, *Journal of the Academy of Marketing Science,* 21(1):1-12.

Zeithaml, V.A. and Bitner, M.J., 1996, *Services Marketing,* New York: The McGraw-Hill Companies, Inc.

Chapter 14

Cognitive Distance:
A Neglected Issue in Travel Behavior

David J. Walmsley
John M. Jenkins

LEARNING OBJECTIVES

By the end of the chapter the reader should be able to:

- Introduce the concept of cognitive distance (subjective distance) and to describe how it differs from real distance
- Identify the factors that have been found to influence the accuracy of estimates of cognitive distance
- Demonstrate the application of methods and analytical tools in studying cognitive distance in tourism settings
- Compare intercity estimates of distance made by visitors and residents in a tourist region in Australia

INTRODUCTION

Distance has an important bearing on many forms of behavior. At the individual level, distance is important in determining how the space around an individual is partitioned into intimate, personal, social-consultative, and public space, no matter where that individual is (Hall, 1959; Sommer, 1969). Likewise, distance has an influence on the scale and content of the territory with which individuals identify (Porteous, 1977).

This chapter was previously published in the *Journal of Travel Research, 31*(1), 1992. Reprinted with permission.

In both cases, the significance of distance is itself culturally influenced: the personal space of Anglo-Saxon (noncontact) cultures is more extensive than that of Latin (contact) cultures, and the security and private domain of "home" territory is demarcated differently in the high walls surrounding dwellings in the Moslem world and in the open-plan landscape of North American suburbia (Rapoport, 1969). Distance, in other words, has both social and personal meaning. Much has, in fact, been written about social distance (in the sense of the degree of separation of different social groups in general social intercourse) and the way in which this is reflected in the structure of cities. For example, the high and commanding residential locations often are occupied by high-status groups. In short, the concept of distance (and the concomitant notions of proximity and separation) are fundamental to an understanding of the functioning of human society.

The influence of distance on human behavior is perhaps most vividly expressed in the way in which the overcoming of distance imposes a major constraint on travel behavior. This "friction of distance" is the basis of the much-used gravity model of travel behavior. According to this model, the likelihood of travel between two places is proportionately related to the size of the two places and inversely proportional to some function of the distance between the places (Jakle, Brunn, and Roseman, 1976). Improvements in transport technology have led some authors to propose that the world is "shrinking" in that the constraint of distance is of diminishing significance as travel becomes quicker and more reliable (see Abler et al., 1977). However, despite air, sea, and land communication becoming quicker (if not cheaper in real terms), and despite improvements in telecommunications that render some face-to-face contacts unnecessary, distance remains an important constraint on travel behavior.

COGNITIVE DISTANCE

A great difference exists between distance measured in objective terms (for instance, in terms of kilometers, time, or monetary cost) and distance as cognized by individuals. Most people, for example, have experienced the sensation that a homeward-bound journey along a particular route seems shorter than an outward-bound journey along the very same route. Most people, too, have encountered the situation where locals in an area, on being asked for directions, give distance estimates that are greatly at odds with real distances. These sorts of anomalies suggest that cognitive distance (the impression of distance formed in the mind) is a topic well worthy of research. Indeed, Cadwallader (1976) has suggested that the subject of cognitive distance is worthy of serious research attention because it influences no fewer than three critical decisions in travel behavior: whether to go or stay, where to go, and what route to take. Despite this, relatively little work has been done on cognitive distance. For instance, a recent review of research on cognition and travel behavior made no mention of the subject (Pearce and Stringer, 1991).

The first reference to the phenomenon of cognitive distance was probably Brennan's (1948) observation that shopping centers in a downtown direction were preferred by consumers to shopping centers in an out-of-town direction, even when the latter were geographically closer. However, it was not until the work of Thomson (1963) that the whole question of cognitive distance received serious attention. Thomson examined the behavior of shoppers in San Francisco and found that their estimates of the distances to shopping centers proved to be exaggerated, with distances to centers that were visited being more accurately estimated than distances to centers that were not visited. Thomson himself did not use the term "cognitive distance," preferring instead "subjective distance." Another term that has been used (particularly in psychology) is "perceived distance." It is important therefore to clarify the terminology. The term "perceived distance" should be used to signify estimation of the distance to a visible object. Therefore, it refers to "the properties of visual space and the factors that affect it: monocular versus binocular vision, depth cues, and familiarity with the object" (Downs and Stea, 1977, p. 140). In contrast, "cognitive distance" involves estimates made in the absence of an object. In such cases, the stimulus is merely the place name (e.g., how far is it from here to the town center?). "Subjective distance" is synonymous with cognitive distance.

Thomson's (1963) findings have been corroborated in a wide variety of situations, using estimates based on straight-line distances, road distances, and travel time. Moreover, Cadwallader (1981) has shown that the degree of fit of the gravity model can be improved if cognitive distance is used instead of real distance. Most of this replication of Thomson's work has shown that short distances tend to be overestimated to a greater degree than long distances. This greater exaggeration of short distances might have something to do with the inertia involved in starting a journey. For example, the effort in traveling two kilometers (deciding to go, preparing to go, and getting the car out or walking to public transport) is almost as great as the effort involved in traveling three kilometers (given that traveling the extra distance requires little effort) (Walmsley, 1988). It might also owe something to the heightened awareness that characterizes the early stages of journeys. It may be, for example, that travelers pay attention to what is happening in the early stages of a journey but gradually become inattentive and perhaps even bored. Because more information has been absorbed about the early part of the journey, that part seems longer (see Lowrey, 1973).

Before the causes of exaggeration of distance are examined, it is important to question whether overestimation, such as that found by Thomson, occurs in all cases. The answer seems to be no. Day (1976), in a study of cognitive distance in Sydney (Australia), found that distances in the city center were exaggerated up to about 1,100 meters, whereafter they were underestimated. He attributed this to 1,100 meters being about the upper limit of the walking range of most people in the city center. Beyond that distance, people tended to use public transport, often the underground railway, which was devoid of environmental stimuli and which, therefore, made distances seem shorter. Similarly, Pocock and Hudson (1978) observed that in London, distances of up to about eleven kilometers were overestimated. Distances beyond that point tended to be underestimated. In Dundee (U.K.), the critical distance was about six kilometers, with shorter distances being overestimated and longer distances underestimated. There is no ready explanation for this phenomenon, except perhaps that the more distant locations were not very well known to the sample in question. In short, the overestimation in cognitive distance is not an inviolate rule. In fact, the only consistent finding in all studies of cognitive distance is the very high variance in the estimates that are made. This suggests that impressions of distance are idiosyncratic. Despite this, most researchers have chosen simply to take the mean of the estimates and to compare these figures with real distances, thereby overlooking the variability in the data. This research strategy is weak in that it tends to overlook the processes by which estimates of cognitive distance are developed.

DISTANCE COGNITION

The question of how people come to estimate distance is a deceptively complex one. Sometimes individuals might be able to estimate distances by noting how long they have traveled on a particular journey and assuming an average speed. At other times they might be helped by prominent road signs. However, for the most part, this is unlikely to be the data source that individuals use, particularly in laboratory-based experiments in which they are asked to estimate distances to a wide variety of places. Briggs (1973) has suggested that at least five different processes, including the two already mentioned, are involved in generating cognitive distance estimates:

1. Calculations based on the amount of energy involved in moving between two points
2. Computation based on knowledge of time and velocity
3. Addition of the perceived distances between points along a route
4. Interpretation of environmental patterns, such as the counting of city blocks or traffic lights (sometimes referred to as the "Manhattan metric")
5. Reliance on maps and road signs

This range of suggestions reflects the fact that most research on distance cognition has been done at the city scale. All five processes might be involved in distance cognition within the city (as suggested by Downs and Stea [1977]), but not all are likely to be relevant at larger scales. For example, Process 3 is likely to be computationally too difficult if subjects are asked to estimate distances in a network of towns, because literally thousands of lines of sight would need to be added together in terms of their perceived distances. Presumably, Processes 2 and 5 are more important in the estimation of long (e.g., intercity) distances. Indeed, Process 5 should be extended to include the "cognitive maps" (sometimes also called "mental maps") that individuals build up in their minds of areas that are too big and too complex to be known in their entirety (Downs and Stea, 1977).

Notions of distance are fundamental to any sort of environmental cognition. In building up a mental map, individuals need to know something about nodes within the environment, the closeness of nodes, the relative location of nodes, and the interlinking paths between nodes (Briggs, 1973). Distance is central to each of these. As a result, "cognitive distance estimates reflect much more than the simple geographical separation between places on the earth's surface. They are one result of the attempt by cognitive mapping to synthesize a variety of spatial experiences" (Downs and Stea, 1977, p. 141). In other words, distance cognition is inextricably related to environmental cognition generally. This raises two intriguing questions that are explored in this chapter: first is the overestimation of distance that characterizes distance cognition at the city scale, also apparent in the estimation of intercity distances at a regional scale. Second is errors in distance estimates influenced by variables such as sex, age, and degree of environmental learning that have been found to be important in environmental cognition generally (see Walmsley, 1988, pp. 11-49). To explore these questions, it is first necessary to know something of the factors that influence the accuracy of distance cognition.

Briggs (1976) has suggested that three sorts of factors influence estimates of cognitive distance: those related to the subject, those related to the stimulus, and those related to the interaction of the subject with the stimulus. Among factors related to the subject, age has been found to be important to the extent that the distance estimation skills of young children improve as they grow older (Matthews, 1981). The influence of sex is less clear. Postadolescent males are perhaps better than females of a similar age at distance estimation, possibly because of socialization rather than biology (Saegert and Hart, 1978), but the evidence for this is not always apparent (Evans, 1980).

In terms of factors related to the stimulus, settings with regular features (e.g., street patterns) tend to be more readily comprehended and their distance relations better understood than irregular settings, with a result that the overestimation of distance is less well marked in the former (Evans, 1980). However, small, densely settled areas with many road intersections can appear much larger than they really are (Walmsley, 1978). There is also evidence that downtown distances are overestimated more than out-of-town distances, possibly because the denser packing of land uses in downtown areas makes those areas seem larger, and possibly because of greater experiential travel times in downtown areas as a result of congestion (Golledge and Zannaras, 1973). Lee (1970), however, has debated this finding and produced evidence that out-of-town distances are more exaggerated, at least in a case study in Britain. This difference might of course merely reflect differences in the imageability and legibility of the towns in question (see Lynch, 1960); Golledge and Zannaras studied distances along a straight flat road, whereas Lee worked in a hilly area (Canter and Tagg, 1975).

In terms of factors related to the interaction between the subject and the stimulus, the attractiveness of the end point of an estimate seems critical. A positive evaluation foreshortens a journey (as in homeward bound journeys seeming shorter than outward bound journeys), and an increase in the "pleasingness" of a location results in a decrease in the mean error of distance estimates (Smith, 1984). The nature of a connecting path can also be important. Paths with more bends seem longer even when they are the same length (Sadalla and Magel, 1980), as do paths with more intersections, possibly because the greater amount of environmental information to be handled requires a greater storage area in the brain (Sadalla and Staplin, 1980a, 1980b).

A CASE STUDY

To investigate whether intercity distance estimates are exaggerated relative to real distance in the same manner as intracity distances, an experiment was undertaken involving tourists and permanent residents on the North Coast of New South Wales, Australia. The venue for the experiment was Coffs Harbour, located approximately halfway between Sydney (563 km) and Brisbane (427 km) (Figure 14.1). The city of Coffs Harbour has a population of about 45,000 and is the center of a thriving tourist trade. Indeed, it has been estimated that the area attracts well over half a million

FIGURE 14.1. The Study Area

visitors a year (New South Wales Tourism Commission, 1987). Other tourist centers are dotted up and down the coastline and the area is widely recognized for its subtropical climate, beaches, rainforests, and banana plantations. As a result of this multiplicity of tourist attractions and venues, the New South Wales state government has attempted to both promote and plan tourist development to the extent of issuing the *North Coast Region Tourism Development Strategy*. This strategy stresses the importance of people moving effectively and efficiently throughout the region to capitalize on the many attractions of the area. In other words, the state government is seeking to promote tourist activity in general by encouraging holidaymakers to visit attractions throughout the region.

Such a strategy can only work, of course, if visitors have an idea of where places are and, in particular, how far away they are. In this connection, it is interesting to note that the Central Mapping Authority of New South Wales has published a map specifically of the region, describing it as the "Holiday Coast." However, this map is not issued free but is sold through at a cost of approximately AUS $4.00 (US $3.00). Free maps are available from motoring organizations (e.g., the National Roads and Motorists Association), but these tend to be either statewide in their coverage or restricted to the environs of individual towns. In short, much of the emphasis in tourist promotion in the region is geared to encouraging patronage of attractions in widely separated locations, and yet very little material is available that instructs visitors about the distances to the locations in question. In the absence of such explicit guidance, visitors are likely to fall back on impressions of cognitive distance in many of their decisions about whether to visit certain places. It is therefore important to discover how accurate distance estimates are, because the success of much of the promotion seems to hinge on the assumption that tourists have a good knowledge of relative location.

The settlement pattern of eastern Australia is such that there are two primary cities and a large number of relatively small settlements. The two major cities (Sydney, population 2,989,070 at the 1986 census; Brisbane, population 1,037,815) were selected as stimuli in the distance estimation experiment because they are the centers from which Coffs Harbour draws most of its tourist trade (see Pigram, 1987). In addition, six other places were selected for use as stimuli: two of these were to the north of Coffs Harbour (Woolgoolga, population 2,346; Grafton, population 16,647), three to the south (Sawtell, population 7,905; Nambucca Heads, population 4,923; and Port Macquarie, population 22,884), and one inland to the west (Dorrigo, population 1,167). The settlement pattern is such that the stimuli used in the experiment could not be of a standard size. Rather, they were selected to give a range of distances from Coffs Harbour. Although small, each of the locations is an easily recognizable settlement. The actual distance from Coffs Harbour to each place is shown in Table 14.1.

Several methods can be used to measure cognitive distance. Subjects can be asked to state how many kilometers it is to certain places, they can be asked to mark the distances to a number of places on a scale calibrated in kilometers, or they can undertake pairwise comparisons. A ratio scale can be used whereby distances are estimated relative to a well-known datum, and inferences about distance can be made from freehand sketch maps. Day (1976) has suggested that the method used makes no difference to the accuracy of the estimates. It is, however, very difficult to isolate the influence of the measurement method because "no matter what type of yardstick we use to express our sense of cognitive distance, the resultant estimates express a complex of feelings about the places themselves as much as they represent a human scaling of simple geographical distance" (Downs and Stea, 1977, p. 142).

Given Day's argument that method is not critical, it was decided to use the simplest of all techniques: individuals were asked to state how far, in kilometers, they thought it was from Coffs Harbour to each of the eight places in question. A total of 115 tourists was selected randomly at motels, resorts, caravan parks, and in the street, thereby giving coverage of all different accommodation types. This group was in no way intended as a sample representative of the half million visitors that pass through the region each year. In addition, thirty permanent residents were randomly selected from dwellings within the city for comparative purposes. Again there was no way in which the representativeness of this group could be assessed. As a result, the two groups (tourists and residents) should be viewed from a statistical perspective as populations rather than samples and therefore analysis focuses on descriptive rather than inferential statistics (see Cadwallader, 1976). Once selected, all subjects were presented with a list of eight place names and asked to write down their distance estimates. They also completed a short questionnaire seeking personal information (sex, age, place of residence, mode of travel, length of stay in Coffs Harbour prior to interview, and the nature of the group [if any] with which they were traveling). If respondents had no idea at all of the distance to a place, they were not pressed to make a guess.

Results

The estimated distance to each location is shown in Table 14.1 for both tourists and permanent residents. The most obvious point to be noted in Table 14.1 is that cognitive distance was in all cases overestimated relative

TABLE 14.1. Estimates of Distance

City	Estimated Distance (km)		% Tourists Unable to Estimate	Standard Deviation as % of Mean		Real Distance (km)
	Tourists	Residents		Tourists	Residents	
Brisbane	445 (+4)[a]	472 (+11)	5	26	33	417
Dorrigo	75 (+17)	71 (+11)	30	48	37	64
Grafton	108 (+30)	94 (+13)	7	62	60	83
Nambucca Heads	65 (+25)	62 (+19)	20	64	32	52
Port Macquarie	168 (+3)	170 (+4)	7	32	25	163
Sawtell	20 (+97)	12 (+20)	13	121	31	10
Sydney	575 (+2)	647 (+15)	5	21	32	563
Woolgoolga	28 (+9)	27 (+4)	17	86	34	26

[a] The figures in parentheses indicate the mean percentage error in the distance estimates. Throughout the table, figures have been rounded to the nearest whole number.

to real distance. In other words, the overestimation of cognitive distance that has characterized studies at the intraurban scale is also apparent at the interurban scale.

Interesting differences emerged between tourists and permanent residents. Generally, tourists were more accurate than permanent residents in estimating long distances (Sydney, Brisbane) but less accurate in estimating short distances (Sawtell, Woolgoolga). Regression analysis showed that the relationship between cognitive and real distance for tourists was as follows:

Cognitive distance = 10.7 + 1.01 Real distance (r = +0.99)

For permanent residents, the equation was:

Cognitive distance = 1. 14 Real distance − 2.64 (r = +0. 99)

These equations mean that tourists overstate cognitive distance relative to permanent residents up to a real distance of about 160 km, whereupon permanent residents overestimate cognitive distance relative to tourists. This is an interesting finding, because 160 km is approximately the range of day trips for residents of Coffs Harbour. In other words, permanent residents tend to be more accurate in the area that they might be expected to know rather well. Beyond this distance, tourists performed better, which is consistent with the fact that many tourists have only recently traveled the road from either Sydney or Brisbane and therefore have more recent experience of the distances in question than most permanent residents.

All the permanent residents felt able to make an estimate of the distance to each of the stimuli. In contrast, there was never more than 95 percent of tourists who felt able to undertake the task, even in the case of Australia's largest city (Sydney). Generally, the proportion unable to make an estimate decreased with an increase in the population of the places in question (r = 0.48) and with increasing distance from Coffs Harbour (r = −0.59). These two variables are of course related because the two metropolitan centers, Sydney and Brisbane, are also the two most distant centers. The implication to be drawn is that big cities are reasonably well known, but that the regional network of smaller places is much less well known despite the attractions such places offer for tourists.

Studies of cognitive distance invariably identify high levels of variance in the estimates. This was certainly the case in the present study. Table 14.1 shows the standard deviation in the estimates of the distance to each place expressed as a percentage of the mean of those same estimates. Tourists exhibited a higher level of variance in their estimates for all places except

Sydney and Brisbane. Again, this probably reflects the fact that these metropolitan areas were home to more than 30 percent of the subjects. For tourists, the standard deviation expressed as a percentage of the mean declined as distance increased ($r = -0.75$). No such significant trend was apparent in the case of permanent residents ($r = -0.19$), indicating that the variance in the estimates for this group was reasonably uniform. A similar pattern emerged when the mean percentage error (a measure of the accuracy rather than the variability of the estimates) was examined for each group: for tourists there was a clear tendency for the mean percentage error to decrease as distance increased ($r = -0.49$). For permanent residents, the correlation was zero. Again, this is evidence that tourists do not have a clear idea of intertown distances on the "Holiday Coast."

It is clear from Table 14.1 that cognitive distance is overestimated relative to real distance and that there are differences between tourists and permanent residents, but that—as always—estimates differed greatly from one person to the next. This raises the question of whether different sorts of people are better at predicting distance than others. Table 14.2 suggests otherwise. Using data for tourists, and pooling estimates for all eight locations, the results show no difference at all in the mean percentage error for males and females. Likewise, there was next to no difference between residents of metropolitan areas and residents of country towns. In contrast, age did show a tendency for accuracy to improve as individuals grew older, presumably because older people have traveled more around the state. Similarly, there was a tendency for accuracy to improve the longer a tourist had been in Coffs Harbour, although the difference was only really apparent when the individuals had been there more than a week. Interestingly, those traveling by car were less accurate in their distance estimates than those traveling by other means (mainly bus). Perhaps the responsibility and effort of arranging one's own travel (rather than public transport) makes distances seem longer. Bus travelers might also benefit from commentaries by coach drivers and tour guides, many of whom might make a point of mentioning distance. Finally, there was an interesting tendency for the accuracy of estimates to vary according to the sort of group to which tourists belonged. Those individuals traveling only with a spouse or partner tended to be least accurate, and those traveling with friends tended to be most accurate, with family groups occupying an intermediate position. Perhaps the extent to which the surrounding tourist attractions (i.e., places up and down the coast) are explored or even discussed as opportunities varied according to group type. Groups of friends might be more adventurous than couples. It might also be that group size is critical: the larger the group, the more discussion there might be before a consensus is

TABLE 14.2. The Mean Percentage Errors in Distance Estimates by Tourists

Variable	Mean Error
Age	
< 30	+27%
31-40	+25
41-50	+19
> 50	+17
Sex	
Female	+23
Male	+23
Place of residence	
Metropolitan	+21
Country town	+22
Days spent in Coffs Harbour prior to interview	
0-1	+28
2-3	+24
4-7	+24
8 +	+6
Mode of travel	
Car	+25
Other	+7
Group	
Spouse/partner	+28
Family	+21
Friends	+11

reached on what places to visit. Members of large groups might therefore come to learn of a wider range of places than couples and family groups.

CONCLUSIONS AND IMPLICATIONS

"The world in the head is a warped and twisted model of the real world" (Downs and Stea, 1977, p. 144), and the high level of variance in distance estimates hints at the many factors that might influence the estimation process. We should not therefore expect to find estimates of cognitive distance conforming to a simple set of relationships. Because a wide variety of experiences can influence cognitive distance, the links between distance estimates and independent variables such as age and sex are likely to be less than clear cut. We should remember too that cognitive distance can be measured in absolute terms (e.g., in kilometers), in ratio terms (e.g., by referring to a well-known and familiar route), and in relative terms (e.g., pairwise comparisons based on assessments of which place is nearer). Absolute terms have been adopted in the present study, despite the fact that most people perhaps "rely largely upon relative judgements, resort to ratio judgements only when finer discrimination becomes a matter of significance, and elect to employ absolute judgement only rarely and, even then, with hesitation, uncertainty and qualification" (Robinson, 1982, p. 284). There is of course no pretense in the present study that, if we could discover the metrics underlying an individual's notions of cognitive distance, we would be able to understand that individual's travel behavior. Too many other predisposing and constraining variables are involved.

The fact of the matter is that "we know relatively little about cognitive distance since it is so unconscious, so automatic that it is relegated to 'second nature' status" (Downs and Stea, 1973, p. 317). The case study reported in this article nevertheless has been valuable in many ways. It has shown that, at the intercity scale, cognitive distance is exaggerated relative to real distance, much as it is at the intracity scale. More important, visitors to a major tourist region have been shown to have fairly inaccurate impressions of the distance to the tourist attractions in the region. The fact that the cognitive distance estimates of tourists were often very much in excess of real distances suggests that patronage levels might well be less than if distance was accurately cognized. Such a conclusion fits well with what is known about the friction of distance in tourist travel. It also suggests that some venues might be substituted for others as foci for travel on the basis of mistaken impressions of distance. This must be considered worrying in a region where an explicit role of government policy is the encouragement of visitation at a variety of places. The main implication to be drawn from the present study is, therefore, that promotional and marketing activity needs to be directed to making tourists aware of real distances.

The results of the study suggest that a high level of variance characterizes the distance estimates of tourists. Thus, different tourist market segments seem not to exist, at least as far as distance cognition is concerned. Attention needs to be directed, therefore, at making all tourists aware of the relative location of attractions.

Presently, tourism promotion committees in each town produce brochures and publicity about their own local areas, but no authority seems to take responsibility for a regional perspective. The main source of information on distances at the regional scale is in fact a map that is available only at a few outlets, at certain times and at a cost. If the regional promotion of tourism is to go beyond exhortations to visitors to travel around, this situation needs to be rectified. The findings of this study suggest that cognitive distance is sufficiently different from real distance to both warrant further study and justify the circulation of promotional literature that explicitly highlights location as well as facilities in the marketing of places.

CONCEPT DEFINITIONS

Cognitive distance (sometimes also called *subjective distance*): The impression formed in the mind of the distance between places that are not directly visible. Such distance estimates are invariably greater than real distance.

Gravity model: A model which proposes that interaction between places is directly proportional to the size of those places and inversely proportional to the distance between the places.

Manhattan metric: The measurement of distance in terms of the number of city blocks rather than in terms of units such as meters.

Mental map (sometimes also called *cognitive map*): The simplified images that people build up in their minds to cope with the information overload that results from a real world that is too big and too complex to be understood in its entirety.

Perceived distance: Estimate of the distance to a visible object.

REVIEW QUESTIONS

1. When was the concept of cognitive distance (subjective distance) first discussed?
2. How can cognitive distance be measured?
3. Why might homeward-bound journeys seem shorter than outward-bound journeys?
4. Why might estimates of short distances be exaggerated more than estimates of long distances?
5. What factors influence the accuracy of distance estimates?
6. Why is there often a high level of variance when a group of people individually estimate the distance to a set of places?

7. Why might residents of the North Coast of New South Wales be better than tourists at estimating the distance to relatively close places (say, up to 80 km)?

8. Are some sorts of people better than others at estimating cognitive distance? Give examples.

9. How might the concept of cognitive distance be usefully applied in other recreational or tourist settings?

10. What are the limitations of studies of cognitive distance with specific reference to the study that forms the basis of this chapter?

REFERENCES

Abler, R., D. Janelle, A. Philbrick, and J. Sommer (1977). *Human Geography in a Shrinking World*. North Scituate, MA: Duxbury.

Brennan, T. (1948). *Midland City*. London: Dobson.

Briggs, R. (1973). "Urban Distance Cognition." In *Image and Environment*, R.M. Downs and D. Stea, eds. Chicago: Aldine, pp. 361-388.

Briggs, R. (1976). "Methodologies for the Measurement of Cognitive Distance." In *Environmental Knowing*, G.T. Moore and R.G. Golledge, eds. Stroudsburg, PA: Dowden, Hutchinson and Ross, pp. 325-334.

Cadwallader, M. (1976). "Cognitive Distance in Intraurban Space." In *Environmental Knowing*, G.T. Moore and R.G. Golledge, eds. Stroudsburg, PA: Dowden, Hutchinson and Ross, pp. 316-324.

Cadwallader, M. (1981). "Towards a Cognitive Gravity Model." *Regional Studies*, 15: 275-284.

Canter, D.V., and S.K. Tagg (1975). "Distance Estimation in Cities." *Environment and Behavior*, 7: 59-80.

Day, R.A. (1976). "Urban Distance Cognition: Review and Contribution." *Australian Geographer*, 3: 193-200.

Downs, R.M., and D. Stea, eds. (1973). *Image and Environment*. Chicago: Aldine.

Downs, R.M. and D. Stea (1977). *Maps in Minds*. New York: Harper and Row.

Evans, G.W. (1980). "Environmental Cognition." *Psychological Bulletin*, 88: 259-287.

Golledge, R.G. and G. Zannaras (1973). "Cognitive Approaches to the Study of Human Spatial Behaviour." In *Image and Environment*, R.M. Downs and D. Stea, eds. Chicago: Aldine, pp. 59-94.

Hall, E.T. (1959). *The Silent Language*. New York: Doubleday.

Jakle, J.A., S. Brunn, and C.C. Roseman (1976). *Human Spatial Behaviour*. North Scituate, MA: Duxbury.

Lee, T.R. (1970). "Perceived Distance as a Function of Direction Within the City." *Environment and Behaviour*, 2: 40-51.

Lowrey, R.A. (1973). "A Method for Analyzing Distance Concepts of Urban Residents." In *Image and Environment*, R.M. Downs and D. Stea, eds. Chicago: Aldine, pp. 338-360.

Lynch, K. (1960). *The Image of the City.* Cambridge, MA: MIT Press.

Matthews, M. H. (1981). "Children's Perception of Urban Distance." *Area*, 13: 333-343.

New South Wales Tourism Commission (1987). *North Coast Region Tourism Development Strategy.* Sydney: NSWTC.

Pearce, P.L. and P.F. Stringer (1991). "Psychology and Tourism." *Annals of Tourism Research*, 18: 136-154.

Pigram, J.J. (1987). *Tourism in Coffs Harbour.* Coffs Harbour, Australia: University of New England Department of Continuing Education.

Pocock, D., and R. Hudson (1978). *Images of the Urban Environment.* London: Macmillan.

Porteous, J.D. (1977). *Environment and Behaviour.* Reading, MA: Addison-Wesley.

Rapoport, A. (1969). *House, Form and Culture.* Englewood Cliffs, NJ: Prentice-Hall.

Robinson, M.E. (1982). "Absolute and Relative Strategies in Urban Distance Cognition." *Area*, 14: 283-286.

Sadalla, E.K. and S.G. Magel (1980). "The Perception of Traversed Distance." *Environment and Behaviour*, 12: 65-80.

Sadalla, E.K. and L.J. Staplin (1980a). "The Perception of Traversed Distance: Intersections." *Environment and Behaviour*, 12: 167-182.

Sadalla, E.K. and L.J. Staplin (1980b). "An Information Storage Model for Distance Cognition." *Environment and Behaviour*, 12: 183-193.

Saegert, S. and R.A. Hart (1978). "The Development of Environmental Competence in Girls and Boys." In *Play: Anthropological Perspectives*. M. Salter, ed. West Point, NY: Leisure Press.

Smith, C.D. (1984). "The Relationship Between the Pleasingness of Landmarks and the Judgement of Distance in Cognitive Maps." *Journal of Environmental Psychology*, 4: 229-234.

Sommer, R. (1969). *Personal Space.* Englewood Cliffs, NJ: Prentice-Hall. Thomson, D.L. (1963). "New Concept: Subjective Distance." *Journal of Retailing*, 39: 1-6.

Walmsley, D.J. (1978). "Stimulus Complexity in Distance Distortion." *Professional Geographer*, 30: 14-19.

Walmsley, D.J. (1988). *Urban Living.* London: Longman.

PART IV: RESEARCH METHODS
IN TOURIST BEHAVIOR

Part IV of this book pertains to the two main methods of conducting tourism marketing research, qualitative and quantitative. While both methods vary substantially, the combination of the two techniques produces perhaps the most efficient outcome. Qualitative analysis, while insightful and valuable, is less rigorous, and its interpretation depends on the subjective judgment of the researcher. Quantitative analysis, as its name suggests, is the measurement, assessment, and interpretation of numerical data by using mathematical or statistical manipulation.

Both methods are discussed extensively in the following two chapters. Chapter 15, by Luckett, Ganesh, and Gillett, analyzes the usefulness of quantitative techniques. Quantitative marketing researchers believe that for a business enterprise to be successful, it must have numerical data on who the customers are, what motivates them, and how they perceive the business and its particular tourism products, as well as what they rate as important versus unimportant in their decision-making processes. The chapter describes two basic techniques to answer these questions, factor analysis and perceptual mapping.

Decrop, in Chapter 16, provides a basic examination of the need and uses of qualitative research methods in tourism. Although this fairly new research method in the tourism industry is used to provide preliminary information for further study by quantitative methods, this does not make it less important. Qualitative research helps marketers understand tourists better through in-depth analyses by interviews, observations, and associative techniques.

Chapter 15

Quantitative Tools in Tourism Research: An Application of Perceptual Maps

Michael Luckett
Jaishankar Ganesh
Peter Gillett

LEARNING OBJECTIVES

By the end of the chapter you should be able to:

- Understand the concept and importance of product positioning
- Identify market opportunities and repositioning strategies
- Understand how marketers identify and implement a marketing strategy using perceptual maps
- Know how perceptual maps can be utilized as a strategic management tool
- Know the role factor analysis plays in creating a perceptual map
- Understand the ideal vector and how it can influence product positioning decisions
- Understand the basic processes of creating a perceptual map
- Know the types of information collected in order to create a perceptual map
- Be able to interpret a perceptual map

INTRODUCTION

After years of school and much hard work, Paul James was ecstatic. He had just been promoted to be the manager of the Desert Sun Hotel and Casino in Las Vegas. The Desert Sun Hotel and Casino is prominently located on the famous Las Vegas strip, surrounded by other famous hotels and casinos. Traditionally, the Desert Sun has done quite well catering to a group of customers locally referred to as the "lone gambler" market. These customers demand and receive a high level of hotel services at cut-rate prices. Paul has realized that there is little to no profit to be made providing these customers with things such as room service, suites, restaurants, or Broadway-type entertainment; however, they are high-stake rollers and bring in significant profits on the casino's gaming tables. Although Paul was just promoted last week, for the past few years, while working as assistant manager, he had begun to notice a different type of customer visiting Las Vegas. These customers are quite different from the traditional lone gambler market because they are largely families on vacation. Paul determined that while the "family market" did not spend significant amounts of money gambling, they did spend a substantial amount of vacation dollars on family-style entertainment, hotel amenities, and restaurants.

The Las Vegas market is extremely competitive. Every year more hotels and casinos are being constructed, with increasingly sophisticated themes to lure consumers and their money. Consumers have also become more demanding and particular in what they expect from a hotel or casino. To maintain and protect the Desert Sun's position within the Las Vegas market, Paul James realizes that it is essential to keep in close contact with his customers. He would like to conduct some market research on the family market consumer as a potential new target market for the Desert Sun. While corporate management seems devoted to the lone gambler segment, Paul is suspicious that the family market segment is being overlooked and wants to explore the potential of this new market opportunity. Among the questions he would like to answer are: How are these consumers different from the lone gamblers? How do they perceive the Desert Sun Hotel and Casino relative to its competition? What do they consider the most important attributes for a hotel and casino? How can Paul position the Desert Sun to appeal to these consumers?

MARKET RESEARCH AS A MANAGERIAL TOOL

As any manager approaches a marketing research question, the number of options available can seem overwhelming. Depending upon the nature of the problem, the amount of time available, access to a consumer sample, and the amount of money available to spend, the choices can become confusing. Essentially there are two basic approaches that can be taken in gathering data to answer marketing questions: qualitative and quantitative.

Qualitative techniques focus on gathering data that are largely descriptive. This descriptive data, while extremely rich and detailed, can be labor intensive to gather, and can often take significant amounts of time to properly execute and interpret. Quantitative techniques focus on gathering data that is statistically oriented. Typically, consumer responses using quantitative methods are limited to responses to survey questions. While both methods enable researchers to draw inferences into consumer markets, each has its own advantages and disadvantages. This chapter illustrates the use of one important quantitative tool managers use to gain insight into making strategic marketing decisions—*perceptual maps.*

CONSUMER PERCEPTIONS AND PRODUCT POSITIONING

Recently Audi has been running advertisements comparing its cars to comparable cars made by Mercedes-Benz and BMW. According to the ads, German automotive experts rated Audi cars ahead of both Mercedes and BMW. . . . *Do you believe that? Probably not. Is it true? Does it matter?* (Ries and Trout, 1993)

The point that Ries and Trout (1981, 1993) are trying to make is that consumer perceptions are powerful, and in the ultimate analysis *marketing is not a battle of products, it is a battle of perceptions.* Perceptions affect the way we behave as consumers, but many times they are not based in reality but rather our perception of reality (Ganesh and Oakenfull, 1996). Consumers make decisions based upon their perceptions, regardless of their accuracy or inaccuracy. It is around these perceptions that marketers must build their competitive strategies.

Positioning is the cornerstone of a firm's marketing strategy. Product positioning is the process of creating a unique position for a company's product within the mind of the consumer. Product positioning benefits a company in many different ways. It allows a company to create a competitive advantage for itself in the marketplace, to create a consistent image for consumers regarding a product offering, and to utilize its particular strengths while seeking specific markets.

Positioning relies on the idea that there are multiple ways in which a product can provide added value to consumers. Seldom will any one product or service be able to provide superior value across all aspects of a product offering. It is simply beyond the economic or physical scope of most companies to provide such an all-encompassing value. A number of avenues exist whereby companies can create a unique image for their own product or service. For example, different chains in the fast-food industry position themselves to create a unique image for themselves. McDonald's is positioned as a 'family fun" restaurant, whereas Wendy's positions itself toward more discerning adults seeking food quality. Product positioning ultimately determines the way in which consumers perceive a company's products or services. Therefore, it is the driving force behind most marketing mix variables: product, price, distribution, and promotion. These elements are used to create a unique and competitively advantageous corporate or brand position in the mind of the consumer relative to the competition. McDonald's reinforces its family positioning strategy throughout its marketing mix. It appeals to families with small children via playgrounds attached to its stores, Happy Meals, the Ronald McDonald character, and constant promotions and tie-ins with popular Disney movie characters. Together these elements reinforce the image of a family restaurant that McDonalds is trying to build.

Important to the development of a coherent and effective positioning strategy is the degree to which each individual element of the marketing mix supports one another. For example, if the manufacturer of an extremely expensive watch sold that watch through a discount retailer, consumer confusion might result from the inconsistencies within the marketing mix or positioning strategy. The thought of paying thousands of dollars for a watch at a discount department store is counterintuitive for the consumer. The same confusion would result if an inexpensive watch of suspect quality were sold exclusively through high-end jewelry stores. Every element of the marketing mix must combine to create a consistent image for a particular product. The product being sold must be consistent with the price, the distribution strategy, and the type of promotional media vehicles chosen.

Positioning is critical to a firm because products that have been tailored to suit a specific market segment generally perform better than products that attempt to attract all market segments. Market segmentation involves breaking a large group of potential customers (i.e., all fast-food eaters) into smaller groups of consumers with similar wants and needs (e.g., hamburgers, fried chicken, tacos, or pizza). The process of grouping similar consumers together is called market segmentation. This allows companies to selectively target specific segments with specialized marketing programs. A product that offers average performance across all segments will generally lose out to products that are tuned to fit the specific needs of particular segments (Czepiel, 1992).

Positioning allows companies to utilize their distinctive competencies to their best advantage. Some companies may have excellent distribution systems and other companies may be well known for their production efficiency and quality, while others may have created unique images through advertising and promotion. Positioning allows companies to play to their strengths and downplay their weaknesses. Wal-Mart is well-known for its distribution and pricing efficiency; Macy's is valued by consumers for its high-quality products and services; Little Caesar's pizza has gained a competitive advantage by using very humorous advertising and creative promotions. Each of these companies has used positioning as a tool to take advantage of its respective strengths. The decisions made when positioning a product will determine which product benefits will be stressed in the promotional campaign and which consumers will be targeted. Consumers evaluate these products based upon the positioning strategy that has been created for them. Wendy's fast-food restaurants identified a segment of the market that wanted low fat, but fast food. The positioning strategy involved developing a line of new products (e.g., baked potatoes, pocket pitas, and salads) to appeal to this market segment and then advertising these new products as healthy fast-food alternatives.

APPROACHES TO POSITIONING

Product positioning is critical to the success of a product or service in the marketplace. The position a brand occupies within the collective consumer mind may determine the ultimate success or failure of the product offering far more than objective product attributes. So, it is important to examine the various methods or approaches that one can use when positioning a product in a competitive environment. Aaker and Shansby (1982) suggest six approaches to a firm's positioning strategy. These include positioning by: (a) attribute, (b) price-quality, (c) use or applications, (d) product user, (e) product class, and (f) the competitor.

Positioning by attribute is perhaps the most commonly used strategy. The idea is to associate your product or service with a desired attribute, product feature, or customer benefit. For instance, the Desert Sun Hotel and Casino could position itself as providing the most value for the money, or as a luxury European-style spa/resort. These may be attributes that have been ignored by competing hotels and casinos in Las Vegas. While increasing the complexity of positioning and implementation, many companies opt to position themselves based upon more than one attribute or benefit simultaneously. Miller Brewing Company successfully marketed its Lite Beer for years under the advertising slogan, "Great Taste—Less Filling." Both of these are benefits that Lite Beer offered consumers.

Other hotels seek to position themselves along the *price-quality continuum.* Hotels adopting this strategy will use the price of their product as an indicator of its quality. The more features a product offers, the higher a product's level of performance, or the more services offered, the higher the price. The Desert Sun may choose to position itself as a premium-priced, full-service hotel and casino that caters to its client's desires. Setting a high price for its suites and services will serve as a perceptual cue to hotel guests that they are getting the best possible service.

Another alternative is to position with respect to a *particular product use or application.* This positioning might be achieved for the Desert Sun in a number of different ways. Hotels and casinos can establish reputations for holding certain types of events, such as championship prizefighting or devoting extensive facilities to hold large conferences. Therefore, whenever a large convention is looking for a place to stage a large trade show, or a boxing promoter is looking to stage the next heavyweight championship fight, the Desert Sun would be positioned to benefit.

Positioning by the *product user* or class of users is also a viable strategy. By associating with a particular social class or celebrity endorser through promotion, hotels can become identified to a certain class or type of user. Caesars Palace is known as a very upper-class casino, while the Hard Rock Cafe seeks out a younger, less socially regarded consumer. Whereas the Rolling Stones may endorse the Hard Rock Cafe, it is far more likely that Frank Sinatra would have endorsed Caesars Palace. Creating strategic alliances with celebrity endorsers can greatly enhance the image or position of the Desert Sun.

Often companies will position their brands according to a particular *product class.* Many low-alcohol beers choose to position themselves with the soft drink product category as opposed to the beer product category. In doing so, they may appeal to an entirely different and much larger group of drinkers. Similarly, the Desert Sun could position itself as a "theme park" attraction instead of a casino, or perhaps as a luxury spa rather than a hotel. By associating with different product classes it can potentially expand or limit its customer base.

The final strategy identified is to *position with respect to a competitor.* Firms may be able to exploit the well-known reputations of market leaders by comparing themselves to these companies. Often this is achieved through comparative advertising, which may demonstrate certain similarities in one or more product attributes between a market leader and the competing firm. The Desert Sun may choose to take out ads in travel magazines that make favorable comparisons for the services and features of its hotel and casino with those of a well-known competitor such as the MGM Grand or the Luxor.

Regardless of the positioning strategy ultimately selected, the results of the positioning effort should be measurable. Just like any other marketing objective a firm may establish, it is important that progress toward the objective be quantifiable at some level. To determine the appropriate positioning strategy for a new product or service, or to evaluate the optimum repositioning approach for an existing brand, the marketer needs to know consumers' current perceptions of existing brands. *Perceptual mapping* is a technique that allows marketers to schematically represent consumer perceptions of competing products or services. There are multiple ways of creating perceptual maps; this chapter will demonstrate the use of one such technique, factor analysis, for creating perceptual maps.

PERCEPTUAL MAPS

A picture is worth a thousand words. Managers use graphs to represent complex sales charts, organizations use charts in their annual reports, and students study tables that summarize complex information in order to better understand some process. Pictures are often used to help reduce a complex set of information or ideas to a more simple structure where one is able to grasp the concepts more quickly (Dolan, 1991). With similar ease, market researchers are able to take "pictures" of consumers' perceptions of a competitive marketplace using a technique called perceptual mapping. These maps, detailing a company's position relative to its competition in a given market, allow managers to make adjustments in their marketing strategy to better serve their customers and hopefully gain market share.

Perceptual mapping allows marketers to create a visual representation of a competitive marketplace, holding a wealth of information in an easily interpretable format. Marketers are able to see how consumers perceive their products, as well as those of their competitors. This allows companies to determine if the positioning strategy they are pursuing for a particular brand is being achieved in the marketplace, i.e., do consumers perceive the product as the company intends it to be perceived? For perceptual mapping to be considered a truly useful managerial tool, a number of conditions must be met. First, it is important of the dimensions upon which the map is based are relevant to consumers when they evaluate that particular product category. Marketers should also know the relative importance of these attributes in the consumer's decision-making process. Second, data must be gathered on a sufficient number of competitors within the market to get an accurate feel for the marketplace. Third, these dimensions need to be actionable. The dimensions upon which perceptual maps are built need to be measurable and controllable by the firm. Some experts argue that many current product positioning models focus too intently on the map itself rather than focusing on how companies can achieve the desired position on that map for their products (Kaul and Rao, 1995).

Perceptual mapping focuses on a product's psychological positioning in the mind of the consumer, not on the actual physical characteristics that the product contains. This does not mean that a product's physical characteristics are unimportant, but rather that these tangible characteristics act as cues upon which consumers form their psychological perceptions. Research has shown that over time the functional characteristics of a product are less important in determining a consumer's product choice. More important in ultimately determining product selection, especially for mature product categories, are things such as a product's image, personality, and brand reputation (Lannon, 1991). The longer a product has been on the marketplace, the more familiar consumers are with the product category. Consumer preferences will change over time as their knowledge of the product category and the competing brands becomes more sophisticated. It is expected that a competitive brand within the product category will contain certain prerequisite product attributes; therefore, consumers base their choices on less tangible elements such as reputation, image, and personality. For example, as the ice cream market matured, a number of companies (e.g., Ben and Jerry's, Häagen-Dazs, Edy's) began to develop a line of premium ice creams to appeal to sophisticated and demanding consumer wants. The personality of Ben and Jerry flavors such as "Chunky Monkey," "Chubby Hubby" and "Cherry Garcia" gave them a competitive advantage created through positioning.

As new products are launched into a competitive marketplace, perceptual maps can become extremely valuable tools because of the insight that they provide into a competitive marketplace both before and after market rollout for a new product. While a new product is being developed, perceptual maps can allow marketers to identify areas that may be void of competition, yet still contain viable consumer demand. These may be ideal areas for the development of new products so as to avoid intense immediate competition. Also, with prior knowledge about one's potential competitors, it is possible to study their marketing strategy, look for potential "chinks in their competitive armor," and position your new product offering to its best advantage. Maps may reveal potential new areas of the market that can be targeted or ways that an existing brand can be repositioned.

Once a new product has been developed, perceptual mapping can be used to assess a firm's positioning efforts. Do consumers perceive the product in the manner the company desires? A company may be attempting to position its new product offering as very similar or contrary to competitive offerings. Perceptual maps can provide key managerial insight into what is working and what needs to be revised regarding a firm's positioning efforts. Perceptual maps may indicate whether marketers need to make adjustments in a brand that is not being perceived as intended.

Finally, in addition to identifying new product opportunities and monitoring a firm's positioning efforts, perceptual maps can help discover what consumers consider their ideal product. This idealized product can provide valuable information when a company is repositioning an existing brand (e.g., creating a new image in the mind of the consumer) that is perceived as outdated. As the old product is being redesigned and new features are being considered, the idealized product, as revealed by a perceptual map, can communicate the direction designers need to take. If a certain product attribute emerges as being very strong in an ideal product, then this product attribute certainly needs to be considered when redesigning or repositioning the brand. This technique can help determine whether a competitive advantage is best sought out through physical product benefits, service issues, or other factors. Consumers may not and often do not value the same attributes as a company's research and development department.

CREATING A PERCEPTUAL MAP

A perceptual map can be created in a number of ways. Perhaps the best and most reliable method is one whereby consumers rate various brands within a product category on a number of relevant product characteristics. The information gathered is presented on a two-dimensional map where all brands are represented. The two dimensions used for the axes on the perceptual map are determined based upon which two factors reveal the most insight into the data. Regardless of the number of original product attributes or factors that are considered, the data is ultimately reduced to the two or at most three relevant dimensions, using factor analysis.

Factor analysis is a generic name given to a class of multivariate statistical techniques whose primary purpose is data reduction and summarization. Broadly speaking, this class of technique examines the interrelationships among a large number of variables and tries to explain these relationships in terms of a few (mostly two) common underlying dimensions, also called factors.

For example, to understand the perceptions and preferences of the family market segment of Las Vegas consumers, a researcher may collect a variety of data on consumer attitudes toward hotels, casinos, entertainment choices, and restaurants. This would result in a tremendous number of variables being examined, making it extremely difficult to interpret the data. By using factor analysis, the researcher is able to reduce the large number of variables gathered into a much smaller number of underlying dimensions or factors. Although these factors are more abstract, they are able to capture and summarize the most important aspects of the information contained in the initial data. To illustrate the power of factor analysis in action, this chapter examines a consumer behavior example in the athletic shoe market.

RESEARCH DESIGN

Due to the complex nature of the hotel and casino market, we use the athletic shoe market as an example. This allows us to consider many of the factors that affect the successful development of a positioning strategy. Specifically, the athletic shoe market is fragmented, with consumers expressing distinct preferences for different product forms (e.g., cross-training, tennis, running, aerobics, hiking, etc.), and with brands clearly targeted to specific segments. Positioning in the athletic shoe industry is based upon identifiable attributes such as comfort, styling, affordability, ease of maintenance, etc., and brand image. Although this example focuses on the athletic shoe market, it is not difficult to imagine similar maps being constructed for the hotel and casino market in Las Vegas.

Instrument Design and Data Collection

Prior to construction of the perceptual map, it is important that consumers are asked the right questions. The researcher should identify the various product attributes (features) based on which consumers compare the various competing brands, before arriving at their purchase decisions. To determine all relevant product attributes and the appropriate competitors, the research process typically begins in an exploratory fashion. One common technique used at this stage is the focus group. Focus groups typically contain six to eight consumers led by a moderator. The moderator directs the discussion of all group members in order to reveal certain information regarding the product category, attributes, and competitors. Through a series of focus groups for this chapter, consumers were asked to talk about the various attributes they sought in a pair of athletic shoes, and the influence of these attributes on their purchase decisions.

Based upon these focus group discussions, a list of product attributes and brands were selected as representative of the overall athletic shoe market. The twelve attributes identified based on the focus groups were: (1) comfortable, (2) good for standing on your feet a lot, (3) cushioning support, (4) has a good fit, (5) very lightweight, (6) affordability, (7) easy to clean, (8) good traction, (9) waterproofing, (10) distinctive brand logo, (11) up-to-date styling, and (12) versatility. The ten brands of athletic shoes included in the study were: Nike, Reebok, Fila, Esprit, Adidas, Airwalk, K-Swiss, L.A. Gear, Converse, and New Balance.

A questionnaire was developed that contained items measuring respondents': (a) level of familiarity with each brand; (b) prior brand usage/purchase behavior; (c) perception of each brand on each product attribute (as measured on a five-point scale, indicating how strongly the respondent agrees or disagrees with statements such as: "_____ (fill in name of a brand) feel very comfortable"); (d) importance of each attribute to the respondent (measured on a five-point scale ranging from extremely important to not at all important); (e) ranking of the ten brands indicating order of preference (1 = most preferred; 10 = least preferred); and (f) demographic information (age, sex, and marital status). A copy of the questionnaire appears in the Appendix of this chapter.

A sample of about 250 consumers was surveyed. Table 15.1 provides some information regarding the basic characteristics of the sample. The consumers' responses were then factor analyzed to examine the relationships between the attributes and to extract the underlying dimensions/factors to plot the perceptual map. Results of the analysis, in the form of a factor loading matrix, can be seen in Table 15.2.

The factor loading matrix is a table that displays the factor loadings (correlations between the original variables and the factors) of all variables on each factor. Each column of the matrix represents a separate factor. The numbers represent the factor loadings for each variable on each factor. The factor loadings indicate the extent to which each product attribute and the individual factors are related. High scores (either positive or negative) indicate a strong relationship, while low scores reflect a small correlation or level of interrelatedness. Factor loadings not only aid in the interpretation of the factors, but also in their labeling.

As can be observed from Table 15.2, the five attributes that loaded highly on the first factor were: comfortable (0.84635), good for standing on your feet a lot (0.85669), cushioning support (0.82822), has a good fit (0.80753), and very lightweight (0.64213). Researchers commonly apply a descriptive name to a factor based upon the relative factor loadings of the product attributes; therefore, the first factor or dimension was named "Comfort." The two attributes that loaded highly on the second factor were distinctive brand logo (0.87583) and up-to-date styling (0.74356), resulting in this dimension being labeled "Distinctive Styling." The third dimension, termed "Maintenance," had two attributes with high factor loadings: easy to clean (0.62812) and waterproofing (0.87328). The attrib-

TABLE 15.1. Sample Characteristics

Demographics:

Sex	%	Age	%	Marital Status	%
Male	55.8%	Less than 20	3.1%	Single	82.5%
Female	44.2%	20-24	71.2%	Married	13.4%
		25-29	13.8%	Divorced	4.1%
		30-34	5.7%		
		Greater than 34	6.2%		

Athletic Shoe Usage:

Athletic Shoe Ownership	%	Pairs purchased in last year	%
1 pair	20.2%	1 pair	50.9%
2 pair	39.2%	2 pair	32.6%
3 pair	21.5%	3 pair	10.1%
4 or more pair	19.1%	4 or more pair	6.4%

ute affordability (0.91436) loaded highly on the fourth and final dimension, termed "Affordability."

The perceptual map (Exhibit 15.1) shows where each brand is positioned relative to other brands, on two of the four factors: "Comfort" (factor 1) and "Style" (factor 2). It is customary to draw perceptual maps on two factors at a time, since a picture with more than two dimensions (three dimensions or more) is difficult to interpret. Perceptual maps can be

TABLE 15.2. Results of Factor Analysis for Athletic Shoes

Product Attribute	Factor 1 Comfort	Factor 2 Distinctive Style	Factor 3 Maintenance	Factor 4 Affordable
Feels comfortable	0.846	0.161	0.108	-0.022
Good for standing	0.857	0.125	0.125	-0.004
Cushioning support	0.828	0.232	0.100	-0.066
Good fit	0.808	0.251	0.143	0.094
Lightweight	0.642	0.167	0.099	0.238
Distinctive brand logo/symbol	0.185	0.876	0.056	0.017
Up-to-date styling	0.178	0.743	0.105	-0.032
Easy to clean	0.152	0.196	0.628	0.267
Waterproof	0.182	0.030	0.873	-0.159
Affordable	0.035	-0.053	-0.043	0.914

drawn based on any two of the factors. Our choice of "Comfort" and "Style" was just to illustrate the usefulness of perceptual maps. The perceptual maps also contain "ideal" vectors (based upon attribute importance responses). The brand positions should be examined with respect to this ideal vector.

INTERPRETING PERCEPTUAL MAPS

An examination of the perceptual map (see Exhibit 15.1) reveals the ten competing brands of athletic shoes rated on the two dimensions. "Comfort" is represented along the horizontal axis and "Distinctive Style" is along the vertical axis. In the upper-right-hand quadrant of the perceptual map only two brands appear, Nike and Reebok, which are the two leading-brands in the marketplace. Both brands are perceived by consumers to have high levels of comfort and a strong distinctive style. Nike is per-

EXHIBIT 15.1. Target Market's Perception of Athletic Shoes
(Comfort versus Distinctive Style)

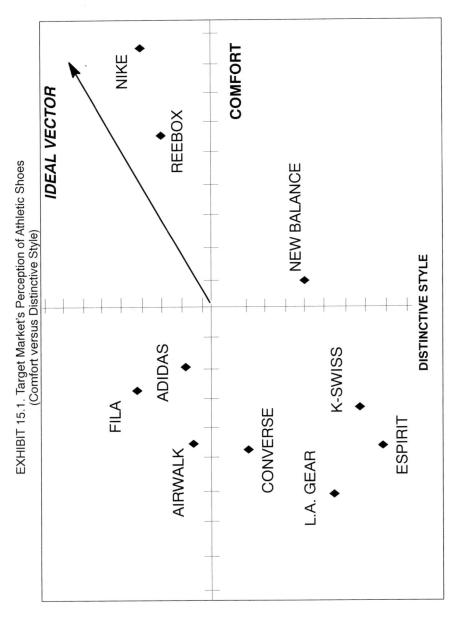

ceived as both more comfortable and having more distinctive styling than Reebok.

Nike and Reebok are also located in the direction of the ideal vector. The ideal vector is constructed by asking consumers how important the various product attributes are to them when purchasing athletic shoes. It represents the consumers' relative preference between the two dimensions and suggests the positioning for an idealized product that consumers would want along these two dimensions.

The lower-right-hand quadrant holds only one brand, New Balance. New Balance is perceived by consumers to be somewhat unstylish and only moderately comfortable. New Balance, if redesigning their existing product line or revamping their promotional strategy, should consider emphasizing the comfort and styling of their shoes to move in the direction of the ideal vector.

Both the upper and lower quadrants on the left-hand side of the perceptual map become more interesting. These quadrants contain the bulk of the competitors in the marketplace. Seven of the ten brands find themselves perceived as marginally uncomfortable. Whereas Fila, Adidas, and Airwalk are seen as being somewhat distinctively styled, Converse, L.A. Gear, K-Swiss, and Esprit are perceived as less than stylish. The proximity of the various brands to one another can indicate the degree to which these brands are perceived as being similar. Brands located closely to one another may be perceived as direct competitors.

CONCLUSION

Despite their relative simplicity, perceptual maps are powerful strategic tools because they allow managers to absorb a tremendous amount of data in a visual format. Perceptual maps intuitively make sense and are able to provide very specific information regarding strategic recommendations for repositioning efforts, new product development, or consumers' ideal level for specific product attributes.

Although perceptual mapping is an extremely powerful heuristic, it does have a number of limitations. Perceptual maps are not dynamic. They represent a static view of a competitive marketplace as a particular point in time and do not provide data regarding how these brands achieved their current positions. To track this type of information, a series of perceptual maps using the same factors would need to be taken over a long period of time. However, while it may be possible to achieve this for a product category for a short period of time, it is extremely difficult to do so over the long run due to the changing nature of consumer ratings. Although companies may use perceptual maps to help make strategic marketing decisions, the maps themselves provide no information on how companies can achieve their desired positions.

Ultimately, perceptual maps are strategic planning tools that must be interpreted and implemented by managers. Despite its usefulness as a managerial tool, no qualitative or quantitative research tool should ever replace the professional insight and experience of a seasoned brand or product manager.

CONCEPT DEFINITIONS

Attribute: A particular feature or characteristic contained by the product.

Comparative advertising: Occurs when one brand's strengths are compared to those of a competitor.

Competitive advantage: A unique strength possessed by one company or brand relative to the competition.

Factor (or *dimension*): A common underlying dimension that captures the essence of a larger group of data.

Factor analysis: A class of multivariate statistical techniques that reduce and summarize data to examine the interrelationships among a large number of variables.

Idealized product: A fictional product created by combining consumer responses to questions regarding their ideal level of certain product attributes.

Ideal vector: Indicates the importance weights the market places on the two dimensions of the perceptual map.

Marketing mix: The controllable elements of a company's marketing efforts, includes the firm's product, price, distribution, and promotion.

Marketing research: The systematic and objective gathering of information for use in marketing decision making.

Market segmentation: The process of subdividing a large market or group of consumers into smaller, more specialized groups of consumers.

Perception: The way an individual selects, organizes, and interprets information to create a meaningful picture of the world.

Perceptual map: A graph displaying consumers' perceptions of product attributes across two or more dimensions.

Perceptual mapping: A technique that allows marketers to visually represent consumer perceptions of competing products or services within a competitive marketplace.

Place: Deals with the distribution of goods from their source to the final consumer.

Price: The money or other consideration given in exchange for the firm's product offering.

Product: The good, service, or idea that is offered by the firm.

Product category: An entire product class or industry.

Product positioning: The place a product offering occupies in a consumer's mind with regard to important attributes relative to competitive offerings.

Promotion: Includes any form of communication with the consumer through advertising, public relations, personal selling, and sales promotion.

Qualitative research: Involves data gathering techniques that focus on gathering data which is largely descriptive and extremely detailed.

Quantitative research: Techniques focusing on gathering statistically oriented data and typically involve gathering consumer responses to survey questions.

Repositioning: Involves changing the image of your product in the mind of consumers from an existing image to a new image using the marketing mix variables.

REVIEW QUESTIONS

1. What are the two major categories of marketing research methods? How do they differ?

2. What is product positioning? Why is it important to companies?

3. How can perceptual maps be used by managers to make marketing decisions?

4. What type of information needs to be collected to create a perceptual map?

5. What role does factor analysis play in the creation of a perceptual map?

6. What are the advantages and disadvantages of the perceptual mapping process?

APPENDIX: ATHLETIC FOOTWEAR SURVEY

name_____

#_____   section 1   2   3   team

Dear Respondent:

This questionnaire is part of a consumer research study conducted in the Department of Marketing, University of Central Florida. We are interested in studying consumers' perceptions of different brands of athletic shoes. Your answers to this questionnaire will provide the information needed in this research project.

Your assistance is very critical to the success of our research project, and much appreciated. The questionnaire will take only a few minutes to complete. Thank you very much for your help!

---

1. How many pairs of athletic shoes do you currently own and use?

   _____
   number of pairs

2. How many pairs of athletic shoes do you buy for yourself in a year?

   _____ _____ _____ _____ _____
   1 pair/year   2 pair/year   3 pair/year   4 pair/year   5 or more

3. What *brand* of athletic shoe do you buy most often? _____

4. Which of the following brands of athletic shoes are you familiar with? Please check all appropriate brands.

   __NIKE   __REEBOK   __FILA   __ESPRIT

   __ADIDAS   __AIRWALK   __K-SWISS   __L. A. GEAR

   __CONVERSE   __NEW BALANCE

5. Which of the following brands of athletic shoes have you owned and used?

   __NIKE   __REEBOK   __FILA   __ESPRIT

   __ADIDAS   __AIRWALK   __K-SWISS   __L.A. GEAR

   __CONVERSE   __NEW BALANCE

The next set of questions concern your perceptions of each brand of athletic shoes on different attributes. Please indicate how strongly you agree or disagree with each of the statements presented below by circling the number (1–5) that best indicates your answer choice.

6. ⸺⸺⸺*feel very comfortable.* (ANSWER FOR EVERY BRAND)

	STRONGLY DISAGREE	DISAGREE	NEITHER AGREE NOR DISAGREE	AGREE	STRONGLY AGREE
(a) NIKE	1	2	3	4	5
(b) REEBOK	1	2	3	4	5
(c) FILA	1	2	3	4	5
(d) ESPRIT	1	2	3	4	5
(e) ADIDAS	1	2	3	4	5
(f) AIRWALK	1	2	3	4	5
(g) K-SWISS	1	2	3	4	5
(h) L.A. GEAR	1	2	3	4	5
(i) CONVERSE	1	2	3	4	5
(j) NEW BALANCE	1	2	3	4	5

7. ⸺⸺⸺*is good for standing on your feet a lot.* (ANSWER FOR EVERY BRAND)

	STRONGLY DISAGREE	DISAGREE	NEITHER AGREE NOR DISAGREE	AGREE	STRONGLY AGREE
(a) NIKE	1	2	3	4	5
(b) REEBOK	1	2	3	4	5
(c) FILA	1	2	3	4	5
(d) ESPRIT	1	2	3	4	5
(e) ADIDAS	1	2	3	4	5
(f) AIRWALK	1	2	3	4	5

(g) K-SWISS	1	2	3	4	5
(h) L.A. GEAR	1	2	3	4	5
(i) CONVERSE	1	2	3	4	5
(j) NEW BALANCE	1	2	3	4	5

8. _____*has cushioning support.* (ANSWER FOR EVERY BRAND)

	STRONGLY DISAGREE	DISAGREE	NEITHER AGREE NOR DISAGREE	AGREE	STRONGLY AGREE
(a) NIKE	1	2	3	4	5
(b) REEBOK	1	2	3	4	5
(c) FILA	1	2	3	4	5
(d) ESPRIT	1	2	3	4	5
(e) ADIDAS	1	2	3	4	5
(f) AIRWALK	1	2	3	4	5
(g) K-SWISS	1	2	3	4	5
(h) L.A. GEAR	1	2	3	4	5
(i) CONVERSE	1	2	3	4	5
(j) NEW BALANCE	1	2	3	4	5

9. _____*has a good fit.* (ANSWER FOR EVERY BRAND)

	STRONGLY DISAGREE	DISAGREE	NEITHER AGREE NOR DISAGREE	AGREE	STRONGLY AGREE
(a) NIKE	1	2	3	4	5
(b) REEBOK	1	2	3	4	5
(c) FILA	1	2	3	4	5
(d) ESPRIT	1	2	3	4	5
(e) ADIDAS	1	2	3	4	5
(f) AIRWALK	1	2	3	4	5

	STRONGLY DISAGREE	DISAGREE	NEITHER AGREE NOR DISAGREE	AGREE	STRONGLY AGREE
(g) K-SWISS	1	2	3	4	5
(h) L.A. GEAR	1	2	3	4	5
(i) CONVERSE	1	2	3	4	5
(j) NEW BALANCE	1	2	3	4	5

10. _____*is very lightweight.* (ANSWER FOR EVERY BRAND)

	STRONGLY DISAGREE	DISAGREE	NEITHER AGREE NOR DISAGREE	AGREE	STRONGLY AGREE
(a) NIKE	1	2	3	4	5
(b) REEBOK	1	2	3	4	5
(c) FILA	1	2	3	4	5
(d) ESPRIT	1	2	3	4	5
(e) ADIDAS	1	2	3	4	5
(f) AIRWALK	1	2	3	4	5
(g) K-SWISS	1	2	3	4	5
(h) L.A. GEAR	1	2	3	4	5
(i) CONVERSE	1	2	3	4	5
(j) NEW BALANCE	1	2	3	4	5

11. _____*is an affordable shoe.* (ANSWER FOR EVERY BRAND)

	STRONGLY DISAGREE	DISAGREE	NEITHER AGREE NOR DISAGREE	AGREE	STRONGLY AGREE
(a) NIKE	1	2	3	4	5
(b) REEBOK	1	2	3	4	5
(c) FILA	1	2	3	4	5
(d) ESPRIT	1	2	3	4	5
(e) ADIDAS	1	2	3	4	5

(f) AIRWALK	1	2	3	4	5
(g) K-SWISS	1	2	3	4	5
(h) L. A. GEAR	1	2	3	4	5
(i) CONVERSE	1	2	3	4	5
(j) NEW BALANCE	1	2	3	4	5

12. _____*is easy to clean.* (ANSWER FOR EVERY BRAND)

	STRONGLY DISAGREE	DISAGREE	NEITHER AGREE NOR DISAGREE	AGREE	STRONGLY AGREE
(a) NIKE	1	2	3	4	5
(b) REEBOK	1	2	3	4	5
(c) FILA	1	2	3	4	5
(d) ESPRIT	1	2	3	4	5
(e) ADIDAS	1	2	3	4	5
(f) AIRWALK	1	2	3	4	5
(g) K-SWISS	1	2	3	4	5
(h) L.A. GEAR	1	2	3	4	5
(i) CONVERSE	1	2	3	4	5
(j) NEW BALANCE	1	2	3	4	5

13. _____*has good traction.* (ANSWER FOR EVERY BRAND)

	STRONGLY DISAGREE	DISAGREE	NEITHER AGREE NOR DISAGREE	AGREE	STRONGLY AGREE
(a) NIKE	1	2	3	4	5
(b) REEBOK	1	2	3	4	5
(c) FILA	1	2	3	4	5
(d) ESPRIT	1	2	3	4	5
(e) ADIDAS	1	2	3	4	5

(f) AIRWALK	1	2	3	4	5
(g) K-SWISS	1	2	3	4	5
(h) L.A. GEAR	1	2	3	4	5
(i) CONVERSE	1	2	3	4	5
(j) NEW BALANCE	1	2	3	4	5

14. _____*has waterproofing (Gore-Tex, etc.).* (ANSWER FOR EVERY BRAND)

	STRONGLY DISAGREE	DISAGREE	NEITHER AGREE NOR DISAGREE	AGREE	STRONGLY AGREE
(a) NIKE	1	2	3	4	5
(b) REEBOK	1	2	3	4	5
(c) FILA	1	2	3	4	5
(d) ESPRIT	1	2	3	4	5
(e) ADIDAS	1	2	3	4	5
(f) AIRWALK	1	2	3	4	5
(g) K-SWISS	1	2	3	4	5
(h) L.A.GEAR	1	2	3	4	5
(i) CONVERSE	1	2	3	4	5
(j) NEW BALANCE	1	2	3	4	5

15. _____*has a distinctive brand logo/symbol.* (ANSWER FOR EVERY BRAND)

	STRONGLY DISAGREE	DISAGREE	NEITHER AGREE NOR DISAGREE	AGREE	STRONGLY AGREE
(a) NIKE	1	2	3	4	5
(b) REEBOK	1	2	3	4	5
(c) FILA	1	2	3	4	5
(d) ESPRIT	1	2	3	4	5

(e) ADIDAS	1	2	3	4	5
(f) AIRWALK	1	2	3	4	5
(g) K-SWISS	1	2	3	4	5
(h) L.A. GEAR	1	2	3	4	5
(i) CONVERSE	1	2	3	4	5
(j) NEW BALANCE	1	2	3	4	5

16. _____ *styling is up-to-date.* (ANSWER FOR EVERY BRAND)

	STRONGLY DISAGREE	DISAGREE	NEITHER AGREE NOR DISAGREE	AGREE	STRONGLY AGREE
(a) NIKE	1	2	3	4	5
(b) REEBOK	1	2	3	4	5
(c) FILA	1	2	3	4	5
(d) ESPRIT	1	2	3	4	5
(e) ADIDAS	1	2	3	4	5
(f) AIRWALK	1	2	3	4	5
(g) K-SWISS	1	2	3	4	5
(h) L.A. GEAR	1	2	3	4	5
(i) CONVERSE	1	2	3	4	5
(j) NEW BALANCE	1	2	3	4	5

17. _____ *is versatile—performs well for almost any activity.* (ANSWER FOR EVERY BRAND)

	STRONGLY DISAGREE	DISAGREE	NEITHER AGREE NOR DISAGREE	AGREE	STRONGLY AGREE
(a) NIKE	1	2	3	4	5
(b) REEBOK	1	2	3	4	5

(c) FILA	1	2	3	4	5
(d) ESPRIT	1	2	3	4	5
(e) ADIDAS	1	2	3	4	5
(f) AIRWALK	1	2	3	4	5
(g) K-SWISS	1	2	3	4	5
(h) L.A. GEAR	1	2	3	4	5
(i) CONVERSE	1	2	3	4	5
(j) NEW BALANCE	1	2	3	4	5

18. We would like to know how important the following characteristics are to you when selecting a brand of athletic shoes. Please indicate how important each characteristic is to you by *circling the appropriate number (from 1 to 5) for each characteristic.*

	EXTREMELY IMPORTANT	VERY IMPORTANT	MODERATELY IMPORTANT	IMPORTANT	NOT AT ALL IMPORTANT
(a) COMFORTABLE	1	2	3	4	5
(b) GOOD FOR PROLONGED STANDING	1	2	3	4	5
(c) CUSHIONING SUPPORT	1	2	3	4	5
(d) HAS A GOOD FIT	1	2	3	4	5
(e) VERY LIGHTWEIGHT	1	2	3	4	5
(f) AFFORDABILITY	1	2	3	4	5
(g) EASY TO CLEAN	1	2	3	4	5
(h) GOOD TRACTION	1	2	3	4	5
(i) WATER-PROOFING	1	2	3	4	5
(j) DISTINCTIVE BRAND LOGO	1	2	3	4	5

(k) UP-TO-DATE STYLING	1	2	3	4	5
(l) VERSATILITY	1	2	3	4	5

19. Please rank the following brands of athletic shoes in your order of preference from 1 through 10, where 1 = *most preferred,* and 10 = *least preferred brand.*

__NIKE __REEBOK __FILA __ESPRIT

__ADIDAS __AIRWALK __K-SWISS __L.A. GEAR

__CONVERSE __NEW BALANCE

Demographics

20. What is your age category? Please check one:

(1)	under 15	_____
(2)	15 - 19	_____
(3)	20 - 24	_____
(4)	25 - 29	_____
(5)	30 and over	_____

21. Please indicate your gender:

(1) Male___ (2) Female ___

22. Please indicate your marital status:

(1)	Single	_____
(2)	Married, no children at home	_____
(3)	Married, with children at home	_____
(4)	Divorced or separated	_____
(5)	Divorced/separated, with children	_____

Thank you very much for your time and cooperation!!!

REFERENCES

Aaker, David A. and J. Gary Shansby (1982), "Positioning Your Product," *Business Horizons* (May-June): 52-62.

Czepiel, John A. (1992), *Competitive Marketing Strategy*, Englewood Cliffs, NJ: Prentice Hall.

Dolan, Robert J. (1991), *Managing the New Product Development Process: Cases and Notes*, Reading, MA: Addison-Wesley.

Ganesh, Jaishankar and Gillian Oakenfull (1996), "A Cross-Cultural Examination of Consumer Perceptions and Preferences: Implications for New Product Introduction and Positioning Strategies," Working Paper, University of Houston, Houston, Texas.

Kaul, Anil and Vithala R. Rao (1995), "Research for Product Positioning and Design Decisions: An Integrative Review," *International Journal of Research in Marketing* 12: 293-320.

Lannon, Judie (1991), "Developing Brand Strategies Across Borders," *Marketing and Research Today* (August): 160-168.

Ries, Al and Jack Trout (1981), *Positioning: The Battle for Your Mind*, New York: McGraw-Hill.

Ries, Al and Jack Trout (1993), *The 22 Immutable Laws of Marketing*, New York: HarperCollins.

Chapter 16

Qualitative Research Methods
for the Study of Tourist Behavior

Alain Decrop

LEARNING OBJECTIVES

By the end of the chapter the reader should be able to:

- Judge the usefulness of qualitative approaches to examine problems related to tourist behavior
- Make trade-off choices between quantitative and qualitative approaches
- Master the major aspects involved in elaborating a qualitative research design
- Think of applications to tourism research where the different data collection techniques could be used
- Contrast the different interview and observation types
- Define what is meant by "depth of analysis" in qualitative research and present the major analysis types
- Explain how codes, memos, and diagrams help in managing and analyzing qualitative information
- Understand how interpretation and triangulation provide trustworthiness of a qualitative study

INTRODUCTION

Researchers who study marketing and consumer behavior in hospitality and tourism have long considered qualitative research as of little value. Largely dominated by positivist thinking, researchers did not see in qualitative inquiry any criteria for a "good" science. In this chapter, we suggest that this is not the case: qualitative research is valuable.

In the first section, we show the usefulness and the need for qualitative approaches to study tourist behavior and we review recent examples from the tourism literature. Next, we present general strategic choices to be made when qualitative inquiry is considered. The focus is on elements that will help in determining how to start and conduct a study. The major data collection techniques are presented in the section on data collection. We both explain and illustrate the basics of primary (interview and observation) and supplementary (review of documents, projective) techniques. In the fourth section, we discuss issues related to the analysis and interpretation of qualitative information. This includes choices about the depth of analysis, activities, and tools to help data management and analysis, and the validation of conclusions via triangulation.

THE NEED FOR QUALITATIVE APPROACHES IN TOURISM RESEARCH

Why Are Qualitative Data Useful?

Today, qualitative methods are widely used in market research and are gaining widespread acceptance in the consumer behavior literature. In travel and tourism research, sociologists and anthropologists have chosen qualitative approaches for a long time. This is not the case for marketing and consumer behavior researchers. Riley (1996) notices that "the majority of tourism marketing research has relied on structured surveys and quantification" (p. 22). Other authors concur with this statement (Henderson, 1991; Peterson, 1994; Riley, 1996; Walle, 1997). This is best explained by the persistence of the domination of the positivist and postpositivist paradigms in tourism marketing research. Researchers feel more comfortable with statistical probabilities than with theoretical conjecture. They prefer to observe an "objective," tangible and single reality, because only then are generalization and prediction possible. The problem is that they often forget that the value of scientific inquiry is not only a question of numbers but also, most particularly, a question of reasoning. They overlook the complexity of many research problems where reality is multiple-faceted and socially constructed. Finally, because of their separation from the informant, they fail to develop a theory that is grounded in people's everyday experiences.

This dichotomy, quantitative versus qualitative, is often associated with the opposition between positivism and interpretivism, and needs clarification. Positivism (and postpositivism) and interpretivism (and constructivism) are general philosophies of sciences. Differences are ontological (the nature of reality), epistemological (the status of knowledge), and methodological (the way to achieve this knowledge). In contrast, the adjectives "qualitative" and "quantitative" originally only pertained to research methodologies. The first implies identifying distinctive observations, and the latter counting similar observations. Some qualitative techniques, such as interviewing, are used both by positivist and interpretivist researchers. Guba and Lincoln (1994) go further by distinguishing five moments in qualitative research, corresponding to as many ways of thinking and performing qualitative inquiry. We conclude that the relevant distinction between paradigms is not one of qualitative versus quantitative but rather one of positivism versus interpretivism. The difference is that interpretivists use verbal and visual data as such, while positivists strive to transform any input data into numbers. Table 16.1 further clarifies the distinc-

TABLE 16.1. Basic Differences Between the Positivist and the Interpretivist Paradigms

Assumptions	Positivism	Interpretivism
Nature of reality	Objective, tangible, single	Socially constructed, multiple
Goal of research	Explanation, strong prediction	Understanding, weak prediction
Focus of interest	What is general, average and representative	What is specific, unique, and deviant
Knowledge generated	Laws Absolute (time, context, and value free)	Meanings Relative (time, context, culture, value bound)
Subject/Researcher relationship	Rigid separation	Interactive, cooperative, participative
Desired information	How many people think and do a specific thing, or have a specific problem	What some people think and do, what kind of problems they are confronted with, and how they deal with them

tion. However, interpretivism is often associated with a qualitative approach (and positivism with a quantitative approach) because interpretivist problems can best be addressed by qualitative methods, and positivist problems by quantitative ones. That is why we often assimilate interpretivism and qualitative research in this chapter.

In consumer behavior, positivist and postpositivist approaches are linked with rational and cognitive models. Teare (1994) suggests that "comprehensive models of consumer decision making are often too complex and/or too generalized to test empirically, indicating that an alternative approach, located much closer to observable consumer behavior, is needed" (p. 38). Other researchers (Dann, Nash, and Pierce, 1988; Brent Ritchie, 1994; Hollinshead, 1996; Riley and Love, 1997) also show the usefulness of a renewed, broader approach to solving marketing problems and thinking about tourism research.

Qualitative methods were originally used to uncover hidden motives of consumption. However, more consumer research problems can be understood better with qualitative approaches, more specifically in those cases where "the gathering of information . . . is too subtle and too complex to be tailored to the structured, standardized techniques and criteria of quantitative research" (Teare, 1994, p. 40). Peterson (1994) also lists possible purposes related to qualitative research in hospitality and tourism, i.e., to develop hypotheses concerning relevant behavior or attitudes, to identify the full range of issues, views, and attitudes of a research problem, and to understand how a buying decision is made.

Review of the Use of Qualitative Methods in Tourist Behavior Research

Until now, interpretivist qualitative approaches have mostly been used from anthropological and sociological perspectives (for a review, see Riley and Love, 1997). In other fields, such as marketing and tourist behavior, "techniques which bear the imprints of logical positivism, statistical investigation, and the scientific method continue to dominate" (Walle, 1997, p. 525). The subordinate and exploratory nature of qualitative research is explicitly mentioned: for most researchers in tourism marketing, qualitative research exists to provide information for developing further quantitative research.

Only in recent years have a few authors used qualitative research designs for studying tourist behavior. Teare (1994) conducted a longitudinal study over a three-year period to investigate the specific case of consumer decision making in the U.K. hotel leisure market, using the grounded-theory approach of Glaser and Strauss (1967). Following the same approach, Riley (1995) examined prestigious travel behavior. Woodside and MacDonald (1994) also gathered qualitative data to support propositions resulting from a general framework of customer choice decisions of tourism services.

Next to these global perspectives on tourist behavior, more specific aspects were qualitatively studied. Recent examples include the study of destination images (Dann, 1996; Bramwell and Rawding, 1996; McCay and Fesenmaier, 1997), motivation (Milman, 1993), travel choices (Stewart and Stynes, 1994; Corey, 1996), tourist satisfaction (Marti, 1995), and tourist consumption experiences (Hartmann, 1988; Marti, 1995; Markwell, 1997; Ryan, 1997).

STRATEGIES OF QUALITATIVE INQUIRY

Framing the Research Question

When starting any research project, it is important to define the problem. In quantitative research, it is very important to narrow it down to a manageable, especially controllable, size. Framing the research question leads to the isolation of hypotheses that will be tested in a deductive way (one tries to support general theories from particular observations). In qualitative research, the framing of the research problem does not have to be so analytical. The process is inductive: theories emerge from particular observations.

Qualitative inquiry starts with guiding hypotheses (in contrast with hypotheses to test) or "sensitizing concepts" (Patton, 1980). These are a few broad research questions that the researcher has in mind, which help in designing the research project, generating questions, and searching for patterns. Framing the research problem is dynamic: the investigator must be willing to revise guiding hypotheses as the study progresses. For example, in the study I conducted on vacationers' decision-making processes, the first idea was to compare tourists' perceptions and preferences for vacation destinations. I quickly realized that the comparison of the two types of judgments could be based on their antecedents (the underlying product attributes and person characteristics) as well as on their consequences (intention to buy and actual purchase). As I found that the relationships between those elements are very complex and dynamic, it became obvious that it would be more fruitful to put them in the broader vacation decision-making process. Perception (or attention) and preference (or attitudes) are indeed key variables in consumers' decisions and behavior. Besides, I realized that destination is only one aspect of vacation decisions, and not always the most prominent one. These considerations led to this broad research question: how do vacation decisions happen?

Although the initial guiding hypotheses do not have to be completely clear, be sure that the hypotheses are researchable. This can be helped by developing a conceptual framework based on existing literature or/and on practical intuitions. Moreover, one must always bear in mind the theoretical or/and practical significance of the research question. Since qualitative research is expensive and time consuming, the study problem must be very worthwhile.

The use of literature is controversial in qualitative research. Some advise that an extensive review of the existing literature on the topic is needed before starting any empirical project. Others present the ideal qualitative researcher as a naive and alert child. We think that although theory blindness must be avoided, over-detailed examination of the literature will lead to preconceived ideas and hypotheses (with respect to variables' intensity and causality) and thus bias data collection. In the premise of the project, we would only review literature on the sensitizing concepts of the study. We would go into more detail during the data collection and interpretation process. Next to literature, theoretical sensitivity can come from other sources such as professional experience, personal experience, and the analytic process (Strauss and Corbin, 1990).

Choosing the Research Methodology

The first objective of this chapter is to show the usefulness of qualitative methods to tourism research. Nevertheless, it should be kept in mind that the choice of a research method is not a question of paradigms but rather a function of the research problem. After having determined "What do I want to investigate?," the researcher must choose the appropriate method.

The basic trade-off is between qualitative and quantitative methodology. The decision depends not only on the nature of the topic to be addressed, but also on the investigator's personal interests. The ideal situation is that of a researcher who is open to and familiar with both qualitative and quantitative methods. A nonpassionate decision is possible depending only on the research questions, but that situation is rare. Personal interest creates an allegiance to a particular paradigm and preference for a particular approach. In my research, I first started considering surveys and multivariate analysis to address the problem of the difference between perception and preference judgments. This choice sounded logical since I had hardly heard about qualitative methods before. After presenting my research project to colleagues, I was told that perhaps a qualitative approach would do the job better. I then decided to immerse myself in the principles of qualitative methods. This did not particularly clash with my personal interests, since I first graduated in modern history. After participation in a doctoral seminar on qualitative methods, I finally realized that an interpretivist qualitative approach was indeed better suited to examine tourists' decision-making processes. Even more factors determine the choice. Table 16.2 provides a checklist of some of the major questions that can influence the choice of an appropriate methodology. In the case of a positive answer to any of these questions, the researcher should consider qualitative methods as a possible way to approach research problems.

The basic distinction of qualitative versus quantitative designs can be nuanced by considering the *level of prominence of the qualitative element* in the research design. Miller and Crabtree (1994) suggest four possible designs: concurrent, nested, sequential, and combination. A concurrent

TABLE 16.2. Checklist for Considering Qualitative or Quantitative Approach

- Is the researcher interested in individualized outcomes?
- Is the researcher interested in examining the process of research and the context in which it occurs?
- Is detailed in-depth information needed to understand the phenomena under study?
- Is the focus on quality and the meaning of the experiences being studied?
- Does the researcher desire to get close to the data providers and become immersed in their experiences?
- Do no measuring devices exist that will provide reliable and valid data for the topic being studied?
- Is the research question likely to change depending upon how the data emerge?
- Is it possible that the answer to the research question may yield unexpected results?
- Does it make more sense to use grounded theory than existing a priori theory in studying the particular phenomena?
- Does the researcher wish to get personally involved in the research?
- Does the researcher have a philosophical and methodological bias toward the interpretive paradigm and qualitative methods?

Source: Henderson, 1991, p. 103.

design involves both qualitative and quantitative research being simultaneously but independently performed on the same topic. At the end, the findings are examined to see if they converge. In a nested design, qualitative and quantitative techniques are directly integrated within a single study in a system of checks and balances to ensure validity. The sequential design limits qualitative research to the exploration of key variables (exploratory research) that need further measurement and inference in a subsequent quantitative phase. In contrast, the qualitative element is prominent in combination or case-study designs. Qualitative findings are used as such (conclusive research) in a contextual approach and local theories are developed. Quantitative data only help to get a better understanding of a particular case.

Completing Yin (1984), Marshall and Rossman (1995) make distinctions among seven research strategies: experiments, surveys, archival analyses, histories, case studies, field studies (ethnographies), and in-depth interview studies. We could locate those strategies on a continuum ranging from highly quantitative (experiments) to highly qualitative (in-depth interview studies). However, we again insist that the choice of an appropriate research strategy does not depend on the qualitative/quantitative dichotomy, but rather on the study's goal and the related research questions. A study can aim at describing, explaining, understanding, and/or predicting events and processes (see Table 16.1).

Designing the Research

There are many possible qualitative research designs. Since innovation and creativity play a major role here, it is impossible to list all alternatives from which the researcher has to choose. Nevertheless, the research design can be facilitated by considering several aspects.

The first important decision of the research design is about *site selection.* A site, or a case, is defined as "a bounded context in which one is studying events, processes and outcomes" (Miles and Huberman, 1984, p. 28). A site can include a wide range of settings, populations, and phenomena. The site selection can involve the decision to focus on a specific setting or place (e.g., the Miami travel trade show), on a particular population (e.g., travel agency customers), or on a phenomenon (e.g., the summer vacation decision-making process). Marshall and Rossman (1995) describe the ideal site as one for which:

1. Entry is possible
2. There is a high probability of variety of processes, people, interactions, and structures of interest

3. The researcher is likely to be able to build trusting relationships with the participants
4. Data quality and credibility of the study are reasonably assured

Identifying the level of analytical interest is also important. Both the social subject (particularly, its size) and the social object deserve attention (Miles and Huberman, 1984). The major alternatives are listed in Table 16.3. Note that the decision is not exclusive: considering the social subject, for example, a particular study could focus both on the individual and the family.

After the site has been selected and the appropriate level of analysis has been determined, waves of subsequent *sampling* decisions are made. In qualitative research, sampling has another connotation as the traditional quantitative tenets of size and statistical representativity. First, sampling is not only about people but may also pertain to type of behavior, events, and processes (see Table 16.3). Second, sampling is not a question of the number of people in the sample, but rather of richness of information. The qualitative researcher strives to record events, and behavior that are relevant to the concept or theory being studied. Hence the notion of theoretical sampling.

TABLE 16.3. Levels of Analytical Interest in Qualitative Research

Social subject	Social object
Individuals	Specific acts and behaviors (what people do or say)
Roles	Events (marked-off happenings)
Relationships	Activities (regularly occurring sets of behavior)
Groups (family, social class, culture . . .)	Strategies (activities aimed toward some goal)
Settings (places or locales within sites)	Meanings, perspectives (how people construe events)
Sites as whole	States (general conditions)
	Process (ongoing flows, changes over time)

Source: Adapted from Miles and Huberman, 1984.

Theoretical sampling consists of consciously adding new cases to be studied according to the potential for developing new insights or for expanding an emerging grounded theory (Glaser and Strauss, 1967). The sample size is not so important. One cannot say how many people will be interviewed at the beginning of the study; the researcher decides to leave the site when theoretical saturation is achieved (the data collected are repetitive and no additional new information is found). This constant search for information-rich new cases makes random sampling irrelevant. Other methods such as purposive sampling (searching people with a specific profile) or snowball sampling (each participant is asked to suggest other people who might participate in the study) are used instead (Patton, 1980). The basic principle is always to get the most comprehensive understanding of a phenomenon. Therefore, both typical and atypical cases are worth investigating. Again, purposive sampling is not limited to people but also involves activities, locations, and time periods.

Issues related to the *researcher's role* are another important consideration in the research design. In qualitative studies, the researcher is the instrument (see Table 16.1) that enters into the life of the informants. This raises several questions that are absent from quantitative research.

One first consideration is about *deploying the self*. The investigator's level of immersion in the site entails four decisions (Marshall and Rossman, 1995):

1. The degree of "participantness": does the researcher participate in the informant's daily life? (from full participant to complete observer).
2. The degree of "revealedness": is the participant aware of the study going on? (from full disclosure to complete secrecy).
3. The intensiveness (amount of time spent in the setting) and extensiveness (duration over time) of the research.
4. The focus of the study: is the research problem specific or diffuse?

A second issue pertains to *negotiating entry*. People are often reluctant to participate in qualitative inquiry because it is perceived as time consuming and intrusive. Moreover, topics to be discussed are sometimes very sensitive. These potential stumbling blocks show the need for carefully planning the entry when designing the research. This means that the researcher shows the usefulness of the project, assures confidentiality, prepares counterarguments, and offers a small gift. However, one should unquestionably respect people's right not to participate in a study.

Third, the researcher should also keep *efficiency* in mind. As qualitative inquiry consumes much time and energy, the question "Is the effort worthwhile?" should be asked when starting any project and selecting any new case.

Finally, self-criticism is much needed. Successful qualitative studies depend most of all on the *interpersonal skills of the researcher.* These skills should lead to building trust, maintaining good relations, respecting norms of reciprocity, and being sensitive to ethical issues (Marshall and Rossman, 1995). A good qualitative researcher is someone who is at ease in the setting, who actively and thoughtfully listens, and who has an empathic understanding of and a respect for the perspectives of others.

Focusing data is a last aspect of the research design. The term is borrowed from Lofland and Lofland (1995). This involves three important activities by the researcher:

1. Envision topics that are possibly relevant to the problem
2. Elaborate questions to ask about those topics
3. Think of questions and themes that will arouse the informant's interest

Because those activities are essentially technical and very specific to any research problem, we do not go into more details here. In addition to Lofland and Lofland (1995), we recommend Patton (1980) as further readings.

DATA COLLECTION

In qualitative consumer behavior research, the palette of data collection methods is very small. We first present the two traditional (primary) families of interview and observation techniques. We then briefly discuss other (supplementary) data collection techniques.

Interview Techniques

As Rubin and Rubin (1995) indicate in the subtitle of their book, qualitative interviewing is the art of hearing data. This requires "intense listening, a respect and curiosity about what people say and a systematic effort to really hear and understand what people tell you" (p. 17). Qualitative interviewing is also called *in-depth interviewing* in contrast with a structured survey interview. In-depth interviewing goes beyond asking questions and listening to people; it entails sharing social experiences.

There are different forms of interviewing. Patton (1980) has identified four variations that range from purely quantitative to purely qualitative:

quantitative interviews with close-ended questions, standardized open-ended interviews, interview guide, and informal conversational interview (Patton, 1980). Only the two last forms are considered in-depth interviews. The interview guide approach is often referred to as a *semistructured* or *semidirective* interview. It lists the topics and issues to be covered but does not specify any particular way and order of asking questions. Informal conversational interviews are also called *unstructured* and *nondirective* interviews since the questions are not planned but rather emerge from the immediate context and are asked in the natural course of interaction (Henderson, 1991).

There are more specialized types of in-depth interviews. Rubin and Rubin (1995) list four alternatives: topical oral histories, life histories, evaluation interviews, and focus groups. Marshall and Rossman (1995) make distinctions among ethnographic, phenomenological, elite, and focus group interviewing. All the interview forms can be encompassed within two broader categories: *"Cultural interviews* focus on the norms, values, understandings, and taken-for-granted rules of behavior of a group or society. *Topical interviews* are more narrowly focused on a particular event or process, and are concerned with what happened, when, and why" (Rubin and Rubin, 1995, p. 28).

The *focus group* is a very popular technique in tourism marketing research. It consists of gathering six to ten people who are unfamiliar with each other, but who share certain characteristics that are relevant to the study problem. The first role of the interviewer is to stimulate discussion and the expression of different opinions, so that the format becomes rather unstructured. The interviewer acts as a moderator by asking questions when necessary to involve everyone in the discussion and to keep the debate focused on the topic.

We do not go into more detail here. Instead, we give tourism research examples for each major interview technique. We advise the frustrated reader to look into Rubin and Rubin's (1995) book. Note that interviewing is often combined with other methods of data collection, such as observation and questionnaires. This is done either for the purpose of triangulation (see the section "Triangulation," and examples in Hartmann, 1988; Markwell, 1997; Wallace and Pierce, 1996), or because interviewing is only exploratory (see Corey, 1996; Nogawa, Yamaguchi, and Hagi, 1996). Whatever the interviewing technique, it is very important to write field notes during and immediately after each interview. These notes describe the setting, the relationship with informants, the direct interpretation of particular words or sentences, personal feelings about what has been done, said, and not said during the interview, and critical remarks about the quality of data or the participation of each interviewee. All field notes are compiled in a "roadbook" that, together with the interview transcripts, will be used for analysis and interpretation. Those observations are especially useful as they cast additional light on the textual content or indicate specific questions that do not directly appear in the transcripts.

Exemplar 1: Unstructured Interviewing

In an example of unstructured interviewing, S. A. Hernandez, J. Cohen, and H. T. Garcia (1996) conducted informal and unstructured interviews using open-ended questions attempting to get hosts to talk freely about a proposed resort. All respondents were initially asked the same question: "What do you think about the proposed Costa Isabela Resort?" (Puerto Rico). This was followed by questions on their expectations of the perceived benefits and costs of the resort. Last, respondents were asked to provide various types of socioeconomic information. Each interview varied in order and specific wording of the questions.

Exemplar 2: Semistructured Interviewing

Alternatively, for the in-depth interviews that would serve as the main data collection method for an unpublished doctoral dissertation (Decrop, 1999) I opted for a semistructured interview. I wanted the informants to speak spontaneously and unrestrainedly, while keeping some structure in the interview, for the following reasons:

1. At the time, I was not a very experienced interviewer. A semistructured interview is preferable for feeling more secure and making sure that all important issues are covered.
2. I used a longitudinal design (I interviewed the same persons three times before the summer holidays and once after). It was important to keep a common base for comparing how answers to a particular question evolved over time.
3. I was limited by practical time and energy constraints. The unstructured interview generally lasts longer and is more complicated to guide and to analyze than the semistructured interview.

So, I started by asking very general questions for "getting in" and making respondents comfortable, such as: Do you like holidays? Have you already thought about your next summer vacation? How do you usually choose your holiday destination? The other questions of the interview guide were used as a kind of checklist and asked only when necessary. Questions were subdivided into three core themes: general holiday behavior, holiday plans for the summer of 1996, and holiday destinations. Finally, I asked a few sociodemographic and lifestyle questions (Decrop, in progress).

Exemplar 3: Focus Group Interviewing

Finally, focus group interviewing was used by McCay and Fesenmaier (1997) in their Riding Mountain National Park (RMNP), Manitoba study examining how content of promotional visuals affects destination image. The data were obtained to serve descriptive, interpretive, and theory-building purposes. The groups also provided relevant physical and perceptual attributes used in constructing scales for the image survey conducted in a subsequent phase. MacKay and Fesenmaier stated, "The qualitative nature of the focus groups also facilitated further description of the visuals beyond their general classifications, thereby helping to yield richer information on the relationship of visuals to image." Focus group members ranged in familiarity with RMNP and were selected using purposive criterion sampling. Free-flowing discussion and individual input was prompted by presenting slides and asking the group to describe the mood or atmosphere, and other images the pictures generated.

Observation Techniques

In qualitative research, observation refers to "the systematic noting and recording of events, behaviors, and artifacts (objects) in the social setting chosen for study" (Marshall and Rossman, 1995, p. 79). Observation means that someone (the researcher) is looking at something or someone else (the informant). Things to be observed are not limited to verbal activities. As Table 16.4 shows, nonverbal behavior, communicational aspects (audience reaction), and global elements (group behavior, body gestures, combined verbal and nonverbal behavior) often give precious clues if not direct insight. Elements of the environment (weather, atmosphere, place, furniture) can also be observed.

The researcher/informant relationship ranges from complete observer (there is no interaction at all) to full participant (the observer participates in the informant's daily life). This distinction poses the question of deploying the self (see the section "Designing the Research"). Note that observation is often used in connection with other methods such as in-depth interviews. This is done either for the purpose of triangulating data (see

TABLE 16.4. What Can Be Observed?

I. Verbal	
A. Tone	Pitch, loudness, intonation
B. Duration	Length of sentence, conciseness
C. Content	Tag questions, phrases of tentativeness (I believe, I guess, I think . . .), apologies, self-denigration, niceties, humor, metaphors, obscenities, parts of speech (verbs, adjectives, pronouns), power language, political and value statements, exhibiting naïveté
D. Silences	Wait time, dramatization
II. Nonverbal	
A. Kinesics	Face, hands, stance, idiosyncrasies, legs
B. Proxemics	Use of space, desk props, spread of territory, control of decor
C. Appearance	Dress, makeup, hair, accessories, facial hair
III. Audience reaction	
A. Distraction	Asides, paper shuffling, off-task behavior, humor, leaving group, body position changes, criticize speech (ask to speak louder . . .)
B. Engagement and feedback	Head nodding, smiling, looking at speaker, eye contact, verbal agreements/critiques, asking questions, body positioning,
C. Interruption	
IV. Macro (global)	
A. Group behavior	Body positioning of groups, arrangement of people map, leadership (formal/informal), defying group norms, structured request for assistance, mirroring body movements
B. Male/female relationships	Amount of time women/men spoke, number of times women/men restructure agenda, how women/men get recognized to speak, proportion of meeting time utilized by men and women, female/male structured commands
C. Global individual behaviors	Hand gestures, indications of agreement, use of objects, courtship behavior
D. Outside primary focus	Taking a break, side comments
V. Combined verbal and nonverbal	
A. Greetings	Touching, verbal salutations
B. Eye pleading with groups	

Source: Adapted from Marshall and Rossman, 1995.

the later section on triangulation) or because of the holistic nature of the research (such as in field and ethnographic research, see Exemplar 4).

Participant observation is a very useful and popular method in tourism ethnography. It is the most comprehensive qualitative method and is often assimilated into field research. Field research consists of systematically collecting data by the social interaction between the researcher and informants in the environment of the latter (Taylor and Bogdan, 1984). This includes observation, informal interviews, and narratives. It is often used in conjunction with other techniques (document analysis, introspection), such as those illustrated by Exemplar 4.

Participant observation is especially appropriate to examine and understand phenomena inside a collective. The method enables catching subtle nuances of attitudes and behaviors and examining social processes over time. This requires the observer to become immersed in the setting. Much time and effort are needed: the observer must enter the group, participate in its life, and become accepted. The researcher must benefit from his or her privileged position to achieve meaning and insight into the problem, while at the same time maintaining an objective, observing capability. Examples of participant observation in tourism consumer research are difficult to find. This is why Exemplar 4 is not directly related to tourist behavior. Participant observation is typically unstructured to maximize the discovery or validation of theory (Denzin, 1978).

Exemplar 4: Field Research/Participant Observation

An example of participant observation was described by T. J. Forsyth (1995), where a researcher immersed himself in the village life of hill people living in Thailand in order to study the effects of tourism on agricultural practices and soil fertility. The researcher studied the Thai language for a year prior to arrival and further enlisted the help of a local interpreter between the Thai and Yao languages. Through the introduction of a local development organization the researcher was able to identify key informants and secure lodging with a group of families living together in a large house belonging to a village leader. The researcher spent a total of six months in the village over several visits, staying a maximum of one month per visit. Both qualitative and quantitative techniques of social research were used, with qualitative participant observation and discussions with villagers considered the most important source of information. During each stay agricultural and touristic activities were observed, key informants were questioned at length, and relevant group discussions were prompted. The researcher waited several weeks before attempting to question anyone other than key informants, and this was done only after villagers were assured that the research was not aimed at assessing illegal activities.

Exemplar 5: Nonparticipant Observation

At the end of March 1996, I made a series of nonparticipant observations at Brussels' holiday trade fair during a four-day period. The task consisted of following visitors of their trade show movements and observing their verbal and nonverbal behaviors. While I was willing to remain a complete observer, an initial contact with potential informants was needed. First, I had to be sure of a right recruitment (I wanted to have all types of decision-making units represented in the sample, i.e., singles, couples, and families). Second, I briefly presented myself and my research project. Third and most important, I asked potential informants whether they minded being followed. Their agreement precluded ethical reproaches later, and made note-taking easier and more detailed. Observations focused on five dominant but not exclusive elements:

1. The setting (place, date, weather, atmosphere in the trade-show hall, etc.)
2. The participant(s) (type and composition of the decision-making unit, sociodemographics, look and mood, etc.)
3. Participants' trade show movements (I indicated their courses on a map)
4. Participants' stops at particular stands (how long, why, is there any interaction, etc.?)
5. The information gathered by the participants (what kind, how much, how detailed, oral or written, etc. ?)

The observation session ended when informants were leaving the trade-show hall. I then asked them a few questions about missing sociodemographic data and current holiday plans and offered them a small gift (Decrop, in progress).

Supplementary Qualitative Techniques

Existing documents ("secondary data") are an important source of information for the qualitative researcher. Reviewing documents involves both heuristic (because gathering the appropriate documents is not always easy) and hermeneutic (analysis of the meaning associated with the document) tasks. Documents can be of multiple types (textbooks, novels, promotional material, minutes of meetings, newspapers, letters). They can be found in libraries, shops, documentation centers, and in personal, institutional, or organizational archives. Next to written material, photographs, films, videos, and music are valuable documents. Most of the time documents are content analyzed and both the verbal and pictorial content is of interest. Semiotic analysis and literary criticism are also used. The analysis of documents is very popular in recent tourism research. The study material includes guidebooks (Bhattacharyya, 1997), photographs (Markwell, 1997), travel diaries (Markwell, 1997), travelogs (Walle, 1996), promotional brochures (Enoch, 1996; Bramwell and Rawding, 1996), committee papers (Bramwell and Rawding, 1996), and journal articles (Jurowski and Olsen, 1995).

Projective techniques are indirect means of qualitative questioning that enable the informant to "project" beliefs and feelings onto a third person, an inanimate object, or a task situation (Haire, 1950). The basic assumption is that the interviewee interprets information on the basis of personal preoccupations, needs, and values, which can be hidden or latent.

Projective techniques are characterized by the ambiguousness of the proposed material (questionnaires, pictures, drawings) or situations (stories, events). The format is quite unstructured: the participant is asked to address questions in his or her own words, with little prompting by the researcher. Many different projective techniques are used in marketing research. In Table 16.5, I list the most popular ones and briefly describe what kind of response the informant is expected to elicit. An example from tourism research literature that combines both sentence completion and drawing elaboration is also given.

Exemplar 6: Projective Techniques

J. Gamradt (1995) used projective techniques during an investigation into Jamaican children's representations of tourism. The instrument employed was a four-page booklet titled the *Mind's Eye Project Activity Book* (MEP). The booklet asked open-ended questions regarding what the children thought about people who visited Jamaica and what the children thought visitors should know about Jamaica. They were also asked to draw a picture of visitors who came to Jamaica from far away. The booklet allowed "a large number of Jamaican children to express their ideas, attitudes, and beliefs about tourists and tourism, their personal aspirations and expectations for the future, and their notions about the qualities that make Jamaica unique" (J. Gamradt, 1995).

TABLE 16.5. Classification of Projective Techniques

Technique	Response Requested

Construction
  Thematic apperception test (TAT)
  Item substitution test
  Photo-driving
	The informant is asked to respond for or to describe a character in a simulated situation.

Association
  Word-association test
  Rorschach inkblot test
  Cloud pictures
  Auditory projective techniques
	The informant is asked to reply to a stimulus with the first word, image, or percept that occurs to him or her.

Completion
  Sentence completion test
  Picture completion study	

Psychodrama	The informant is given an incomplete expresion, image, or situation and asked to complete it however he or she chooses.

Source: Adapted from Green, Tull, and Albaum, 1988.

ANALYZING AND INTERPRETING DATA

In qualitative research, data collection, analysis, and interpretation are deeply interwoven. The output (descriptions and meanings) of the first collected data serves as an immediate input for further data collection. The decision to stop gathering data is also guided by concurrent analyses (to see when saturation is reached). The attentive reader will have noticed that I have already mentioned several methods and tools of analysis in the previous sections.

Depth of Analysis

In qualitative analysis, data are words or pictures. The advantage of this type of data is that they fit more closely to informants' thoughts and behavior. But they have a major disadvantage in comparison with quantitative data (i.e., numbers): they are much more complicated to process. Words and pictures can have more than one meaning. That is why it is important to interpret them in their full context.

There are many ways to analyze qualitative data. We do not want to list all possible methods and techniques because it is not what matters here (for more details, see Miles and Huberman, 1984; Denzin and Lincoln, 1994). The basic decision is about the depth of analysis: do we "only" want to describe data or also to infer propositions from it? After Strauss and Corbin (1990), we distinguish three alternatives, depending on how much interpretation there should be.

Straight description involves the pure statement of the phenomenon under study. The goal is to give a faithful account of informants' view of reality (what happened, what and who was involved, etc.) without any analysis and interpretation by the researcher. The resulting qualitative descriptions, or *reports*, are written in a narrative form, sometimes reporting an activity in detail, sometimes giving a more holistic picture of the phenomenon.

Analytic description involves reducing and arranging the gathered material to make sense and structure of it. This leads to accurate or "thick" descriptions, which are the product of the researcher's presentation of what is being studied. Illustrative material (text quotations, pictures, and so on) is displayed to give an idea of what the observed world is really like. The researcher's interpretation (which varies in level of abstraction) of that descriptive material is meant to represent a more detached conceptualization of that reality. *Case studies* are a typical example of analytic description. This involves focusing data collection and analysis on specific cases (individuals, groups, phenomena) within their real-life context in order to get a comprehensive, systematic, and in-depth insight into these cases. Data can be of any type: interviews, observation transcripts, field notes, documents, quantitative data, and so on. There can be one or multiple cases, one or multiple units of analysis (Yin, 1984). Case studies are very popular in tourism research.

Building a *local theory* is an even more inferential alternative. Interpretation is not limited to descriptions and conceptualizations, but also aims at connecting concepts to form a theoretical rendition of reality. The emerging local theory is not only used to explain that reality but also provides a framework for action. Building a local theory involves both inductive and logical analysis. Inductive analysis means that categories, patterns, and themes emerge from the data rather than being imposed before data collection and analysis. Categories help break up the complexity of reality into parts. The resulting typologies can be constructed in two ways. In the first, the analyst uses the categories generated by the informants themselves ("emic" approach), while in the second, the researcher develops terms to describe categories and patterns for which the informants did not have labels ("etic" approach).

Logical analysis is the highest-order step in the inductive process. It pertains to cross-classifying the different dimensions "to generate new insights about how the data can be organized and to look for patterns that may not have been immediately obvious in the initial, inductive analysis" (Patton, 1980, p. 314).

The *grounded theory* approach (Glaser and Strauss, 1967; Glaser, 1978) is a typical illustration of logical analysis and is characterized by the following basic principles:

- Concurrent data collection and analysis
- Theoretical sensitivity: think descriptively, analytically, interpretatively, and critically at the same time
- Evolving technique: categories and theory evolve as long as new material is gathered and analyzed
- Coding procedures (see below) lead the way to the final formulation of an explanatory framework that fits emerging theory
- Asking of questions and making of comparisons

In recent years, a few authors have used the grounded-theory approach to examine problems in tourism behavior (Teare, 1994; Riley, 1995; Hernandez, Cohen, and Garcia, 1996; Decrop, in progress). Connell and Lowe (1997) have recently reviewed the application of inductive methods in tourism and hospitality management research.

Activities and Tools

Qualitative researchers are often overwhelmed with information. Different activities and tools help them in creating order out of chaos. A first task, especially when working with large chunks of text, is to reduce it (selecting relevant elements in the gathered material) and organize it (to ease storage and retrieval). Useful information must also be displayed, analyzed, and synthesized. Interpretation and verification, i.e., giving meaning and soundness to findings, are the paramount qualitative activities. Be aware that these activities are not sequential but often occur concurrently. They are helped by coding the transcripts of the gathered material (field notes, interviews, observations). Writing memos and constructing matrices and diagrams are other profitable techniques to support data management and analysis.

Codes

Coding represents "the operations by which data are broken down, conceptualized, and put back together in new ways" (Strauss and Corbin, 1990, p. 57). A code is an abbreviation or a symbol given to a chunk of text (a paragraph, a sentence, or even a single word) for classification or categorization (Huberman and Miles, 1994). An important remark is that besides text chunks, nonverbal and nontextual attitudes such as hesitations or signs of emotions can also be coded. There are many procedures for coding that range from "customized" informal systems to more formal procedures (Glaser, 1978; Spradley, 1979; Bogdan and Biklen, 1992; Lofland and Lofland, 1995). Eventually, it is not the method that matters but rather obtaining easy access to the data.

Strauss and Corbin (1990) suggest three types of coding: open, axial, and selective. *Open coding* is considered the first level of coding, which pertains to the conceptualization and categorization of data. Miles and Huberman (1984) call it the descriptive level. Text chunks are given "etiquettes" and are classified. Axial coding is more inferential: connections between emerging categories are made following this paradigm model:

(A) CAUSAL CONDITIONS → (B) PHENOMENON →
(C) CONTEXT → (D) INTERVENING CONDITIONS →
(E) ACTION/INTERACTION STRATEGIES →
(F) CONSEQUENCES.

Selective coding is not basically different from axial coding since it also consists of linking and connecting different categories. But this is done at a higher, more abstract level of analysis. A few "core" categories are selected and systematically related to other categories. After that, the problem is to validate these relationships and to fill in categories that need further development.

Memos

Memos represent the written form of our abstract thinking about data (Strauss and Corbin, 1990). In qualitative analysis, it is advisable to write a memo each time we feel it necessary to interpret in more depth what is going on and to explain it consistently at a more conceptual level. Writing memos pertains to codes, research activities, and theories:

1. Code memos are written for problems related to the categorization of data, the relationships between variables, and theoretical intuitions.
2. Operational memos contain indications about directions to follow in later interviewing, analyses, or interpretations (potentially interesting comparisons, questions that deserve special attention, ideas to follow up on, etc.).
3. Theoretical memos pertain to the definition and explanation of (at least potentially) important categories and concepts. Relevant literature is referenced.

Diagrams and Matrices

Diagramming is a very useful way of classifying, displaying, and synthesizing qualitative information. In the end, diagrams represent "an unencumbered graphic version of the theory available to aid others in visualizing and comprehending your theory as well as assist you to keep the relationships clear when writing" (Strauss and Corbin, 1990, p. 220).

Matrices are a special case of diagrams. Other examples are flow charts and sets. While there are no fixed canons for constructing a matrix, functionality should always kept in mind. Miles and Huberman's (1984) message is to "think in terms of matrices, and invent a format that will serve you best" (p. 211). However, these authors give a checklist of questions guiding choice:

1. Descriptive versus explanatory intent: Do I want to report data as they are or to infer some interpretation from them?
2. Single- versus multiple-site data: Am I focusing on phenomena attached to a single research setting/case or to several settings/cases from which reasonably comparable data have been collected?
3. Ordered versus nonordered: Do the matrix's successive rows and columns represent any logical order (according to intensity of a variable, time, role of participants, sites, etc.) or "only" the different descriptive categories, one by one?
4. Categories of variables: What is the analytical level of interest (social subject, social object; see Table 16.3)?
5. Cell entries: What level and type of data will you enter in the matrix cells? Alternatives include: direct quotes, text extracts; summaries,

paraphrases or abstracts; personal explanations; ratings or summarized judgments.

For all of the previous elements, combinations are possible such as illustrated by Exemplar 7.

Exemplar 7: Summary Sheets

To keep a global view in the longitudinal process of gathering and analyzing information about vacationers' decision-making processes, I constructed a summary matrix for each decision-making unit of my sample. Rows represent the major aspects of holiday projects (position in the decision-making process, content, and situational factors) and of envisioned destinations (consideration set, situational factors, and gathered information). Columns correspond to a time line where the four periods of interviews are placed in a sequential order. I filled in one column each time the decision-making unit had been interviewed. It is easy to notice that my summary sheets contain both descriptive and interpretative elements. These matrices were useful for three reasons:

1. I could use the summarized data as an input for questions in later interviews.
2. I could follow the evolution of the holiday projects and the evoked destinations.
3. Finally, these sheets help analysis when making comparisons both within and between cases.

Practical Advice

I close this chapter by giving a few comments on how to use the previous tools practically. First of all, any recording (tapes, field notes, etc.) should be extensively transcribed. The raw material should be listened to, read, or contemplated again and again in order to become immersed in the data.

Coding is usually done by writing in the left margin of the transcripts, placing slashes between text chunks, or underlining quotes with different colors. Cutting, piling, and indexing are used in later coding phases. Note that the textual unit of analysis can be a paragraph, a sentence, a string of words, or even single words. Line-by-line analysis is also sometimes used (especially with computer programs). Memos are better written on index cards and then piled and sorted. Matrices and diagrams are best displayed on one sheet, even if that sheet covers a wall. The number of variables must not be exaggerated. Decomposition and hierarchization improve the visual presentation.

Until recently, all those operations were done by hand. Today, several computer software programs such as *The Ethnograph, NUD-IST,* or *ATLAS/ti* help in qualitative data management and analysis. Weitzman and Miles (1995) give a good description of the functionalities of twenty-four programs. Despite the usefulness of those programs for retrieving and coding text and building conceptual networks, a substantial number of researchers still prefer the old pencil and scissors technique because they need to stay immersed in their data.

Triangulation

The major critique raised against qualitative approaches is their lack of scientific rigor and of generalizability. Both reliability and validity are brought into question since Cronbach's alphas and probabilistic predictions cannot be determined. In the section, "Why Are Qualitative Data Useful?" I already defended the usefulness of qualitative data. Here I present criteria by which the soundness of a qualitative study can be judged. First, it is important to notice that trust is established by paying attention to the general methodology and not only to the results. Lincoln and Guba (1985) have developed four precise criteria that parallel the quantitative terminology:

1. Credibility (internal validity): How truthful are particular findings?
2. Transferability (external validity): How applicable are the research findings to another setting or group?
3. Dependability (reliability): Are the results consistent and easily reproduced?
4. Confirmability (objectivity): How neutral are the findings (in terms of whether they are reflective of the informants and the inquiry, and not a product of the researcher's biases and prejudices)?

All those criteria are operationalized by *triangulation,* which means verifying qualitative information by looking at the same phenomenon from different angles. Denzin (1978) identifies four basic types of triangulation. By combining data, investigators, methods, and theories, triangulation opens the way for richer and potentially more valid interpretations.

Data triangulation is the use of a variety of data sources in a study. There are several ways to achieve this. First, different types of material can be collected (see the section "Supplementary Qualitative Techniques").

Second, a broad range of informants can be examined (see the section "Designing the Research"). Finally, the same persons or phenomena can be observed at different points in time. In so doing, all kinds of comparisons are possible.

Method triangulation entails the use of multiple methods to study a single problem. In my research, for example, I used projective techniques to gather holiday information in another way than through asking direct questions. After the first interview, I suggested that one person in each decision-making unit should close his or her eyes and describe in his or her own words one typical day out of the next summer holidays. After the second interview, I asked informants to show me a few photographs of their last summer holidays and to comment on them. Along with interviewing and projective techniques, I also decided to observe vacationers in settings that are less obtrusive for the decision maker than a discussion at home. Sessions of nonparticipant observations were held at a holiday trade fair (see Exemplar 5) and in a travel agency.

Theoretical triangulation involves using multiple perspectives to interpret a single set of data. Confronting emerging hypotheses with existing theories (no matter whether they are based on quantitative and qualitative approaches) and searching for alternative explanations help make conclusions more robust.

Investigator triangulation is concerned with using several different researchers to evaluate the same body of data. Besides the investigator's own subjectivity, gender, race, and culture can bias qualitative analysis. This type of triangulation is very demanding in effort and time; the best solution is to work as a team. I could add a fifth type of triangulation that is very relevant for tourism research: *interdisciplinary triangulation*. Interpretations would become richer and more holistic if investigators and theories from different disciplines (psychology, sociology, anthropology, marketing, geography) are all used to study one problem.

SUMMARY AND CONCLUSIONS

Qualitative research often frightens researchers. It frightens beginners because it proposes no fixed methodology to follow. It frightens quantitative researchers because it allows no strong predictions. It frightens lazy people because valuable material can be huge. In this chapter, I have shown that, while partly founded, these fears are balanced by greater promises. A qualitative approach is strongly recommended in tourism for studying motivations, attitudes, and behavior, for understanding how decisions are made and how tourist experiences are lived. Techniques such as in-depth interviewing and participant observation bring the investigator much closer to informants' daily-life reality. Methods such as case studies and grounded theory allow in-depth, and thereby potentially more valid, analysis of the phenomenon under study. Tools such as codes, memos, and diagrams offer considerable help in reducing, organizing, and synthesizing high piles of data. Triangulation further contributes, ensuring a qualitative study's soundness, and refuting positivists' reproach that it is not "good" science.

CONCEPT DEFINITIONS

Case: A bound context in which one is studying events, processes, and outcomes.

Case study: The systematic examination of a specific case in its real-life context.

Code: An abbreviation or a symbol given to a chunk of qualitative data for conceptualization and categorization.

Field research: See Participant observation.

Focus group: A qualitative interview technique in which a group of persons are brought together to debate about a particular topic.

Grounded theory: A theory that is inductively derived from the study of the phenomenon it represents.

Guiding hypotheses: See Sensitizing concepts.

In-depth interview: A qualitative, open-ended interview method for pursuing a subject in-depth, operating in a discovery mode, and creating interaction with an individual.

Memo: The written product of abstract thinking about qualitative data.

Observation: The systematic noting and recording of events, behaviors, and objects in the social setting chosen for study.

Participant observation: A qualitative method in which data are systematically collected by the social interaction between the researcher and informants in the milieu of the latter.

Projective techniques: Indirect means of qualitative questioning in which informants' beliefs and feelings are "projected" onto a third person, an inanimate object, or a task situation.

Sensitizing concepts: Broad research questions that provide a basic framework highlighting the importance of certain kinds of events, activities, and behaviors.

Setting: A physical place or location where a population or a phenomenon can be observed.

Site: See Case.

Theoretical sampling: Sampling method based on concepts that have proven theoretical relevance to the evolving theory.
Triangulation: The process of verifying qualitative information by looking at the same phenomenon from different angles.

REVIEW QUESTIONS

1. Explain in which instances qualitative approaches are more appropriate than quantitative approaches for dealing with problems in tourism behavior.
2. What is meant by "guiding hypotheses" or "sensitizing concepts"?
3. List and briefly discuss the criteria on which the choice of an appropriate research methodology should be based.
4. Discuss the problem of selection and sampling in qualitative tourism research.
5. Imagine and explain one original example in tourism behavior in which interview and observation could be used together.
6. What are the goals and characteristics of projective techniques?
7. Compare straight description, analytic description, and local theory as methods to analyze qualitative material.
8. Explain how you would code in order to develop a grounded theory.
9. Next to codes, what additional help do memos and diagrams bring to the qualitative analyst?
10. Name Lincoln and Guba's four criteria by which the trustworthiness of a qualitative study can be evaluated and explain how these criteria are operationalized by triangulation.

REFERENCES

Bhattacharyya, D.P. (1997). Mediating India: An analysis of a guidebook. *Annals of Tourism Research*, 24, 371-389.
Bogdan, R.C. and Biklen, S.K. (1992). *Qualitative research in education: An introduction to theory and methods*. Boston: Allyn and Bacon.
Bramwell, B. and Rawding, L. (1996). Tourism marketing images of industrial cities. *Annals of Tourism Research*, 23, 201-221.
Brent Ritchie, J.R. (1994). Research on leisure behavior and tourism—State of the art. In R.V. Gasser and K. Weiermair (Ed.), *Spoilt for choice. Decision making processes and preference change of tourists: Intertemporal and intercountry perspectives* (pp. 2-27). Thaur, Germany: Kulturverlag.

Connell, J. and Lowe, A. (1997). Generating grounded theory from qualitative data: The application of inductive methods in tourism and hospitality management research. *Progress in Tourism and Hospitality Research, 3,* 165-173.

Corey, R.J. (1996). A drama-based model of traveler destination choice. *Journal of Travel and Tourism Marketing,* 5 (4), 1-22.

Dann, G.M. (1996). Tourists' images of a destination—An alternative analysis. *Journal of Travel and Tourism Marketing,* 5 (1/2), 41-55.

Dann, G., Nash D., and Pierce, P. (1988). Methodology in tourism research. *Annals of Tourism Research,* 15, 1-28.

Decrop, A. (in progress). Where will we go this year? Consumers' decision-making processes revisited through an ethnography of vacationers. Unpublished doctoral dissertation, University of Namur, Belgium.

Denzin, N.K. (1978). *The research act: A theoretical introduction to sociological methods.* New York: McGraw-Hill.

Denzin, N.K. and Lincoln, Y.S. (Eds.). (1994). *Handbook of qualitative research.* Thousand Oaks, CA: Sage.

Enoch, Y. (1996). Contents of tour packages: A cross-cultural comparison. *Annals of Tourism Research,* 23, 599-616.

Forsyth, T.J. (1995). Tourism and agricultural development in Thailand. *Annals of Tourism Research,* 22, 877-900.

Gamradt, J. (1995). Jamaican children's representations of tourism. *Annals of Tourism Research,* 22, 735-762.

Glaser, B. (1978). *Theoretical sensitivity.* Mill Valley, CA: Sociology Press.

Glaser, B. and Strauss, A. (1967). *The discovery of grounded theory.* Chicago: Aldine.

Green, P.E., Tull, D.S., and Albaum, G. (1988). *Research for marketing decisions.* Englewood Cliffs, NJ: Prentice Hall.

Guba, E.G. and Lincoln, Y.S. (1994). Competing paradigms in qualitative research. In N.K. Denzin and Y.S. Lincoln (Eds.), *Handbook of Qualitative Research* (pp. 105-117). Thousand Oaks, CA: Sage.

Haire, M. (1950). Projective techniques in marketing research. *Journal of Marketing,* 14, 649-656.

Hartmann, R. (1988). Combining field methods in tourism research. *Annals of Tourism Research,* 15, 88-105.

Henderson, K.A. (1991). *Dimensions of choice: A qualitative approach to recreation, parks, and leisure research.* State College, PA: Venture Publishing.

Hernandez, S.A., Cohen, J., and Garcia, H.L. (1996). Residents' attitudes towards an instant enclave resort. *Annals of Tourism Research,* 23, 755-779.

Hollinshead, K. (1996). The tourism researcher as a bricoleur: The new wealth and diversity in qualitative inquiry. *Tourism Analysis,* 1, 67-74.

Huberman, A.M. and Miles, M.B. (1994). Data management and analysis methods. In N.K. Denzin and Y.S. Lincoln (Eds.), *Handbook of Qualitative Research* (pp. 428-444). Thousand Oaks, CA: Sage.

Jurowski, C. and Olsen, M.D. (1995). Scanning the environment of tourism attractions: A content analysis approach. *Journal of Travel and Tourism Marketing*, 4 (1), 71-95.

Lincoln, Y.S. and Guba, E. (1985). *Naturalistic inquiry.* Beverly Hills, CA: Sage.

Lofland, J. and Lofland, L.H. (1995). *Analyzing social settings: A guide to qualitative observation and analysis.* Belmont, CA: Wadsworth.

Markwell, K.W. (1997). Dimensions of photography in a nature-based tour. *Annals of Tourism Research*, 24, 131-155.

Marshall, C. and Rossman, G.B. (1995). *Designing qualitative research.* Thousand Oaks, CA: Sage.

Marti, B.E. (1995). Marketing aspects of consumer purchasing behavior and customer satisfaction aboard the Royal Viking Queen. *Journal of Travel and Tourism Marketing*, 4 (4), 109-116.

McCay, K.J. and Fesenmaier, D.R. (1997). Pictorial element of destination image formation. *Annals of Tourism Research*, 24, 537-565.

Miles, M.B. and Huberman, A.M. (1984). *Qualitative data analysis: A sourcebook of new methods.* Beverly Hills, CA: Sage.

Miller, W.L. and Crabtree, B.F. (1994). Clinical research. In N.K. Denzin and Y.S. Lincoln (Eds.), *Handbook of Qualitative Research* (pp. 340-352). Thousand Oaks, CA: Sage.

Milman, A. (1993). Maximizing the value of focus group research: Qualitative analysis of consumer's destination choice. *Journal of Travel Research*, 32 (Fall), 61-64.

Nogawa, H., Yamaguchi, Y., and Hagi, Y. (1996). An empirical research study on Japanese sport tourism in sport-for-all events: Case studies of a single-night event and a multiple-night event. *Journal of Travel Research*, 35 (Fall), 46-54.

Patton, M.Q. (1980). *Qualitative evaluation methods.* Beverly Hills, CA: Sage.

Peterson, K.I. (1994). Qualitative research methods for the travel and tourism industry. In J.R. Brent Ritchie and C.R. Goeldner (Eds.), *Travel, Tourism, and Hospitality Research: A Handbook for Managers and Researchers* (pp. 487-492). New York: John Wiley and Sons.

Riley, R. (1995). Prestige worthy leisure travel behavior. *Annals of Tourism Research*, 22, 630-649.

Riley, R. (1996). Revealing socially constructed knowledge through quasi-structured interviews and grounded theory analysis. *Journal of Travel and Tourism Marketing*, 5 (1/2), 21-40.

Riley, R.W. and Love, L.L. (1997). The state of qualitative tourism research. Unpublished working paper.

Rubin, H.J. and Rubin, I.S. (1995). *Qualitative interviewing: The art of hearing data.* Thousand Oaks, CA: Sage.

Ryan, C. (1997). Tourist experiences, phenomenographic analysis and neural networks. Unpublished working paper.

Spradley, J.S. (1979). *The ethnographic interview.* New York: Holt, Rinehart and Winston.

Stewart, S.I. and Stynes, D.J. (1994). Toward a dynamic model of complex tourism choices: The seasonal home location decision. *Journal of Travel and Tourism Marketing*, 3 (3), 69-88.

Strauss, A. and Corbin J. (1990). *Basics of qualitative research: Grounded theory procedures and techniques.* Newbury Park, CA: Sage.

Taylor, S.J. and Bogdan, R. (1984). *Introduction to qualitative research: The search for meanings.* New York: John Wiley.

Teare, R. (1994). Consumer decision making. In R. Teare, J.A. Mazanec, S. Crawford-Welch, and S. Calver (Eds.), *Marketing in Hospitality and Tourism: A Consumer Focus* (pp. 1-96). London: Cassell.

Wallace, G.N. and Pierce, S.M. (1996). An evaluation of ecotourism in Amazonas, Brazil. *Annals of Tourism Research,* 23, 843-873.

Walle, A.H. (1996). Habits of thought and cultural tourism. *Annals of Tourism Research,* 23, 874-890.

Walle, A.H. (1997). Quantitative versus qualitative tourism research. *Annals of Tourism Research*, 24, 524-536.

Weitzman, E. and Miles, M.B. (1995). *Computer programs for qualitative analysis.* Thousand Oaks, CA: Sage.

Woodside, A.G. and MacDonald, R. (1994). General system framework of customer choice processes of tourism services. In R.V. Gasser and K. Weiermair (Eds.), *Spoilt for Choice. Decision Making Processes and Preference Change of Tourists: Intertemporal and Intercountry Perspectives* (pp. 30-59). Thaur: Kulturverlag.

Yin, R.K. (1984). *Case study research: Design and methods.* Beverly Hills, CA: Sage.

PART V: TOURIST BEHAVIOR

The chapters in this section describe the varied types of travel and travelers. The authors analyze and compare the behavior of tourists of different ages, nationalities, and lifestyles in regard to vacation destination selection, the activities they engage in while on vacation, and other similar factors.

Douglas and Douglas, in Chapter 17, analyzed the behavior of cruise passengers and found that different cruises are suited for different people, as are most types of vacations. Their study examined three different vessels and concluded that their passenger profiles differed in such important features as age, socioeconomic and cultural background, cruise experience, and consumer expectations. The concept of a typical cruise "society" or "cruise culture" is not borne out by their study. While they found some similarities in cruise consumer behavior, there were also a significant number of differences, which well outweighed the similarities.

In Chapter 18, the effect of the nationality of tourists on their touristic behavior is analyzed by Pizam in a series of studies conducted among British, Korean, Israeli, and Dutch tour guides. As expected, the tour guides in all four studies perceived significant differences in the behavior of tourists of different nationalities.

In a study that concentrated on the effect of age on tourist's behavior, Javalgi, Thomas and Rao compared the behavior of older travelers to those of younger age, which is reported in Chapter 19. As expected, the researchers found substantial differences between the two groups. Yet, surprisingly it was found that many older travelers do not vacation for the sheer purpose of rest and relaxation.

This leads us to believe that lifestyle and the stage of a person's family life cycle play a substantial role in when, how, where, and even if travel occurs. The chapters written by Lawson (Chapter 20) and Lawson, Thyne, Young, and Juric (Chapter 21) prove that these characteristics have a substantial effect on tourist behavior and influence the amount of money spent while vacationing. For example, it has been well established that certain tourists prefer outdoor or sporting activities while others prefer to vacation with the family or indoors. Not surprisingly, personal lifestyle characteristics play a determining role in this preference.

Last, but not least, the travel behavior of older women is examined in a study conducted by Hawes (Chapter 22). This study found that though older (50-plus) women shared some common sociodemographic characteristics such as higher education and higher incomes, and the majority of them disliked big-city vacations, they nevertheless varied significantly in terms of excitement and adventure seeking as well as other touristic preferences.

In conclusion, the chapters in this section make it clear that many factors influence the way consumers behave if and when they decide to travel on vacation. "If" is used here because even the decision to travel at all also varies with the lifestyle, nationality, family life cycle, age, and gender.

Chapter 17

Cruise Consumer Behavior: A Comparative Study

Ngaire Douglas
Norman Douglas

LEARNING OBJECTIVES

By the end of the chapter the reader should be able to:

- Describe the historical and current development of cruising as a tourist activity
- Analyze the nature of the relationship between types of cruise ships and types of passengers
- Understand the motivations of tourists who choose to cruise
- Determine the similarities and differences between on-board activities on three different cruise ships
- Describe the participation and behavior of passengers in various activities

HISTORICAL BACKGROUND

In 1844 Arthur Anderson, cofounder of the Peninsular and Oriental Steam Navigation Company (P&O), advertised the first sea voyage that could justify the description "cruise"; that is, a round trip for the purposes of pleasure and recreation rather than simply a method of transport. The route took passengers from England around the Mediterranean and home again, stopping at a number of ports with organized shore excursions in each. It was a significant event in tourism history for at least two reasons: it initiated affordable, organized, pleasure-motivated sea travel, and it

369

introduced English travelers, in greater numbers than ever before, to warmer shores. Only three years earlier Thomas Cook had organized his famous first group excursion by rail, thus ensuring his place in history as the founder of popular tourism. Over the next century, rapid developments in maritime technology led to the extensive growth of passenger shipping for both transport and recreational purposes, while increases in leisure time assisted the growth of tourism. In many parts of the world passengers on ocean cruises were the first tourists, establishing host-guest relationships that became the basis of much later developments in large scale tourism (Douglas and Douglas, 1997a, 1997b).

CRUISING IN THE 1990s

One hundred and fifty years after the pioneer efforts of Anderson and Cook, tourism is the world's largest industry and cruising one of its most dynamic components. Ocean cruising shows consistent growth of between 10 and 12 percent annually and accounts for some five billion dollars in annual investment. Many of the cruise sector's major features have been detailed in reports by Peisley (1989, 1992, 1995) and Cruise Lines International Association (1995), but, except for some statistical details, these have paid scant attention to what is arguably cruising's most significant feature—the passengers. However, to provide some overall context for this study, which concentrates on cruise consumer (i.e., passenger) behavior, some of the main points of these studies may be summarized here.

In the late 1990s, the industry worldwide is dominated by eight principal cruise lines of which three, Carnival, Royal Caribbean, and P&O, have emerged as leaders. Increased investment in new and larger ships, corporate mergers, and ever more vigorous product promotion suggest that the three leaders will draw further away from the smaller companies, some of which may vanish completely.

The demand by major companies for larger ships is overwhelming. Between 1995 and 1998, of twenty-eight ships purchased by or on order from major cruise lines, twenty-three were over 40,000 gross registered tons (GRT: a measurement of capacity, not of weight), with passenger capacities of more than 1,000; four of them of 100,000 GRT and capacities of 3,000. Two of the latter have been added to Carnival's fleet and one to P&O's fleet, which also added two vessels of 77,000 GRT, while Royal Caribbean's fleet has been increased by five vessels of 70,000 GRT or more, further emphasizing the dominance of these three lines.

Cruise destinations are dominated by the Caribbean, which accounts for more than 50 percent of the North American market and is increasing in popularity with passengers from the U.K. and Europe generally. Other destinations pale by comparison, with the next most popular location, the Mediterranean, attracting only a little over 9 percent of the North American market, Alaska accounting for just under 8 percent, and the South Pacific for only 2.2 percent of that market. Caribbean dominance of the market is expected to increase with the probable location there of most of the new and larger vessels.

The popularity of the Caribbean as a cruise destination reflects other significant features of the industry: the overwhelming importance of the North American (preponderantly U.S.) market and the popularity of short cruises—those from two to eight days—which account for 90 percent of the market. Cruises of nine days or more appear to have declined in popularity since the late 1980s.

LITERATURE AND RESEARCH METHOD

Compared with the proliferation of studies on other aspects of tourism, there is a limited number of formal studies of the cruise sector, although the activity has always encouraged an abundance of anecdotal and visual material. Formal studies to date have generally concentrated on the supply side, with passing reference to demand (Plowman, 1992; Peisley, 1989, 1995), or have examined cruise ship influence on destination development (Lawton and Butler, 1987; Douglas and Douglas, 1997a). Foster's (1986) case study undertaken on a specialist ship in the South Pacific was distinctive in that it applied other research techniques and interpretive skills to passenger motivation and behavior. A special edition of the *Journal of Tourism Studies* in December 1996 was a significant attempt to focus attention on this sector of tourism, filling a much needed bibliographic role as well as bringing together a useful collection of cruise-related studies on history, economic impacts, and motivation. Despite its long history and its significance to the development of leisure travel, however, cruising has been largely overlooked by tourism researchers.

This chapter examines the behavior of passengers on three ships on cruises with three different itineraries and describes the similarities and differences. As lecturers regularly engaged on a number of cruise ships for over a decade, the authors have had excellent opportunities to study both passengers and crews in a wide variety of situations. For this study the research techniques incorporated participant observation as well as structured interviews with ships' staff members. Company statistics and passenger profiles were used to confirm observed patterns and trends in behavior (Ryan, 1995, p. 97). Although participant observation may raise ethical issues about disclosure and privacy rights of respondents, the authors agree with Foster (1986) that the use of such research tools as tape recorders and structured questionnaires would introduce elements of constraint with fellow passengers which would be counterproductive. In the experience of the authors, they would be even more counterproductive if used with crew. Video and still camera records, however, were maintained because their use was not seen as atypical behavior. Senior staff, including captains, pursers, and cruise directors, were routinely informed of the purpose of interviews and conversations prior to their taking place. Other informants such as bar staff, waiters, and room stewards were freely engaged in conversation in the same way as they might have been with regular passengers.

SHIPS OF THE STUDY

Island Princess, Fairstar, and Crystal Symphony

Three ships were selected for this study, significantly different from each other in terms of size, age, quality, target market, and passenger profile. Some details of their history, physical features, facilities, and passenger capacity will help to make the analysis of passenger behavior more meaningful, as each ship offers a different product and, thus, attracts a different clientele. In view of the emphasis placed on the American market in studies of cruising, it was decided to include a ship that had little if any association with American passengers or their presumed needs but whose target market was almost entirely Australian, or perhaps Antipodean, since *Fairstar* (withdrawn from service in early 1997) was marketed also in New Zealand.

Island Princess entered service in February 1972 as *Island Venture*, undergoing a change of name at the time of its acquisition by Princess Cruises. With a GRT of 19,907 and a passenger capacity of 717, it is not only the smallest of the three ships studied here, but of a size that may well become obsolete, if the present trend toward "megaships" continues. It is a sister ship to *Pacific Princess*. The two ships have acquired the status of tourism legends as a result of the TV series *The Love Boat* and the assimilation of the series' title into the marketing campaign of P&O, which acquired Princess Cruises in 1974. "It's more than a cruise; it's the Love Boat," runs the slogan used to promote *Island Princess*—indeed all ships bearing the Princess brand name—many years after the series ended. However, the regular screening of episodes from the series on the in-cabin video systems on Princess ships helps to reinforce the legend, as does the frequent playing of the series' theme tune by ships' orchestras, although now almost no resemblance exists between those parts of the Love Boat shown in the TV series and the ships themselves.

Passenger facilities on *Island Princess* include—in addition to the dining room—two small outdoor swimming pools, fitness center, library, beauty salon, four bars, multipurpose shop/boutique, photographers' shop, one show lounge and one other general-purpose lounge, film theater, and casino with both gambling tables and slot machines. Officers are mostly (but no longer entirely) British. The crew is generally described as "international" and may include Americans and British (mostly as bar staff), Filipinos (mostly as bar staff and cabin attendants), Pakistanis (as deck hands or maintenance staff) and, increasingly, Iberians and Eastern Europeans as dining room waiters or assistant waiters. The days when Italians, because of their tradition of service, all but monopolized dining room staff positions appear to be over.

In *Berlitz Complete Guide to Cruising and Cruise Ships* (Ward, 1992) *Island Princess* was rated at four stars plus in a rating system in which the maximum award was five stars plus. However, at the time of writing, the ship was beginning to show signs of age and wear, although refurbishment in 1992-1993 had recast it "in the style of the newer, more elegant vessels" (Slater and Basch, 1996). In *Fielding's Worldwide Cruises 1997* (Slater and Basch, 1996) *Island Princess* received a three-star rating out of a maximum of six stars. Its relatively small size has made the vessel one of the most versatile cruise ships in the world, and it has cruised a number of locations with equal success. Its size has also helped to encourage a high degree of relaxed camaraderie among passengers and between passengers and staff, which is not always present on larger vessels.

Fairstar (originally *Oxfordshire*) entered service in February 1957 as a troop carrier, but saw little of this activity before its conversion to immigrant vessel and subsequently to cruise ship. It had a GRT of 23,764 and—in its final manifestation—a passenger capacity of 1,598. From 1974 it was used almost exclusively to cruise the South Pacific, following a well-established itinerary and marketed aggressively by its owners, Sitmar, as the "Funship," during which time it established a reputation for economy, informality, high spirits, and casual sexual encounters. Both the ship and its parent company were acquired in 1988 by P&O, which modified *Fairstar*'s established itinerary by adding some "exclusive," lesser-known Pacific Island ports, but were obliged to maintain its reputation for boisterous good times almost intact, having attempted with little success to modify its image.

Passenger facilities included a casual coffee shop/snack bar (with surcharge) in addition to two dining rooms; outdoor swimming pool; fitness center; several bars, including one (the Sharp End Bar) in which graffitists were encouraged to write or draw on wall space intended for this purpose; two shops, the larger of which was the only genuinely duty-free outlet on any of the ships studied in this article; show lounge; large film theater; no library—a feature which helped to add to the abundance of jokes about the quality of its passengers—beauty salon; photographers' shop; casino consisting mainly of slot machines, more of which occupied space in other parts of the ship; and children's playroom, staffed on most cruises. The ship's officers were Italian—a legacy of the association with Sitmar—and its crew "international," although service staff were mainly European and Indonesian. With a relatively large passenger capacity, a number of four-berth cabins (marketed as the "Friendly Fours") and even some six-berthers (though these were generally unused in its later years), sixty-eight cabins without en suite facilities, small, awkwardly designed bathrooms in most others and many cabins whose walls provided only minimal soundproofing, *Fairstar* constantly disclosed its history as troop and immigrant ship, despite frequent refits. It was the only ship studied here on which it was impossible to avoid noise (from roistering passengers or the ubiquitous PA system) at any time of the day in any of the public areas, open or enclosed. It was also the only one on which the disco was vigorously active every night of the cruise. For all that, its reputation helped make it one of modern cruising's great success stories during its twenty-three years of service in the Pacific, until its retirement in early 1997. It was rated three stars by Berlitz, which drew attention to its generally crowded conditions and its "lack of finesse," but added, "Who cares?" (Ward, 1992).

Crystal Symphony, with a GRT of 50,000 and a passenger capacity of 1,010, entered service in May 1995 and may be regarded as one of the new generation of floating resort hotels, displaying in many respects features more common to land-based resorts than to ships. The vessel features a large hotel-style lobby with winding staircase, shopping arcade ("Avenue of the Stars") rather than a single multipurpose shop, business center with the latest computers, specialty restaurants (with no surcharge) in addition to the main dining room, and spacious passenger accommodations with marble-lined bathrooms. Many also have private verandas. *Crystal Symphony* contains activity rooms for both young children and teenagers, but they are evidently staffed only on certain sailings. The vessel's film theater is closer in appearance to a traditional cinema than those on the other two ships and its library more capacious and much better equipped. Of its two swimming pools, the larger is considerably bigger than any on the other two ships. The casino, operated by the Caesar's Palace organization and named accordingly, is the largest and most opulent of the three vessels studied and contains 125 slot machines in addition to eleven tables. In keeping with the traditions of Las Vegas, casino patrons receive free drinks at the casino's bar, one of eight bars on the ship.

Passenger space ratio (arrived at by dividing GRT by passenger capacity) is 27.7 on *Island Princess* and 14.8 on *Fairstar*, compared with a generous 52.08 on *Crystal Symphony*. The vessel was rated six stars by Fielding, which commented: "Big ship cruising doesn't get any better than this" (Slater and Basch, 1996). Officers are Norwegian and Japanese, while staff are "international," although with a seemingly smaller number of Filipinos and Indonesians than were encountered on the other vessels. Although built in Japan and owned by the Japanese NYK (Nippon Yusen Kaisha) Line, *Crystal Symphony* (together with its elder sister *Crystal Harmony*) is marketed chiefly in the United States and attracts an older and considerably higher income group than the other two ships. The history of the Crystal ships is a good deal briefer than that of the other ships in this study: it might be said that while they quickly acquired a reputation for style and outstanding service, they have not yet established an identity that completely distinguishes them from several of the other large, new vessels. In the world of cruising, the development of a ship's persona—gained partly from promotional imagery and partly from passenger experience—can be crucial to its success, even to its survival.

PASSENGER PROFILES

Tourists who choose cruises are seeking experiences that are different from those they would have in resorts, cities, land-based tours, and theme parks. Although cruise operators have been claiming this all along according to their own observations and data, Moscardo et al. (1996) applied multidimensional scaling analysis to a Canadian leisure survey with over 12,000 responses and concluded that cruise passengers chose the experience for the following reasons:

- Sense of romance
- Good value for money
- Excellent dining
- Quality entertainment
- Access to water-based activities
- Variety of destinations
- Opportunity to visit international destinations in controlled and organized way
- Safety

While several of these attributes can be identified with a number of other types of holidays, the last two are extremely significant in understanding the spectacular growth in demand for cruising, particularly when looking at the market. North Americans (especially U.S. citizens) are by far the largest market segment and while they are undoubtedly frequent travelers, they are also nervous ones. In times of international crises such as the Gulf War in 1991, regional conflicts, or terrorist activity, Americans fear being the target, even if unwittingly. They are not particularly adventurous in terms of culinary and cultural experiences, often preferring the opportunity to observe or sample cautiously without large-scale commitment. To these problems and perceptions of international travel the cruise ship apparently provides a solution. The self-contained environment is fully secured, with patrolling security staff, scanning machines for luggage and people, and extremely limited access via a single, constantly guarded gangway.

The formal entertainment on vessels catering to the U.S. market is determinedly American, with many guest performers recognized by passengers for their appearances on American television. The stage presentations are often based on famous Broadway shows or employ familiar techniques. The more patriotic the productions, the better they are received. One such production, *America's Music*, a Princess Cruises specialty, regularly receives a standing ovation accompanied by tears of pride and joy. Catering is designed around the nutritional requirements and expectations of Americans and it is entertaining for non-Americans to watch each other try such culinary challenges as waffles and maple syrup for breakfast. While dinner menus often adopt special themes—Italian Night, French Night, South Seas Night, for example—on American Night the dining room may reverberate with group renditions of *God Bless America*, while the small contingent of non-Americans looks on bemused. In foreign ports, well-planned shore excursions are available with English-speaking guides and air-conditioned buses, permitting passengers a quick, controlled, trouble-free experience of the most significant sites before they return to the comfort zone of the ship. Tomorrow may be another day, but it will be similarly organized. In short, for an increasing number of vacationers the cruise ship is the ideal total holiday experience.

Consumers who choose the *Island Princess* are generally of mature age and well-traveled, experienced cruisers who display a distinct preference for smaller ships. They regularly identify the more friendly atmosphere and the "cozy" ambiance as important factors along with the efficiency and quality service attitude of the crew. They are frequently repeat passengers and staff recognize them, thus cultivating a feeling of esteem and value. Their own familiarity with the ship complements this as well as adding a perception of control of the situation. This is considerably more difficult to achieve on the much bigger ships. The Southeast Asian schedule studied here is quite expensive compared to many other routes, particularly when connecting flights are factored in. Passengers, therefore, tend to belong to higher income brackets than on cruises closer to home. The Asian ports are, for most, at the extreme end of a continuum of cultural experiences; passengers who choose these cruises are more curious than many of their compatriots. Children are rare on these itineraries and no special facilities are provided for them. More visible are the indicators of wealth and displays of the floating resort experience. Gold glitters in a variety of forms and clothes decorated in nautical motifs dominate shipboard fashion, although to some extent this form of dress identification characterizes most cruising—and many resort—experiences.

Although the majority of passengers are couples, there are usually enough widows and divorcees on board to ensure that unaccompanied males are significantly outnumbered and that any male who can dance is in constant demand. Unlike Crystal Cruises and other lines, which address this gender imbalance by providing male hosts, on *Island Princess* passengers are more inclined to make up groups among themselves that accommodate their needs. Americans made up almost 80 percent of the passenger list on the cruise studied, with Canadians and British most prominent among the remainder.

Fairstar passengers were distinctive for a variety of reasons. P&O's publicity was directed at "average Australia," that is, low- to middle-income earners. A small contingent of New Zealanders was usually on board. On a typical cruise about 65 percent of passengers were cruising for the first time and almost 50 percent of passengers were age thirty years or under. This large percentage of young, predominantly single people contributed significantly to the ship's reputation as a place for constant partying. It was not unusual for early morning deck walkers to find the deck chairs fully occupied by sprawling, sleeping, hungover "party animals," the term popularly used by the ship's entertainment team (see Figure 17.1).

Staff in the purser's office and entertainment division were mainly Australian, a factor that contributed significantly to the nature of host-guest relationships. Australia does not possess a traditional service culture, a fact that was evident in relations between passengers and crew. Egalitarianism characterized communication, and this was evidently preferred by passengers. Passenger dress was decidedly casual; even the time-honored captain's cocktail party was a less dressy affair than those experienced on other ships where evening wear and formality prevail. It was not unknown for young men to embark on a *Fairstar* cruise with nothing but the clothes they were wearing, having been assured by their travel agents that a pair of

FIGURE 17.1. *Fairstar's* "Party Animals" Sleep Off the Effects of the Previous Night.

Photo: Norman Douglas.

shorts and a T-shirt were all that was required. Invariably, however, they found themselves directed to the shop for the compulsory purchase of long trousers and shirt to wear to dinner (Douglas and Douglas, 1997b).

For many the shipboard opportunities were the primary attractions, the ports of call all but incidental. The younger set, in particular, attracted by the budget fares, responded enthusiastically to the ship's reputation for informality. Until P&O disallowed the practice, young males not infrequently embarked with their own cases of beer; sometimes these made up the bulk of their luggage. The ship's spatial arrangement permitted the public areas preferred by the party animals to be sufficiently distant from those preferred by families and couples so that *Fairstar* could satisfy the entertainment requirements of most passengers. The raucous reputation of the Australian cruise market has long been an issue for P&O. The authors have been on ships such as *Canberra* on positioning voyages and watched the crew remove quality fittings, replacing them with lesser items. "We're getting ready for the Australian cruise season" was their response to queries about these activities (see Figure 17.2). For all its idiosyncrasies,

FIGURE 17.2. Cartoonist Benier Interprets the Australian Cruise Season

"Dunno—but I seem to remember the Captain getting a bit sensitive about 4 a.m. . . ."

Source: P&O Archives, Sydney, Australia.

Fairstar will long be missed by Australians, and attempts by P&O and other lines to introduce more up-market products have not been overly successful to date.

At quite the other end of the market spectrum is *Crystal Symphony*. The majority of the passengers are financially successful couples between ages forty-five and seventy with a median age of sixty. Young children are not common. The gentleman host program (lampooned in the recent film *Out to Sea*) ensures that a noticeable contingent of unattached women frequents the lounges and the dance floors. The hosts work hard on a number of activities throughout the ship and are obliged to comply with very strict rules of behavior. Despite the occasional comments inspired by their presence, this is definitely not a gigolo service. Americans make up over 90 percent of the passengers with the remainder from Canada, Japan, South America, and Europe. Currently, more than 50 percent are repeat Crystal clients and most of the others are experienced cruisers with other lines. The nature of many itineraries, in which ports of call are kept to a minimum and days at sea maximized, is indicative of consumer preference—it is the shipboard experience rather than the shore excursions that people find most appealing. This may be regarded as the only feature common to *Fairstar* and *Crystal Symphony* passengers. Terms such as "luxurious," "soothing," "choice," and "celebrities" sprinkled throughout the line's promotional literature act like magnets to well-to-do people seeking the "ultimate cruise experience." The atmosphere on board resembles that of an exclusive country club (see Figure 17.3) more than a floating resort and the highly trained, impeccably presented staff provide discreet and quality service accordingly. Industry sources informed the authors that with the demise of the prestigious Royal Viking Line, Crystal Cruises determinedly targeted not only experienced ex-Royal Viking staff, but also the passengers who may once have cruised with Royal Viking, offering them a similar experience, even to such services as the host program (Personal communication, 1997).

PASSENGER BEHAVIOR

Although the concept of a single "cruise culture" has been suggested (Foster, 1986), the experience of these authors has been that this is no more sound than the concept of a single "tourist culture." There are necessarily basic experiences and activities common to all cruises that involve the participation of either all or the great majority of passengers (embarking, eating, and disembarking are the most obvious ones), but there are also a significant number of variations in the attitude and behav-

FIGURE 17.3. Quiet Time in *Crystal Symphony*'s Palm Court

Photo: Norman Douglas.

ior of passengers, not only between one ship and another but among passengers on the same vessel, and these may be attributable to age, socioeconomic, or cultural factors which are by no means submerged within a common "cruise culture."

Rather than discussing passenger behavior on each of the above ships separately, this study finds it preferable to identify the activities and experiences associated with cruise ships and under a number of headings compare behavior among the three ships.

ARRIVAL AND EMBARKATION

Because of the scattered locations of the world's major cruise centers (e.g., Singapore, Hong Kong, Fort Lauderdale) a majority of passengers on each cruise have already undertaken a journey—often over a long distance by plane—in order to reach the ship. A number of consequences follow: they are frequently tired by the time they embark, the tiredness aggravates the feeling of disorientation common on entering the distinctive environment of a cruise ship, and their conversation for the first few days is likely to turn on such topics as the length of their journey to the ship and/or the discomfort experienced during it, the unfortunate fate of their luggage or their extraordinary feeling of relief at finding that it had not suffered misfortune, and the quality of the accommodations that they have been allocated on the ship. If conversations heard at random are any guide, an unreasonable number of passengers seem to experience the temporary loss of at least one piece of baggage and a significant number appear disenchanted with the size or appointments of their cabins. However, this last feature was more evident on *Island Princess* than on *Fairstar*, where the cost of the cruise seemed commensurate with the budget-quality accommodations, or *Crystal Symphony*, where the vessel's elegant fittings and generous cabin space would have made complaints seem churlish.

The first activity on any cruise likely to involve all passengers is the safety drill required by international maritime law, in which shortly after embarkation passengers are required to report to assigned muster stations with the life jackets provided in their cabins to be instructed by members of the ship's company in the safety and emergency procedures. Remarkable as it has seemed to the authors, some passengers choose not to attend these brief demonstrations (rarely lasting longer than fifteen to twenty minutes), and others appear reluctant to take them seriously. Jokes about *Titanic* are inclined to be whispered audibly during the demonstration and the phrase "abandon ship," which occurs during the instructions, provokes a good deal of uneasy laughter.

MEALS

Since the great majority of cruises depart from their port of embarkation in the late afternoon or early evening, the next large-scale activity engaging the participation of passengers is their first meal—dinner. It is fair to say that on a cruise ship food probably becomes a far more significant part of one's daily routine than it might otherwise be; this aspect is not only displayed in the promotional literature but acknowledged at considerable length in a number of guides to cruising and cruise ships. Under the section "Cruise Cuisine," Berlitz devotes over eight pages to the various aspects of shipboard meals (Ward, 1992). Fielding offers seven pages that include "Tips on reading a shipboard menu" and a discussion of ship sanitation inspections—usually involving correct food storage (Slater and Basch, 1996). Since all meals on board are invariably included in the price, passengers are inclined to take full advantage of them. Fielding includes advice on "How to Avoid Pigging Out at Sea."

The amount of food offered has become a standard quip in the repertoire of cruise directors and guest comedians, besides being a regular topic of conversation among passengers. It is possible on many ships to begin eating at about 7 a.m. and continue almost unchecked until past midnight, if one takes into account not only the scheduled dining room meals but also the snack bars, afternoon (and sometimes morning) teas, and latenight buffets. If the quality of food varies considerably from one cruise ship to another, the enthusiasm for eating displayed by most passengers does not. Absences from table are a sound indication, not that the absentees are being sensibly cautious about the extent of their food intake, but that they are seasick and unable to eat at all.

Meals taken in the ship's dining room, however, also offer interpersonal experiences that can be regarded as essential to the cruise. At the first meal passengers may meet others for the first time, perhaps establishing friendships that will last for the duration of the voyage or longer; perhaps deciding to request a change of table before the next dining room meal. Passengers will also meet their waiter and assistant waiter for the first time (this may be the first formal encounter with any members of the ship's company), thereby establishing another sort of relationship, one in which the waiter's performance is likely to be strongly motivated by the anticipation of reward—a tip—at the end of the cruise. The number of cruise ships that discourage tipping or build it into the fare are very few indeed. Far more frequently passengers are instructed both verbally and in writing not only how they should go about it, but also how much they should tip. *Fairstar* was one of the few exceptions to this universal principle.

PASSENGER ACTIVITIES

Once the ship is under way, the range of activities offered to passengers throughout the day and night is extensive, and may be categorized as organized, that is, those requiring direction from, or interaction with, at least one member of the cruise staff (for example, supervised deck game competitions, aerobics, dance instruction, and lectures) (see Table 17.1); and unorganized, that is, those requiring no direction from or interaction with a member of the cruise staff (for example, sunning, reading, promenading, and unsupervised deck games) (see Table 17.2). With the exception of those generally small vessels that emphasize the expeditionary aspects of cruising, the range of organized activities on days that the vessel is at sea is great enough to keep passengers involved for almost all their waking hours. Although a full range of activities is offered only on sea days, a smaller choice is offered on days when the ship is in port, to cater

TABLE 17.1. Selected Organized Activities: Level of Consumer Participation

	Aerobics	Bingo	Lectures*	Craft Classes	Bridge Instruction	Evening Shows
Island Princess	M	H	M to H	L	M	H
Fairstar	M	H	N/A	L	N/A	H
Crystal Symphony	M	H	M to H	L	H	H

*Other than port briefings

H = high level of participation

M = medium level of participation

L = low level of participation

N/A = absent or not applicable

TABLE 17.2. Selected Unorganized Activities: Level of Consumer Participation

	Sunning	Deck Games (unsupervised)	Shopping	Cinema	Casino	Disco
Island Princess	M	L	H	L	M	L
Fairstar	H	L	H	M	H	H
Crystal Symphony	L	L	L to M	L	M	N/A

H = high level of participation

M = medium level of participation

L = low level of participation

N/A = absent or not applicable

to those passengers who choose to stay on board. These activities and other relevant daily information are listed in the ship's newspaper, compiled by the cruise director and usually delivered to passenger cabins on the previous evening. Passengers consult it keenly.

The levels of participation recorded in the tables are based—following discussions with appropriate members of the respective cruise staffs—on an assessment of participation considered representative of the activity. Thus, while twenty-four passengers might represent a medium level of participation in aerobics, crafts, or bridge, that figure would represent a very low level of participation in bingo or show attendance. Conversely, a representative bingo or show audience—perhaps 200 to 300—would be unthinkable for an activity such as crafts.

A number of inferences may be drawn from the tables. Traditional cruise pursuits, such as deck games (e.g., shuffleboard, deck quoits), once the mainstays of daytime activities, have declined in popularity, a development that may be related to changes in ship design and consequent limitations of open deck space (see Figure 17.4). Cinema attendance appears to have suffered a similar fate, even though the facilities are usually excellent and the films screened are mainly first-run theatrical films. Craft classes seem to attract very few. These features were not only common to the three ships studied here, but have been observed on at least five other cruise vessels experienced by the authors. Observations about shopping, evidently as much a recreational pursuit on a cruise ship as on a land-based vacation, are qualified here by the fact that *Crystal Symphony* had, in addition to its multipurpose shop, at least two other outlets, which specialized in such items as resort wear, glass, porcelain, and jewelry. Paintings and art prints were also available for sale, though they were displayed gallery style in a wide passageway rather than in a shop. Compared with the multipurpose shop, these specialty outlets appeared to do very little business indeed, perhaps reflecting their price structure. *Fairstar*'s high participation level in shopping strongly reflected both the genuinely duty-free status of the shop and the nature of the merchandise sold: cameras, audio, video, and other electronic equipment and perfumes represent traditionally sought-after duty-free items among Australian travelers.

Participation in casino gambling was higher on *Fairstar* than on the other ships, because its casino featured mainly slot machines in low denominations, and Australian consumers are far more used to slot machines than any other gambling device. Casino staff on *Island Princess* generally agreed that the consumer participation level was usually much higher in other cruise locations (particularly the Caribbean and the Mexican Riviera) than on the cruise studied here. "They attract more of the

FIGURE 17.4. Deck Games on *Island Princess;* Limited Participation

Photo: Norman Douglas.

Vegas crowd," we were told by a number of staff (personal communications, 1996). However, based on regular observations of the casinos on both *Island Princess* and *Crystal Symphony,* it would be easy to form the opinion that—with the exception of blackjack—table gambling was declining in popularity, since there was very little consumer involvement in roulette or craps (see Figure 17.5). Bridge playing under the supervision of instructors evidently appeals to generally older, higher-income groups than those represented by *Fairstar*'s typical passenger complement: *Crystal Symphony*'s bridge lounge was regularly full of enthusiastic players.

Attendance at lectures varies considerably according to the topic, the time of day, and the verbal skills of the lecturer. On the cruise studied, *Fairstar* presented no lectures at all. *Crystal Symphony,* on the other hand, may have six or more lecturers per cruise, including specialists whose subjects might range from drama criticism to finance and investment to regional history and culture, and celebrity guests whose subjects are their own experiences or those of their celebrity friends. On all cruises that

FIGURE 17.5. Shipboard Casino; Little Interest in Roulette

Photo: Norman Douglas.

feature it, bingo—played at least once a day on sea days—is by far the most popular organized daytime recreational activity.

The most popular nighttime activities by any measure are the cabaret-style or production shows that are now a well-publicized feature of many cruise ships. There are sound reasons for their popularity. For many passengers they represent an essential aspect of an evening out—"dinner and a show" at no extra charge—their quality is generally highly professional and, importantly, they have no, or very little, competition from any other activity during their time of presentation. Shows on *Island Princess* and *Crystal Symphony*, presented in lounges designed essentially for their staging, typically attract capacity attendance—several hundreds. Production shows were not a feature of *Fairstar*'s entertainment, which emphasized cabaret of the type usually associated with Australian sporting clubs, from whose ranks many of its entertainers were drawn. Like the others, however, they attracted capacity—occasionally standing room only—audiences. It is fair to say that on all three ships consumer satisfaction with the shows was of a high level.

PORTS

The itinerary of a cruise is one of the most significant reasons for its success, although it is by no means the sole or even the major determinant. Some cruise locations perennially attract a greater number of people than others, and many of these people are evidently happy enough to have cruised the same area and seen more or less the same ports of call several times. The Caribbean attracts by far the greatest number of passengers in any given year, to the extent that many of the larger vessels going into service will be permanently positioned in that region. However, in the late 1990s there is barely a major waterway in the world to which a cruise ship of some kind has not been, and as the Caribbean becomes more congested, other regions are almost certain to experience an increase in cruise traffic.

ITINERARIES TRAVELED FOR THIS STUDY

Island Princess: Singapore, Koh Samui (Thailand), Bangkok, Saigon (Ho Chi Minh City), Brunei, Kota Kinabalu, Manila, Shekou (Canton), Hong Kong.

Fairstar: Sydney, Amedee Island (New Caledonia), Nouméa (New Caledonia), Lifou (New Caledonia), Port-Vila (Vanuatu), Sydney.

Crystal Symphony: Apia (Western Samoa), Savusavu (Fiji), Port-Vila (Vanuatu), Sydney.

The itineraries studied here attract far fewer cruise passengers overall than the Caribbean or the Mediterranean, indeed are still regarded as novelties by the Americans who make up the majority of passengers on both *Island Princess* and *Crystal Symphony*. *Fairstar*, on the other hand, cruised a well-worn route in the Western Pacific for much of its twenty-three years in the region, while occasionally pioneering less frequented ports of call. Except for the authors, there were no passengers on the former two ships who had previously experienced these cruise itineraries. On *Fairstar*, however, there were more than fifty who had cruised with the ship more than once and hence would have experienced previously at least three of the four ports of call.

On port days, passengers may generally choose between participating in organized shore excursions, going ashore independently, or remaining on the ship, an option not infrequently accepted by the elderly or disabled, especially if the prospects ashore appear daunting as a result of weather conditions or sociopolitical and cultural factors. In Bali and the Andaman Islands, for example, the authors have observed passengers stepping tentatively ashore, only to return to the ship on the same tender because they felt threatened by vendors or were otherwise discomfited. It is not uncommon for some passengers to proceed no further than the wharf, especially if souvenir stalls are accessible there. Why else would one spend thousands of dollars journeying from the United States to, say, Phuket in Thailand, except to buy a cheap souvenir or to attempt to obtain a $10 copy of a designer wristwatch for $8?

If a generalization may be permitted, it is that destinations displaying evidence of wealth and ostentation are more attractive to American passengers than those that appear economically depressed, no matter how historically or culturally significant the latter may be. On Mediterranean cruises, Monte Carlo is regularly rated a favorite destination. Similarly, Singapore, Brunei, and Hong Kong were of greater appeal to *Island Princess* passengers than Koh Samui or Kota Kinabalu. Saigon is an interesting exception in this context. Americans, apprehensively encountering Vietnam as tourists, often seem surprised at the manner in which they are received. The unexpectedly hospitable reception influences their attitude considerably, making them well-disposed toward the sort of city they would normally instinctively dislike. On the other hand, among some passengers, Saigon—with its bustle, crowds, pollution, and chaotic traffic—provoked the most negative reaction of any port on that itinerary.

Fairstar's constant success and its number of repeat passengers, despite its generally predictable itinerary, indicated strongly that for the majority of passengers the ship itself was the major attraction, the ports of secondary importance. Indeed, one of the regular ports, Nouméa—the capital of a French Pacific territory—regularly received poor ratings in passenger surveys, with passengers advancing a number of reasons ranging from its expensive nature to the "arrogance" of locals and the consequent difficulties of communicating with them. Yet out of thirty-four cruises in *Fairstar*'s 1996 calendar, Nouméa appeared in twenty-six (P&O Holidays 1995), a reasonable indication that its presence on an itinerary offered little disincentive to passengers, even to those experiencing the itinerary for the third or fourth time. However, far greater passenger satisfaction was evident at the "unspoiled" island of Lifou, which offered little more in the way of diversions than a beach and a barbecue, and at Port-Vila, for many years a favorite port on *Fairstar*'s itinerary. At Lifou passengers needed to spend nothing at all, since food and drinks were brought from the ship, while at Port-Vila, cheap souvenirs, ease of communication, and relatively easy beach access made the port consistently popular. These aspects of consumer preference reflect strongly the nature of *Fairstar*'s passengers and the socioeconomic backgrounds of the majority.

The example of Port-Vila provides a valuable contrast between passenger behavior on *Fairstar* and *Crystal Symphony,* since the latter also called there on the cruise studied. A far greater number of passengers from *Fairstar* than from *Crystal Symphony* took the small shuttle buses from the wharf into town in order to look around independently, while a greater number of passengers from *Crystal Symphony* took the organized tours. This illustrates the generally cautious attitude of American travelers toward unfamiliar locations. Information given them on the ship in both written and spoken form may well have provided many *Crystal Symphony* passengers with their first-ever details of the small South Pacific republic, particularly of a Melanesian society. Although the ship had called earlier at Savusavu in Fiji, weather conditions discouraged a considerable number of passengers from going ashore and personally encountering other black Pacific Islanders. "Are they Africans, or what?" one female passenger asked the authors, observing ni-Vanuatu on Port-Vila's wharf and illustrating the considerable geographic and cultural distance that separates the United States from the islands of the Western Pacific. On the other hand, Vanuatu's proximity to Australia makes it a popular and familiar destination for Australians, both as package holiday and cruise port. Australians are unlikely to confuse Melanesians with Africans.

CONCLUSION

This study began by outlining the historical context of cruising and its rapid growth in the 1990s to illustrate its place in the development of tourism as a whole. More than any other kind of tourism, cruising offers traditional activities—deck games, bridge, passenger talent concerts—alongside modern diversions such as discos, production shows, and lessons in computer awareness. The element of tradition is strongly maintained also in promotional material that frequently suffuses verbal descriptions of modern facilities with nostalgic images, a technique which evidently appeals to many consumers. Cruise ships offer far more choices now than ever before, which may reflect both the growing difficulty in keeping consumers occupied and the growing competition within the industry.

In any meaningful discussion of consumer behavior in cruising, a variety of factors must be taken into account. These include the size and physical aspects of the cruise vessel and the amenities it provides, the type of passengers it attracts, the on-board activities it features, and the nature of the cruise itinerary.

The concept of a typical cruise "society" or "culture" is not borne out by the study. Although there are some similarities in cruise consumer experiences and behavior, there are also a significant number of differences that well outweigh the similarities. Even the experience of a shared environment (the ship) is strongly qualified by the attitudes and expectations that consumers carry on board as part of their baggage. These reflect the consumers' national, cultural, and socioeconomic backgrounds and their age levels, factors that will not only influence the type of ship chosen, but will influence their behavior and their response to certain conditions and activities on the ship itself. There is little in common among *Island Princess* passengers, *Fairstar* passengers, and *Crystal Symphony* passengers except that they are all on a cruise.

CONCEPT DEFINITIONS

Cruise: A journey by sea solely for pleasure and recreation, which was originally in the form of a round trip, i.e., beginning and ending at the same place. However, a great number of cruises no longer follow this original principle, beginning and ending in different places, with the vast majority of passengers flown to and from the ship as part of the overall cruise package.

Cruise director: The individual on all cruises who is responsible for the organization and presentation of on-board activities and entertainment. Although not involved in operational matters, he/she generally holds officer rank, and on some ships is the fourth ranking officer.

Destination: A term meaning the predetermined end of a journey or voyage, but which is often used in cruising to refer to the ports of call; e.g., "a five-destination cruise," or even the region in which the ship cruises, such as the Caribbean, Mediterranean, South Pacific, etc.

Itinerary: The route and ports of call on a cruise.

Passenger: The consumer on a cruise ship, someone who has paid a fare for the experience. As cruise ships begin more and more to resemble resorts, passengers are sometimes referred to as "guests."

Shore excursions: Optional activities, usually involving a tour, offered to passengers at each port of call. They are not generally included in the cruise fare and may last from a few to several hours.

REVIEW QUESTIONS

1. How does the cruise experience differ from land-based package holidays?

2. Why do people choose to cruise?
3. Can you describe how the nature of a specific cruise product determines the type of activities offered on board?
4. Does the physical design of a ship influence the choice of activities provided? How?
5. If you could choose to go on one of the cruise ships described, how would your choice reflect your own tourist consumer background and behavior?

REFERENCES

Cruise Lines International Association (CLIA) (1995). *The Cruise Industry: An Overview*, New York, Cruise Lines International Association.

Douglas, N. and Douglas, N. (1997a). P&O's Pacific, *Journal of Tourism Studies*, 7 (2), 2-14.

Douglas, N. and Douglas, N. (1997b). Farewell Fairstar, Ciao Canberra, *Signals*, 34, 21-23.

Foster, G. M. (1986). South Seas Cruise: A Case Study of a Short-Lived Society, *Annals of Tourism Research*, 13: 215-238.

Lawton, L. J. and Butler, R. W. (1987). Cruise Ship Industry—Patterns in the Caribbean 1880-1986, *Tourism Management*, December, 329-343.

Moscardo, G., Morrison, A. M., Cai, L., Nadkarni, N., and O'Leary, J. (1996). Tourist Perspectives on Cruising: Multidimensional Scaling Analysis of Cruising and Other Holiday Types, *Journal of Tourism Studies*, 7 (2), 54-63.

P&O Holidays (1995). *The Time of Your Life* (Cruise Calendar), Sydney, P&O Holidays.

Peisley, T. (1989). The World Cruising Industry in the 1990s, *EIU Travel and Tourism Analyst*, 6, 5-18.

Peisley, T. (1992). The World Cruise Ship Industry in the 1990s, *EIU Special Report* No. 2104, London, Economics Intelligence Unit.

Peisley, T. (1995). Transport: The Cruise Ship Industry to the 21st Century, *EIU Travel and Tourism Analyst*, 52, 24-25.

Plowman, P. (1992). *From Emigrant Ships to Luxury Liners*, Sydney, University of New South Wales Press.

Ryan, C. (1995). *Researching Tourist Satisfaction: Issues, Concepts, Problems*, London and New York, Routledge.

Slater, S. and Basch, H. (1996). *Fielding's Worldwide Cruises 1997*, Redondo Beach, CA, Fielding Worldwide Inc.

Ward, D. (1992). *Berlitz Complete Guide to Cruising and Cruise Ships*, New York and London, Berlitz Publishing Company.

Chapter 18

Cross-Cultural Tourist Behavior

Abraham Pizam

LEARNING OBJECTIVES

By the end of this chapter the reader should:

- Understand the effect of nationality and culture on tourist behavior
- Have a broad grasp of the limitation of cross-cultural research
- Be familiar with various cross-cultural studies in tourism
- Understand that local residents and tourism practitioners perceive that tourists of different nationalities behave differently
- Have a general understanding of the usefulness of realizing that tourist behavior is not only affected by motivation, demographics, and lifestyle but also by culture and nationality

TOURISM AND CULTURE

Culture is an umbrella word that encompasses a whole set of implicit, widely shared beliefs, traditions, values, and expectations that characterize a particular group of people. It identifies the uniqueness of the social unit, its values and beliefs (Leavitt and Bahrami, 1988). Like nations, organizations, industries, and occupational groups have cultures too. Though, for the most part, these cultures have been neither extensively documented nor properly classified, the few case studies and short descriptions that were made enable us to draw the conclusion that they do exist. Thus we can speak of the cultures of physicians, lawyers, engineers, and computer programmers, to name just a few (Kunda, 1991; Couger et al., 1990). Some researchers such as Nash (1978) and Tyagi (1989) have suggested that tourists too have a culture of their own.

If these arguments are correct, tourists of various nationalities possess simultaneously both "touristic cultures" (i.e., the culture of group tourists, conventioneers, backpackers, etc.) and "national cultures." The question then must be posed as to what extent are touristic cultures relatively free of national cultures, and would be universally reflected in the behavior of all tourists regardless of nationality, or are they subjugated to national cultures and would therefore vary from one to another?

THE CONVERGENCE-DIVERGENCE DEBATE

The evolution of multinational companies has been characterized by a growing conflict between the advocates of the convergence and the divergence hypotheses. Proponents of the philosophy of global organizations, products, and brands (convergence) such as Levitt (1983) state that economies, organizations, and markets are becoming more and more homogeneous. Arguments that support the convergence process are based either on the contention that some normative systems of economic structure, organizational design, managerial processes, and marketing processes are universally superior or that they are technologically indispensable. These individuals argue that convergence is a process induced by industrialization, which is based on science and technology, two supranational processes, which are independent of governmental forms and national cultures. Through trade, imitation, economic aid, and military channels, there is a worldwide diffusion of industrial technology from developed to developing nations (Pizam, 1993). "The worldwide diffusion of technology creates a 'logic of industrialism,' since it sets up a range of tasks and problems. The pressure toward efficient production will ensure that the most effective ways of tackling these common tasks will be adopted worldwide. As this process continues, organizations tackling the same tasks, in whichever culture, will become more and more alike" (Open University, 1985). Researchers supporting the convergence hypothesis argue that "individuals, irrespective of culture are forced to adopt industrial attitudes such as nationalism, secularism, and mechanical time concerns in order to comply with the imperative of industrialization" (Okechuku and Yee, 1991). Customers have common preferences; differences are disappearing. Hence companies do not have to look for differences among the desires of customers but for commonalities (Levitt, 1983; Ohmae, 1989). Summarizing the convergence-divergence debate, Child (1981) suggests that "the controversy in the debate is most of the times due to the level of analysis of the studies. Most of the studies concluding convergence focus on macro level issues such as the structure of the organization and its technology, while studies concluding divergence analyzed micro level issues such as behavior of people within the organization" (p. 354). Pizam (1993) agrees with Child's conclusions and observes that in the hotel sector national culture has little impact on the organizational structure but significantly affects the behavior of its people.

Scholars who support the divergence process argue that economies, organizations, and markets have always been, still are, and always will be culture bound, rather than culture free. Therefore we should not expect to see any convergence in managerial and marketing practices or consumer behavior across different cultures, since these depend on the implicit model prevalent in a particular culture. The models in turn are generated by the mental programming occurring within each culture. Change in managerial and marketing practices, or in consumer behavior, will develop slowly and will always be induced by a change in culture first. Researchers such as Douglas and Wind (1987) consider convergence in consumer behavior across countries to be just a myth. Despite the fact that some companies target global customer segments, numerous other companies adapt their product lines to the specific characteristics of individual markets. Advocates of this view claim that divergence remains both in the demand and in the supply of services. Often this divergence is based on the cultural differences in the countries across the world (Douglas and Wind, 1987).

In the past two decades, the international tourism industry has been a part of the convergence-divergence debate as well. On one hand there was the trend toward standardization of services (convergence). Uniform quality standards of service evolved because tourist businesses wanted to compete on the international market with high-quality products/services and low prices. On the other hand there was and still is a growing belief that standardization of tourist services is undermining the very attraction of the destination and decreases competitiveness in the international market. The tourist product is losing its unique cultural characteristics, which are normally associated with certain destinations.

CROSS-CULTURAL OR NATIONAL CHARACTER RESEARCH

The study of differences across nations can help to solve the controversy over the degree to which marketing elements should be standardized globally. First, cross-cultural research can help to discern similar patterns among consumers and decision makers in different countries. In this way it can contribute to a rational basis for global thinking Second, through the identification of multimodel patterns at the national level, more rational segmentation and market niching strategies can be suggested (Clark, 1990). From a managerial perspective, the choice between adaptation and standardization across markets must explicitly consider the differences and similarities in consumer behavior for a particular setting (Dawar and Parker, 1994).

Differences in consumer behavior have been studied in both direct and indirect ways. Whereas direct research is based on empirical measurement of actual differences, indirect research focuses on the judgment and perceptions of other people about the behavior of consumers (Pizam and Sussman, 1995). The effect of national characteristics on consumer behavior has been investigated in several studies. Researchers such as Boote (1983), Onkvisit and Shaw (1987), Synodynos, Keown, and Jacobs (1989), and Grunert (1990), to name just a few, analyzed national consumer values as viable segmentation variables for promotional objectives. For example, Boote (1983), in studying consumer values in the United Kingdom, Germany, and France, came to the conclusion that the underlying value structure in each country appeared to bear both similarities and differences. Grunert (1990) also investigated the differences in values of consumers in Germany, the United States, Norway, and Canada and found several significant cross-cultural variations in values.

CROSS-CULTURAL STUDIES IN TOURISM

Until recently the role of national cultural characteristics in determining tourist behavior has not been paid much attention in tourism research. However, the examination of cultural differences is especially relevant to the tourism industry for several reasons. First, the industry has experienced a growing internationalization in the past decade. Hence, considerable attention has been given to the globalization discussion and the relevance of cultural diversity. Second, cultural characteristics are especially relevant in tourism because they are vital to the attractiveness of the product itself. Finally, tourism is a service industry where people from different nationalities meet.

Studies that examined the effects of national cultural characteristics on tourist behavior have been conducted by either direct or indirect methods. Using the indirect method, researchers tried to describe and catalog the various perceptions that residents and entrepreneurs in tourist communities had of tourists of various nationalities. By the direct method, researchers have tried to empirically discover what if any differences *actually* exist in the behavior of tourists of various nationalities.

To begin with indirect methods, a number of studies show that in many tourist destination areas residents have been found to differentiate tourists by nationality. For example, Brewer (1978), in a study conducted in San Felipe, Baja California, Mexico, suggested that local residents have "general" stereotypes of all Americans, which lead to "specific" stereotypes that apply to American tourists. The traits attributed to Americans were caution, calculation, purpose, and care with money. These traits were used to explain the observable actions of American tourists and helped to create "specific" tourist traits, which were applied to individual transactions between locals and American tourists (Brewer, 1984, p. 492).

General and specific views of tourists were found in other destinations as well. Boissevain and Inglott (1979) observed that the Maltese characterized Swedish tourists as misers, and French and Italians as excessively demanding. Pi-Sunyer (1977) found that Catalans stereotyped English tourists as stiff, socially conscious, honest, and dependable. Other studies found that residents of tourist destinations perceived the tourists as different from themselves in a variety of behavioral characteristics and lifestyles. For example, in a Vienna Center-sponsored study (Pizam and Telisman-Kosuta, 1989, p. 86-88) of seven samples of residents in tourist communities in Yugoslavia, Wales, Spain, Hungary, Bulgaria, Poland, and Florida, it was found that in destinations where the majority of the tourists were foreigners (Yugoslavia, Spain, and Hungary) the residents perceived the tourists as very different from themselves in a variety of characteristics such as general behavior, attitudes toward nature, religiousness, manner of spending leisure time, and morality. On the other hand, in destinations that were frequented mostly by domestic visitors (Poland and Wales), the residents perceived only minimal differences between themselves and the tourists. Similarly, Wagner (1977), in a study of charter tourism to the Gambia, noted that the locals saw Scandinavian tourists as a "clearly demarcated group, whose dress, behavior and life-style set them apart" (p. 43).

People in the tourism trade have also suggested that tourists of different nationalities behave in different ways. For example, Japanese travelers have been described by the trade press as "always traveling in groups and marching off in steps, reminiscent of primary school students . . . they bow to everybody they meet, are indefatigable photographers and usually spend heavily" (Cho, 1991). Koreans have been portrayed as having implacable loyalty to their sociocultural identity and unwilling to accept anything that has little in common with the Korean way of living. They insist on going to Korean restaurants while abroad, are fond of traveling to Asian countries that are based on Confucian philosophy as Korea is, and prefer to travel in groups rather than individually (*Business Korea,* 1991).

As far as direct methods are concerned, Szalai (1972), in a minute-by-minute account of everyday living patterns of people from twelve different countries, measured the amount of time spent in thirty-seven primary activities. Later on, Ibrahim (1991) used the same instrument to study a sample of Egyptians. In comparing the results obtained in both studies, Ibrahim found a significant variance in the amount of leisure time among nations. Ibrahim suggested that this variance is not necessarily caused by economic factors but mainly by the value system of a society. Following Szalai, other recreational researchers conducted similar cross-cultural studies that analyzed the difference in patterns of recreation among different nationalities. Such studies were conducted by Rodgers (1977), who analyzed patterns of participation in sport and problems of encouraging mass participation across eight countries, and by the Council of Europe (1985). All of these studies noted differences in the leisure behavior of various nationalities.

Some geographers such as Ritter (1987, 1989), Holzner (1985), and Groetzbach (1981, 1988) have also noted, from their own structured observations, marked differences between tourists of different nationalities.

For example, Ritter noted that Japanese tend to travel in groups and take shorter holidays than Europeans. He attributed this behavior to Japan's more collectivist culture where separation from the group is viewed as painful and dangerous to psychic well-being.

Holzner (1985), as quoted by Ritter (1987), identified a few basic traits of the American culture that in his opinion have influenced the leisure and travel behavior of Americans. These traits are love of originality, desire to be near nature, freedom to move, individualism, and social acceptance. "Americans like to spend holidays in a simple way in the wilderness which they try to preserve. Love of newness and desire to be near nature prompt their visits to national parks and national monuments" (Ritter, 1987, p. 5).

Groetzbach (1981, 1988) analyzed the differences between the travel behavioral patterns of Muslims and Arabs as compared to those of Europeans. He claimed that "everywhere the Oriental style of tourism was markedly less active, and more socially gregarious than the European style" (Ritter 1989, pp. 9-10). Barham (1989), too, noted the lack of activity preferred by the Arabs in general. "In Jordan, like in most Arab societies, the main motive for excursions is recreation which usually means absolute relaxation called 'raha.' Any physical activity is against the aim of this motive" (Barham, 1989, pp. 37-38).

In the United States, the now-defunct U.S. Travel and Tourism Administration (USTTA, 1984a, 1984b) conducted a series of surveys among potential Japanese, Australian, United Kingdom, West German, and French vacationers. The study found significant differences among the above nationalities on vacation preferences and on the importance of various factors in choosing a destination. Woodside and Lawrence (1985), in a study examining the benefits realized from traveling to Hawaii, noted a significant difference between Canadian, American, and Japanese visitors. Richardson and Crompton (1988) found significant differences between the patterns of vacation travel of English and French Canadians.

Sheldon and Fox (1988), in a study that examined the cross-cultural differences in the importance of food service in vacation choice, found that for Japanese as compared to Canadian and American tourists, food service had a stronger influence on their destination choice. Last, Yiannakis, Leivadi, and Apostolopoulos (1991) in a study comparing Greek and American male and female tourists' role preference found that within the nationality group, sex differences were relatively small in the American sample, and large in the Greek sample. The authors suggested that the observed differences between the sexes in the Greek sample could be attributed to the more traditional social structure of Greek society and the greater sex-role demarcations between the sexes (Yiannakis, Leivadi, and Apostolopoulos, 1991, pp. 35-36).

More recently, the present author in cooperation with a number of colleagues from the United Kingdom (Pizam and Sussman, 1995), Israel (Pizam and Reichel, 1996), Korea (Pizam and Jeong, 1996), and Holland (Pizam, Jansen-Verbeke, and Steel, 1997) conducted a series of four studies intended to explore further, using an indirect method of assessment, the explanatory value of nationality in regard to tourist behavior. To do this the investigators set out to identify the perceptions that British, Israeli, Korean, and Dutch tour guides had of tourists of different nationalities, and to test whether there were significant differences by nationality in these perceptions. All studies controlled for tourists of a certain type—group tourists participating in escorted motor-coach tours. It was hypothesized that for most tourist behavioral characteristics under study, the tour guides would perceive significant differences by nationality between these tourists.

OBJECTIONS TO CROSS-CULTURAL/NATIONAL RESEARCH

Some objections have been made to studying behavior across nations. Peabody (1985) listed several objections to this type of research. First, he claims that generalizations about people and nations are not possible and even if they were, they would be overshadowed by variations within national groups. Second, judgments about nations are too often based on indirect experiences. Finally, the assessment of national characteristics is often biased by ethnocentrism.

Dann (1993) criticizes the practice of using nationality as a sole discriminating variable for explaining the differences found in the behavior of tourists. Dann's criticism is based on four observations: (1) the fuzzy nature of these variables, (2) the globalization of our world, (3) the cosmopolitan nature of generating societies, and (4) the pluralistic nature of receiving societies. The above observations bring Dann to the conclusion that:

> tourism is now well and truly a global phenomenon in the hands of multinational corporations which pay scant attention to the national boundaries circumscribing either host or guest . . . for this reason, it becomes more appropriate to employ alternative approaches to the analysis of tourism. (Dann, 1993)

While the present author agrees with Dann's observations about the difficulties encountered in dealing with national cultures, I contend that:

> National cultures have an important intervening effect on tourist behavior. This is especially true in the case of *perceived* nationality differences where residents or tourist-entrepreneurs tend to hold specific stereotypes of tourists based on their nationalities, regardless of their country of birth, ethnic background and country of origin. (Pizam and Jeong, 1996, p. 282)

The view that studies about national differences have significant value is further reasserted by Clark (1990) who suggests, first, that evidence about cross-national differences does exist; second, that these differences can be observed and recorded; and third, that these observed differences have a significant bearing on the behavior of both consumers and marketing decision makers.

As previously indicated, many cross-cultural studies often find both differences and similarities in consumer behavior across countries. Peabody (1985) refers to these as partial differences rather than complete differences across nations. We basically agree with Peabody's observation that both differences and similarities can be found in the behavior of tourists.

OBJECTIVE

The objective of this chapter is to summarize the results of the British (Pizam and Sussman, 1995), Israeli (Pizam and Reichel, 1996), Korean

(Pizam and Jeong, 1996), and Dutch (Pizam, Jansen-Verbeke, and Steel, 1997) studies and confirm the explanatory value of nationality, in regard to tourist behavior. This will be accomplished by showing that tour guides of four different nationalities perceived a significant difference in the behavior of tourists of different nationalities.

METHODOLOGY

Samples

British Tour Guide Study

A mailed questionnaire was sent to every member (289 in total) of the British Guild of Guides residing in London. The questionnaire and its attached letter asked respondents who regularly guided groups of Japanese, French, Italian, or American tourists—the most frequent tourist nationalities on guided motor-coach tours in London—to complete a questionnaire for each of the above nationalities only if they had sufficient experience with them. Return responses were received from 123 subjects who completed a total of 252 questionnaires, an average of two questionnaires per respondent.

Israeli Tour Guide Study

The sample consisted of 400 Israeli tour guides randomly selected from a total of 1,683 guides registered with the Ministry of Tourism. Only those tour guides who regularly guided groups of American, British, French, or German tourists—the most frequent tourist nationalities on guided tours in Israel—were asked to return the completed questionnaires. Respondents were asked to complete a separate questionnaire for each of the above nationalities only if they had sufficient experience with them. Of the 400 individuals who were mailed the survey, 124 returned one or more completed questionnaires for a net response rate of 33 percent. The 124 respondents completed a total of 251 questionnaires, an average of 2.02 per respondent.

Korean Tour Guide Study

The sample consisted of eighty-six Korean tour guides who regularly guided groups of Japanese and American tourists—the most frequent tourist nationalities on guided motor-coach tours in Korea—and Korean tourists on escorted motor-coach tours outside Korea. The tour guides' names and business addresses were obtained from Seoul-based Korean travel agencies that specialize in inbound and outbound escorted motor-coach tours. Since mail questionnaires have an extremely low completion rate in Korea, it was decided to conduct the study via personal interviews. One hundred tour guides were personally approached and asked to participate in the study by completing a separate questionnaire for each of the above-mentioned three nationalities only if they had sufficient experience with them. Of the 100 subjects approached, 86 agreed to participate and completed a total of 130 questionnaires, an average of 1.5 questionnaires per respondent.

Dutch Tour Guide Study

The sample consisted of 200 Dutch tour guides randomly selected from a list provided by the National Tour Guides of The Netherlands (GUIDOR) and several small tourist organizations. Only those tour guides who regularly guided group tours of Japanese, French, Italian, or American tourists—the most frequent tourist nationalities on guided motor-coach tours in Holland—were asked to return the completed questionnaires. Respondents were asked to complete a separate questionnaire for each nationality only if they had sufficient experience with them. Of the 200 guides who were mailed the survey, sixty-three returned the questionnaires, for a return rate of 31.5 percent. The sixty-three respondents completed a total of 159 questionnaires, an average of 2.52 per respondent.

Instrument

To identify behavioral characteristics of tourists while on guided tours, a group of twelve experienced British tour guides were gathered for a two-hour focus group session. Throughout the session the issues of perceived behavioral similarities and differences between tourists were discussed, and a listing of various kinds of typical tourist behavioral characteristics was produced.

Twenty of the most significant typical behaviors were incorporated in a questionnaire that was used in all four studies. Each behavioral characteristic was listed on two extremes of an anchored semantic differential scale ranging from 1 through 5. Tour guides were asked to circle for each statement a number from 1 to 5, which represented their opinion on the extent to which the characteristic *in general* was typical for the nationalities under study.

The following twenty characteristics were listed in the questionnaire:

The numbers [5] and [1] next to each statement represent a 1-5 scale, where 5 = the left-side statement, 1 = the right-side statement, and 2, 3, and 4 are in-between.

Interact with other tourists [5]	Keep to themselves [1]
Socialize with other tourists [5]	Avoid socializing [1]
Congregate with tourists from other nationalities [5]	Congregate only with tourists from same nationality [1]
Travel in groups [5]	Travel by themselves [1]
Take long trips [5]	Take short trips [1]
Buy souvenirs [5]	Do not buy souvenirs [1]
Buy gifts for F&R at home [5]	Do not buy gifts for F&R at home [1]
Trust tourist-trade people [5]	Suspicious of tourist-trade people [1]
Interested in people [5]	Interested in artifacts [1]
Prefer local foods & drinks [5]	Avoid local foods & drinks [1]
Visit places in loose and unplanned manner [5]	Plan their tours rigidly [1]
Shop constantly [5]	Do not shop at all [1]
Bargain at shopping [5]	Pay asking price [1]
Want to see the "real thing" [5]	Satisfied with "staged" attractions/ events [1]
Adventuresome [5]	Safe [1]
Active [5]	Passive [1]
Interested in novelty [5]	Interested in familiar things [1]
Take photographs [5]	Do not take photographs [1]
Write letters/postcards [5]	Do not write letters/postcards [1]
Knowledgeable about the destination and prepared [5]	Not knowledgeable about the destination and unprepared [1]

Statistical Analyses

To test the hypothesis about perceived differences by nationality, eighty (twenty characteristics × four studies) one-way analyses of variance with post hoc multiple comparisons (Student-Newman Keuls multiple range test) were conducted to determine which of the nationalities' means were significantly different from each.

RESULTS

British Tour Guide Study

An examination of the differences between the perceptions of the four nationalities—Japanese, French, Italians, and Americans—on each of the twenty behavioral characteristics showed that two of the characteristics, "Novelty versus Familiarity," and "Knowledge About the Destination," failed to demonstrate any significant differences among the four nationalities. In these respects, the British tour guides perceived that the Japanese, French, Italians, and Americans were all alike. On the other hand, the variables of "Interacting," "Socializing," and "Photographing" showed differences between each nationality and all other nationalities. As far as these behavioral characteristics were concerned, it was possible to conclude that the tour guides perceived the Japanese, French, Italian, and American tourists to be totally unlike each other. In the remaining fifteen variables, the data showed various differences between pairs of nationality groups ranging from a minimum of three out of six possible pairs, to a maximum of five out of six. A summary of the differences showed that according to the perceptions of the tour guides, Japanese tourists were the most distinct with 70 percent differences between themselves and the rest, followed by Americans with 68 percent, French with 67 percent, and Italians with 62 percent.

To summarize the findings for this study, the one-way analysis of variance found that in an absolute majority of the characteristics there was a significant difference in perceived behavior among the four nationalities, lending support to the general hypothesis that tour guides would see significant differences by nationality. Furthermore, an analysis of the perceived similarities and differences between each of the four nationalities discovered that in the British tour guides' perceptions the Japanese were the most distinct among the four, while the Italians were the most like the other nationalities.

Israeli Tour Guide Study

As was the case in the British study, the results indicated that in 90 percent (18/20) of the researched behavioral characteristics Israeli tour-guides perceived a significant difference between the French, German, British, and American tourists. For only two behavioral characteristics—"Trip Planning" and "Letter Writing"—nationality was not perceived to play a role and all tourists were thought to behave alike. The behavioral characteristics on which the greatest differences by nationality turned up were "Buying Souvenirs," "Shopping," "Buying Gifts," and "Photographing." On these variables, with the exception of the French-British pair, each nationality was perceived as different from each other nationality.

As to similarities and differences between nationalities, the Americans were perceived to be the most distinct and the French the most similar to other nationalities. A pair comparison found that the tour guides perceived the French and British to be the most similar to each other in their behavior, followed by French and Germans, French and Americans, and culminating with British and Americans, who were perceived to be the most dissimilar. The results for the pairs similarities contradict to a certain extent the results obtained in the British tour-guide study, were the French and American pair was perceived as the most dissimilar.

Korean Tour Guide Study

An examination of the differences between the Korean tour guides perceptions of the three nationalities—Japanese, Koreans, and Americans—on each of the behavioral characteristics confirms our previously stated hypothesis that the number of behavioral differences by nationality will be significantly larger than the number of similarities. Out of the twenty behavioral characteristics, only two—"Interact versus Socialize" and "Authenticity versus Staging"—showed no significant differences between the three nationalities. In these respects, the tour guides perceived the Japanese, Americans, and Koreans to be alike. On the other hand, the variables of "Trip Length," "Food Preference," "Adventuresome versus Safe," "Novelty versus Familiarity," "Photographing," and "Letter Writing" showed differences between each nationality and all other nationalities. As far as these are concerned it is possible to conclude that the tour guides perceived the Japanese, American, and Korean tourists to be totally unlike each other. In the remaining twelve, the data showed various differences between pairs of nationality groups ranging from one to two out of three possible pairs.

A summary of the differences showed that according to the perceptions of the tour guides, American tourists were the most different from the rest (77.5 percent differences), followed by Koreans (70 percent), and Japanese (57.5 percent). The pairs that were perceived to be most similar to each other were Japanese and Koreans (50 percent difference), followed by Japanese and Americans (65 percent differences). The most dissimilar pair were Koreans and Americans (90 percent difference).

Dutch Tour Guide Study

Differences were found between all four nationalities (Japanese, French, Italians, and Americans) on eighteen out of twenty behavioral characteristics. Only two characteristics—"Trust Tourist-Trade People" and "Letter Writing," showed no significant differences between the four nationalities. The largest amount of differences was found in the variables "Socialize," "Interact," "Groups," and "Trip Length." The smallest number of differences was found in the variables of "Food Preferences" and "Shopping."

As to similarities and differences between nationalities, the Americans were perceived to be the most distinct—as was the case in the Korean and Israeli studies—and the Italians the most similar to other nationalities. A pair comparison found that the tour guides perceived the Italians and Americans, as the most similar to each other in their behavior, followed by French and Italians, Japanese and French, Japanese and Italians, Japanese and Americans, and culminating with French and Americans, who were perceived as the most dissimilar. The results for the pairs similarities confirm the results obtained in the British tour-guide study, where the French and American pair were also perceived as the most dissimilar.

CONCLUSIONS

The basic postulate of the four studies was that national cultures have a moderating effect on tourist behavior. This was tested in the context of group tourists on escorted motor-coach tours, and by analyzing the perceptions of British, Israeli, Korean, and Dutch tour guides regarding the differences and similarities between tourists of different nationalities. The results indicated that in 90 percent (18/20) of the researched behavioral characteristics the tour guides perceived a significant difference in behavior among tourists of different nationalities.

The results of these studies confirm to a certain extent the results obtained in previous studies such as Brewer (1978, 1984), Boissevain and Inglott (1979), Pi-Sunyer (1977), and Wagner (1977), which demonstrated that local residents and tourism employees perceive that tourist behavior is affected by national culture.

Therefore we suggest that if future research supports the findings of this study with tour guides and tourists of other nationalities, and in different touristic situations, it would be accurate to conclude that from a *subjective* point of view tourists are perceived to vary not only according to their motivation, demographics, and lifestyle, but also according to their nationality. Therefore, nationality counts.

LIMITATIONS OF THE STUDIES

All of the aforementioned studies have several limitations. First, because they portray the *subjective* perceptions that particular samples of British, Israeli, Korean, and Dutch tour guides possessed of tourists of different nationalities, these studies should be considered exploratory. Though there might be some similarity between these stereotypes and the tourists' actual behavior, until this is proven empirically with actual tourists, we do not claim that these opinions are either an objective representation of the tourists' actual behavior, nor that the results of these studies could be generalized to other tourist populations. Second, despite the fact that the perceptions of Dutch tour guides regarding many behavioral characteristics of American and Japanese tourists have been found to be identical or or very similar to the perceptions of British, Korean, and Israeli tour guides, we cannot claim yet that the opinions of tour guides can be used as a proxy for observing or recording the actual behavior of tourists. For this to occur we must have significantly more evidence from many more tour guides of various nationalities. Third, because the study was not designed to measure the effect of other factors such as lifestyle, motivation, demographics, etc. on tourist behavior, it is impossible to claim that nationality is a determining factor in tourist behavior. At best, it is only possible to portray nationality as a moderating variable. Fourth, because this study was limited to a particular type of tour guides, namely those who specialize in escorted motor-coach tours, it is not possible to generalize its findings to other tour guides (e.g., tour guides who are based in one location such as a tourist attraction) or other tourism professionals.

CONCEPT DEFINITIONS

Convergence advocates: Scholars who believe that economies, organizations, and markets are becoming more and more homogeneous and therefore organizations and consumers are becoming more alike.

Cross-cultural research: The study of differences across nations for the purpose of determining whether similar patterns exist among consumers and decision makers in different countries.

Culture: An umbrella word that encompasses a whole set of implicit widely shared beliefs, traditions, values, and expectations which characterize a particular group of people.

Direct methods of cross-cultural research: Methods of research aimed at discovering what if any differences actually exist in the behavior of tourists of various nationalities.

Divergence advocates: Scholars who argue that economies, organizations, and markets have always been, still are, and will always be culture bound rather than culture free. Therefore we should not expect to see any convergence in managerial and marketing practices, or consumer behavior across different cultures, since these depend on the implicit model prevalent in a particular culture.

Indirect methods of cross-cultural research: Methods of research aimed at describing and cataloging the various perceptions that residents and entrepreneurs in tourist communities have of tourists of various nationalities.

Perception: The process by which an individual selects, organizes, and interprets information to create a meaningful picture of the world.

Tour: A prearranged journey to one or more destinations.

Tour guide: A professional escort who conducts a travel group.

Tourist behavior: The study of why and how tourists buy specific products and services, act in certain ways, and make certain decisions.

REVIEW QUESTIONS

1. Discuss the main points in the convergence-divergence debate and how these are reflected in the tourism discipline.
2. What are the differences between the perceived and actual differences in consumer behavior by nationality?
3. Cite two studies that proved that tourists of different nationalities behave differently, and two others that showed that tourists of different nationalities are perceived to behave differently.
4. Describe the main objections to cross-cultural research. Who were the subjects in the four studies conducted by Pizam and colleagues and why were these subjects chosen?
5. What were the main conclusions reached by the author from the four studies conducted in Britain, Israel, the Netherlands, and Korea?

REFERENCES

Barham, N. (1989). Winter Recreation in the Jordan Rift Valley. *Tourism Recreation Research,* 14 (2): 33-39.

Boissevain, J. and P. Inglott (1979). Tourism in Malta. In E. De Kadt, ed., *Tourism: Passport to Development?,* Oxford, UK: Oxford University Press.

Boote, A.S. (1983). Psychographic Segmentation in Europe. *Journal of Advertising Research*, 22 (6): 19-25.

Brewer, J. (1978). Tourism Business and Ethnic Categories in a Mexican Town. In V. Smith, ed., *Tourism and Behavior*, Williamsburg, VA: College of William and Mary.

Brewer, J. (1984). Tourism and Ethnic Stereotypes: Variations in a Mexican Town. *Annals of Tourism Research*, 11 (3): 487-502.

Business Korea (1991). The Way of Korean Traveling, Koreans Are So Strange? *Business Korea*, 9 (2): 29.

Child, J. (1981). Culture Contingency and Capitalism in the Cross-Cultural Study of Organizations. In L.L. Cummings and B.M. Staw, eds., *Research in Organizational Behavior*, Vol. 3, Stanford, CT: JAI Press, 303-356.

Cho Sun-Young (1991). The Ugly Koreans are Coming? *Business Korea*, 9 (2): 25-31.

Clark, T. (1990). International Marketing and National Character: A Review and Proposal for an Integrative Theory. *Journal of Marketing*, 54 (4): 66-79.

Couger, J.D., H. Adelsberger, I. Borovitz, M. Zviran, and J. Motiwalla (1990). Commonalities in Motivating Environments for Programmer/Analyst in Austria, Israel, Singapore and the U.S.A. *Information and Management*, 18 (2): 41-46.

Council of Europe (1985). *Evaluation of the Impact of Sports for All Policies*. Strasbourg: The Council of Europe.

Dann, G. (1993). Limitations in the Use of Nationality and Country of Residence Variables. In D.G. Pearce and R.W. Butler, eds., *Tourism Critiques and Challenges*, London: Routledge, 88-112.

Dawar, N. and P. Parker (1994). Marketing Universals: Consumers' Use of Brand Name, Price, Physical Appearance and Retailer Reputation as Signals of Product Quality. *Journal of Marketing*, 58 (2): 81-95.

Douglas, S. P. and Y. Wind (1987). The Myth of Globalization. *Colombia Journal of World Business*, 22 (4): 19-29.

Groetzbach, E., ed. (1981). *Freizeit und Erholung als Probleme der vergleichenden Kulturgeographie*. Regensburg, Germany: Eichstater Beitrage 1.

Groetzbach, E. (1988). Erholungsverhalten und Tourismusstile am Beispiel Orientalischer Lander. In W. Ritter and G. Milelitz, eds., *Berichte und Materialien*, Berlin: Institut für Tourismus, Freie Universitat.

Grunert, S.C. (1990). Consumer Values in West Germany. Underlying Dimensions and Cross-Cultural Comparison with North America. *Journal of Business Research*, 20 (2): 97-107.

Holzner, L. (1985). Stadtland USA. *Geographische Zeitschrift*, 75 (4): 192-205.

Ibrahim, H. (1991). *Leisure and Society: A Comparative Approach*. Dubuque, Iowa: Wm. C. Brown.

Kunda, G. (1991). *Engineering Culture: Culture and Control in a High-Tech Corporation*. Philadelphia: Temple University Press.

Leavitt, H.J. and H. Bahrami (1988). *Managerial Psychology*. Chicago: University of Chicago Press.

Levitt, T. (1983). The Globalization of Markets. *Harvard Business Review*, 83 (3): 92-102.

Nash, D. (1978). An Anthropological Approach to Tourism. *Tourism and Economic Change Studies in Third World Societies*, 7: 133-152.

Ohmae, K. (1989). Managing in a Borderless World. *Harvard Business Review*, 67 (3): 152-161.

Okechuku, C. and W.M.V. Yee (1991). Comparison of Managerial Traits in Canada and Hong Kong. *Asia Pacific Journal of Management*, 8 (2): 223-235.

Onkvisit, S. and J.J. Shaw (1987). Standardized International Advertising: A Review and Critical Evaluation of the Theoretical and Empirical Evidence. *Columbia Journal of World Business*, 22 (3): 43-55.

Open University (1985). *Technology: A Second Level Course, Managing in Organizations, Block V: Wider Perspectives, Unit 16: International Perspectives*, Milton Keynes, UK: Open University Press.

Peabody, D. (1985). *National Characteristics*. Cambridge: University Press.

Pi-Sunyer, O. (1977). Through Native Eyes: Tourists and Tourism in a Catalan Maritime Community. In V. Smith, ed., *Hosts and Guests: The Anthropology of Tourism*, Philadelphia: University of Pennsylvania Press.

Pizam, A. (1993). Managing Cross-Cultural Hospitality Enterprises. In P. Jones and A. Pizam, *The International Hospitality Industry*, New York and London: Wiley, pp. 205-225.

Pizam, A., M. Jansen-Verbeke, and L. Steel (1997). Are All Tourists Alike Regardless of Nationality? The Perceptions of Dutch Tour-Guides. *Journal of International Hospitality, Leisure and Tourism Management*, 1 (1): 19-40.

Pizam, A. and G.H. Jeong (1996). Cross-Cultural Tourist Behavior: Perceptions of Korean Tour-Guides. *International Journal of Tourism Management*, 17 (4): 277-286.

Pizam, A. and A. Reichel (1996). The Effect of Nationality on Tourist Behavior: Israeli Tour Guides' Perceptions. *Journal of Hospitality and Leisure Marketing* 4 (1): 23-49.

Pizam, A. and S. Sussman (1995). Does Nationality Affect Tourist Behavior? *Annals of Tourism Research*, 22 (2): 901-917.

Pizam, A. and N. Telisman-Kosuta (1989). Tourism As a Factor of Change: Results and Analysis. In J. Bystrzanowski, ed., *Tourism As a Factor of Change: A Socio-Cultural Study*, Vol. II, Vienna: European Coordination Centre for Documentation in Social Sciences.

Richardson, S.L. and J. Crompton (1988). Vacation Patterns of French and English Canadians. *Annals of Tourism Research*, 15 (4): 430-448.

Ritter, W. (1987). Styles of Tourism in the Modern World. *Tourism Recreation Research*, 12 (1): 3-8.

Ritter, W. (1989). On Deserts and Beaches: Recreational Tourism in the Muslim World. *Tourism Recreation Research*, 14 (2): 3-10.

Rodgers, H.B. (1977). *Rationalizing Sports Policies*. Strasbourg: Council of Europe.

Sheldon, P. and M. Fox (1988). The Role of Foodservice in Vacation Choice and Experience: A Cross-Cultural Analysis. *Journal of Travel Research,* 27 (3): 9-15.

Synodynos, N., C.F. Keown, and L.W. Jacobs (1989). Transnational Advertising Practices: A Survey of Leading Brand Advertisers in Fifteen Countries. *Journal of Advertising Research,* 29 (2): 43-50.

Szalai, A., ed. (1972). *The Use of Time: Daily Activities of Urban and Suburban Residents in Twelve Countries.* The Hague, Netherlands: Mouton and Co.

Tyagi, A.K. (1989). Tourist Culture in India: Insight and Implications. Unpublished PhD dissertation, Syracuse, NY: Syracuse University.

USTTA (1984a). *A Survey of Potential Vacation Travelers to the U.S. from Britain, West Germany, and France,* conducted by the Gallup Organization, for the USTTA. Washington, DC: United States Travel and Tourism Administration.

USTTA (1984b). *A Survey of Potential Vacation Travelers to the U.S. from Australia and Japan,* conducted by the Gallup Organization, for the USTTA. Washington, DC: United States Travel and Tourism Administration.

Wagner, U. (1977). Out of Time and Place: Mass Tourism and Charter Trips. *Ethnos,* 42 (1): 38-52.

Woodside, A. and J. Lawrence (1985). Step Two in Benefit Segmentation: Learning the Benefits Realized by Major Travel Markets. *Journal of Travel Research,* 24 (1): 7-13.

Yiannakis, A., S. Leivadi, and Y. Apostolopoulos (1991). Some Cross-Cultural Patterns in Tourist Role Preference: A Study of Greek and American Tourist Behaviors. *World Leisure and Recreation,* 33 (2): 33-37.

Chapter 19

Consumer Behavior in the U.S. Pleasure Travel Marketplace: An Analysis of Senior and Nonsenior Travelers

Rajshekhar G. Javalgi
Edward G. Thomas
S. R. Rao

LEARNING OBJECTIVES

By the end of the chapter, students should be able to:

- Explain why the senior market has now been "discovered" by travel and tourism marketers
- Summarize the relevant travel-related research on the senior market
- Outline the demographic differences among consumers in the following age groupings: under fifty-five, fifty-five to sixty-four, and sixty-five and older
- Differentiate between senior and nonsenior pleasure travelers with respect to types of pleasure trips taken
- Outline the differences among the three age segments studied with regard to the travel-related behaviors exhibited
- Discuss the marketing implications of the findings of the study

INTRODUCTION

Travel and tourism marketers face a highly competitive environment brought on by the changing demographics of the U.S. population, the most significant change being the growth in size of the older segment of the

This chapter was previously published in the *Journal of Travel Research, 31*(2), 1992. Reprinted with permission.

population. Consumers age fifty-five and over represent one of the fastest growing segments of the population (Shoemaker, 1989; Waldrop, 1989). This demographic market segment has been variously labeled as the "older market," the "mature market," and the "senior market" (Shoemaker, 1989; Lazer, 1985; Allan, 1981). The term used in this study is "senior market" because it appears to be preferred by most of those who make up this market (Shoemaker, 1989).

Regardless of the terminology used, consumers ages fifty-five and older are a demographic "discovery," the importance of which will extend through the 1990s and beyond for two reasons—market size and market potential. In terms of market size, an estimated 59 million people in this country will be ages fifty-five and over by the year 2000 (Hawes, 1988; *Technology and Aging in America*, 1985). Currently, within this consumer group, the 28 million people sixty-five years old and older constitute 11.9 percent of the population. This sixty-five-and-over age group has been growing at twice the rate of the population as a whole and is projected to reach 64.6 million by the year 2030 (Lumpkin and Hunt, 1989). Waldrop (1989) notes that the "household boom and bust will continue in the 1990s—look for rapid growth in the forty-five-to-fifty age group and a decline in the number of households headed by twenty-five to thirty-four-year-olds." The number of households headed by people ages thirty-five to forty-four grew 38 percent between 1980 and 1988 as the baby boom generation entered this age bracket, making it the fastest growing segment.

In terms of market potential, the senior market of persons ages fifty-five and older possesses a relatively large share of all discretionary dollars because this market segment traditionally has fewer major bills—investments in home and family have been made and their children no longer depend entirely upon them (Blazey, 1987; Anderson and Langmeyer, 1982). England (1987) notes that "Americans over sixty-five are the second richest age group in the U.S. society. Only those Americans in the next-oldest age bracket, from fifty-five to sixty-five, are better off." The assets of the aged are now nearly twice the median for the nation.

With regard to seniors and the pleasure travel market, evidence suggests that people over the age of fifty-five account for some 80 percent of all vacation dollars spent in the United States; these people travel more often, tend to go longer distances, and stay away longer than any other age group (Shoemaker, 1989).

Despite an increasing interest in senior consumers and the implications of their market size, economic potential, and desire to travel, relatively little is known about their actual travel behavior in the pleasure travel marketplace. For travel-related service providers to meet the needs of the senior market, it is necessary to achieve a greater understanding of the pleasure travel behavior of seniors and the basic differences between seniors and nonseniors in the pleasure travel marketplace. The present study focuses its attention on the consumer behavior of seniors in this marketplace.

RELATED RESEARCH

Recently, the consumer behavior of the senior market has become an increasingly important area of interest to various public policymakers and researchers. Guinn (1980) examined older people as a recreational user group, but limited his work to recreational vehicle tourists. In a more focused age-specific travel-related research study, Tongren (1980) investigated the over-sixty-five market (pre- and postretirement). His findings revealed that the older market group engaged in a distinct preretirement travel-planning phase and a detailed postretirement information-searching and travel execution (or implementation) phase. Tongren suggested using different promotional programs for effectively targeting pre- and postretirement individuals.

Anderson and Langmeyer (1982) presented a profile of the differences and similarities between travelers under the age of fifty and those over fifty. Their study, based on a sample of 826 households in the Dayton Standard Metropolitan Statistical Area, indicated that the over-fifty travelers preferred nonhectic, preplanned pleasure trips for rest and relaxation or for visiting relatives; the under-fifty group also tended to travel for rest and relaxation, but was more likely to participate in outdoor recreational activities or to visit commercial amusement facilities.

A handful of other recent studies have focused on the mature market. Hughes (1985) emphasized the size, attractiveness, and heterogeneity of this market, while Supernaw (1985) noted that retired people give travel the highest priority for their retirement years. Blazey (1987) examined the differences between participants and nonparticipants in a senior travel program, while Vincent and De Los Santos (1990) focused on the senior winter traveler to Texas. In this latter study, for example, it was reported that nearly 70 percent of all "winter Texans" (visitors to Texas who stay for at least one month during the winter season) come from the Midwestern states, and the climate and friendliness of the local people are the two most important attractions when choosing a winter vacation place.

At least two observations can be made from the review of literature. First, it seems clear that the mature market is not homogeneous and that age has been used as a demographic variable to segment this market. Second, relatively little is known about the travel behavior of senior consumers in the pleasure travel marketplace, and the literature suggests that more research is needed to identify and describe the travel preferences of mature consumers, particularly with regard to the types of pleasure trips taken and the characteristics of the trips (e.g., the modes of transportation, the types of accommodations used, and the like) (Tongren, 1980). Vincent and De Los Santos (1990) support this view by noting that "because of the growth in numbers and wealth of America's senior population, continuing research is needed on effective strategies for its segments."

STUDY OBJECTIVES

The study reported here investigated the travel behavior of senior and nonsenior groups in the pleasure travel marketplace. The three specific age groups considered were: under-fifty-five, fifty-five to sixty-four, and sixty-five and older. These particular groups were chosen because they conform to age groupings often reported in other sources. In this study, we refer to the fifty-five and older groups as the senior market and the under-fifty-five group as the nonsenior market. Within the senior segment, those sixty-five and older are referred to as the elderly.

The specific study objectives were:

1. to present demographic information on the senior and nonsenior market segments;
2. to determine the types of pleasure trips taken by senior and nonsenior travelers; and
3. to determine the differences in travel-related characteristics (i.e., the mode of transportation, the type of accommodations used, and the use of package travel and travel agents) between senior and nonsenior pleasure travelers.

By building on previous research, this study seeks to improve the knowledge base concerning the senior and nonsenior segments of the pleasure travel marketplace.

METHODOLOGY

The study reported here used data collected in a research project sponsored by Tourism Canada. This comprehensive study of the perceptions, preferences, and travel-planning behavior of U.S. pleasure travelers utilized personal interviews to gather information from some 9,000 travelers in late 1985.

To be included in the study, respondents must have been at least sixteen years old and have taken at least one pleasure trip during the three years preceding the study. A "pleasure trip" was defined as a trip that required the respondent to travel more than 100 miles one way, spend at least one night away from home, and use commercial accommodations and/or transportation. For those interested, a much more detailed discussion of the data collection procedure has been published elsewhere (Taylor, 1989).

The respondents were asked to provide information on the types of trips they had taken, the mode of travel, and the accommodations used. They were also asked whether they had used a commercially available packaged trip and whether they had used a travel agent for making any of the arrangements.

For the purposes of the present study, the trip types were defined as follows (Taylor, 1989):

1. Visit to friends/relatives—a trip where the primary purpose is to spend time with friends and/or relatives
2. Close-to-home leisure trip—a trip to a place close to home where one can enjoy facilities related to a beach, lake, seashore, or park
3. Touring vacation—a trip by car, bus, or train through areas of scenic beauty and cultural and general interest
4. City trip—a journey to a city where one can shop, visit museums, enjoy entertainment, dine, attend plays or concerts, or just stroll around and enjoy the city
5. Outdoor vacation—a trip to a natural area where one can engage in activities such as camping, hunting, fishing, hiking, or rafting
6. Resort vacation—a journey to a resort or resort area where a wide variety of recreational activities, amenities, and facilities are available nearby or on the premises
7. Cruise—a trip on a cruise ship where one enjoys all on-board activities and planned stops at points of interest along the way
8. Trip to theme park, exhibition, or special event—a trip taken primarily for the purpose of visiting a major theme park, exhibition, or special event such as a Super Bowl, a world's fair, or the Olympic Games

RESULTS

The following discussion focuses first on a comparison of selected demographics of senior and nonsenior pleasure travelers. Then, information pertaining to the other study objectives is presented.

Demographics of the Segments

Table 19.1 contains a summary of the demographic information collected.

Education

As shown in Table 19.1, clearly there appears to be a significant association between the educational categories and the three age segments ($\chi^2 =$ 233; $p < .001$). Members of the under-fifty-five group appear to be somewhat more highly educated than their senior counterparts, at least in terms of years of formal education completed. However, this will most likely change in the future as the better educated baby boomers move into the senior age groups. Furthermore, trends in the environment, such as the increased use of state-of-the-art technology, will compel citizens to have better education to adapt to the changes.

Of the individuals responding to this survey, approximately one-third of the senior consumers indicated that they had completed vocational training or high school; among the elderly (sixty-five and older), almost 25 percent reported having completed some college or having received a college degree. Another 5 percent had attained a graduate degree. Over 47 percent of the nonseniors indicated that they had completed some college or beyond.

Income

The elderly generally face a decrease in income upon retirement and their income remains relatively fixed. The measure of association between the income levels and the three groups is highly significant ($\chi^2 = 284$; $p < .001$). Table 19.1 shows that slightly less than 10 percent of the elderly placed themselves in the over-$40,000 income category; a higher percentage of members from the fifty-five to sixty-four group reported their income in this category. Some 23.5 percent of the under-fifty-five segment is in this income range. Just over 25 percent of the respondents from the under-fifty-five and the fifty-five to sixty-four segments reported income between $20,000 and $29,999. Close to 44 percent of the responding elderly members noted that their incomes were under $15,000, a much higher percentage than in the other two age brackets.

Employment Status

As shown in Table 19.1, employment status is significantly related to the three age categories or segments ($\chi^2 = 186$; $p < .001$). Of the sixty-

TABLE 19.1. A Comparison of Selected Demographic Characteristics of Senior and Nonsenior Pleasure Travelers

CHARACTERISTICS	AGE		
	Under-55 (N = 3,277) (%)	55-64 (N = 601) (%)	65 & Older (N = 687) (%)
EDUCATION:			
Grade 8 or less	.9	8.0	13.3
Some vocational or high school	15.8	15.0	18.6
Completed vocational or high school	28.0	34.2	30.3
Professional/technical training	6.8	7.7	7.5
Some college or university	23.6	17.8	14.6
Graduate college/university	15.5	10.4	10.1
Graduate work	8.4	6.9	5.6
$\chi^2 = 233; p < .001$			
INCOME:			
Under $15,000	13.6	18.0	43.8
$15,000 to $19,999	10.7	10.6	16.5
$20,000 to $29,999	25.9	25.7	21.5
$30,000 to $39,999	26.3	17.8	8.6
$40,000 or more	23.5	28.0	9.6
$\chi^2 = 284; p < .001$			
OCCUPATION:			
Employed full time	61.6	36.8	4.2
Employed part time	13.5	9.4	6.0
Retired	1.4	31.7	72.1
Temporarily unemployed	4.2	1.5	0.4
Homemaker	16.3	15.5	16.2
Other	3.0	5.1	1.1
$\chi^2 = 186; p < .001$			

five-and-above segment, 72 percent indicated that they were retired, compared to just less than 32 percent of those in the fifty-five to sixty-four group. Only 1.4 percent of the under-fifty-five group were retired.

Over 60 percent of the under-fifty-five category and almost 37 percent of the fifty-five to sixty-four age grouping indicated that they were employed full time. Part-time employment was higher for the under-fifty-five group compared to the seniors. The percentage of respondents indicating their occupation as homemaker was similar across the three groups (in the 16 percent range).

Types of Pleasure Trips Taken

Table 19.2 contains information on the types of pleasure trips taken by seniors and nonseniors. Overall, Table 19.2 appears to reveal that a linear relationship exists between the age groupings and the types of trips recently taken. That is, for some trip types, members of the youngest group are more likely to have taken a trip of the type in question, with the fifty-five to sixty-four age group members being less likely to have taken the trip type and the sixty-five-and-over travelers being least likely to have taken the trip type. In other cases, the reverse is true, with the youngest group being least likely to have taken the trip and the oldest group being most likely to have taken the trip type.

In general, the under-fifty-five group was slightly more likely ($p < .05$) than one or both of the other groups to have taken a close-to-home pleasure trip, a city trip, an outdoor vacation, a resort vacation, and a trip to a theme park. The seniors were more likely to have taken a trip to visit friends and/or relatives, a touring vacation, or a cruise.

The largest percentage difference appears to be in the outdoor vacation category, where just over 24 percent of the under-fifty-five travelers had taken such a trip, but only 14.8 percent of the fifty-five to sixty-four group and 8.9 percent of the sixty-five-and-older group had taken such a trip ($p < .01$). This type of pleasure vacation may be more appealing to nonseniors because these younger age group members are more likely to want to engage in a variety of heavy physical activities, including skiing, hunting, and hiking.

As one would expect, a trip to a theme park, exhibition, or special event is more popular among the under-fifty-five segment ($p < .01$) and a cruise trip is more preferred by seniors ($p < .05$). Theme park trips are obviously more appealing to the nonsenior market because many members of this segment are likely to have children still at home. On the other hand, the seniors have "empty nests" and are freer to take cruise trips with their spouses.

TABLE 19.2. A Comparison of Pleasure Trip Types of Senior and Nonsenior Pleasure Travelers[a]

Pleasure Trip Type	Nonsenior Group Age Under 55[b] (N = 3,277) (%)	Senior Group Age 55-64 (N = 601) (%)	Age 65 and Older (N = 587) (%)
A visit to friends/relatives	57.6	61.1	64.5
A close-to-home leisure trip	36.5	31.8	24.8
A touring vacation	20.8	26.9	29.1
A city trip	22.0	17.7	16.8
An outdoor vacation	24.1	14.8	8.9
A resort vacation	20.2	15.8	16.1
A cruise	1.5	4.5	6.5
A trip to theme park	14.4	7.5	7.2

[a] Respondents were asked about the number of trips of each type they had taken.
[b] Except for "visit to friends/relatives," there was a significant difference (at the .05 level or beyond) for all comparisons of proportions between the nonsenior group and one or both of the senior groups. Comparisons between the proportions for the two senior groups revealed a significant difference (at the .001 level) on two trip types (i.e., the "close to home leisure trip" and the "outdoor vacation").

Travel-Related Characteristics

The third objective was to investigate how each of the three segments differ regarding various travel-related characteristics, including mode of travel, accommodations used, and the use of package travel and travel agents for arranging accommodations. These elements were chosen as they provide important pieces of information to decision makers in the travel and tourism industry (Taylor, 1989). Table 19.3 presents this information.

Transportation Mode

Table 19.3 shows that the most preferred means of travel overall is the automobile. However, it is interesting to note that a linear relationship

TABLE 19.3. A Comparison of Travel-Related Characteristics of Senior and Nonsenior Pleasure Travelers

Travel Characteristics	Nonsenior Group Age Under-55[b] (N = 3,277) (%)	Senior Group	
		Age 55-65 (N = 601) (%)	Age 65 and Older (N = 587) (%)
MODE OF TRAVEL[a]			
Automobile	73.7	65.4	58.3
Plane	16.9	20.7	22.4
Train	1.4	1.1	1.6
Bus	3.8	6.9	17.1
Truck/Van/R.V.	9.0	10.6	9.3
Other	2.7	3.9	5.4
ACCOMMODATIONS[a]			
Home of friends/relatives	22.4	20.5	23.8
Hotel	25.2	24.6	27.7
Motel	30.4	39.0	38.9
Campground/trailer park	17.2	12.8	11.1
Cottage	3.6	2.6	2.9
Other	7.4	5.9	7.4

USE OF PACKAGE TRIP

	Yes No	Yes No	Yes No
Was this a package trip covering both transportation and accommodations?	11.0 89.0	16.8 83.2	23.9 76.1

$$\chi^2 = 101; \ p < .001$$

	Yes No	Yes No	Yes No
Did a travel agent book the transportation accommodations, or any part of this trip?	14.4 85.6	20.4 79.6	26.1 73.9

$$\chi^2 = 77.63; \ p < .001$$

[a] Multiple responses.

appears to exist with regard to the mode of travel and the three age groupings. While for the under-fifty-five group members, the automobile is clearly the most preferred means of travel, the popularity of this travel mode drops as the age of the respondents increases. Bus travel, on the other hand, is not a popular mode compared to an automobile or plane, but the older the respondent, the more likely they were to have used this mode of transportation for a pleasure trip.

These findings are consistent with previous research (e.g., Anderson and Langmeyer, 1982) and can easily be interpreted when we integrate the additional information that many members of the under-fifty-five age group travel with children (and the automobile is the most flexible and inexpensive mode of travel for families). Many of the over-fifty-five group (or seniors) travel as members of packaged tours, which cover both transportation and accommodations, and such tours are likely to incorporate travel by bus and/or plane.

Use of Package Travel

As noted in Table 19.3, the measure of association between the use of package trips and the three segments was statistically significant ($\chi^2 = 101$; $p < .001$). While fewer than one-fourth of the trips taken by the respondents were packaged trips, Table 19.3 clearly suggests that when package trips are taken, they are preferred more by seniors than nonseniors ($p < .001$).

It is also evident that the members of the elderly group prefer packaged trips more than the members of the fifty-five to sixty-four group. This is consistent with the findings of Alderman (1989), who notes that "a large percentage of older travelers have incomes under $20,000 and are looking for travel they can afford. They provide the industry the opportunity to design and operate budget travel experiences for mature travelers."

When asked whether a travel agent had booked the transportation, accommodations, or any part of the trips taken, the percentage of affirmative responses from the senior group was higher than the percentage from the nonsenior group ($p < .001$) (see Table 19.3). Because the percentage of use of travel agents was higher than the percentage of use of package tours for all age groups, it is evident that travel agents are used to make arrangements for other types of trips.

Accommodations Used

Like the transportation mode used by pleasure travelers, another important element of tourism marketing information is the type of accommodations used. Table 19.3 reveals that hotels and motels clearly dominate the accommodation preferences of both the senior and nonsenior groups. It is interesting to note that close to 40 percent of both the fifty-five to sixty-four and over-sixty-five groups prefer motels compared to some 30 percent of the nonseniors ($p < .01$).

As was discussed earlier, senior travelers in the pleasure market appear to go for packaged trips and tend to make both transportation and accommodation arrangements with a travel agent. It is likely that the use of commercial accommodations in the form of hotels and motels is higher for the members of the senior market partially because of this greater preference for packaged trips.

Almost equal percentages of responding members from the three age segments indicated that they stayed in the homes of friends and/or relatives ($p < .10$). Table 19.3 also shows that the use of campgrounds and trailer parks is higher for the nonsenior segment, with the fifty-five to sixty-four and sixty-five-and-older groups indicating equal preferences for these types of accommodations. Cottages are not really popular with any groups, but appear to be used slightly more by the nonseniors.

IMPLICATIONS AND CONCLUSIONS

The information presented in this study may be helpful to travel marketers and various other parties interested in formulating marketing programs aimed at senior and nonsenior pleasure travelers. As one would expect, some demographic differences exist between the two groups of pleasure travelers studied.

As revealed by the study, the nonseniors are currently a better-educated group than the seniors. Those with better formal educations also are likely to be better educated as consumers. That is, they are more likely to engage in a detailed information search process before making a purchasing decision, using comparison shopping as a standard practice. Thus, marketers to the nonsenior group should probably approach the market with more and better consumer-oriented information about their travel-related products and services, including the use of comparative advertising methods.

It is important to bear in mind that the nonsenior consumers of today are the senior consumers of tomorrow. So future promotion and advertising programs directed at seniors may need to be more sophisticated and more consumer-information-oriented than currently is the case.

Clearly, today's seniors tend to be on relatively fixed incomes at a level much below that of the nonsenior group. This means that they are price sensitive in their shopping behavior, including shopping for travel-related products and services. Thus, seniors seem to prefer package travel in greater percentages than nonseniors. Travel marketers who wish to target senior travelers may find that an increased emphasis on travel packages will help capture a bigger share of this market. Furthermore, seniors are more likely than nonseniors to use travel agents for making travel arrangements. Therefore, travel and tourism marketers should make sure that they are effectively utilizing travel agents in their marketing programs aimed at senior travelers.

The employment-status variable has marketing implications in that retired persons (primarily seniors) have more leisure time for travel than do their nonretired counterparts. However, as was pointed out previously, seniors also have lower income levels than nonseniors (and nonretired persons). Thus, marketers attempting to develop a travel-package mix for seniors should emphasize discount pricing in a package that also involves travel for longer periods of time and/or for greater distances than packages for nonsenior travelers. While developing such a travel package, it is strategically vital to recognize that the nonsenior grouping is not homogeneous. For instance, within the nonsenior market, families with children and families without children may look for different package mixes.

In addition to selected demographic differences, the findings also revealed a number of similarities and differences between the two groups in actual travel behavior. The most common type of pleasure trip taken by both groups studied was the trip to visit friends and/or relatives. This would appear to be a type of pleasure trip that has not been specifically targeted by travel marketers for a number of reasons. For example, such trips are very personal to the trip takers; they could involve travel to a virtually unlimited number of destinations; and such trips often involve the travelers in staying for one or more nights with friends or relatives rather than seeking commercial accommodations. However, this could present an opportunity for travel marketers to convince such travelers to change the patterns typically followed in the past.

For example, the new group of low- and medium-priced motels could attempt to convince those visiting friends and relatives that it is better to stay in one of their motels than to stay with friends and relatives, especially if the price is attractive. In their advertising, they could point out that staying in a motel provides the traveler with more independence, is less disruptive to those being visited, and gives everyone a better chance to get a good night's sleep, especially if those being visited are somewhat cramped for space. Senior travelers who visit friends and/or relatives may even be targeted directly by such an appeal because they may be most likely to appreciate budget accommodations and they may also like to have a break from the friends and relatives, especially those with many small children.

The findings of the study also revealed a number of types of trips where differences existed in preferences between the senior and nonsenior groups. The nonseniors were more likely than seniors to have taken a close-to-home pleasure trip, a city trip, an outdoor vacation, a resort vacation, and a trip to a theme park, exhibition, or special event. Seniors were more likely to have taken a cruise or touring vacation. Marketers obviously should design travel and tourism marketing programs to respond to these differences. Family-oriented travel programs and services should be targeted to the nonsenior segment while travel involving greater distances or longer periods of time should be marketed to seniors.

Differences were also noted between the two groups with regard to travel-related characteristics. Although a majority of both groups use the automobile as the mode of transportation for pleasure trips, nonsenior travelers are somewhat more likely to do so. Senior travelers are more likely than nonseniors to travel by bus or airplane. Marketers with travel products and/or services that could benefit automobile travelers can target both groups, perhaps with more emphasis on families traveling by automobile. Seniors might be better targeted by those wishing to capitalize on the speed and convenience of air travel or the economy and leisurely pace of traveling by bus.

In the area of accommodations, it is clear that those marketing accommodations at campgrounds and trailer parks should concentrate on nonsenior travelers, while those offering other types of accommodations may target either or both groups.

Seniors are more likely than nonseniors to buy trip packages covering both transportation and accommodations, but the majority of pleasure trips are not of this type. Those who wish to market packaged trips obviously would look first to seniors, but they may also wish to do something to create a higher level of demand for such trips among the members of both groups. Appeals to seniors should probably emphasize the lower cost and higher security of packages versus more independent travel, while nonseniors, who have less leisure time, may be attracted to the convenience of having someone else make all the arrangements for travel.

With respect to the use of a travel agent for making travel arrangements, seniors were more likely to use travel agents than were nonseniors. Thus, those interested in reaching pleasure travelers through travel agents would target the senior group first. But, because the overwhelming majority of pleasure travelers do not use travel agents, the opportunity exists to create a higher level of demand for travel agent services among both groups.

Perhaps what is needed is more informative advertising designed to make all consumers aware of the services that travel agents provide and the fact that such services typically do not carry a direct cost to the consumer.

In conclusion, this chapter has identified a number of areas in which senior pleasure travelers differ from their nonsenior counterparts. The present study is also an initial step toward establishing an understanding of the need for developing effective pleasure travel marketing programs aimed at the senior and nonsenior markets. There clearly is a need for additional research, especially in the area of market segmentation, to better understand the needs and wants of the senior group in the pleasure travel marketplace. As the senior market continues to grow in the 1990s and beyond, unprecedented marketing opportunities will prevail for those who will accept the challenge.

CONCEPT DEFINITIONS

Elderly market: Consumers ages sixty-five and older, a subset of the senior market.

Heterogeneity: The quality of being heterogeneous or nonuniform; a heterogeneous market is a group of consumers exhibiting a wide variety of characteristics and/or behaviors.

Homogeneous market: A group of consumers exhibiting similar characteristics and/or behaviors.

Nonsenior market: Consumers under fifty-five years of age.

Packaged trip: A pleasure trip arranged by a tour promoter that typically includes transportation, lodging, and a preplanned itinerary.

Pleasure travel market: Consumers who engage in nonbusiness travel of a personal nature, such as vacations, visits to friends or relatives, and the like.

Senior market: Consumers ages fifty-five and older.

REVIEW QUESTIONS

1. What are the factors that have led travel and tourism marketers to "discover" the senior market? Why is this a lucrative market now and for the immediate future?

2. What were the major findings of related research studies mentioned in this chapter?

3. What are the major demographic differences among consumers in the three age groupings included in this study?

4. What type of pleasure trip was taken most frequently by the senior and nonsenior travelers included in this study? For each age grouping covered, what other types of trips were most often taken? How can we explain the relationships that exist between the age groupings and the types of pleasure trips taken?
5. What were the preferred modes of travel for each of the age groups studied? What differences exist among the groups? How can these differences be explained?
6. What were the patterns of use of package travel among the age groups studied? What differences exist among the groups? How can these differences be explained?
7. What were the preferences in the types of accommodations used for pleasure travel among the three age groups studied? What differences exist among the groups? How can these differences be explained?
8. What are the marketing implications of the findings of this study? What kind of marketing programs and services should travel and tourism marketers design to serve today's senior and nonsenior markets? Based on the demographic trends and travel-related behavior patterns noted in the chapter, what marketing opportunities will there be in the senior travel market in the next ten to fifteen years?

REFERENCES

Alderman, Barbara (1989), "Travel by Seniors," *Travel and Tourism Executive Report*, 9 (April), 1-8.

Allan, Carol (1981), "Measuring Mature Markets," *American Demographics*, 3 (March), 13-17.

Anderson, Beverlee B. and Lynn Langmeyer (1982), "The Under-50 and Over Travelers: A Profile of Similarities and Differences," *Journal of Travel Research*, 20 (Spring), 20-24.

Blazey, Michael A. (1987), "The Differences Between Participants and Non-Participants in a Senior Travel Program," *Journal of Travel Research,* (Summer), 7-12.

England, Robert (1987), "Greener Era for Gray America," *Insight* (March), 8-11.

Guinn, Robert (1980), "Elderly Recreational Vehicle Tourists: Motivation for Leisure," *Journal of Travel Research*, 19 (Summer), 9-12.

Hawes, Douglas K. (1988), "Travel Related Lifestyle Profiles of Older Women," *Journal of Travel Research,* (Fall), 22-32.

Hughes, William (1985), "The Mature Travelers," in *The Battle for Market Share: Strategies in Research and Marketing,* Proceedings of the Sixteenth Annual Conference, Travel and Tourism Research Association, Salt Lake City, UT: Business of Economic and Business Research, Graduate School of Business, University of Utah, 281-285.

Lazer, William (1985), "Inside the Mature Market," *American Demographics,* (March), 24-25, 49-50.

Lumpkin, James R. and James B. Hunt (1989), "Mobility as an Influence on Retail Patronage Behavior of the Elderly: Testing Conventional Wisdom," *Journal of the Academy of Marketing Science,* (Winter), 1-12.

Shoemaker, Stowe (1989), "Segmentation of the Senior Pleasure Travel Market," *Journal of Travel Research,* (Winter), 14-21.

Supernaw, Scott (1985), "Battle for the Gray Market," in *The Battle for Market Share: Strategies in Research and Marketing,* Proceedings of the Sixteenth Annual Conference, Travel and Tourism Research Association, Salt Lake City, UT: Bureau of Economic and Business Research, Graduate School of Business, University of Utah, 287-290.

Taylor, Gordon D. (1989), "The United States Pleasure Travel Market," *Journal of Business Research,* 18 (August), 1-79.

Technology and Aging in America (1985), Washington, DC: U.S. Congress Office of Technology Assessment, OTA-BA-264, June.

Tongren, Hale N. (1980), "Travel Plans of the Over-65 Market Pre- and Post-Retirement," *Journal of Travel Research,* 19 (Fall), 7-11.

Vincent, Vern C. and Gilbertro De Los Santos (1990), "Winter Texans: Two Segments of the Senior Travel Market," *Journal of Travel Research,* (Summer), 9-12.

Waldrop, Judith (1989), "America's Households," *American Demographics,* (March), 20-27.

Chapter 20

Patterns of Tourist Expenditure and Types of Vacation Across the Family Life Cycle

Robert Lawson

LEARNING OBJECTIVES

By the end of the chapter the reader should be able to:

- Understand the potential role of the family life cycle in tourism market segmentation
- Be aware of the potential advantages and disadvantages of using the family life cycle for segmentation
- Understand how stages of the family life cycle can be linked to destination choice
- Understand how patterns of holiday expenditure may vary across the stages of the family life cycle
- Understand how patterns of vacation behavior may vary across the stages of the family life cycle

INTRODUCTION

The family life cycle (FLC) is an established concept in the literature used to describe and explain consumer behavior. Briefly, the FLC desribes how, from the time it is first formed by marriage until the death of the last

This chapter was previously published in the *Journal of Travel Research, 29*(4), 1991. Reprinted with permission.

partner, the family passes through alternative phases of relative want and plenty. This cyclical effect is caused mainly by the arrival and dispersal of children and then later by retirement and old age.

The focus of this study was the relationship between the FLC and patterns of tourist behavior. Because of the more discretionary nature of expenditure on vacations, tourism is an area where theoretically behavior should be strongly related to the stage of the FLC. Observation of business practices in some sectors, such as the U.K. package holiday industry and the New Zealand approach to the Japanese market, indicates that the FLC is being used in an implicit way; however, businesses tend not to distinguish the concept from segmentation on the basis of age. Further, they do not always comprehend the full multidimensional scope of the FLC with its representation not only of age but also marital status, age of children, employment status, size of traveling group, and availability of discretionary income (Lawson, 1989; NZTP, 1985, 1987).

This lack of clarity in understanding and applying the concept of the FLC is compounded by a lack of supporting empirical work in consumer behavior and tourism marketing literature. Specific studies on the relationship between tourism and the FLC are very limited. Plog (1972) analyzed the vacation aspect of family travel across junior, mid-, and mature status families, and Cosenza and Davis (1981) examined differences in vacation decision making over the FLC. However, most assumptions about the relationship between tourism and the FLC seem to be founded upon general reviews of consumer behavior over the FLC (Wells and Gubar, 1966; Reynolds and Wells, 1977; Stampfl, 1978). Probably the most important study is that by Wells and Gubar, who divided the history of a family into nine possible phases and highlighted how the bachelor, newly married, full nest III, and empty nest I stages of the life cycle are the particularly important periods for heavy expenditure on leisure and tourism.

STUDY BACKGROUND AND CONTEXT

During the 1980s, the growth in tourism in New Zealand was quite spectacular. In New Zealand's list of foreign exchange earners, the tourism industry moved from seventh place in 1980 to first place in 1988, and the number of overseas visitors is forecast to reach one million by 1991 (NZTP, 1986). This will represent a 100 percent increase from 1984. The country trades mainly on its primary assets with "outstanding scenery making it one of the world's most beautiful countries" (New Zealand Tourism Council and NZTP, 1984). International visitors to the country are drawn mainly from Australia, North America, and Great Britain but the highest areas of growth are from Southeast Asia, Scandinavia, and selected other countries of Western Europe.

Interest in detailed examination of life cycle relationships with tourism arose because of the difficulty of finding common effective segmentation criteria to describe this international and multicultural mix of tourists. The normal criteria that the New Zealand industry has applied are those listed by Meidan (1984) in his review of tourism marketing: country of origin, age, sex, and purpose of visit. Efforts to find better classification variables have focused particularly on psychographics, since they purport to provide some representation of the benefits sought by consumers. Two particular problems have been encountered in trying to apply psychographics to international visitors. First, the systems (such as VALS) are based on American cultural values and do not adapt easily even to the Australian or New Zealand situation, let alone the Japanese or Malaysian. Second, psychographics are individual constructs. This can present problems in trying to relate them to group behavior such as family vacations. It has been noted that American husbands and wives traveling abroad often belong to two different psychographic segments (Pyszka, 1987). Such a dichotomy within a traveling group can obviously cause real practical problems for the marketer attempting to use lifestyle as a basis for segmentation.

A priori reasoning suggests that if common ground can be found to describe consumers from many different cultures it is most likely to occur in demographic statistics. Evidence for demographic convergence is available which would suggest that the life cycle could be uniformly applicable, assuming that it distinguishes tourist behaviors effectively (Kumagai, 1984; Safilios-Rothschild, 1989).

Data were provided for the research by the New Zealand Tourist and Publicity Department, which made available the database from its 1986 survey of international visitors to New Zealand (NZTP, 1986). This database contained data from 4,123 questionnaires completed at airports as visitors left New Zealand. Those visitors reporting business or conferences as their primary motive for visiting New Zealand were excluded from the analysis, leaving a total of 3,426 cases. Besides personal data on the respondents, information was collected on all aspects of their vacations in the country, including accommodation, activities, expenditures, transport, and length of stay.

The results of the data analysis are discussed in three general areas:

1. The distribution of tourists entering New Zealand according to the stage of FLC
2. Expenditure on different elements of vacations across the FLC

3. Differences across the life cycle in the type of holiday, taken as described by the activities pursued, amount of traveling done, type of accommodation used, and length of stay

DISTRIBUTION OF FLC OBSERVATIONS

Information on the traveling group, ages of the group members, occupation, and the number of people in the group in paid employment made it possible to construct a life cycle variable for 60.3 percent of the 3,426 cases used in the analysis. The life cycle constructed had eight categories and was based essentially on the scheme devised by Wells and Gubar (1966). Three slight alterations were made to their classification:

1. The break between full nest I and full nest II was defined at the age of five, not six, for the youngest child. This more accurately accommodated the critical point regarding starting of school among the countries in the sample.
2. Possible nondependent children were included with dependents in full nest III, i.e., families with older children.
3. No allowance was made for solitary survivors still within the labor force. The numbers in this group were too small and too poorly defined in the survey to consider a separate classification.

Under this classification the frequencies of visitors entering New Zealand by stage of FLC were as shown in Table 20.1. The composition of the 1,359 cases not classified according to the life cycle was as follows: lone tourists, 784; couples, 155; pairs (friend or relative), 345; groups of friends, 72; special interest groups, 3.

The 420 cases in the last three of these groups fall entirely outside the scope of the FLC since the traveling group could not be equated with the family unit. Also, there were numerous missing observations on age, which meant that it was not possible to classify a further 66 cases in the first two groups above. The remainder of the cases not classified into this life cycle framework were childless couples in the thirty-five to forty-four age group (135) and lone tourists between the ages of twenty-five and sixty-five (738).

If the possibility of solitary survivors under sixty-five (from the Wells and Gubar structure) is excluded, neither of these groups has a place within the traditional concept of the life cycle and could only be incorporated by using the kind of revised structures discussed by authors such as

TABLE 20.1. Distribution of FLC Observations

FLC Stage	Description	Frequency	Percent
0	Not classifiable	1,359	39.8
1	Young single (under 25)	312	9.1
2	Young couples (no children)	392	11.4
3	Full nest I (with preschool children)	51	1.5
4	Full nest II (school-age children)	192	5.6
5	Full nest III (older children, possibly nondependent)	165	4.8
6	Empty nest I (still working, no children)	587	17.1
7	Empty nest II (retired)	262	7.6
8	Solitary survivor (retired)	106	3.1
		Total 3,426	**100.0**

Source: The 1986 International Visitors to New Zealand Product Survey.

Murphy and Staples (1979) and Gilly and Enis (1982). These revisions have attempted to update the life cycle concept to take account of changing demographic trends, particularly in procreation and divorce. Data did not allow for some of these modifications to be considered, for example those relating to single-parent families. Other proposals relating to the inclusion of people who remain single or couples who remain childless were rejected, since they do not conform to the concept of the FLC as "a processual model of family growth development over time" (Bristor, 1985). The concept was designed to illustrate the economic and sociological effects of preparenthood, parenthood, and postparenthood roles on a family group, and the inclusion of such groups as "double income, no kids" (DINKS) does not conform with its basic theoretical foundations. For example, couples who remain childless do not go through the same pattern of financial cycles that underpin many of the economic aspects of life cycle theory. This is the suggested reason why the extended coverage models have been shown not always to offer improved explanation of behavior (Wagner and Hanna, 1983). The best approach with such groups would seem to be that followed by Zimmerman (1982), who produced three alternative structures for conventional families, childless couples, and remaining singles. However, this is not a real option when working solely with cross-sectional data, and in consequence it was decided to remain with a conventional framework, even though this reduced the coverage and hence relevance of the life cycle to the total visitor market.

Of the 2,096 cases classified into life cycle groupings, 1,819 (88.0 percent) came from one of five following countries—Australia, Canada, Japan, the United Kingdom, and the United States. This proportion is consistent with the total survey sample. Referring to demographic data for these five major countries made it possible to calculate the approximate expected frequencies for the distribution of life cycle observations that could be classified (Murphy and Staples, 1979; Kumagai, 1984; Lawson, 1988). The expected frequencies were then used in a simple chi-square test to examine the significance of the observed distribution. The results are shown in Table 20.2.

It can be seen that only the empty nest II category at all approximates the expected frequency. All the full-nest stages and the solitary survivor category are underrepresented, while the remainder score more highly than would be expected on the basis of the distribution of observations from the sample countries. The important stages in terms of frequencies of arrivals are identical to those highlighted earlier by Wells and Gubar (1966). These stages can be explained by a number of factors, all related to FLC theory, when one considers the nature of a New Zealand vacation as a relatively expensive acquisition involving long-haul international flights. Part of the explanation is undoubtedly due to physical constraints associated with children and old age, but the distribution also conforms exceed-

TABLE 20.2. Observed and Expected Frequency of FLC Cases

FLC Stage	Number of Cases	
	Observed	**Expected**
1	312	55
2	392	95
3	51	375
4	192	519
5	165	227
6	587	203
7	262	264
8	106	329

Chi-square = 3509.83; significant at p .0000, 7 d.f.

ingly well with the life cycle pattern of financial cycles and the availability of money for discretionary expenditure. The one exception to this is the lower than expected full nest III figure. A possible explanation for this may be that, despite full nest III being one of the optimum financial periods for most families, there is still not enough discretionary finance around for the four or more full international flight tickets required for the holiday. Later analysis of holiday expenditures by stage of life cycle possibly confirms this interpretation, since tourists in this group were overall the largest spenders and the greatest proportion of their expenses were incurred in relation to airfares.

THE FLC AND VACATION EXPENDITURE

Expenditure data in the International Visitors Product Survey were recorded in nine different categories: accommodation, travel inside New Zealand, meals, arranged tours, shopping, entertainment, miscellaneous items (anything not otherwise classified), total expenditure within New Zealand, and total holiday expenditure including air fares and other costs before arrival. Data were analyzed by group and per capita; the main results are detailed in Tables 20.3 and 20.4. Comparison of the tables gives an indication of how the varying sizes of group represented by the different stages of the life cycle influence expenditure.

Life cycle theory suggests that discretionary expenditure will be high during stages one and two and fall sharply at stage three, before rising steadily through to stage six, where it will peak. Stages seven and eight will see a decline as financial constraints tighten after retirement and more expenditure is committed to items associated with health and security. This general trend can be observed in many of the expenditure classes in both Tables 20.3 and 20.4. Per capita expenditure on meals follows the sequence exactly, while many others, such as travel and total expenditure in New Zealand, are very close to that pattern.

Except for miscellaneous expenditure and per capita expenditure on tours, all results are statistically significant. The results contain some exceptions to the general trend, which deserve comment. First, young singles and empty nest I have the highest levels of per capita expenditure on accommodation (stages one and six). The latter is easily understood in the context of the FLC. The next section confirms that they are heavy users of more expensive accommodation options. The accommodation expenditure figure for young singles has to be taken in the context of the average length of stay in the country. On a per capita per day basis it is fourth highest behind young couples, empty nest I, and empty nest II.

TABLE 20.3. Average Holiday Expenditure by Category

Category	Expenditure for Family Life Cycle Stage								f	Sig.
	1	2	3	4	5	6	7	8		
Accommodation	$165[a]	249	207	243	384	309	241	111	5.95	.0000
Travel	140	323	295	368	342	292	208	84	10.81	.0000
Meals	156	325	328	458	503	380	310	136	19.66	.0000
Tours	52	111	48	131	161	111	114	59	4.88	.0000
Shopping	271	554	394	454	641	452	378	316	8.00	.0000
Entertainment	87	40	155	26	41	26	21	15	9.49	.0000
Miscellaneous	67	97	60	134	143	110	46	33	1.43	.1875
Total N.Z.	913[b]	1,702	1,496	1,831	2,200	1,666	1,350	764	24.56	.0000
Grand Total	$2,436	5,059	3,245	6,054	8,786	5,569	6,278	3,414	30.96	.0000

[a] Figures are New Zealand dollars, rounded to the nearest dollar.
[b] Categories do not sum to total because of missing observations.

TABLE 20.4. Average Holiday Expenditure Per Person by Category

Category	Expenditure for Family Life Cycle Stage								f	Sig.
	1	2	3	4	5	6	7	8		
Accommodation	$165[a]	123	87	61	111	155	120	111	4.52	.0001
Travel	140	161	98	96	98	146	104	84	3.19	.0023
Meals	156	162	99	115	144	190	155	136	4.92	.0000
Tours	52	56	15	33	47	56	57	59	1.37	.2144
Shopping	271	276	134	116	190	226	189	316	6.12	.0000
Entertainment	87	19	51	7	12	13	10	15	23.37	.0000
Miscellaneous	67	49	15	33	42	54	23	33	1.21	.2916
Total N.Z.	913[b]	851	490	468	648	832	674	764	10.47	.0000
Grand Total	$2,436	2,524	1,104	1,566	2,539	2,783	3,139	3,414	11.69	.0000

[a] Figures are New Zealand dollars, rounded to the nearest dollar.
[b] Categories do not sum to total because of missing observations.

Second, per capita shopping expenditure figures emphasize three groups: young singles, young couples, and solitary survivors. In the case of young singles, this is probably a reflection of length of stay; $271 represents 29.7 percent of total expenditure in New Zealand and as a percentage is comparable with full nest III and within 1 to 2 percent of most groups. On a per capita basis, young couples spend a slightly higher percentage of their within-New Zealand expenditure in this category (32.4 percent). This group has a significant number of Japanese tourists (80 out of 392), who are recognized by the industry as being heavy spenders on shopping. The most remarkable shopping figure is that for stage eight, the solitary survivors, shopping makes up 41.4 percent of their expenditure in New Zealand and largely explains the rise from stage seven to stage eight in total expenditure in New Zealand. Analysis of vacation type shows this group to contain many elderly British tourists spending time with families who have moved to New Zealand. Advice from an industry expert suggests that this result may represent expenditure by doting grandparents on their Kiwi grandchildren.

Third, entertainment expenditure is the one category that shows little relationship to the generally expected life cycle pattern. The per capita figures show little variation except for young singles and full nest I. High expenditure by young singles is understandable, but not by full nest I. The standard deviations associated with the full nest I entertainment figures are huge (e.g., $710.56 on a mean of $155.85) and the results are heavily influenced by a small number of very high observations. If six cases are dropped from this category, the overall mean for the remaining forty-five falls to $68. Clearly little emphasis should be placed on the full nest I entertainment figure.

Fourth, the pattern for overall total expenditure per capita is slightly at odds with expectations from life cycle theory as it rises through the final two stages. The explanation for this has to be related to airfares as the major component of this category. Obviously the origin of the tourist will explain some of the variation, with very-long-haul British visitors spending more than closer tourists representing other life cycle stages. Also, more elderly people may be prepared to trade up in order to achieve a higher degree of comfort on long flights.

HOLIDAY DIFFERENCES OVER THE FLC

Data on holiday activities, accommodation, and transport were all nominally scaled, and simple cross-tabulations were used to look for differences over the FLC. Length of stay and number of locations visited were ratio-scaled and were analyzed by analysis of variance. Unfortunately, measurement of the significance of the relationship between the FLC and the holiday type measures was difficult because of small cell sizes, making the chi square test on the cross-tabulation inappropriate. Analysis of some items in the survey, such as the use of commercial homes, and participation and spectatorship in sports such as basketball, bowls, marathons, and soccer, was not attempted because of low overall frequencies. Also, the small number of observations in the full nest I category caused some problems even where overall frequency levels were high. Of the fifty-five cross-tabulations completed, only the following proved significant at .05 or better where the effective frequency of cells with fewer than five observations was less than 5 percent:

a. Activities—use of cinemas, nightclubs, hangis (meals prepared in a traditional Maori way using an earth oven heated by hot rocks), Maori concerts, spa pools, jet boats, and museums
b. Travel—use of friends and relatives, hire cars, tour operators
c. Accommodation—use of friends and relatives, hotels

The analysis of variance of the FLC against length of stay produced an f value significant at .0000, and that on the number of locations visited a value significant at .0005.

Table 20.5 gives a summary of the findings from the analysis. It shows where attributes in particular life cycle stages deviated considerably from the mean value for the total sample of FLC observations. Thus the features described in the table do not reflect absolute levels of activities or other features, but the entries reflect variations between the life cycle stages.

Young Singles

The variations given in Table 20.5 show that young singles stay a long time in the country (average thirty-four nights as opposed to the overall average of twenty nights) and are highly active. Reference was made in the previous section to their relatively high level of spending on entertainment. In other ways young singles were seen to be average to low spenders, which is confirmed by a high dependence on friends and relatives and restricted traveling within the country. Even the reference to domestic flights fits this pattern since it suggests many of them traveled directly from Auckland or Christchurch to their main destination in the country. Also, internal flights booked as a supplement to international flights can be fairly cheap. To summarize, the key words that seem to be associated with young singles' holidays are "cheap" and "active."

TABLE 20.5. Differences in the Nature of Vacations over the FLC

Travel		Accommodation		Activities		Duration
Young Singles						
+	domestic flights	+	motor camps	++	rafting	++length of stay
++	friends and relatives	++	friends and relatives	+	jet boating	
++	buses	− −	hotels	++	sports (skiing)	
−	visiting national parks			+	sports watching (rugby)	
				++	entertainment (plays, concerts, cinema, others)	
Young Couples						
++	tours	+	motor camps	++	rafting	− length of stay
+	hire cars			+	jet boating	
+	taxis			++	spas	
++	visiting national parks			+	sports (skiing)	
+	locations visited			+	tours	
−	friends and relatives			−	Maori concerts	
				−	hangis	
Full Nest I						
++	friends and relatives	++	friends and relatives	− −	rafting	
− −	hire cars	− −	hotels	− −	museums	
− −	visiting national parks			− −	tours	
−	locations visited			− −	Maori concerts	
				− −	hangis	
				+	spas	
Full Nest II						
+	friends and relatives	− −	hotels	−	rafting	
−	hire cars			+	spas	
				−	museums	
				− −	tours	
				+	sports watching (rugby)	
				−	Maori concerts	
				−	hangis	
Full Nest III						
+	tour operators	−	hotels	++	jet boating	
+	hire cars			−	museums	
				+	sports (golf, fishing)	
				+	sports watching (horse racing)	
				+	cinema	

TABLE 20.5 (continued)

Travel	Accommodation	Activities	Duration
Empty Nest I			
++ tour operators	++ hotels	+ Maori concerts	− length of stay
++ hire cars	− − motor camps	+ hangis	
++ taxis		++ museums	
		++ tours	
Empty Nest II			
+ tour operators	+ commercial farms	− − rafting	
+ taxis	− − motor camps	− − jet boating	
++ visiting national parks		− − spas	
+ locations visited		++ museums	
		++ Maori concerts	
		++ hangis	
Solitary Survivor			
+ tour operators	++ friends and relatives	− − rafting	+ length of stay
++ friends and relatives	− − motor camps	− − jet boating	
− visited locations		− − spas	
		++ fishing	
		+ concerts	

Key: The ++ or − − shows that involvement in that characteristic deviated in that life cycle stage by more than 50 percent from the overall level of involvement. A + or − represents a 25 percent deviation. As an example, the use of spa pools was recorded by 31.2 percent of the sample. FLC stages recording over 46.8 percent usage of spas have been designated ++ (young couples); between 39 percent and 46.7 percent are designated + (full nest I and full nest II); between 23.5 percent and 38.9 percent there is no designation (young singles, full nest III, and empty nest I); between 15.7 percent and 23.4 percent are designated − (empty nest II); and below 15.6 percent is − − (solitary survivor).

Young Couples

The variations described for the young couples mainly seem to reflect the Japanese "honeymoon" market referred to earlier. Table 20.5 depicts this group as short duration (average sixteen nights, and it is known from the industry that the Japanese tours are often only seven or ten nights) but highly organized, with a lot of prearranged tours and a higher than average number of places visited. Indications do exist of an alternative holiday profile for some members of this group with the use of hire cars and motor camps. This probably represents a more independent non-Japanese element. In total, the group is an active segment but without a large entertainment element. The overall pattern suggests that the New Zealand vacation is probably an important holiday in the lifetime of these people, and something not to be repeated in the near future; thus they put a great deal into the vacation and see as much of the country as possible in a short time. Key words to describe this holiday pattern may be "short" and "full."

Full Nest I

The small full nest I group in the sample appears to be the most homogeneous of all the groups. They are closely tied in with visiting friends and relatives and the constraints imposed by small children are easy to discern in their lack of activities. Consequently they do little traveling within New Zealand and participate in few of the normal tourist activities. Over all the different activities, entertainment, and sports covered in the survey, this group recorded the lowest levels of involvement. This finding regarding entertainment levels throws even more doubt on the freakish expenditure figure recorded for this group. The impression given is very much one of a "relax with Granny" vacation.

Full Nest II

In many ways, the full nest II stage follows the same pattern as full nest I, but the deviations in terms of reliance on friends and relatives and low activity levels are not so exaggerated. This accords well with the theory of the life cycle and reflects the loosening of child and financial constraints from the preceding stage. Therefore this group, even with an average length of holiday a couple of days less than the full nest I group, visits an average of 7.5 locations (also the overall mean number) compared to the average of 5.0 for the preschool families. Activities such as whitewater rafting are, not surprisingly, still outside the potential of the family, but other interests can be pursued with more vigor and the children appear to be old enough to stand or sit through a rugby match. Rather than relaxing with Granny, this group may be the "keep Granny busy" segment.

Full Nest III

The further relaxation of income and child constraints can be seen in the full nest III stage. Activity levels are continuing to rise, although parents still apparently have difficulties persuading children to go to museums. Through the use of hire cars, tours, and hotels one can discern the improvement of the financial situation of the family, an interpretation compatible with the results from the expenditure analysis. Of all the life cycle segments, this seems to be the most difficult to summarize. Full nest III are "busy holiday people" but there are few really distinctive traits or patterns differentiating them from the average.

Empty Nest I

Conversely, the patterns with empty nest I seem very clear. This group are similar to young couples in a number of ways. The average length of stay is low (sixteen nights) yet the number of tours taken is high. The use of taxis, hire cars, and hotels reflects the fact that this is the life cycle stage where the family is supposed to be in its optimal financial situation. Activity levels are not high in absolute terms and the composition has changed distinctively from earlier stages to give an emphasis on more sedentary and "cultural" pastimes. This group seem to be seeking a "comfortable New Zealand experience."

Empty Nest II

Patterns emerging in the empty nest I stage seem to follow through naturally to the penultimate stage of the FLC. In empty nest II, the average duration of the holiday moves back to nineteen nights (only one below the overall mean). This may reflect the lack of a time constraint on vacations as the couple moves into their postretirement period and the increase in length of stay is accompanied by an increase in locations visited. At a mean of nearly 8.5, this group has the highest average for the number of locations visited. At the same time, the indications of affluence in the use of hire cars and hotels are no longer present, while the age associations concerned with the lack of using motor camps and participating in white-water rafting, jet boating, and even hot water spas are obvious. Like the empty nest I stage, the activities that are participated in reflect the sedentary and "cultural." This is perhaps the group seeking the "relaxing New Zealand experience."

Solitary Survivors

The same indications of the age constraint as outlined above also show through in the solitary survivor stage. However, in other ways the profile is very different. This group has the second longest stay (mean twenty-seven nights), but it visits an average of only just over 5.5 places in New Zealand. Like the other single tourists, the solitary survivors are primarily in New Zealand to visit friends and relatives and, apart from a little gentle fishing in some of New Zealand's famous and beautiful salmon and trout rivers, their interests and activity levels are low. The VFR gives a different aspect to the empty nest I group and there is no corresponding emphasis on the "cultural" side of things. The keywords for this holiday group may be "relaxation with the grandchildren."

CONCLUSIONS

It has been shown throughout the discussion that the discernable trends in the type of vacation taken fit life cycle theory quite well. The patterns of vacation taken accord well with the results of the expenditure analysis and support the financial cycles aspect of FLC theory. The social orientation of young singles is evident. The constraints imposed by young children at full nest I, and to a lesser extent at full nest II, are also clear to see and so is the correlation between activities and the age of adult members of the group.

It has not been possible to validate every relationship with statistical tests of significance, but it is relevant that the effective significance tests from the ANOVAs and cross-tabulations did cover items from all four types of holiday attribute (accommodation, activities, travel, and length of stay) as well as expenditure. Moreover, the analysis revealed strong and consistent patterns of tourist behavior through the stages of the life cycle, which it is believed are of potential use for marketers in formulating segmentation strategies. This is particularly important in the context of a small country such as New Zealand, where niche marketing is always going to be essential. Use of good segmentation tools should allow the tourism industry to construct a series of products compatible with the environment and culture on which the industry depends so heavily. Also, good segmentation ensures that promotional efforts are carefully directed toward target audiences. Levels of awareness and knowledge of New Zealand as a tourist destination are very low in many parts of the world and the country cannot afford to waste the limited resources available for overseas promotion in undirected efforts.

In practical terms, the big advantages offered by the FLC are twofold. It is relatively easy for marketers to identify life cycle stages of tourists. Also, the concept can apparently be applied across visitors from different countries. However, the caveat must always be given regarding the potential coverage of the market obtainable through the FLC. Other, simpler segmentation variables such as age, sex, and income may be universally applied while, based on demographic evaluations quoted earlier, the FLC is never likely to cover more than 80 percent of the tourism market.

CONCEPT DEFINITIONS

Family life cycle: Refers to the progressive stages through which individuals and families proceed over time. It describes patterns of relative want and prosperity experienced by family members.

Market segmentation: The process of partitioning the heterogeneous market into segments based on important characteristics. The goal is to facilitate development of unique marketing programs that will be most effective for these specific segments (Lawson et al., 1996).

REVIEW QUESTIONS

1. What advantages and disadvantages can be seen in employing the family life cycle as a segmentation variable in the context of international tourism?
2. How is the family life cycle linked to destination choice in the context of an international long-haul destination, such as New Zealand?
3. What are the major links shown between holiday expenditure and different stages of the family life cycle?
4. What are the major links shown between holiday behaviors and different stages of the family life cycle?
5. If you were responsible for the international marketing of New Zealand as a tourist destination, which two life cycle stages would you select as potentially the most important target markets and why?

REFERENCES

Bristor, J.M. (1985). Consumer behavior from a contemporary philosophy of science perspective: An organizational framework. *Advances in Consumer Research, 12,* 300-304.

Cosenza, R.M. and Davis, D.L. (1981). Family vacation decision making over the family life cycle: A decision and influence structure analysis. *Journal of Travel Research, 20* (2), 17-23.

Gilly, M.C. and Enis, B.M. (1982). Recycling the family life cycle: A proposal for redefinition. In A. Mitchell (Ed.), *Advances in consumer research* (pp. 271-276). Ann Arbor, MI: Association for Consumer Research.

Kumagai, F. (1984). The life cycle of the Japanese family. *Journal of Marriage and the Family, 46,* February, 191-204.

Lawson, R.W. (1988). The family life cycle: A demographic analysis. *Journal of Marketing Management, 4* (1), June, 13-32.

Lawson, R.W. (1989). Family life cycle. In S.F. Witt. and L. Moutinho (Eds.), *Handbook of tourism management* (pp. 147-151). Englewood Cliffs, NJ: Prentice Hall.

Lawson, R.W., Tidwell, P., Rainbird, P., Loudon, D., and Della Bitta, A. (1996). *Consumer behaviour in Australia and New Zealand.* Sydney: McGraw-Hill Book Company.

Meidan, A. (1984). The marketing of tourism. *The Services Industries Journal, 4* (3), November, 166-186.

Murphy, P.C. and Staples, W.A. (1979). A modernized family life cycle. *Journal of Travel Research, 6*(1), 12-22.

New Zealand Tourism Council and NZTP (1984). *New Zealand tourism: Issues and policies,* Wellington, New Zealand: NZTP.

NZTP (1985). *Japan travel market report—a guide to the Japan/New Zealand travel trade.* Wellington, New Zealand: NZTP.

NZTP (1986). *Forecasts of international visitor arrivals in New Zealand to 1991.* Wellington, New Zealand: NZTP.

NZTP (1987). *Some recent changes in tourism patterns in New Zealand.* Wellington, New Zealand: NZTP.

Plog, S. (1972). Developing the family travel market. In Travel Research Assoc., *The values of travel research: Planning, techniques and applications* (pp. 209-221). Third Annual Conference Proceedings (August 13-16), Quebec.

Pyszka, R.H. (1987). Psychographic market segmentation: The VALS approach. *Proceedings of the Tourism Research Forum.* July 1-3 1986, Wairakei, New Zealand. Wellington, New Zealand: NZTP.

Reynolds, F.D. and Wells, W.D. (1977). *Consumer behavior.* Chapters 3-7. New York: McGraw Hill.

Safilios-Rothschild, C. (1989). Theoretical aspects of the family systems of the less and more industrialized countries: Are all family systems converging? *Proceedings of the International Population Conference, 3* (pp. 119-129). New Delhi: IUSSP.

Stampfl, R.W. (1978). The consumer life cycle. *Journal of Consumer Affairs, 12,* 209-219.

Wagner, J. and Hanna, S. (1983). The effectiveness of family life cycle variables in consumer expenditure research. *Journal of Consumer Research, 10,* December, 281-291.

Wells, W.D. and Gubar, G. (1966). The life cycle concept in marketing research. *Journal of Marketing Research,* November, 355-365.

Zimmerman, C.A. (1982). The life cycle concept as a tool for travel research. *Transportation, 11,* 51-69.

Chapter 21

Developing Travel Lifestyles: A New Zealand Example

Robert Lawson
Maree Thyne
Tracy Young
Biljana Juric

LEARNING OBJECTIVES

By the end of the chapter the reader should:

- Understand the concept of lifestyles and some of the theoretical problems that have been associated with their development
- Be aware of the means/end structure and the domains to be considered in a travel lifestyle study
- Understand the advantages and disadvantages of using lifestyles as a form of market segmentation
- Appreciate how lifestyle segments are formed on the basis of complex clustering procedures that require some degree of interpretation skill
- Understand how each of the segments should form a unified and coherent pattern of attitudes and behaviors
- Understand how differences between segments may be identified in all areas of destination choice, activities, accommodation, transport, and prepurchase and purchasing behavior

BACKGROUND AND INTRODUCTION

The term "style of life" was first coined by Alfred Adler over fifty years ago, to refer to the goals that people shape for themselves and the means they employ to reach them (Lazer, 1963). This simple explanation still provides a useful description of what we mean by "lifestyle" when using the term to analyze consumer behavior. Lifestyles are employed as a method of market segmentation that offer marketers particular advantages. Because they are related to the goals that people set for themselves, they provide marketers with an understanding of the motivational forces that drive behavior. Consequently, compared to most market segmentation methods, they can give added insight for the development and management of the marketing mix, particularly for product development and promotion strategies.

Despite these clear managerial advantages, lifestyles have never really become established as a preferred method of segmentation. There are several reasons for this, which are both practical and theoretical in nature:

1. Lifestyles require extensive and expensive information on consumers. They are based on a wide array of information about many dimensions of a consumer's life. This approach is more demanding and complex than, for example, data on age, family life cycle, or nationality, which are sometimes employed as the only criteria in segmentation studies.

2. Even though most companies in the 1990s would have access to computing hardware and would be able to afford the appropriate statistical programs, the actual analysis of the data requires knowledge of advanced statistical techniques.

3. Beyond the accepted general definition of lifestyles, there are many different interpretations of exactly what is entailed in the concept. As an example, the relationship between the terms "lifestyle" and "psychographics" is not at all clear. In some cases the terms seem to be used interchangeably (Wells, 1975), while other authors view them as quite separate (Craig-Lees, Joy, and Browne, 1995). Other interpretations define psychographics as the research process that may be used to generate lifestyle segments (Lawson et al., 1996). None of these are easy to accept as definitive positions. In 1975 Wells noted that he found thirty-two definitions of psychographics in twenty-four articles. This same point about a lack of standardization was still being argued by Plog in his 1987 review.

4. Another concept that is ambiguously related to lifestyles is values. Values have a well-defined heritage within the psychology literature (Rokeach, 1968; Schwartz, 1992) and this has not always been incorporated into understandings of lifestyles, even when terms describing individual values are often used to explain key dimensions of particular lifestyle segments. The most prominent example relating the two concepts are the VALS profiles (SRI International, 1989).

5. A further complication, which this chapter mainly seeks to address, is that lifestyles have been accepted as appropriate concepts at two distinct levels. First, general consumer lifestyle segmentations aim to give a holistic view of all the domains of consumer behavior relevant to an individual (Morgan, 1994; SRI International, 1989; Faris, Lawson, and Todd 1996). Second, the term "lifestyles" has been accepted as an appropriate definition for segmentation within specific product domains. The two product areas where this has particularly occurred are food (Grunert et al., 1996) and travel or tourism (Abbey, 1979; Hawes, 1988). At the general level, this content and structure of lifestyles research has been guided by the AIO (Activities, Interest, and Opinion) schedules that were defined in the early 1970s (Plummer, 1974; Wells and Tigert, 1973). However, the content and structure at this product level have not received such meticulous attention. Consequently, while some authors have tapped into general approaches such as VALS (Shih, 1986), most lifestyles research is characterized by ad hoc studies using individually created survey instruments that offer differential coverage of this topic area (Taylor, 1986; NZTP, 1989; Pitts and Woodside, 1983; Schewe and Calantone, 1978; Hawes, 1988).

6. Some of the conceptual problems associated with lifestyles, and discussed in the previous points, are reflected in a number of critical papers that have examined reliability and validity in this research (Boote, 1980; Lastovicka, 1982; Lawson, 1991). Reliability issues are the most likely ones to be addressed and some attention may be paid to content validity but little attention is paid to underlying constructs or issues such as the stability and discriminant validity of the segmentation process.

STUDY DEVELOPMENT

This study was done not for the purely theoretical reasons of attempting to address some of the issues listed above, but as a way of investigating a larger problem of understanding how the growth of international visitors to New Zealand has affected the nature of the domestic market. In the ten years between 1986 and 1996 the number of international visitors to New Zealand more than doubled to reach 1.4 million (New Zealand Tourism Board, 1996). Evidence has been gathered from other studies on residents' attitudes (Lawson et al., in press) and usage of walking trails in national parks (Kearsley et al., 1996) that at least some New Zealanders may be modifying their own travel behavior in response to these pressures. Furthermore, no publicly available information on the domestic New Zealand market has been collected since the late 1980s, following a restructuring of the government department responsible for the tourism sector. Considering the purposes and strengths of lifestyle profiling, it was chosen as the method by which we could offer a current picture of the domestic market, useful to local businesses and regional tourism authorities. In addition to this, it was thought that lifestyle profiling would be the most insightful way to identify which parts of the domestic market are most likely to be affected by growth and crowding from international visitors. The project was funded by a grant from the New Zealand Foundation for Science, Research, and Technology.

CONCEPTUALIZING TRAVEL LIFESTYLES

Grunert et al. (1996) approached the issue of generating food lifestyle profiles from a strong conceptual foundation centered on the notion of a means-end chain (see Figure 21.1). The concrete attributes and product categories represent the final product likely to be purchased by consumers, that is, the means by which they attain their goals. These are linked through more generic quality dimensions to purchasing motives and ulti-

FIGURE 21.1. Grunert's Model of Food Lifestyles

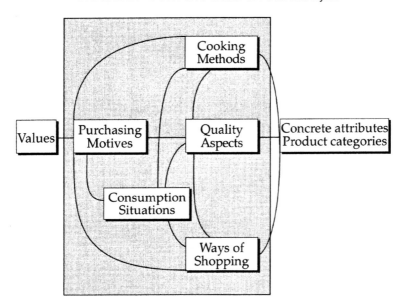

Source: Grunert et al., 1996, p. 48.

mately values as the final goals. For example, a person who seeks an exciting life as an important end state or value may manifest this in terms of exploration motives. These lead the individual to seek stimulation through new events or circumstances (McGuire, 1976). In turn, they may lead to assessments of product quality through generic dimensions such as risk or exclusivity, and are finally manifested in the price paid, choice of supplier, or final product chosen.

The means-end chain, therefore, provides a central structure around which to define lifestyles and it relates well to Adler's original explanation. However, it is clear that this central process will be modified by individuals according to consumption situations and will correlate with other associated behaviors. In particular, an important factor of lifestyle analysis in consumer behavior is that it describes not only consumption but also purchase. In the case of Grunert's portrayal of food lifestyles, changing the consumption situation by the time of day or the social setting for the meal will have impacts on quality aspects, way of shopping, and cooking methods. For example, providing dinner for your boss from work and his or her partner may mean that the appearance and quality of the food is more important. This may affect the way of preparing the food, and even a decision to buy from a specialist such as a butcher, maybe with a personal recommendation to reinforce the quality, as opposed to choosing a prepacked item from the supermarket. A food lifestyles segmentation must be able to account for such tendencies and identify related patterns in all these areas. Therefore, in Grunert's conceptualization, the boundaries defining lifestyles should be embraced within the components covered by the shaded box in Figure 21.1.

If this structure is applied to travel and tourism, there are many obvious comparisons. The means-end chain remains at the center, linking the values with particular destination attributes (Figure 21.2). As with food consumption situations, one can parallel different types of holidays according to the time of year, occurrence of public or school holidays, or weekend breaks versus long vacations. Likewise, there are many ways of shopping for travel and tourism products. Different purchasing methods will involve different amounts of prebooking; usage of different intermediaries, for example travel agents or visitor centers, if any intermediary is used at all; and different payment methods ranging from cash to credit cards, traveler's checks, or prepaid vouchers.

The more difficult comparisons with the food model come with the disaggregation of the product itself and the preparation. This is not quite so straightforward as in the food model, but a similar dichotomy is expressed in literature on service quality, including studies in travel and

FIGURE 21.2. A Model of Travel Lifestyles

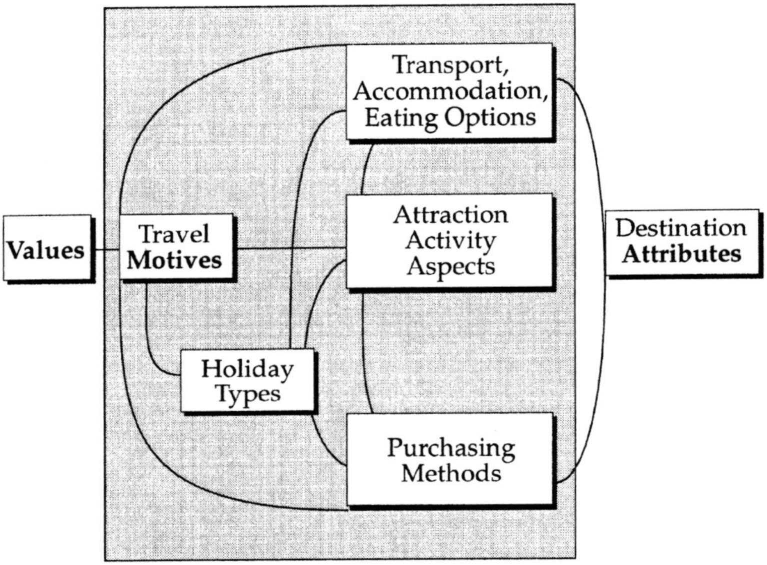

tourism (Gronroos, 1990). This dichotomy draws a distinction between functional and technical (or instrumental and expressive) product/service attributes. Again the distinction between means and ends become appropriate. In most cases the choice of a particular cooking method is the means to achieve a particular end for this final food product. The same arguments may be expressed for the essential role of accommodation, transport, and eating options in tourism, while the attraction and activity aspects may be seen to relate to the core dimensions of the product. Of course, one may find examples where this distinction is not sustained and perhaps the core attraction is an accommodation experience, such as staying at a luxury hotel. But the same may be identified in a food lifestyle situation where, for example, the fondue or stone grill becomes most important because of the preparation. However, distinctions between these components of vacations are not new and, if required, additional justification can be sought from the tourism motivation literature, which identifies pull factors associated with destinations (Dann, 1981). These are primarily associated with attraction and activity aspects and can be seen to support the general structure of the means-end chain at the center of our model. Indeed Todd (1997) has pointed out that the tourism motivation literature is riddled with studies that do not effectively differentiate between true motivations, reasons expressed in "intermediate level" terms, such as "to get a tan," and the destination attributes themselves. The means end chain provides an effective and simple framework for clarifying those issues.

DEVELOPING A LIFESTYLE MEASUREMENT INSTRUMENT

After reviewing the content of previous studies on travel lifestyles, a series of twelve in-depth interviews were conducted. These interviews were constructed using laddering techniques, which are designed to uncover the stages of a means-end chain (Reynolds and Gutman, 1988). This method starts by asking people to describe a particular behavior and then probes beyond this by asking why each event took place and ultimately why the issues were important to them. The different dimensions of the vacation that were covered in the interviews were defined from Woodside and MacDonald's (1993) model of vacation decision making, which provides a comprehensive description of the different decision areas involved in tourist behavior:

- Purchasing behavior
- Motivations / reasons to travel
- Choice criteria—determining type of destination chosen
- Travel behavior—including transport, accommodations, and dining habits, as well as attractions and activities
- Personal values

The in-depth interviews (lasting between thirty and ninety minutes) were conducted with individuals contacted at random from the local telephone directory, and included both males and females and a cross-section of ages and occupations. After twelve interviews had been conducted it was clear that the last three or four interviews had yielded little in the way of new motivations and attitudes, and a decision was made to stop at that point. The interviews were transcribed and content analyzed according to the generic levels presented in Figure 21.3. As an example, one of the respondents discussed the physical activity of boogie boarding down sand hills. This was associated with the abstract attributes of fun and excitement and eventually traced back to terminal values associated with self-esteem through the chain shown.

The findings from this lengthy process were compared to the literature for obvious anomalies or shortcomings in coverage before constructing

FIGURE 21.3. An Example of a Means/End Structure

Generic Levels	*Example*
Terminal Values	Self-Esteem
	↑
Instrumental Values	Self-Confidence
	↑
Psychosocial Consequences	Social Acceptance
	↑
Functional Consequences	Keeping Fit
	↑
Abstract Product Attributes	Fun and Excitement
	↑
Concrete Product Attributes	Physical Activity (boogie boarding down a sand hill)

Source: Grunert et al., 1996, p. 47.

the questionnaire. The content areas of the questionnaire are summarized in Table 21.1. For practical reasons within the context of a large questionnaire, it was decided to represent values using the LOV scale, which was developed as an efficient approach to measuring values specifically for the context of consumer behavior (Beatty et al., 1985). After several iterations involving pretests with a small group of individuals, a questionnaire involving 266 questions was pretested in the local community, in February 1997. The final version of the questionnaire was mailed out during March and April 1997 to 3,700 people chosen from telephone directories throughout New Zealand. As an incentive to respond, three "mystery weekends" were offered as prizes to be drawn from those returning completed questionnaires. Usable responses were obtained from 1,703 of the 3,586 individuals who received the survey. This meant that the effective response rate was 47.5 percent (see Table 21.2).

To check for representativeness, the sample was compared against information from the 1996 New Zealand Census. There were three identifiable differences between the sample and the census, which affected gender, age, and ethnic background. The first two of these were probably due to the use of telephone directories as the sampling frame. The sample compared well to other census data on all other factors, including income, marital status, and household composition.

The first difference reflected an overrepresentation of males in the sample (62 percent to 38 percent). However, this is not a cause for concern

TABLE 21.1. Summary of Questionnaire Content

Question subject	Details about the question	Number of questions
Details of last holiday	When did you last travel? Where did you travel? Travel companions Holiday planning	Eight
Main reasons for travel	Being with people Things to do Personal reasons Special features of a place General reasons	Sixty-three
Information sources used	Main sources of information used when planning the holiday	Thirteen
Attractions and activities actually completed (with booking and purchasing methods included)	Attractions General activities Adventure activities / Sports	Fifty-three
Dining habits	Where did you mainly dine?	One
Transportation	Type of transport used Reasons for choosing main modes of transport	Twenty-one
Accommodations	Type of accommodation used Reasons for choosing that type of accommodation	Twenty-three
Payment methods and expenditures	Main methods of payment Estimate of how much money was spent	Twenty
Trends and changes in travel behavior	Do you travel more, less, or as often as you did five years ago? Considering distance from home, where do you usually travel?	Five
Avoidance of destinations	When traveling in New Zealand or overseas, what places would you avoid and why?	Twenty-four
Tourism in New Zealand	General questions regarding opinions on tourism in New Zealand	Fourteen
Values	LOV scale	Nine
Demographics and classification data	Age Gender Marital status Race/ethnic group Education Employment Income	Twelve

TABLE 21.2 Summary Survey Statistics

Sent	Returned— wrong address	Effective Sample size	Returned— completed	Effective response rate
3,708	122	3,586	1,703	47.5%

in the final analysis because gender does not vary in any meaningful way across the segments identified. For example, the largest proportion of males in any segment was 66.5 percent and the smallest 60.5 percent. The second skew in the sample related to a smaller proportion of eighteen-to twenty-one-year-olds in the sample than in the population. Obviously, fewer people in this age range are householders with separate telephone entries. This age group is particularly associated with one of the travel lifestyle segments (described below as outdoor adventurers) and this shortfall in the sample should be considered when reflecting on segment sizes. No age group was correspondingly overrepresented.

The last skew, and almost certainly not a result of the sampling frame, is the smaller number of responses from the Maori and Pacific Islander ethnic groups. These two groups together account for approximately 15 percent of the population and only about half that number identify themselves as belonging to one of the two groups in the sample. This is consistent with response patterns to other surveys (Faris, Lawson, and Todd, 1996) and is found across personal and telephone surveys as well as those administered by mail. Uncertainties with the English language may be associated with nonresponse in these groups, but it is also believed that there is a cultural norm that does not identify individual and written questionnaires as appropriate mechanisms for offering feedback.

DATA ANALYSIS

In the first instance, an exploratory factor analysis was undertaken to identify the main underlying dimensions in the motivations and reasons data. The purpose of this was to aid interpretation of the clusters and the potential factors discriminating among the lifestyles groups. The factor analysis used principle axis factoring (PAF) as the extraction technique and Oblimin as an oblique rotation. PAF was chosen since it focuses on the shared variance in the data and the oblique rotation allows the factors to be correlated as opposed to orthogonal techniques such as Varimax (Hair et al., 1995). The solution extracted fourteen factors that together explained 58.4 percent of the variance. This can be regarded as a high percentage for a PAF extraction. Only the final factor was difficult to interpret and name since the two issues of safety and climate are not necessarily related. The remaining factors were very easy to understand and the reliabilities associated with them were generally good. The summary is presented as Table 21.3.

TABLE 21.3. Summary Results of the Exploratory Factor Analysis

Factor	*Reliability*
Actualization/Learning	.744
New Experiences	.877
Physical Adventure	.817
Sporting Activities/Interests	.557
Extended Family and Roots	.637
Closeness and Proximity	.799
Being with Immediate Family	.632
Socializing (new people and friends)	.566
Shopping	.792
Accessibility and Price	.718
Escapism	.796
Favorite and Familiar Places	.749
Business and Work Related	.654
Safety and Climate	.733

Cluster analysis was performed on the same set of variables using k-means methods. To estimate how many clusters might be appropriate, hierarchical cluster analysis using Ward's method was run on two randomly selected subsamples of approximately one hundred cases. In both trials the dendrograms illustrated that the most likely number of clusters lay between four and six. K-means was applied for all three options and the solutions were checked for stability by saving the cluster centers and rerunning the analysis. Reverse discriminant analysis (i.e., forecasting the cluster membership from the original variables) worked well for the five- and six-group solutions (94 percent and 93 percent correct classifications respectively) but less so for the four-group solution (86 percent). Profiling of the cluster solutions showed the six-group solution to be the most preferred. It gave the clearest appreciation of the different motives and attitudes differentiating between the lifestyle segments and was more clearly associated with the ratings from the LOV scale. Also, this solution gave distinctly more statistically significant results when related to the behavioral variables in the data, including activities carried out on holiday, accommodation and transport choices, information search, booking options, and payment methods. Part of the profiling gives the demographic characteristics of the clusters. Many of these relationships were either fairly weak or complex to interpret. For example, some segments were spread across both high and low income and age groups with little representation in the middle ranges. The clearest links with any demographic variable were found with the family life cycle. Information on age, marital status, employment status, and ages of children was used to construct a family life cycle classification based on that proposed by Gilly and Enis (1982). The six segments are summarized in the next section.

CLUSTER DESCRIPTIONS

Outdoor Adventurers (13 Percent)

Outdoor adventurers vacation to experience new things, to take part in physical activities, and just to enjoy themselves. They like a challenge and want a holiday that will improve their mental and physical well-being. This is reflected in the self-fulfillment and excitement values, which this group considers important. Being respected is also an important value to the outdoor adventurers. They travel extensively throughout New Zealand but seldom go overseas. This group finds themselves traveling at least as often if not more than they did five years ago. This is because they have more time and money as well as more interest in traveling. Outdoor adventurers generally travel with others, usually their spouses or partners and sometimes with friends or other family members. Outdoor adventurers seek simplicity in their travels.

Reasons for Traveling

Outdoor adventurers enjoy meeting people when they travel. They like to vacation with their friends and think it is important to go to a place where the local people are friendly. They also want a change from their jobs, and the holiday they choose needs to offer them the chance to experience some adventure and excitement. They think it is important that they rediscover themselves and build their self-confidence while on holiday. They are keen to experience wilderness and nature in its natural state. However, they are not so interested in visiting places such as zoos or wildlife parks. They also enjoy beautiful scenery and visiting out-of-the-way places. The opportunity to experience a simpler lifestyle is a priority, as is the authenticity of the experience. Outdoor adventurers feel it is important to see their own country before traveling overseas.

Destination

In New Zealand the main places visited by outdoor adventurers include the following regions: Nelson/Marlborough, Northland/Auckland, the West Coast, Canterbury, Otago, and Southland/Fiordland. The average number of times they crossed Cook Strait in the past five years was 2.6, making them the most frequent group of interisland travelers. They generally dislike popular places at peak times, and tourist resorts. The main reason they give for not wanting to visit a particular New Zealand destination is overall crowding. An important reason they give for not traveling overseas is that they want the money they spend to stay in New Zealand.

Planning and Expenditure

Outdoor adventurers are independent travelers and rarely go on organized tours. They are planners though, spending between one and six months planning their holidays. Half of them gather information about their destinations before they leave home. The sources of information they use include their own knowledge of a place, maps, word of mouth, and sometimes Visitor Information Centers. Once there, they usually participate in activities without booking. They generally pay for their holiday expenses with cash or eftpos (electronic funds transfer at point of sale) and, at $49 per person per day, the median spending is just below the sample average of $55.

Attractions and Activities

As would be expected, outdoor adventurers enjoy spending time outdoors. They are an active segment and like to take part in a variety of pastimes over the course of their holidays.

Visit national parks	Visit local architecture
Go for short bush walks	Go on scenic boat cruises
Visit natural attractions	Observe wildlife in its natural habitat
Visit historic sites	Take photos

Visit gardens
Visit wineries
Visit the beach
    and go swimming

Go fishing or tramping
Play cards and board games
Read books and magazines

Overall, a relatively small number of people in the total sample participated in the following activities; however, almost all who did are outdoor adventurers.

Cycling
Mountain biking
Rock climbing

Mountain climbing
Snow skiing
Participate in water sports

Air sports
Caving
Jet boating

Accommodations and Dining Habits

About half of the outdoor adventurers stay at campgrounds, some stay in backpackers' places, and a few stay in holiday homes. Their main reason for choosing these types of accommodations is location and to a lesser extent the price, and the quality they offer. Some get free accommodation, for example by staying in family holiday homes. Most outdoor adventurers take their own food with them on holiday. They also buy food at the supermarket and then cook it themselves. If they do not do this, then they eat at cafes or friends' houses.

Transport

The outdoor adventurers usually take their own cars on holiday. Some fly, but not many. They are the highest users of ferries as a method of transport. The overall number of hitchhikers in the sample is very small; however, all of them are in this segment. Outdoor adventurers choose their transport based on convenience and freedom.

Demographics

Over half of the outdoor adventurers have professional training or university qualifications; most are employed full time. Of this segment, approximately 30 percent are either single or divorced, which makes this the segment with the greatest proportion of single people. In family life cycle terms this segment is most associated with bachelor I (young singles) and second with bachelor II (singles ages thirty-five to sixty-four). Only about a quarter have children under the age of eighteen. The majority earn between $30,000-$59,000 per household. They are the largest group of housing renters compared to other segments.

Sports Devotees (20.7 Percent)

This group loves to watch and/or play sports. This is their primary motivation for traveling. The sports devotees usually vacation in New Zealand, but those who travel overseas go to Australia or the United States. While on holiday this group does little other than watch, or take part in, the sports event they have planned their trip around.

Reasons for Traveling

The sports devotees will travel to watch or participate in a special sporting event; for example to take part in the Masters Games, or to watch an event such as the America's Cup or a netball or rugby test. Sport is their main motivation to travel.

Destination

Within New Zealand the sports devotees travel to Northland/Auckland, Waikato/Bay of Plenty, and Canterbury. These are not unexpected choices since these regions are the main centers for many sporting activities in New Zealand.

Planning and Expenditure

The majority of sports devotees travel with their spouses or family group, although more people in this group travel either alone or with friends. This group is also different from other segments in that they are most likely to have their destination choice prearranged by a club or organization. Consequently, some of this group use organized tours, although most sports devotees still travel independently. Generally this segment spends less than two months planning a trip. They feel that they have all the information they need about a destination from their own knowledge. In the rare event that sports devotees pursue activities unrelated to sport, they do not book in advance. Payment for holiday activities, accommodation, and transport is by cash, eftpos, or check, and the median amount of money spent is $52 per day, which is close to the sample average.

Attractions and Activities

All of the following activities are undertaken by sports devotees, although they are less frequent participants than members of other segments.

Visit shopping malls	Do some general sightseeing
Take photographs	Dine out
Watch TV	Go for walks around town
Go for a day trip in the car	

Accommodations and Dining Habits

Sports devotees' accommodation is often free because most of them stay with friends or relatives. Alternatively some stay at motels, because of the location of the accommodation. Since this group stays with family or friends they usually eat with them too. They also buy food from the supermarket to eat while on holiday.

Transport

The sports devotees choose their method of transport for convenience. The majority of them take their own cars when going on holiday, while some travel by train.

Demographics

A quarter of this segment is between forty-five and fifty-four years of age, with a further quarter over sixty-five. The first of these age ranges is often when children are leaving home, and many sports devotees indicated that this gave them an increased opportunity to travel. In life cycle terms, this is clearly shown in a high incidence of full nest III and bachelor III (solitary survivors) in this segment. The other life cycle stage with a high representation in this segment is bachelor I. Interestingly, both the younger and older life cycle stages are involved with participation and spectatorship and it would seem that discretionary income and time are more important than age as underlying facilitators for this segment. A third of the group have university qualifications or professional training, although almost half have only the lowest level of secondary school qualifications, while those in work are mostly employed in skilled or highly skilled jobs. Reflecting this split in age and employment status, most of the group have an income of less than $40,000, but there is also 10 percent of the segment who earn over $100,000. This split is consistent with some of the other clusters in the sample and reflects the growing discrepancy between the "Haves" and the "Have Nots" that is occurring in many societies, including New Zealand.

Fun-Loving Holidaymakers (14.4 Percent)

Fun-loving holidaymakers like to experience new things. They consider fun and entertainment to be very important reasons for going on holiday. However, it is interesting that they also seek familiarity in their holiday experience and prefer to visit places where people speak the same language. They enjoy planned shopping trips and think that a holiday is a good reason to have the spending spree they feel they deserve. Fun-loving holidaymakers generally like to have a good time and enjoy themselves. This is evident in the values they consider most important: fun, excitement, a sense of belonging, being well respected, and a sense of accomplishment. Almost half of the fun-loving holidaymakers travel more now than they did five years ago. The reasons for this are that they have more money, more time available, and more interest in traveling. About three-quarters of this group traveled overseas for their last holiday, although only one-third of them say they would usually travel overseas.

Reasons for Traveling

It is important for this segment to visit a place where the local people are friendly. The things that they want out of a holiday destination include the following: safety, a warm and predictable climate, good local cuisine, and the availability of first-class accommodations. However, they still expect to receive value for money. They also need a wide variety of activities available to participate in.

Destination

It is important that the destination they choose is easily accessible. They also rate the recommendation of a destination, from a friend or travel agent, as being an important part of their choice. Fun-loving holidaymakers often travel overseas; their destinations mainly include Australia and the Pacific Islands. When they are not taking an overseas holiday they travel within the island where they live. They are the least frequent group of travelers across Cook Strait, with an average number of only 1.5 crossings in the past five years. The little travel they do in New Zealand takes place predominantly in the Northland/Auckland region or in Waikato/Bay of Plenty.

Fun-loving holidaymakers avoid cold places. This is reflected in the destinations they travel to, for example Australia and the Pacific Islands. Few in this segment choose to visit the South Island.

Planning and Expenditure

Fun-loving holidaymakers usually travel with their spouses or partners. They go on more organized tours than any other group. Almost a third of them went either exclusively on a package tour, or used some combination of independent travel and organized tour for their last holiday. The majority of fun-loving holidaymakers spent between one and six months planning their holidays. Over half of them gathered the information they needed before they left home. Their most important sources of information were brochures and the travel agent. Most of this group prebooks the activities and attractions they visit while on holiday. This is normally done directly with the provider, although they also use travel agents to help with prebooking before leaving home. Once at the destination they often use booking facilities available through the hotel or motel. Payment for activities, accommodation, and transport is generally by prepaid voucher or traveler's check. Transport arrangements are normally made through a travel agent and, at $142, their daily expenditure per person is the highest of all segments and almost three times the sample median.

Attractions and Activities

Fun-loving holidaymakers are very busy on holiday, with many of the activities they enjoy being based in cities.

Visit museums and art galleries
Visit zoos and wildlife parks
Watch a cultural performance
Visit an historic site
Visit a casino
Visit fun parks and amusement parks
Visit national parks
Go to a concert
Go to the theater

Go to shopping malls/
  visit street markets
Do some general sightseeing
Take photographs
Go to the beach and go swimming
Watch TV
Go for walks around town

Go on a scenic boat cruise
Send postcards
Dine out
Visit pubs and nightclubs
Visit craft shops
Participate in water sports
Go for a day trip, driving

Accommodations and Dining Habits

This group stays predominantly in motels or hotels. The reasons for this choice are quality, price, and comfort. Because they are staying in motels and hotels, fun-loving holidaymakers generally eat out at cafes and restaurants.

Transport

Almost half of this group travels between cities by airplane. Fun-loving holidaymakers are also rental car users and some of them travel by bus. The fun-loving holidaymaker chooses a method of transport because it allows better sightseeing. Price is also important along with quality, convenience, and comfort.

Demographics

The fun-loving holidaymakers are mainly over thirty-five years of age, and most are married or living with a partner, although about 20 percent are single or divorced. Most fun-loving holidaymakers are in the bachelor II or childless couple phases of the life cycle and very, very few fall into either full nest III or the retired segments. Over a third of them have either school certificates or trade certificates. Most work full time and about 60 percent occupy skilled or highly skilled positions. The majority of people in this segment earn between $30,000 and $59,000 per household.

Education Seekers (16.8 Percent)

Education seekers travel to learn and gain knowledge. They like to meet people and to learn something that will be useful to their careers or businesses. As a group they are concerned with the following individually based human values: self-fulfillment, excitement, self-respect, and accomplishment. Education seekers vacation mainly with their spouses or in family groups and they are one of the segments most likely to undertake international travel.

Reasons for Traveling

Education seekers' main motivation for travel appears to be learning and knowledge. They enjoy a holiday that includes any sort of learning experience, and meeting people is very important to them. The special features that the education seeker looks for in a destination include: a sense of history, cultural differences, an authentic experience, and natural attractions. They like to visit places that friends and family have never been and to go to special out-of-the-way places to see something unique. It is also important for them to see the most they can in the time available, while on holiday.

Destination

When education seekers travel they tend to travel further abroad than other groups, mainly going to the United States, Europe, and the United Kingdom. Likewise, holidays within New Zealand may also involve greater distances, and chosen destinations included South Island locations such as Nelson, the West Coast, Canterbury, and Otago. Education seekers generally avoid tourist resorts, and prefer to visit areas of historical interest.

Planning and Expenditure

Education seekers make destination choices themselves and in consultation with their partners. Nearly a quarter of this group travels wholly or partly on organized tours. This can be anything from an all-inclusive ten-day bus tour to a short guided tour. Many of the education seekers do a lot of planning for their holidays, with some spending over a year gathering information before they travel. Most get this information via word of mouth, for example from friends, family, and travel agents. Other important information sources for this group are Visitor Information Centers and maps. This group has a higher use of credit cards than other travel lifestyle segments, when paying for holiday activities. They are also high users of traveler's checks, which is understandable given their overseas travel patterns. At $79, their median daily expenditure per person is the second highest of all the segments.

Attractions and Activities

Education seekers participate in a wide variety of activities while on holiday.

Visit museums and art galleries
Visit zoos and wildlife parks
Visit a natural attraction
See a farm show
Go to live theater and concerts
Observe wildlife in natural habitat
Visit gardens
Write postcards
Go sightseeing and take
  photographs
Dine out
Go for short bush walks

Visit national parks
Go for walks around town
See a cultural performance
Visit cultural and historic sites
Go on a boat cruise
Visit a winery
Visit shopping malls
  and street markets
Visit local craft shops
Visit local architecture
Go for a day trip in the car

Accommodations and Dining Habits

In New Zealand, education seekers usually stay in motels or campgrounds. When traveling overseas the majority of this segment stay in hotels, booked through their travel agents. The main reasons for their accommodation choice are price, quality, and location. When education seekers are on holiday they buy their own food, eat with friends and family, and dine out at cafes.

Transportation

Education seekers use a more varied range of transport options than those in other lifestyle segments, with more widespread usage of air travel, rental cars, ferries, and trains.

Demographics

Education seekers are one of the older groups, with more than half of the respondents being fifty-five or older. Almost all of the education seekers are married or living with their partners but less than a quarter of them still have children living at home. Overall, they have fewer children than any other segment. Membership of the education seekers segment is almost totally confined to the following five life cycle stages: young couples, childless couples, full nest III, bachelor II, and empty nest. In terms of educational qualifications this group is split. Many are reasonably well educated, with over one third having polytechnic qualifications, trade certificates, or professional training, but another third have only school certificates or school exams. Despite the mix of educational qualifications, members of this group are more likely to have highly skilled or professional jobs. This may well be a reflection of their age, as this segment started working at a time when formal qualifications were not considered as necessary as they are today.

Special Family Occasions (20.7 Percent)

The main reason why special family occasion travelers go on holiday is to visit friends and family for a special occasion. Social contact is important to this group, as they value keeping in touch with friends and relatives. Most of this group say they travel less than they did five years ago. The reasons for this include the lack of money and time, but it may also reflect a decreasing emphasis on the extended family within modern society (Faris, Lawson, and Todd, 1996). Special family occasion travelers generally vacation within New Zealand and they travel interisland more often than average. This is largely a "noncommercial" segment who make little use of the traditional tourism infrastructure. For example, they organize their own holidays, use their own cars for transport, and stay with friends or family.

Reasons for Traveling

This group's main motivation to travel is to visit friends and family for a special occasion, such as a wedding, birthday, or anniversary. They also like to visit the place where their family came from.

Destination

Special family occasion travelers vacation more in New Zealand than overseas, but when they do travel overseas they tend to visit Australia. This reflects the strong demographic ties between the two countries. In New Zealand they mainly travel to important population centers, such as Auckland, Waikato, and Canterbury.

Planning and Expenditure

This group makes destination choices themselves, with their partners, or in consultation with relations. Many of the special family occasion segment travel independently, with nearly a quarter of the group traveling alone. Most special family occasion travelers plan for their holidays from one week to two months before and few feel that they need to seek any information about their destinations. They mainly pay for transport by cash or eftpos, but they are more likely to use checks than any other group. Accommodation is usually free because many of this group stay with friends or relatives. Overall, this segment have a lower than average level of daily expenditure at $45, most of which is attributed to transport costs.

Attractions and Activities

This segment travels for the purpose of taking part in special family occasions, and they only tend to participate in a few other activities.

Visit gardens
Write postcards
Watch television

Visit shopping malls
Visit street markets

Accommodations and Dining Habits

The majority of special family occasion travelers stay with friends or family, mainly because this type of accommodation is available. Special family occasion travelers tend to dine at the homes of friends or relatives. Otherwise they eat out at family restaurants.

Transportation

Nearly all of the people in this group travel in their own cars, while others choose to travel with friends in their cars. Special family occasion travelers are also ferry users. Their main reasons for choosing these types of transport are convenience, freedom, and comfort.

Demographics

Most of this segment falls into one of two distinct age groups. Nearly a third of this segment is over sixty-five and there are also a significant number of widowed people in the special family occasion group. However, the majority in this segment falls into a thirty-five to fifty-four age range and are married with children under the age of eighteen. Both these age groups represent stages of life when anniversaries become more significant and travel is more likely, to attend events such as weddings and christenings among following generations. Nearly half of those who are working are in skilled or semiskilled employment, with an annual household income of less than $39,000. Special family occasion travelers are a lower-income segment in comparison to other groups.

Kiwi Family Holidays (14.4 Percent)

This group enjoys traveling with the immediate family. The values that are important to them include: fun, self-respect, self-fulfillment, and a sense of belonging. The Kiwi family holiday segment prefers to travel to destinations relatively close to home.

Reasons for Traveling

The Kiwi family holiday group's main travel motivations are to be with family when traveling, or because a friend or family member wants to go to a particular destination. One important aspect that they look for in a holiday destination is children's attractions. They are also looking for a change from their jobs, some rest and relaxation, and to escape from their everyday routines. In addition, the Kiwi family holiday group enjoys: revisiting favorite places, going somewhere familiar, and a warm and predictable climate. They choose destinations that are easily reached, not too far from home, and that have good roads and highways.

Destination

The Kiwi family holiday group predominantly spends their vacation time in New Zealand. Because they vacation close to home, their destination choices are scattered widely across even parts of New Zealand including: Northland, Taupo/Tongariro, Waikato/Bay of Plenty, Nelson/Marlborough, and Central Otago.

Planning

The majority of this group travels as a family and almost all travel independently, as opposed to a prearranged package tour. This segment generally does not put much time into planning their holidays, with nearly half spending less than four weeks organizing their trips. The majority feel they know enough about the destination they visit from their own past experience and knowledge. Kiwi family holiday travelers pay for their holidays mainly with cash or eftpos, and they book accommodations directly with the company. This group has the lowest expenditure per person per day of all segments ($26). Food and accommodations are the major items.

Attractions and Activities

As you would expect, a Kiwi family holiday includes many outdoor and group activities:

Visit natural attractions
Visit the beach
Play cards or board games
Go for day trips in the car
Go for a short bush walk
Water-based sports

Reading
Go swimming
Read books and magazines
Play golf
Go fishing
Horseback riding

Accommodations and Dining Habits

Just over one-quarter of the Kiwi family holiday group stay at their holiday homes, one-quarter stay at campgrounds, and a few rent houses. The main reasons for these accommodation types are: price, quality, location, and comfort. This group tends to take their own food, or buy food from supermarkets at the destination.

Transportation

Nearly all of this group use their own cars; the main reasons are freedom and convenience.

Demographics

Three-quarters of the Kiwi family holiday group are in the thirty to forty-nine age bracket and, as would be expected, they are heavily represented in the full nest I and II stages of the family life cycle. Indeed, when single parents are included, almost 70 percent of this segment fall within these two life cycle stages. Two-thirds of this group, have either professional or highly skilled jobs, and this is the largest family group, with almost two-thirds having children still at home. Nearly one-quarter of this group earn over $100,000; this makes them the highest income segment.

DISCUSSION AND CONCLUSIONS

The only previous attempt to profile travel lifestyles in New Zealand was a commercial study conducted on behalf of the New Zealand Tourism and Publicity Department in 1989 (NZTP, 1989). That study also resulted in six segments being identified but methodologically it followed a process of "tacking on" a series of travel motivation and attitude questions to a more general AIO schedule. Not surprisingly, the results are quite different and only one of their segments (Pleasure-Seeking Holidaymakers) shows any strong relationship to the segments produced in this study. This contrast emphasizes the problem discussed earlier about the lack of good conceptual foundations for the topic resulting in inconsistent and noncomparable results.

In all the previous literature, the most similar-looking set of segments to those identified in our study were produced by Rusk and Schott (1977). They were investigating U.S. visitors to Canada and in a very short paper summarized six segments as follows. The possible parallel groups from our study are noted in brackets at the end of the description. One distinguishing feature of our study is the separation of friends and relatives into different groups, while traditional descriptions, such as that of Rusk and Schott, do not discriminate.

1. "The nonactive visitor"—seeks familiar surroundings where they can visit friends and relatives and disinclined to participate in any activities. (special family occasions)
2. "The active city visitor"—familiar surroundings where they can visit friends and relatives but takes on sightseeing, shopping, cultural, and entertainment activities. (fun-loving holidaymakers)
3. "Family sightseers"—new vacation places to treat children and provide an enriching experience. (No direct parallel to this group, but it could describe the small number of the education seekers with families. It made up only 6 percent of Rusk and Schott's sample.)
4. "The outdoor vacationer"—seeks clean air, rest and quiet, and beautiful scenery. Many are campers, and recreation facilities are important. Children are an important consideration. (Kiwi family holidays)
5. "The resort vacationer"—interested in things such as water sports, good weather, and popular places with a big-city atmosphere. (fun-loving holidaymakers)
6. "The foreign travel vacationer"—looks for new places with foreign atmospheres to obtain exciting and enriching experiences. Accommodation and service are more important than price. (education seekers)

Obviously, not all segments are reflected in the comparisons, but considering the different methodologies it is exciting that there seem to be so many similarities between two studies which are twenty years and two continents apart, even if they are both modern Western societies. This reinforces a belief, based on the work on food lifestyles completed by Grunert et al. (1996), that if the conceptual development is secure, then lifestyles may be transferable across cultures with an appropriate measurement instrument. We believe that the fundamental aspects of the means/ end approach and the surrounding domains established for this work are appropriate to travel and tourist behavior in any cultural setting.

Within the context of a single chapter it is not possible to provide tables of vast amounts of empirical data that underpin the descriptions of the segments. However, it is important to emphasize that the lifestyle segments in this study provide excellent discrimination on many aspects of holiday behaviors and choices. The activities undertaken by the different groups are very distinct, and the full lifestyle profiling offers much more information than is contained in purely behavioral-based segmentation studies (e.g., Morrison, Hsieh, and O'Leary, 1994). Types of destination and accommodation choices are also very distinct between the segments. Transport choices are perhaps the least well defined because of the general lack of variation in types of transport used. Private cars predominate for travel within New Zealand and all overseas travel involves flying. Even so, there are still some significant variations in features such as ferry usage between the two main islands. Other features that show clear differences between the segments are the length of planning horizons, the amount of information search, the amount of prebooking, and payment methods. In the last category, the use of traveler's checks, credit cards, and prepaid vouchers are all clearly associated with particular segments, as noted in the discussion.

One area where relationships are less clear is between the travel lifestyle segments and demographic characteristics. In many ways this is a "two-edged" result. The fact that we have good relationships with many aspects of tourist behavior and weak ones with most demographics emphasizes how much more a lifestyle approach has to offer managers for interpreting the marketplace and planning product developments and other marketing activities. Conversely, because so much customer data held by operators is in the form of demographic information, it means that it is more difficult to use the knowledge contained in this type of analysis. By far the strongest relationships between the lifestyle segments and any demographic variable is with stages of the family life cycle. This is an interesting finding because it can be used to support other approaches to lifestyles generated by sociologists (Chaney, 1996), who view them as a consumption-defined construct that has replaced social class as a way of stratifying society. The means/end approach used to hinge this and Grunert's work in food lifestyles operationalizes this central notion of consumption. Also, since family life cycle stages are recognized as varying considerably in the different resources (income, time, age, and ability) that support consumption activities, one might expect to find clear associations between lifestyles and the life cycle. Part of our plans for future work involves revisiting the same sample of respondents in 2002 and developing longitudinal research that might help understand significant relationships between the two concepts.

CONCEPT DEFINITIONS

Cluster analysis: A technique for grouping individuals or objects into clusters so that objects in the same cluster are more like one another than they are like objects in other clusters (Hair et al., 1995).

Lifestyles: Patterns of living that both influence and reflect a person's consumption behavior (Lawson et al., 1996).

Market segmentation: The process of partitioning the heterogeneous market into segments based on important characteristics. The goal is to facilitate development of unique marketing programs that will be most effective for these specific segments (Lawson et al., 1996).

Means/end chain: A hierarchy of concepts that allows researchers to link specific behaviors to general values held by consumers (Grunert et al., 1996).

Values: Centrally held and enduring beliefs that guide actions and judgments across specific situations (Rokeach, 1968).

REVIEW QUESTIONS

1. What are identified as the main problems in the use of lifestyles to analyze consumer behavior?
2. What does the chapter propose as the central principles about which lifestyles should be defined?
3. Develop a hypothetical means/end structure for (1) sunbathing on the beach, (2) a religious pilgrimage, and (3) bungee jumping.
4. Identify areas where you believe lifestyles show important differences in travel behavior. Support your choices with particular examples from the chapter.

5. Place yourself in the position of either (1) a manager wishing to investigate options for outbound tourism from New Zealand, or (2) an operator with capital to develop a tourism product in New Zealand. Show how the information contained in the chapter could be used to develop an appropriate marketing strategy. Evaluate what other information would be required to implement your strategy.

REFERENCES

Abbey, J.R. (1979). "Does Life Style Profiling Work?" *Journal of Travel Research* Summer: 8-14.

Beatty, S., Kahle, L., Homer, P., and Misra, S. (1985). "Alternative Measurement Approaches to Consumer Values: The List of Values and the Rokeach Value Survey." *Psychology and Marketing* 2(Fall): 181-200.

Boote, A.S. (1980). "Psychographics: Mind Over Matter." *American Demographics* April.

Chaney, D. (1996). *Lifestyles*. London, Routledge.

Craig-Lees, M., Joy, S., and Browne, B. (1995). *Consumer Behaviour*. Sydney, John Wiley and Sons.

Dann, G. (1981). "Tourists Motivation: An Appraisal." *Annals of Tourism Research* 8: 187-219.

Faris, F., Lawson, R., and Todd, S. (1996). *New Zealand Towards 2000—A Consumer Lifestyles Study*. Dunedin, New Zealand, University of Otago.

Gilly, M.C. and Enis, B.M. (1982). Recycling the Family Life Cycle: A Proposal for Redefinition. In *Advances in Consumer Research*, Vol. 9, ed. A. Mitchell. Ann Arbor, Michigan, Association for Consumer Research.

Gronroos, C. (1990). *Service Management and Marketing: Managing the Moments of Truth in Service Competition*. Toronto, Lexington Books.

Grunert, K.G., Baadsgaard, A., Larsen, H.H., and Madsen, T.K. (1996). *Market Orientation in Food and Agriculture*. Boston, Kluwer Academic Publishers.

Hair, J.F., Anderson, R.E., Tatham, R.L., and Black, W.C. (1995). *Multivariate Data Analysis with Readings*. Englewood Cliffs, NJ, Prentice Hall.

Hawes, D.K. (1988). "Travel Related Lifestyle Profiles of Older Women." *Journal of Travel Research* Fall: 22-32.

Kearsley, G., Higham, E., Coughlan, D., and Thyne, M. (1996). Perceptions of Social and Physical Impacts upon New Zealand's Back Country Environments. *Towards a More Sustainable Tourism*, Dunedin, New Zealand.

Lastovicka, J.L. (1982). "On the Validation of Lifestyle Traits: A Review and Illustration." *Journal of Marketing Research* 19: 126-138.

Lawson, R. (1991). *What Is Psychographic Segmentation? A Comparison Between General Consumer Analysis and Product Specific Analysis*. New Horizon Conference, The University of Calgary.

Lawson, R., Tidwell, P., Rainbird, P., Loudon, D., and Della Bitta, A. (1996). *Consumer Behaviour in Australia and New Zealand*. Sydney, McGraw-Hill Book Co.

Lawson, R., Williams, J., Young, T., and Cossens, J. (in press). "A Comparison of Residents' Attitudes Towards Tourism in Ten New Zealand Destinations." *Tourism Management.*

Lazer, W. (1963). Lifestyle Concepts and Marketing. In *Towards Scientific Marketing,* ed. S. Greyser. Chicago, American Marketing Association.

McGuire, W.J. (1976). "Some Internal Psychological Factors Influencing Consumer Choice." *Journal of Consumer Research* 2: 302-319.

Morgan, R. (1994). *The Roy Morgan Values Segments.* Sydney, The Roy Morgan Research Centre Pty. Ltd.

Morrison, A.M., Hsieh, S., and O'Leary, J.T. (1994). "Segmenting the Australian Domestic Travel Market by Holiday Activity Participation." *The Journal of Tourism Studies* 5(1): 39-56.

New Zealand Tourism Board (1996). *Tourism in New Zealand: Strategy and Progress.* Wellington, New Zealand, NZTB.

NZTP (1989). "Domestic Travel Segmentation Study." *NZTP Domestic Research Series 1989* 24: 105.

Pitts, R.E. and Woodside, A.G. (1983). "Personal Value Influences on Consumer Product Class and Brand Preferences." *Journal of Social Psychology* 119: 37-53.

Plog, S. (1987). Understanding Psychographics in Tourism Research. In *Travel, Tourism and Hospitality Research,* eds.. B.J.R. Ritchie and C.R. Goeldner. New York, Wiley: 203-213.

Plummer, J. (1974). "The Concept and Application of Lifestyle Segmentation." *Journal of Marketing* 38.

Reynolds, T.J. and Gutman, J. (1988). "Laddering Theory, Method, Analysis and Interpretation." *Journal of Advertising Research* February/March: 11-31.

Rokeach, M.J. (1968). *Beliefs, Attitudes and Values.* San Francisco, Jossey Bass.

Rusk, B.M. and Schott, M. (1977). *Marketing Canada as a Vacation Nation Evaluating the Creative Implementation of a Benefit Market Segmentation Study: Keeping Segmentation Current.* Chicago, Moving Ahead with Attitude Research.

Schewe, C.D. and Calantone, R.J. (1978). "Psychographic Segmentation of Tourists." *Journal of Travel Research* 16(3): 14-20.

Schwartz, S.H. (1992). "Universals in the Content and Structure of Values: Theoretical Advances and Empirical Tests in Twenty Countries." *Advances in Experimental Social Psychology* 25: 1-61.

Shih, D. (1986). "VALS As a Tool of Tourism Market Research: The Pennsylvania Experience." *Journal of Travel Research* Spring: 2-11.

SRI International (1989). *VALS 2.* Menlo Park, CA, SRI International.

Taylor, G.D. (1986). "Multidimensional Segmentation of the Canadian Pleasure Travel Market." *Tourism Management* September: 146-153.

Todd, S.J. (1997). S*elf-Concept and Tourist Motivation: An Empirical Examination of the Association Between How Tourists Feel and How They Travel.* Department of Marketing. Dunedin, University of Otago.

Wells, W.D. (1975). "Psychographics: A Critical Review." *Journal of Marketing Research* 12(May): 196-213.

Wells, W.D. and Tigert, D.J. (1973). Activities, Interests and Opinions. In *Perspectives in Consumer Behaviour,* eds. H. Kassarjian and T. Robertson. Englewood Cliffs, NJ, Prentice Hall: 162-176.

Woodside, A.G. and MacDonald, R. (1993). *General System Framework of Customer Choice Processes of Tourism Services.* Institute of Tourism and Service Economics International Conference, University of Innsbruck.

Chapter 22

Travel-Related Lifestyle Profiles of Older Women

Douglass K. Hawes

LEARNING OBJECTIVES

By the end of the chapter the reader should be able to:

- Understand the travel-related lifestyle profiles of elderly female travelers
- Gain an appreciation of the size and market power of the over-fifty population group
- Understand the approach-avoidance paradigm in tourist decision-making
- Briefly examine tourist motivation factors
- Understand what changes in female travel-related preferences occur with advancing age
- Examine how the lifestyle profiles of older women who have traveled overseas differ from those of older women who have not
- Examine the impact of travel-related attitude dimensions among older women travelers and how these attitudes affect media usage

INTRODUCTION

The United States is unquestionably becoming an older and more affluent society. In 1984 the median age in the United States was 31.3, compared to 29.8 a decade earlier (U.S. Department of Commerce, 1975,

---

This chapter was previously published in the *Journal of Travel Research, 25*(4), 1993. Reprinted with permission.

p. 31; 1985, p. 25). As of July 1, 1984, an estimated 28 percent of the female population in the United States was fifty years of age or older. Older households also tend to be more affluent: the mean 1984 household income of those households headed by someone ages fifty-five to sixty-four was $32,056, while the median for all households was $24,094 (U.S. Department of Commerce, 1985, pp. 24, 26, 452).

By the year 2000, an estimated 59 million people in this country will be ages fifty-five and over (*Technology and Aging in America,* 1985, p. 39), and they will have substantial buying power.

The total over-fifty crowd in 1984 numbered some 82.1 million; this group controlled 50 percent of the U.S. population's discretionary income and 77 percent of financial assets. Today's over-fifties represent a market of $866 billion a year (Linden, 1986, p. 4).

Fabian Linden (1986), veteran consumer researcher for the Conference Board, sums up the relevance of this market segment for marketers in general and travel marketers in particular:

> Today's 50-and-older are not only better educated than past generations of older people, they are also robust because of their awareness of the need for preventive health care. In addition, by all major economic measures—current income, financial assets, and net worth—today's older people are substantially better off than those who came before them. They are involved in more activities and they have more interests than previous generations, making them a promising market for luxury goods and services and quality merchandise. (p. 6)

Travel researchers McIntosh and Goeldner (1984,) have also noted increased travel by people sixty-five and over, commenting that if "this trend continues, the travel potential of this group cannot be overlooked" (p. 252). Rosenfeld (1986) supports this view: "Older Americans travel more frequently, go longer distances, stay away longer, and rely more on travel agents than any other segment of the population" (p. 38).

RELATED RESEARCH

In recent attention to the mature traveler, or the "gray market," Hughes (1985) stresses the size, attractiveness, and heterogeneity of this segment, while Supernaw (1985) suggests that retired people give travel the highest priority for their retirement years (pp. 287-288). Crissey (1980) stresses that the many "active affluents" among those fifty and over are looking for unique learning experiences via participation—that chronological age has little inherently to do with fitness to travel.

Research on the segment presented in this chapter has been limited. Van Doren (1981) merely calls attention to the growth in the older age brackets, both up to and over sixty-five years. Guinn (1980) examines older people as a recreational user group, but limits his study to the recreational vehicle tourist.

More focused age-specific travel-related research has been reported by Tongren (1980), who found that while respondents generally traveled less than they had anticipated, some three out of every four retirees used some type of travel service (p. 9). Tongren found distinct preretirement planning and postretirement (more detailed) search and execution phases of travel preparation, and suggested different promotional strategies for effectively reaching pre- and postretirement travel shoppers (p. 11).

Anderson and Langmeyer (1982) give support to under- and over-fifty age-based segmentation of the travel market. The major group profile differences they found seemed "to center on reasons for travel, the planning of travel and the cost of travel" (p. 23). Over-fifties were found to prefer nonhectic, preplanned, group-based, leisurely travel and were significantly more likely than under-fifties to prefer air travel.

Other related research appears to fall under two general topics of motivation and satisfaction. The underlying motivation to travel has been studied by Cohen (1972, 1979, 1984), who has evolved a typology of tourist roles and expedencies based on a presumed desire for variety, novelty, and strangeness, albeit in varying degrees: "motivation for travel is now increasingly understood in terms of how it relates to the individual's long-term psychological needs and life-plans; intrinsic motives such as [Maslow's] self-actualization seem to be particularly important" (Cohen, 1984, p. 377).

Dann (1981, 1983) and Iso-Ahola (1982) have conducted a protracted discussion of tourist motivation. Tourism is seen as motivating because it is basically a liberating opportunity; in fact, however, Dann has identified seven different approaches to tourist motivation, which suggests a lack of agreement on the parameters of the concept. Iso-Ahola (1980, 1982) focuses on the social-psychological underpinnings of tourist motivation, including the approach-avoidance conflict dimension of the decision process. Pearce (1982) supports this approach-avoidance paradigm, particularly in the context of Maslow's hierarchy of needs:

> Tourists are attracted to holiday destinations because of the possibility of fulfilling self-actualization, love and belongingness needs, and

physiological needs in that order of importance. When one considers the avoidance side of the motivational paradigm, a concern with safety is the predominant feature, with additional emphasis being placed on the failure to satisfy psychological needs, love and belongingness needs, and self-esteem needs (p. 129).

The second general research thrust bearing upon this chapter addresses satisfaction. The two streams of research are clearly linked, at least conceptually, since motivation is a precursor to behavior and satisfaction is a related consequence of behavior: "satisfaction is the comparative measurement of the event and its expectations, and the latter is *based* on motivation. Consequently, it makes little sense to study satisfaction in isolation from motivation" (Dann, 1981, p. 203).

Lounsbury and Hoopes (1985) found that, among other variables, overall vacation satisfaction was most strongly related to satisfaction with relaxation and leisure, and somewhat less strongly related to satisfaction with escape opportunities, marriage and family satisfaction, and level of educational attainment. The linkage between vacation (or leisure activities in general) satisfaction and satisfaction with retirement life has been noted by Mobily et al. (1984), Romsa, Bondy, and Blenman (1985), Dorfman, Kohout, and Heckert (1985) (especially with regard to the importance of social involvement/integration on retirement satisfaction), and Riddich and Daniel (1984). This latter study specifically focused on older women, including retirees.

All of these studies support the activity theory of aging, in which successful aging is seen to be a direct function of maintaining middle-age activity levels or substituting new activities for those that must be relinquished (Riddich and Daniel, 1984, p. 137). The tendency "for aged people to persist with the same relative levels of activities and attitudes as they grow older" had been noted at least as far back as 1968 (Palmore, 1976). These findings are in disagreement with the disengagement theory of aging, which states that successful aging is a process of withdrawal, restructuring relationships, and reducing activity (cf. McIntosh and Goeldner, 1984, pp. 142, 172).

FOCUS OF THE STUDY

The study reported here examined the travel-related lifestyle profiles of women ages fifty and over grouped by five-year age brackets, i.e., fifty to fifty-four, fifty-five to fifty-nine, sixty to sixty-four, sixty-five to sixty-nine, and seventy and over. The particular age brackets chosen are somewhat arbitrary, but conform to age groupings often reported in other sources. As a coincidence, the Ns in each of the five selected groups are all generally close to 100.

This chapter focuses on the following questions:

1. What are the general travel-related lifestyle patterns of each of the five selected age groupings of women?
2. What changes in female travel-related preferences occur with advancing age?
3. What differences exist in lifestyle profiles between older women who have traveled overseas and those who have not?
4. Are there underlying attitudinal dimensions, relative to travel, either within or across these age groups? If so, what are the components of those dimensions and the relationship of the dimensions to media usage?

RESEARCH METHODOLOGY

The study reported here used data taken from a representative nationwide sample of 1,650 households surveyed by Market Facts, Inc. (Chicago) for the author and several of his colleagues during the late spring of 1984. The overall study was designed generally to replicate a similar one conducted by the author in the late spring of 1973. The households surveyed were selected from Market Facts' 60,000-plus household Consumer Mail Panel (CMP), and the sample was balanced on five variables so that the household demographic composition closely paralleled the continental civilian adult noninstitutionalized population as defined by the U.S. Census Bureau's Current Population Survey in March 1983. The five balancing variables were geographic region, population density, total annual household income (TAHI), household size, and age of female head of household.

The female head of household (CMP member) received a sixteen-page pink questionnaire booklet, while the male head (if present) received an eight-page white booklet. Two follow-up reminder postcards were sent out at two-week intervals. The questionnaire had been extensively pretested in conjunction with the 1973 study; new questions in this study were pretested by the author in his local community.

The 1,650-household sample contained 872 households in which the female head indicated she was married and 778 households in which the female head indicated she was not married. The male questionnaire was sent to the 872 "married" households. A total of 1,090 female questionnaires were returned for an overall response rate of 66 percent. Of these,

605 returns came from "unmarried" households (78 percent return rate), and 485 returns included both a female and a male questionnaire (56 percent return rate).

ANALYSIS

The analysis pattern below underlies the results discussed in the following section.

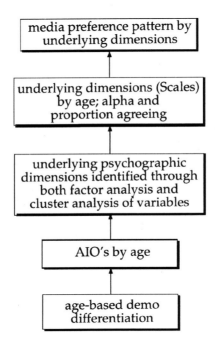

After starting with demographic profiling, the analysis examines travel-related psychographic dimensions of the five age groups. Both R-type factor and cluster analysis were then used to seek out underlying travel-related dimensions within the larger set of variables. These dimensions were codified into three scales, which were then examined across age categories. Finally, the scales were linked to media preferences to permit targeting of marketing messages to those agreeing with the basic premise of the scale.

RESULTS

Since Market Facts has a complete demographic file on each CMP household, it was possible to compare respondent and nonrespondent households. With only two expectations, the differences between the initial sample respondents and nonrespondents did not exceed 5 percent in any demographic variable category. The initial sample tracked the national quota within a maximum difference of 2.6 percent. With regard to household size, the largest difference was between respondents and nonrespondents in the single-member household category; 11.3 percent more single women returned the questionnaire than did not.

There was a slight upward age bias in that older women tended to be overrepresented among the respondents. There were nearly 16 percent more respondents in the sixty-and-over age group than nonrespondents, although in the middle years the difference between the two groups does not exceed 6 percent. At the youngest ages, nonrespondents exceeded respondents by nearly 10 percent. This is not unexpected given the typical level of activity in the younger years.

Table 22.1 displays the demographic profiles of the five selected age groups. The different groups were relatively evenly distributed within each of the geographic areas. Roughly half of each age group completed their formal education with high school, and half had some (or completed) college. The fifty to fifty-four and sixty-five to sixty-nine groups each had about 10 percent more high-school-only women and 10 percent fewer "some college" women than the other three groups. Most of these women below the normal retirement age of sixty-five were either in the "other" category (essentially "not specified," i.e., not presently employed outside the home) or were employed in clerical or kindred occupations. A surprisingly large percentage of those employed (as much as 30 percent of those fifty to fifty-four) were in professional or managerial roles. Roughly one-fifth of the women in each age group identified themselves as full-time homemakers. From 47 to 62 percent of those below age sixty-five indicated they were employed full time; another 8 to 10 percent were employed part time.

As one would expect, household size declines with increasing age, although even in the youngest age group two-fifths indicated a household size of only two. Half the women were married and a third of those in the youngest age group were divorced. The prevalence of divorce in younger generations is reflected in the continued decline in divorced women in succeeding age groups.

The women in these five groups could be classified as living in middle-income households. Half or more of each age group had total household incomes in 1983 of between $15,000 and $40,000 per year. The expected

TABLE 22.1. Demographic Profile of Women in the Five Selected Age Groups (Percents)

	Age: 50-54 (n=97)	55-59 (n=96)	60-64 (n=125)	65-69 (n=110)	70 & up (n=106)
Geographic					
New England	4%	4%	6%	6%	5%
Mid-Atlantic	20	15	16	15	18
E. No. Central	17	23	23	22	26
W. No. Central	7	8	11	8	8
South Atlantic	18	13	13	13	18
E. So. Central	8	6	5	6	2
W. So. Central	8	10	9	7	6
Mountain	4	4	3	5	5
Pacific	14	17	14	18	13
Education level					
8 yrs. grade school or less	4	0	2	1	3
1-3 yrs. high school	8	5	7	16	10
4 yrs. high school	51	43	42	42	40
1-3 yrs. college	24	37	31	22	18
4 yrs. college	9	4	9	10	14
5-8 yrs. college	4	12	8	10	15
Occupation					
Professional worker	13	16	14	3	4
Manager/administrator	17	10	6	5	2
Clerical & kindred	26	29	30	11	3
Sales	5	2	1	4	1
Craftsmen & kindred, operatives, transport, laborers, farm workers	4	4	3	0	0
Service workers	8	5	2	2	1
Other or not employed	25	33	43	76	90
Employment status					
Works for someone else full time	53	53	41	11	5
Temp. unemployed	3	3	2	0	1
Self-employed	9	2	6	3	2
Works for someone else part time	10	8	8	10	3
Retired & not employed	2	7	19	55	66
Disabled & not employed	2	3	3	2	0
Full-time homemaker	21	23	22	20	24

	Age: 50-54 (n=97)	55-59 (n=96)	60-64 (n=125)	65-69 (n=110)	70 & up (n=106)
Household size					
1	20	35	35	31	42
2	40	43	47	56	51
3	25	14	8	8	6
4	13	5	6	2	1
5 or more	2	3	4	3	1
Marital status					
Married	51	50	51	57	49
Widowed	11	12	18	26	38
Divorced	34	28	23	7	3
Separated	2	2	2	2	0
Never married	2	7	6	7	9
Total household income (1983)					
$10,000-14,999	18	11	20	27	25
$15,000-19,999	13	19	15	18	23
$20,000-24,999	12	20	17	13	13
$25,000-29,999	10	6	10	10	3
$30,000-39,999	17	17	16	8	13
$40,000-49,999	10	9	8	6	3
$50,000 and over	6	7	3	3	2
Population density/degree of urbanization					
Non-MSA	27	28	26	29	26
Central City (50K-500K)	5	12	12	10	9
Outside CC (50K-500K)	10	14	12	14	14
Central City (500K-2M)	14	13	12	13	12
Outside CC (500K-2M)	18	13	14	16	21
Central City (2M & up)	8	9	11	12	8
Outside CC (2M & up)	18	13	13	6	11

increase into percentage falling into the lower income categories, as age increases, is clearly evident. The vast majority of women in all age groups live in suburban or exurban locales.

Psychographic Profiling

Although it is appropriate to first profile potential market segments on demographics, that alone is but a skeleton. A common way to enhance such skeletal descriptions is with lifestyle measures, often psychometrically developed through activity-interest-opinion, or AIO, statements. These statements are usually phrased in such a way that they can be answered on a five- or seven-point agree-disagree Likert scale. Earlier research by the author had shown the utility of psychographic profiling of travelers (Hawes, Blackwell, and Talarzyk, 1977).

Initially the author selected the seventeen distinctly travel-related AIOs from the 151 AIOs on the survey questionnaire. The remaining sixteen statements were culled from separate intercorrelation matrices for each of the five age groups on the basis of being the most highly correlated (.30 or greater) with one or more of the initial seventeen statements for three or more of the age groups. These were then used in the factor and cluster analyses discussed in conjunction with Table 22.5. The full wording of the selected thirty-three AIO statements is shown in Table 22.2; the statements are paraphrased in subsequent tables.

Table 22.3 shows the proportions of women in each age category agreeing with the seventeen distinctly travel-related AIOs on the survey instrument. Since the focus is on travel-related attitudes and behavior, the responses to the remaining sixteen statements are not presented. Differences between age groups that are statistically significant at the .05 level or greater (Z-test, two-tailed) led to several inferences about the differences between age groups.

Women fifty to fifty-four are less likely to have traveled overseas than women over sixty; further, those between fifty and sixty-four are less likely to have done such traveling than those seventy and older. It is somewhat surprising that the biggest jump just barely missing statistical significance) is between the sixty-five to sixty-nine and the seventy-and-older groups. A priori, one would have predicted a major discontinuity in the data between sixty to sixty-four and sixty-five to sixty-nine, given the customary retirement age of sixty-five.

When asked if they would like to take a vacation overseas, however, women in the fifty-five to fifty-nine group were significantly more interested in doing so than those in any other age group. Similarly, those in this age group were significantly more likely than those in any other age group to express a desire to vacation in Canada, Mexico, or the Caribbean and, along with the fifty to fifty-four age group, significantly less likely than older ages to feel satisfied with their present leisure-time activities. Perhaps this reflects the pressures of employment. This age group and those over seventy were also significantly more likely to have traveled to these locations than were the other groups.

TABLE 22.2. Full Wording of Activity-Interest-Opinion Statements Used in Analysis

1. I have traveled overseas.[T,D(*)b]
2. I would like to take a vacation overseas.
3. I would like to take a vacation in Canada, Mexico, or the Caribbean.[T]
4. I have traveled to Canada, Mexico, or the Caribbean.[T]
5. Basically, I'm satisfied with my present leisure-time activities.
6. On a vacation, I just want to rest and relax.[L]
7. A cabin by a quiet lake is a great place to spend the summer.[L]
8. Our family travels together quite a lot.
9. When it comes to my recreation, time is a more important factor than money.
10. When it comes to my recreation, money is a more important factor than time.[D]
11. Vacations should be planned for the children.[L]
12. A "travel-now-pay-later" vacation is wrong.[L]
13. I like to spend my vacation in or near a big city.[L(*)]
14. I would like to live in a foreign city, like Paris, for a year.[T]
15. On my vacation, I like to experience the uncertainty of not knowing what I will encounter from day to day.
16. On a vacation, it is better to drive on side roads than on superhighways.
17. On my vacation, I like to get away from mechanization and automation.
18. Credit cards make it too easy to buy things I may not really need.[D]
19. I would rather use a credit card than pay cash.
20. I am satisfied with my present financial situation.
21. Our family income is high enough to satisfy nearly all our important desires.[D(*)]
22. I like excitement.[L(*)]
23. I like to serve or eat unusual dinners.
24. I really enjoy life.
25. I have enough leisure time.
26. People express their real selves in their leisure-time activities.
27. My leisure time tends to be boring.[D]
28. I would like to take a lesson in my favorite sport.[T]
29. I would rather spend a quiet evening at home than go out to a party.[L]
30. I watch television more than I should.[D]
31. Television is our primary source of entertainment.[D]
32. My choice of brands for many products is influenced by advertising.
33. I often shop from a Sears, Penney's, or Ward's catalog.[L]

---

[a] These statements were responded to on five-point Likert scales anchored by "strongly agree" and "strongly disagree." The order in which these statements are listed here does not reflect their order on the questionnaire; they were scattered among 118 other such statements.

[b] Letter superscripts refer to the scale (T = traveler, D = dreamer, L = laid back) of which the AIO statement is a component variable. (*) means the scoring of the statement was reversed for that particular scale. See Table 22.6 and attendant discussion.

TABLE 22.3. Percentage of Women in Each Age Category Agreeing with Selected Travel-Related AIO Statements[a]

AIO Statement	Age: 50-54 $(n=97)$	55-59 $(n=96)$	60-64 $(n=125)$	65-69 $(n=110)$	70 & up $(n=106)$
Have traveled overseas	25%[b]	33%	38%	40%	52%
Like to vacation overseas	51	71	62	55	56
Like to vacation in Can., Mex., Car.	70	84	70	62	68
Have traveled to Can., Mex., Car.	43	59	50	56	62
Satisfied with L-T activities	54	46	70	76	78
On vacation, rest and relax	65	52	53	61	40
Cabin by a quiet lake	69	70	67	64	64
Family travels together	42	47	42	47	43
Time more important than money	46	47	40	40	44
Money more important than time	34	27	41	41	42
Vacations planned for kids	40	37	39	42	40
"Travel now, pay later"	62	57	58	61	60
Vacation in/near big city	21	23	36	26	24
Live in Paris for a year	28	31	34	22	21
Like uncertainty	43	45	54	56	51
On vacation, drive on side roads	53	51	57	66	59
On vacation, get away from it all	45	58	46	58	40

[a] Percentage represents combination of "strongly agree" and "agree somewhat." Definite yes/no-type statements were typically answered either "strongly agree" or "strongly disagree."

[b] For significance at the 5 percent level or greater (Z-test, two-tailed), the difference between any two percentages in a row must be equal to or greater than 5-7 points for all combinations, except those involving the 60-64 group, and over the range from 20 percent to 80 percent. The smaller difference is significant at the 20-30 and 70-80 base percentage levels, while 6-7 points difference is needed in the range between 35 and 65 base percentage points. Comparisons involving the 60-64 age group requires a difference of approximately one percentage point less to be significant, i.e., 4-6 points (Downie and Heath 1974, pp. 181-187).

Elaborating upon the first four statements, Table 22.4 shows that, by and large, previous exposure to a "foreign" setting predisposes one to want to return. Travel begets travel, or at least whets the appetite for more travel to locations previously visited (either on business or on vacation). In all age groups, the percentage of those indicating they would like to travel to a foreign location and who had traveled to the area earlier was greater than the

TABLE 22.4 Relationship Between Previous Travel Experience to an Area and Desire to Vacation There

	50 & up (n=534)	50-54 (n=97)	55-59 (n=96)	60-64 (n=125)	65-69 (n=110)	70 & up (n=106)
Have traveled overseas and would like to take a vacation overseas	157/202 (78%)[a]	31/53 (67%)[c]	29/32 (91%)[a]	35/47 (74%)[b]	37/44 (84%)[a]	40/55 (73%)
Have not traveled overseas and would like to take a vacation overseas[d]	89/162[e]	18/40 (45%)	21/34 (62%)	24/42 (57%)	15/27 (56%)	11/19 (58%)
Have traveled to Canada, Mexico, or the Caribbean, and would like to take a vacation in Canada, Mexico, or the Caribbean	232/286 (81%)	37/42 (88%)[a]	52/57 (91%)[c]	49/62 (79%)	42/59 (71%)	52/66 (79%)[b]
Have not traveled to Canada, Mexico or the Caribbean, and would like to take a vacation in Canada, Mexico, or the Caribbean.[d]	109/168 (65%)	22/38 (58%)	20/25 (80%)	31/43 (72%)	21/36 (58%)	15/26 (58%)

[a] Difference between "have" and "have not" significant at .01 level or greater (Z-test, two-tailed).
[b] Difference between "have" and "have not" significant at .05 level.
[c] Difference between "have" and "have not" significant at .1 level.
[d] It is recognized that having traveled and liking to travel both answered on a five-point agree-disagree scale form at least a four-cell matrix if the "undecideds" are combined with the "disagrees." However, the interest here is in the two cells described in the table. In all cases, if the "undecideds" are separated from the "disagrees," the percentages in the two other cells in the matrix (based on "would not like to take a vacation overseas/in Canada, etc.") are quite small.
[e] The two denominators do not add up to the figure at the head of the column due to omission of the "undecided/no opinion" (middle) category of response. Applies to all columns.

percentage so indicating who had not previously been to the area. In nine of the twelve pairs, the "have traveled" percentage was statistically significantly greater than the "have not," with five of those nine at the 1 percent level.

Returning to Table 22.3, a rather unusual pattern is noted on the sixth statement. Both the women fifty to fifty-four and the immediately postretirement group sixty-five to sixty-nine are significantly more interested in resting and relaxing on a vacation than those between fifty-five and sixty-four and those over seventy. Could the ten years prior to retirement (age sixty-five) represent a surge of energy for many, leading to a burnout around sixty-five and a consequent desire to take it easy, only to be followed by a resurgence of energy after seventy?

Roughly two-thirds of each age group like the idea of a cabin by a quiet lake as a summer retreat. The differences between this and the preceding statement within the fifty-five to sixty-four age groups can only be explained by differences in perspective. What is appropriate for a two- to three-week vacation may not be the ideal were a full summer vacation available.

Approximately two-fifths of each age group indicate that their family travels together quite a bit, that time is more important than money (or the converse), and that vacations should be planned for the children. There is one exception, however. Women in the fifty-five to fifty-nine age group (possibly reflective of household high-earnings years) are significantly less likely to feel that money is more important to them than time.

Approximately three-fifths of the women in each age group felt that a travel now, pay later vacation is wrong. This compares with 56 percent of all women in this study, and 64 percent of a similarly balanced female sample in a survey conducted by the author in 1973 (Hawes, Blackwell, and Talarzyk, 1976, p. 68). Apparently there is still significant reluctance in the population to go into debt by using credit for leisure-time pursuits. As noted in the earlier article, this reluctance continues to pose marketing difficulties for travel and leisure organizations.

Most of the women in each age group were not interested in either spending their vacations in or near a big city or living in a foreign city for a year. For inexplicable reasons, the sixty to sixty-four age group was the most interested in the big-city environment—significantly more so than those over sixty-five in both cases, and more interested in spending their vacations in or near a big city than any other group. At best, however, this represented only about a third of the women in that age group. Perhaps vacation expectations and fantasies peak in the years immediately prior to the nominal retirement age of sixty-five.

Finally, between 40 and 60 percent of the women in each age group prefer uncertainty, prefer side roads to super highways, and like to get away from mechanized or automated society on a vacation. In each of these three cases, one age group stands out from the other four in a statistical sense, but no apparent significant pattern is evident.

Factor and Cluster Analyses

Table 22.4 suggests that managerially meaningful differences exist between respondents who had traveled and those who had not insofar as desire to travel goes. One way of further expanding on the travel-related profile differences within each age group is to determine whether the AIO statements (and selected demographic variables) form differentiating structures, on composite underlying dimensions, within each age category. One of several techniques for doing this is R-type exploratory factor analysis.

The objective of this stage of the analysis is to determine whether there are any underlying dimensions (within and/or across the age groupings) among the AIO statements and selected demographics that are not immediately evident from an examination of the full set of variables within each age category. This is an appropriate use of R-type factor analysis (Stewart, 1981; Bieber and Smith, 1986). This is not an attempt to develop clusters of respondents (Stewart, 1981).

The results of a six-factor varimax (orthogonal) rotation factor analysis of the full set of thirty-three AIO statements (plus the five demographic variables of education, occupation, household size, marital status, and income) for each of the five age categories is shown in Table 22.5. Six factors were selected for rotation based upon the convergences of the criteria of eigenvalues ≥ 1.00, variance explained (≥ 5 percent), and the screen tests (Rummel, 1970, pp. 357-365). Table 22.5 displays only those distinctly travel- and/or leisure-related factors within each age group; other factors consisted of secondary dimensions unrelated to this analysis. The labeling of each factor indicates the hierarchical number of the factor, the postrotation variance explained, and the percentage of cases loading strongly on that factor (factor score ≥ 1.0). The loading of each significant variable (loading $\geq .35$) on the factor is given in parentheses after each paraphrased variable.

The factors appear to indicate several common underlying dimensions relative to travel and leisure, both across all five age groups and within each age group. One dimension reflects a strong vacation travel orientation (both having traveled and wanting to) and is generally associated with singleness or small household size, activeness, acceptance or liking of excitement and uncertainty, higher income, and education. This would certainly appear to confirm generally accepted stereotypes.

TABLE 22.5. Results of R-Type Factor Analysis of AIO Statements Across and Within Each Age Group

Across all 5 groups (n = 534)

#1 (31%/27%)	#2 (26%/28%)	#3 (17%/24%)	#4 (13%/24%)
Satisfied with present finances (.66)	Like to take a vacation o/s (.71)	TV is primary source (.58)	Cabin by a quiet lake (.62)
Have enough leisure time (.58)	Like to live in for. city (.57)	Watch more TV than I should (.51)	On vacation, rest and relax (.43)
Satisfied with present leisure time (.57)	Like to vacation in Can., Mex., Cari. (.50)	Money more important than time (.47)	On vacation, want to get away (.40)
Family income is high enough (5.4)	Like excitement (.44)	My Lt tends to be boring (.41)	Rather spend quiet evening at home (.36)
Occupation (.41)	Have traveled to Can., Mex., Cari. (.38)	Family income high enough (−.39)	
Age (5 groups, −.62)	Like to serve/eat unusual dinners (.38)	Time more important than money (−.35)	
	Would like a lesson in favorite sport (.36)		
	Have traveled o/s (.35)		

Age 50-54 (n = 97)

#1 (31%/22%)	#2 (19%/27%)	#4 (13%/21%)	#5 (12%/19%)
Satisfied with present Lt (.55)	Like to vacation o/s (.69)	Cabin by a quiet lake (.50)	I have enough Lt (.59)
Time more important than money (.53)	Like to live in for. city (.59)	Watch more TV than I should (.43)	Like to vacation in big city (.36)
Satisfied with present financial situation (.50)	Like to vac. in Can., Mex., Cari. (.58)	Credit cards make it too easy (.42)	I like excitement (.323)
Family income high enough (.46)	Like to experience uncertainty (.49)	On vacation, want to get away (.40)	Time more imp. than money (−.41)
Have traveled o/s (.45)	Rather spend a quiet evening at home (−.34)	Family income is high enough (−.38)	On vac., drive on side roads (−.46)
I enjoy life (.44)			
Have traveled to Can., Mex., or Cari. (.42)			
Travel now/pay later is wrong (−.41)			
TV is primary source of entertainment (−.49)			
Money more important than time (−.57)			

Age 55-59 (n = 96)

#2 (24%/20%)	#3 (22%/22%)	#4 (14%/25%)
I really enjoy life (.69)	Would like to take a vac. o/s (.58)	Cabin by a quiet lake (.56)
Satisfied with present Lt (.57)	Would like to take a vac. to Can., Mex., Cari., (.59)	Better to drive on side roads (.39)
Family income is high enough (.50)	Have traveled o/s (.51)	Family travels together (.38)
Satisfied with present financial situation (.49)	Would like to live in a for. city (.40)	On vac., want to rest and relax (.37)
Occupation (.37)	Have traveled to Can., Mex., Cari. (.36)	I like excitement (−.38)
Vacations should be planned for kids (−.38)	Total household income (−.39)	Like to vac. in/near big city (−.43)
My Lt tends to be boring (−.40)	Education (−.48)	Choice of brand influenced by adv. (−.51)
	I have enough leisure time (−.48)	

Age 60-64 (n = 125)

#1 (27%/27%)	#3 (20%/22%)	#4 (15%/25%)	#5 (12%/23%)
TV is primary entertainment (.56)	Like to serve/eat unusual dinners (.64)	Cabin by a quiet lake (.68)	Like to vac. o/s (.65)
Education (.52)	Like to experience uncertainty (.55)	Rather spend quiet evenings (.656)	Like to vac. in Can., Mex., Cari. (.51)
Watch too much TV (.43)	Like excitement (.50)	On vac., want to rest and relax (.49)	Money more imp. than time (.48)
Like to live in a for. city (−.34)	On vac., drive on side roads (.47)	Rather use credit card than cash (−.36)	Like to live in a for. city (.34)
Like to take a vac. o/s (−.34)	Like a lesson in favorite sport (.42)	I like excitement (−.42)	Time more imp. than money (−.39)
Household size (−.35)	On vac., want to get away (.37)		
Have traveled o/s (−.40)	Like to live in a for. city (.36)		
Have traveled to Can., Mex., Cari. (−.54)			

TABLE 22.5 *(continued)*

Age 65-69 (n = 110)

#1 (31%/29%)	#2 (21%/28%)	#4 (11%/22%)
Like to live in a for. city (.66)	Watch too much TV (.67)	Cabin by a quiet lake (.57)
Like to take a vacation o/s (.60)	TV is primary entertainment (.64)	Rather spend a quiet evening at home (.48)
Like to take a lesson in fav. sport (.53)	On vac., want to rest and relax (.42)	On vac., want to rest and relax (.46)
Like to vac. in Can., Mex., Cari. (.50)	Money more imp. than time (.34)	On vac., want to get away (.46)
Have traveled overseas (.43)	Am satisfied with present financial situation (−.32)	Express real self in Lt acts (.39)
Household size (.34)	Have traveled overseas (−.42)	Like to vac. in/near big city (−.34)
Marital status (− .38)		

Age 70 & up (n = 106)

#1 (30%/28%)	#3 (17%/22%)	#4(13%/29%)	#6 (10%/22%)
Watch too much TV (.60)	Would like to vac. in Can., Mex., Cari. (.82)	Express real self in Lt acts (.65)	Have traveled overseas (.48)
TV is primary entertainment (.58)	Would like to vac. overseas (.64)	Like to serve/eat unusual dinners (.49)	On vac., drive on side roads (.36)
Leisure time tends to be boring (.57)	Would like a lesson in favorite sport (.50)	Like to live in a for. city (.47)	Have traveled to Can., Mex., Cari. (.36)
Money more imp. than time (.46)	Have traveled to Can., Mex., Cari. (.38)	I like excitement (.42)	Education (−.64)
On vac., want to rest and relax (.44)	Household size (.37)	Like to vac. in/near a big city (.40)	
Cabin by a quiet lake (.39)		Watch TV too much (.38)	
My choice of brands influenced by adv. (.39)			
Credit cards make it too easy to buy (.35)			
Would like to take a vac. o/s (− .39)			

The second dimension indicates an acceptance of vacation travel, but essentially of the domestic, unhurried, "unexciting," quiet and relaxing, rural variety. This group would appear to be less affluent and more concerned with indebtedness than the first. These two types of travel-oriented groups would appear to support Wohlers and Etzel's (1985) findings on stimulation seekers and avoiders.

A third dimension seems to reflect an orientation in which vicarious thrills and wishing or dreaming substitute for the real thing. For these people, television is their primary source of stimulation and exposure to foreign locales.

One of the most significant findings from this factor analysis is the extremely low loadings (or strongly negative loadings) of the two television statements on the two "traveler" factors. This suggests that using television advertising to reach actual and potential travelers may not be as cost effective as other media such as print and outdoor.

Finally, one factor seems to reflect a rather nebulous "generally satisfied" dimension. The respondents who load heavily on this factor are concentrated in the two lowest age groups and would appear to be satisfied with both their financial situation and leisure time, but do not have any strong preferences built up regarding their vacation options. Since these women are in the preretirement age groups (their husbands, if they are married, may be nearing retirement), they may represent a "swing" market segment that can be interested in nondomestic travel.

At the other extreme of the age range, the statement, "People express their real selves in their leisure time activities," comes into play with relatively strong loadings. This suggests not only an acceptance of post-retirement leisure time, but an awakening to creative and self-development possibilities. The author suspects that this dimension may be the counterpoint to the generally satisfied, but not "into" leisure time dimension in the two youngest age groups.

In summary, then, the factor analysis seems to indicate three major underlying dimensions within this group of travel and leisure-related AIO statements that transcend the five age groups selected. The factor analysis has reduced the thirty-eight variables to three underlying dimensions of attitudes and behavior toward travel and related leisure-time pursuits. These dimensions may be potentially viable market segments. They can be labeled "traveler," "laid back," and "dreamer" based on the discussion above.

As both a check on the findings of the factor analysis and as a further elaboration in the analysis schemata, a hierarchical clustering-of-variables analysis using BMDP (Dixon, 1983) was performed (routine PI M, using correlation as the measure and average linkage). Such analysis methodology is also appropriate for exploratory purposes to ascertain how many, if any, distinguishable groups of variables (stimuli, attributes, etc.) exist in a data set (Bieber and Smith, 1986).

Without presenting the six-cluster dendograms here, let it be noted that the clusters supported (at reasonably high levels [short distances] and with very similar groupings of variables, as noted in the next section) the results of the factor analysis. The cluster analysis did show, however, several other variables that were strongly associated with the core statements of each of the three scales, but which did not come through clearly from the factor analysis alone. In that sense, the cluster analysis proved a useful adjunct to the primary dimensionalizing capability of the factor analysis.

Travel-Orientation Scale Development

The next step in the analysis involved generating separate scales for each of these three apparent underlying dimensions. Intercorrelations, author's judgment, several iterations of the factor analysis (both orthogonal and oblique), and the results of the cluster analysis led to selection of six to nine AIO statements to make up each scale. These are indicated in Table 22.2 by the superscript T (traveler), L (laid back), or D (dreamer) for each of the indicated scales. An average agree/disagree score across each of the statements in a given scale was computed. This has the advantage (over a cumulated score) of allowing interpretation of the relevant scores in the same metric as the original scale items (Hull and Nie, 1981, p. 257).

The reliability of each scale as applied to each age group was determined through the calculation of Cronbach's alpha, (Hull and Nie, 1981 p. 248ff) for each of the fifteen combinations; also, each scale was applied to the whole sample. Nunnally (1978) states that the primary way to make tests more reliable is to make them longer (the precision of the reliability estimate being directly proportional to the number of items in the test). Interestingly, he alludes to twenty-item tests (scales) as "short." He further indicates that, in the early stages of research, reliabilities of .50 or .60 are considered "modest" and scales with such reliability "will suffice" (p. 226).

On that basis, the reliabilities of the three scales in Table 22.6 appear to be quite good, given that they were only six- to nine-item scales. Scale "laid back" seems to be the weakest when applied to the fifty to fifty-four age group. The other scales tend to increase (or remain the same) in reliability as they are applied to older age groups. Overall, the "traveler" scale has the highest reliabilities across all age groups, with the other extreme of "dreamer" second and the intermediate category of "laid

TABLE 22.6. Proportion Agreeing with Each of the Three Scales, and Cronbach's Alpha (α) Across All Age Groups and Within Each Age Group

Age grouping	N	"Traveler"[b]	(Alpha)	"Laid Back"[c]	(Alpha)	"Dreamer"[d]	(Alpha)[e]
Across all							
5 groups	(534)	33%[a]	(.69)	34	(.57)	22%	(.59)
50-54	(97)	25	(.68)	37	(.47)	31	(.63)
55-59	(96)	41	(.59)	39	(.58)	27	(.58)
60-64	(125)	33	(.68)	35	(.53)	19	(.52)
65-69	(110)	24[c]	(.67)	33	(.63)	20	(.65)
70 & up	(106)	41	(.77)	27	(.57)	13	(.66)
average:		33%	.68	34%	.56	22%	.61

	"Traveler"			"Laid Back"			"Dreamer"		
Across all									
5 age	α	Delete	α'	α'	Delete	α'	α'	Delete	α'
groups	.69	–	–	.57	–	–	.59	–	–
50-54	.68	–	–	.47	–	–	.53	#27	.54
55-59	.59	#28	.62	.58	#6	.65[f]	.58	#1	.59
60-64	.68	–	–	.53	#11	.56	.52	#21	.58[g]
65-69	.67	#4	.70	.63	#12	.65	.65	–	–
70 & up	.77	–	–	.57	#29	.59	.66	#21	.69

[a] Proportion scoring below 3.0 as an average composite score on the AIO variables in the scale using a 5-pt. agree-disagree scale. See p. 257 of *SPSS Update 7-9* (Hull and Nie, 1981) for algorithm used in computing composite scores.

[b] Within scale percentage differences between the age groups of 50-54/65-69 and 55-59/70 and up significant at 1% level (Z-test, two-tailed): between "across all 5"/60-64 and 55-59/70 and up significant at 5% level: between 50-54/65-69 and "across all 5"/60-64 significant at 5% level.

[c] Within scale percentage differences between 70 and up and 50-54/55-59 significant at 5 percent level.

[d] Within scale percentage differences between 70 and up and "across all 5." J50-54, 55-59 significant at 1 percent level: between 50-54 and "across all 5"/60-64/65-69 significant at 5 percent level.

[e] Effects of deleting one scale item (per numbered list in Table 22.2) correlating the least with the overall scale on resultant Cronbach's alpha (α). α' represents the increased alpha.

[f] Deleting item/AIO *6 raised the proportion agreeing with the "Laid Back" scale in that age group from 39 percent to 62 percent.

[g] Deleting item/AIO *21 raised the proportion agreeing with the "Dreamer" scale in that age group from 19 percent to 45 percent.

back" third. A footnote to the table indicates the increase in the scale reliability coefficient for each age category, which occurs if the scale item correlating the least with the scale is removed from the scale for that age category. This also happens to represent the maximum alpha possible based on any number of item deletions from the initial pool of scale items. Again the "traveler" scale is seen as the most robust, with the other two scales approximating the same level of robustness except for one age category on each scale where the deletion of one item noticeably improved the alpha. This information is provided to the interested reader who might wish to use these scales on specific age groups from fifty years of age up.

Across all the age groups, approximately one-third of the respondents agreed with both the "traveler" and "laid back" scales, and 22 percent agreed with the "dreamer" scale. From a marketing perspective this suggests a substantial market segment already predisposed to nondomestic travel and another equally large segment (the "laid backs") who might be induced to broaden their travel horizons if the destination can be portrayed as a location for quiet, tranquility, rest, and relaxation, and away from big-city and high-tech accoutrements. Wohlers and Etzel (1985, p. 293) point out that several researchers have indicated that sensation seeking declines with age. This would appear to be supported by the significantly declining percentages of respondents agreeing with the "traveler" scale over the age groups from fifty-five to fifty-nine to sixty-five to sixty-nine. However, the seventy-and-up group is as likely to agree as the fifty-five to fifty-nine group!

Media Preferences

Finally, again from a marketing perspective, the magazine and television preferences of adherents to the three lifestyles would be useful to know in developing promotional and media strategy. Table 22.7 presents the proportion of respondents agreeing on each of the three composite scales who (a) "subscribe to or read regularly" each of the indicated magazines, and (b) "like very much" or "like somewhat" each of the indicated television program types.

The media preferences shown in Table 22.7 appear to confirm accepted stereotypes. Women interested in foreign travel disproportionately read *National Geographic, Newsweek, Smithsonian,* and *U.S. News and World Report* and tend not to read *TV Guide* as compared to the "laid back" group. Similarly, "travelers" are more likely to read *Bon Appetit, National Geographic, Newsweek, Smithsonian, Time,* and *U.S. News and World Report,* and are less likely to read *Good Housekeeping, Ladies' Home Journal,* and *TV Guide* than the "dreamers."

TABLE 22.7. Proportion Agreeing with Each Indicated Scale Who "Subscribe to or Read Regularly" Each Magazine, and Who "Like" (Like Very Much or Like Somewhat) Each Type of Television Program

Medium	Scale		
	"Traveler"	"Laid Back"	"Dreamer"
	(280)[b]	(337)[b]	(212)[b]
Magazine[a]	%	%	%
AARP Bulletin[l]	45	46	40
American Legion	7	6	5
Better Homes and Gardens	43	42	41
Bon Appetit[h]	14	10	7
Business Week	3	2	1
Changing Times	11	10	9
Consumer Reports	18	17	17
Cosmopolitan	5	6	7
Discover	4	3	2
Elks Magazine[f]	2	4	5
Family Circle	52	55	53
Field and Stream	3	3	3
Glamour	4	2	2
Golf Digest	1	1	1
Good Housekeeping[f]	33	34	39
Ladies' Home Journal[f]	28	31	35
McCall's[l]	36	31	38
Modern Maturity[l]	42	44	35
Money	5	5	6
National Enquirer	10	13	18
National Geographic[c,h,j]	37	32	24
New Woman	1	3	4
Newsweek[c,g]	17	13	11
Parents	1	0	1
People	16	15	18
Penthouse	1	1	1
Playboy	3	2	2
Popular Mechanics	4	5	5
Popular Science	2	2	3
Prevention	12	12	10
Reader's Digest	60	61	59
Redbook	12	15	15
Self	3	3	2
Smithsonian[d,h]	14	8	5
Southern Living	16	13	14
Sports Illustrated	3	3	4
Sunset	7	7	10
Time[g]	15	13	9
True Story	3	5	5
TV Guide[d,h]	25	33	38

TABLE 22.7. *(continued)*

	Scale		
	"Traveler"	"Laid Back"	"Dreamer"
Medium	(280)[b]	(337)[b]	(212)[b]
Magazine[a]			
U.S. News and World Report[d,g]	15	10	9
Us	2	2	4
VFW Magazine	3	3	3
Woman's Day	43	43	41
Workbasket	15	19	16
Television program types	%	%	%
Westerns[e,h]	44	56	60
National or world news programs	89	86	76
Police shows[g,h]	46	46	55
Music and dance[e,h]	74	65	64
Religious programs[d,h]	38	45	50
Sports[d,g]	53	45	44
Variety shows, "specials"	77	75	72
Quiz or game shows[g,i]	66	69	75
Plays[e,h]	76	66	64
Horror movies[c,h]	11	16	21
Concerts[e,h]	62	45	41
Talk shows or interviews[e,h]	70	58	60
Daytime or evening serials[j]	48	45	55
Business and finance programs[e,h,k]	28	19	11
Music videos	18	15	15
Mystery or suspense shows	62	57	60
Educational programs[e,h]	81	71	69
Romance or love stories[g,k]	58	54	67
Cooking programs	57	55	57
Gardening or home improvement programs[f]	56	52	48
Major motion pictures (on TV)	87	85	90

[a] Listed magazines include the top 25 magazines plus 20 selected others from those ranked 26-60 on the list of "100 leading A.B.C. Magazines" (based on combined circulation per issue) for the first six months of 1983 (Magazine Publisher's Association, 1983).

[b] Numbers in parentheses are those scoring below 3.0 as an average composite score on the scale this reflects "strongly agree" and "somewhat agree." See footnote a of Table 6.

[c] Difference between "traveler" and "laid back" scales significant at 10% level (Z-test, 2-tailed).

[d] Difference between "traveler" and "laid back" scales significant at 5% level.

[e] Difference between "traveler" and "laid back" scales significant at 1% level.

[f] Difference between "traveler" and "laid back" scales significant at 10% level.

[g] Difference between "traveler" and "laid back" scales significant at 5% level.

[h] Difference between "traveler" and "laid back" scales significant at 1% level.

[i] Difference between "traveler" and "laid back" scales significant at 10% level.

[j] Difference between "traveler" and "laid back" scales significant at 5% level.

[k] Difference between "traveler" and "laid back" scales significant at 1% level.

The television program type preferences show even more dramatic differences between the groups than the magazine preferences. Sixteen of the differences between "travelers" and either "laid backs" or "dreamers" are significant at the 1 percent level or greater, whereas only five of these same group-to-group differences are significant at the same level among the magazines.

By comparison with the other two groups, "travelers" are most likely to watch national and world news programs, music and dance, plays, concerts, talk shows or interviews, business and finance programs, and educational programs. They are slightly more likely to watch sports than "laid backs" and "dreamers," and are significantly less likely to watch westerns, religious programs, and horror movies than members of the other two groups. They are somewhat less likely to watch police shows, quiz or game shows and romance or love stories than are the "dreamers." All in all, "travelers" prefer more intellectual, upscale, sophisticated television programming, which intuitively would seem to be in line with their more worldly orientation.

CONCLUSIONS AND IMPLICATIONS

This report has attempted to discern or clarify the travel-related lifestyle profiles of women over fifty years of age. Given the current size of the over-fifty female market segment and the fact that women tend to live longer than men, this group is and will continue to be an important target market for the travel industry. The results reported here suggest that there are useful marketing implications in the three profiles developed.

The limitations inherent in this study concern the representativeness of the older segment of the Market Facts panel, the typical caveats associated with mail questionnaires, the particular AIO statements that were used, and the atheoretical, descriptive nature of the research. However, the following conclusions appear reasonable:

1. Women in the fifty-five to fifty-nine age group constitute an age-based segment with high interest in traveling overseas.
2. The best future customers are past customers: previous exposure to foreign travel predisposes one to want to return.
3. Three of the five age groups, including the seventy-and-over group, were not primarily interested in resting and relaxing on a vacation, suggesting that the common stereotype of lower energy over fifty is misleading.
4. The Puritan ethic lives; roughly 60 percent of the women studied do not support the notion of travel now, pay later vacations.

5. Big-city vacations or travel hold less appeal than alternatives to women in these age groups.
6. The general profile of women with a travel orientation is what one might predict: higher education and income levels, small household size, activeness, and acceptance of the uncertainty involved in travel.
7. Travelers differ markedly; some like excitement and adventure, some prefer predictability, and some are content with vicarious experiences and fantasizing with television. Roughly a third of the respondents fell into each of the first two groups, while about a fifth of the respondents agreed with the "dreamer" scale.
8. Television would not appear to be an appropriate medium to reach the two traveler groups ("traveler" and "laid back"). Specific print media are likely to be more effective; if television is used, more upscale, intellectually stimulating programming would be appropriate. Western and religious programs do not attract many "travelers."

The importance of these findings lies both in a confirmation of other studies' results on the characteristics of travelers to areas outside the United States and in further developing the profile of older American women travelers. This group apparently has not been widely studied in this context.

These findings clearly suggest that many older women, even many over seventy, have the energy and desire to do active things. Tinsley and Tinsley (1986) cite several studies showing moderately high correlations between overall life satisfaction factors and leisure-activity participation. Older women seem to be cognizant of that relationship. Ruth Ziff of Doyle Dane Bembach has stated that people sixty-five and older "do not think of themselves as having one foot in the grave. . . . They describe themselves in positive terms: 'prime of life,' 'mature,' 'best years of their lives.' [Advertisers] should treat these people in advertising and marketing as useful, competent, confident, coping individuals with a zest for life and a desire to be self-sufficient and active" (ACLI, 1986, p. 8).

These findings also suggest that television may *not* be the best way to promote travel packages and destinations to experienced travelers, although "dreamers" may be a good potential segment for travel-related advertising on television (however, they may show initial interest but not follow through). Further research is needed to explore the efficacy of pursuing the "dreamer" segment.

The action suggested by these findings is to further expand the profiles of these three groups, verify the results on other samples, examine older males in the same context (as well as male-female pairs), and reexamine the utility of television advertising as a primary media-mix element in trip package and destination marketing.

CONCEPT DEFINITIONS

Age-based segmentation: Grouping people on the basis of age categories.

AIO statements: Short statements reflecting activities, interests, and opinions of people. These are the three basic broad categories of lifestyle measures when the statements are responded to on an agree-disagree scale.

Approach-avoidance paradigm: The theory that some goal objects can bring about simultaneous desires to move both toward and away from that object, thus bringing about cognitive conflict.

BMDP: A set or package of computer-based statistical analysis routines developed at UCLA.

Cluster analysis: Multivariate statistical analysis procedures for classifying objects or people into some number of mutually exclusive and collectively exhaustive groups on the basis of two or more classification variables. Ideally, the resultant clusters should exhibit high internal homogeneity and high external (between-cluster) heterogeneity.

CMP (Consumer Mail Panel): A nationwide panel of many tens of thousands of households around the United States who have agreed to answer periodic questionnaires dealing with a wide variety of their consumption patterns. It is operated by Market Facts, Inc. of Chicago.

Cronbach's alpha: A reliability coefficient used in evaluating multiple-item additive scales. It ranges from zero to one, with higher values indicating that all the items in a multiple-item scale "hang together" well and address the same underlying dimension or issue.

Dendrogram(s): A graphical representation in the form of a tree diagram of the results of a clustering procedure in which the vertical axis consists of the objects or individuals, while the horizontal axis shows the number of clusters formed at each step of the clustering procedure.

Eigenvalues: In matrix algebra, an eigenvalue is a latent root of a characteristic equation. Here, it is used as a rule of thumb for limiting the number of factors extracted from the data to those with eigenvalues greater than unity.

Gray market: A term used to refer to the market segment of mature (generally over 50, sometimes over fifty-five) consumer.

Intercorrelation matrix (or matrices): A display (rows × columns) of the correlation coefficients (measures of association) between all possible pairs of variables.

Lifestyle profile: A summary description of the pattern of living and spending of time, money, and energy of a specific group of people.

R-type factor analysis: A statistical analysis process for identifying a set of dimensions that are latent (not easily observed) in a large set of variables. Factor analysis is a generic name given to a set of multivariate statistical methods whose purpose is the condensing of the information contained in a number of original variables into a smaller set of fundamental constructs or dimensions assumed to underlie the original variables.

Satisfaction: A postconsumption evaluation that a chosen alternative meets or exceeds expectations.

Scree test: An approach used to identify the optimum number of factors that can be extracted from the data. One plots the latent roots (eigenvalues) against the number of factors in the order of their extraction, and evaluates the resulting curve for the point where it first begins to become horizontal. The number of factors at this point is assumed to be the optimal number; any more contribute very little to the understanding of the data.

Variance: The variance of a variable is the mean of the sum of the squared deviations of its values from the overall mean of the values of that variable. In factor analysis, one looks for factors that "explain" the greatest amount of the variance in the factors used in the analysis.

Varimax rotation (in factor analysis): A particular method of deriving factors that are mathematically independent ("orthogonal" or at 90 degrees to each other, graphically) that has been found to give a relatively clearer and more stable separation (and hence interpretation) of the factors.

Z-test, two-tailed: A statistical test for the significance of the difference between two percentages for uncorrelated data. Two-tailed refers to the fact that it is a nondirectional test where it is of no concern whether the sample mean is larger or smaller than the population mean.

REVIEW QUESTIONS

1. What major dimensions of travel and leisure attitudes came out of the factor analysis of the data? Briefly describe the major differences between these three major dimensions or groupings of female travelers.

2. Which of these three groupings proved to be the most robust (meaningful) across the age categories used, and how was this determined?

3. What percentage of respondents "agreed with" each of the three scales of female travelers?
4. Which magazines, of those included in the study, did women interested in foreign travel tend to read?
5. How effective might television be as a medium to reach actual and potential travelers, based on this study?
6. What types of television programs was the "traveler" group most likely to watch?
7. How would you describe the general profile of older women with a travel orientation? From your own personal experience/observations, would you agree with this profile? Why or why not?
8. Do you think that the findings regarding the effectiveness of television as a medium to reach travel-oriented older women would hold true if the study were done today?

REFERENCES

ACLI (1986). *Data Track* (January). Washington, DC: Social Research Service, American Council of Life Insurance.

Anderson, Beverlee B. and Lynn Langmeyer (1982), "The Under-50 and Over-50 Travelers: A Profile of Similarities and Differences." *Journal of Travel Research,* 20 (Spring), 20-24.

Bieber, Stephen L. and David V. Smith (1986), "Multivariate Analysis of Sensory Data: A Comparison of Methods," *Chemical Senses,* 11(1), 19-47.

Cohen, Erik (1972). "Toward a Sociology of International Tourism," *Social Research,* 39, 164-182.

Cohen, Erik (1979). "Rethinking the Sociology of Tourism," *Annals of Tourism Research,* 6 (Jan./Mar.), 18-35.

Cohen, Erik (1984), "The Sociology of Tourism: Approaches, Issues, and Findings," in Ralph H. Turner, Editor, *Annual Review of Sociology,* 10, Palo Alto, CA: Annual Review, Inc., pp. 373-391.

Crissey, Yvonne (1980), "Over Forty-Nine: The Active Affluent," in *Research and the Changing World of Travel in the 1980's.* Proceedings of the Eleventh Annual Conference, The Travel Research Association, Salt Lake City, UT: Bureau of Economic and Business Research, Graduate School of Business, University of Utah, pp. 127-142.

Dann, Graham M.S. (1981). "Tourist Motivation: An Appraisal," *Annals of Tourism Research,* 8, 187-219.

Dann, Graham M.S. (1983), "Comment on Iso-Ahola's 'Toward a Social Psychological Theory of Tourism Motivation,'" *Annals of Tourism Research,* 10, 273-276.

Dixon, W.J. (1983), *BMDP Statistical Software,* Berkeley, CA: University of California Press.

Dorfman, Lorraine T., Frank J. Kohout, and D. Alex Heckert (1985), "Retirement Satisfaction in the Rural Elderly," *Research on Aging*, 7 (December), 577-599.

Downie, N. M. and R. W. Heath (1974), *Basic Statistical Methods*, Fourth Edition, New York: Harper and Row.

Guinn, Robert (1980), "Elderly Recreational Vehicle Tourists: Motivations for Leisure," *Journal of Travel Research*, 19 (Summer), 9-12.

Hawes, Douglass K., Roger D. Blackwell, and W. Wayne Talarzyk (1976), "Attitudes Toward Use of Credit Cards: Do Men and Women Differ?," *Baylor Business Studies*, 7 (Nov./Dec.), 57-71.

Hawes, Douglass K., Roger D. Blackwell, and W. Wayne Talarzyk (1977), "Psychographics Are Meaningful (. . . Not Merely Interesting)," *Journal of Travel Research*, 15 (Spring), 1-7.

Hughes, William (1985), "The Mature Traveler," in *The Battle for Market Share: Strategies in Research and Marketing*. Proceedings of the Sixteenth Annual Conference, Travel and Tourism Research Association, Salt Lake City, UT: Business of Economic and Business Research, Graduate School of Business, University of Utah, pp. 281-285.

Hull, C. Hadlai and Norman H. Nie (1981), *SPSS Update 7-9*, New York: McGraw-Hill.

Iso-Ahola, Seppo E. (1980). *Social Psychological Perspectives on Leisure and Recreation*, Springfield, IL: Charles C. Thomas.

Iso-Ahola, Seppo E. (1982), "Toward a Social Psychological Theory of Tourism Motivation: A Rejoinder." *Annals of Tourism Research*, 9, 256-262.

Linden, Fabian (1986), "The $800 Billion Market," *American Demographics*, 8 (February), 4ff.

Lounsbury, John W. and Linda L. Hoopes (1985), "An Investigation of Factors Associated with Vacation Satisfaction," *Journal of Leisure Research*, 17, 1-13.

Magazine Publishers Association (1983), "100 Leading A. B. C. Magazines," Statistics Sheets Nos. IH, 2H, and 3H. New York: Magazine Publishers Association.

McIntosh, Robert W. and Charles R. Goeldner (1984), *Tourism Principles, Practices, Philosophies*, Fourth Edition, New York: John Wiley and Sons, Inc.

Mobily, Kenneth E. (1984). "Factors Associated with the Aging Leisure Repertoire: The Iowa 56+ Rural Health Study," *Journal of Leisure Research*, 16, 338-343.

Nunnally, Jum C. (1978). *Psychometric Theory*, Second Edition, New York: McGraw-Hill.

Palmore, Erdman B. (1976), "The Effects of Aging on Activities and Attitudes." in Cary S. Kart and Barbara B. Manard, editors, *Aging in America: Readings in Social Gerontology*. Alfred Publishing Company, Inc.

Pearce, Philip L. (1982), *The Social Psychology of Tourist Behavior*. New York: Pergamon Press, Inc.

Riche, Martha Famsworth (1986). "Retirement's Lifestyle Pioneers," *American Demographics*, 8 (January), 42-44ff.

Riddich, Carol C. and Stacy N. Daniel (1984), "The Relative Contributions of Leisure Activities and Other Factors to the Mental Health of Older Women," *Journal of Leisure Research*, 16, 136-148.

Rosenfeld, Jeffrey P. (1986). "Demographics on Vacation." *American Demographics,* 8 (January), 38-41ff.

Rummel, R.J. (1970), *Applied Factor Analysis*. Evanston, IL: Northwestern University Press.

Stewart, David W. (1981), "The Application and Misapplication of Factor Analysis in Marketing Research," *Journal of Marketing Research*, 18 (February), 51-62.

Supernaw, Scott (1985), "Battle for the Gray Market" in *The Battle for Market Share: Strategies in Research and Marketing*, Proceedings of the Sixteenth Annual Conference, Travel and Tourism Research Association. Salt Lake City, UT: Bureau of Economic and Business Research, Graduate School of Business, University of Utah, pp. 287-290.

Technology and Aging in America (1985), Washington, DC: U.S. Congress, Office of Technology Assessment, OTA-BA-264, June.

Tinsley, Howard E.A. and Diane J. Tinsley (1986), "A Theory of the Attributes, Benefits and Causes of Leisure Experience," *Leisure Science*, 8, 1-45.

Tongren, Hale N. (1980), "Travel Plans of the Over-65 Market Pre and Postretirement," *Journal of Travel Research*, 19 (Fall), 7-11.

U.S. Department of Commerce (1975), U.S. Bureau of the Census. *Statistical Abstract of the United States, 1975*, 96th ed., Washington, DC: U.S. Government Printing Office.

U.S. Department of Commerce (1985), Bureau of the Census. *Statistical Abstract of the United States, 1986*, 106th Edition. Washington, DC: U.S. Government Printing Office.

Van Doren, Carlton S. (1981), "Outdoor Recreation Trends in the 1980's: Implications for Society." *Journal of Travel Research*, 19 (Winter), 3-10.

Wohlers, Russell G. and Michael J. Etzel (1985), "Vacation Preferences as a Manifestation of Optimal Stimulation and Lifestyle Experience," *Journal of Leisure Research*, 17, 283-295.

Summary and Conclusions

Abraham Pizam
Yoel Mansfeld

As we indicated in our Introduction, the aim of this book was to increase the reader's understanding of the process by which tourists make travel decisions and purchase travel goods and services. Understanding tourists' needs and the "why" and "how" of tourist behavior is the foundation of effective tourism marketing.

By now, we hope that the reader is familiar with:

- The basics of tourist motivation
- The intention to visit and the destination selection process
- The importance of dividing the market into identifiable segments and satisfying the unique needs of each segment
- The role that personal, social, environmental, and marketing communication stimuli play in affecting buying behavior
- The factors that cause satisfaction or dissatisfaction with the travel experience

More specifically, the twenty-two chapters in this book presented the reader with theoretical essays, research results, and case studies that discussed such issues as:

- How to determine in advance whether a tourism product/service will appeal to potential tourists and at what price level it should be offered
- The use of means-end theory in destination choice
- The stages through which tourists pass in making a vacation destination decision
- The role played by image in destination selection
- The differences between the interpretivist and constructivist approaches in analyzing the vacation decision-making process
- The need for developing new typologies of tourists

- How families make vacation decisions, and what role each family member plays in this decision
- The importance and role of various sources of information on travel decision making
- The differences between the "proportionality" and the "similarity hypothesis" models in explaining consumer choice
- How the combination of the price and quality of new products introduced into the market affect the decision-making process of the consumer
- How to maintain and increase tourist loyalty
- What techniques are available for "destination image assessment" and "image modification" and what their strengths and weaknesses are
- How expectations form in the minds of tourists and how one studies these
- What service quality theory is and how this theory can help anticipate customer satisfaction
- What cognitive distance is and its effect on destination selection
- What perceptual maps are, and how they are created and interpreted
- What qualitative research techniques are available for studying tourist behavior
- Why people choose to cruise and how the physical design of a ship influences the choice of on-board activities provided
- The effects of nationality and culture on tourist behavior
- How senior and nonsenior tourists differ in their pleasure travel
- The effect of family life cycle on destination choice and tourist behavior
- How travel lifestyles can be used in tourism marketing segmentation
- The travel-related lifestyles of elderly women travelers

It is our hope that this book will lead to a greater understanding of consumer behavior in tourism and create a heightened interest in, and appreciation of, this important domain.

Index

Page numbers followed by the letter "e" indicate exhibits; those followed by the letter "i" indicate illustrations; and those followed by the letter "t" indicate tables.

HAWORTH HOSPITALITY PRESS
Hospitality, Travel, and Tourism
K. S. Chon, PhD, Executive Editor

THE PRACTICE OF GRADUATE RESEARCH IN HOSPITALITY AND TOURISM edited by K. S. Chon.

THE INTERNATIONAL HOSPITALITY MANAGEMENT BUSINESS: MANAGEMENT AND OPERATIONS by Larry Yu. "The abundant real-world examples and cases provided in the text enable readers to understand the most up-to-date developments in international hospitality business." *Zheng Gu, PhD, Associate Professor, College of Hotel Administration, University of Nevada, Las Vegas, CA*

CONSUMER BEHAVIOR IN TRAVEL AND TOURISM by Abraham Pizam and Yoel Mansfeld. "A must for anyone who wants to take advantage of new global opportunities in this growing industry." *Bonnie J. Knutson, PhD, School of Hospitality Business, Michigan State University*

LEGALIZED CASINO GAMING IN THE UNITED STATES: THE ECONOMIC AND SOCIAL IMPACT edited by Cathy H. C. Hsu. "Brings a fresh new look at one of the areas in tourism that has not yet received careful and serious consideration in the past." *Muzaffer Uysal, PhD, Professor of Tourism Research, Virginia Polytechnic Institute and State University, Blacksburg*

HOSPITALITY MANAGEMENT EDUCATION edited by Clayton W. Barrows and Robert H. Bosselman. "Takes the mystery out of how hospitality management education programs function and serves as an excellent resource for individuals interested in pursuing the field." *Joe Perdue, CCM, CHE, Director, Executive Masters Program, College of Hotel Administration, University of Nevada, Las Vegas*

MARKETING YOUR CITY, U.S.A.: A GUIDE TO DEVELOPING A STRATEGIC TOURISM MARKETING PLAN by Ronald A. Nykiel and Elizabeth Jascolt. "An excellent guide for anyone involved in the planning and marketing of cities and regions. . . . A terrific job of synthesizing an otherwise complex procedure." *James C. Maken, PhD, Associate Professor, Babcock Graduate School of Management, Wake Forest University, Winston-Salem, North Carolina*

Order Your Own Copy of
This Important Book for Your Personal Library!

CONSUMER BEHAVIOR IN TRAVEL AND TOURISM

_____ in hardbound at $69.95 (ISBN: 0-7890-0610-3)

COST OF BOOKS_____

OUTSIDE USA/CANADA/
MEXICO: ADD 20%_____

POSTAGE & HANDLING_____
(US: $3.00 for first book & $1.25
for each additional book)
Outside US: $4.75 for first book
& $1.75 for each additional book)

SUBTOTAL_____

IN CANADA: ADD 7% GST_____

STATE TAX_____
(NY, OH & MN residents, please
add appropriate local sales tax)

FINAL TOTAL_____
(If paying in Canadian funds,
convert using the current
exchange rate. UNESCO
coupons welcome.)

☐ **BILL ME LATER:** ($5 service charge will be added)
(Bill-me option is good on US/Canada/Mexico orders only;
not good to jobbers, wholesalers, or subscription agencies.)

☐ Check here if billing address is different from
shipping address and attach purchase order and
billing address information.

Signature_____

☐ **PAYMENT ENCLOSED: $**_____

☐ **PLEASE CHARGE TO MY CREDIT CARD.**

☐ Visa   ☐ MasterCard   ☐ AmEx   ☐ Discover
☐ Diners Club
Account # _____

Exp. Date _____

Signature _____

Prices in US dollars and subject to change without notice.

NAME _____

INSTITUTION _____

ADDRESS _____

CITY _____

STATE/ZIP _____

COUNTRY _____ COUNTY (NY residents only) _____

TEL _____ FAX _____

E-MAIL_____
May we use your e-mail address for confirmations and other types of information? ☐ Yes   ☐ No

Order From Your Local Bookstore or Directly From
The Haworth Press, Inc.
10 Alice Street, Binghamton, New York 13904-1580 • USA
TELEPHONE: 1-800-HAWORTH (1-800-429-6784) / Outside US/Canada: (607) 722-5857
FAX: 1-800-895-0582 / Outside US/Canada: (607) 772-6362
E-mail: getinfo@haworthpressinc.com
PLEASE PHOTOCOPY THIS FORM FOR YOUR PERSONAL USE.

BOF96

Learn how to increase your share of the hospitality and tourist business with the information and advice offered in these books!

Take 20% Off Books! Special Sale

CONSUMER BEHAVIOR IN TRAVEL AND TOURISM

NEW!

Over 500 Pages!

Edited by Abraham Pizam and Yoel Mansfeld
This extraordinary book packages the various issues and aspects of consumer behavior in travel and tourism in the form of a textbook to be used by both students and practitioners. Each chapter includes learning objectives, main concept definitions, and review questions.
$69.95 hard. ISBN: 0-7890-0610-3.
Text price (5+ copies): $49.95.
Available Spring 1999. Approx. 540 pp. with Index.
Features case studies, tables/figures, concept definitions, and a bibliography.

LEGALIZED CASINO GAMING IN THE UNITED STATES

NEW!

Over 250 Pages!

The Economic and Social Impact
Edited by Cathy H. C. Hsu, PhD
Provides a comprehensive overview of the history, development, legislation, and economic and social impacts of riverboat, land-based, and Native American casino gaming.
$49.95 hard. ISBN: 0-7890-0640-5.
Text price (5+ copies): $24.95.
1999. Available now. 256 pp. with Index.
Features tables and figures.

THE INTERNATIONAL HOSPITALITY BUSINESS

NEW!

Over 400 Pages!

Management and Operations
Larry Yu, PhD
You'll find a complete analysis of the complex issues hospitality managers face when they are assigned overseas, including international hospitality firms' policies regarding development strategy, organizational structure, marketing, finance and accounting, and human resource management.
$79.95 hard. ISBN: 0-7890-0559-X.
Text price (5+ copies): $39.95.
1999. Available now. 418 pp. with Index.

Textbooks are available for classroom adoption consideration on a 60-day examination basis. You will receive an invoice payable within 60 days along with the book. If you decide to adopt the book, your invoice will be cancelled. Please write to us on your institutional letterhead, indicating the textbook you would like to examine as well as the following information: course title, current text, enrollment, and decision date.

WE'RE ONLINE!

Visit our online catalog and search for publications of interest to you by title, author, keyword, or subject! You'll find descriptions, reviews, and complete tables of contents of books and journals

http://www.haworthpressinc.com

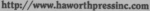
The Haworth Hospitality Press
new trends in lodging, tourism & foodservice management
An imprint of The Haworth Press, Inc.
10 Alice Street, Binghamton, NY 13904-1580 USA

HOSPITALITY MANAGEMENT EDUCATION

NEW!

Over 250 Pages!

Edited by Clayton W. Barrows, EdD, and Robert H. Bosselman, PhD
Focuses on the academic aspect of hospitality—the mechanisms of hospitality education programs, their missions, their constituents, and the outcomes of their efforts.
$49.95 hard. ISBN: 0-7890-0411-0.
Text price (5+ copies): $34.95.
1999. Available now. 286 pp. with Index.
Features case studies, tables/figures, a list of organizations, Web site/Internet addresses, and exhibition details!

THE ROLE OF THE HOSPITALITY INDUSTRY IN THE LIVES OF INDIVIDUALS AND FAMILIES

NEW!

Over 225 Pages!

Edited by Pamela R. Cummings, PhD, Francis A. Kwansa, PhD, and Marvin B. Sussman, PhD
This book will teach you how to better meet the needs of guests at the national or international level while learning how the industry affects employees and their lives outside of work.
(A monograph published simultaneously as Marriage & Family Review, Vol. 28, Nos. 1/2.)
$49.95 hard. ISBN: 0-7890-0524-7.
$24.95 soft. ISBN: 0-7890-0526-3. 1998. 247 pp. with Index.

FUNDAMENTALS OF LEISURE BUSINESS SUCCESS

NEW!

A Manager's Guide to Achieving Success in the Leisure and Recreation Industry
Jonathan T. Scott, MBA
You'll have the benefit of 20 years of actual experience in the leisure and recreation field at your disposal, so you can master the importance of contemporary business management and techniques.
$39.95 hard. ISBN: 0-7890-0445-3.
Text price (5+ copies): $19.95. 1998. 189 pp. with Index.
Features case studies, tables and figures, a glossary, a list of organizations, and a bibliography.

MARKETING YOUR CITY, U.S.A.

A Guide to Developing a Strategic Tourism Marketing Plan
Ronald A. Nykiel, PhD, and Elizabeth Jascolt, MHM
You'll discover how easy it is to market your hometown to potential tourists. You'll find a simple, surefire strategy proven to bring out the charm and beauty of any town, anywhere.
$29.95 hard. ISBN: 0-7890-0591-3.
$19.95 soft. ISBN: 0-7890-0592-1. 1998. 126 pp. with Index.
Features tables/figures, 10 work forms to assist you in creating a marketing plan, and a bibliography.

HOW CONSUMERS PICK A HOTEL
Strategic Segmentation and Target Marketing
Dennis J. Cahill, MBA, MA
"A concise overview of consumer behavior, intertwining marketing theory with ways in which to implement the theory."
—Book News
$39.95 hard. ISBN: 0-7890-0139-X.
$19.95 soft. ISBN: 0-7890-0184-5. 1997. 164 pp. with Index.

MARKETING ISSUES IN PACIFIC AREA TOURISM
Edited by John C. Crotts and Chris A. Ryan
Since many of these countries are becoming not only generators of tourist demand but also new tourist receiving areas, this book covers both inbound and outbound markets.
(A monograph published simultaneously as the Journal of Travel & Tourism Marketing, Vol. 6, No.1.)
$39.95 hard. ISBN: 0-7890-0029-6.
$14.95 soft. ISBN: 0-7890-0310-4. 1997. 114 pp. with Index

GEOGRAPHY AND TOURISM MARKETING
Edited by Martin Oppermann, PhD
Covers diverse geographical aspects of tourism marketing from "modern" promotion channels such as the Internet to "traditional" ones such as brochures.
(A monograph published simultaneously as the Journal of Travel & Tourism Marketing, Vol. 6, Nos. 3/4.)
$39.95 hard. ISBN: 0-7890-0335-X.
$19.95 soft. ISBN: 0-7890-0336-8. 1997. 186 pp. with Index.

RECENT ADVANCES IN TOURISM MARKETING RESEARCH
Edited by Daniel R. Fesenmaier, PhD, Joseph T. O'Leary, PhD, and Muzaffer Uysal, PhD
Explores exciting new approaches to conducting tourism marketing research and presents applications which will help you develop and implement new tourism marketing strategies in your business.
Over 250 Pages!
(A monograph published simultaneously as the Journal of Travel & Tourism Marketing, Vol. 5, Nos. 1/2/3.)
$45.00 hard. ISBN: 1-56024-836-X. 1996. 279 pp. with Index.

CALL OUR TOLL-FREE NUMBER: 1–800–HAWORTH
US & Canada only / 8am–5pm ET; Monday–Friday
Outside US/Canada: + 607–722–5857

FAX YOUR ORDER TO US: 1–800–895–0582
Outside US/Canada: + 607–771–0012

E-MAIL YOUR ORDER TO US:
getinfo@haworthpressinc.com

VISIT OUR WEB SITE AT:
http://www.haworthpressinc.com

Take 20% Off Books! Special Sale

Order Today and Save!

TITLE	ISBN	REGULAR PRICE	20%-OFF PRICE

- Discount good only in US, Canada, and Mexico and not good in conjunction with any other offer.
- Individual orders outside US, Canada, and Mexico must be prepaid by check, credit card, or money order
- In Canada: Add 7% for GST after postage & handling.
- Outside USA, Canada, and Mexico: Add 20%
- MN, NY, and OH residents: Add appropriate local sales tax

Please complete information below or tape your business card in this area.

NAME _____

ADDRESS _____

_____

CITY _____

STATE _____ ZIP _____

COUNTRY _____

COUNTY (NY residents only) _____

TEL _____ FAX _____

E-MAIL _____
May we use your e-mail address for confirmations and other types of information? ( ) Yes ( ) No. We appreciate receiving your e-mail address and fax number. Haworth would like to e-mail or fax special discount offers to you, as a preferred customer. We will never **share, rent, or exchange** your e-mail address or fax number. We regard such actions as an invasion of your privacy.

POSTAGE AND HANDLING:	
If your book total is:	Add
up to	$29.95	$5.00
$30.00 – $49.99	$6.00
$50.00 – $69.99	$7.00
$70.00 – $89.99	$8.00
$90.00 – $109.99	$9.00
$110.00 – $129.99	$10.00
$130.00 – $149.99	$11.00
$150.00 and up	$12.00

- US orders will be shipped via UPS; Outside US orders will be shipped via Book Printed Matter. For shipments via other delivery services, contact Haworth for details. Based on US dollars. Booksellers: Call for freight charges. • If paying in Canadian funds, please use the current exchange rate to convert total to Canadian dollars. • Payment in UNESCO coupons welcome. • Please allow 3–4 weeks for delivery after publication. • Prices and discounts subject to change without notice. • Discount not applicable on books priced under $15.00.

☐ **BILL ME LATER** ($5 service charge will be added).
(Bill-me option available on US/Canadian/Mexican orders only. Not available for subscription agencies. Service charge is waived for booksellers/wholesalers/jobbers.)

Signature _____

☐ **PAYMENT ENCLOSED** _____
(Payment must be in US or Canadian dollars by check or money order drawn on a US or Canadian bank.)

☐ **PLEASE CHARGE TO MY CREDIT CARD:**
☐ VISA ☐ MASTERCARD ☐ AMEX ☐ DISCOVER ☐ DINERS CLUB

Account # _____ Exp Date _____

Signature _____
May we open a confidential credit card account for you for possible future purchases? ( ) Yes ( ) No

The Haworth Press, Inc.
(28) (18) 04/99 BBC99
10 Alice Street, Binghamton, New York 13904–1580 USA